THOMAS MORE

THOMAS
✥ MORE

A BIOGRAPHY

RICHARD
MARIUS

VINTAGE BOOKS
A DIVISION OF RANDOM HOUSE
NEW YORK

GRATEFUL ACKNOWLEGMENT IS MADE TO THE FOLLOWING FOR
PERMISSION TO REPRINT PREVIOUSLY PUBLISHED MATERIAL:

UNIVERSITY OF TORONTO PRESS: EXCERPTS FROM THE *COLLECTED
WORKS OF ERASMUS.* VOL. 3, COPYRIGHT © 1976; VOL. 4,
COPYRIGHT © 1977; VOL. 5, COPYRIGHT © 1979. ALL ©
BY THE UNIVERSITY OF TORONTO PRESS. USED WITH PERMISSION.
YALE UNIVERSITY PRESS: EXCERPTS FROM *TWO EARLY TUDOR
LIVES,* ED. RICHARD S. SYLVESTER AND DAVIS P. HARDING,
COPYRIGHT © 1962; *THE YALE EDITION OF THE COMPLETE
WORKS OF ST. THOMAS MORE.* VOL. 4, *UTOPIA,* ED. EDW. SURTZ,
S. J., AND J. H. HEXTER, AND VOL. 5, *RESPONSIO AD LUTHERUM,*
ED. J. M. HEADLEY, TRANS., SISTER SCHOLASTICA MANDEVILLE,
COPYRIGHT © 1963 BY YALE UNIVERSITY; VOL. 3, PART 2, *LATIN
POEMS,* ED. MILLER, BRADNER, LYNCH, AND OLIVER, COPYRIGHT
© 1984 BY YALE UNIVERSITY. USED WITH PERMISSION.

LIBRARY OF CONGRESS CATALOGING IN PUBLICATION DATA
MARIUS, RICHARD.
THOMAS MORE.
REPRINT. ORIGINALLY PUBLISHED:
NEW YORK: KNOPF, C1984.
BIBLIOGRAPHY: P.   INCLUDES INDEX.
1. MORE, THOMAS, SIR, SAINT, 1478-1535.
2. STATESMEN—GREAT BRITAIN—BIOGRAPHY.
3. CHRISTIAN SAINTS—ENGLAND—BIOGRAPHY.
4. GREAT BRITAIN—HISTORY—HENRY VIII, 1509-1547.   I. TITLE.
[DA334.M8M275   1985   942.05′2′0924 [B]   85-40156
ISBN 0-394-74146-3 (PBK.)

THIS BOOK IS DEDICATED

TO THE MEMORY OF MY FRIEND

RICHARD S. SYLVESTER

AND IN HOMAGE TO MY FRIEND

MILTON KLEIN

OF

THE UNIVERSITY OF TENNESSEE

CONTENTS

Illustrations follow pages 134 and 294.

*Source references will be found in the notes at the
end of the book, located by page number and an
identifying phrase from the text.*

ACKNOWLEDGMENTS

A BIG BOOK creates big personal debts for any author. I cannot repay all the debts I owe for this book, but I can at least acknowledge some of them.

To no one is my obligation greater than to my editor, Ann Close. To detail all her work on this book would require a book almost as large. She asked relentlessly intelligent questions, and she always made me think of the general audience of intelligent and educated people I hope will read the work. She kept me (I trust) from being either obscurely pedantic or patronizingly obvious. She also weeded out some heavy clumps of verbiage. And she never once lost patience through three major drafts of the manuscript.

Robert Gottlieb believed in the book before he ever saw a page of it and supported it and me far beyond the original deadline. Erasmus would have called him a Maecenas; More would have enjoyed his company.

My colleague David Sacks gave the first draft of the manuscript an astonishingly close reading and made dozens of valuable suggestions, especially relating to English government in the sixteenth century. Professors John Headley, Walter Kaiser, and Thomas White also read that enormous, chaotic first draft and commented helpfully on it. My colleagues Terry Shaller and Jay Boggis read chapters of the work and talked about them with me, and my good neighbor in Widener Library, Professor Gwynne B. Evans, read the chapter on More's *History of King Richard III*. While I was working on the book, I read parts of it as lectures at Villanova University, Agnes Scott College,

Gannon University, Thomas More College, Marshall University, the University of Mississippi, the University of Rhode Island, Brown University, and Yale University and received many helpful comments after these presentations.

My conversations about More with Nicholas Barker, G. R. Elton, Stephen Foley, John Guy, the late Davis Harding, J. H. Hexter, Ralph Keen, Lee Cullen Khanna, Dan Kinney, Thomas Lawler, James Lusardi, Louis Martz, Frank Manley, Clarence Miller, Joe Trapp, and the late Warren Wooden have gone on through the years and have been immeasurably valuable in forming my opinion of the man and his times.

The late Richard S. Sylvester, executive editor of *The Yale Edition of the Complete Works of St. Thomas More*, helped me with my dissertation, *Thomas More and the Heretics*, and when I had received my Ph.D. at Yale in 1962, brought me on as an editor of the edition. He was a scholar of unmitigated energy, loyalty, and generosity. He died in 1978, but his legacy lives on in the hearts of those he loved and helped and especially in those of us who came to Thomas More through him and remained with More longer than we dreamed we would.

Yet inevitably anyone who works at any subject as long as I have worked with Thomas More comes to some independent judgments and disagrees with his dearest and most respected friends. I have deliberately avoided making this book a running scholarly debate that would appeal only to specialists in the field. But it is worth saying that I take a minority view of many issues. I think that More and Erasmus were profoundly different and that their famous friendship was not nearly so close as modern liberal Catholics yearn for it to have been. I also believe that the religious revolution of the sixteenth century involved much more than conflicting interpretations of how people might win eternal salvation. I think it arose partly out of a profound skepticism about Christianity itself and that many people who battled and burned each other over dogma were fighting away a horrendous doubt that God ruled in His creation.

There are many other places in this book where I have disagreed with my friends, and no one should read my appreciation of them as their certification of my arguments.

My secretary, Amelie Ratliff, helped much in the preparation of the final manuscript, and by her cheerful, efficient magic regularly reduced tornados in our office to zephyrs and gave me time to write.

To others, mercifully uninterested in Thomas More, I owe perhaps my most profound debts. My wife refused to let Thomas More make our house a mortuary during these past years and frequently declared a moratorium on my writing and got me away from it for a while. My three sons remained delightful and delightfully unimpressed. Their attitude was: "The More the merrier"— or perhaps: "The More the Marius." And I gratefully acknowledge the sustaining laughter and good talk of E. T. Wilcox, Burriss Young, Douglas Price, Susan Lewis, Douglas Bryant, Bob Kiely, Kiyo Morimoto, Donald Stone, Donald Fanger, Stephen Williams, and my dear and special friends Jean and David Layzer, and Connie and Ralph Norman. Perhaps I owe my greatest debts to my brother John.

RICHARD MARIUS
Cambridge, Massachusetts
December 21, 1983

INTRODUCTION

BIOGRAPHERS of Thomas More have always praised him and made him an example for their own times. This exemplary mood was set by the first biographical account we have of him, that written by Erasmus of Rotterdam in a letter to young Ulrich von Hutten of Germany in 1519, when More was in the prime of life.

Erasmus makes one negative comment—the observation that although More loved music, he did not have a good singing voice. Otherwise Erasmus gives us a detailed and laudatory description of a paragon a little past forty, a member of the royal council of King Henry VIII, a family man, a devout Christian layman, a scholar, friend, and wit.

His More works hard at affairs of state but has time to read classical literature. He is a paterfamilias—demanding, upright, and gentle. He is a courtier, a man born for friendship and friendly to all. He hates idleness, silly games, gambling, and ostentation. He loves simplicity and virtue. He drinks wine mixed with water and often drinks water alone—although with proper modesty he tries to hide his abstemious ways. His health is good without being robust, his complexion radiant without being ruddy, his hair dark without being black, his eyes blue-gray and speckled, his height neither short nor tall, his body almost perfectly formed.

Erasmus casually passes on the report that More pondered a religious vocation but burned to marry and so decided to become a good husband rather than a bad priest. He also relates some details about the composition of *Utopia*,

More's most famous work, and makes the guarded comment that its style is uneven because More wrote the first part some time after the second.

It is altogether a careful portrait of a vigorous man living well in the world of secular affairs—the world Erasmus thought was the best stage for good Christians. He tells us that More especially liked eggs—a detail about the simple pleasures of the body that would never have appeared in the ethereal lives of the medieval saints who, in popular conception, lived only to be holy and lived on as little as they could, eating the coarsest food possible. Erasmus took the Christian doctrine of creation seriously; he believed that God had made the whole world and not merely the churchly part of it and that by living justly within that world, men and women served their creator better than any monk could do in the isolated cloister.

Erasmus wrote again about More in later years in other letters, usually with extravagant praise. He sent the painter Hans Holbein over to England to be introduced to English high society by More. More started Holbein off by having him paint the More family; so indirectly at least it is to Erasmus that we owe the stunning portrait that is on the cover of this book and most books about More. Obviously Erasmus hoped that people would think highly of him because he enjoyed the friendship of an important man like Thomas More. There was always something self-serving in Erasmus's flattery, and he and More were far from being intimate. But the details he presents about More are worthy of scrutiny, and at heart his admiration of the Englishman was sincere.

A few others wrote about More while he lived, but it was his death that made his life truly important and called forth the biographies that formed an enduring image of the man in English history. The publicists of Henry VIII came swiftly to press with justifications for More's execution. Devout, orthodox, enraged Catholics—some who had never seen More in the flesh—rushed into print defenses of his sanctity, defenses intended to blacken the reputation of Henry VIII before the public and posterity. The consequence was the creation of much ambiguity about More in the public mind for the first twenty years after his death.

In 1553 Mary Tudor, daughter of Henry VIII and his rejected first wife, Catherine of Aragon, came to the throne of England bent on returning her nation to the embrace of the Catholic Church from which her father had torn it. More, the most eminent martyr for the old faith, became an object of intense interest and admiration. In 1557, the year before Mary died, More's nephew William Rastell published the great folio edition of More's English works. Dominating this huge work were More's angry religious polemics that tried to answer every attack the Protestant heretics made against the Catholic Church while annihilating the heretics themselves in an acid flood of vituperation. For the purposes of Mary and those around her who shared her vision of an England restored to the ancient church, no book could have better served than this one, done by a believer faithful unto death.

Some 157 copies of this beautiful book survive today in libraries in Europe and America. John Foxe, who in 1563 published the first edition of his *Acts and Monuments of the Martyrs* to show Elizabethan Englishmen the horrors of popery, said that in his time the works of More still did much damage— a hint of their continuing influence. But we look in vain for substantial literary proof that people read More's polemics for long. People did read *Utopia,* and they read More's *History of King Richard III,* which was incorporated almost verbatim into Edward Hall's great *Chronicle* of English history that first appeared in 1548 and was subsequently plagiarized by other chroniclers until Shakespeare made a historical play of it. But the polemical works fell into almost total oblivion.

That More's own life did not suffer a similar fate is largely to the credit of his adoring son-in-law William Roper, who married More's eldest and most beloved child, Margaret, in 1521. About 1557 Roper wrote the splendid short biography of More that has been the heart of every More biography written in English until now.

Roper had an unpleasant side. He was a litigious, grasping man like a great many others of his day. He had some kind of falling-out with his father and was slighted in the elder Roper's will. Son Roper disputed the will until Parliament itself, the supreme court of England, ruled in his favor and gave him a larger share of the estate than his father had intended. After More died, Roper went to court against Dame Alice, More's widow, about some property. At the end of his little biography, he breaks off his moving account of More's life and death to protest with unseemly indignation that the crown and Parliament had robbed him and his wife of property More had tried to transfer to them by putting it in trust. He was for a time, shortly after he married Margaret, a vehement Protestant and wanted to preach the new gospel from Germany. It is not hard to see him as one of the zealots churned up in every tumultuous age, finding in religious conversion a pinnacle from which they may scorn the mob below.

But whatever Roper's character, he loved his father-in-law, and his book is saturated with that devotion. He had lived in More's house for sixteen years. English families commonly sent their sons to live in other households for a time. Roper apparently joined the More family as part of this custom, and in time he married Margaret. She died in 1544. Roper lived the rest of his life without marrying again—apparent testimony to an unusual devotion in an age when women died young and men married often. Roper's More is a saint, although Roper, like Erasmus, is free of the crude miracle-mongering found in conventional saints' legends. He wrote at a time when stories including miracles would not be believed by the educated, and he did not tell them. His aim throughout was to prove that his father-in-law was "a man of singular virtue and of a clear, unspotted conscience." Doubtless he expected More to be canonized by the pope.

Roper's most valuable information came from his personal recollections. More told him many stories, and he witnessed part of More's final ordeal, although he did not attend the trial and execution. The biography takes up fewer than sixty pages in a modern edition; by far the greater part of it considers the last five years of More's life. Roper does not mention *Utopia*.

Roper's More is always calm, always in command of the scene if not of events. Roper claims never to have seen him "in a fume" and gives us a brave, unruffled Christian, doing his duty without wavering and without seeking reward, a Thomas More always doing the right thing merely because it is right, a stoic combining in himself the virtues of devotion, selflessness, sacrifice, and self-control that fifteen hundred years of classical and churchly tradition had held to be supreme among men. Roper's biography is consummate Renaissance art, giving us an ideal man against whom to measure the stature of lesser beings.

But good art is not necessarily good history, and when Roper can be checked, he is often found to be wrong. Sometimes when he cannot be proved in error, we suspect that he has erred because what he tells us is implausible. In his work there is no effort to analyze More, only the desire to prove him above reproach. Roper's is a family history, a literary epitaph designed by one who loved his subject, written for those who also loved him. Such works are devotions, and they seldom show warts and wobblings, but perhaps just because the work shows More in such a mellow and heroic light, it became the most influential thing ever written about him.

So it is ironic that Roper did not mean for this book to be a full-scale biography or even for it to be published. It was rather a sketch, a source to be used for a larger and more comprehensive biography to be written by a family friend, Nicholas Harpsfield. After More's execution in 1535, Harpsfield shared exile on the Continent with other Catholics, including the physician John Clement and his wife, Margaret Giggs, More's ward and adopted daughter and the only member of the family circle to see him die. When Mary came to the throne, Harpsfield and the other Catholic exiles returned to England, where he became archdeacon of Canterbury, closely associated with Reginald Pole, Mary's Archbishop of Canterbury, the leading power under the queen in seeking to bring England back to the papal communion. Harpsfield collected information and documents, including many letters which have since been lost, and Roper wrote down his recollections so that Harpsfield might use them in writing the official biography.

Harpsfield's manuscript was completed in time to be presented as a New Year's gift to Roper in 1557 or 1558. For some reason we do not know, the book was not printed. Mary died in November 1558. Elizabeth came to the throne and led her people into a secularism with Protestant trappings that proved enduring. Harpsfield's book languished in manuscript until it finally saw the dim light of scholarly publication in 1932. (Roper's *Life* was first printed in 1626.)

Thus centuries of delay kept a large audience from enjoying a brilliant example of Renaissance historiography. Harpsfield had read and absorbed Roper, and he incorporated Roper's work verbatim when it was fitting. He knew many people who had known More, and he used their recollections along with Roper's. He had read More's works and what he could find already written about More. The result is a big book that feels reliable, especially since in several places Harpsfield gently corrects Roper's errors.

But Harpsfield shared Roper's purpose—to prove that More had been a saint. The same is true of the third sixteenth-century biography worthy of mention, that done in Latin by Thomas Stapleton in 1588 and the only one of the three to be published in that century. Stapleton, born in 1535, the year of More's death, found refuge from Elizabeth's Protestantism by fleeing with other Catholics to Douai in Burgundy, then under the rule of the Spanish Hapsburgs. He wrote voluminously against the Protestants under the common assumption of the time that polemical pages were like soldiers and that the side that produced the greater number would win the war.

His life of Thomas More was part of a book he named *Three Thomases*. The other two were Thomas the apostle and Thomas Becket, the English Archbishop of Canterbury murdered by henchmen of Henry II in 1170. So, like Roper and Harpsfield, Stapleton made a plea for More to be canonized; throughout the book we find comparisons of More and various saints, and Stapleton clearly believed that More belonged in their company.

Stapleton used Roper, but the plan of his book is his own. He had many sources, including some of More's letters. Several of these he preserved in full within his text, perhaps translating them from More's English into Latin. Like Harpsfield, he incorporated anecdotes of friends who remembered More, anecdotes which had lost nothing in years and years of telling. Stapleton loved a good story, and at times, we suspect, he tells a tale too well.

Stapleton and Harpsfield are both valuable sources. They were clerics, trained in the Scholastic method, accustomed to quoting their authorities and to making conclusions agree with the evidence. It is easy to forget how important the Scholastics were to the development of the Western mind, especially since moderns have absorbed the contempt for the Scholastic theologians that burns in the writing of many famous Renaissance figures. Erasmus detested them for their theological arguments, and More wrote once that the *Sentences* of Peter the Lombard—one of the first Scholastics of the twelfth century— was like a Trojan horse from which vain questions came forth to vex Christendom. The Scholastics conceived their task to be to reconcile reason and faith and to free Christian dogma from contradictions that might cause doubt about the validity of the Christian religion. They sought truth by posing questions, and some of their theological questions seemed ridiculous or even blasphemous to the ordinary run of humankind.

But in their favor it may be said that the Scholastics believed that human reason was a friend to the Christian faith. They exalted God, but they also exalted the human mind, and they wanted to arrive at truth by a systematic exploration of whatever data they could find. Their questions might at times have been extreme, even foolish, but they were hardly as extreme as the superstitious excesses of the gullible popular piety. Like More and Erasmus and other devotees of the new learning of the Renaissance, the Scholastics believed in quotation, in the authority of learned men who had written previously on a subject, and in trying to make disparate chunks of evidence agree with one another. In the thirteenth century, Thomas Aquinas did his best to assemble every contrary argument to every proposition he espoused, tried to treat those arguments fairly, and tried to reconcile the contradictions. Though they themselves seldom wrote history, their tools were essential to writing history, the rescue of the past from legend, fancy, and oblivion, and historians like Harpsfield and Stapleton demonstrate an important use of Scholastic mental equipment in their building of biography. Compared to the wildly supernatural medieval saints' stories, their biographies of More are down-to-earth, believable, and judicious. They are much better sources than Roper for those parts of More's life that Roper did not observe.

The Spanish Armada lost its battle with the weather in the same year that Stapleton's book appeared. Mysteriously enough, the pope did not canonize More, although a couple of later and unreliable biographies kept up the effort to prove that he was a saint.

More's story fell into the hands of Protestant writers, who despite their willingness to throw him an occasional good word, usually viewed him as one who started on the road to reform and then turned back. Still, he was never forgotten, and his reputation was never entirely black among the English people. They admired his courage but usually abhorred his cause. He stood on the losing side of the great struggle for English nationhood, and the English people have been notoriously uninterested in the virtues of the defeated.

In the nineteenth century, the English religious mood changed. From the time of the Romantics at the beginning of the century, England was awash in the euphoric love for the medieval. Ivanhoe had been a Catholic, after all, and so had the Black Prince, Edward III, King Arthur, and the Knights of the Round Table. The Catholic Church seemed to belong in a pre-industrial, peaceful England without the misery and grime of the age of slums and factories. In time the Oxford Movement and the conversion of John Henry Newman to Rome gave the Catholic Church a renewed place in the realm, and the bleak, bloody world portrayed by Charles Darwin helped drive many yearning and frightened souls into the arms of a venerable tradition that promised certainty and buried doubt in liturgy and general indignation against modernity.

In this warm, moist climate of sentiment, interest in Thomas More flowered again. In 1867 Frederick Seebohm published his lively book, *The Oxford Reformers,* in which John Colet, who had been dean of St. Paul's, and Erasmus and More all received generous adulation. Seebohm made it seem that these men were in perfect accord and that they would have been perfectly at home in the genteel English drawing rooms of Victorian England. It was perhaps just this fault that made his work so popular. He presented historical figures as if they belonged in the present. However, his measured style was an antidote to the excessive Romantic mythmaking that rendered history glorious but unreal; Seebohm was one of those historians who, like Ranke in Germany and Burckhardt in Switzerland, tried to make history plausible while keeping it lively.

In 1886 Pope Leo XIII beatified More—a step that in modern times normally precedes canonization. Then in 1891, the first and best of the modern biographies appeared, written by T. E. Bridgett, an English priest, born to a dissenting family but inspired by Newman and converted to the Catholic Church. Like most converts, he felt himself required to convert others, and he wrote several books intended to banish the legend of an evil Catholicism and to make the ancient church understandable and desirable to the generality of educated Englishmen. Among them was a biography of More's fellow martyr Bishop John Fisher of Rochester. Bridgett laboriously gathered More's works, and he read everything he could about More, including many of the manuscripts buried in the vaults of the Public Record Office in Chancery Lane. He loved theology, and he understood More's religious works and conveyed their broad outline to his readers—though he saw them through the warped lens of the First Vatican Council and the Council of Trent, which took place long after More died.

Bridgett's aim, like that of all the other More biographers, was to prove that More had been a saint. He also tried his best to be accurate. He took at face value Roper's estimate of More's character, and he never asked profound questions; but without Bridgett's work the course of More studies as they have since developed would have been retarded. He tried to tell a complete story, to put More's life together from all the sources he could gather, and he saw the importance of all More's works, even the religious ones that have so little appeal to moderns. He was the first modern scholar to see how varied More's life was and how that variety makes him much more interesting as a figure caught between the Middle Ages and the Renaissance.

In 1935, four hundred years after his martyrdom, More was finally canonized by Pope Pius XI. In that same year—with Hitler in power in Germany,

Mussolini in Italy, and Stalin in Russia—Professor R. W. Chambers of the University of London brought out the biography that has become the standard work. Chambers wrote in an irenic spirit about a Thomas More who gave his life rather than submit to a tyrant. Since Chambers himself was not Catholic, he felt himself liberated from the dogmatic religious preoccupations that had colored attitudes about More for many centuries. He wrote in the mood of liberal English schoolmasters who held all religions to be good as long as one did not become excessively serious about any of them. He began by comparing More to Socrates and proceeded in an effort to prove that More represented the best in English medieval life. Chambers had read everything, it seems, that had been written about More from the sixteenth century on, and he attacked all the attacks and defended all the defenses.

Finally this cloying, unrelenting, often unthinking defense of More in every particular is irksome. Chambers, above religious dogma himself, wrote his entire book without giving any serious consideration to More's theology, his hatred of heretics, and his fear of hell. At times, as when Chambers justifies his snow-white estimate of More's character by quoting the praise of Jonathan Swift, he is simply silly. His unbearably chatty style condescends to serious readers, and those who approach Chambers's book today are likely to come to pray and stay to mock.

Since Chambers's times, several have tried their hands at More biography; the best has been the work of E. E. Reynolds, who in 1968 published *The Field Is Won*. Reynolds took advantage of the flourishing of More studies since Chambers, and he did a competent job of putting together a solid, readable book that combines enormous admiration for More with simple common sense. His account is pedestrian; he knew More's works but did not use them much, and he is long on simple narration and short on interpretation.

The present book tries to find the More of history buried under the pyramid of praise heaped over his name in recent times. It is an effort to discover the living being behind the glorified mummy wrapped in gold and embalmed with adulation that has become a museum piece rather than a man. It has been made possible by the steady progression of great blue volumes in *The Yale Edition of the Complete Works of St. Thomas More*, published by Yale University Press, and with which the present author has been associated almost since the inception of this enormous project in 1958. It is the first full-length biography to try to take into account what all of More's works may tell us about all of his life.

Biographers are always hooked on a dilemma. On the one hand, biography is possible only if we assume that nearly all people share many human qualities identifiable in all ages—pride, love, ambition, generosity, hypocrisy, greed, whatever. On the other, biography is worthwhile only when we can locate those peculiar qualities that set someone off from the masses and make him worthy of special attention. To emphasize too much the common qualities may isolate an individual from his own time and place and make him unreal; to stress too much the peculiar qualities may make him so remote that we lose interest in him quickly.

More shared many common qualities. He appreciated wit in others and was wonderfully witty himself. We can still laugh with him. He loved the sensuous life, and he had a vivid imagination about the physical world, a power of observation that made him notice telling details. He was the greatest English storyteller between Chaucer and Shakespeare. His delight in the particular and in the observation of human traits would have made him a fine novelist had he lived later, when novels replaced theology in ordering the moral universe. Yet sometimes his fear of death and hell was so powerful that his life became a prison from which he longed to escape, and he believed that worldly pleasures were traps to ensnare his soul. Shut up in the Tower of London, waiting for death, he made a striking metaphor of God our jailer who keeps us locked in "this whole broad prison the world." Then he lamented that he had enjoyed the world as much as he had.

He was ambitious, but he did not want people to know that he was. He loved the praise of the crowd and worked hard to create a public image of himself as a man who took no care for what people thought of him. Yet he hated criticism and responded furiously whenever attacked. He was gregarious, but he felt a contrary pull to solitude, loving isolation and serenity, and he never overcame his early longing for the unambitious, remote life of the cloistered monk he might have been, the monk he always thought he should have been. He worked hard to seem humble. But he always wanted to be somebody, and he always tried to make the public imagine that high position had been thrust upon him only because great and wise men insisted that his talents were too large to be hidden. Few people have enjoyed greater success in advertising their humility.

He seemed to fight a wearing battle to resolve the conflict between powerful sexual desire and the guilty conviction of his conscience that sexuality was tainted and often damnable and that people who married were never as pure as those who abstained. (It is remarkable to note that the three important modern biographers of More have all been unmarried Englishmen and that the worrisome sexuality of their subject is hardly reflected in their pages.) He was a Renaissance man, acquainted with a wide variety of knowledge, but he believed that a few great ideas gave meaning to life. They happened to be thoroughly medieval ideas, and when they were threatened, he could and did descend into deceit, hatred, and murderous rage—as most of us can and do when the very ground of our being is threatened and when we are not sure of ourselves. He could be a devoted and generous friend; he could also be an ugly and implacable enemy.

At the end—like all of us who live long enough—he had to decide whether the convictions he had always professed had been worthwhile or whether his earlier days—the books he had written, the ideals he had espoused, and the choices he had made—had all been sound and fury. He had to meet death in a way harmonious with his own best estimate of what his life had been, as we all must do if we are to die at peace with ourselves. His own act of self-validation turned out to be a martyrdom that he did his best to avoid but that he had to accept if he was to see any coherence between the course of his life and its end. As with all martyrs who are not insane, it may be argued that he died not for what he believed but for what he wanted to believe.

These inner conflicts are not uncommon in any age, and these and other qualities in More's life come on us at times with what Edmund Wilson called "the shock of recognition," so that, like the characters in a good novel, Thomas More seems suddenly contemporary, somebody we know or somebody we have known. Biographers love those qualities that bind a man in one age to men in all the ages, for they help in the belief that to study the life of a great figure in the past is to learn something important about our own lives in the present. Good biography can never be simple entertainment; the resonances we feel as we strum the lyre of the past must carry some wisdom—perhaps indefinable —that we crave in our own chaotic world.

But obviously biographies are about individuals living in a certain time and a certain place. Thomas More lived some 21,000 days between 1478 and 1535, a confused and threatening epoch of prodigious change when nothing seemed certain and no one could make clear sense of experience. The major substance of this book is about the More who lived in that time.

It was the time when the Renaissance was first making an impression in England. The Renaissance stream, bearing its great cargo of classical culture from Greek and Roman antiquity, was pouring heavily into the Middle Ages and changing forever the course of Western civilization. The Renaissance did not obliterate the Middle Ages, as an earlier generation of cultural historians supposed. Rather the mingling of waters from these different sources produced a new stream combining both, and in the running together produced danger-ous eddies, lethal whirlpools, and gargantuan crosscurrents. More was swept along in the stream, thrilling at times to its progress, carried under at last by its contradictions.

For those who know More's life best, the most puzzling thing about him is that he did not become a priest or perhaps a monk, devoting all his days to the quest for salvation. The testimony of Erasmus, seconded by Roper and confirmed by the rigorous spirit of his voluminous and vehement religious works, makes it clear that More considered a religious vocation and turned back. He gave it up because he wanted a wife.

In his letter to Hutten, Erasmus praised More for this choice of matrimony over priesthood. Erasmus did not think much of priests, and he never supposed that virginity carried any special virtue. Most scholars of More's life have passed over the matter with equal ease, and few have contemplated the deep inner conflict that More's decision cost him, the burden of guilt that a man of his own uncompromising temperament felt at bowing to the demands of the flesh. I believe it was the ruling drama of his life. More always thought he should have been a monk or a priest, and his character was formed by his decision to take a wife, which in turn inexorably drove him to assume a public career. His profuse public modesty becomes annoying to a habitual reader of his works, but we may believe that his frequent assertions that publication or high office was thrust upon him represented something he wanted to believe about himself. He might have chosen the solitary religious life had not over-powering forces kept him from doing so. We feel less guilty when we can suppose that we have no choice.

His glory has always been the outward serenity and courage with which he faced death. Had he not died so nobly, we would not remember him so well. His outward tranquillity was the reflection of a curious inner detachment. He was in the world, a public man, driven by an ambition that would justify the decision he had made, driven also by the need to provide a good living for the large household that marriage had given him. But always he struggled for assurance that he might escape the judgment of God for his impurity of soul, and this inner battle made all the external things a little less important. He never had the driving interest or genius in administration that marked Thomas Wolsey, his predecessor as Lord Chancellor, or Thomas Cromwell, who in More's tenure of office became the real power behind the throne of Henry VIII. The best administrators are able to throw themselves single-mindedly into the task of managing things, and More could never be single-minded about governance and power. He was distracted by concern for his own soul and with a darkness that always threatened to consume him. In some remark-able ways he resembled his older contemporary Leonardo da Vinci—brooding, otherworldly, sensual, preoccupied with too many tasks and beset by his inabil-ity to finish great works, unable to make a clear distinction sometimes between ideal and fantasy, a man who made a much stronger impress on history by the power of his imagination and by the force of his character than by the strength of his practical accomplishments.

He was a melancholy man as well as a witty one—by no means a contra-diction, for both attributes were products of his attitude toward the world. Humor often arises from a certain detachment from everyday affairs, because the humorous person has built an ideal world in his mind that makes the real world with all its pomp and circumstance and posturings a bit absurd. Mel-ancholy is the common sense of those who know that no matter what tri-umphs the real world of time and place may bring, they are never quite enough to satisfy the deepest longings of hearts that reach impossibly for perfection.

For More the insufficiency and the detachment worked together to create the irony that became the blade of his wit—a wit that makes it difficult for a biographer, who cannot always tell when More speaks seriously and when not. His mind turned not only to ironic utterance but also to the recognition of irony in events; his works are filled with tales of those who said and did things without recognizing a meaning to their words and deeds that others could see and ponder. More's own life was beset by ironies that a man of his deep introspection saw well enough. At the end, even his death was irony—he a layman offering his head in witness to the unity of the English church with all Christendom, a unity quickly forsaken by all the English bishops save one, his fellow martyr John Fisher.

He was a complex, haunted, and not altogether admirable man. We may assume that he endured a lifelong inner torment because of the contradictions in his character and his experience. His fury at the Protestant heretics— particularly at their teaching, followed quickly by practice, that priests and nuns could marry—has a touch of hysteria about it, and although we may exonerate him from old charges that he tied heretics to a tree in his yard at Chelsea and beat them, he was if anything inclined to an even greater savagery against them, for he cried for them to be burned alive, and he rejoiced when some of them went to the fire. This fury was not a bizarre lapse in an otherwise noble character; it was almost the essence of the man.

Yet he seduces biographers. We all end by liking him. That in itself is one of his mysteries. The present book is yet another effort to explore that character and to fit the disparate pieces together to provide a coherent picture of the man and his times. I have never supposed that the tantalizing gaps in the evidence and the general ambiguity of the sources can be so mended that any biographer may write a book about Thomas More that will provide agreement in every particular. Nor has my purpose been to include every detail known about More. The best biographers try to take into account the various kinds of evidence and to shape a portrait that arises from a discerned unity, although inconsistencies must remain. The evidence has not led me to suppose that I can shape a Thomas More without spot or wrinkle or one who fits the image that most earlier students have cast of him. But it has made me suppose that I can provide readers with a man of flesh and blood and mind, able to take a place in his real world and in ours.

THOMAS   MORE

1

THE BEGINNINGS

THOMAS MORE was born early in the morning of February 7, 1478, in the city of London, where he would spend his life and meet his death.

He was always a Londoner, a city man to the marrow of his bones, and he neither liked nor understood rural life and rural ways. We have a letter from him written about 1504 to his older friend John Colet, dean of St. Paul's Cathedral. Colet is in the country. More thinks he is wise to be there. The city is a place of wickedness, says young More. No matter where you go, you find feigned love and the honey poison of flatterers, and there are always hatred, quarrels, and the din of the market. "Wherever you turn your eyes, what else will you see but confectioners, fishmongers, butchers, cooks, poulterers, fisherman, fowlers, who supply the materials for gluttony and the world and the world's lord, the devil? Houses block out light and hide us from the heavens."

But in the country, young More says, Colet can live among simple people who do not know the deceits of the city. Out there "wherever you cast your eyes, the smiling face of the earth greets you, the sweet fresh air invigorates you, the very sight of the heavens charms you. There you see nothing but the generous gifts of nature and the traces of our primeval innocence."

Despite these lugubrious conceits, More is not announcing his flight from the city; he is instead begging Colet to return to it. We have here a youthful effusion in the bucolic tradition of the later Middle Ages in which every city writer felt himself obliged to praise the pure simplicity and peace of the countryside—where in fact misery abounded and order was kept only by the stern, often cruel force of the landed nobility and the laws of the king. The bucolic ideal itself was rooted in ancient monastic piety, which More knew and revered, a piety that valued retreat into the country from the wicked city, and we find St. Basil writing a letter in the fourth century that might have been a model for this studied production of More's pen.

More was to spend the first forty-five years of his life near the center of London. He loved the city and served it well, and London formed his mind and his heart.

His London would have seemed unbearably small and dirty to us. Our first large artistic representation of the city—a painting by a Flemish artist—dates from 1549, just over a decade after More died, and we may suppose that the city we see from the brush of the artist is pretty much the London More knew. St. Paul's Cathedral with its square Gothic tower stands atop Ludgate Hill at the place where Christopher Wren's high-domed St. Paul's stands today. But in the middle distance fields roll down to the old London wall, and a brisk walker might have traversed the distance between the cathedral and the open country in less than a half hour. Londoners strolled in the green fields on Sundays in good weather to "recreate themselves," as John Stow, a later chronicler, said; they would have had no trouble in getting home to supper.

Except for the broad Strand, the streets are narrow, irregular, and sometimes overhung with the timbered-and-plastered upper floors of bulky houses. The streets are unpaved, and we may suppose that they became stinking bogs in the steady rains of the London winter. From Westminster to the Tower, the town reclines along the wide river Thames, alive with boats and ships and spanned by London Bridge on its arches of stone, crossing into the village of Southwark, where Chaucer's pilgrims began their journey to Canterbury almost a century before More came into the world. The shops of London Bridge hang precariously over the busy river.

About 40,000 souls lived within the city, and since they dwelled so close together, citizens knew each other, and the city as a whole possessed a communal spirit that bound the populace together—especially its ruling classes. Later on More in his *Utopia* depicted an ideal commonwealth where cities were extended families. Although we should not idealize his London, we may say that his Utopia came from his own ideal of what London might be.

The same names crop up again and again in the records of the time. The great holidays were civic affairs with processions and banquets in the streets and bonfires at night in the fields beyond. Executions at Tyburn were intended to enlighten the community, and for many years a bouquet of flowers was customarily given to felons marched through the streets to the gallows near the present Marble Arch as if to signify the gratitude of the city for the edifying spectacle in which the condemned were about to play the leading part. Crowds gathered eagerly to view the remarkable sight of violent judicial death, and how men died was talked about in the town. The occasional fires that devastated the wooden city were communal calamities and provoked communal measures to prevent them, communal action to rebuild when they had burned themselves out.

London was ruled by a merchant aristocracy that fluctuated with the generations. Wealth and reputation—not blood and land—were the keys of entry into this ruling class, although once within, prosperous and yet insecure burghers did their best to act like aristocrats, to get themselves land and titles, and to trace out their genealogies. When wealth departed, so did position. A merchant might go into business with as little as ten pounds for capital, and he might become rich in a couple of decades. His children after him might live like lords, and both he and they could expect to serve as aldermen and perhaps even as mayors of the city. Then something—bankruptcy, bad luck, or the death of the family in the main line—would overtake aspiration, and the family would vanish. The same wheel of fortune spun for the nobility; it is rare to be able to trace any family more than three generations.

So it is not surprising that we lose track of More's family swiftly once we go back before his father. His grandfather seems to have been a baker named William More. When William died, he left a claim of eighty-seven pounds against the Earl of Northumberland. An artisan could live on ten pounds a year, and nearly three centuries afterwards an Irish painter assured young Samuel Johnson that one could live in London on thirty pounds a year—and this after a whopping inflation in the sixteenth century. To be owed eighty-seven pounds in the fifteenth century and by an earl, no less, was a sign of place in the world.

The profession of baker was honorable without being distinguished. No baker became mayor of London during the fifteenth century. Drapers and mercers, fishmongers and even skinners achieved this high dignity with mechanical regularity and served out their one-year terms in the pomp and (probably) the pomposity the office required. These were wealthy men, belonging to the great livery companies that controlled politics in the city; bakers were of an indefinably lower order. When we find them in the records, it is usually because they were locked in the public stocks for selling at the standard price bread of less than the standard weight. They were not incorporated until 1509, meaning that Londoners throughout the Middle Ages saw them as a socially inferior class. Even in the nineteenth century, Dickens has Herbert say to Pip in *Great Expectations*, "I don't know why it should be a crack thing to be a brewer, but it is indisputable that while you cannot possibly be genteel and bake, you may be as genteel as never was and brew. You see it every day."

The example of William More shows that bakers could become prosperous. They had natural ties with the brewers; both dealt in grain. A prosperous baker might provide an attractive match for the daughter of a brewer. However it was, William More the baker came into contact with John Joye, brewer, and married Joye's daughter Johanna. John More, Thomas's father, was the eldest child of this union.

William died in 1467 when John was only sixteen. Evidence is that John's grandmother on his mother's side was a strong woman, resolved to see that things turned out well. She married again after her first husband died, and she took a hand in John's affairs when he was too young to take charge of them himself. He was put to the study of law. It may be to her resolution that John More owed the education and the direction that got him his remarkable career.

For many families in trade, the law offered a ladder that allowed sons to climb in the world. Society was becoming ever more complicated, and so were the laws that held it together. A vigorous and able young lawyer might expect to keep company with the great and be seen by the many. The More family, bourgeois by this time and having attained something, was resolved to have more. It depended for its place in the world on its talents. A son sent to the law might achieve great things for the family as a whole; at least his success might reflect on those who had made it possible. So John More went to the law—as did Thomas Wolsey, his countryman and contemporary, and Martin Luther in Germany, and countless others.

John More grew up during the last years of Henry VI. Henry was either insane or feebleminded—at this remove it is difficult to say which; but he was incapacitated enough to require a regent to direct the kingdom. Richard, Duke of York, first claimed this right, tracing royal descent from Edmund, Duke of York and fourth son of Edward III, and before long claimed the throne himself. Thus began thirty years of the desultory civil war that Sir Walter Scott was to name "The Wars of the Roses."

Richard was not popular among the nobles, and when he died in battle at Wakefield in 1460, few mourned his passing. His eldest son, Edward, picked up the claim to the throne and asserted it with unquenchable vigor. Edward was young, vigorous, handsome, and brave. His most obvious sins—gluttony and fornication—were those the English have always found easy to forgive in their kings, and he had a great talent for advertising himself. After much toil, tribulation, exile, and danger, he became king as Edward IV, and by 1471 he was firmly on the throne.

Somehow through all this confusion, John More rose in the world. He won the favor of Edward IV and with it a coat of arms giving him official status as a gentleman. When he died in 1530 at the age of seventy-nine—a marvel of old age in the century when Montaigne said that most men died before they were thirty-five—he left a bequest to have masses sung for Edward's soul. He did not mention Henry VII or Henry VIII in this charity. John More felt some bond of affection and gratitude to Edward, although the reason remains a mystery.

Edward was king when John More married Agnes Graunger, the daughter of Sir Thomas Graunger, in 1474. Graunger was also a lawyer, a man of enough substance to be elected sheriff of London in November 1503. John immediately began to produce a family, and he kept careful memoranda of the births of his children, writing them down in the blank leaves at the back of a manuscript copy of Geoffrey of Monmouth's *History of the Kings of Britain* —a book that seemingly had no appeal to his son since it was filled with tales of mythological chivalry of a sort that Thomas More supposedly scorned.

The first child was Johanna, born in March 1475. Next was Thomas, born apparently in 1478. The birthdate is debatable because John More wrote a memorandum saying that "on the Friday next after the Feast of the Purification of the Blessed Virgin Mary, between two and three in the morning, was born Thomas More, son of John More, gentleman, in the seventeenth year of King Edward, the Fourth after the Conquest of England." Later he scribbled the additional information: "to wit, the seventh day of February." The seventeenth year of King Edward IV ended on June 28, 1478, but in 1478, February 7 fell on Saturday. What does John More's discrepancy mean? Probably only that like most people he considered a new day as beginning at dawn and not at midnight and that when he wrote his original record he thought of his son as being born on Friday night. Later, in correcting himself, he added the date February 7, in the realization that his son had been born after midnight. In general, the evidence seems to stand for a date of 1478, but the issue now and then occasions debate.

Thomas was probably named for both Thomas Graunger and Thomas Becket, but it is hard to say, since Thomas was by far the most popular name in England at the time. Next was Agatha, born in January 1479; she apparently died young. Thomas's younger brother John was born in June 1480 and lived long enough to be mentioned as a scribe by Erasmus in 1511. We find no mention of him after that. In September 1481, a brother Edward was born and probably died soon after. A sister Elizabeth was the last child in the family, born in 1482. She eventually married John Rastell, a bizarre and unstable man, converted to Protestantism by John Frith, one of Thomas More's adversaries in religion. Rastell seems to have died in prison, poverty-stricken, in 1536, leaving only a house to Elizabeth. It was his son William Rastell, always a loyal Catholic, who wrote a biography of Thomas More (preserved in fragments) and performed the monumental service of printing the great 1557 folio edition of More's English works.

Johanna and Elizabeth were still alive when John More made his will in 1527. Thomas seems to have kept close ties with them throughout his life, although any correspondence between him and them has been lost. In 1519 he mentioned in a letter that he had made a visit to Coventry to visit his sister. We may presume that this was Johanna, but we cannot be sure. We may suppose that such a journey, requiring a fair amount of effort, illustrates the interest More had in keeping his family ties.

Agnes More seems to have made little impression on her famous son though she probably lived on until 1499, if a funeral monument transcribed by the English antiquary John Weever in 1631 did indeed belong to her. He never mentioned her in any of his surviving works. Although it was customary to name daughters after women in the father's family, More did not name a daughter for his mother, and he does not have much to say about mothers in any of his works except when he speaks again and again of the Catholic Church as mother of all the faithful.

John More was another matter. Thomas adored him. In the fashion of the times, Thomas composed an epitaph for himself still visible in Chelsea Old Church, where More prepared a family tomb, one that his bones were not destined to occupy. Here he calls his father "civil, gentle, innocent, meek, merciful, just, and pure." The joining of adjectives suggests an intense feeling, and all More's reports of his father confirm that sentiment.

John More told funny stories, and Thomas repeated them—a son doing honor to a beloved father by telling his tales after him. John More made fun of women. He told the story of the ignorant and prejudiced female who learned to her horror that the Virgin Mary had been a Jew. "So help me God!" she cried. "I shall love her the less for that as long as I live."

Embedded in this story is a certain gentleness toward Jews, rare for the age. John More thought people could be absurd in their hatreds, and the wit of his little tale turns not against the Jews but against a silly woman unable to imagine that Jews could be the source of anything good, even the Savior. So perhaps it is to him that we owe the startling fact that we find no hostile remark or metaphor about contemporary Jews in all the works of Thomas More. True, the Jews had been expelled from England years before, and in More's time their synagogue, which had been the home of one of London's mayors for a while, was falling into decay. Englishmen did not often see Jews and may not have been much aware of them. Still, proverbial utterances castigating the Jews abounded: "As false as any Jew." "It would make a Jew repent." "As vile as a Jew." "For pity had he no more than a Jew." And "Worse than a Jew." Shakespeare's Shylock demonstrates that Englishmen could still hate Jews in the barbarous style of most Christians of the time; it happened that Thomas More did not.

Like his father, Thomas usually saw women as foolish creatures and expected little of them. Thomas is remembered for his deep affection for Margaret, his eldest child, and in an age when most men saw little reason for educating women, he procured tutors for his daughters and had them instructed in classical languages and wisdom. Fatherly affection aside, he was always ready to mock women, and his tales of female foolishness quickly become tedious to the modern ear. The only time he was ever likely to praise a woman was when he put her in contrast to a man whose vices and ignorance were notorious. Then, by bringing a woman forward as a virtuous example, fictional or real, he made the man's wickedness all the more striking. "Even a woman," he seemed to be saying, "is better than this ignorant or evil man."

John More was much the same, having little good to say of wives and women in general. He said that getting married was like putting a hand into a sack of snakes and eels, seven snakes to the eel, and trying to draw the eel out without looking. Even considering the delicacy of eels to the English palate, we do not find the image comforting. He also said that there was only one wicked wife in the world and that every man knows she is his own.

But John More put his hand into the sack four times, and his last wife survived son Thomas by several years. John More's motives were probably not sentimental. After Agnes, his wives were widows who evidently had substantial possessions. He must have seen marriage as a business proposition as well as a bodily comfort. At least he did not let love run away with his head and make him marry a woman without purse or property. That he had no children by any wife except Agnes must mean that these women were close to the end of the childbearing years when he married them; perhaps they were even older.

John More was devout enough for a lawyer. His will shows his piety to have been conventional and sincere. He provided, in essence, two scholarships, one for a student in divinity at Oxford and another for such a student at Cambridge. Each man, "being a good and virtuous scholar" and also being a priest, was to receive five pounds a year for seven years for praying for John More's soul and for the souls of various friends and relatives, including, as we have noted, Edward IV. He wanted his funeral made with an eye to cost and "not too pompously performed." His executors were to give forty pounds in charity to the poor, to maids who had no dowries, to prisoners, and to his poor kinfolk. He left forty pounds for the repair of a stretch of highway near the town of North Mimms, where the More family held some land. "Also I will that the sum of forty marks which I received of Richard Clowdisley be spent also in making and mending of the said way for the soul of me and the same Richard."

A mark was about thirteen shillings; we do not know what this sum from Richard Clowdisley represented—perhaps repayment of a debt—and we do not know what relation Clowdisley had to the highway near North Mimms. But it is striking that John More regarded repairs to the highway as a help to his soul, a mingling of civic charity and private salvation that may throw some light on Thomas More's *Utopia* with its teaching that citizens were virtuous when they supported the community life and with its monks who worked on bridges and roads.

John More also left money for a yearly obit, a mass said for his soul, to be kept for him in the church of St. Lawrence Jewry for ten years after his death, and he expressed the wish that the four orders of friars say a dirge, a requiem mass, and thirty other masses for the repose of his soul. He obviously did not share the contempt for friars that would shortly sweep them out of England.

Still, John More's piety had a skeptical side. He could laugh at the credulity of the mob and the deceits of superstition. One of his best-remembered tales was of a false miracle exposed by good Duke Humphrey of Gloucester, uncle to and briefly regent for Henry VI.

Henry's madness took the form of an obsessive religiosity. He lived like a monk, often dressing in a monk's cowl. When his wife presented him with a son, the future Prince Edward, destined to be butchered at Tewkesbury, he is said to have declared that the child must have been conceived by the Holy Ghost. (Others supposed a more earthly paternity!) He loved to go on pilgrimages to shrines where the bones and other relics of saints were preserved like talismans for the good of the faithful. His favorite shrine was St. Albans in the rolling green hills just north of London where lay the bones of England's earliest martyr. (The English scorned the claim of Cologne that it possessed the bones of the true St. Albans, who, the Germans said, was not an English martyr at all.)

In the midst of the festivities of a royal visit, a beggar, claiming to have been born blind, suddenly announced that he could see, his vision restored by the relics of the saint. The bells of the churches rang in celebration of the miracle. A *Te Deum* was sung in the grand old church that still houses the decaying wooden tomb of Duke Humphrey himself.

The duke, in charge of the royal progress, summoned the beggar. Was he really blind from birth? Indeed he was, said the beggar. His wife, tramping through the countryside with her husband, solemnly affirmed the lie. (Whether she was there or not, John More could hardly spin a yarn without including a deceitful woman.) Duke Humphrey advised him to give all the glory to God. Then, in a deeply studious way, Duke Humphrey peered into the beggar's eyes and seemed to become skeptical. "I believe you very well that you were born blind," he said at last. "For me thinketh you cannot see well yet."

The beggar, suddenly confident of victory, said, "Yes, sir! I thank God and His holy martyr. I can see now as well as any man."

"Then what color is my gown?" said the duke. The beggar told him and did the same for the colors of all the gowns around him. Whereupon Duke Humphrey had him locked in the stocks. For, as Thomas More explained years later, "though he could have seen suddenly by miracle the difference between diverse colors, yet he could not so suddenly tell the names of those colors." The tale is one of John More's stories that lingered on in English life; Shakespeare used it in *Henry VI Part Two*.

So John More loved a laugh, and nearly everyone who commented about Thomas More agreed that he, too, was a man of marvelous wit. The wit annoyed Edward Hall. Said he of More, "For undoubtedly he beside his learning had a great wit, but it was so mingled with taunting and mocking that it seemed to them that best knew him, that he thought nothing to be well spoken except he had ministered some mock in the communication."

Hall knew More, having served in the Parliament of 1529, which More, newly Lord Chancellor, opened, and there may have been a grain of truth in his judgment that More's humor always had a mock to it. Tensions make people prone to laughter; we have a tradition of gallows humor in the West to which More himself contributed. And for a bourgeois family, straining to hold its place against a myriad of threats, imagined and real, laughter was one way to relieve the stresses of life. But the service of humor does not always make it pleasant to others. More's wit could be gentle and whimsical, but it was often sharp. Sometimes it was savage.

John More's legal career succeeded so well that about 1518 he became a judge on the King's Bench, the most distinguished common-law court in the realm below the great court of Parliament. Thomas More—even as Lord Chancellor—never failed in greeting his father to go down on his knees to ask the old man's blessing, a blessing in which the father placed both hands on the son's head, much as in the ritual of ordination. Englishmen took such forms seriously; a father's curse was one of the most terrible punishments anyone could imagine. Age was authority in the sixteenth century, and More's deep reverence for his father showed a general habit of mind that offered a way of managing uncertainty. If the authority of experience can be trusted, there may be in respect for age a way of fending off questions that might otherwise overwhelm.

A council of fathers governed Thomas More's mythical island common-wealth, Utopia. If father knows best, a group of fathers meeting together should be almost infallible. There was a stubborn strain of authoritarianism in More that embarrasses some of his modern admirers. Having never revolted against his own father, he could be merciless to those who dared to rebel against the surrogate fathers that every society raises as a standard of order in the world.

There was perhaps even a darker side to this relation between John More and his famous son, though this is only speculation. John More had enjoyed stunning success, and he expected his son to succeed. We have the testimony of Erasmus that More might have pursued a career in liberal studies had his father not thrust him into the law. John More's ambitions for Thomas seemed every bit as strong as those of Hans Luther for his son Martin.

The Freudians tell us that such a father may create in his son—especially in the eldest son—an overpowering superego, a force that drives the young man to set impossible goals for himself and torments him afterwards when he cannot achieve them. Throughout Thomas More's life we find a man driven to use every moment in the most profitable way he can. He detested idleness and all the sports that idle men invented to kill time. A family tradition, reported by Stapleton, held that he slept only four or five hours a night and that he made his bed on the ground or on planks and used a chunk of wood for a pillow. Such was his defense against the deadly sin of sloth, which he treated again and again in his later devotional works. He would not pause to write unnecessary letters; in those he did write, we find his continual complaint that he was too busy. He often signed letters "In greatest haste." He relentlessly educated his children and both his wives, making his first wife thoroughly miserable by his dogged insistence that she improve her mind. His *Utopia* is a rigorous textbook on how to use time, how to avoid wasting a moment, how to squeeze some lasting good out of every second.

Time was the discovery of the Renaissance, for this was the first period when time was seen as constantly slipping away, something rare and precious to be controlled and preserved. It was then that the first mechanical clocks came into use. One appears in the Holbein sketch of More and his family. During the Renaissance the clocks of the Italian cities began striking all twenty-four hours of the day, and men used children or fame to ward off or to mitigate the devastating effects of time. More was in this mood; time was for him always the most precious possession, and it was wickedness to use it poorly. Heaven was everlasting time.

The consequence of such demands may be depression or even melancholia —another of the afflictions noted increasingly as the sixteenth and seventeenth centuries drew on. From More's earliest days we find a man brooding over death, and the melancholy of his temperament comes through all his works like some hard, black stain that wit could neither cover nor eradicate.

His polemical works burn with an unrelenting fury which, like his laughter, may have been the release of a fire kept seething too long inside. The stupendous Holbein portrait done about 1527 shows us in part a conventional pose, a man who aims to look the part he plays in the world, wearing the golden chain of Tudor knighthood—dignified, sober, wise. But no other Holbein portrait shows a figure so brooding, with so much on his mind, with so many things to do that he must hold a little book with both hands as if to keep himself from jumping up and going back to work. More's right arm in this likeness does not truly rest on the little table beside him; it merely touches a corner. The figure is stiff, tense, leaning very slightly forward, impatient. More probably did not sit for long. Holbein made a quick study (which we have) and from it executed the portrait while the subject plunged back into the hurly-burly of the world. It is hardly a surprise that at the end of his life More complained frequently about pains in his chest: he was virtually a clinical model of a man prone to heart attack from the rigors of his incessant drive.

It was a condition that might have been aggravated by another quality we have noted in More, his inability to devote himself heart and soul to any one task. He worked hard, but in the end had no great accomplishment on the public scene as Wolsey had before him and Cromwell did after him. And John More—doubtless feeling some of the same compulsions about time that obsessed so many others in that age—was probably the principal source of the similar compulsion in his son.

Yet the most important gift of John More to his son was a comfortable life in a comfortable home, a life with prospects. It was not a boon that a son in that miserable and tumultuous epoch could take for granted, and Thomas's awareness of the misery of the common lot as he portrays it in *Utopia* must have made him grateful for what his father gave him—a chance to find his own place in the world, free from the fatal destiny of poverty.

Thomas More was not ungrateful for the complex legacy of his father. When John More died at last in 1530, Thomas held the old man in his arms and kissed him and wept.

2

FROM EARLY LIFE
TO THE INNS OF COURT

T<small>HOMAS MORE</small> lived his first twenty-two years in the fifteenth century, and his character was formed by that time. The details of his youth that are known for certain could be set down on a single page. The times must have left their mark, and his associations must have influenced him, but we can only speculate about how important this or that event, this or that person was to his development as a man.

His growing up seems to have been orderly enough. When his mother died, his father presented him with at least three successive stepmothers. We are not sure when these stepmothers married John More or when they died. Erasmus says More loved them all, including the fourth wife, Alice Clarke, whom John More married when Thomas was already on the verge of middle age. But they seem, like his mother, to have left little impression on him. Though in his epitaph he praises his second wife, Alice Middleton, for her affection toward his children by his first, he never mentioned, so far as we know, any affection shown by these stepmothers to him.

We can only guess at the relations More had with his mother. Depictions of Madonnas show that mothers held their babies, but there is not much evidence that mothers were especially close to their sons in later childhood or adolescence. As an adult, More did furious battle against his own sensual appetites and regarded it as a defeat when his longing for a wife made him give up his aspirations to be a priest. He did his best to atone. He beat himself with whips. He wore a coarse hair shirt next to his skin. Here he may have been following his namesake Thomas Becket, who flagellated himself and wore a hair shirt that, as a contemporary chronicler noted approvingly, swarmed with vermin. He was abstemious in food and drink, always seeing the flesh as a beast to be tamed. He was horrified when Luther and other heretics taught that priests and nuns could marry. The Middle Ages wobbled between the excesses of hot sensuality and cramped virginity. Mothers were usually remote figures and many unprepared boys met women intimately for the first time in a shock of sudden and shattering lust.

At the appropriate time, John More sent young Thomas to St. Anthony's School in Threadneedle Street. The school may have been a bargain: John Stow, whose *Survey of London* appeared in 1598, called St. Anthony's a "free school." It was attached to St. Anthony's Hospital, a sort of nursing home where a dozen old men were cared for, apparently much in the style of the Barchester establishment described by Anthony Trollope in *The Warden*. Stow said that St. Anthony's produced the best scholars of any school in London, and that the students—like bright boys from the beginning of time —had a reputation for being an unruly lot.

There Thomas More would have started learning the *trivium* of the seven liberal arts that stood at the base of all medieval education. The *trivium* included the rudiments of Latin grammar, logic, and skill in debating. Stow tells us that students from all the schools in London held debates in St. Bartholomew's churchyard on the eve of St. Bartholomew's Day and that the boys from St. Anthony's usually won the laurels. Sound heads in an urban age recognized the importance of being well spoken, and the man who could make a good speech was almost certain of rising in the world, especially if he had something to say. Civic orations were part communication, part spectacle and entertainment. In Renaissance Latin, the word *orator* translated to the English word "ambassador," for good speaking in public was a major requirement for any embassy. We often forget that one of More's great distinctions in his own time was that of being a fine speaker and that he was often an official orator for his city and his king. He probably got his first taste of public discourse at St. Anthony's.

Latin grammar was necessary to everything else, especially to the study of English. The notion that people should be able both to read and to write English caught on during the fifteenth century, but students studied English only as they needed it to translate Latin. English-Latin grammars and English-Latin dictionaries appeared in the fifteenth century for the first time, so that as young people learned Latin, they invariably learned something about their mother tongue. It has been frequently noted that men like Thomas More who were among the first able to write a wide-ranging, flexible, and accurate English prose had all been schooled carefully in Latin.

Logic helped students put a discourse together so that it made sense and did

not contradict itself. Young scholars learned the classic Aristotelian syllogism
with its method of relating a minor premise to a major premise so that some
relation between the two was established in a conclusion: All men are mortal;
Socrates is a man; Socrates is mortal. Young debaters used syllogisms to advance their own arguments, and if their foes advanced false syllogisms, the
skilled youth could detect the flawed argument. More told of Caius the poet
of Cambridge who could not delude a boy into accepting this syllogism: My
ass has two ears; you have two ears; therefore you are my ass.

While More was in school, following the trail to learning blazed by medieval
Scholastics who taught that education was a slow, methodical, and logical
process, the times were in great flux. Printing came to England in the baggage
of William Caxton, who set up a press in Westminster about the time More
was born. More's generation was the first in England to consider printing a
normal part of life. Although no one could foresee the magnitude of the
revolution printing would bring, More prized the craft and counted it one of
the great inventions of the Western world. When he described, in 1516, the
gifts Europeans might offer an advanced civilization like that of Utopia, he
mentioned Greek literature and the printing press.

The age witnessed much building, especially of churches and country
houses, and some members of the merchant class raised urban dwellings of
great magnificence. Yet in general the economic life of England presented an
aspect of decay and uncertainty. Nine-tenths of the English people lived on
the land, dependent on the annual autumn harvest, and virtually enslaved by
toil. In the 1480s, the harvests were generally bad; in the 1490s, generally good;
and in the first decade of the new century, mixed. Prices fluctuated wildly with
the success and failure of the harvests. Recurrent cycles of plague had, in the
previous century, killed off a huge number of the country laborers, and great
parts of the English landscape threatened to return to primeval wilderness.
Many towns complained of depopulation and dearth. John Russell, bishop of
Lincoln and Lord Chancellor of the Realm under Richard III, prepared a
speech for Richard's Parliament in 1483 condemning the "sloth and negligence of the landlords," which, if not checked, would mean that "cities and
towns should fall into extreme decay and ruin."

Yet, although much work should have been available, beggars swarmed the
streets, and vagabonds, roaming the highways, made travel unsafe for the
solitary. Thomas More, like most of his countrymen in authority, always had
a passion for order. That passion was born of the sense that disorder could break
out any minute, and More was not alone in his willingness to prescribe strong
medicine to purge the economic ills of the times.

Political events in More's childhood were as turbulent as the social changes.
Edward IV died in April 1483, when he was hardly forty. He had known no
moderation in the bodily pleasures, had grown fat and unhealthy, and probably

died of heart failure. The next two years are among the most talked about and least understood of English history, and Thomas More remains the source of much of the talk and writing about them.

Edward left two sons, a twelve-year-old named Edward and a boy of ten named Richard. Almost immediately the dead king's younger brother, Richard, Duke of Gloucester, seized the children, shut them up in the Tower of London, and began to rule as Lord Protector. By July he had made himself king as Richard III, and by the end of the summer the little princes in the Tower had vanished, never to be seen again.

More believed Richard killed them. Later, in his *History of King Richard III,* he recalled a story his father had told him. On the April night when Edward died, one William Mistlebrook, an auditor for Edward IV, came rapping at the door of a man named Potter living in Red Cross Street in Cripplesgate, not far from the house where John More lived with his young family. On being let in, Mistlebrook reported that the king was dead. "By my faith, man," said Potter, "then will my master the Duke of Gloucester be king."

The story in itself does not prove that Richard was already plotting to seize the throne. More knew as much and said so. Such dark confidences exchanged in the middle of the night were rather a sign that people who knew Richard found in him no room for human sympathy or natural affection. They thought he was a man who would be king. John More, by telling the story much later on, indicated that he believed Richard was guilty as charged for the crimes laid against his name by posterity. Here, as in so many other things, More's opinions were inherited from his father.

Whether guilty or innocent of the murder of the little princes, Richard could not stir enthusiasm for himself among the English people. In early August 1485, Henry Tudor landed at Milford Haven with a small force. He possessed only a shadowy claim to the English throne, but his claim gained substance as other rivals to Richard fell away. So it was that on Bosworth Field on Monday, August 22, with the issue in doubt, Richard—on horseback—flung himself at Henry Tudor to hack him to death in single combat. Instead he was cut down.

Richard's last furious charge—his sword rising and falling against his massed foes, killing some of them, almost reaching Henry—has the wild glitter of chivalry about it. No one—not even Thomas More—ever doubted Richard's courage. He was here the stalwart king seeking a duel with the leader of his adversaries in a way often promised but never performed by so many kings at war in those gallant times. Richard would do the deed; the issue of arms would be decided by the two men most concerned with the fray. But Henry Tudor was no chivalrous knight. His bodyguard did its duty, and Richard died, swarmed over by efficient swordsmen who had the good sense to leave chivalry shut up in books.

An old story holds that Richard's golden crown, which he insisted on wearing into battle, was discovered after his fall, hanging on the branch of a hawthorn bush. It was placed on the victor's head, and Henry Tudor, having been acclaimed on the field by the cheers of his army, rode down to London as King Henry VII. Little Thomas More, age seven, must have been in the crowd that greeted the new monarch in the streets of the city, and during Henry's reign, More—who came to detest him—grew to be a man.

Henry VII was as prudent in rule as he had been in war. He avoided foreign entanglements and foreign conflicts and worked to make his throne secure. He was good with money. When he came to power, he had had no experience in financial affairs, but he gathered around himself eager and energetic associates who could collect and count. They made no startling innovations in administration. But they did make the old ways work as no one had made them work before. He was avaricious—perhaps pathologically so—and deeply suspicious of the English nobility, which, he knew, was as indifferent to him as it had been to Richard III. He demanded huge recognizances from many nobles to ensure their good behavior, and his attainders against the persons and property of some great men of the realm kept them all in fear. He was quick to strike anyone he suspected of treason, and as he grew older his distrust of the world deepened. Thomas More thought he was a tyrant; many other Englishmen glumly agreed.

But Henry brought stability to England. He managed to collect his taxes and his fines and to impose his bonds on the nobility and to crush several revolts and to keep the grudging allegiance of his people and to succeed at last in dying in bed. He founded the powerful dynasty that was to rule England throughout the sixteenth century. His remains lie in the tomb that received them when he died, marked by a strikingly lifelike effigy done by Torrigiano in the magnificent fan-vaulted chapel that Henry added to Westminster Abbey. That they have lain undisturbed for so many centuries is tribute to his enduring achievement.

Henry brought not only political stability but economic prosperity for merchants and artisans, and under his rule England became a force to be reckoned with by continental powers. England also became an object of considerable curiosity to foreigners, especially the Italians, whose maritime powers stretched their sea lanes naturally to an island nation.

About the year 1500 some travelers from Venice—probably merchants—visited England. One of them—probably a secretary—wrote a long memorandum of their journey to his employer. It remains, although the names of both scribe and patron have been lost. Through its pages we can view young Thomas More's civic world and catch a glimpse of the proud, hurrying society of the reign of Henry VII.

The writer was astonished at the wealth displayed in London, especially in the shops of the goldsmiths and silversmiths in the Strand. He claimed never to have seen such an abundance of these precious metals anywhere else. He noted that the English were deeply religious, and he catalogued the wealth of their shrines, especially that of Thomas Becket at Canterbury, the greatest of all. But he grumbled that the English people were prone to heresy.

Evidently he had run into some who spoke well of John Wycliffe and ill of the pope. Wycliffe, England's most famous heretic, had been dead since 1384, but his memory endured and his followers were still active. He had been an Oxford don disenchanted with the elaborate philosophical speculations about theology current in his time, speculations that had led many to doubt that reason and faith were compatible. Wycliffe read St. Augustine and the Bible, and against the Aristotelians prevailing in the schools who taught that God can be known by the study of creation, he taught that knowledge is a gift of God and that before we can know anything at all, God has to implant ideas in our intellect.

He was a great preacher in both Latin and English, and deep in his soul ran the streak of English puritanism that emerged for good during the Protestant Reformation. He hated the vices of the clergy, especially those of the monks and the begging friars, by then generally mocked. (Wycliffe was a contemporary of Chaucer.) He believed that a Christian government should judge clergymen who do not live up to their profession, and he taught that it is far better to read the Bible than to obey the pope. The papacy at the beginning of his life was in exile from Rome, installed at Avignon on the Rhone and widely believed by Englishmen to be the willing tool of the king of France. Before Wycliffe died, the Great Schism had rent the Catholic Church, and two popes—one in Rome and another at Avignon—were hurling fiery anathemas at one another, much to the scandal of the devout, who believed that the true church was the seamless garment of Christ. Wycliffe taught that the true church was not an institution but a spiritual communion. Not stopping with a denunciation of the papacy, he also rejected the Catholic teaching of transubstantiation, the belief that the bread and the wine in the mass are changed into the actual body and blood of Jesus, so that no bread and no wine remain although the elements continue (by a double miracle) to taste, look, feel, and smell like bread and wine. He was forced to leave Oxford, but protected by John of Gaunt, the powerful third son of Edward III, he died of natural causes. His followers were savagely persecuted by the Lancastrian government of Henry IV, John of Gaunt's son, who in seizing the throne from Richard II helped justify his usurpation by becoming a scourge of heretics.

The memory of Wycliffe ran deep in the English people, and neither Henry IV nor the Catholic authorities could eradicate it. Some of Wycliffe's associates had translated the Bible from the Latin Vulgate into English. Both the government and the bishops had done their best to suppress the book, but

manuscript copies circulated surreptitiously almost everywhere, especially in
the South. The Lollards, as Wycliffe's disciples were called, found a ready
hearing among isolated country folk and also among many merchants in London. It was probably from the merchants, who believed that the church
drained money out of England, that the Italian visitor got wind of heresy.

All in all, the Italian admired England but disliked the English. He thought
them insufferably arrogant and narrow:

> They think that there are no other men than themselves, and no other world
> but England. And whenever they see a handsome foreigner, they say that he
> looks like an Englishman and that it is a great pity that he should not be an
> Englishman, and when they partake of any delicacy with a foreigner, they ask
> him whether such a thing is made in *his* country.

But what offended his good Mediterranean heart most was the apparent lack
of affection of the English toward their children. When children were seven
or nine years old at the most, their parents sent them to live with other families,
making them servants to the masters of the houses where they went to live.
When these Venetians inquired as to the reason for this unnatural act, they
were told that children learned manners better in the households of others. But
the writer thought that the English were merely greedy, that they wanted to
enjoy all the comforts of life and felt they could be served better by the children
of others than by their own.

Whatever the reason, John More followed the custom of the times and sent
his son Thomas to a man who could help shape his career. John More did
exceptionally well by his son; about 1490 he placed the boy in the household
of John Morton, Lord Chancellor of the Realm, Archbishop of Canterbury,
and soon to be a cardinal of the church. If a boy had any promise, here was
the man who might see to it that the promise would have some chance of
fulfillment.

Historians have not been kind to John Morton. There is no good biography
of him, and a cloud hangs over his name. Writers searching for other things
have glimpsed his sturdy form tramping through the yellowing records of the
past, and when they have looked hard enough at him to make a judgment, it
has generally been harsh. The late Paul Murray Kendall, the greatest modern
defender of King Richard III, wrote of Morton, "Like many another man of
the century, he had espoused the church only to rise."

Professor Kendall's judgment has a touch of modern moralizing and incom-
prehension about it. Kendall belonged to our world, a world where the secular
and the religious have become so distinct that he was unable to see how the
religious and the political man could live devoutly together under the same skin
as was possible in the Middle Ages. Morton was indeed political; there can be

no doubt about that. He had a talent for intrigue and survival, and his contemporaries do not recall him often at his prayers.

When he emerges from the obscurity of youth, we find him devoted to the dying cause of Henry VI of the House of Lancaster. He was with that king's resolute wife, Margaret of Anjou, at the battle of Tewkesbury in 1471. There the army fighting in Henry's name was massacred, and the boy said to be Henry's son was chopped down trying to run away. Shortly afterwards Henry himself was put in the Tower and murdered. With his death it seemed that the House of Lancaster had come to an ignominious end.

It is not impossible to see a religious motive in Morton's loyalty. Kings were made by God. In Morton's world, rebellion against a divinely installed king was akin to blasphemy, worthy not only of death but also of eternal hell. Morton made his sacrifices for the Lancastrian cause; he was not a reed bent by the wind. He was more than once in exile, in poverty, and in danger of death. He tasted the bitterness of isolation and humiliation in France, but in travail and in danger he never flagged in his devotion as long as any chance remained that Henry VI might keep his throne.

Although rebellion was in theory a crime against God, theologians had to reconcile their authorities with their experience. What if a rebellion succeeded, as did that of Edward of York, and the old king was put away and killed? God must have had some purpose in such events or else they were incomprehensible. So the rebel who succeeded and established himself on the throne and defeated all his adversaries was seen to be God's tool in the mysterious march of Providence through history. And after Tewkesbury, when Edward IV was king and Henry dead, Morton made his peace with events. The new king gave him amnesty. Edward was not vengeful, and he could recognize a good man when he saw one. His judgment was vindicated; Morton served him well and loyally tried to serve his children after him.

Richard's usurpation put Morton in lethal peril. In More's *History of King Richard III*, written over a decade after Morton's death, the bishop is one of the chief actors in the drama. Richard, making his lunge for the throne, placed Morton under arrest and handed him over to Henry Stafford, Duke of Buckingham, for safekeeping. Buckingham conspired with Richard to thrust the two young sons of Edward IV out of the succession to the throne and perhaps to kill them. Then, in the autumn of 1483, only months after Richard had been crowned king, Buckingham himself led an insurrection. But the rivers flooded, he could not get his troops together, and his uprising became a fiasco. He was swiftly taken and summarily beheaded at Salisbury.

Morton escaped to the Continent and eventually joined Henry Tudor, who, through his mother, Margaret Beaufort, had inherited Lancastrian blood—an inheritance tainted with bastardy but enough to revive Lancastrian hopes in Henry's person and finally to grant those hopes both throne and crown. During their common exile, Morton managed to get Henry word of a plot intended to rob him of both liberty and life. Morton's swift messenger was Christopher Urswick, a young priest who loved to ride and hunt, then an agent acting for Margaret Beaufort. Urswick later became a friend to Thomas More, and he must have been a major source for More's *Richard III.* Urswick delivered the message, and Henry galloped to safety. So it is not surprising that when Henry triumphed, the wily and loyal bishop should become his most important councillor.

More admired Morton and praised him extravagantly in both *Richard III* and *Utopia.* He closed *Richard III* by showing Morton beguiling Buckingham into the rebellion that cost the duke his life and sent Morton fleeing over the Narrow Seas to labor patiently for another and more successful candidate for the throne. He had been willing to believe that Edward IV had been a tool of God in the overthrow of Henry VI. But he could not believe that Richard was anything other than a usurper, and in the complex Christian theology of the time, people believed that a usurper could be killed on sight.

According to Roper, the boy Thomas More impressed the old man as much as the old man impressed the boy. "This child here waiting at table, whosoever shall live to see it, will prove a marvelous man." Such was his judgment on the young More, though like so many stories in Roper's *Life,* this one has the smack of legend about it. Roper told it; biographers routinely repeat it. Where did Roper get his information? Did someone tell John More what the bishop had said, and did John More then proudly repeat the story in the family so that Roper could hear it? Or did More tell this story about himself?

We should linger a moment over this last question. Roper tells another story that biographers always repeat when they write of More's stay in Morton's household. At Christmastime, when wandering actors put on plays and pageants, young Thomas More often stepped in among the players and made a part for himself better than theirs, causing the spectators to marvel at his precocious wit and skill.

The actors must have been disconcerted by the impromptu appearance of this brash and clever boy among them. Biographers have always been admiring. For this biographer it is worth saying that this youthful intervention on a public stage is typical of all More's life, for he was always making himself a stage and acting on it for an audience. In two of the dialogues that he wrote, *Utopia* and *A Dialogue Concerning Heresies,* he appears under his own name. In both he is careful to show his own important place in the world, his role as royal servant —a busy man engaged in important business. In *A Dialogue of Comfort Against Tribulation,* composed as he faced imprisonment and death, he appears transparently disguised as "Anthony," a saintly old man sick in Hungary and awaiting the coming of the Great Turk. He composed this work for his family and his closest friends; the name Anthony is that of one of the most famous suffering saints in Christendom, one who wrestled with demons in the desert. So at least part of the consistent family tradition of More's sanctity, a tradition lovingly expounded by Roper, Harpsfield, Stapleton, and the lesser men who came after them, was encouraged by More himself, playing out his role on the stage he made of his work. He was also a good father to his children, and in various public utterances he took pains to let educated Europeans know what a good father he was. At the end of his life he brilliantly turned the scaffold into a stage and played his part to the multitude that came to see him die.

When we read Roper with an eye to his sources, we find stories that, if true, could only have come from More's own mouth. It is possible that John More passed on Cardinal Morton's praise, but other things are less easy to explain away. At this remove, More looks like a man always self-consciously performing, seeking to play a role that others must admire and cheer.

To mention this startling consistency is hardly to condemn him. Classical education, revived in More's time, made much of education by example. Classical literature is filled with stories of good men to be imitated and bad men whose examples are to be shunned. The lives of the virtuous were paraded before the young with a view to providing a standard of virtue. The inevitable consequence of such instruction for those who take it seriously is to make the virtuous young aspire to be examples themselves, to translate life into a story that others can tell.

Such an exemplary life must be a public life according to classical wisdom. Yet More, spending two years at an impressionable age in the household of the Archbishop of Canterbury—surely going down with Morton time and again to Canterbury itself, watching the ancient liturgy of the church unfold in candlelight, plainsong, procession, and bells under the resounding arches of the grand old cathedral, surrounded by priests, seeing monks at their prayers —must have been drawn into the enthralling spell of medieval piety. The years with Morton, short as they were, are the most likely origin of the profound devotion to God and church that was to mark the rest of his life, although, of course, a young boy with another temperament might have emerged from this experience in another direction.

More took seriously all the eternal truths that the sensuous rituals of the church signified, stirring the mind to rise from performance of the liturgy to the perfection of the deity and the divine realm. He was to become a man of detailed and vivid imagination with a talent for telling a story unsurpassed between Chaucer and Shakespeare, and although it is the fashion to compare him, as Chambers does, with Socrates and Swift, it is probably closer to the mark to group him with John Bunyan and James Joyce, given their startling and terrifying power to evoke heaven and hell but especially hell. So More with his love for the dramatic was caught up in a much more exalted play than a

pageant put on by wandering actors at Christmastime, a pageant in which he
was always talented enough to make a part for himself to the delight of an
audience. The drama he would have seen under Morton's tutelage was that of
sin and redemption, of life and death, of doom, bliss, and damnation, God and
Satan. A sensitive boy, lonely, exiled from home, his mind teeming with images
raised in him by what he saw and heard, he was drawn to devote his life to
the devout contemplation of God in preparation for death.

But that same child loved praise and the admiring attention of people
around him. Throughout his life he loved to repeat the good things others said
about him, and he was always given to public displays of humility. He wore
his robes carelessly as if to show that high office had not gone to his head. He
made much of his dislike of the gold chains of office, and he wore them only
when necessary, but he did let people know that he had to wear them, and
Holbein painted him with a huge one around his neck. He yearned in published
letters for simplicity and lamented his involvement in the affairs of court that
kept him from the life of contemplation and study. Yet every time he had a
chance for advancement and for a busier life, he took it. He said that he did
not really want to publish his books, that friends urged publication upon him,
or that admirers published his books against his will and without telling him
what they were going to do. But when any critic attacked his writing, he
defended it furiously, sometimes almost hysterically, and we know some of the
efforts he took in revising and publishing. He wanted people to think he did
his duty only because it was his duty and not because he expected a reward
from it. Yet his rewards were great, and he lived well, prosperous if not wealthy.
When he was rewarded, he dutifully and loudly protested his unworthiness—
which was one way of letting people know he had been rewarded. Always we
see in him the young boy who used to step in among the players and make
a part for himself while the audience applauded. The yearning to please God
on the one hand and an audience on the other must have been one of the
causes of the tension in him we have already noted.

He was never ambiguous about his love of John Morton, and we may surmise
that Morton loved young Thomas More in return; most people who knew
More well did love him. It is tempting to see the old archbishop, his battles
done, success in his hands and nothing left to hope for, emotionally adopting
the bright young boy, giving him the love and the attention that he could never
give any children of his own, telling tales about the past.

Roper tells us that it was Morton's influence that caused More to go up to
Oxford. Morton had always been interested in the quiet university spread out
in its little town on the upper Thames. If Morton had his way, More probably
went to Morton's college, Balliol. A much later family tradition held that he
lived at Canterbury College. The records that would solve this unimportant
mystery have long since vanished.

More probably enrolled in the faculty of liberal arts about 1492, when he was fourteen, the normal age for such study. Roper said that John More always kept his son on a strict allowance. We may suppose that John More was like many mercantile city people then and now, pushed to the limit of his resources by the burden of keeping his status in a world where status counted for everything. He had to make a public display of his wealth in London to get people there to have confidence in him, and he probably had little left over to send to a son—invisible to the public—at Oxford.

Thomas More became a great success, able to sustain a large household in comfort. Yet he was always to make much of simplicity, condemning the lust for wealth that marked his world. Similar tastes have frequently been expressed by similar men. Here again John More probably shaped his son's life. On the one hand, Thomas heard a lot about money and felt himself compelled to make a lot of it if he was to please his father. But he was also compelled to wonder why the world must be so. In his *Utopia* he was to rebel in literature against a bourgeois style of life that he could not rebel against in his daily world.

He later recalled Oxford as a place of habitual discipline and penury. Roper tells of a little conference More had with his family after he resigned the office of Lord Chancellor in 1532. He wanted his dependents to know what the loss of his income meant. He hoped all of them could continue living together, he said, though now life would be hard, and they would all have to help. He was sure that they could manage by living more simply. He reviewed his life from Oxford to the king's court, and he suggested that they could go back down that ladder step by step as necessity compelled them. They could descend to the stage of Lincoln's Inn, where More had concluded his study of law, and if they could not maintain that level, he said, they could go on down to the fare of the New Inn, where he had begun his legal education. If that, too, proved impossible for them, they could "descend to Oxford fare, where many grave, learned, and ancient fathers be continually conversant. Which, if our power stretch not to maintain neither, then may we yet, with bags and wallets, go abegging together, and hoping that for pity some good folk will give us their charity, at every man's door to sing *Salve Regina*, and so still keep company and be merry together." We should note that he could imagine nothing but begging to be lower than Oxford fare.

More would have continued, at Oxford, the studies in grammar, logic, and rhetoric he had begun at St. Anthony's, and he would have gone on to the *quadrivium*, the other four liberal arts. The *quadrivium* comprised the four mathematical disciplines—arithmetic, music, geometry, and astronomy. These mathematical studies stayed with More, though he did not make them the core of his interests. He knew enough arithmetic to keep his accounts, and he knew enough music to sing in the choir at church, where chant and plainsong required much skill. This kind of music was done in a spirit of prayer, and he delighted in it to the end of his days. In his letter to Hutten in 1519, Erasmus wrote of More's love of music, somewhat ungallantly adding (as we have seen) that More had no natural gift as a singer. More tried to teach his second wife how to play on the virginals—an instrument of the time somewhat like our zither and supposed to be fitting for chaste women because it could be played at home.

Geometry meant Euclid, who had flourished in the third century before Christ. He remains the bane of all struggling high school students who are required to prove that the square of the hypotenuse of a right triangle is equal to the sum of the squares of the other two sides. His great textbook, *The Elements*, was often published after the invention of printing, and he became popular in the sixteenth century everywhere in Europe, his printed work becoming a basis for the great mathematical revival of the times.

But Euclid had always held a firm place in medieval education. His work was appealing not only because it was practical but also because of the philosophical reflection that it inspired. Euclid seemed to lead men as close to certainty as the human mind could come. It seemed impossible to doubt his principle that parallel lines can never meet or his axiom that the opposite angles made by intersecting straight lines are equal. In the *Paradiso* Dante uses an image from Euclid's geometry to illustrate divine knowledge.

Later, in defending the Catholic faith against the heretics, More was to say that faith was not the same as Euclid's geometry. His declaration reflected the ancient paradox in the problem of knowledge: the more important things are to us, the less sure we can be of them. He attempted to break the paradox by lifting faith to a superior place above reason and by putting religion beyond the doubts that reason can raise.

Astronomy meant Ptolemy of Alexandria, whose work, done in the second century after Christ, brought together the scientific wisdom of the classical world on the heavens. Ptolemy set up an enormous and beautiful machine that turned, not according to the whims of the gods, but according to mathematical principles. His world was a globe hanging magnificently still in the midst of a universe that, by our reckoning, was tiny. The sun, the moon, the planets all wheeled in distinct hollow glass spheres around the earth. Beyond all these spheres was the final globe that held the fixed stars, and beyond that, so Christian interpreters of Ptolemy thought, was heaven itself, glowing with the blue empyrean fire.

More later puzzled over one of the standard theoretical problems of Ptolemy's view of the world. If a hole could be bored through the center of the earth, would a stone dropped into the hole come to rest in the middle, hanging like the earth itself with no visible means of support? More's mind ranged over a great field of playful speculation; apparently he liked to toy with riddles like these among his friends.

He knew the stars. Roper tells us that Henry VIII loved to take More up to the roof of the palace, probably Greenwich, where the Royal Observatory is today, and there talk with him about the stars and the planets in their courses. But More ridiculed astrology—the study of the motions of the stars to discern what they might reveal about events on earth—a branch of astronomy that flourished with belief in Ptolemy's closed universe.

People in More's day retained the ancient awe and mystery that the stars had long inspired in those who looked skyward and wondered at the stately progression of the heavenly bodies across the circle of space. Before cities were artificially illuminated at night, a profound darkness fell on the earth with the departure of the sun, and even urban dwellers felt an intimacy with the heavens that we can scarcely appreciate. Many Christians believed that since God had set the stars in their courses, He must have a purpose for them. Man was given dominion over the earth. God ruled the heavens, and God did nothing in vain; heaven and earth had innumerable connections. If people would only look devoutly, they could find a divine sign in almost anything. The stars turned in courses mathematically described centuries earlier by Ptolemy, and astronomers versed in Ptolemy could predict with astounding accuracy dramatic celestial events such as conjunctions of the planets and eclipses of the sun. It seemed reasonable to suppose that the stars controlled or influenced human destiny. Astrologers believed that if they knew the moment a child was born, they could predict his fate just as they could predict conjunctions and eclipses.

More was somewhat unusual in that he rejected astrology as a silly and pernicious superstition, although he was not alone. Many were already scoffing at astrology because the predictions of rival astrologers often contradicted each other, and all astrologers were frequently wildly wrong. Long before More, St. Augustine of Hippo (350?–430) had mocked the astrologers of the later Roman Empire, pointing out, for example, that identical twins—supposedly born under the same heavenly signs—often had markedly different fates. Augustine also believed that astrologers blasphemed God by pretending to know things that God alone could know. More, believing always that human beings must take some responsibility for their fates, would have rejected astrology for its determinism, though his main comments about the "science" were merely that it was foolish and wrong.

We cannot precisely measure the influence of Oxford on More, for we know so little of his stay there or of the university in his time. We always find a part of him that was critical and amused at the mindless enthusiasms of the masses. Astrology was one of those enthusiasms, and it seems plausible to suppose that at Oxford he ran into astrological zealots and others who ridiculed them. Universities of that time would have seemed unbearably stuffy and theological to us, but at their dull worst they were places where people debated ideas and learned something of the nature of evidence.

More important, Oxford may have created the traditionalist frame of mind that we discover in so much he wrote, although his own temperament might have made him a traditionalist wherever he had gone to school. In 1518, writing as an irate alumnus, he castigated the university for lagging behind Cambridge in Greek studies. Some students and dons, calling themselves "Trojans," had banded together to banish Greek from the school. Oxford was more conservative than Cambridge, and it resisted passionate enthusiasms for novelties. We may detect here a spirit of resistance to any movement that lacked the support of long tradition, and—paradoxically enough—this sense may have communicated itself to More, who, though he accepted Greek, still imbibed Oxford's fundamental spirit. At Cambridge, new ideas—such as Greek and heresy—found a more congenial welcome.

He spent only two years at Oxford, forced to leave (so Erasmus tells us) by his father, who feared that he might enter liberal studies rather than the law. A life in liberal studies would have meant a university career, and since all dons were clerics, such a career would have meant priesthood. Obviously John More demurred at that prospect, since, like Martin Luther's father, he had his own plans for his brilliant son. More returned to London to read law, first at the New Inn, and then, after two years of study, at Lincoln's Inn.

The Inns of Court were all located within an easy walk of the place where the Strand today intersects the Kingsway at the busy half-moon of urban clutter and noise known as the Aldwych. Lincoln's Inn is still there, changed like the rest of London from More's time, though law students still come and go in transit from classroom to court, and the place preserves something of the spirit of busy leisure that it must have had when Thomas More, still an adolescent boy, walked through its gates for the first time.

We know almost everything we do of the Inns of Court in More's time through the great work of Sir John Fortescue written about 1470, *De laudibus legum anglie*, "On the Glories of the English Laws." Fortescue explained the origin of the Inns and described the life that went on in them, and in his work we hear a voice that echoes in Thomas More's works and in the stories told about him.

The chief reason for the Inns, said Fortescue, was that the language of the universities was Latin whereas the language of the courts in England was law French—that curious amalgam of English and French that was one of the cultural relics of the Norman Conquest. The Inns were located near the royal courts so students could see the law in operation.

Fortescue noted that tuition at the Inns was expensive—as much as thirteen pounds, six shillings, and eight pence a year. He remarked proudly that the poor could not afford such a sum and that the merchant class would not spend its money so. Consequently, he said, hardly anyone was to be found learned in the laws of England who was not of noble birth. From what we know of John and Thomas More, it is clear that Fortescue exaggerated. When he wrote *De laudibus*, he was in exile with Henry VI in France, where nobility counted for everything, and he painted the English lily to impress his French hosts and perhaps to keep up the spirits of his fellow Englishmen in a foreign land.

His depiction of the Inns has its charming side, for he described the academy that was part of every Inn. Here young boys learned to sing, to play harmonies, and to dance, and they learned noble manners—probably meaning the elaborate drills of courtesy that delighted the upper classes of the time and served, like some arcane grammar, to set them off from lesser beings who knew nothing of noble delicacy. The complex elaboration of such manners at the end of the Middle Ages has its counterpart in the petrified rituals of the dying Austro-Hungarian Empire and, as has often been remarked, it indicated a lessening of confidence that nobility was self-evident, by virtue of birth alone. Nobles had to be taught to act nobly, but if noble behavior could be taught, could not anyone learn it? And could not anyone who acted nobly be considered noble? The issue was argued to no certain conclusion at the time.

Fortescue says that boys at the Inns read scripture and the chronicles of the history of England. Like his son, John More passed through this regime, and as we have seen, he owned a copy of the most famous chronicle of all, Geoffrey of Monmouth's *History of the Kings of Britain*. History was important to English lawyers because their common law was so different from the Roman civil law everywhere in vogue on the Continent, and they believed that its superiority was demonstrated by the superiority of their past, which they covered with the trappings of a glorious mythology—a mythology that Henry VIII was later to use to enormous effect when he tore England away from the Roman Catholic communion presided over by an Italian pope with supposedly supranational authority.

Every Inn was, so Fortescue says, a school for the cultivation of virtues and the elimination of vice, and the sense of community in all of them was so great that the worst punishment anyone could imagine was to be excluded. Sometimes, he says, nobles sent their sons to the Inns just for the education the Inns afforded, not with the thought that the sons might enter the law. It is a view of education much gentler and more humane than we find in most medieval schools, especially those on the Continent. We find none of the sadistic brutality that Luther often mentioned when he spoke of the schooling of the young in Germany and none of the senseless hardship and harshness that Erasmus recalled from his brief stay at the College of Montaigu at the University of Paris. It is possible that the gentleness of his own education in the Inns almost unconsciously influenced Thomas More when he considered the education of his own children.

We must stay a while with Fortescue. Thomas More was a lawyer, and in his view the law was ordained not merely to punish and to keep order but to bring justice and equity to the citizens of the commonwealth. Law did punish, of course, and when More faced the onslaught of Protestant heresy, he cried as loudly as anyone else for the law to crush offenders and save society. But it is equally clear that the law for him was as grand for its liberties as it was for its penalties. The English were a practical people, seldom lingering over the philosophy that lay behind their law. Fortescue is one of the very few who tried to explain its guiding principles, and in his thought we find sources for More's own.

Fortescue's attitude toward the law has been called "clerical," and in a way it was. He tells us that the law is a holy thing and that teachers of the law are a kind of priesthood, that all laws promulgated by men are in truth decreed by God. Happiness, he says, is the end of all human desire, and Stoics and Epicureans alike agree that nothing can be pleasurable without virtue. So all true happiness must include virtue, he says. Laws give justice, and justice makes people happy. But since original sin destroys our appetite for virtue, those who seek the good embodied in the law do so by divine grace and not by human strength alone. Laws, he says, come to us as a favor of God; he meant that they were part of God's grace—like salvation itself.

The ideas are commonplace in general theological considerations of law in the Middle Ages, and a great many clerics were trained in the law, evidence of its close connection with theology. Thomas Wolsey was one such priest; Martin Luther was another. Fortescue's book might have been the source of a needed rationale for Thomas More, who wanted a sacred vocation, even if he could not become a priest, and found in the law—prodded along by his father—a divine realm where he could serve God.

Fortescue assumed that there was a natural law, as did most legal thinkers in his time. The idea of natural law is simple enough: it is the sense in us of right and wrong that we know through the higher powers of the intellect. All intelligent beings can supposedly agree on its principles even without special revelation from God. Natural law comes to us because we are created in the image of God, and to believe in natural law is to hold that with most ethical problems we are able to look at all sides and make a decision in keeping with a universal standard of right and wrong.

In practice natural law is hard to apply to individual cases. Christian theories of natural law usually hold that it is the golden rule: "Do unto others as ye would that they do unto you." Such sentiments are noble enough, but they are not helpful in deciding if a contract is valid or if a will is fair to the heirs and fair to the society at large or if a title to land is genuine. So there must always be some agency to bring the natural law down to cases, and for the Middle Ages and for Sir John Fortescue, that agency was custom. So it was also for Thomas More.

Medieval people honored custom because they assumed that God involved

Himself in the ordinary events of life. For all but the most doubtful philosophers, this assumption meant that God ordered a world that made sense. Human life had a purpose, and human society was shaped by God's intentions. The world groaned in sin, but God had not cast off His creation, and He was guiding it to redemption. Those who would be saved were the obedient.

But obedient to what? To the doctrines of the church, of course. Obedience to the laws of society was also required. Even in the days when Rome was persecuting them, most Christians believed they should be good citizens of the empire and reported that they prayed for it regularly. Christians obeyed all laws except those that came into direct conflict with their faith. Even then the Christian did not rebel against authority. Since God had ordained that authority, there must be some reason for it, and Christians must accept it even if they could not understand God's purposes.

So it became a normal habit in the Middle Ages to grant custom the status of law and to believe that all laws agreed with custom. Once any act was thought to be customary, it was likely to be considered unchangeable. The peasant who gave a goose to his master at Christmas was likely to bind his children and their children for generations to make the same gesture if the master took the gift as custom and conveniently forgot that there had been a time when it had not been so. By the days of Fortescue, Parliament made statutes that put custom aside in favor of new laws, but the prevailing sentiment seemed to be that statutes cleansed society of inexplicable deviations from honest custom. Or else statutes clarified the spirit of tradition and made the law apply to particular and seemingly unprecedented cases. The reverence for custom remained strong. Both Henry VIII and Thomas More thought that the very gestures of the priests in the mass had been given to the apostles by Christ and handed down through the church. They could not imagine anything so blasphemous as to suppose that human beings had ever started making holy gestures on their own, apart from the will of God.

On the Continent custom was complemented by the Roman law, known from the great Code of Justinian, the *Corpus iuris civilis.* Custom was important in the regions where Roman law held sway, but practitioners of the Roman law held that the most perfect expression of law came from the mouths of the Roman emperors. These lawyers assumed that custom was authoritative, but they also believed that not everybody knew what custom was. In dubious cases, somebody had to define custom, and in the Roman law, that somebody was the emperor. It was easy in the Roman law to assume that the monarch spoke with the voice of God.

But in England the Roman law never took hold, and Fortescue's work praises English common law especially for the limits it placed on kings. Here was law defined by judges as they heard cases. Or, if we are to adopt Fortescue's fiction, it was the law known to judges by their knowledge of custom and applied to cases that came to hand.

Fortescue believed English customs were older than those of any other Christian people, accepting wholeheartedly the myth, stirringly recounted by Geoffrey of Monmouth, that England had been founded by Brute and his band, who fled to Albion after the fall of Troy. In England, as Albion became, these hardy contemporaries of Aeneas and the other builders of Rome had lived in a rich good land in isolation and purity—a kind of Utopia, we might say. The customs of the English law were thus much older than the Roman law, and because of their great antiquity, these English customs were closer than any others to the natural law given to humankind by God at creation. The English, living in their demi-paradise, had leisure enough to give their law a degree of perfection that was lacking in France, cursed by endless war.

All this may strike us as quaint and unreal, but Fortescue believed it, and we may assume that most people who taught the law to Thomas More believed it, too. We could say that to Fortescue and to the English legal tradition, natural law, with the reason it comprised, was a placid lake filled with pure water and that judges dipped calmly into the lake when they ruled on their cases and cleansed away problems with eternal and infallible justice.

Fortescue's esteem for these judges was unbounded. He advised young Prince Edward—Henry VI's son, who was to perish at Tewkesbury—not to trouble himself to learn the English law in any great profundity. The king should rather leave hard study of the law to his Serjeants-at-Law, carefully selected legal scholars, the most skilled in England on the subject of law and equal, so Fortescue boasted, to any doctor of any university. The king's duty was to see to it that the law was upheld, but he should neither make law himself nor act as judge in any case, "for none of the kings of England is seen to give judgment by his own lips."

More shared this faith in the judges of England. His father was one of them, as we know, and in 1503 John More became a Serjeant-at-Law. Much later on Thomas More would declare, with some passion, "For in good faith I never saw the day yet, but that I durst as well trust the truth of one judge as of two juries." Since juries were composed of local men who had to go on living in the community after a trial which they helped adjudicate, they were often subject to intimidation, and since they were not themselves educated in the law, they often brought in decisions directly contrary to both custom and statute.

So More's confidence in judges was justified on the practical level, but it also fitted the temper of his mind, which gave authority to the learned and the deliberate. He later addressed himself to many of the issues of English legal practice, and although he never stated the matter so baldly, he always acted as if judges were always fair and the accused always guilty—until he came to the legal revolution of Henry VIII that cost him his own life.

But the most important thing that Sir John Fortescue or the English law taught Thomas More was that kings are limited in the power they may exercise justly. More was to have a remarkable record of opposition to the kings of his own lifetime; in fact, the only king he did not oppose in some way, literary or otherwise, was Edward IV, who died when More was only six! Fortescue taught that kings were limited, that they could not make law; they were, he said, as subject to the law as they were to the sacraments, and if they made laws against the sacred rules of custom, the English people had every right to disobey them.

In Fortescue's mind, bad kings were bad for many reasons. But their great symbolic wickedness was to seize the property of subjects for ignoble purposes. Bad kings tried to tax without the consent of Parliament, and they tried to keep their people poor. Fortescue prefigured in a remarkable way John Locke's dictum that government existed only to assure its citizens of life, liberty, and property, and in Fortescue's mind, possessions were necessary if one was to be fully a person. Without property, men were reduced to servitude, and slaves were not whole men able to take the responsibility for right and wrong that was necessary for Christian civilization.

There is a grand humanity in Fortescue's view of the law. English law uses no torture, he says; English law demands clear proof of guilt. Otherwise the accused must go free, and in one great sentence that deserves to be repeated he says, "I should indeed prefer twenty guilty men to escape death through mercy than one innocent to be condemned unjustly."

Did More read Fortescue, or were Fortescue's opinions simply in the air, as it were, to be absorbed by anyone who studied the law with certain propensities of mind? We cannot tell. So much of the law as it was taught in the Inns was simply craft—knowing how to make pleadings, how to obtain writs, how to tell the difference between a felony and a lesser crime, how to interpret contracts, how to tell what was a true boundary, and so on. We can only say that much in More calls Fortescue to mind and that it is plausible to assume that the study of the law provided some direction in forming the habits of thought that become so clear when the evidence allows us to see More's mind in his actions and his books. Not the least of the influences of the law would be the sanctity of old tradition on which the common law of England and law in general was assumed to rest.

About 1501 More finished the formal study of law and became an "utter barrister," a complete lawyer, we would say, and began his own practice. It is a period when we begin to have a considerable number of details about his life, and what we see suggests a storm that never entirely calmed in him.

3

PRIESTHOOD
OR MARRIAGE?

T HERE IS much to suggest that the years between 1501 and his
marriage in 1504 or 1505 marked a spiritual crisis for Thomas More.
In his 1519 letter Erasmus wrote that More thought of being ordained but that
he could not shake off his desire for a wife, that he decided he would become
a good husband rather than a bad priest. Stapleton said that More thought of
becoming a Franciscan friar.

Roper tells us that before his marriage More "gave himself to prayer and
devotion in the Charterhouse of London, religiously living there without vow
about four years." Erasmus, who detested monks, makes no mention of this
stay, but he does say that More engaged in vigils, fasting, and prayer there.
Most modern scholars, puzzled at the thought that the monks of the Charterhouse might have taken in boarders, think that More may have lived in the
neighborhood and shared in the daily services of the monastery. We do not
know.

More always venerated the Carthusians. Erasmus wrote as if monks were
nearly always hypocrites, and he spent much of his energy trying to keep from
being sent back to the monastery where he had taken vows as a youth. More
mocked the bad monk, but he spoke as if he longed for the monastery all his
life, and he would always recall the Carthusians and remember that some
monks were saintly.

The Carthusians were grave and devout and spent much time in prayer,
solitude, and silence. Their stern boast was that their order had never been

reformed because it had never fallen into corruption. When the Reformation came, no monastic order showed itself more willing to suffer agony and cruel death for the old faith. Even if he did not live within their sprawling compound, More's daily sharing of their rituals left him deeply stirred by their austere piety. He was of their temper, and he certainly believed that theirs was the surest way to heaven.

His decision to marry must have been agonizing. Today it is hard even for devout Catholics to understand how completely the cult of virginity captivated the church of the Middle Ages. From the beginning, Christians prized virginity above matrimony. A deep sexual asceticism runs through much of the New Testament. It is remarkable that Jesus, called a rabbi and springing from a Judaism that considered men hardly men unless they were married, should have remained, apparently, without a wife. He commended those who had made themselves eunuchs for the kingdom of heaven. Two centuries later, Origen of Alexandria took this praise of eunuchs literally and castrated himself so he might serve God without the temptation of lust. Later interpreters were not so literal, but they thought these strange words of Jesus meant that priests should abstain from sex and make themselves figurative eunuchs. Paul was hostile to women in general though not always in particular. Given the uncertainty of the times and the supposed near return of Jesus, he thought it better for everyone to remain single like himself, though he conceded that it was better to marry than to burn. To the Corinthians he allowed marriage as a substitute for fornication, but he suggested that husband and wife might agree to abstain from sexual intercourse during special periods of devotion.

Paul's combination of antipathy and grudging acceptance remained the view of the church. Marriage was permitted, and in time matrimony became a sacrament, but virginity was thought far superior. Augustine wrote that marriage was once commanded of the people of God because it was necessary to propagate the holy race; now, he said, it was only a remedy for human weakness and a consolation for human frailty. Even before Augustine an early pope wrote that marriage for priests was a pollution that they could not allow themselves; he implied that it was a pollution for the laity, too, but to them it was permitted because they were lesser beings. Marriage gave men and women carnal pleasure of a sort thought revolting by theologians who had rarely if ever experienced it. Jerome, the translator of the Vulgate and a contemporary of St. Augustine's, said that anyone who loved his wife too much might be damned, and he advised sexual intercourse without passion and only for the procreation of children. The church always held that the only justification for marriage was the production of children, and many church fathers cautioned husbands not to lust after their wives and not to use them as whores.

As the centuries passed, fantastic stories of heroic saints proliferated, and nearly all of them included tales of startling virginity or amazing abstinence by married people. More read the stories and repeated some of their miracle tales in one of his polemical religious works against heresy in which he defended with all his might the veneration of saints. In *The Golden Legend,* a medieval collection of stories he knew well, we find the tale in which the apostle Thomas appears in the room where a young man has taken his bride to consummate their union. Thomas tells the young couple that purity is the queen of all the virtues, the one that leads to eternal salvation. "Virginity is the sister of the angels," he says, and he makes clear that "pollution," by which he means any kind of sexual intercourse, in marriage or out of it, leads directly to hell. So the couple abstains; the bride becomes a martyr, the husband a bishop.

All this is nonsense to us, and we must realize that in every age, popular piety —of which *The Golden Legend* is an example—is more extreme than the formal theology of the church. Still, many devout Christians did believe that sexuality was a slide into hell, and More seems to have been one of them.

His inner anxiety over the desires of the body could hardly have been relieved by a series of public lectures he gave on *The City of God* by Augustine of Hippo soon after finishing his legal studies. Augustine was always his favorite saint, the writer who more than anyone else influenced the shaping of his mind. He knew Augustine almost by heart, and *The City of God* is more often quoted in his works than anything else in the Augustinian corpus. More spoke in the church of St. Lawrence Jewry, probably at the suggestion of William Grocyn, the rector. These lectures brought More into public notice for the first time, and they made a great impression. Erasmus mentioned them, and so did Roper; all the other sixteenth-century biographers did the same.

We have no idea what More said, but we know Augustine and *The City of God.* Augustine towered over the Latin Middle Ages. He defended the church against infidels, pagans, and heretics, and he was the first major theologian to teach that secular government should force people to be good Christians. He wrote Bible commentaries, and he tried to make paradoxical doctrines like the trinity and predestination seem plausible to the educated citizens of the dying Roman Empire. He believed that all sensuality was evil. He wrote against Julian of Eclanum:

> What sober-minded man would not prefer to take food, dry or moist, without any stinging carnal pleasure, if he could, as the air he draws in and lets out into the surrounding air by inhaling and exhaling?

In 1519, when Erasmus described More's abstemious nature, he probably— without quite knowing it himself—gave us a man whose views on sensual pleasure were much like St. Augustine's; it was not that the pleasures of the senses were harmful merely when they were taken in excess; they were a sign of wickedness merely by their being, and the Christian should limit indulgence in them as much as possible.

The worst of the sensual sins, according to Augustine, was sexuality. As a Christian who believed in the doctrine of creation, he had to believe that marriage and childbearing accomplished a divine purpose since society required a steady supply of new life to take the place of the old that died. But since sexual intercourse was almost impossible to isolate from intense sensual pleasure, he could not view sexuality without a certain loathing, and at times he came very close to saying that sexual intercourse is a sign of our depravity. He had had a mistress when he was young. When he became a Christian, he put her away, although he had had a son by her, Adeodatus, whose name means "gift of God." His primary view of Christian salvation was that it was redemption from sensuality, which, if indulged in unchecked, would lead the soul directly to hell. He never ceased to exhort Christians to chastity, by which he meant abstention from sexual intercourse, and even when he praised marriage, he took care to say that virginity or abstinence was a higher state. Always, in his view, the man who succumbed to the sensuality of marriage was inferior to the person to whom God gave the gift of surmounting passion.

Absorbed as he was in Augustine's work, More would have been saturated with the teaching that those who fall to sensuality will continue their plummeting into hell itself. That he lectured on Augustine at this time would indicate that he was seriously contemplating entry into the priesthood. It was quite common for young men knowledgeable in the law to study theology and become clerics. Many of More's friends were clerics; John Colet, whom he deeply revered, was learned and puritanical and thought that even the vergers who took care of church buildings should be restrained from sexual intercourse by vows of chastity. Colet's devotion to virginity would certainly have communicated itself to the younger man who admired him so much. In the normal course of things, More might have been expected to be ordained. Instead he married.

Stapleton says that More feared "even with the help of his practices of penance that he would not be able to conquer the temptations of the flesh that come to a man in the vigour and ardour of his youth," and so "he made up his mind to marry. Of this he would often speak in after life with great sorrow and regret, for he used to say that it was much easier to be chaste in the single than in the married state."

In a work he did about the time that he made his decision to marry, we can find evidence of the brooding his choice inspired in him. This was a translation of a biography of Pico della Mirandola done by Pico's nephew, Giovanni

Francesco. More presented his little work as a New Year's gift to Joyce Lee, the daughter of an old family friend, who had just entered the convent of the Poor Clares, whose house was not far from the Tower. The Clares lived withdrawn from the world in a life of extreme simplicity, prohibited by the rules of their order from receiving any material gift; so More gave Joyce Lee a spiritual present.

In his translation More made a few minor changes from the Latin original, but they are insignificant. The importance of his effort is that he thought enough of Pico and the book about him to make the translation and to give it to a woman friend who had entered a religious vocation.

Stapleton says that early in his life More made Pico his ideal because Pico had been a learned and devout layman. Obviously much in Pico's life would have appealed to More. Pico was an extraordinarily learned Italian, deeply devout, abstemious, noble, diligent, and prolific with his pen. One of his most important beliefs was that human beings have free will and can choose whether they will rise toward God or sink toward the beasts. He mocked astrologers for their determinism, because he found the dignity of man to lie in the soul's capacity for choice and in its ability to ascend to God through the great chain of being that knits creation together.

More would have seen Pico as an example of the Christian life he might live himself—warmhearted lay piety, at home in a cultured world. But when Pico died, aged thirty, in 1494, he was a disciple of Girolamo Savonarola, then preaching sternly against the vanity of art and other forms of idle worldliness and predicting the imminent end of the world. After Pico died, so Giovanni Francesco said, Pico appeared to Savonarola in a dream, his body suffused with fire. He was in purgatory, and the fire was his punishment for refusing a religious vocation and remaining a layman. More faithfully translated the story; it must have given him somber reflections.

Gloomier yet would have been the recollection that, though a layman, Pico remained unmarried. He fled both marriage and worldly business in the proud palaces of stately lords, More's translation says. In jest Pico said that if he had to choose one over the other, he would take marriage, thinking there was less jeopardy in that than in service to princes.

Pico's poetry is deeply melancholy, as if it might be presumptuous to suggest that anyone might enjoy the sensual world; in that respect it is in rebellion against the sensual nature of poetry of the later Middle Ages in which versifiers endlessly propounded the delights of color and growing things and the bliss of earthly love. More translated Pico's verse with great skill and with much greater feeling than he discovered in himself when he wrote poetry of his own. His own sensuality was always half tamed at best, but his melancholic temperament brought him easily to the melancholy of Pico, who had managed to raise gloom to a pious art. Here are some lines, in More's translation:

This wretched life, the trust and confidence
Of whose continuance maketh us bold to sin,
Thou perceivest well by experience
Since that hour, in which it did begin,
It holdeth on the course and will not lin [wait]
But fast it runneth on and passen shall
As doth a dream or shadow on the wall.

Consider well that every night and day
While that we busily provide and care
For our disport, revel, mirth and play
For pleasant melody and dainty fare
Death stealeth on full slyly and unware [unperceived].
He lieth at hand and shall us enterprise [grasp]
We know not how soon or in what mannerwise.

These are Pico's thoughts, faithfully rendered by More, and they are More's thoughts, too. But either shortly before or shortly after he wrote them, he married.

The wife he chose was Jane Colt, the eldest daughter of a family friend who lived in the country. Roper tells us that More continued his attendance at the Charterhouse monastery "until he resorted to the house of one Master Colt, a gentleman of Essex, that had oft invited him there." John Colt was a prosperous man who had three daughters, and Thomas More would naturally impress a father with daughters to wed. Roper's "until" is significant; it looks as if More's stay at the Charterhouse came to an end as a direct consequence of the persistent invitations of Master John Colt to come to the country and meet his daughters. Probably John More urged his son to go ahead. However that may be, More went and met the young women, "whose honest conversation and virtuous education provoked him there specially to set his affection." Roper's sentence is a little confusing; it sounds as if More gave his affection to all three of them. Maybe he did. For a young, passionate man accustomed to four years of relative isolation in the company of Carthusian monks, the sudden proximity of available young women must have been a shock, and Roper suggests that More's clerical aspirations caved in before the general "affection" stirred up in him by this meeting.

Roper says that More liked the second daughter better than he did Jane, the eldest. But he thought it would be a shame for the firstborn not to be married first; so he resolved to fancy the eldest and framed his desire toward her. Little by little he succeeded, and they were married.

We must suppose that Roper got this tale from More himself. There is no reason to think that Margaret, More's eldest daughter and Roper's wife, was

ignorant of it. In that light the story is rather cruel, though Roper told the tale
to illustrate the kindness of his father-in-law, and that is probably why More
told it himself. Here again he seems to be a man on a stage he has made, acting
out a part he has chosen before the world.

The story may also represent something else—the feeling in More that the
first reason for having a wife was sexual necessity. Then almost any wife would
do, and once the wedding was over, a strong and resolute man with virtue on
his mind could shape his wife's character according to his own tastes.

Erasmus, writing of More years before Roper put pen to paper, supports this
view. He said that More married a young girl, untrained and having no
experience but the country, so he could make of her what he wanted. He had
her instructed in literature and trained in all kinds of music. Erasmus may even
tell us something in addition to what this letter reveals. In his colloquy called
"Marriage," he tells of a young man who married a girl of seventeen who had
never spent any time outside the country home of her parents. Her very
simplicity impressed the youth because he imagined that he could train her to
match his own taste. He taught her literature and music, and when they had
been to a sermon, he made her repeat the words of the preacher to see if she
had understood them and remembered them.

The girl rebelled! She answered her husband's insistence with tears, and
sometimes she beat her head against the floor. The husband, unable to do
anything with her, suggested a visit to her father in the country. Off they went,
the bride delighted to go home. Once there, the husband left her with her
mother and her sisters and went hunting with the father. He asked the question: What could he do to make his wife obey? The father counseled a good
beating. The husband demurred. He would prefer that the father use his skill
or his authority; he did not want to beat his wife into submission.

The father did his part; he drew his daughter aside, and he reminded her
of how ugly she was, how crude, how often he had feared that he could not
find her a husband. With much effort he had found the girl a man who would
delight even a beautiful and talented woman, a man who would scarcely think
her fit to be a servant if he were not so kind. She was rebelling against this
princely fellow. The father then seemed ready to beat her; he may have drawn
back his hand as if to strike her. The daughter went down on her knees and
begged forgiveness. She also fell on her knees before her young husband and
begged him to forgive her, too. Ever afterwards she was a perfect wife, doing
everything her husband wanted, no matter how lowly it might be. In a few
years they loved each other, and the girl congratulated herself for her good luck
in marrying such a man.

Modern scholars note the similarity between the opening of this colloquy,
published in 1523, and the description by Erasmus in 1519 of More's marriage
to Jane. They assume that the story of this husband and his weeping young

wife is a true account of the relation between Thomas More and his first wife. They may be right; if More told Roper how he came to marry Jane in the first place, he might well have told Erasmus how he made her a good wife. But the artistic imagination always decorates reality, and perhaps it is an error to read the little dialogue by Erasmus as literal history.

The attitude of the husband in the colloquy is indeed like that of Thomas More toward women in general. They are most virtuous when they are submissive to the authority of a good man. The husband in the colloquy shows the relentless drive for improvement that we find always in More, a man who could not bear to waste a minute. Even his pleasures were intended to instruct, and we may be driven to reflect that in this aspect he often sounds rather like an eighteenth-century Methodist born out of his time.

Poor Jane must have taken an emotional beating in her marriage even if her husband did forgo his legal right to beat her with his fists. She died in 1511 after bearing him four children—Margaret, Elizabeth, Cecily, and John. She was twenty-three. More loved her in his way. In the epitaph he composed for the tomb that was never to hold his bones, she was his "dear little wife."

He married again within a month. His second wife, Alice Middleton, widow of a London merchant, was already in full maturity, six years older than he. By all accounts she was quarrelsome, petty, ignorant, and even stupid, and there is nothing to suggest that she was sexually attractive. Harpsfield calls her "aged, blunt, and rude," implying that she was so when she married More. More made her the target of many unkind jokes, though in his epitaph he praised her.

Why did he marry her, and why so soon after Jane's death? Her husband had left her considerable property when he died, and both More and his father saw marriage as an economic union—as did nearly everybody in that time. People did not marry for love; as the colloquy of Erasmus shows, they hoped to love each other only after they had lived together for a time.

Still, his haste seems almost indecent, and his biographers have puzzled over it; at times they seem embarrassed by it. They usually explain it by More's desire to have a mother for his children, and this must have been part of his decision. Dame Alice brought a daughter with her—also named Alice—so she had some experience with children, and, as we have seen, More praised her for giving loving attention to his offspring. She was, by our standards, probably more manager than mother, for she took over the household, and More wrote her as one might write to a good steward. She apparently had a sharp eye for accounts, ridding the house of parasitic guests who stayed too long. Andrea Ammonio, friend to both More and Erasmus, fled the premises after some kind of encounter with her, and he wrote ungallantly to Erasmus of the "hooked beak of the harpy." If More sought a good manager, he found one.

He may have had another motive in marrying Alice—the continuation of his lifelong struggle against sexuality and desire. We have noted his observation that it was harder to remain chaste as a married man than as a single person. He must have had in mind the ability of married men to satisfy their sexual longings whenever they wanted, and he took to heart the consensus of the church fathers who held that sex for pleasure alone—even with one's wife— was a sin. Early Christians, responding to their general horror of sex, frequently took vows to abstain from sexual intercourse even if they were married. Sexual intercourse after menopause was a questionable act. And it is just possible that More married his second wife with this early Christian abstinence in mind. The doctors of the church had debated the validity of any second marriage, and the debate had gone on for centuries, finally settling to a grudging consensus that second marriages were valid for Christians though not signs of valiant faith.

Menopause at that time, as now, came when women were about forty-five, but many women reached it earlier, and Dame Alice may have already passed through menopause when More married her. At the very least she was near the end of her childbearing time. Had More married a younger woman, a person of his temperament might have justified habitual sexual relations with her by the hope of fathering other children. But sexual intercourse with a woman after menopause could only be for the sexual pleasure that the church fathers had condemned so vehemently. In Augustine's eyes, using a wife merely for pleasure was to make her a whore. It is quite unlikely that a man of More's devout and ascetic disposition would have indulged in sexual intercourse with a woman who could not give birth. His four children by Jane Colt were born one after another about as quickly as human biology permits, seeming to testify to his own regular sexual activity for as long as his marriage to her lasted. He married Dame Alice when he was only thirty-three—not far beyond the height of his sexual powers, and if he then began to abstain completely from sex, we may understand a little better the hair shirt, the whips, the vigils, and his later horror at the Protestant approval of clerical marriage.

His marriage with Dame Alice, then, was probably a quiet and unobtrusive way of living a life of sexual abstinence while he remained in the world to do his duty to his children, to his father, and to society at large. He always believed that the natural man sought pleasure for the body but that the true Christian sought pain and punishment in this life for sins that had to be punished somewhere, either in this world or in the world to come. His marriage to Dame Alice may have been a continuing penance.

He may also have used Dame Alice to cancel a revived longing for priesthood or the monastic life. As he himself later pointed out, a man could become a priest after his first wife died, but a second marriage closed the sacrament of ordination to him forever. Paul had written that a "bishop" could be the husband of one wife; the church interpreted this text to mean "no more than one." A man who had been married twice was, by canon law, a "bigamist," even if his first wife had very properly died and left her husband a widower; no bigamist could be a priest.

More loved his children, and his sense of responsibility for them was enormous, but they might have been provided for had he chosen the priestly vocation when Jane died. Her family was well-to-do, and it is unlikely that More would have married her without receiving a substantial dowry, which he might have returned on condition that it be used for the support of his children. John More was also prosperous enough to help his grandchildren should his son have chosen to be ordained—though the elder More would have been irate at the thought. The lure of priesthood in such circumstances must have become once again beguiling, and More's later ruminations as to why he could not be a priest—ruminations that in context seem gratuitous—may reveal this prospect suddenly presented a second time by the death of his wife in 1511. His quick marriage to Alice Middleton may well have been a way of slamming a door that had suddenly flown open years after he thought he had shut it forever with his marriage to the young Jane Colt.

Whatever may have been the cause of the union, it is clear that after 1511 his two marriages, his children, his growing household, and his offices fixed him irrevocably on the public stage. He might retain the wounds left over from his decision to forsake the priesthood, and from time to time these old wounds might cause an ache in his bones. But he was to be a public man, and he set about to make himself a public career.

4

PUBLIC CAREER
TO 1515

THOMAS MORE'S public career was to be made and unmade in his service to the Tudor house. The association began early. Erasmus came to England for the first time in the summer of 1499, and somehow he and More were thrown together. Erasmus was always subject to attacks of loneliness and gloom, and perhaps someone thought that witty young More would cheer him up. One morning when Erasmus was staying with his patron Lord William Mountjoy, More came by and took him for a walk. It was probably a Sunday, when Londoners regularly took walks in the country, and without telling Erasmus where they were going, More led him over to Eltham Palace.

At Eltham the younger children of Henry VII were being brought up. Arthur, heir to the throne, was at Greenwich a few miles away with the king and queen. In Eltham Palace, Henry, the eight-year-old Duke of York who by the accident of Arthur's early death would become Henry VIII, presided over his two sisters, who would both become queens, one of France and one of Scotland.

More brought a little gift, something he had written, probably a poem to honor the prince. Erasmus was embarrassed and annoyed. He had not known that they would be visiting a king's son, and he did not happen to have an offering in his pocket.

The two visitors were invited to stay for the midday meal. Henry and his sisters would probably have been seated on a raised platform at the end of the hall. More and Erasmus and others as well would have eaten at tables spread in the center of the hall under the magnificent hammer-beam ceiling that endures yet at Eltham.

During the meal Henry sent word down by a boy that he expected something from Erasmus. Erasmus went back to his lodgings and with excruciating toil hacked out a long poem in three days, praising Henry VII and England and the royal family and everything else that Erasmus could think of. (He later said that this effort so taxed him that for years afterwards he neither wrote poetry nor read verse; judging from this poem, we can say with some certainty that his retirement from verse represents no great loss to the poetic art.)

The story shows that More was no stranger to the royal family. He had no trouble at all gaining access to Eltham and to the young prince, with whom he was obviously already acquainted. We may surmise that he was a regular caller. He and his friend were invited to stay for dinner. Surely such a privilege was not granted to everyone who came by! It would be clear to anyone who cared to notice—and Erasmus cared to notice these things—that More had connections, even as a student, and that he was on his way up in the world.

The connections obviously came from his family, both from John More and Thomas Graunger, More's maternal grandfather. The smallness of England meant that a hardworking king showed himself often and took care to know the important people of the realm, seeing his kingdom as a kind of extended family with himself the father of all. John More and Thomas Graunger were obviously important men, and it is not surprising that young Thomas More should have made the acquaintance of royalty, although we do not know exactly how it came about.

Like most Englishmen, More showed a lively interest in the spectacle of royal appearance. The first surviving letter that we have from his pen was written about November 1501 to his friend John Holt, a Latin teacher who had been for a time, after More had gone to Oxford, chief tutor to the boys in the household of Cardinal Morton at Lambeth Palace, the archbishop's London residence. More's letter is in the formal epistolary style with which the young learned to phrase their thoughts in Latin. It has the smack of an exercise; in it he reports his studies of the classics and announces that he has begun to learn Greek. He also mentions that he has been attending lectures given by William Grocyn.

At the end he gives a long comment on the arrival of the Princess Catherine of Spain to marry Arthur, Prince of Wales. She "lately made her entry into London, amid a tremendous ovation," he says. "Never to my knowledge has there been such a reception anywhere." He comments on the splendor of the English nobles who greeted her but mocks the shabbiness of her entourage of Spaniards. Some of these retainers were barefoot, he says. Some were hunchbacked. They looked like "Pygmies from Ethiopia." He praises the princess herself and closes with a conventional bit of Latin epistolary effusiveness: "She thrilled the hearts of everyone; she possesses all those qualities that make for beauty in a very charming young girl. Everywhere she receives the highest of praises; but even that is inadequate. I do hope this highly publicized union will prove a happy omen for England."

It was, of course, an omen of disaster for Thomas More. Arthur was a sickly child, perhaps tubercular like his father. He may have been diabetic. He had passed his days in study, and in a time when every prince had to be praised for something, he was praised for knowing the classics. No one commended him for his looks or his strength. Most of his contemporaries—including Thomas More—kept such a discreet silence about him that we know him hardly at all.

He was not quite fifteen; Catherine was a little older. They were splendidly married on Sunday, November 14. It was the day of St. Erkenwald, an especially beloved English holy man and one venerated by Thomas More. He had built Barking Abbey near London in Saxon times, and More told one of the familiar stories about him and apparently believed it. When one of the roof beams was found too short, St. Erkenwald miraculously stretched it to just the right length. Arthur, shorter by a head than his bride, must have seemed pale and thin compared to her ruddy health. But perhaps with divine help he might be stretched to fit.

On the morning after the wedding night, Arthur got up and called for drink, saying that he had been all night in the midst of Spain and that the trip had made him dry. Such at least was the tale told long afterwards by several witnesses when Henry VIII wanted with all his heart and soul to prove that Arthur had consummated his union with Catherine. Even if the tale was true, it might have been only a boy's braggadocio, meant to hide the awful fact that he could not perform. By April 1502, Arthur was dead, and Catherine maintained then and for the rest of her life that Arthur had been too feeble with his illness to have sexual intercourse with her and that he left her a virgin. Thomas More had little to say about Queen Catherine, at least in his written works that survive, but he obviously always believed her. He would have seen the young couple pass in splendor through the streets of London, and from the way Arthur looked, More probably drew his own conclusions.

Young Henry, Duke of York, was now heir to the throne from which he had seemed debarred by his older brother. Deferred for a while was an issue only slightly less momentous than the death of Arthur: What would happen to the Spanish alliance that Henry VII had so laboriously put together and sealed by the marriage of his son to a Spanish princess?

By the summer of 1503 that question seemed settled. Henry, now Prince of Wales, was promised in marriage to Catherine. He was twelve years old. A promise was not the fact, but it was a commitment.

The marriage required a papal dispensation. The canon law of the church forbade a brother to marry the widow of a dead brother. The church's rule here rested on an obscure text, Leviticus 20:21: "If a man takes his brother's wife, it is impurity. He has uncovered his brother's nakedness; they shall be child-less." Interpreters of this text reasoned that it could not be merely a prohibition of adultery between a man and his sister-in-law; the penalty for adultery was not childlessness but death by stoning. The church was always apt in picking up divine restraints about marriage because the sexual relations in marriage were so dangerous. So it construed this text to forbid just the kind of marriage that Henry VII and the Spanish royal house now wanted the pope and the world to accept.

The pope, as Vicar of Christ, claimed the right to dispense with some decrees of the canon law when there seemed to be good reason for doing so. Everyone agreed that some parts of the canon law were less important than others; Thomas More later wrote, correctly enough, that the canon law was only a collection of decrees and that the decrees had no authority greater than their source. If a rule of the canon law had been made originally for some practical reason or for some reason special to the times, the pope or tradition might dissolve the rule for some other practical reason or if the times changed. No one believed that a pope could dissolve a direct divine command intended to stand forever; a pope could not, for example, sanction blasphemy.

But the book of Leviticus was of a different order from the ten command-ments or the teachings of Jesus or Paul. In addition to commands about marriage and adultery, Leviticus issued injunctions to Jewish priests about how to wring the neck of a chicken, how to detect leprosy, and how to know and avoid "unclean" animals, including rabbits. It forbade men to have intercourse with their wives during menstruation, and it forbade a priest to touch any dead body, even that of his father or mother. If any book of the Bible did not seem fully binding on Christians, it was Leviticus. More himself seldom mentioned it in his later voluminous works, although he spilled much ink in defending the right of the church to set aside many of the commandments of the old law of the sort that fill Leviticus. It seems clear at least that he never believed that anything in the book of Leviticus could stand between Henry VIII and a valid marriage with Arthur's widow. Three hundred years earlier the church had revised the rules of kinship within which marriage could take place. It seemed that a pope might easily enough assume the power to dispense with any rules about marriage that rested on the authority of Leviticus alone.

The dispensation was granted by Pope Julius II, elected to the papal office in the latter part of 1503. Julius had two passions—art and politics. He was responsible for engaging Michelangelo to paint the frescos in the ceiling of the Sistine Chapel, and Michelangelo also did the mighty seated Moses that served as the principal decoration for Julius's tomb. The greatest political desire of this pope was to drive the French out of Italy, where they had been coming and going with plundering armies since 1494. Julius needed allies, and both Spain and England were habitual enemies of France. A marriage treaty between them perfectly served the pope's interest, and so after some delays to be sure that everything was done with the proper forms, he granted his official consent to the projected marriage.

Even with the dispensation, Henry VII and his son hesitated. It was not until after the elder Henry died in 1509 that the young man who now became Henry VIII married the Spanish princess. Some Englishmen still doubted the pope's power to dispense with any rule relating to the marriage. William Warham, who became Archbishop of Canterbury in 1503, objected to the union. More's later official life brought him fairly close to Warham, but there is no evidence that Warham's misgivings had any effect on More or anyone else at the time.

More continued to act as spectator to the royal house. On February 11, 1503, Elizabeth of York, daughter of Edward IV, sister to the little princes in the Tower, and queen to Henry VII, died. The court astrologer, an Italian, had predicted a few months earlier that she would live to be eighty. Her death at thirty-seven seems to have cost him his job.

More wrote twelve lugubrious verses to mourn her death; his poem is painfully conventional, but people were expected to take lessons from the doings of royalty, and More did his best. In his verses the dead woman bids farewell to her family one by one without managing to say anything memorable. The real theme of the poem is not so much the queen's death but death itself and the vanity of earthly things. In it we find echoes of the morality play *Everyman,* so popular among all classes in that morbid time. More approached the subject of death with the alacrity finality always inspired in him, a trait that endured all his life. One verse will give the flavor of the whole:

> If worship might have kept me, I had not gone.
> If wit might have me saved, I needed not fear.
> If money might have helped, I lacked none.
> But O good God what availeth all this gear?
> When death is come, thy mighty messenger,
> Obey we must; there is no remedy.
> Me hath he summoned, and lo now here I lie.

The most interesting thing about these lines is that More's pen was causing him an itch. That fact marks him off as different from the great majority of English lawyers, who have never been prolific writers. It would also be interesting to know the audience for whom More intended the verses. Were they only a private meditation? Or did he make them as an offering to the grieving family, perhaps to the young Henry? He could very well have meant them to teach a moral lesson to the heir to the throne, especially since More at this time had heavily imbibed the idea that education was a way to virtue and that the most important obligation anyone had to a young prince was to see that he was well taught. If he did offer the poem—in 1503, when he was staying at the Charterhouse, observing the pious rituals of the monastery, and considering a clerical vocation—it probably reflects the conflict between his longing for the contemplative life and his hankering for a public place. People who wrote to kings or princes expected notice in return, and these mournful verses look as if More was keeping his hand in the public water even while he considered retreat.

Much like his rueful lament for Elizabeth of York were some verses he wrote about the same time for a "book of fortune," a sort of manual used, it seems, in a parlor game. Here the theme was the common one of meditation on the vagaries of chance in this life. The wheel of fortune slowly turns; those who are high are brought low. Those who wallow in the pit may be carried up and exalted. Fortune called on the high and the mighty not to be arrogant and advised the lowly not to despair.

> And though in once chance fortune you offend
> Grudge not thereat but bear a merry face.
> There is no man so far out of her grace
> But he sometime have comfort and solace,
> Nor none again so far up in her favor
> That is full satisfied in her behavior.

The sentiments are conventional. We may assume that the game played with these stanzas fitted the requirement for games in More's *Utopia* written over a decade later. It taught the players wisdom about life; at least it seemed to do so, and people could play it without believing that they were wasting time.

In these days, too, More wrote a little farce in verse called "A Merry Jest how a Serjeant would Learn to Play the Friar." It has been suggested that young Thomas composed the piece for recitation at a feast given in London in 1503 when John More was made a Serjeant-at-Law and Thomas Graunger, More's maternal grandfather, became sheriff of London.

As we have seen, a Serjeant-at-Law was a member of an elite group of lawyers from whom the judges of the common law were chosen. John More's election to such a position at about age fifty marked his steady rise in the world. More wrote of a different kind of serjeant, a lower, part-time officer of the courts who earned a small fee for delivering summonses and making arrests. In this piece the serjeant pretends to be a friar to gain entry into a house where a debtor is hiding. The false friar finds his man and places him under arrest, only to be thoroughly beaten by the women of the household. The verse is doggerel, and if it was read after dinner with great zest and many gestures, it was probably funny to men who had eaten well and drunk a lot of wine. We may suppose that the scholarly Serjeants-at-Law laughed heartily at the spectacle of a petty officer, too clever for himself, getting a thrashing from a maid and a housewife.

Of greater interest is the presence of the king himself at the feast along with the mayor and the aldermen of London and many of the nobles of the realm. The occasion would have given the youthful More a chance to shine before many notables, and it seems to have been after this feast that Master Colt invited the eligible young man down to the country to meet his marriageable daughters, perhaps having heard from important people how clever he was.

For a time after this More's career passes into shadow. Roper tells us that he was elected to the Parliament called by Henry VII in 1504. It is the fashion now to doubt this story because many think that he was too young for such service in that year. The records of the Parliament have vanished, and Roper's account is the only source we have for More's participation. Yet there are many reasons to believe it.

More was indeed young—about twenty-six—but old enough to be considered a mature man by the people of the time. He was an eloquent speaker; his lectures on *The City of God* had won him a certain fame. He had in addition been by this time a reader at Lincoln's Inn, proof that his fellow lawyers believed in his competence. His family connections were good, and he would have been a logical choice to represent the city in Parliament.

Henry called the Parliament to get money. He found the Commons in a grumbling mood. By this time he had developed his long-enduring reputation for gouging the English people, and his avarice bordered on lunacy. He sought to wring every shilling he could out of every law and custom that offered any chance for gain. Now he tried to collect from Parliament the ancient feudal dues supposedly owed a medieval king as tribute for the knighting of his eldest son and for the marriage of a child. His daughter Margaret had been married to James IV of Scotland only the year before, but Arthur had been knighted in 1489, and by the time Parliament was asked to contribute to his knighthood, the young prince had been rotting in the grave for two years.

Henry also seems to have wanted to start a survey of landholdings for the entire realm to produce an up-to-date version of the Doomsday Book that would allow more effective taxation. It is the sort of thing all local governments now have at their disposal, but the prospect created great antipathy among those whose property would become the object of royal scrutiny. In the end he had to settle for a parliamentary grant much smaller than the sum he had requested.

Roper says that the person who spoke most eloquently against the king's bill was young Thomas More, whose arguments were such "that the king's demands thereby were clean overthrown, so that one of the king's privy chamber, named Master Tyler, being present thereat, brought word to the king out of the Parliament House that a beardless boy had disappointed all his purpose." Roper may have exaggerated, for Henry did get a tax from this Parliament and all his purpose was not disappointed. It is likely that More made a speech; he was always making speeches, he did oppose taxation, and he would have expressed vigorously the sentiments of those who did not want to bend to the king's demand. With his talents, his speech was probably quotable and memorable.

Roper says that Henry was furious and sought revenge, and that the royal wrath first fell on John More. The king engineered a quarrel with the judge and clapped him in the Tower until the older More paid a fine of a hundred pounds—reason enough, we may suppose, for John More to have neglected Henry VII's soul in his will. Although Roper is the only source for this story, it is the kind of thing we know Henry did with some regularity. The judge was probably accused of violating some old law, the hundred pounds a fine for the offense. Thomas More later condemned such practices by kings when he wrote his *Utopia*.

Roper says that the king was not satisfied with striking at More's father but also wanted vengeance against the man responsible for opposing his bill in Parliament. To this end he enlisted the aid of Richard Fox, bishop of Winchester, the richest bishopric in Christendom after the see of Rome. After Morton's death, Fox became Henry VII's chief political adviser. Now he feigned the role of mediator, telling More that he should confess his fault to the king and beg forgiveness. The bishop's chaplain, Richard Whitford, gave More a friendly warning. Fox, he said, would not scruple to put his own father to death if he could thereby please the king; More should beware.

The point was touchy. More, speaking his mind in Parliament, was acting on an unwritten English tradition that members of Parliament were at liberty to oppose the king among themselves in formal session so long as they did so with proper respect. Had More confessed that opposition was a fault, even a crime, Henry could have punished him by the evidence of More's own mouth. It was this that Whitford sought to avoid. Perhaps More did not need Whitford's advice, for he was always a jealous guardian of parliamentary sovereignty, and it would not have been lawyerly of him to call one of the greatest of English traditions a fault.

Roper tells us that More was so anxious that he considered leaving the country. In 1515 when he wrote Martin van Dorp of the University of Louvain in defense of Erasmus, More mentioned that he had studied for a time in Paris and Louvain about 1508. That year is a little late to flee wrath engendered in 1504, yet More's journey abroad might be explained simply by assuming that Henry VII did not immediately pick the quarrel with John More. The king could have bided his time for three or four years until he discovered him in a vulnerable spot—Roper's sense of chronology is notoriously loose. That event might then have caused Thomas More to cross the Narrow Seas to look for refuge. He tells Dorp that he was in neither Paris nor Louvain for a long time, but it is hard to say what a "long time" means. It might have been long enough to assure himself that Henry was not going to move further against him, long enough perhaps for John More to have raised enough money for the hundred-pound fine and to buy his release from the Tower.

In April 1509, Henry VII died. More greeted the old king's demise with rejoicing. In a Latin poem he wrote for the coronation of Henry VIII he cried, "This day is the end of our slavery, the fount of our liberty, the end of sadness, the beginning of joy." Henry VIII would be a king "to cleanse every eye of tears and to substitute praise for a long moaning." The nobility would no longer be oppressed, he said. The merchant would no longer be deterred by taxes; all people could once again show their possessions without fear of having them stolen by the government. Informers could be ignored.

It is a pretty grim account of the reign of the first Tudor, and his bitterness toward Henry VII is so evident in these verses that years later when he published them in a collection of "epigrams," a Frenchman, Germanus Brixius, accused him of disloyalty to the crown. Yet the verses were clearly written to be presented to Henry VIII, and what must be the presentation copy is still extant. More must have known what others have surmised, that there was no love lost between the old king and the new one. The tribulations More had endured under the father may in fact have endeared him to the son.

Henry VIII ascended the throne when he was not quite eighteen—the age of today's college freshman. He had spent the early years of his life in relative isolation and neglect, trotted out from time to time to play a supporting role in the drama of his brother's life. When Arthur and Catherine married, Henry led the bride into mass at St. Paul's and then out again to the great ceremonial dinner given by the mayor and the aldermen of London to honor the princely couple. Once Arthur was dead, young Henry was brought to his father's side but guarded so closely that a Spanish envoy said he might have been a virgin daughter. Apparently he was not allowed to speak except to answer his father's questions, and he was not allowed to see anyone unless his father gave permission. Nor was he given anything to do; Henry VIII came to the throne without having ever performed any of the tasks by which Princes of Wales have learned to be kings.

When he did succeed to the crown, Henry and England with him rejoiced. To show that his reign would be liberal, the young king at once locked up his father's chief financial advisers, Richard Empson and Edmund Dudley. They were charged with imposing a tyranny of taxation on the English people, and great was the rejoicing when the two were summarily tried, condemned, and beheaded. Stapleton tells us that Thomas More watched as the two men were led to their deaths on Tower Hill and that Dudley spoke to him, recalling the Parliament of 1504. Had Thomas More confessed his "fault" to the king after that Parliament, Dudley said, the king would surely have put him to death.

Henry set his coronation for Midsummer Day, Sunday, June 24, a holiday when bonfires were set in the streets and the rich set out tables of food and drink and praised God for His blessings throughout the year. On Midsummer Eve, doors were decorated with greenery and flowers, and oil lamps were hung out to burn all night long. People dressed gaily and marched through the city singing, accompanied by drums and stringed instruments, horns, and the soft piping of recorders.

Thomas More greeted the new king as a savior. Henry VIII would "wipe away all tears." People were beside themselves, More wrote; they leaped for joy. They crowded every space just to see the king, and they ran to look at him again and again. As for young Henry, More said he was perfect for the part, taller than anyone else, and very strong. "There is fiery power in his eyes, beauty in his cheeks as is typical of roses."

More believed that Henry had been well taught, having a liberal education to match his liberal gifts. The new king was bathed, said More, in the Castalian fount—the clear, cold spring that gushes out of Mount Parnassus at Delphi, said by the ancients to convey the wisdom of all the Muses. The queen was a fit match. "She is descended from great kings," More said, "and she will be the mother of kings as great as her ancestors. . . . Your fruitful queen will give you a male heir in a short while, a protection in unbroken line who shall be supported on every side." There was always in More a tendency to think that if he wrote things vigorously, they must be true.

More was probably redeemed from obscurity by the death of the old king, and he now entered upon a period of great activity. Roper gives us an impression of a man continually busy in the public service; we know also that More had a private law practice, although we know almost nothing about it.

Erasmus told Hutten that More tried to get his clients to settle their cases out of court, implying that More's motive was Christian charity. But sensible lawyers in every age would say that judges should be the last resort in any case simply because no one can predict what they will do. More's practice probably dealt in the main with civil cases, and in commercial suits the aim of all parties was to reach a quick settlement and to avoid tying up money in litigation that could better be spent in trade. Some guilds required that members submit their disputes with each other to the guild for settlement before they went to court. From what we know of More's wit, his tact, and his gift for friendship, we may suppose he did well in getting angry parties to sit down together to reconcile their differences without litigation.

He also served as an undersheriff of London, a post he held from 1510 until he joined the royal council and started collecting fees from the king in 1518. With a father and a father-in-law who were prominent judges and popular citizens of London, he would have naturally been in line for public office when a vacancy turned up. It was his first experience as a judge. Erasmus tells us that More presided over a court that sat only on Thursday mornings. John Guy, the best student of More's public career, says that this was the Sheriff's Court and that it assumed general jurisdiction over "ordinary assault and violence, minor wrongdoing, debt, account, covenant, defamation, and disputes over bonds and obligations." Apparently the court was conducted with a minimum of formality. Plaintiff and defendant each paid three shillings as costs for the hearing. Considering that in English law a man could be hanged if he stole more than a shilling, we may assume that three shillings was a goodly sum, and we can appreciate the delight of Londoners if, as Erasmus tells us, More refused to accept these fees. "By this behavior," Erasmus told Hutten, "he won the deep affection of the city." Well he might, for if a man aspired to be something in London, the affection of the populace could do him no harm. Guy points out that the undersheriff helped represent the city in the royal courts at Westminster and that his fees for these services must have made up a large share of the income of four hundred pounds that Roper attributes to More in these years. It appears that the office was significant and that More used it well.

In November 1511, Andrea Ammonio, the Italian humanist we have mentioned earlier as a guest in More's house until Dame Alice chased him out, wrote to Erasmus that More daily saw the Archbishop of Canterbury, William Warham. What this means is a bit unclear. Warham was by now Lord Chancellor, and More's business with him probably had to do with the Chancellor's Court at Westminster, where More would have seen him in cases involving the city. Daily contact was not intimacy; More wrote to Warham with the effusive respect required in addressing an honored man who was both Archbishop and Lord Chancellor, but his only surviving letter to Warham reveals no evidence of real closeness. More's position was certainly important enough to bring him to the continual notice of influential people, and his performance was good enough to make his superiors think of him when they needed a man. He worked hard, and although his ambition to enter the royal council was probably natural and already alive in him, for the moment he did his duty and waited.

He lived in London's midst, nourished by London, serving London, and in the process serving himself and the needs of his household. In the meantime, Henry VIII, settling down in his reign, began making plans to unsettle Europe. In a clumsy and incompetent way he started a series of wars with France. War required a vast expansion of diplomacy and a much more complicated government. A complicated government meant that new men must be found for royal service. Thomas More was clever enough to have made his way up in the world even in peace, but as things turned out, his rise to prominence accompanied the great changes in English government brought about by Henry's attempt to renew the Hundred Years' War.

The story of Henry's wars has been often told; it is a confusing tale, and there is no need to dwell on it, although it may be useful to sketch the outline. Henry believed that his natural enemy was France because the English and the French had been fighting each other for centuries. In war, as in so many other things, Henry was a traditionalist. He went to war not merely with the dream of taking land back from France but also because people in his age believed that a king was not truly great unless he led men into battle. Henry VII had been wise in this regard; he had fought his war, and his triumph over Richard III was sufficient to let him live out the rest of his days in peace and to save both his money and his realm.

But cautious kings often engendered warlike sons. Henry VIII, kept so long under the strict control of his parsimonious and severe father, yearned for the fame and exuberance of war. In 1511 he pushed through Parliament a statute ordering every man in England to desist from unlawful games such as tennis and bowling; Englishmen were to amuse themselves by practicing archery. Every man "not lame, decrepit, or maimed" and under sixty years of age was to practice continually with the long bow and to keep a bow and arrows in his house. Only priests, monks, judges, and barons of the exchequer were excepted. More may have been excused from this obligation because he was a judge of sorts, serving as undersheriff. But we should recall how detailed were the military provisions in his *Utopia* and how important archery was to the Utopian army. He may have taken his turn at the butts along with everyone else and kept his required bow and arrows at home.

In the spring of 1511, Henry, "ever desirous to serve Mars," as Edward Hall admiringly said, sent troops to Spain to help his father-in-law Ferdinand in a putative crusade against the Moors, who still harassed Spain from the Mediterranean. Henry's army sailed from Plymouth in May and landed in Cadiz in June 1. The English soldiers did not do well. Hall blamed drink. The English, he said, were not used to the "hot wines" of Spain. They became ungentlemanly in the Spanish whorehouses. They broke down hedges and plundered orchards and vineyards, and they ate Spanish oranges before they were ripe. We may suppose a militant case of general diarrhea. Spanish and English soldiers fell to fighting one another. Ferdinand called off his crusade, and after only sixteen days the English packed up and came home. The expedition had done the Moors no harm and Henry no good. But its failure did not dull his appetite.

A year after the first English debacle in Spain came another. Again Henry made an alliance with Ferdinand, this one against France rather than the

Moors. Again an English army sailed to Spain and landed in the middle of
June. Hall, whose mind turned to culinary explanations of great events, explained the subsequent disaster by saying, "The Englishmen did eat of the
garlic with all meats, and drank hot wines in the hot weather, and did eat all
the hot fruits that they could get, which caused their blood so to boil in their
bellies that there fell sick three thousand of the flux, and thereof died eighteen
hundred men." Once more discipline departed from the army as diarrhea
descended upon it.

Ferdinand had summoned Henry to fight France. As reward, England was
to recover her ancient possession of the beautiful hill country of Guienne with
its lovely towns built against the lower folds of the Pyrenees. But again Ferdinand left the war and abandoned the English. He had used them only as a
diversion against the French while he occupied Spanish Navarre, the last
territory south of the Pyrenees not already in his hands. His troops took
Pamplona while the French held back, waiting to see what the English would
do. The English did nothing but wait for Spanish horses and mules to haul
English cannon and supplies into battle. When the animals did not come, the
English packed up and went home.

These paltry affairs, virtually forgotten now, may have been among the most
important events in the history of the times, not for their military accomplishment but because they elevated Thomas Wolsey to be the king's chief minister
and the most powerful force in English policy until his precipitous fall in 1529.
Wolsey had been the king's almoner, in popular fancy at least an officer
important in assuring the eternal salvation of the king's soul since the almoner
was charged with giving alms to the poor in the king's name; the rich were
supposed to give alms if they were to have any hope of entering the kingdom
of heaven. Wolsey was much more proficient at giving advice. In Henry he
had a willing listener—perhaps because he was a genius at rephrasing the king's
fancies to repeat them back to his sovereign disguised as wise counsel.

He was already involved enough in the expedition of 1512 to be blamed by
many for its failure. But he was not fully in charge, and others could be blamed
for the poor discipline of the English army and the insufficiency of its weapons.
(One commander reported that of 8,000 bows, not 200 were sound.) He had
enjoyed some success in fortifying the northern borders against the Scots,
directing that enterprise from London and showing himself a man capable of
getting things done. Now he moved to the heights.

Wolsey was essential to Thomas More's career, since had Wolsey disapproved of him, More could never have become a royal councillor. The two
worked together for many years. Wolsey was always the superior and More the
underling, and in the custom of the times, More flattered him continually.
When Wolsey fell in 1529, More succeeded him as Lord Chancellor and
turned vehemently against him. The two were unlike in personality, but in

other ways remarkably similar. Both were devoted to the Catholic Church, and both believed passionately that it was a mortal sin for kings to rule or restrict the spiritual authority of the church, which had been granted by God. Both were loyal servants to their king, and both were destroyed by their master in the end. Both at the last regretted the ambition that had compelled them to forsake a life of spiritual solitude to grasp at fame and fortune in the world. Both were ambitious, although Wolsey's ambitions as well as his successes were far greater than More's, and he did not as often as More make public professions of his humility. Both had a vindictive streak that came to light when they faced serious opposition from anyone but their king, although both could be magnanimous toward petty foes who could do them no real harm. Both were loving parents.

Wolsey's origins were lower than More's, and we may see in the difference in their personalities the difference in their backgrounds. Wolsey was born in Suffolk, the son of a butcher of Ipswich, about 1473. The butcher's trade was considered contemptible. For sanitary reasons most large cities in England and Europe required butchers to do their slaughtering outside the city walls. In More's island of Utopia, only slaves could be butchers. His narrator tells us, "They do not allow their citizens to accustom themselves to the butchering of animals, by the practice of which they think that mercy, the finest feeling of our human nature, is gradually killed off." Wolsey never quite shook off his origins. A fierce little poem in 1528 cried:

> This is a great presumption
> For a village butcher's son
> His authority so to advance . . .

Wolsey was intelligent, high-spirited, gregarious, and affable—like Thomas More, the kind of person Henry VIII, delighting in hearty souls, loved to have around him. His intelligence brought him notice and got him to Oxford, where he made a brilliant showing that won him friends in high places who were quickly impressed by his energy, discretion, and wit. He never wavered in his lunge for the top, and once there never hesitated to destroy anyone who threatened his place at the pinnacle of power.

Without Wolsey we cannot imagine what More's life would have been. Yet Wolsey interests us not only for his contribution to More's career but also for the contrast that he affords to More himself, a contrast that stands out over all their similarities. Wolsey loved administration, loved the public life, loved pomp and circumstance, and loved power. We have already noted that More lacked Wolsey's aggressive delight in administrative matters, his gift for grand solutions. Although people may debate the wisdom of Wolsey's policies, no one doubts his immense and almost implacable influence on English government and English life. There is no real evidence that More ever had any influence at all. Wolsey loved the baton of command, the swagger of authority. But though More was incessantly busy, he was always uneasy with power, and his mind was that of the eternal staff sergeant rather than the field marshal.

Wolsey enjoyed huge success at first, and he developed the hubris that seems to be the downfall of all great manipulators: he imagined that he could do anything, that no obstacle could withstand his energy and his persuasions, and that by the relentless exercise of charm, flattery, ruthlessness, and intelligence, he could always make people do what he wanted. His failures finally became so enormous that in retrospect his successes have the quality of mirage about them. Yet there is truth in the remark of his first and best biographer, his "gentleman usher" George Cavendish, who, writing in the wake of all the changes that came after Wolsey died, said, "In my judgment I never saw the realm in better order, quietness, and obedience than it was in the time of his authority and rule, nor justice better administered with impartiality."

Now, in 1512, Wolsey rose as war minister because, despite his setbacks, Henry remained resolved to have his war with France. Throughout the summer of 1512, English and French ships skirmished in the Narrow Seas between the two realms. On August 10, 1512, the *Regent*, carrying seven hundred men and at one thousand tons the greatest ship of Henry's navy, tangled with the French ship *Cordelière* off the coast of Brittany. The tangling was quite literal, since the naval tactics of the day required fighting ships to grapple each other and to send marines swarming over the sides to battle like infantrymen on a floating field. Someone started a fire; it spread to the powder magazines, and both ships went up in flames "within the turning of one hand," as Thomas Wolsey wrote in an account of the scene to his friend, Bishop Richard Fox. The only survivors were a few French sailors who knew how to swim. English sailors were even then apparently possessed of the superstition that for a seaman to learn to swim was to ask the gods for shipwreck.

The event was awesome and perhaps tragic. At least it evoked the tragic muse. In France, a scholar-priest, Germanus Brixius, was set upon by a serious attack of epic verse and displayed his violent poetic pox in a little book called *The Burning of the Ship Cordelière*, marked by effusions of elegiac praise for Hervé de Porzmoguer, captain of the *Cordelière*, who went down with his ship.

Brixius suffered from a bad case of Virgil. His poem recalls the prodigious delight in battle and color that marks the *Aeneid*. The French adore their homeland. Bows are bent; battle-axes slice through the foe; the sun is darkened by arrows. The cries of fighting men mount toward heaven. The French under their valiant captain are victorious over the fainting English—who nevertheless fight bravely. Hervé is in the midst of the fray, and Brixius describes his valor in words that the poet thought must compare with Virgil's verses that describe the victory of Aeneas over the Etruscans. But despite Hervé's courage, the flames devour the two ships and their men, and Brixius, like some Joseph Turner born out of his time, delights in the joys of describing a great conflagration. The poem is much more an exercise in ardent expression than it is an attack on the English.

Thomas More must have read these verses when they appeared early in 1513. He was, like everyone else, caught up in the pleasures of Henry's wars, and he took the poem as an insult against the valor of the English nation. In reply he wrote a string of stinging little epigrams mocking Brixius and his work. Here Brixius is a liar and a fool. He deserved to have been on the *Cordelière* himself, "amidships—so that he might know the whole story more accurately."

> As for the statements that Hervé struck some enemies down with javelins through their temples, thrust his sword through the abdomens or ribs of others, in other cases severed heads with ax-blows to the neck, pierced the shoulders and flanks of others, and as for his bravely striking down with his shield the hurtled missiles of the enemy and returning them to their source—all this is beyond the reach of understanding, how one man could fight with so many weapons, and that while one arm was burdened with a shield. Unyielding nature herself contradicts this battle. I think that in this passage you omitted something. For when you represented heroic Hervé fighting indiscriminately with four weapons and a shield, perhaps the fact slipped your mind, but your reader ought to have been informed in advance that Hervé had five hands.

Brixius has stolen all his good lines from the ancient poets, More says. Brixius has claimed that Hervé was the equal of the two Decii, father and son, who in separate battles against the enemies of ancient Rome, died valiantly to inspire their fellow citizens with their courage. Says More, "And yet there is the difference: The Decii died willingly; Hervé, because he could not avoid it." There are other epigrams, equally insulting to Brixius, equally strong for England.

More did not publish these epigrams until 1518. For whom were they intended when he wrote them? Doubtless they were meant for the king himself. This was still the same Thomas More who presented a little gift of writing to Henry in 1499 at Eltham and who gave Henry flattering verses for the coronation of 1509. More's epigrams against Brixius were meant not only to make Henry laugh but also to show More's support for Henry's military enterprise. Every modern biographer has assumed that More opposed these foolish continental wars, but there is no evidence that he did while they went on, and these epigrams and several other utterances of his show that in this as in most other things, More was unwilling or unable to oppose his king.

So the war went on, and Henry went off to France with his army in the summer of 1513 and had a wonderful time. Old Kaiser Maximilian, the Habsburg Emperor of the Holy Roman Empire of the German Nation, joined him as an ally, saying effusively flattering things and receiving twenty-five pounds a day in wages from the English king. In such ways did the treasure gathered by Henry VII melt away. Henry's army captured Thérouanne at the end of the summer, and at his order, the walls, the gates, and the towers that enabled the city to defend itself were torn down. When the king departed, English looters set fires, and much of Thérouanne burned.

Back in England, the Scots saw an opportunity and, sticking to their Aulde Alliance with France, invaded England. James IV of Scotland was married to Henry's sister Margaret, but a woman belonged to her husband and not to her brother, and the kinship of royal houses through marriage seldom led to peace between realms. James led his army below the Tweed, and because he was brave and foolish, he set his troops an example by carrying in his hand a sword he meant to use. Early in September he collided with an English army led by the old Earl of Surrey on a little rise of ground called Flodden in the bare Cheviot Hills near the river Till. There the Scots were slaughtered and their king slain. It was the greatest English land victory of the century, but it was not won by England's king, and Catherine, his queen, who had promised to defend the realm in his absence, sent a message accompanying "the piece of the King of Scots coat which John Glyn now bringeth," saying in gentle irony that must have stung: "In this your Grace shall see how I can keep my promise, sending you for your banners a King's coat."

The Earl of Surrey was Thomas Howard, who had fought courageously for Richard III at Bosworth Field. His father, John, first Duke of Norfolk, had steadfastly served the house of York, and at Bosworth led the van of Richard's army and died for Richard's cause. The son was imprisoned for three and a half years after Bosworth, but on his release from the Tower in 1489, proved his loyalty to the Tudor house by putting down a rebellion in Yorkshire, where the Yorkist cause still smoldered against Henry VII. After Flodden, he received his father's old title and became Duke of Norfolk.

His son, Thomas Howard the younger, became Duke of Norfolk himself when his father died in 1524, and much later on William Roper called him Thomas More's "singular dear friend." Elizabeth, daughter of the victor of Flodden, was married to Sir Thomas Boleyn, an able diplomat in the king's service. In the summer of 1513, their daughter Anne was about six years old.

Thomas More followed the war with an interest shared by most informed Englishmen. After Flodden, he composed a moralistic epitaph for Scotland's fallen king:

> It is I, James, King of the Scots, brave and ill-starred enemy of a friendly power, who am interred beneath this sod. Had my loyalty been equal to my courage, the sequel with its shame for me would not have happened. But, alas, I must

not boast and I will not complain—therefore, I shall say no more. And I hope, O chattering infamy, that you may be willing to keep silent. You kings (I was once a king myself) I warn not to let loyalty become, as it often does, a meaningless word.

A few days after Flodden, Henry's army took the city of Tournai, much larger than Thérouanne. Wolsey had been made its bishop even as the English army still camped before its walls. In October, Henry came home wearing the laurels of his triumphs. He could imagine that he had revived the victorious spirit of Henry V, and he could dream of other campaigns culminating in the eventual glory of the crown of France itself, the goal for two centuries of his forebears. More composed an epigram on the surrender of Tournai:

Valiant Caesar first conquered you in your might, Tournai, but not without disaster to both sides. Henry, a king both mightier and better than Caesar, has taken you without bloodshed. The king felt that he had acquired honor in taking you, and similarly you yourself felt it no loss to be taken.

Neither the epigram about the death of James nor that about the conquest of Tournai is bloodthirsty, but they are both patriotic. In his epigrams against Brixius, More's patriotism is as virulent as any during the time, and he is much less preoccupied with the evils of war than he is with the reputation of English warriors. He shared fully in the English nationalism observed with such annoyance by the Italian visitor mentioned earlier, and he seems much less the pacifist than modern scholars have made him.

Henry's victories in France were as ephemeral as a morning mist in summer. Within a year he had made peace with King Louis XII, and in token of his good will, he sent his sister Mary to be Louis's third wife. (Young Anne Boleyn was dispatched with her to be a serving maid and to learn good manners at the French court.) The great war with its great aims had dissolved into a game of chivalry, and Henry discovered that even with the organizing genius of a Thomas Wolsey, war was far too expensive to be waged for long. France was too large, too well organized, too nationalistic to accept an English conquest or an English king. Maximilian had no money and no power to help. Ferdinand of Spain backed out of the alliance he had sworn on his honor to uphold. The English king, smarting with wrath against his father-in-law, was left to face his French foes alone, and he had sense enough to see that they were too much for him. So he cut his losses and allowed Louis to pay a ransom for his cities, and after a decent interval of a few years, they went back to French rule.

To Englishmen with ties to the merchant class, Henry's war must have been a debacle, not because it was cruel but because it disrupted trade, drained the treasury, and put the country in danger of higher taxes—all for nothing but military spectacle. Both More and his father were members of the Mercers' Company, one of the great London mercantile associations that ruled the city. With such associates More had reason to have second thoughts about the war, not for its bloodshed, but for its stupidity.

Throughout 1513 and 1514 he continued his busy life as lawyer and under-sheriff, keeping a practice of his own and serving London as a responsible good citizen. Occasionally he served on royal commissions of the peace to see to the good order of the nearby countryside, but most of his business was with the city. He was a member of the commission that looked after London Bridge and of another that took care of the sewers. Roper says that he was twice reader at Lincoln's Inn, "which is as often as ordinarily any judge of the law doth read." Twice, Roper says, More represented the London merchants in disputes with the German merchants in the Steelyard, the trading enclave near the bridge where the Hanseatic League had a concession. If Roper is correct in saying that More was making at least four hundred pounds a year in this period, he was a man of substantial wealth.

It was probably for his standing in the city that on May 7, 1515, More was commissioned by Henry VIII to go on a diplomatic mission to Flanders to renegotiate commercial treaties England had made with that region during the reign of Henry VII. More accompanied Cuthbert Tunstall, Richard Sampson, Thomas Spinelli, and John Clifford.

Tunstall and Sampson were members of the king's council, and for the next fifteen years Tunstall would be one of More's closest friends. He was a bastard, and like Thomas Wolsey, he was saved from obscurity by the power of his intellect and by the liberal spirit of the medieval Catholic Church that scorned no man for his origins as long as his mind and energy were quick and safe. Tunstall's father acknowledged him and sent him to Oxford about 1491. Although he was four years older than Thomas More, the two may have met at the university, since they were there at the same time. Tunstall afterwards took a degree in the Roman law from the University of Padua. The Roman law and canon law were spiritual siblings, and it was not at all uncommon for English churchmen to study both. Padua, in the sphere of Venice, was a noted center of Aristotelian learning, and it had a reputation for theological and philosophical radicalism as well as a tradition of independence in the face of papal pretensions.

Tunstall, however, was a conservative, and once back in England from Italy, he rose rapidly in the conservative ecclesiastical climate fostered by Archbishop William Warham, whose chancellor or chief executive officer Tunstall became. His knowledge of the Continent, his discretion, and his ability to give a speech made him a good diplomat, used on occasional missions by Henry VIII. He would become bishop of London in 1522, and he was always to be one of the most respected churchmen in the realm. In the end his friendship with More could not endure the strain of Henry VIII's divorce, but until that time—still distant in 1515—he was More's closest intellectual confidant.

Spinelli was an Italian in Henry's service, a man very much like Andrea Ammonio and other learned Italians who put their learning to work for the Tudors. Spinelli had served the king before as an agent to Flanders. Clifford was the "governor of the merchants of the English nation," a kind of consul general in Flanders. More was called a squire, meaning simply that he was a gentleman, an "esquire," a leading citizen, although one without a title of nobility.

The Flemish connection was the most important part of English trade. To the great weaving cities of Flanders, England sold both wool and unfinished cloth. From these cities, until her own industrial age, she bought garments that had been dyed and finished by the craftsmen of the Flemish towns. She also bought luxury goods that came into Flanders from Italy, Spain, and the rest of the Mediterranean. As a member of the Mercers' Company, More represented the mercantile interests of London.

By the middle of May, More was installed in Bruges, still an ocean port then, although because of the silting up of its harbor, it was already giving way rapidly to Antwerp, the greatest of the Flemish ports and the doorway to English commerce.

The negotiations went slowly; time lay heavy on More's hands. What we remember from this visit is not the political and diplomatic necessity that took him to Flanders, but the fact that it was there that he wrote his *Utopia*, the first work of the Renaissance in England that was to become known all over Catholic Europe.

5

THOMAS MORE
AND THE RENAISSANCE

W E H A V E already seen that many of Thomas More's earliest friends were Englishmen who had been to Italy, there to absorb something of the new learning of the Renaissance. No writer has ever defined "Renaissance" to the satisfaction of everyone who has studied its legacy. It is wise to start with what the term "rebirth" meant to the people who first used it: they meant the rebirth of the art of Greek and Roman antiquity, an artistic flourishing created by Italian painters, sculptors, and architects who first learned to duplicate and then to go beyond the technical proficiency of the classical age.

To most educated Europeans, the fascination of painting and sculpture lay in its realism. Sculptors freed what looked like real human bodies from the imprisonment of stone, and both painters and sculptors captured expressions that often revealed character and temperament in so universal a fashion as to make us believe even today—certainly with some illusion—that we know people like that.

More's own sense of the visual arts never went beyond that level. Like Erasmus, he expressed amazement that painters could capture the appearance of things with astonishing fidelity. When More had Holbein do drawings and paintings of his household, he must have felt that he was getting his money's worth because the likenesses were so true to life. We have become so accustomed to this technical proficiency that we can scarcely appreciate the astonishment and admiration it created among those who saw it first—just as we cannot appreciate the reaction of the first movie audiences who thought that the dramas they witnessed on the flickering screen were live.

It is not far from this simple delight in the realism of art to the pleasures Renaissance men took in classical literature. In the first letter we have from More, written when he was twenty-three, he tells his friend John Holt, "You ask how I am doing in my studies. Wonderfully, of course; things could not be better. I have shelved my Latin books, to take up the study of Greek."

To men like More, classical literature seemed more real, more a part of the common human experience than the high-flown theological puzzles of the Scholastics, which seemed so far from normal thought as to be ludicrous. There was cause for such sentiments. Few of us read medieval literature nowadays, but the Greeks and the Romans continue to have a devoted and often vociferous audience. The reason is simply that when we read Plato or see *Oedipus Rex* or *Medea* performed on the stage, the universality of their characterization makes us feel that we already know these passions and these ideas, that they make explicit a lesson that we have somehow already learned, that in short we not only perceive but recall. We may suppose that the discovery of this literature in the Renaissance provided a comforting reality to those who took it up in the face of the distant abstraction of much medieval thought.

Renaissance artists developed perspective, the illusion that as we look on a two-dimensional surface covered with a painting only a few millimeters thick, we are looking through a window onto a scene where the figures have the solidity of three dimensions. Renaissance historians began to perceive the difference between their own times and the past they described—a distance scarcely known in the Middle Ages, when Mary appeared in the garb of an urban matron, the soldiers of the Roman Empire in medieval armor, and Herod and David in the array of medieval kings. Then the past faded into a vague folk memory where men and women of antiquity were no different from the people one saw in the throng of a feudal procession. Once the difference between past and present was recognized in the Renaissance, the aim of historians became to re-create the past in words, to make it live again for readers. The talents of the good historian were directed both to reality and proportion, to a recognition of what makes good evidence and to a perception of how it should be gracefully fitted together to tell a story.

More's own literary preoccupations shared the passion of visual artists for harmonious arrangement and instructive realism—for artists and literati both studied the past to edify the present. The goal of edification was harmony. The literary scholars of the Renaissance (we call them "humanists," a name they did not use for themselves) had absorbed from Plato and the classical philosophical tradition the belief that the good, the beautiful, the divine were all joined, perhaps identical. Literati like More, interested in reform in church and secular life, aspired to make society harmonious and to keep in careful balance the various rival communities in the commonwealth and the rival passions and needs of individual human beings. In their ideal world, citizens lived orderly lives, and the professions of society and its conduct were in symmetry with each other. It was the flaw of such reformers to exclaim at the aesthetic delights of projected reforms rather than to engage in the hard political work to bring reform about.

Yet this aesthetic impulse created a new sensibility, and Thomas More shared it and shared also the special turmoil of the collision of medieval and Renaissance. A thesis of this biography is that until his imprisonment More suffered the severe inner conflict of a deeply divided soul. Perhaps the fundamental cause was that he struggled to combine medieval piety with the invincible temptations of Renaissance secularism.

We should be careful to avoid the easy assumption that the Middle Ages represented only an otherworldly piety and that Renaissance secularism was identical to the irreligious, casual atheism of modern secular society. Many elements of medieval sensibility continued into the Renaissance and still persist because they seem to be inextricably bound up with the human condition. Medieval thinkers, including both artists and theologians, wanted symmetry and harmony as much as Thomas More ever did.

The conflict was over how that harmony might be attained. In the twelfth century, St. Bernard of Clairvaux and Abelard fought a furious battle over the relation of reason and faith in theology. Abelard was an early medieval Aristotelian, enthralled as Aristotelians tend to be with the vision of classifying and systematizing all knowledge by means of the cool certainty of logic. Aristotle believed that by the orderly arrangement of data acquired by the senses, we can understand everything worth knowing and that all things that can be known are parts in a grand system with neither contradictions nor flaws, an intelligible system where reason permeates the world. His could be called the great unified field theory held for centuries, and since the demise of the Aristotelian faith in the unity of all knowledge—a demise evident by the eighteenth century—we have not had a substitute for it in Western thought, not even in mathematics.

Abelard believed that the gift of reason came from God and that it was intended by God to draw reasoning humankind back to Himself, that reason was what Aristotle said it was—the faculty of the mind to begin by doubt and then to proceed, a step at a time, with what could be known, to build a system with all the parts in perfect harmony with one another, the harmony itself open to the human mind.

Bernard was much closer to what Thomas More later became—suspicious of reason, hostile to any presumption that men might penetrate the secret mysteries of the Almighty. Bernard wanted rapture—an aesthetic emotion— that lifted the soul from the love of self to the complete love of God, a love that filled the soul with bliss, conveying an intuitive certainty far richer than intellectual understanding, a direct experience that was a foretaste of heaven itself. His comments on the Old Testament book called the Song of Solomon, which he loved to expound, may serve for his definition of religion:

> A canticle of this kind, fervor alone can teach; it can be learned only through experience. Those who have experienced it will recognize this. Those who have not experienced it, may they burn with desire not so much to know as to experience.

His ideal of the beauty of God and the divine destiny of the soul reduced reason and Aristotelian logic to a servile place because he thought that to ask searching questions of the faith was to court eternal danger to the soul. He could see no beauty at all in the systematic inquiry that Abelard so much admired and so eloquently taught. Bernard thought it was all blasphemy. He ridiculed also the elaborate convolutions of the Gothic architecture, new in the twelfth century and flowering across northern Europe with its stained glass and high arches that let light pour into the sanctuary, with its gargoyles and other monstrous figures that medieval architects made part of the only architectural form that ever tried to embrace the universe. Bernard would have understood perfectly the physical simplicity of worship that Thomas More imagined in Utopia, where the churches were dark within because the Utopians thought that "excessive light makes the thoughts wander," but that dim light leads the soul to true worship.

Thomas Aquinas, best known of the great Scholastic thinkers after Abelard, followed Abelard's road to Aristotle and so combined piety with questioning that he won a lasting place for Aristotelian logic in theology. Aquinas found beauty in the intellect and labored to build a theological system in which all the apparently contradictory things Christians believed were carefully reconciled and the whole was fitted together in a unity of diversity that, as many have noted, corresponded to the architectural unity of the Gothic cathedrals.

Bernard's spiritual disciples never surrendered their conviction that it was essential to love God and dangerous to try to understand Him. Bernard's truest followers were the Franciscans, whose order, if we are to believe Thomas Stapleton, Thomas More aspired to join. The partisans of human reason defended their quest by encircling their work with a rhetoric of piety that made the intellectual search for God a way of praising Him. These professions were entirely sincere; of that there can be no doubt. But their energy must have come in part from the need such thinkers felt to justify their fascination with logic to those who found Christianity more an affair of the heart than the head.

Yet both the Scholastic way of Abelard and Aquinas and the mystical way of Bernard depended on an aesthetic sense. We must suppose that the philosophical theologians building their great systems felt some of the same emotions known by artists at work on successful creations. A good argument is not merely convincing; it is beautiful. Perhaps only the philosophically inclined can understand such a statement, but they are surprised that it is not self-evident to others. Bernard, Francis of Assisi, and others in their fervent train spoke continually of the beauty of holiness. So the aesthetic ideal hardly fell on Europe suddenly and without warning in the Renaissance; it merely changed its form.

Other things as well continued from the medieval spirit. Both the Renaissance and the Middle Ages took emotional sustenance from old books and old traditions. Thomas More received his early education in the seven liberal arts under the common faith that all human knowledge about creation had been set down a long time ago and that study meant learning for oneself what had been known before by someone else. The medieval doctors of the church claimed to expound a tradition that ran back to Christ himself, a tradition that faithfully handed down beliefs and practices that had been used by the Savior and by his immediate followers in the primitive church. Novelty was abhorrent. Thomas Aquinas and the other Scholastics never intended to use Aristotelian logic to deliver something new to Christian Europe; they meant only to show that everything Christians had believed from the beginning could be made to harmonize, to be systematized.

But perusal of ancient texts increasingly available after the invention of printing revealed some startling and disquieting items. The texts had been corrupted in their passage across the centuries. Some things had been added, some books had been forged, the medieval grasp on antiquity was shown to be much less certain than Aquinas and others had supposed.

We have spoken of the lack of historical consciousness in the Middle Ages. Medieval scholars did believe in history; they did not think that life was an endless cycle; they saw time drawn out in a line from creation to redemption. But although they believed in history, they did not have much sense of the historical. They knew that one thing happened after another, and they left us innumerable chronicles that set down the events of successive years, often going all the way back to Adam. What these chroniclers and their readers did not perceive was that whole patterns of culture changed with time and that the great events of history were only part of a vast and continuous shifting in the way men and women lived and thought. The medieval histories recorded the great events but remained oblivious of the change.

As Renaissance artists and sculptors studied Greek and Roman statuary, they perceived that customs of dress had changed. The excavation and study of Roman ruins revealed that architecture had changed. Close attention to texts revealed that the shape of life itself had been altered with the slow revolutions of the centuries. The transmission of texts had been a part of this relentless transformation. As Renaissance scholars came to see how different the present was from the antiquity that absorbed their minds, they could see that the texts were different, too. Above all, the text of scripture had been corrupted, and the texts of the fathers of the church were found to be riddled with errors.

The Middle Ages and the Renaissance were at one in their veneration of the ancient and the traditional. But the Renaissance humanists discovered that the medieval perception of the ancient was badly flawed and that many beliefs and practices supposedly old and sacred were in fact novelties, possibly not sacred at all, possibly the product of human contrivance and even of human perversion.

This discovery of gigantic change—so full of common sense to us because our world changes with terrifying rapidity—was met with a combination of pessimism and hope. It was one thing to discover that the usages of medieval chivalry had been unknown to the Greeks and the Romans; it was quite another to ponder the poverty and the simplicity of the primitive church and to compare it with the wealth and complexity of the church of the later Middle Ages.

Many devout souls in the Renaissance believed that the steady accretion of novelty to the text of scripture was a satanic corruption and that the world stood on the edge of doom because it had forsaken the original inspiration of God. Many humanists—including Erasmus and sometimes Thomas More— thought that the Scholastic philosophy based on Aristotle was one of these corrupting novelties. But the trouble was not limited to texts and traditions. Somehow the entire society had become corrupt, and no one could tell where the corruptions would end short of the horrible advent of Antichrist and the spilling out of the wrath of God upon the earth.

From this prodigious sense of the depravity of the age was to come the Protestant Reformation, fed by the printing press, an invention that made the formal pessimism of intellectuals the common property of literate Europeans. Serious writers had to be gloomy in print if they were to be respectable and read. Thomas More adopted this formal gloom and made it the background of nearly everything he wrote; unlike others, he believed it.

The traditional Christian style has always been to bemoan the wickedness of the present and to look back nostalgically to the good old days when life was supposed to have been purer and people more saintly. Unfortunately, when we examine those supposed golden ages, we find people in them complaining about the decay of their times and looking back to other good old days: Renaissance Christians looked back to the fathers of the church; the fathers of the church—perplexed and frequently furious at the divisions in the church of their times—to the New Testament. The later books of the New Testament bemoaned a corrupt and heretical church; even Peter and Paul quarreled over the true meaning of the gospel, Judas betrayed Christ, and Peter denied his master. Thomas More, idealizing Christian antiquity, scarcely perceived that rather than making an acute observation about his own times, he was falling into a habit of centuries. In the Renaissance, this habit of gloom became a cry of moral misery echoing through the world. It is well enough for us to argue now that the moral and intellectual state of the church in the Renaissance was probably better than it had been for two centuries. People like Thomas More, John Colet, Erasmus of Rotterdam, and Martin Luther thought that the church was in miserable shape and that reform had to come if society was to endure.

Why was this sense of corruption so strong if the corruption itself was no worse than it ever had been? As we have indicated, part of it was literary habit, a habit both fed on and nourished by the printing press. Yet there is something else here, and we must wonder if the sense of corruption in the church became so strong because intellectual doubts about the legitimacy of Christianity itself became so profound. It may well be that educated Christians demanded reform in the church with such passion because they were trying to find some hold on a faith that seemed to be dissolving in their hands. If reason could no longer support faith, perhaps purity could.

By More's time the synthesis Aquinas had made between reason and faith had broken down—if indeed that synthesis had ever truly existed. The subject was still fervently debated. Many of the ridiculous problems that More and Erasmus mocked when they mocked Scholastic theology arose from efforts to make some common dwelling for reason and faith in the Christian community. Could God have been incarnate in a stone? Why not, if He was all-powerful! God did not have to order the world or to reveal Himself in the ways He has chosen; He could have chosen other ways, utterly different from the ones He has used. Reason must admit such things once it accepts the omnipotence of God. But then reason lost all hope of proving that faith and reason went hand in hand or that there was an Aristotelian intelligibility to the universe. The universe was not the way it was because it was permeated with reason; it was the way it was solely because God had willed it so. The effect was to remove God a vast psychic distance from the earth, to feel as if perhaps He might be something other than what the Christian church claimed He was.

The debates about faith and reason were carried on with foolish subjects—as More and Erasmus both attest. Yet they were fought with such intensity that they must give us pause. Martin Luther was not preoccupied with mere moral questions; he struggled mightily to affirm the existence of the benevolent, loving personal God of the ancient Christian faith. He could do so only by launching a revolution, a revolution that was a passionate, uncompromising, often hateful effort to make affirmations in a world of doubt.

Most were not so strong. The reforming Catholic humanists, including Thomas More, nourished a desperate optimism, the hope that all might be well if Christians could only penetrate the obscurity that had gathered over European letters during what Petrarch called the "dark age" and rediscover and re-create a world where people lived unselfishly, in a society of virtue, proving Christianity true, not by dead logic, but by living example. They supposed that if the literature of the classical world, which included primitive Christianity, could be uncovered in its textual purity, it might help reform and purify Christian Europe in much the same way that clearing the accumulated debris of centuries from around a buried ruin had often revealed a breathtaking and inspiring beauty that had impelled artists to make creations of their own. Here and there we find examples of frivolous learning in the Renaissance, and the frivolity of customs was a continual complaint of the times. But most striking to us in our own age of frivolity is to feel, by dipping into the books of the time, the deep, anxious yearning that swept scholars like Erasmus and literati like More along in the conviction that ancient study was modern salvation.

Italy was the source of this new learning about old things. The most important of More's friends who went there to study was John Colet, born about 1467, member of a family powerful among the merchants of London. In his travels in Italy as a youth, he may have met Marsilio Ficino, the Florentine polymath who translated all of Plato's extant dialogues from Greek into Latin. At least Colet and Ficino corresponded, for we have some of their letters. Both were imbued with the Neoplatonic vision of the distinction between soul and body. Neoplatonists believed that all life should be a process of climbing from the seen to the unseen world and that the soul was strengthened against its enemy, the body, by proper education. To them reason was not a way of solving logical problems but a way of dominating the passions of the body and purifying the soul.

In 1497 Colet gave a series of lectures at Oxford on Paul's Epistle to the Romans. He created a sensation. Instead of suffocating his audience with quotations from medieval commentaries as Scholastic lecturers habitually did, he swept away centuries of turgid and often fantastic pedantry and went directly to the text itself. (At least he went to the Latin text of the Vulgate; despite his admiration of Plato and Ficino, Colet never learned Greek.) What he gave his entranced auditors sounds a little like the expository preaching of Puritan divines later on in Britain and America, although unlike most of them, Colet interpreted Paul as a thoroughgoing Platonist very much like Colet himself. Erasmus wrote in 1499, "When I hear my Colet, I seem to be listening to Plato himself."

Colet dealt boldly with the teaching of divine predestination that leaps out of Romans to stun and trouble those possessed of the comfortable notion that God always does what human beings think is fair. No human wisdom can understand God's ways. Why did God harden Pharaoh's heart as Paul says He did? Colet says we cannot know. The point is that God knows what He is doing even if we do not; our duty is to adore rather than to question. Colet was sure Christians knew enough about God to live better lives, and morality to him was the most important element in Christian life.

The doctrine of predestination was yet another way of confounding reason. More did not easily accept the doctrine, although like most orthodox Christians who ponder it at length, he was finally driven to embrace it. He was never a Platonist except in the general sense that Platonic rhetoric about death as liberation and the immortality of the soul influenced most Christian thought in the sixteenth century. But Colet embodied a piety and a learning that deeply impressed More, and he was a preacher of such power that More was quoting his sermons long after Colet died in 1519. Colet was also one of that powerful group of scholars who believed that education was the surest way to reform. In 1504 he became dean of St. Paul's Cathedral, and in a few years he established St. Paul's Grammar School, dedicated to teaching young boys literature and Christian piety. William Lily became his first high master, charged with supervising 153 students. The Mercers' Company, to which More and Colet belonged, was given financial responsibility for the school.

Colet wanted the young to read Christian authors and to learn good Latin, which to him was classical Latin. He hated the barbarous Latin of the medieval theologians, speaking of it in his characteristically forceful way: "I say that filthiness and all such abuse which the later blind world brought in, which more rather may be called blotterature than literature, I utterly banish and exclude out of this school and charge the Masters that they teach always that [which] is the best and instruct the children in Greek and reading Latin [by] reading unto them such authors that have with wisdom joined the pure, chaste eloquence."

Colet's zeal for the Bible and for reform based on the simplicity of the primitive church drew Lollards to his sermons and also got him into trouble with the authorities. Bishop of London Richard FitzJames accused him of heresy, but Colet's reputation and his powerful friends prevented the bishop's charges from getting anywhere. If Erasmus is to be believed, Colet disparaged pilgrimages and the relics of saints. FitzJames accused him of preaching against images. Certain it is that Colet stormed against the clergy for worldliness and other corruptions.

More also met William Grocyn, the first Englishman to teach Greek in his own land. Grocyn had been born about 1449, so that he was around forty when he went to Italy in 1488. He came back in 1490 and was lecturing on Greek at Oxford when More was a student there, though we do not know if they met then. The first certain knowledge of their acquaintance comes from More's letter to John Holt in November 1501, where More mentions that Grocyn is instructing him in Greek, and adds the news that Grocyn was lecturing on *The Celestial Hierarchy* of Dionysius the Areopagite.

These lectures represent a great moment in Renaissance scholarship. Dionysius was thought to have been the Athenian converted by the sermon preached by the apostle Paul on Mars Hill, the "Areopagus," just below the Acropolis. He was supposed to have been the first bishop of Athens, and his works were revered by medieval scholars only slightly less than the Bible itself.

To us *The Celestial Hierarchy* is a strange book, unreadable and seldom read. Dionysius considered the order of spiritual beings and classified them in ranks. The heavenly realm was a pyramid; the higher one got, the more authority, but the fewer there were of each class. At the apex was God, dwelling alone in His stupendous and almighty eternity. One approached this God through an ascent of the soul.

The Celestial Hierarchy appeared to give divine sanction to the hierarchies that existed on earth, for it was thought that earth should duplicate heaven as much as possible. In the church there should be lay people at the bottom, then various orders of minor clergy, common priests, bishops, archbishops, and finally, in the Western church, the pope at the top. In secular society there should be peasants, burghers, knights, lords, kings, and an emperor who should rule over all the inhabited world. It was in the spirit of Dionysius that Thomas Aquinas declared that the general inequality of things was from God.

And it was in the same spirit that medieval thought in general held to a rigid view of a stratified society. People were born in the status God intended them to have, and those who tried to climb above their origins—like merchants— were viewed with suspicion and sometimes with outright hostility because they seemed to be trying to undo the orderly and serene harmony that God had set for the world. Kings were kings because God made them so. Peasants bent their backs in the fields because God intended them to labor when He caused them to be born. Bishops could not be born bishops, but when the bishop's miter was offered to a priest, he had to refuse it three times. This litany of refusal was meant to be a sign that he was not rising out of personal ambition but in response to the call of God.

By the time Grocyn began lecturing on *The Celestial Hierarchy*, a few critics had begun to say that the work was a pious fraud. Years later Erasmus wrote that Grocyn began by attacking critics of the work but ended by seeing that they were right. He saw that whoever "Dionysius" was, he could not have been a contemporary of Paul the apostle.

We do not know the line of argument that led Grocyn to his conclusion; he was a great teacher, but he did not publish, and only a short letter of his has survived. We do know what others said, and we may surmise that some of Grocyn's arguments were the same. They noticed that though early Christians were always quoting each other, they never quoted Dionysius, supposedly converted by Paul. Nor was there any mention of him by Cyprian, who died in 258; or by Jerome, who died in 420; or by Augustine, who died in 430. The work was written in Greek, and when Renaissance scholars learned Greek and began to study Dionysius, they discovered words coined long after the New Testament was written. Once people began reflecting on these oddities, the conclusion was inescapable that the book was a forgery. It is now the nearly unanimous opinion of scholars that it was written about the beginning of the sixth century after Christ.

More must have witnessed Grocyn's conversion to the view that *The Celestial Hierarchy* was not to be trusted. When Luther came crashing onto the European scene, many Catholics—including More's friend and later fellow martyr John Fisher—used Dionysius to refute him. More never did; Grocyn's lessons endured.

But a larger issue than Dionysius was at stake; namely, the value to be placed on history and the sense of history itself. If the books by Dionysius, so long revered in the church, were forgeries, who could say that any of the medieval doctors of the church could be trusted? If the church had erred in the faith it had placed in Dionysius, could it not have erred on many other important things as well?

As we have seen, Scholastic thought in the later Middle Ages was built on the assumption that all the things Christians believed, whether commanded in the Bible or sanctified by tradition, could be finally arranged in a grand system without contradictions. Scholastics worked for generation after generation trying to make this systematic statement of theology, weeding out apparent contradictions and puzzles by using Aristotelian logic. The underlying conviction in this patient enterprise held that the labor of commenting on texts through the centuries had to add up to something. The Scholastics accepted the sacred quality of tradition—the record of what the church had believed and practiced since its founding by Christ—more than did the Renaissance humanists with their predilection for original sources and their dislike of Scholastic problems. (All the humanists did not scorn Scholasticism, but most of them did.) The Scholastics did not think that God would allow generations of their scholarship to go to waste; saints like Thomas Aquinas could not have labored in vain. Everyone agreed that their work was incomplete, but the Scholastic view of history was a kind of dialectic in itself, that one generation of scholars worked, that the next took their work and reacted against it and produced a synthesis that became in its turn the material for another generation of scholars to test and revise. In time a great edifice of reason would resolve all the contradictions, or it would at least succeed in bringing about a unity of assumption about the faith, granting to the church a seamless garment of things to be believed.

Now, in their distinct ways, Colet and Grocyn undermined the belief that the wisdom of the church was cumulative. Grocyn at least intended no such thing; unlike most students of Greek at the time, he was devoted to Scholastic theology. He loved Aristotle and spoke of Plato only with contempt. But whatever his intent and his affections, he was making matches to burn the woods. The discovery that Dionysius's works were forgeries contributed to a growing skepticism about some parts of the church's tradition, a skepticism not helped by the continuing revelation by scholars that many other books supposedly written by ancient fathers were in fact later impostures. Just as the harmony between faith and reason became more problematical, the demand for a morally reformed church grew more intense. If Christian faith could not be somehow validated by reason, and if long traditions could be proved wrong, it was all the more important that the church, with its claim to hold the keys of the kingdom, should be proved true by the pure moral example that a reformed priesthood and purified practice could provide.

More's devotion to Grocyn continued. In his letter to Colet written about 1504, he told his absent friend that until his return, "I shall pass my time with Grocyn, Linacre, and our dear friend Lily, the first as you know the sole guide of my life (in your absence), the second my master in learning, and the third the dearest partner of my endeavors." We have noted that More gave his lectures on Augustine's *City of God* in the church of St. Lawrence Jewry, where Grocyn was, at the time, vicar.

As an important sidenote, we should mention that Grocyn was also tutor to William Warham and kept close ties to him after Warham became Archbishop of Canterbury. More probably came to Warham's attention through Grocyn. Although we cannot prove that Warham influenced More or his career, we can say with some confidence that his would have been a voice raised in favor of More's entry into royal service when the opportunity came.

In the letter to Colet, More also mentions Thomas Linacre and William Lily —other ties to the Renaissance. Linacre had been to Italy, staying for about six years, longer than anyone else More would have known. Like Tunstall, he had been to Padua, where Aristotle was avidly studied for his medical lore as well as for his philosophy. Linacre took a medical degree. At Padua, Aristotelianism had led some to doubt the immortality of the soul; at least they doubted that immortality was plausible to reason. So it is probably from both Linacre and Tunstall that More took his knowledge of such ideas, knowledge that crops up several times in his writing.

Linacre came back to Oxford sometime during the 1490s, and in 1499 he had some responsibility for introducing Erasmus, then visiting England, to the study of Greek, although Grocyn may have taken the lead in this tutoring. After years of receiving the income from ecclesiastical preferments—the grants of their day that allowed scholars the leisure to pursue their bookish interests —Linacre was ordained in 1520 and gave up his medical practice. He died in 1524 from the complications of kidney stones—one of the horrors of the time. More was one of the trustees of a bequest Linacre made to found a lectureship in medicine at Oxford. For some reason it was not established until well over a decade after More's death.

Lily was also a student of Greek, and the partnership More mentions in his letter to Colet may have been the friendly rivalry More and Lily set for themselves in translating Greek epigrams into Latin. The products of their joint labors were published with other epigrams by More in the third edition of *Utopia* in 1518. Lily had been on a pilgrimage to Jerusalem, and he had stayed for some time on Rhodes. More may have taken from him the tale of the miraculous thorn of Rhodes which bloomed out with a fresh rose on every Good Friday, a tale More told as proof that miracles still happened in the world under the auspices of the Catholic Church.

Lily returned from his pilgrimage by way of Italy and stayed there to study for a time. He has always been renowned for his simplified Latin grammar, developed for the boys at St. Paul's Grammar School, through which centuries of English children learned the mysteries of the eight parts of speech and the delights of *amo, amas, amat,* as well as the ablative absolute. He was the natural choice of Colet to be the first high master of his school.

It is hard to make sensible generalizations about these friendships and their influence on More. They took place against a background of general intellectual quickening throughout Europe and the conviction that good learning led to good living. The common denominator of these friendships is Greek— knowing it well as Lily, Linacre, and Grocyn did, or believing in its value as Colet did. All these friends were older than More; Colet was born about 1467, Lily perhaps a year later, Linacre about 1460, Grocyn about 1449. More delighted in their company and in pleasing them just as he delighted in his own father's company and in pleasing him. Whether we can make anything of this fact is hard to say.

The men themselves represented the contradictions of the age—contradictions we find in More. As we have seen, Colet seems to have regarded pilgrimages and relics as superstitions or, at least, unnecessary, but Lily made the arduous and dangerous journey to Jerusalem, a pilgrimage Christians took because in the Holy Land relics were everywhere. Colet held the Scholastics in contempt, but Grocyn read them with devotion. Linacre and Grocyn loved Aristotle; Colet was a Platonist.

More vehemently defended pilgrimages and relics, but so far as we know never went on a pilgrimage himself and never had anything to say about his own seeking out of relics, though he does mention with appropriate reverence some handkerchiefs supposedly hemmed by the Virgin, handkerchiefs that came to light accidentally and that he saw. He wrote conventionally against Scholastic questions and just as conventionally called Aquinas "the flower of theology." He used Platonic rhetoric now and then, but he was much more an Aristotelian in spirit, and he was not in any formal sense a philosopher.

These contradictions are worth noting as proof—if any were needed—that the term "Renaissance" does not hold a universal meaning. For many the new learning meant a pathway into reform, but the shape of that reform remained vague and general, fixed on the faith that if people knew a lot, they would be better for their learning, giving education pride of place over action, which these men never spelled out very well. Knowledge involved associations with other scholars and pleasure in their company, and so these men pursued it, unaware—as people are always unaware—that they were sharing in a gradual and accumulating movement that would make the world a far different place from what they wanted or imagined.

The Renaissance spirit looked backward to Greece and Rome and to ancient and supposedly superhuman knowledge set down in books reverently rediscovered, edited, printed, and read throughout Christian Europe by people thirsty for pure learning and swift reform. But in 1492 an Italian mariner in the service of the monarchs of a newly united Spain put to sea in three flimsy ships to sail in search of a western passage to the riches of the East.

Late on the night of October 12, a Spanish sailor scanning the moonlit ocean caught the glimmer of man-made light shining out of the dark and wakened his ship and then the tiny fleet with his cry of "Land! Land!" Thomas More was at Oxford; the great world around him went on in its seemingly eternal routines, and when news of the discoveries of Columbus circulated in Europe, people seemed most interested in reports that the natives of those lands out there went around naked. The stories of nakedness were more than erotic; Adam and Eve had been naked in the Garden of Eden before the fall, and some minds were naturally stirred with the supposition that these strange new peoples had somehow escaped the corruptions that plagued old Europe.

Columbus was a humanist in his way; he had unshakable faith in the classical wisdom encapsulated by Ptolemy, who believed that the world was a much smaller ball than it really is. So Columbus could never understand that he had stumbled onto a new world—a world unknown to the wise Greeks and the learned Romans. Finally, another Italian, Amerigo Vespucci, sailing along the coast of South America, making observations of latitude, comparing them with bearings taken by sailors who had sailed to India and China around the horn of Africa, realized that here was a continent undreamed of by antiquity.

The political and social revolutions provoked by the discovery of America are well known. It has been less frequently observed that Columbus effectively demolished the intellectual supposition that everything worth knowing had been known to Greece and Rome and that the surest way to wisdom was to discover and study ancient books.

The Renaissance myth of the golden age held that the distant past was perfection and that the best any society could do was to imitate something that had been done long ago and that the only worthwhile learning was to recapture the lore of a book that was centuries old. Now the location of the golden age in time began to shift, and increasingly it came to be an age yet to be attained, something glimmering in the future, making all the past of less account. The idea of progress slowly and irrevocably replaced a reverence for tradition. And people were moved, almost unconsciously at first, to renounce all the past as something that should be shaken off, and life began to resound with the tramping feet of a world marching forward into novelty and to what it assumed would be glory.

6

MORE AND ERASMUS

THE GREATEST SCHOLAR of the Northern Renaissance was Erasmus of Rotterdam, and he first came to England in 1499 while More was still a student at Lincoln's Inn. The two met and became friends. It is a commonplace to say that their friendship was one of the jewels of the Renaissance, and Erasmus himself declared again and again until the end of his life his affection and admiration for his English friend. They shared a love of Greek and the belief that a sound education in the best classical literature could create a sound piety in the present and help reform the church. Both were great talkers and apparently they had some memorable conversations.

Erasmus was born in 1467 or maybe two or three years later. He was the bastard son of a Dutch priest, and he always felt ashamed of his ignoble origins. His parents died when he was young, and his guardians put him in the Augustinian monastery at Steyn. Later he claimed that his guardians spent his inheritance and forced him to take monastic vows to be rid of him. Certainly nothing suggests that Erasmus became a monk to save his soul. He was always rather pleased with himself, rather sure that people did not treat him as well as he deserved. He never exhibited any sentiments like those of Martin Luther, another Augustinian monk, who took the cowl out of guilty torment for his sin and out of fear of damnation. If Erasmus ever felt guilty about anything, he was singularly quiet about it.

He was lonely in the monastery. His letters from the period ache with a desire for love—saccharine letters to other young men, begging them for love, protesting that they ignored his outpourings of devotion. Perhaps these letters were merely the effusions of a misplaced Latinity, for the Latin epistolary style lends itself to hyperbole and to expressions of emotion that sound embarrassing when translated into English.

In 1493 a larger world opened abruptly. The bishop of Cambrai, Henrik of Bergen, planned a trip to Rome, where he hoped to receive a cardinal's hat. He needed a good Latin secretary to accompany him; someone suggested Erasmus. The abbot of Steyn seems to have jumped at the chance to attach one of his own to the staff of a bishop, and he gave Erasmus leave to go, expecting the young man to return to the cloister and to the quiet ways of the monastic routine after his service to the bishop ended. Erasmus never went back except on infrequent visits that in a few years ceased altogether.

The bishop never made his Roman journey, but he was impressed enough with Erasmus to send him to the University of Paris to study. Erasmus lived in the dismal College of Montaigu (the sharp mountain), where later John Calvin and Ignatius Loyola studied. He hated the diet of bad fish and the hard discipline, and he thought his teachers were barbarians. After a year or so, he left.

The bishop lost interest in him. To make a living he became a tutor. One of his charges was a young Englishman named Thomas Grey. For a time they shared rooms, but Grey's guardian became suspicious that they might be too intimate, and he threw Erasmus out. Erasmus wrote heartbroken letters to Grey, lamenting the loss of their companionship. Then he got another job, this one tutoring William Blount, Lord Mountjoy, distinguished in England for his military virtues. Mountjoy wanted a fashionable humanist education in the classics, and he invited Erasmus to visit England in the summer in 1499. There the young Dutchman, at a loss for friends, purpose, and place in the world, met Thomas More.

Several legendary accounts have come down to us of how they met; none of them can be true. They did meet, but we do not know how, and nothing much came of their meeting at first. More was about ten years younger than Erasmus, although the difference in age would have been no barrier to friendship given More's tendency to choose older friends. But More was studying law, a discipline that Erasmus disliked and mistrusted, and his piety was more profound than that of Erasmus, especially at that time.

Still they got on. Erasmus had reason to be impressed, both for More's precocious learning and for his important associations. We have mentioned the incident at Eltham—the two new friends setting out on a walk, coming to Eltham Palace, asked to remain for dinner with the young Duke of York, later Henry VIII. Writing to an English friend in December of that year, Erasmus praised England extravagantly and lauded the friends he had made there. He had never been so pleased by anything, he wrote. The climate was most pleasant and healthful, and there were so many learned in Latin and Greek that now he had no need to go to Italy, he said, except for the pleasure of seeing it. "When I hear my Colet, I seem to hear Plato himself. As for Grocyn, who is not amazed at his complete mastery of disciplines? What is sharper than the judgment of Linacre, what higher, what more refined? When did nature ever fashion a temper more gentle, more sweet, or more happy than that of Thomas More? Now why should I recite the rest of the catalogue? It is amazing to see how thickly this standing grain of ancient letters now ripens to Harvest."

Here Erasmus is already reaching behind the Scholastic tradition, which bored him, to bask in the ideal virtues of the classical world, and he sees More as a member of a company of older and learned men. He remarks not on More's learning, but on his disposition, obviously a temperament that stirred something in Erasmus, at that time in his life yearning for the affection of young men.

We have one letter from him to More from this period, a short note written from Oxford on October 28, 1499. Erasmus had gone there to live in the local house of the Augustinian order and to share in the life of the university, perhaps drawn by Grocyn and Linacre, who could teach him Greek. Erasmus begs More for letters. He wants so many that they would break the back of an Egyptian porter. (Egyptian porters were legendary for their strength since, presumably, they had lofted the stones to build the pyramids.) The note is like the other effusions Erasmus habitually wrote to men whose friendship he craved in these years, and we have no evidence that More replied.

Erasmus stayed in England until after the first of the year, when he went back to the Continent. He had managed to collect twenty pounds during his English visit—a handsome sum, enough to support him for months. But Henry VII had decreed that currency could not be taken out of the kingdom—in an effort to prevent a shortage of precious metals for internal trade. Erasmus did not know the law. His twenty pounds was confiscated; he thought he had been robbed, and he was furious. None of his friends could or would undo his loss. He brooded for years over that lost little treasure, and Henry VII, whom he had praised as "My Apollo, the father of the age of gold," now became a despot.

Erasmus did not return to England until 1505. In the meantime he and More did not correspond. Erasmus was making a name for himself, publishing books that More must have admired. In 1500 he brought out his *Adages*, a collection of wise sayings from the Greek and Roman world. The book demonstrated his prodigious learning and indefatigable scholarly energy, and it was devoured by an age hungry for classical learning. Its proverbs and epigrams revealed the flavor of daily life, the aspirations deemed worthy by the ancients, and perhaps above all, the intense preoccupation of classical writers with the active life and the virtues possible to men struggling in the political arena. The

Adages danced away from dogmatic balderdash and portrayed a simpler world where the ideal of art was life, not Scholastic theory, where goodness lay in reason, tolerance, measure, and duty rather than in ceremony, creeds, miracles, and doctrines. The *Adages* presented proverbial wisdom, unaided by divine revelation, and seen all together in one large book, they gave an optimistic impression of what human nature could achieve with the proper education and good will. The work was to go through many editions and to be expanded from a few hundred citations to many thousands. Students used the *Adages* to spice up their own writing and speaking, and with this one work Erasmus became a name among those who read Latin easily in Britain and on the Continent.

By 1505 Erasmus had also published a little devotional work, largely unnoticed at the time, called *The Enchiridion*, the "handbook" or "dagger" of the Christian knight. It came out in 1503, was read only by a small circle, and through the years gathered force like a stone rolling down a mountain and clattering against other stones ready to fall. Within two decades it had passed through thirty editions and had been translated into French, Dutch, Spanish, and German. Translated into English, supposedly by William Tyndale, *The Enchiridion* probably contributed more to the origins of English Puritanism than any other book except the Bible itself. Within a hundred years after Erasmus died, Protestant Pilgrims had landed on the shores of Massachusetts in the New World, dedicated to the rigorous simplicity and the union of the Christian and secular life that he had espoused in *The Enchiridion*.

Here Erasmus put forward a warm and simple piety of the heart, disparaging ceremonies, pilgrimages, the veneration of saints, and even some of the extreme forms of the cult of the Virgin Mary. He wanted to create purity and simplicity in the inner person because he was sure that a pure heart could generate good deeds without a cluttered liturgy.

He did not, of course, condemn all liturgical practices, but in this book he shows a detachment from the liturgy and from the observances of popular piety that set him apart from the spirit of Thomas More. More could not have objected to Erasmus's contention that true faith was a matter of the heart; but while Erasmus nearly always condemned ritual observance as physical ceremony detracting from true piety, More always saw the liturgy as an aid to devotion. Erasmus fixed on the worst in popular religious practice with its concentration on forms and things; More recognized the worst but never took the worst for the whole.

More would have disagreed also with the Erasmian teaching that laymen were not inferior to priests in their standing before God. The notion could mean many things. If Erasmus meant that both priests and lay persons had to confess their sins before God and repent and seek salvation, he was uttering only a theological commonplace. If in the vagueness of his language he was suggesting that the priestly order was not superior to the lay estate, he was making a revolutionary pronouncement. Fortunately for him—unfortunately for scholars of his work—he managed to write evasively enough to avoid letting us know precisely what he did think, and Thomas More could have read the work as nearly everybody did at the time without being shocked by it.

Erasmus was thoroughly conventional in some things. He objected to anything that gave bodily pleasure merely for the sake of pleasure. In discussing the incest committed by the daughters of Lot with their father, he says, "As a matter of fact, I would unhesitantly excuse your wedlock less than their incest if, in marriage, you aim not at having children but at gratifying your lusts." It was a conservative, Augustinian position; Erasmus was not so modern that he could unleash sexuality, even within marriage.

The Enchiridion is a calm and measured book sprinkled on almost every page with classical allusions that show the unity Erasmus saw in classical culture and Christian virtue, and the little book marks a conversion of sorts. The Erasmus we know before it was an aimless, wandering scholar, looking for fortune, for purpose, and for fame. With *The Enchiridion* we find a Christian philosopher who believed in living in the world without any great preoccupation with salvation in a life to come. True Christianity is to be self-disciplined, learned, meek, loving, and simple. He is not far from saying that the good Christian is the good citizen, and so it was that the ideas in *The Enchiridion* represented a quiet and enduring revolution in how educated and urbane people defined the nature of true religion.

This secular religion of Erasmus was partly formed by his increasing loathing of the monastery and his horror at the prospect of having to return there. His piety was always shaped by his desire to prove to others and perhaps to himself that a good Christian was better off outside the monastery than within its walls, which enclosed, in his view, a community predominantly ignorant, churlish, envious, and self-righteous. He wrote copiously about piety, but no evidence shows that he was especially pious himself. He wrote to put in the best possible light the scholarly life in the secular world that he had chosen for himself against his monastic vows. Such a statement is neither to reproach him nor to denigrate *The Enchiridion;* it is only to suggest that his ideals evolved from the dialectic between his old life in the cloister and the life that he had almost accidentally discovered in Greek, Latin, and classical learning.

On his second trip to England, Erasmus began a closer association with Thomas More, although we still know maddeningly little about their relations with each other. They entered into a friendly competition to translate some of the dialogues of Lucian of Samosata (125?–190?) from Greek into Latin.

The task was in keeping with a common desire to make Greek wisdom available to a Latin-reading public. Lucian would seem an unlikely interest for two Christians, since he was bawdy, sometimes obscene, always skeptical of supernatural religion. He taught that most popular religious beliefs were nonsense, and he wrote dialogues that mocked the superstitions of his day. He disbelieved in the immortality of the soul and scorned those who believed that something of us lingers after death. Luther, looking later for any weapon to use in attacking Erasmus, accused him of "stinking of Lucian." John Colet would almost certainly have excluded Lucian's work from his school at St. Paul's, since his statutes for the establishment banished pagan works of "filthiness and abuse."

But there was much in Lucian that Renaissance Christians could admire. He hated pretense, vanity, and hypocrisy. By mocking the old gods, he prepared the way for Christianity without knowing what he did. At least Christians looking for some excuse to enjoy him could see him in that light. Luther thought that all the Greek and Roman philosophers might go to hell because they had taken pride in their own wisdom without humbling themselves before God. But someone with the universalist spirit of Pico or Erasmus, seeing all good inspired by Christ, whether Christ was known by name or not, could appreciate Lucian.

Besides, Lucian was funny. He loved irony. In his dialogues people do the most ridiculous or fantastic things without any sense that they are doing anything surprising. He was a great deadpan comic, reminding moderns a little of Art Buchwald or Pogo or the Doonesbury cartoons. Thus Lucian allowed people with an educational bent—like More and Erasmus—to use him to combine learning and virtue with pleasure.

More admitted that Lucian had flaws—his rejection of immortality, for example. In this, More said, he was like Democritus, Lucretius, Pliny, and others in the ancient world. But, More asked, "what difference does it make to me what a pagan thinks about those articles contained in the principal mysteries of the Christian faith? Surely the dialogue will teach us this lesson: that we should put no trust in magic and that we should flee superstition, which obtrudes everywhere under the guise of religion. It teaches us also that we should live a life less distracted by anxiety, less fearful, that is of any gloomy and superstitious untruths."

These lines are taken from More's dedication of his translations of Lucian to Thomas Ruthall. They offer a fine example of the medieval Christian justification for reading pagan authors—a view that the Middle Ages and the Renaissance held in common from the church fathers in the classical world. The pagans may still be read even if they are ignorant of Christian revelation. (Here More classifies the immortality of the soul as a gift of Christian revelation; his later creations, the Utopians, would believe firmly in immortality though they had never heard of Christ.) Lucian assaulted superstition, and since superstition is always with us, attacks on it are always worthwhile, and we can learn from them.

Superstition is the belief that religion is magical, that the divine power can be harnessed and directed by outward acts without reference to any internal condition of the heart, just as we can turn on a light with a physical motion without consideration of any moral quality. The superstitions More has in mind are the fantastic tales attached to the lives of Christian saints, tales crowded with pointless wonders and unbelievable happenings. These fantasies have grown out of the "common herd," according to More's scornful analysis, people persuaded that truth cannot stand on its own but must be upheld with lies. "They have not shrunk from defiling with their tales that religion which Truth itself established and which it intended to consist of truth unadorned; and they have not considered that fables of this kind, so far from helping at all, do more deadly harm than anything else. . . . Wherefore I have often suspected that a large portion of such fables has been concocted by certain crafty, wicked wretches and heretics whose object was partly to amuse themselves by the thoughtless credulity of the simpleminded (rather than the wise), partly to undermine trust in the true stories of Christians by traffic in mere fictions." Christians should believe all the miracle stories they read in the Bible, More said; others they should treat with caution. He seems thoroughly caught up in the same spirit that had inspired Erasmus to write *The Enchiridion:* religion was not an affair of magic and fantasy; true religion was devotion to Christ, a faith of the heart.

Why did he mention gloom, fear, and anxiety as the product of saints' tales? We may have here his own reaction to those tales when he decided to marry. We have already noted that stories of the stupendously heroic resistance of the saints to sexual intercourse were current in most such legends. A devout and sensitive young man, wanting to marry, but reading these stories, perhaps hearing them from the pulpit, would have naturally reproached himself severely because he could not live up to their ideal of sexual purity. His translations of Lucian, published just after his beloved daughter Margaret was born, may have represented a counterattack against the anxiety he felt for his married condition and the opportunity it gave him to have sexual intercourse anytime he wanted.

Among the works More translated from Lucian was a declamation meant to mock the Sophists of Lucian's day, those clever men who boasted of their ability to debate any side of any issue, delighting in spinning endless silly arguments out of trivial questions—much like some of the Scholastic theologians.

Lucian proposed the case of a town ruled by a tyrant. On the books is a law promising a reward to anyone who kills such a tyrant. A man, wishing to collect the reward, enters the tyrant's stronghold to slay him but finds the tyrant's son and kills him instead. Running away, he leaves his sword in the son's body. The tyrant comes on the corpse, and despairing at the loss of his child, seizes the sword and kills himself. Lucian's declamation supposedly comes from the son's killer, a Sophist, who steps forward to argue that since he has been responsible for the tyrant's death, he deserves the reward.

More and Erasmus amused themselves by entering a little contest with each other to see who could write the better declamation in refutation of Lucian's Sophist. Such exercises were thought educational by rhetoricians in the classical world; More and Erasmus engaged in a literary sport thousands before them had enjoyed. More, always the actor, happily cast himself in the role of the opposing lawyer before a jury of the townspeople. He demonstrates a thorough knowledge of the forms of classical rhetoric, especially Ciceronian discourse, and he shows his ability to hang on to an argument and to wring out of it everything a good lawyer could imagine. The modern editor of the piece believes that readers in the sixteenth century liked it, but to us its wit is quite dead.

Some interest may be gleaned from More's description of the tyrant—a man "cruel and violent by nature," allowing his people no freedom, holding power so passionately "that he has trampled on the laws of men, scorned those of the gods, [and] had no respect for life." The tyrant is "puffed up by pride, driven by the lust of power, impelled by greed, provoked by thirst for fame." And, says More, "certainly tyranny is always a violent and fearsome thing." Erasmus noted in 1519 that More had early conceived a hatred of tyranny; by the time he translated Lucian and wrote his declamation, he had already run afoul of Henry VII because of his opposition to Henry's tax measures. His interest in tyranny may have arisen in that experience and flowered in his translation of Lucian.

The translations by More and Erasmus were published in Paris in 1506. More's dedicatory letter to Thomas Ruthall was addressed to a bright young clergyman with a political bent, rising in the world, in 1506 a secretary to Henry VII and in a position to say a good word for young More when a good word was needed—as apparently it was. Erasmus nearly always dedicated his books to men of power and influence whose help he thought he could use, and he wrote dedicatory prefaces to many of his individual translations of dialogues. Erasmus's declamation to match More's was addressed to Richard Whitford, chaplain to Richard Fox, bishop of Winchester. It was Whitford, according to Roper's story, who warned More not to apologize to Henry VII for speaking against the tax bill in the Parliament of 1504.

Erasmus wrote to Whitford that he had written the declamation at the urging of Thomas More. But we have already noted that the humanists habitually claimed that they wrote in response to the urging of others, and it is hard to know if we should take Erasmus literally here. He praises More for many virtues and comments that if More commanded him to jump, Erasmus would jump. He mentions that Whitford has said that More and Erasmus were more alike than twins—a comment habitually quoted by those who believe that

More and Erasmus agreed with each other in all the important things. Unfortunately we do not know enough about Whitford to know how well he judged his friends.

The Lucian translation went through seven editions in More's lifetime, probably because Lucian became so popular that people wanted to read him. Since the translations by More and Erasmus were always included in the same volume, we may assume that the name of Erasmus on the book helped its sales as he became increasingly famous. More himself must have been somewhat interested in these editions, but he never mentioned them in anything that survives from his pen after his early dedication to Ruthall.

Erasmus went back to the Continent in June, and after a couple of months in Paris, where he probably saw the Lucian book through the press, he went to Italy. In September he was made a Doctor of Theology in Turin. We do not know how this degree came about. He seemed a little ashamed of the lowly origin of this honor; Turin was not a great university, not even a very good one, and Erasmus always implied that he had received his doctorate from the far grander university of Bologna.

He went to Bologna as soon as he could, and there he witnessed for himself the effects of those accidents of history that had made the pope not only the Vicar of Christ but also a prince of Italy. Bologna was at war with Pope Julius II through the summer and fall of 1506. In November the city opened its gates to a papal army headed by the pope himself. Julius entered in a triumphal procession, carried richly dressed on a ceremonial throne. Erasmus saw the triumph. He had already become a devotee of Christian pacifism, and he was disgusted at seeing the supposed Vicar of Christ looking more like Caesar than the meek Messiah whose triumph had been in sacrifice rather than in arms. Afterwards he was to court the favor of popes; but he always hated Julius II and his memory. Both he and Thomas More shared a grinding ambiguity about the place of the papacy in the church.

Erasmus lingered in Italy for three years, bringing out a second edition of the *Adages* from the magnificent press of Aldus Manutius of Venice. He had profited from his study of Greek to add many wise sayings from Greek literature. The new edition of the *Adages* still did not make Erasmus rich, although the work did add greatly to his already considerable fame. In 1509, when Henry VII died and young Henry VIII ascended exuberantly to the throne, Erasmus was ready to heed a summons from a monarch who might become his patron. The summons came through Lord Mountjoy in England, who had listened to the new young king extol learning. To Mountjoy, Henry spoke of his yearning to be a better scholar. Mountjoy replied that scholarship was not expected of a king; rather a king should encourage those who were scholars. Henry replied, "To be sure, for without scholars we should hardly continue to exist."

Mountjoy took the king's words for sterling and wrote a rapturous letter to

Erasmus. Or he probably had his clever Latin secretary, Andrea Ammonio, write a letter in his name, praising extravagantly the advent of the new king. If Erasmus could see the joy of the people over Henry, he would not be able to contain his own tears of rejoicing. "The air laughs, the earth exults, all things are filled with milk, honey, and nectar." He begged Erasmus to come to England at once; he would find bountiful patronage from a king eager to support scholars. It must have seemed to Erasmus that his dedication of the *Adages* to Mountjoy had at last brought a reward that would allow him to continue his life of learned leisure.

He set out from Rome in July 1509. We know nothing of his journey, and we know as little about his arrival in London. The reason for our ignorance is a strange lacuna in Erasmus's correspondence. We have a fair number of his letters from before 1509; from 1511 to the end of his life we have a torrent of his correspondence, permitting us to know his movements and thoughts better than those of any other man of his age. But from the summer of 1509 until the summer of 1511, an eerie silence settles over his life. Not a scrap of any letter he wrote during these years has survived; nor do we have anything written to him.

We do know that once in London, Erasmus spent some time at the house of Thomas More, by this time a comfortable establishment in Bucklersbury Street. There he wrote his most enduring work, *The Praise of Folly.* He always wrote in Latin, and the Latin title of the book, *Moriae Encomium,* spoken aloud sounds as if it could mean "In Praise of More," or "encomium mori." (More himself made frequent puns on the Greek meaning of his name—"fool" or "stupid.") Erasmus, taking advantage of the obvious pun, dedicated the work to More, and in a prefatory "letter" begged him to defend both *The Praise of Folly* and its author. In 1519 in his letter to Hutten, he claimed that More had caused him to write and publish *The Praise of Folly.* Again, he may have been following the Renaissance convention in which writers pretended that they had been coaxed into fame.

The work itself is a great tour de force, an ironic masterpiece. Erasmus takes the voice of Folly, the wise fool in cap and bells, a woman whose foolishness is made all the clearer by her sex. The conventions of the time required that women speak wisely only if they seemed to be joking, pretending to be fools.

Folly claims that she is responsible for nearly everything in human life—for the love men have for themselves, for the happiness of husbands who believe that whorish wives are faithful, for old women who simper and flirt and pretend that they are still young, for the pleasures of grammarians who pother through moldy manuscripts searching for words unknown to common readers, frantically scouring grammar books written by rivals to see if their own sovereign rule over the parts of speech is threatened. Folly lives in poets, in hunters, and in fools who imagine themselves wise, and Folly is the master of those who write books.

There is a higher folly, and at the end of this little declamation—for that is what *The Praise of Folly* is—Erasmus turns back to the strain in the New Testament that held the Christian to be foolish in the opinion of the worldly-wise. Christ attacked those whom the world thought clever. "But he seems to have taken the greatest delight in simple people, women, and fishermen. In fact, even on the level of animal creatures, Christ is most pleased with those who are farthest removed from the slyness of the fox. Hence he preferred to ride on an ass, when if he wished, he could have mounted on a lion's back with impunity." The true Christian "flees from whatever is related to the body and is carried away in the pursuit of the eternal and invisible things of the spirit."

So at its end *The Praise of Folly* becomes a work of mystical devotion, progressing in the Renaissance spirit from irony and pleasure to sobriety and instruction. This much of the work would have delighted More.

But in the midst of all the lighthearted banter comes a vitriolic blast against the theologians and monks who by their wickedness bring scorn and shame on the church they profess to serve. Folly mocks the Scholastic theologians who debate nonsensical questions: Is it possible that God the father hates the son? Could God have become incarnate in a woman, in the devil, in an ass, in a cucumber, in a piece of flint? And if God had become incarnate in a cucumber, could the cucumber "have preached, performed miracles, and been nailed to the cross"? As we have seen, these questions—ridiculous as they were—had a place in the debate on the relation of faith and reason. If God was all-powerful, He could do all things. Could God become incarnate in a cucumber? The devout were supposed to answer, "Of course He could." But unless they were logicians, the devout were more likely to laugh—or to be disgusted. Erasmus had gone beyond the place where these questions could be taken seriously. To him these painful debates on the omnipotence of God and the insufficiency of reason were silly obstacles to true piety, a foolish effort to satisfy vain curiosity, and through Folly's mockery, Erasmus was harking back to the ancient belief that it was death for men to apply their wisdom to the secrets of the gods.

He was willing to admit that a few virtuous theologians did exist. But when Folly speaks of monks, she makes them all bad, in Erasmus's continuing efforts to make his readers believe that monks were so wicked that no virtuous man —like himself, for instance—could afford to consort with them. Folly depicts monks as illiterates, bound to the slavish devotion to nonsensical rules that produce a hypocritical display of piety without any substance of true godliness. They hear confession and babble the solemn secrets of the confessional to anyone who will listen. They are drunkards and womanizers, and they preach ridiculous sermons. Folly has apparently never encountered a virtuous monk, and in her descriptions of their vices, she loses entirely the genial spirit of tolerant twitting that fills the rest of the book.

The Praise of Folly appeared in print in 1511. Erasmus tried to lead people to believe it was published against his will and without his knowledge. The little declamation was immensely popular, passing through some forty editions while Erasmus lived, and, before the sixteenth century was over, it had been translated into every major European tongue. Erasmus loved it and went on tinkering with the text through the seven editions that came out under his auspices. (In the absence of copyright laws, any printer could pirate a popular work; and most things Erasmus wrote were pirated.)

The theological suppositions of the book were as startling as its rhetoric; Thomas More must have studied them with some ambivalence. Folly not only attacked Scholasticism with its Aristotelian dialectic put to work for theology; she attacked the very notion of the systematic reasoning that travels from effects back to causes and orders the world in a great pattern discernible to the careful human mind. She taught that there is a substance in all of us that cannot be explained by reason or controlled by it no matter what our positions or pretensions. We are what we are, and our essential being will leap out no matter how hard we try to hide it. That essence is spontaneous and unpredictable, and it lays waste the grand system of Aristotelian logic and assaults the careful distinctions of the Aristotelian mentality with its wish to demonstrate the perfect order of all things. Aristotle himself is mocked as "the god of our master-doctors."

Erasmus did not, of course, demolish Aristotle, for Aristotelian learning enjoyed a vigorous, if autumnal, flowering throughout the Renaissance and lived on to plague Galileo a century after Erasmus. But *The Praise of Folly* is an implicit critique of the expectations of Aristotelian theology and its view of learning and life. In the critique the great unease of the age vibrates, an unease hardly visible in Erasmus but ruling Thomas More's view of himself and the world.

Aristotelian learning took time, and an unspoken assumption of Aristotelianism is that there is time enough to know everything. Aquinas worked all his life showing the harmonies of religion, politics, economics, ethics, and philosophy—and died with his great *Summa theologiae*, the sum of theology, unfinished. The best word on Aristotelian Christianity was uttered by Dante in the *Comedy* when he relegated complete knowledge to paradise. Neither Aquinas nor any other Scholastic theologian would ever have dared believe that complete knowledge was available to mortals this side of the heavenly realm; but they had prodigious expectations for what was possible to the human mind if people only kept at the task of discovery.

Always the mystical tradition espoused by St. Bernard survived with its conviction that it was much better to know God than to know about Him. The tradition lives on in *The Praise of Folly*, although without the emphasis on ecstasy that Bernard had taught. Erasmus was suspicious of ecstasy and temperamentally unsuited to extremes. Yet he comes close to ecstatic language in the conclusion of *The Praise of Folly* where he describes those who sometimes experience "a certain flavor or odor" of the immortality of the soul. "And this, even though it is like the tiniest droplet by comparison with that fountain of eternal happiness, nevertheless far surpasses all pleasures of the body, even if all the delights of all mortals were gathered into one." The people who experience such bliss "when they come to themselves . . . say they do not know where they have been, whether in the body or out of it, whether waking or sleeping. They do not remember what they heard or saw or said or did except in a cloudy way, as if it were a dream. All they know is that they were never happier than while they were transported with such madness."

No evidence shows that Erasmus ever experienced a state like this himself, and although Thomas More was deeply devout, his temperament was not suited to the ecstatic mysticism that Erasmus here describes. Erasmus used a rhetorical praise of mystical experience to support his view that dogma should be kept to a minimum and that ceremonies could easily become pernicious. The Christian should love Christ and his neighbor, and that love was the essence of the Christian life. More's view was something else; he held that Christians must believe the dogmas of the infallible church before Christian love could be active.

Folly's world moved according to the unfathomable essence of things, and people acted according to the impulses of the heart and not by calculation; the way to the good life was to make sure that those impulses of the heart were in tune with Christ, who meets us not as logician but as a person offering continuously a divine love that no one on earth really deserves. It was a statement of the limits of the human intellect, made by the greatest intellectual of the sixteenth century.

In *The Praise of Folly* Erasmus is only a step from the later conviction of Protestants like William Tyndale that when the heart was pure, good works naturally followed like a shadow cast by the sun. The Christian should begin the devout life by seeking purity, not by trying to amass a heap of supposedly virtuous acts in the belief that he might then claim some debt from God.

The relation of *The Praise of Folly* to Thomas More in 1511 is difficult to assess. The frivolity and radicalism of the work are opposed to the spirit of his own works. The unanimous judgment of scholars has been to take Erasmus at his word and to assume that the two men happily shared the piece as it was being written. One modern writer even has Erasmus reading the manuscript aloud to More. The evidence for such a happy scene is lacking, and what we do know is subject to a far different interpretation.

Erasmus obviously wanted More to like the book, and he tells one story in *The Praise of Folly* that clearly refers to his younger friend.

> I know a certain man named after me who gave his bride some imitation gems, assuring her (and he is a clever jokester) that they were not only real and genuine but also that they were of unparalleled and inestimable value. I ask you, what difference did it make to the girl since she feasted her eyes and mind no less pleasantly on glass and kept them hidden among her things as if they were an extraordinary treasure? Meanwhile, the husband avoided expense and profited by his wife's delusion, nor was she any less grateful to him than if he had given her some very costly gifts.

The story is in keeping with More's habitual tendency to mock women and to regard them as foolish creatures. It agrees with More's comment in *Utopia* that "the Utopians wonder that any mortal takes pleasure in the uncertain sparkle of a tiny jewel or precious stone when he can look at a star or even the sun itself." The wife in question would have been Jane Colt, and it makes us sympathize with her. The story itself is the sort men might exchange over a convivial dinner. But it does not prove intimacy between the two men, and the warm letter that Erasmus wrote dedicating *The Praise of Folly* to More cannot be taken as evidence that he had shared the work with his friend before it was published. We have noted the habit of Erasmus of dedicating books to men he thought might help him; he did not ask permission to make these dedications, which usually appear as effusive "letters" placed at the beginning of the work.

Erasmus did stay in More's house, but we do not know for how long. He said that he wrote *The Praise of Folly* there and that the work occupied him for a week. He probably told a small untruth about the time he spent on the book; he wanted it to seem that he was a genius and that he had not meant anything especially serious in composing it. Did he stay longer than a week? Was his stay with More uninterrupted, or did he come and go? Did More even know he was writing the book? We cannot tell. When his correspondence takes up again after the two-year gap, we find Erasmus on his way to Paris, where, during his two-month sojourn, *The Praise of Folly* was printed. At Dover he wrote to Andrea Ammonio, who was living at More's house, sending More warmest greetings. He had left some books in his little room at More's; he asked Ammonio to have More see to it that the books were returned to Colet.

In May 1511, while Erasmus was still in Paris, Ammonio wrote, "Our sweetest More with his affable wife, who never mentions you without praying for your good, and his children and indeed the whole household are doing exceedingly well." Jane, the "affable wife," died only a few weeks after Ammonio wrote these lines.

By the end of the summer Erasmus had returned to England. From then until the summer of 1514, he remained there, residing most of the time in Cambridge, but occasionally visiting London. He was unhappy with Cambridge, and he was without funds. He wrote to Colet and to John Fisher, but neither could give him much. His correspondence with Colet was regular and lively, but it was not intimate.

Real intimacy he reserved for Ammonio. Ammonio was witty, learned, and generous. He knew Greek, and he liked to write letters, although he complained that he could not keep up with the epistolary pace of Erasmus. Ammonio now occupied a position of some importance; he had left Mountjoy's service to become Latin secretary to the king. To him Erasmus poured out his soul, complaining continually. Ammonio sent him wine, encouragement, and cheerful letters full of hopes for preferments that never materialized. The two of them indulged themselves in one of the oldest pleasures of foreigners thrown together in an alien land—they berated the natives to one another. For Erasmus, Cambridge was the slough of despond, and Ammonio was his only firm ground. Mountjoy seemed to have forgotten him; Henry VIII ignored him.

More and Erasmus seldom communicated. Ammonio acted as their intermediary. Having lived for a time in More's house, he departed for the College of St. Thomas soon after More's sudden marriage to Alice Middleton. In October 1511, he wrote from St. Thomas, "I am no better off in my opinion than I was with More. I do not see the hooked beak of the harpy, but I am offended by many other things, so that I do not know, as God may love me, how I am going to live in England." On one occasion Erasmus wanted to know if More had delivered a letter to Warham; Ammonio wrote that More was burdened with affairs and that he did not think it wise to trouble him at this time. More must have delivered the letter, Ammonio said, since he and Warham saw each other every day.

John More, Thomas's brother, served on occasion as a courier between Ammonio and Erasmus, and in November 1511, Erasmus wrote to Ammonio to ask him to get Thomas More to have his brother transcribe something Erasmus had written. Though Cambridge was a university town, said Erasmus with bitter irony, no one could be found to make a decent fair copy of anything.

Some say that the correspondence between More and Erasmus in those years has been lost. Such a thing is hardly likely. Erasmus zealously squirreled away letters sent him by the great and the near-great; he would hardly have discarded letters from More. In his *Farrago* of 1519 he published 333 letters by himself and various correspondents—an effort to show those doubtful about his Greek New Testament that he had many important friends. He included his correspondence with Ammonio (who was dead by then) and his letters to and from many other Englishmen, including the first letter he had written to Thomas More, in October 1499. No letter between More and Erasmus appears from the period of Erasmus's stay in England from 1509 to 1514. The tone of the letters Erasmus wrote Ammonio and received in return suggests that More was a somewhat distant figure, not hostile, not unfriendly, but by no means close.

In October 1511, Erasmus did stay at More's house during a brief visit to London. He wrote later to Ammonio, lamenting that he and Ammonio had missed each other, and in passing gives a picture of life in the More household that is at variance with that commonly assumed by writers on the subject. He had thought that Ammonio was not there, for when he had knocked at Ammonio's door, he had received no reply. But later, from his own room, he heard a clatter of hoofs in the courtyard. He was writing something. Thomas Linacre was with him, and he asked Linacre to see who it was. Linacre reported that Ammonio was departing; so Erasmus barely missed his friend and wrote to express his deep regret.

All this suggests that the More house was what houses were for all public men at the time—symbols of their public life. Men aspiring to prominence in London made gifts of wells and conduits to the city or provided dowries for poor maids and furnished food for prisoners and otherwise demonstrated their sensibility to the corporate life of the community. They made their houses expressions of the same spirit. Much later, when he was a member of the royal council and when England was suffering a dearth of grain, More sent word that he was feeding a hundred men a day at his house. In 1598, John Stow recalled that Thomas Cromwell, Henry VIII's great secretary, had fed three hundred beggars from his house. Such deeds affirmed a certain place in the world for the men who performed them. It seems that a part of such benevolence in More's case was to keep a visiting scholar as a guest—as he had kept Ammonio and perhaps Linacre.

But guests were not necessarily intimate with the master of the house. Obviously More kept several people at the same time, and they had their separate rooms. His wife—first Jane and then Dame Alice—would have looked after the needs of the visitors, for it was a wife's duty to be a steward in her husband's place in such matters. It is not surprising that Jane should have remembered Erasmus with pleasure, for he was unfailingly charming to women. Nor is it odd that Dame Alice should have lost patience with her husband's guests. Jane was a country girl of little experience, only about twenty-three when she died; Dame Alice was a mature woman, the widow of a prosperous London merchant, and she had a sharp eye for accounts and a sharp tongue to match.

The importance of all this is to recall that most of our assumptions about the relation of More to *The Praise of Folly* arise from our view of how it would be to keep a guest in our house who wrote a book punning on our name and then dedicated the book to us. But these familiar assumptions, set in our own small homes, are not apt for the sixteenth century or for Thomas More, whose large house helped him fulfill many official and quasi-official obligations.

We have noted that in 1519 Erasmus wrote to Hutten that More had caused him to write *The Praise of Folly*. But in the dedicatory letter to More affixed to the book itself, Erasmus says that he began writing the work to amuse himself on the long journey from Italy to England. In a letter to Martin van Dorp of Louvain, a letter appended to most editions of *The Praise of Folly* published after 1515, Erasmus said that he began to write the book in More's house because he was laid up with a kidney ailment and had nothing else to do. He showed it to several friends—he does not say More was one of them —and claims that they urged him to go on with it. These accounts are not beyond reconciliation, but the effort at reconciliation becomes strained.

Still, More's relations with Erasmus after *The Praise of Folly* was published must give pause. Erasmus spent some miserable years in Cambridge and London; no evidence exists that More did anything to make life easier for him or that he ever wrote him. No appreciation from More's pen is extant for *The Praise of Folly* until 1515, when More was driven to defend it by events to be discussed in their place. Erasmus had to leave England in 1514 because he could not find a patron. Nothing suggests that he thought More, by this time a fairly wealthy and influential man, would either give him money or help find someone who would. No record tells us that Erasmus felt any reluctance at leaving Thomas More in 1514 or that he even bade him goodbye.

It is just possible that More was offended by *The Praise of Folly* and embarrassed at having his name so conspicuously attached to the work. The book is unlike anything More ever did himself. It is too lighthearted in some respects, too critical of church practices in others. The attack on monks and Scholastic theologians is broader and sharper than anything More ever wrote about them; he was always happy to laugh at erring monks and ridiculous Scholastics, but he was also at pains to show that though some monks might be vile, monasticism was a precious institution. Erasmus, pushed to the wall by dangerous men sniffing for heresy, tried to save himself by claiming that he only pointed out the abuses, that he did not condemn monasticism itself. Yet clearly he had to be forced to say a good word for it whereas More invariably came forward voluntarily to say that good monks and good theologians far outnumbered the bad. All his life he retained a nostalgia for the monastic ideal that Erasmus did not share.

Erasmus mocked the worship offered to saints to induce them to grant some favor; More defended such practices. Erasmus did not condemn all miracles, but he scoffed at the credulity of the masses. More berated that credulity, too, as we have seen in his Lucian translations, but even in *Utopia* he vigorously upheld the belief that God continually performed miracles in the world.

It may be that Erasmus wrote the work at first in the playful spirit that, he always said, impelled him to begin it. Perhaps he did read it to a number of friends who laughed and encouraged him to go on with it—without expecting him to publish it. Perhaps some of them told him that he could not publish it without reprisal from the authorities. His dedicatory letter to More clearly indicates that Erasmus expected the book to be attacked:

> For there will probably be no lack of quarrelsome quibblers who will attack it unjustly, some as too light and frivolous for a theologian, some as more biting than is compatible with Christian moderation.

Erasmus defends the book himself, then closes his letter by asking More to defend it. His own defense may have been directed partly toward those English friends who thought *The Praise of Folly* was suitably amusing for an inner circle of the cognoscenti but that it would not do at all to cast it abroad in print.

Erasmus went to Paris, as we have seen, for a couple of months in the summer of 1511, and while he was there *The Praise of Folly* was printed in the shop of Gilles Gourmont. We cannot suppose that his journey was unconnected with the publication of the book. Yet it was seen through the press not by Erasmus himself but by a young Englishman, Richard Croke. This *editio princeps* has been called "This shabby first edition" by *The Praise of Folly*'s latest and greatest editor. But Erasmus himself was so far from condemning Croke that in September 1511 he urged John Colet to send Croke a little money. It could be that Croke was Erasmus's agent and that Erasmus stayed away from the press himself so he could tell his cautious English friends that he had not been responsible for giving the work to the world. Possibly he supposed that once it was in print, his English friends would have to accept it, and his letter shows that he hoped More would defend it if necessary.

While the printing was in progress, More's young wife died. Erasmus returned to find him preoccupied, perhaps annoyed at *The Praise of Folly* and the reckless and unauthorized use of his name, immersed in business, and perhaps also sunk in a sober religious mood reminiscent of the days when he debated whether to enter the priesthood or to marry. If More was at all close to his brother John, who probably died at about the same time Jane did, he must have borne a double burden of melancholy, and the frivolity of *The Praise of Folly* may have been an annoyance that he chose to ignore as much as he possibly could. In September, Erasmus wrote Ammonio, "I should be most wicked if I did not forgive More since he is occupied with such serious matters." The "serious matters" probably relate to Jane's death and More's subsequent quick marriage to Dame Alice. But why is Erasmus forgiving More? For being miffed at the publication of *The Praise of Folly?* Or merely for neglecting his friends? Whatever the reason, the letter supposes a distance that was not overcome as long as Erasmus remained in England.

There was no open quarrel. Later on Erasmus described More's way of relieving himself of an uncongenial associate: "If by chance he falls on someone whose vices he cannot mend, he sends him away as the occasion permits, dissolving friendship, not breaking it." When he wrote these words in 1519, his friendship with More was as strong as it ever was. But it is possible that they were a reflection of something he had himself experienced during the Cambridge years after he had thrown *The Praise of Folly* into the world with More's name indissolubly chained to it.

7

THE HISTORY OF
KING RICHARD III

ALTHOUGH MORE was absorbed with his public career in these years, a hankering for the life of letters evidently burned within. It found its first major expression in his *History of King Richard III,* perhaps the finest thing he ever wrote. It is his only historical work, and it is so different from other works of his that some scholars still doubt that he wrote it, although the general consensus is that he did. Its influence and the controversies it has engendered have been vast.

More would have been surprised. Although he wrote versions in both Latin and English, he never finished either, and the book remained unpublished in his lifetime. Yet it is the first long piece of his prose left to us other than the translation of Pico's life, and in it we find the mature man, a genius at setting a scene, a wizard at depicting character, a believer in a fundamental order of things that gave events meaning and provided a moral context that allowed reasonable men to recognize virtue when they saw it and to condemn vice on the intuitive perception of the vicious act.

It is a dark tale, the history of a villainous king who let nothing stand before his headlong rush to power. More lived through the days he describes, although he was only a child, no older than seven, on the August morning when Richard galloped to his death at Bosworth Field. He may have recalled Richard parading through the streets of London, and he must have heard stories from his loquacious father about the brief, violent reign of the usurper. Perhaps his fascination with Richard was partly a means of dealing with memory, of reaching into the dimness of his own recollections to find something hard and enduring in the way a man in middle age will sometimes visit the distant house where he was born, trying to bring the haunting phantoms of childhood back to reality.

More's *History* was later incorporated into Edward Hall's great *Chronicle* of 1543, and Hall's work was copied over by Holinshed in 1577. More's book was first independently published from a holograph in the Rastell edition of More's English works in 1557. (Rastell's headnote telling us of the holograph is the strongest external evidence we have of More's authorship.) Shakespeare took the story up from these sources and added some details, and his monstrous villain, slinking and grinning about the stage, is the King Richard III Thomas More gave to the world.

Reaction to such a persistent tradition was inevitable. To many, Richard III has become an abused saint, crucified by hearsay. No one saw him kill the little princes in the Tower. His coronation, attended by the greatest lords and ladies in the realm, was splendid. Laws passed in his brief reign were good. The portrait of him done by an unknown artist and preserved in the National Portrait Gallery shows a sensitive face. (It is a sixteenth-century copy of a vanished original, perhaps taken from life.) So for some it is an article of faith that the real villain in this story is Thomas More, who slandered Richard and made him a caricature of tyranny. More is seen as just another Tudor propagandist, grossly inaccurate, deluded, malicious, and deluding.

But More's account is only one of several written about Richard III by Richard's contemporaries, and none of them is flattering to the usurper king. Some of these histories were—like More's own—left in manuscript and published long after the writers had died. They can hardly be interpreted as self-conscious efforts to flatter the Tudors. There are many contradictory details in the several accounts, and we will never pierce the veil to know exactly what happened in that confused and darksome time or read clearly the motives of all the actors in a drama now dead for centuries. All we can do is build a plausible reconstruction, leaving it to readers to decide whether what is plausible to at least one observer is plausible to others.

Like all historians in the Renaissance, More wrote to teach a moral lesson —here, the nature of tyranny, the wicked conduct and self-seeking that kings should avoid if they are to be good. He was also preoccupied with one of the great dilemmas of the day: How did one preserve and respect a good office, necessary for the rule of a dangerously unstable society, while condemning the bad officer? His story errs in some names, and he makes other obvious mistakes. He left some names blank in the version of his history that his nephew William Rastell faithfully reproduced in 1557, intending no doubt to go back and fill them in. But on the whole the history stands up remarkably well, and there is every reason to assume its basic reliability. He had, as we know, lived in the

house of Bishop Morton, a major character in *The History of King Richard III.*
John Morton was a prejudiced witness, having worked for Richard's doom and
ending as the chief counselor to Henry VII. But More knew many others as
well, including his father, who had lived through those same days: Christopher
Urswick, who had been in exile with Morton, and very probably the elder
Thomas Howard, second Duke of Norfolk and victor at Flodden, one of
Richard's most valiant supporters. Since More did not publish his work or even
finish it, it is hard to make the charge of "Tudor propagandist" stick, and he
seems throughout his tale to sift the evidence in a genuine effort to find the
truth. The work is polemical of course—a polemic both against Richard and
against tyranny. But it is the most dispassionate of all the polemical works that
More ever wrote.

The story as More tells it can be briefly summarized. When Edward IV died
in 1483, he left two little sons, Edward, Prince of Wales, age twelve, and
Richard, Duke of York, age nine. The dead king's younger brother, Richard,
Duke of Gloucester, conspired with the Duke of Buckingham, Henry Stafford,
and William Lord Hastings (More calls Buckingham "Edward" and Hastings
"Richard") to seize Prince Edward, who had been residing at Ludlow Castle,
the traditional station of the Prince of Wales. Young Edward had been under
the tutelage of Anthony Earl Rivers, the brother of Elizabeth Woodville—
Edward IV's queen—and her son by her first marriage, Richard Grey, Marquis
of Dorset. Richard exploited the fears of his cohorts that the queen's family
might use the child king to destroy enemies that included themselves. Richard
and Buckingham intercepted Rivers and Grey at Northampton, and put them
under arrest. Richard had them beheaded later without trial. The child king
was brought by Richard and his fellow conspirators to London, where, they
discovered, Queen Elizabeth had gone into sanctuary in St. Peter's Church at
Westminster Abbey with the little Duke of York. As long as she could keep
him safe, she knew, she protected her other young son as well. But Richard,
Buckingham, and Hastings persuaded the council of regency that the right of
sanctuary should not be granted to a child who had committed no crime.
Confronted with the prospect of seeing her child forcibly removed, Elizabeth
gave him up, and the two boys were locked away in the Tower.

Meanwhile Richard moved relentlessly toward usurpation. He decided that
Hastings, devoted to the children of Edward IV, would not follow him to
usurpation and murder. So he trumped up a charge of treason against this loyal
lord and had him summarily beheaded. He then alleged that his dead brother,
Edward IV, was a bastard, thereby impugning the good name of his own
mother, who was still alive. Richard also argued that Edward's marriage to
Elizabeth Woodville was invalid because Edward had previously vowed to
marry another woman. Consequently the little princes in the Tower were
bastards, and the young Edward V had no right to the throne of England.

Buckingham became Richard's chief agent in getting London to accept him as king, and so it was done. To assure his own security, Richard saw to it that the little princes in the Tower were smothered to death in their sleep. But now the colleagues in the conspiracy began to fall apart. Buckingham felt mistreated. He had become the keeper of John Morton after the judicial murder of Hastings, and he was incited by the wily bishop to rebel against the new king. Right here More's *History* breaks off.

This is history in the classical mode of Thucydides or Tacitus; it is the first true work of Renaissance historiography done by an Englishman, a lean, fast-moving narrative intended not only to teach the major lessons More has in mind about tyranny and public office but also to instruct his readers in the vagaries of fortune and the evils of presumption. Here is Lord Hastings on his way to the Friday-morning council meeting where Richard has resolved to kill him before lunch. Not dreaming of his fate, he runs into an old acquaintance whom he had seen in the same place at a time when, deeply out of favor with Edward IV, Hastings had feared for his life. Now he says:

> In faith man I was never so sorry, nor never stood in so great dread in my life as I did when thou and I met here. And lo how the world is turned. Now stand mine enemies in the danger . . . and I never in my life so merry, nor never in so great surety.

To make sure we don't miss the point, More shouts it at us: "O good God, the blindness of our mortal nature! When he most feared, he was in good surety; when he reckoned himself surest, he lost his life, and that within two hours after."

Sometimes a single incident provokes More to teach several lessons. Edward IV had a beautiful mistress, Jane Shore, beloved by Hastings and taken over by him after Edward's death. More, calling her "Shore's wife," finds in her example both proof of how earthly beauty dissolves into corruption and sure evidence for the ingratitude of human nature. She was beautiful and generous, he says, but now she is forgotten because, at the time More writes, she is "old, lean, withered, and dried up, nothing left but wrinkled skin and hard bone." His description has many affinities to the funerary monuments of the time that showed female bodies in hideous decay. The original motive, and one surely shared by More, was to point out how quickly bodily grace passes away so that onlookers might think more soberly of the eternal soul and its destiny. But by More's time, artists and writers alike seemed to depict corruption for corruption's sake and to take a melancholy delight in recounting the details of physical disintegration.

Shore's wife never used her favor with the king to harm any man, More says, but "where the king took displeasure, she would mitigate and appease his mind;

where men were out of favor, she would bring them in his grace; for many that highly offended, she obtained pardon." Now she is utterly neglected, in "beggarly condition, unfriended and worn out of acquaintance." "For men are accustomed," More says, "if they have an evil turn, to write it in marble, and whoso doth us a good turn, we write it in dust; which is not worst proved by her, for at this day she beggeth of many at this day living, that at this day had begged if she had not been."

Despite his occasional digressions, More's narrative always returns to his major character, Richard himself. Richard's depravity lies in his fierce ambition that has long since corrupted all his natural human feelings, making him a monster. More has no sympathy for the dilemma that Richard's modern defenders have, with some truth, put strongly forward: Had the young princes escaped his power, Richard's property, position, and life would have been endangered by the queen mother and the ambitious and ruthless men around her. For More, Richard's danger is only smoke, and he gives us a villain much like Shakespeare's Iago, doing evil continually only because evil is his nature.

Richard was born, More says, by cesarean section and came into this world feet first. The point made is that Richard arrived in the world in the same posture that men are carried out to their graves, implying that the usurper's life was a kind of death. He and many of his educated readers would have recalled that Nero had been born of cesarean section and that eventually Nero had murdered his own mother. A graver crime against nature could scarcely be imagined, and it was in keeping with the unnatural birth with which he had perversely entered the world.

More readily admits that Richard was brave and that he never lost a battle through lack of courage. But, says More, giving us the key to Richard's nature, "he was close and secret, a deep dissembler," humble in expression and arrogant in his heart, outwardly friendly "where he inwardly hated," not hesitating "to kiss whom he meant to kill. He spared no man's death whose life withstood his purpose." The physical ugliness of the man was in perfect keeping with the spiritual ugliness of his hideous heart.

Although More has been criticized for inventing these details to prove Richard's ugliness, they did not in fact originate with him. What is surprising is to find More, who later vehemently attacked Luther's doctrine of predestination, seemingly here at least making Richard's character a matter of fate, destined from birth and sealed by appearance. He was influenced in part by the rhetorical mode that held good kings to be handsome and bad kings to be hideous—a style prevailing in the fairy tales most of us recall from our youth. More, devoted as he was to his own family, probably found the most horrifying perversity in Richard's bloodthirstiness against his close kin. And it was easy for More the moralist and lesson-giver to suppose that a villain of such unnatural lusts would have had an unnatural appearance.

More's favorite literary device was always irony, and his *History of King Richard III* abounds with it. He develops Richard's hypocritical character through a collection of ironies that illustrate the contradictions between Richard's professions and his deeds.

For example, there is Richard's public behavior with its effusive and hypocritical meekness. More puts in Buckingham's mouth a stirring speech delivered in the Guildhall, trumpeting the wickedness of Edward IV, the bastardy of his children, and the perverted claim of Richard to the throne. After a few hirelings toss their hats in the air and shout "King Richard! King Richard!" the conspirators take this shoddy performance as sufficient acclamation for granting Richard the crown. The next day the mayor, the aldermen, and the chief citizens "in their best manner appearelled" are led by Buckingham to Baynard's Castle, where Richard is staying. Richard pretends that he has no idea why they are coming to him in such numbers and affects to fear that they may mean him harm (this from the most fearsome man in England!). He will not descend to them but stands on a gallery overhead while Buckingham shouts up their wishes.

Richard, in a great show of humility, rejects their offer of the throne. Then, as he and Buckingham had carefully devised, Buckingham whispers among the crowd and calls back that if Richard will not take the throne, they must seek someone else since they are all resolved that the heirs of Edward IV will no longer reign over them. Thereupon Richard makes an abject speech accepting the crown.

More likens the performance to a stage play and makes a telling pun on the word "scaffold," which then meant a raised platform where plays could be performed before the age of theaters as well as where executioners might practice their bloody art:

> And in a stage play all the people know right well that he that playeth the sultan is perhaps a shoemaker. Yet if one should be so foolish in an inopportune way to show what acquaintance he hath with him and call him by his own name while he standeth in his majesty, one of his tormentors might chance to break his head, and worthily so, for marring of the play. And so they said that these matters be kings' games, as it were, stage plays, and for the more part played upon scaffolds, in which poor men be but the lookers-on. And they that be wise will meddle no farther.

More puts special ironic stress on this fawning and hypocritically humble mask that Richard presents to the public, a mask that momentarily hides Richard's single-minded and ruthless appetite for power. Since Richard's story is, in some sense, one we already know when we begin our reading of More, just as we know the story of Othello, Iago, and Desdemona before we see the play, our impulse is to cry warning the moment we come on these expressions of obsequious humility. And when Richard adopts the title of "Protector" over the little boys whom he will slaughter, we are brought to the tragic. Yet More never allows us to rise far from scorn for Richard's wallowing servility in public. He mentions the way Richard saluted everyone he saw in the streets on his way home from the Court of the King's Bench, where he had granted amnesty for any offense against him. (We are reminded of how Louis Philippe, the last king in France, got down out of his carriage to shake hands—his own protected by gloves, of course—with commoners he encountered in the streets of Paris.) More's comment is sharp: "For a mind that knoweth itself guilty is in a manner humbled to a servile flattery."

Then there is Richard's war against sexual offenders, a war waged by the perpetrator of usurpation, mendacity, and murder. A charge against Hastings is that on the night before his murder he slept with Jane Shore and that he had been guilty of vicious living and the inordinate perversion of his body with many others. And when Hastings is dead, Richard forces Jane Shore to walk through London in public penance for her adulteries, "going before the cross in procession upon a Sunday, with a taper in her hand," dressed only in her outer petticoat. Richard impugns the sexual purity of his own mother. He claims that Edward's children are bastards. And in Buckingham's speech in the Guildhall, we find a furious litany of attack on Edward IV for his many sexual sins:

> For no woman was there anywhere, young or old, rich or poor, whom he set his eye upon, in whom he anything liked, either person or appearance, speech, pace, or countenance, but without any fear of God or respect of his honor, murmur or grudge of the world, he would importunely pursue his appetite and have her, to the great destruction of many a good woman and great dolor to their husband and their other friends, which being honest people of themself so much regard the cleanness of their house, the chastity of their wives and their children that they would prefer to lose all that they have rather than have such a villainy done them.

Buckingham's speech was obviously coached by Richard, and the usurper is, ironically enough for one sodden with wickedness, claiming the throne by reason of his purity!

These ironies make Richard's tale exactly the kind of story that would be thoroughly appealing to More's devout temperament. More could never resist teaching the lesson that things are seldom what they seem to be, that the most careful plans of human beings often come to nothing because a profound current of irony pours across the uncharted ocean of worldly life and casts all of us where we do not dream of going.

Other characters become almost as vivid in More's offering. Buckingham is splendidly drawn—a hearty, witty, garrulous, impetuous figure, ruthless in his ambition, magnificent in his duplicity, yet somehow fatally lacking in substance, so that he is led by others like some great bull coaxed into the slaughterhouse with a handful of straw. More thinks that when the usurpation began, Buckingham did not know where it would end, but that once the princes were in custody, Richard revealed the rest of his purpose to the duke, without whom he could not hope to succeed, and drew him on into the conspiracy.

Buckingham, for all his outward bluster, is in More's account a fearful man, and he is convinced by Richard that the two of them have already offended young Edward V to the point that they cannot turn back. If Edward should now assume power on his own, Buckingham would be in lethal danger, for, according to Richard, the king would never forget what had been done to him when he was powerless. But Richard also makes it clear to Buckingham that the duke would be in equally grave danger should he oppose Richard, whose present power and ruthlessness—as well as his spies—pose a mortal threat to anyone Richard sees as an enemy. "These things and such like, being beaten into the Duke's mind, brought him to that point that where he had repented the way that he had entered, yet would he go forth in the same; and since he had once begun, he would stoutly go through. And therefore to this wicked enterprise which he believed could not be undone, he bent himself and went through, and determined that since the common mischief could not be amended, he would turn it as much as he might to his own commodity."

At the end, Bishop Morton, left with Buckingham for safekeeping, uses Buckingham's flawed character to provoke the duke to rebellion. In More's closing scene, just before breaking his history off, he has Morton and Buckingham discussing Richard, now king. Buckingham has praised Richard; Morton relates some of his own history, recalling his loyal service to Henry VI and afterwards to Edward IV, but stops in midsentence when he begins to discuss Richard, as if he would not say something for fear of being misunderstood. Buckingham genially insists that Morton continue. And in the last passage in More's book, the bishop says, "In good faith, my lord, as for the late protector, since he is now king in possession, I purpose not to dispute his title. But for the weal of this realm whereof his grace hath now the governance and whereof I am myself one poor member, I was about to wish that to those good abilities, whereof he hath already right many little needing my praise, it might yet have pleased God for the better store to have given him some of such other excellent virtues meet for the rule of a realm, as our Lord hath planted in the person of your grace."

Buckingham did rebel in the autumn of 1483, for reasons that have always been obscure. His uprising collapsed. The duke was taken and summarily beheaded at Salisbury, pleading for one last interview with Richard—which was denied. It appears that More read his impetuous and unstable character well.

The women in More's story are well done. We have mentioned Jane Shore; there are two others, the queen mother, Elizabeth Woodville, and Elizabeth Lucy, a foolish deceived woman with whom Edward IV was said to have contracted marriage before he wed Elizabeth Woodville.

In the queen, More gives us a mother driven to desperation by events she cannot control, a powerless creature bent on protecting her own children from the wickedness she alone discerns in the Protector. (More can fairly be accused of distortion here; in her own days as England's queen, Elizabeth Woodville was cruel, arrogant, greedy, and deadly even to the little children of those she considered her foes.)

When Richard and his council demand the release of the little Duke of York from sanctuary, Queen Elizabeth appeals to the quality of mercy in her tormentors and finds none. But in the fervor of her appeals and in the depths of her grief, she attains, in our eyes, a heroic and tragic stature. "The law of nature," she protests, "wills the mother to keep her child." We know all along that Richard's iron heart is not to be melted by such a plea, so we see in her sad figure almost the archetypal mother who can only weep while war, famine, pestilence, and death consume her sons.

In the end, when she realizes that her cause is hopeless and that she must give up her younger son, she utters a long monologue filled with resigned grief. Since she cannot protect him herself, she can only call on the lords who have come to fetch him away, lords blind to the Protector's evil, and she begs them to pledge their honor to keep the boy safe: No matter what anyone says, she could keep him safe in sanctuary. She knows that there are some people out there who hate her blood so much that if they thought any of it ran through their own veins, they would cut themselves to let it out. Ambition for a kingdom knows no kindred. One brother has killed another for such a prize. And may nephews trust an uncle? As long as they are apart, each of her children is defense for the other "and each of their lives lieth in the other's body. Keep one safe and both be sure, and nothing for them both more perilous than to be both in one place. For what wise merchant adventureth all his good in one ship? All this notwithstanding, here I deliver him, and his brother in him, to keep into your hands, of whom I shall ask them both afore God and the world." If these lords cannot vow to protect this child, they should leave him with her, she says. They say she fears too much; she thinks that they do not fear enough. "And therewithall she said unto the child: 'Farewell my own sweet son; God send you good keeping. Let me kiss you once yet ere you go, for God knoweth when we shall kiss together again.' And therewith she kissed him and blessed him, turned her back and wept and went her way, leaving the child weeping as fast."

As we have already noted, women exist in More's works either to show how good and sensible some of them are in comparison to wicked men, or else to play a comic role. More often used to the full the literary convention of the times that made women a signal that the audience should be prepared to laugh, much as black actors (and whites in blackface) were once used in American plays. So we have Elizabeth Lucy in the *History,* a pole away from the tragic figure of Elizabeth Woodville.

Elizabeth Lucy had a child by Edward IV. Edward's mother, the dowager Duchess of York, was furious with him for marrying Elizabeth Woodville and claimed, so More says, that the marriage was invalid because Edward had promised to marry Elizabeth Lucy. Elizabeth Lucy was thereupon interrogated by a panel of judges and asked if the charge was true. Under oath she said that the king had never made such a promise explicitly. "Howbeit, she said his grace spoke so loving words unto her that she verily hoped he would have married her, and if it had not been for such kind words she would never have showed such kindness to him to let him so kindly get her with child." More's point was not mere comedy; it was to show that the charge had been made and refuted long before Richard and his cohorts brought it up. Yet the story does let him mock a foolish woman.

More's eye for detail is one of the most compelling literary qualities of his *History.* At Northampton, where Richard, Buckingham, and their henchmen intercept Earl Rivers, they feast merrily with him in the evening, but after he has happily and without suspicion gone off to bed, they conspire against him until nearly dawn. Early the next day, says More's Latin text, they move against the earl while his servants are still snoring. When Rivers, Thomas Vaughan, and others friendly and familiar to the child king are snatched away, the boy weeps—an unkingly gesture but one fitting for the child the king is. More says it made no difference. It is a small detail that prepares us to be outraged when this weeping and helpless child is smothered to death in the Tower at Richard's command.

When the queen mother goes into sanctuary, we find a brilliant description of the turmoil of servants hurrying in with chests, coffers, packs, and bundles while the queen mother sits apart on the rushes that cover the floor, "all desolate and dismayed," and while outside the Thames fills with boats manned by Richard's servants. Richard at the Friday-morning council that will end in the murder of Hastings looks cheerfully over at Bishop Morton and says, "My lord, you have very good strawberries at your garden in Holborn; I require you, let us have a mess of them." Since it is Friday, a good Catholic can eat no meat, and the detail of Richard's request for strawberries underscores his hypocrisy.

Jane Shore blushes as she carries her taper through the street in penance for adultery. She is far more virtuous than Richard, who is beyond any sense of shame. At the Guildhall, Buckingham makes his infamous speech, claiming the bastardy of the children of Edward IV and of Edward himself, demanding an answer from the assembly as to whether Richard should be king. More says, "At these words the people began to whisper among themselves secretly [so] that the voice was neither loud nor distinct, but as it were the sound of a swarm of bees." In nearly every scene More combines details like these with pithy lessons to be learned from the story, so that, together, details and lessons give us a morality play. To us the most compelling function of these sharp and memorable details is the Proustian one of making us aware of the striking power of small things to elicit whole scenes.

The greatest public interest in More's *History of King Richard III* has been the one least interesting to a biographer. It is this: How accurate is the work? Richard's modern defenders have assaulted More as a slanderer and a simple liar, believing it necessary to impugn More's character to extol that of Richard III. These people have leaped on the obvious inaccuracies of parts of the tale to argue that the whole is in error. It is true that More gets things wrong—the Christian names of Hastings and Buckingham, for example. He errs as well in dates and in some other things. Richard and Buckingham in some accounts accused Edward IV of making a marriage contract with one Eleanor Butler. More does not mention her but gives instead the humorous tale of Elizabeth Lucy, who hoped that the king might wed her if she permitted him to bed her.

Obviously, too, the long speeches in the work were composed by More for rhetorical effect. He was following a tradition as old as Thucydides, allowing historians to put words to fit the occasion into the mouths of leading characters. The line between history and literature was not as sharply drawn then as it is now, and More fell into the habit of centuries. We should recall that he had had occasion to talk to a great many eyewitnesses of the events he reports and that the underlying substance of the long speeches may be accurate. This is especially true of Buckingham's speech in the Guildhall.

Of greatest interest is More's portrayal of Richard's character. Here the modern literature is immense, though much of it is trivial. Some things that Richard's defenders can hardly deny speak powerfully against him. He had Hastings summarily executed. Paul Murray Kendall, Richard's ablest modern champion, does his best to mitigate Richard's crime even in this calculated bloodiness. "The speed with which Hastings was hustled to the headsman was perhaps prompted by Richard's fear that if he paused to reflect, he would be unable to commit the deed." But the *Great Chronicle of London*, written a few years after Richard's reign, expressed a more realistic appraisal and the conviction that informs the work of Thomas More: Hastings's execution was "done without process of any law or lawful examination."

Even Professor Kendall could hardly claim that Richard's command to execute Earl Rivers, Richard Grey, and Thomas Vaughan was hurried up lest Richard feel too soft to do the deed. Beheading was the means by which traitors were usually put to death, and the manner of the executions might allow the common folk to suppose that Hastings and the others were guilty as charged. But nothing could hide from thoughtful men the truth as More saw it many years later, that Richard "caused them hastily, without judgment, process, or manner of order, to be beheaded, and without other earthly guilt but only that they were good men, too true to the king and too nigh to the queen."

More's delineation of Richard's character shows a striking consistency, and it seems dubious that he manufactured this coherence out of whole cloth. Richard's loathing of sexual sins is remarkable, and although More stresses this part of his character merely to show that Richard is a hypocrite, the force and constancy of Richard's animadversions against sexual offenses is striking.

His attacks on his mother's morals are more than striking; they are shocking. He claimed that both Edward IV and George, Duke of Clarence, Richard's older brothers, were not sons of his father. In fact the surviving iconographical records show that both Edward and George were fleshy and blond and that Richard was slender and dark. Edward had been born at Rouen in Normandy in the spring of 1442 when the Hundred Years' War was drawing to an end and the English were losing. There had been gossip about a certain archer named Blayborgne who was said to have shot Edward's mother with an arrow not tipped with steel. The slander was widely circulated. An Italian visitor, Dominic Mancini, was in England in 1483 and wrote an account of the usurpation of Richard III that came to light only a generation ago. He claimed that Edward's mother, Cecily of York, told people that Edward IV was a bastard when she became enraged over his sudden marriage to Elizabeth Woodville.

Such an outburst by the queen mother herself may not seem credible at first reading. But then we recall the formal declaration of Queen Isabeau of France, wife to the mad King Charles VI a century before More wrote his *History*, claiming that her son Charles VII was not fathered by her lawful husband, broadcasting doubts about the succession to the French throne that were finally resolved only by the witness of Jeanne Darc, who got her information from angels. So we cannot reject out of hand the report of a maternal confession of adultery, and we cannot dismiss the possible effects of such a confession on a brooding son who might believe only himself legitimate, as Richard obviously did.

More thought these and all of Richard's other condemnations of sexual impurity were merely perverse and reported them as such. But the sincerity of Richard's scruples is more probable than not. The age knew its melancholiacs who wallowed in the infinite details of sin and gloomily counted the costs of their own wickedness and ranted against the wickedness of others. Richard may represent those who desperately yearned to find meaning in the universe, for if God punishes sin in overt and unmistakable ways, the demonstration of coherence in the world may be stronger than the questionable demonstrations of mere logic. Martin Luther was born in November of the same year that Richard usurped the throne of England; his scrupulosity created the greatest religious upheaval in Christian history. Scrupulosity was an affliction well known to priests and occupied a prominent place in the confessional manuals intended to help confessors deal with various sorts of penitents. More himself made mention of it, and his own preoccupation with sex in his works may have represented a form of it. It may be that we understand Richard best if we interpret him, not as More did, a man consumed by wicked ambition, but rather as a self-appointed prophet of God commissioned to make right the sins of his family, which, so the Bible says, might be visited on children to the third and fourth generations unless someone atones for them.

More took Richard's attacks on the legitimacy of his kin as hypocritical slanders; Richard may have seen them as confession. But even if More's interpretation was askew, the consistency of his portrait testifies to determined research, and willy-nilly he gives us a more satisfying and coherent image of Richard than the king's many modern apologists have managed to create.

By far the most controversial part of More's *History* is his account of the murder of the little princes. His tale has passed through Shakespeare into common currency, and it is so stark, so poignant, and so terrible that it has naturally drawn hard rebuttal by modern revisionists.

In the summer of 1483, the little princes disappeared forever; that much is certain. Did Richard have them killed? More, writing a generation afterwards, said that even in that late time some wondered if the children had perished in the days of Richard III. So he acknowledged speculation—revived in modern times—that the little princes may have survived Richard only to be done to death by Henry VII, Richard's conqueror. But although he detested Henry VII (a fact that those who claim More to have been a Tudor propagandist always forget), More had no such doubts about the fate of the children. He was sure that they had been murdered shortly after Richard usurped the throne and that Richard commanded the deed; he was almost certainly right.

Richard had the most obvious reasons for wanting them dead. He had lived through a tumultuous civil war that had been enough to teach him that powerful men were always itching to rally around a standard of revolt. If such a flag could be raised for a prince of the blood royal to restore him to a rightful throne, noblemen with great lands, great debts, and empty wallets might readily spring to arms, looking for the main chance in the change of kings. Richard never appears to have felt secure on his throne; his swift, lawless, and lethal moves against those who threatened him are enough to show that he was capable of murder if by murder he could rid himself of the mortal danger he must continually face as long as the little princes remained alive.

More's account of the crime itself is open to doubt. He said it was engineered by Sir James Tyrell, a man longing for a way to rise in the world. Richard, on a progress from London to Gloucester, had tried to get Sir Robert Brackenbury, who More says was Constable of the Tower, to kill the princes, but Brackenbury refused. While the royal party stopped at Warwick, a page proposed Tyrell's name one night shortly after Brackenbury's refusal. Richard was at the moment having a bowel movement, More says, but he arose at once, hitched up his breeches, and went to get Tyrell out of bed. Sir James was willing.

The next day Sir James rode up to London with a letter from Richard to Brackenbury, giving Tyrell charge of the Tower for the night. More here makes a critical error, probably because he was himself deceived. Robert Brackenbury did not become Constable of the Tower until July 17, 1483. Before that date, the Tower was in the charge of John Howard, one of Richard's most intimate friends. John Howard was the father of Thomas Howard, the victor at Flodden, and the grandfather of the Duke of Norfolk, who was, in Roper's words, Thomas More's "singular dear friend." This John Howard was made Duke of Norfolk on July 28, 1483, and it is of some interest that Richard, the little Duke of York and brother to the child king, Edward, was also Duke of Norfolk, having been married to Anne Mowbray—who had already died, age nine, bequeathing to her equally young husband the vast Mowbray estates. Her deceased father had been Duke of Norfolk, and the title accompanied—or could accompany—the Mowbray lands. John Howard had every reason to want the little princes dead since he was, by an act of Parliament passed in 1478, next in line for this inheritance should Anne Mowbray die without heirs. Since Anne had died, her heir was her young husband, and should he die, John Howard's fortune would be made.

Professor Kendall scorned More's assertion that Brackenbury, who would not kill the little princes himself, had handed the Tower over to Tyrell surely knowing what was intended. So it would seem. But More's error in identifying the Constable of the Tower offers an interesting conjecture—that he got this part of the story from the victor of Flodden and that he was here simply misled. Thomas Howard would have been happy to mislead a young historian in the interest of protecting the Howard family name and helping to cover up the close association of that family with the usurper.

John Howard would have been unlikely to take such an important step as murder without some command from Richard III. And it was this warrant, it seems, that Tyrell brought into London from Warwick, where Richard rested, perhaps supposing that distance from the deed would clear him of suspicion. By More's account, Tyrell used a couple of thugs named Miles Forest and John Dighton, who smothered the children in their blankets around midnight. People slept naked in those days, and the two nude bodies were laid out on the bed so that Sir James might inspect them. He ordered them to be buried at the foot of a staircase, fairly deep in the ground under a pile of stones. More had heard that they were later moved to another place, but no one knew where. And Tyrell could then have ridden back out to Warwick to assure Richard that the princes were dead.

Such is More's account, and some details seem much too good to be true. Anyone reading More's version will see that he was himself uncertain about many parts of the story. But is it to be rejected entirely? Probably not, especially if one of his informants was the elder Thomas Howard or even Howard's son, the Thomas Howard who was the Duke of Norfolk while More was Lord Chancellor, handing on a tale that his father had passed on to him.

In 1674 two small skeletons were found in a wooden box buried ten feet under a small staircase that workmen were removing from the White Tower. They were thought to be the bones of the little princes, and King Charles II (who had his own reasons for being offended at the murder of kings) had them placed in a great urn designed by Sir Christopher Wren and enshrined in the chapel of Henry VII in Westminster Abbey.

In 1933 the urn was opened, and the bones subjected to medical examination. The medical evidence confirmed that the skeletons were of male children of the ages of the little princes in 1483. Their discovery under a staircase is a remarkable corroboration of at least one part of More's story. His belief that the skeletons had been moved after the initial burial may derive from a deceit perpetrated on him by the Howards, who would have had no reason whatsoever to direct people to the burying place of the little princes, thereby resurrecting questions along with the bodies, questions that could do the Howards no good at all.

Professor Kendall launched a volley of objections to More's story of Sir James Tyrell's guilt. His most important argument is that Sir James never made the admission of guilt that More claims he did. Tyrell had served Richard, survived him, and become one of the few of Richard's followers to hold important office under Henry VII. (The elder Thomas Howard was, of course, another.) In 1502 he was suddenly executed for treason, and More claimed that while he lay in the Tower awaiting the headsman's ax, he confessed to the murders.

Professor Kendall asked why Henry VII did not give wide publicity to this confession. Why was Tyrell not given an opportunity to speak it publicly on the scaffold, as criminals sometimes did for the edification of the crowd looking on? Kendall says that Henry could only have profited from telling the world both that the princes were really dead and that Richard III was guilty of their deaths. And why, asked Professor Kendall, were the bones not dug up and displayed? Polydore Vergil, a humanist Italian, like Ammonio in the service of Henry VII, wrote a laudatory history of England at the king's commission. He made Richard out to be a wretch and drew Tyrell, whom he also identifies as the murderer, as a reluctant worker of Richard's will. But he says nothing of any confession by Sir James in the shadow of death.

These are heavy questions, and they may indeed be enough to bring down what Kendall calls "More's fine circumstantial tale," although they do not disprove More's principal contention that Richard was guilty of commanding the children to be killed.

Sir James was a courtier in Richard's household. More says that he had a "high heart and sore longed upward, not rising yet so fast as he had hoped." Though Kendall thinks that Tyrell did have a position of confidence and that Richard needed no page to suggest the man's name, we may not so easily dismiss More's account. No evidence shows that Tyrell was intimate with Richard or that he shared in the great decisions of king and council. And a man we observe casually every day can be transformed in our own eyes when someone mentions his name in a connection that has not occurred to us. Richard might easily have failed to see Sir James as a murderer of children, and Tyrell, then captain of the king's henchmen, might as easily have aspired to rise yet further in the world.

Tyrell did rise under Richard, and in 1485 he was captain of Guisnes Castle, the stronghold that guarded the last outpost of England on the Continent, the city of Calais. There he remained undisturbed after Henry Tudor took the throne, and when he did depart from Guisnes, it was to become a royal councillor. He held many offices, and he rode in the lists to celebrate the elevation of Henry's second son, the later Henry VIII, to the title Duke of York in November 1494.

It would not be surprising if Tyrell had been dissatisfied with the rewards Richard had given him after 1483, and if he had begun to communicate with young Henry Tudor in exile in Brittany, waiting his chance. Somebody had to assure Henry that the little princes were out of the way; otherwise all his labor against Richard would have been nonsensical. Henry was not one to lay his life on the line for restoring Edward V to the throne. Had he not known that the princes were dead, he would hardly have maneuvered to engage Richard as far to the north of London as he did in the campaign that ended at Bosworth in the summer of 1485. He would not have dared take the risk that someone might release young Edward from the Tower and proclaim him king while Henry was on his way down to the city. His enterprise and his plan of attack make sense only if we assume that he knew beyond any doubt that the little princes had been eliminated.

Nothing in Henry's character lets us suppose that he would have dissolved in moral outrage had Tyrell sent him word that the princes were dead and that Tyrell was certain of their demise because he had engineered the deed. Tyrell might very well have represented the murders as something done for Henry's sake, or he could have claimed that he was forced into the act by Richard and perhaps by John Howard. (Since Howard died fighting valiantly for Richard at Bosworth, we may exculpate him from conveying any information about the murder of the princes to Henry Tudor.) Such useful information would have brought about other exchanges of views, and if Henry and Tyrell were not friends by 1485, they might well have enjoyed the relations cemented by the advantages one greedy man hopes to gain from another.

Tyrell's confession in 1502 might have been partly religious, an effort to prepare his soul for eternity, and it would have included his communication with Henry about the murder of the princes and perhaps some information about the role of John Howard in the business. Tyrell's subsequent honors, as well as the considerable favor John Howard enjoyed after Henry released him from confinement, would have been demonstration enough to all that Henry had approved of both doer and deed. So the confession was hardly something Henry would have wanted spoken to the public.

Henry was never popular, and his son Arthur had died only a month before Tyrell climbed the steps of the scaffold. The alliance with Spain was jeopardized by Arthur's death. General knowledge of the early collusion between Henry and Tyrell would have brought odium on Henry at home and perhaps diplomatic disaster abroad, especially if such a revelation had led to a renewed outbreak of rebellion.

If John Howard and perhaps his son Thomas had been implicated in the murders, the estates that had come to the Howard family through the death of the little Duke of York might have been in jeopardy. Both John and Thomas had been up to their necks in the conspiracies that had brought Richard to the throne. Though Thomas More does not name him, calling him only a "mean knight," the future victor of Flodden was sent by Richard to fetch Hastings to the Tower on the Friday morning that Hastings was judicially murdered, and he could have been the only source for the stories that More tells of the doomed lord on his way to that fatal encounter with the usurper. The involvement of the Howards with Richard had been pushed to the background by 1502, and no one in authority could have seen any sense in calling attention to it again. It would have been much better to do what was done —shut the matter up, to give out later, as Henry did, that Tyrell had confessed but to give no detailed account of the confession, to make no investigations and no recriminations, and to leave the little princes undisturbed until time had swept away their political significance forever.

More's version of events and especially his lurid story of the death of the little princes retains its central place in any consideration of Richard III, and it has often been made a measure of More's own integrity. As we shall see soon enough in his account of the Richard Hunne case, More was not above wrenching a historical tale around to make it prove what he wanted it to prove. Yet unlike the willful distortions in the Hunne case, *The History of King*

Richard III offers a consistent, detailed, and plausible version of events, one not published in his lifetime and consequently less open to the charge of malice that More's accusers have made. In its general outline, More's story also enjoys the advantage of agreeing substantially with much other evidence from the time.

The most important question a biographer can ask of *The History of King Richard III* is not about the work's accuracy but rather about what it can tell us of More's mind. Here we find two essential and enduring subjects that preoccupied him until his death—the nature of the English church and the nature of God.

More's view of the church becomes evident in the long discussion about the right of sanctuary after the queen mother has taken the little Duke of York into the precincts of Westminster Abbey, where he is safe from English law. At the end of the Middle Ages, the right of sanctuary was one of the most vehemently debated legal issues in English life—one to be swept away by the Reformation of Henry VIII, except in the case of debtors, for whom sanctuary remained until the eighteenth century.

Sanctuary rested on the ancient claim of the Catholic Church to be free from the authority of the secular government, and in England sanctuary was considered a liberty of the church recognized by Magna Carta. The theory behind sanctuary was that as the soul was superior to the body, so the church was superior to earthly governments and their laws. Part of the church's freedom was that clergymen should not be tried in secular courts except for high treason; another was sanctuary. Some churches, including Westminster Abbey, were designated places of refuge. If someone accused of crime could get into such a church, the political authorities had no right to come in and take him out.

English lawyers believed that the source of all law was the wisdom of God; we have seen as much in our discussion of Fortescue. They were wrestling with the growing power of the secular government and the contradiction inherent in the notion that God's law for churchmen was one thing but God's law for everyone else was another. Churchmen clung to their ancient liberties, including sanctuary, but the clerical estate was becoming increasingly unpopular, and priestly claims to be outside the jurisdiction of the secular authority enjoyed less and less support in the general public as respect for secular government increased.

In More's *History,* Buckingham speaks powerfully against sanctuary, adding the crafty argument that sanctuary is not for innocents, like the young Duke of York, who have committed no crime. The queen mother argues that sanctuary is granted by God's law for anyone in danger, that it is not merely to protect accused criminals. As it happened, young Edward V was born in sanctuary, where the queen mother had fled when her husband had been temporarily driven into exile abroad. No tyrant, More has her say, had ever been so devilish as to violate sanctuary in England. And as a student of Augustine's *City of God*, More would have known that the queen mother's definition of sanctuary had an ancient validity, since Augustine reports with satisfaction that Christians who fled into churches during the Sack of Rome in 410 were spared by Rome's invaders, the Goths.

Assuming, as we must, that More composed these speeches partly from hearsay and partly from what he thought should have been said, it seems clear enough that he supported the right of sanctuary as a necessary liberty of the church but that he also thought that the practice should be reformed. The issue would continue to haunt him, since it was related to his own profound conviction that to be the agency of divine revelation in the world, the church had to be free.

Another deep conviction of More's life, revealed in *The History of King Richard III*, is the place of irony not only in events but in the nature of human beings in the world. He loved irony as a literary device, but behind the literary convention is the sense of a mysterious world directed by a fathomless God whose acts often seem meaningless and whose ways can never be understood. Irony may become a religious tool, used in much the same way we find it in classical Greek dramas such as *Oedipus the King*. The efforts of men to avoid the fate ordained for them are the very instruments of bringing that fate about. The moral lesson to be learned from this irony in human purpose is abiding humility before the will of the gods and their inscrutable purposes. Or the will of the Christian God.

The sense of God's awesome mystery informs the comments Morton makes to Buckingham in the last scene of the *History*. It is a part of the doctrine of Providence that More, like Jacob wrestling with the angel in the dark, was to struggle to comprehend during the blackest moments of his life. The question was this: What part does God play in human events? Do the actors on the earthly stage have any choice in their destiny? Or have their lines been written for them by an implacable and unknown power, and are their fates as inexorable as the conclusion of a play created before they were born?

Morton considers divine Providence almost casually in the review of his own career. Had the world gone as he wished, he tells Buckingham, the son of Henry VI would have ruled in England and not King Edward IV. "But after that God ordered him to lose it and King Edward to reign, I was never so mad that I would with a dead man strive against the quick." Accepting God's judgment, Morton served as chaplain to King Edward. And he would have been glad, he says, had Edward's son succeeded to the throne. "Howbeit, if the secret judgment of God have otherwise provided, I purpose not to spurn against a prick, nor labor to set up that God pulleth down."

Morton starts to speak of Richard but breaks off. Buckingham must persuade him to continue. Morton protests that it is dangerous to speak of princes because they can find fault where none is intended, illustrating his reluctance with a little fable. It is as good a summary as we have of how More defined tyranny, the focus here of the discussion about divine Providence.

A lion proclaimed that on pain of death no horned beast should abide in the forest. On hearing this news, an animal with a lump of flesh in its forehead fled. The fox, seeing him run, asked him why. The animal replied that he fled out of fear of the lion's proclamation. "What a fool you are!" the fox said. "You can stay here well enough. The lion did not mean you. That is no horn on your head."

"I know that well enough," said the beast, "but if he call it a horn, where am I then?"

The meaning was clear: Richard was a lion whose will crushed the restraints of law, and when the law could be replaced by whim, no man was safe, no matter how innocent. Buckingham could recall that Hastings was a traitor only because Richard said he was. In a world where law was dead and the prize went to him most swift to shed blood, Buckingham could suppose that he had better strike first to avoid first being struck. The laggard, the weak, the loyal, and the confident were soon gone in Richard's merciless universe.

Morton's aim in More's account is to provoke Buckingham to rebellion. If Buckingham succeeds, Morton and others like him will bow to God's will for the kingdom—another way of saying that a successful rebellion would be accepted by the English people and that the victor over a tyrant like Richard need not fear prolonged opposition from the people.

Morton's view had become almost a commonplace in England since the deposition of Richard II less than a century before Richard III usurped the throne. It has a stark and terrible side. In it, human beings become instruments —often unwitting—to accomplish a purpose known only to God. The Christian must believe that God knows what He is doing, no matter how chaotic, violent, or wicked the particular acts of God seem to be or what strange consequences they bring. Morton declares that he will not dispute Richard's title because Richard is a king in possession of the throne; it must follow that if another king comes into possession, Morton will not dispute his title either. God's will is what happens, and what happens is God's will. It is a view of divine omnipotence and direction that allows men to do anything they want so long as they win, for they are but tools of God's plan for the world.

Here is a doctrine that More later condemned with all his might when Luther and Tyndale offered it in the guise of predestination and presented it not as an explanation for the rise and fall of kings but as a means of comforting the common folk in their daily life.

We should recall that Morton in this scene is trying to gull Buckingham and that More reports Morton's speech without making a judgment on its underlying supposition. One school of criticism holds that we must never assume that characters in a drama express the beliefs of the author. Yet passion and conviction throb through this passage, and it is striking that the dialogue meets with no rebuttal by More, the author, who throughout has commented on the words and deeds of his characters, making sure that readers get the moral lessons to be learned in the events he records. Morton's speech to Buckingham and its circumstances offer an ambiguity suitable to the elusive nature of the subject under discussion—God's role in the apparent chaos that reigns in creation. It is a fitting place for More's *History of King Richard III* to end.

The general paradox of the work—the possibility that kings who should be shepherds to their flock could become devouring wolves—became one of the great paradoxes of More's life. He lived in a disorderly, violent world, and in such a world, kings were looked upon as the only sure bulwark against chaos. God had ordained kingship, and He ordained kings to rule, an ordination symbolized by the anointment by a bishop at the king's coronation. Shakespeare had his Richard II declare:

> Not all the water in the rough rude sea
> Can wash the balm off from an anointed king;
> The breath of worldly men cannot depose
> The deputy elected by the Lord.

And More would always hold the common medieval view that rebellion against the Lord's anointed was mortal sin. Yet what did Christians do when they found themselves ruled by one like Richard, almost the incarnation of wickedness? The traditional answer was to submit up to the point where conscience demanded resistance and then to resist passively unto death. Such was More's belief; and such became his life to martyrdom. But it was a hard paradox nevertheless, and it is easy enough to trace More's thoughts from the tyranny of Richard III to the ideal of the republic of virtue, existing without kings, in *Utopia*. Men had to live under the authority given to them by the Providence of God for whatever mysterious purpose God chose. But clearly More thought that in an ideal world this authority would be vested in the community of citizens and not in a single man who might so easily use it to deprive citizens of life, of liberty, and of property.

Why did More not finish the book and publish it? The late A. F. Pollard's suggestion is undoubtedly the right one: When More wrote, too many important people were still around who had been compromised by their relations with Richard. We have already mentioned the Howards. Pollard noted that More wrote as if the Howard family scarcely existed—perhaps because he got much of his information from them and certainly because nothing he could have written about their equivocal role during Richard's reign would have been flattering.

In 1514 and 1515, while More was writing, the third Duke of Buckingham, Edward Stafford, was still powerful, a violent and impetuous man, much like his father, and immensely popular in London. The blood royal ran in his veins because he was descended from Edward III, and in 1521 Henry VIII would bring him to the block on a trumped-up charge of treason. His sudden fall would be a morality play to the age—one that More himself would comment upon. Had his father's rebellion against Richard III succeeded, he would not have been mere Buckingham but Prince of Wales, perhaps king already. The notion ate at him, and he died in part because he made some kingly remarks that were reported to Henry VIII. In 1515 he would most certainly have objected to the publication of a book that resurrected the treachery and folly of his father.

The widow of the second Duke of Buckingham was Catherine Woodville, sister to Elizabeth Woodville, Edward IV's queen. After the triumph of Henry VII, she married Jasper Tudor, the king's uncle, who became Duke of Bedford. And after Jasper Tudor died in 1495, she married Richard Wingfield, a diplomat at the height of his power and influence when More was writing his *History*. The younger Thomas Howard, who would become the third Duke of Norfolk, Thomas More's friend and later a judge at More's trial, was married to a daughter of the third Duke of Buckingham, and although he tired of her and treated her abominably after her father's execution left her friendless in 1521, the alliance of the Howards and the Staffords was strong when More wrote. Altogether the Buckingham connection represented a powerful constituency in England, not one to be affronted by a man with a career to make and in need of influential friends.

More makes fun of Elizabeth Lucy, gullible enough to admit Edward IV to her bed in the hope that he might marry her. The child born of that illicit union was Arthur Plantagenet, later Viscount Lisle, born about 1462, a hale fellow, good friend and sporting companion to Henry VIII, brave soldier in the French campaign of 1513, a man strongly fixed in the world with the aid of his powerful connections, not one to insult and anger with a public recollection of his mother's passion and absurdity.

Any publication of More's *History of King Richard III* would have damaged beyond repair his prospects for royal service, and he knew it. He did not finish the work, and he had no thought of printing it, although it did circulate in manuscript. Edward Hall incorporated much of it into his *Chronicle* long after most of the principals in the story were safely dead. Then Rastell printed More's original English version in 1557. The Latin text appeared much later.

One final literary judgment remains to be made on More's *History of King Richard III*. It is the first work in Western literature with a dissembling hypocrite as the major protagonist. Other hypocrites had made their appearance, especially in classical histories like those of Tacitus and Suetonius, whose works More had absorbed before he wrote his own. But no one before More dwelled with such concentration and with such quiet horror on hypocrisy itself. To Thomas More, Richard III was the sort of king Judas Iscariot might have become had he had the chance.

More obviously believed what he wrote. But it is tempting to see in More's loathing and fascination for Richard's hypocrisy an almost subconscious tableau of how some Renaissance men regarded their own experience in the world. If the well-known melancholia of the age had any major source, it was the uncertainty of things and the way appearances gave the lie to reality. Martin Luther was to raise this sentiment to become the apex and binding knot of his theology, making paradox rule the universe. What seemed to be God's blessing was really curse, for the man comfortably at ease in Zion is in fact doomed to hell. The torments of conscience were the Christian's first sign that he was predestined by God to salvation. Men are most free when they seem most bound; the supposed Vicar of Christ is in fact the Antichrist; apparent miracles of God at the shrines of saints are really delusions of Satan.

Luther's doctrines had such wide appeal because they seemed to correspond to something in the common experience of humankind at the time. It is not so very far from them to the reasoning of Niccolò Machiavelli that the successful prince must study to give an appearance that belies reality, and that beneath the appearance, the ruler must work with another world—the world of naked power. Nor is it so very remote from Luther's paradoxes to consider the worried banter about those who would be courtiers in Balthasar Castiglione's famous *Book of the Courtier.* This book, translated into every major European language during the sixteenth century and issued in edition after edition, taught men to keep up appearances in a world where appearances were everything, and it includes the advice that courtiers should never wrestle with peasants since the peasants might beat them, thus destroying a fine and necessary illusion that allowed those of noble blood to claim that they were justly installed in their superior places. The Neoplatonic effusions of Pietro Bembo in that same book suppose that this world with all its material beauties is only a symbol, fleeting and unreal, of the true beauty. That beauty is unity with God in the transcendent and eternal realm where the material has no place. A true kiss, says Bembo, is not a bodily act of physical passion but rather the pouring of one soul into another through the mouth which grants the soul its expression.

So here is a current of the Renaissance running against the artistic realism that we have noted earlier, a realism in literature and in the visual arts that conveyed a world closer to common experience than the abstractions and elevations of medieval thought and art.

The Aristotelian Scholastics believed in a reason inherent in the nature of things. They pursued that reason with words that became more difficult of definition as the problems they considered became more abstract and as thinkers tried to patch over the inadequacy of their systems with ever more subtle arguments. Yet always the desire of the Scholastics was to show that ordinary reason had a place in systematizing Christian doctrine and in leading the mind to respect it.

Aristotelianism begins with a reliance on the truth of sense experience, a faith in feeling, tasting, touching, hearing, and—above all—seeing. This confidence in the senses offers the comforting assurance that the world we experience is truly real and that it exists, as Thomas Aquinas saw it, in full harmony with the eternal world existing above the senses and above the knowledge we can gain from them. Aquinas believed that we ascend through reason and pass on to faith in a harmonious and unbroken journey, a journey we can embark upon only because God gives us grace in our human nature. Part of that grace is that God allows our intellects to absorb true information through the senses.

With the Renaissance, the common sense at the heart of Aristotelianism was sometimes lost in the abstractions generated by the philosophical and theological debates about the relations between reason and faith. But the underlying conviction, fostered by centuries of Aristotelianism in the Christian Middle Ages, that the physical world was valuable in itself and open to human understanding remained a permanent part of Western civilization. Paradoxically enough, this cultural heritage of Aristotelianism contributed to the public acceptance of the realism of artists in paint and stone as well as the related down-to-earth stance of writers like Erasmus. There is a world that is what it seems to be; we would do well to understand it better and to appreciate it more. That proclamation might have been spoken by many an artist and many a humanist in the period.

Erasmus's *The Praise of Folly* provides a humorous attack on the supposed rationality of the world. More's preoccupation with the dissembling hypocrite Richard III goes much further and reveals a terror not found in the playful mockery of Erasmus. In Richard's awful world, things were *not* what they seemed; they were exactly the opposite. Seeming good was really wickedness; safety was destruction; benevolence was malice. If the human intellect should be prey to an essential irony in nature that prevents any natural perception of truth, where could people go for meaning and certainty? As that question ate through the sensibilities of the age, many souls turned with all the greater passion to a quest for certainty, for some infallible authority that would make up for the lack in human nature.

So More's horror with Richard III represents a side of the general terror of the times toward the illusions of what seemed to be. Luther's devotion to an infallible and sufficient scripture and More's equal devotion to an infallible and sufficient church represent another. The determined realism of artists and humanists may have been an effort to tame the wildness of nature with the certainties of art.

But in *The History of King Richard III* More gives us a record of human experience that by the overwhelming power of its details flattens the reasonable expectation that we can depend on what we perceive. Events destroy theory; history defies abstraction. And his *History* questions by its blunt, demanding factuality the supposition that human events cohere and that the wise may discover merely by observing a divine purpose and rationality in the world. God has His purposes; Morton and More would stake their lives on that belief. But no one can tell merely by looking what those purposes are. The only certainty lies in the trust that the God we submit ourselves to will ultimately bring the world and His people to a good end.

8

THE RICHARD HUNNE
AFFAIR

IN EARLY DECEMBER 1514, while Thomas More was laboring on *The History of King Richard III*, the body of one Richard Hunne was found hanging by the neck in a cell of the Lollards' Tower, the prison kept by the bishop of London in St. Paul's Cathedral. When the news of Hunne's death spread through the city, Londoners exploded in a murderous howl of outrage against the clergy and especially against the bishop, Richard FitzJames, and his chancellor, Dr. William Horsey. The anticlerical citizens believed FitzJames and his cohorts had murdered Hunne and tried to make the death look like suicide.

The Hunne affair with its rabid insurgency of laity against clergy sounded the first blast of the trumpet for the Protestant Reformation in sixteenth-century England. It aroused the passions of both clericals and anticlericals, and fifteen years after Hunne died, Thomas More felt obligated to resurrect the affair in his *Dialogue Concerning Heresies*, written to defend the English church. More's account of the case was the first extended report of it to see print, and along with *The History of King Richard III*, it has often been made a test of More's integrity. Here it is impossible to avoid the conclusion that More distorted the facts to uphold the official view of the church that Hunne was a heretic and a suicide.

More lent to his account his own authority as an eyewitness, saying he knew the case "from top to toe." He said he was present during many of the official examinations of the affair, that he had talked to nearly everyone involved except Hunne himself. He says with some pride that he was in St. Paul's on the day Hunne, already dead, was judged a heretic. Yet for all this bold talk, More was strangely elusive about some of the most important details in the case, and he twisted others in an urgent desire to absolve the clergy of wrongdoing.

A biographer of Thomas More must be troubled by the Hunne case, not only for the shadow the affair casts on More's integrity but also because the case itself and More's report of it are divided by fifteen of the most turbulent and important years in European history. The danger of heresy to the Catholic Church made the Thomas More of 1529 a much less reliable witness than the More of 1515 might have been. A strictly chronological biography would present the case and, later, in its proper place, More's account of it. But it seems better to treat the affair itself and More's version of it together here, since his later effort to justify the clergy shows how critical the Hunne case was to the period and how threatening were some of its implications to the church in England.

The facts of the case are buried under centuries of debate and conjecture, and like the deaths of the little princes in the Tower, Hunne's end will be forever a mystery.

Hunne was a merchant tailor of London, a man of good reputation, "a fair dealer among his neighbors," More said, conceding that "of his worldly conversation among the people I have heard none harm." More said Hunne was worth a thousand marks; that would translate into a yearly income of about 650 pounds, and—if true—it would have made Hunne a wealthy bourgeois.

In March 1511, Hunne's son Stephen died at the age of five weeks. The body was taken to St. Mary's Church in Whitechapel for burial. Priests received a fee called a "mortuary" for such services. The old rule was that the priest should have a piece of the property owned by the deceased. The custom was not unlike the law of heriot, by which at death a tenant was required to forfeit to his lord a valuable piece of property. The forfeiture was a symbol of the status of the tenant, an acknowledgment that he did not own the land he worked and that his family must make some show of dependence to the lord. The rule could be financially and symbolically hard. It seemed to mean that the chief matter in the tenant's death was the inconvenience suffered by the lord, who must be compensated for his loss of a human chattel. Peasant tenants felt not only impoverished but degraded by the custom, and whenever they presented grievances to their masters in the later Middle Ages, heriot was always high on their lists.

John Wycliffe had vigorously condemned greedy priests who had demanded mortuaries in his day. The complaint against such fees was general in Europe; they seemed especially harsh since priests often refused to perform funerals unless they were paid for their spiritual services, depriving the poor of the consolation of religion when it was most needed.

Thomas Dryfield, a priest at St. Mary's, demanded a mortuary from Hunne's child, the "bearing sheet" that the child had been wrapped in for his christening, an article of little value in itself. More, describing the case years afterwards, and wishing to prove that Hunne was proud and perverse, pointed out that Hunne could easily have afforded to surrender the small piece of clothing. But the symbolic importance of the bearing sheet was enormous, since payment of the mortuary signified the subservience of laymen to the priesthood of the Catholic Church. Hunne refused to let the sheet go.

His argument was, on the surface, a technical one. By the custom of English common law—a custom observed to this day in lands where that law retains its power—a corpse can own no property. Hunne maintained that the bearing sheet did not belong to the dead child and that the priest could not have it. In effect Hunne was asserting the sovereignty of the English common law over the canon law of the church, since the canon law had long recognized the validity of mortuaries. Hunne was using a small piece of cloth to attack the ancient dominion of the clergy over the lay estate.

The issues to embattled churchmen were terrifying. As we have observed, a fiery anticlericalism smoldered just under the surface of English society. (It is just possible that the peculiarly vehement anticlericalism of the English common people represented a lingering memory of the Norman Conquest, sanctioned by a Roman pope.) John Wycliffe and his Lollard movement had strengthened and preserved the old hostility, and Wycliffe's passionate tracts against the property holding and immorality of the Catholic priests still circulated vigorously in manuscript across England. The very religiosity of the English people contributed to their hatred of a clergy unable to embody the piety the common folk yearned to see in those charged with the mechanisms of salvation. The only bulwark of the church against this furious anticlericalism lay in the traditional ecclesiastical liberties confirmed by Magna Carta, one of which removed the church from the jurisdiction of the secular law. The liberties came from God, the theologians said, although by this time Englishmen knew that the practical enjoyment of them depended on the king's good will, and that a king driven by outraged public opinion might limit those liberties or abrogate them altogether. Throughout the fifteenth century English kings and the papacy had enjoyed good relations; now it was possible that a king might court popularity by moving against clergymen considered unworthy of their ordination. Hunne's case threatened the legal place of the church in English society.

Dryfield sued Hunne for the mortuary in the Bishop's Court, the ecclesiastical tribunal where all legal cases pertaining to the church were supposed to be tried under canon law. Bishop FitzJames must have pushed Dryfield to prosecute. To let the matter drop would have been to acquiesce in a blatant and perhaps irreparable assertion of the superiority of secular law over the church.

In May 1512, the case was heard before Cuthbert Tunstall, recently made chancellor to the Archbishop of Canterbury, William Warham, and perhaps already a close friend of More's. Naturally Tunstall ruled in favor of Dryfield. But Hunne was persistent. More said he was "high minded and set on the glory of a victory" and "that he trusted to be spoken of long after his days and have his matter called Hunne's Case." Clearly Hunne understood the issue at stake, and he saw his chance to strike hard against clerical privilege. He sued the priest in the common-law courts with a charge of violating the Statute of Praemunire. Suddenly the English church found itself drawn into mortal battle with the English government and with the secular laws of the English people —precisely the conflict that Henry VIII would later open anew and one he would win, bringing with his triumph all the dire consequences that anguished and devout clergymen could foresee in the Hunne affair of 1515.

The Statute of Praemunire had first been passed by Parliament during the reign of Edward III. It was intended as a weapon against the French popes of the fourteenth century, in exile from Rome and dwelling in Avignon just beyond the borders of France, favoring the French in the Hundred Years' War. The statute was born of the incipient nationalism that created this bit of doggerel verse at the time:

> Now that the pope has become French
> And Jesus has become English,
> We shall see who does more,
> The pope or Jesus.

The aim of the Statute of Praemunire, first enacted in 1353, was simple enough —to prevent the church courts from robbing the common-law courts of jurisdiction and to prohibit appeals to the pope in matters that might better be decided in England. It kept anyone from suing in a church court in a cause where the common law provided a remedy. No one intended to deprive church courts of their traditional jurisdiction over spiritual matters such as heresy, marriage, and divorce. But the statute left to the king the definition of those matters that the pope and the church could not touch with the canon law. Most particularly, the Statute of Praemunire meant that the king claimed the right to assign the income from church offices—meaning that a bishop appointed to an English diocese against the royal will might be forbidden to collect any income—and that only royal courts could handle the disputes that might arise with such patronage.

Such were the theory and the practice behind the statute, but because the law was seldom applied, no one quite understood what it meant. Kings and popes had a common interest in staying at peace with one another; neither was popular enough in England to risk a quarrel that might make people take sides. So the statute remained on the books, subject to whatever the English government and the English king wanted to make of it, which was generally nothing at all.

Hunne knew enough law to get himself into trouble. He intended to prove that a spiritual court had no right to make him surrender his child's mortuary when, by the rules of common law, the dead child owned nothing, not even a bearing sheet. Dryfield, by suing him in the spiritual court, was guilty—so Hunne hoped to prove—of seeking to evade the rightful jurisdiction of the common-law courts. Under the penalties of praemunire, the priest was liable to have all his goods confiscated by the crown, and he himself could be flung into prison for as long as it pleased the king to keep him there.

Hunne apparently filed his suit under praemunire early in 1513. About the same time, he filed suit for slander against a priest who refused to let him hear mass in December 1512. Sometime later—we do not know when—FitzJames brought formal charges of heresy against Hunne. Probably the bishop meant no more at first than that it was heresy to assert the superiority of a secular court over a spiritual court, for such a claim necessarily meant that the place of the priestly order in Christian society was turned upside down. But then other evidence may have turned up to show that Hunne's supposed heresies were deeper and more obvious than the authorities had imagined. When Hunne was dead, Londoners claimed that the bishop had charged him with heresy only because the church feared the charge of praemunire. To the London populace, it seemed that the church was ready to shout "heretic" at anyone who criticized the clergy or resisted the greed of priests, and to many in the city, Hunne was not a heretic but a potential martyr, a good man persecuted by wicked clergymen.

More always believed—or said he believed—that the clergy's charges against Hunne were well founded and that the man had been a heretic, a Lollard holding John Wycliffe's beliefs. Weavers and cloth merchants counted radical thinkers among their numbers in all parts of Europe, and it may be that Hunne —an example of a general phenomenon—had indeed wandered beyond the boundaries of orthodoxy. In 1511 on the eve of Hunne's troubles, several heresy trials had taken place in the South of England, and some Lollards were burned —among them five in Kent sentenced to the stake after conviction by Archbishop Warham. Many others confessed and abjured and so saved themselves from the fire. The authorities had every reason to suspect heresy in a contumacious merchant tailor apparently resolved to bring down clerical power, especially if a whisper of clandestine meetings with Lollards blew across his name. Lollards gathered at night to read the Bible and to listen to heretical expositions by lay ministers. Hunne looks, from this distance, like a man who thought he had considerable support from friends, who encouraged his resistance and cheered his pluck, and More believed that among these friends were heretics "that were wont to haunt those midnight lectures."

We do not know exactly when Hunne was arrested by the bishop's officers and thrown into the Lollards' Tower. He may have been imprisoned for several months before he was interrogated by FitzJames and officers of the Bishop's Court on Saturday, December 2, 1514. Afterwards he was locked up for the weekend. Early in the morning of Monday, December 4, he was found hanging in his cell, dead.

Now the complications arise that test More's veracity when he later describes the case in his defense of the Catholic Church against heresy. A coroner's inquest found that Hunne had been murdered. The coroner and his jury were city officials, for murder was an affair for the magistrates of London, even if committed within the sacred precincts of the bishop's prison. Edward Hall reproduces some—perhaps all—of the records of the inquest in his *Chronicle*. If the coroner's report is genuine, the evidence is clear that Hunne was murdered, and it is also clear that More's version of the Hunne case is a distortion of events.

By Hall's account, Thomas Barnewell, the coroner, put a jury together on Tuesday, December 5, a jury made up of twenty-four leading citizens. Bishop FitzJames was later to call them "false, perjured caitiffs," a charge that stirred up even fiercer anger among Londoners. Thomas More disagreed with the jury's verdict, but he was too much of a Londoner himself to impugn the integrity of the jurors. Diplomatically, he said, "I cannot think but that the Jury which were right honest men found the verdict as in themself thought in their own conscience to be truth," and yet in his own mind, said he, he believed they were wrong.

FitzJames and his men could see the dangerous drift of things. They pushed on with their case against Hunne for heresy—something they could do under the canon law even though Hunne was dead. An English translation of the Bible was said to have been in Hunne's possession. More later claimed that he saw it and that Hunne had written notes in its margins about the heresies it contained, proving, he said, "what naughty minds the men had, both he that so noted them and he that so made them." More claimed not to recall the "specialities of the matter nor the formal words as they were written," but he did remember that the prologue of the Bible had condemned the mass.

Arthur Ogle argued many years ago that the charges against Hunne—that he called the pope "Satan" and "Antichrist," that he condemned papal indulgences and the veneration of images, that he declared that lords and prelates pursued unmercifully the true preachers of God, and other accusations—were lifted out of the prologue to the English Bible attributed to John Wycliffe and that the large Bible displayed at the trial did not belong to Hunne at all but was planted evidence. Ogle believed that he had found the very Bible used to trump up the charges, and he also conjectured that when it was displayed at Hunne's trial before an immense assembly, More did not examine it closely but rather accepted as fact what the clergy claimed was there—heretical comments in the margins done in Hunne's own hand.

It is strange indeed that More, whose interest in heresy was so manifest by the time he wrote and whose memory was so demonstrably keen, should be so vague on just what it was that Hunne believed! Yet it is clear that the bishop and other clergymen were committed to the effort to prove Hunne a Lollard and to make it seem that whatever the cause of his death, he deserved to die. If he was a heretic, nothing was too bad to believe about him, and it would seem correct to assume that a heretic in despair at being found out might have killed himself.

Such was always More's view, and in his 1529 *Dialogue Concerning Heresies,* he confined himself to a probability: It was much likelier to him that Hunne had killed himself than that the bishop's agents had murdered him. In *The Supplication of Souls,* written a few months afterwards, More said flatly that Hunne "hanged himself for despair, despite, and for a lack of grace." In a time like our own, when jailers routinely remove the belts of new prisoners to keep them from hanging themselves, More's view seems plausible. More said that Hunne knew that his suit in praemunire had failed and that he was in despair, seeing that "in the temporal law he should not win his spurs," and that, in addition, his secret heresies had now come to light, so that "he began to fall in fear of worldly shame." Suddenly the proud man who had expected to humiliate the clergy found himself locked in prison, at times with a heavy iron collar around his neck, facing a dismal future. The shock of such a turnaround might have been enough to drive even a strong man to suicide, and something about Hunne's acts—the refusal of the mortuary, the suit in praemunire by a man belonging neither to the government nor to the nobility—smacks of an impulsive, driven personality that could not brook defeat.

It is important to remember that even if Hunne had been condemned for heresy, he could have recanted, carried a faggot in sign of penance, and suffered no further consequences except possibly ridicule. Only if he had been caught a second time in heresy would he have been burned. It is a puzzle within a puzzle, and much depends on Hunne's character, which, at this distance, we cannot know except through the bare chronicle of his acts in the charges against him and in More's prejudiced account. More himself seems to have a certain preoccupation with suicide; he discusses it briefly but with praise in his *Utopia,* and he devotes several pages to it in his *Dialogue of Comfort,* written when he was imprisoned in the Tower—pages that would appear to show him wrestling with the idea for himself. Perhaps he was disposed to think Hunne killed himself no matter what the evidence showed.

More was present on December 16 when Hunne was formally tried for heresy in the Chapel of Our Lady at St. Paul's. Hunne was duly condemned; his property was forfeit to the crown, for no one condemned for heresy or treason was thought fit to leave an estate to his family. In a world where families were considered extensions of the father in a way inconceivable to us now, a wife and children who might otherwise have enjoyed Hunne's legacy now had to suffer for his ignominy. Four days after the trial, Hunne's body was burned at Smithfield. John Wycliffe's body had been dug up and burned when he was posthumously convicted of heresy a century earlier, and it must have seemed fitting that Hunne's corpse suffer the same fate.

If FitzJames had hoped to end the affair by precipitate action, he was swiftly jolted out of his illusions. The coroner's jury went doggedly on with its investigation. At one time a coroner's jury might have been overawed by the church's condemnation for heresy of a corpse that was the subject of an inquest and simply dropped the case. Thomas More clearly thought that that should have happened; he believed that the Bishop's Court had full jurisdiction since a mortuary was involved, and mortuaries were to him a spiritual matter. But the coroner's jury—representing London and civil justice under the common law —had arrived at the quite modern and practical view that murder had been done and that whatever a bishop and his court might say, the representatives of the people had to seek the truth about the deed.

According to Hall's record of the inquest, Hunne was discovered hanging fully clothed with his bonnet on his head, suspended by a black silk belt of a sort that ran around a robe and tied in front. His face was in repose. Apparently the body was left hanging in place for a day while the coroner's jury was selected and sworn in. (This long hanging seems somewhat bizarre, and if no guards were posted to see to it that no one disturbed the evidence, the coroner's jury could have been tricked; yet surely if the evidence had been rearranged, rumors would have flown, and More in his active role in city life would have heard them and used them later as vital evidence to support the bishop and the other clergy implicated in the case. That he does nothing of the kind is further reason to accept Hall's report of the inquest.) When someone pushed the body, it fell out of the noose. The silk belt had not been knotted around the neck but had simply been tied in a loop with one end of the loop run through an iron staple set in the wall and the other circling Hunne's neck. The body was held in the loop by some links of chain hanging from the staple and thrown across the loop at the back of Hunne's head—hardly the sort of thing a suicide might have arranged for himself.

Hunne's wrists showed the marks of having been bound, although they were loose when the body was found. A reasonable conclusion would be that the marks of the binding would have been erased by the normal circulation of the blood had Hunne been alive when the bindings were removed. Nor was the only stool in the room situated near enough for Hunne to have stood on it before he hanged himself. Hunne's neck showed rough marks, and the jury did not believe that the soft silken belt they had found around his neck could have inflicted such damage.

By far the most compelling evidence for murder was that Hunne's face and body were clean of any discharge. In the nineteenth century, after the reformers of the Enlightenment had tried to bring about less cruelty to prisoners, hangmen tried to kill their clients by a quick drop that broke the spinal cord with such rapidity that all muscular activity ceased in an instantaneous death. Well known to professional hangmen of all times was that a victim of slow strangulation was bound to bleed from the nose and the mouth and to discharge bowels and bladder in the struggle against the noose. But even the quick drop used by the nineteenth-century hangmen seldom succeeded in avoiding the mess. Suicides today who hang themselves are still almost always found in a fouled condition.

Hunne's jacket was discovered clotted with blood but folded nearby. A pool of blood was found on the floor some distance from where he was hanging.

A plausible story of Hunne's death by foul play may be deduced from this inquest. Hunne was surprised in his sleep and killed—perhaps garroted with some rough instrument like the chain found hanging over the silken belt behind his neck when the body was discovered. His hands were probably bound when he was put in the cell, so that he could not defend himself. He bled profusely on his jacket, which he was wearing for protection from the damp cold of the English December. At some point he was wrestled out of the bed and flung onto the floor, where the hemorrhaging continued, for in strangulation the heart continues to beat for several moments after breathing has stopped. Because Hunne was in a horizontal position when he died, he was less likely to have discharged his bowels than a man who swings and kicks in a noose. His murderers, working swiftly, may have stripped off his bloody jacket out of some misplaced squeamishness or because they did not want to stain their own clothes as they heaved Hunne's body up into their makeshift noose.

All this is compelling if not conclusive evidence against suicide. There is more.

The jailer of the Lollards' Tower was one Charles Joseph. On the day Hunne's body was found, he fled into sanctuary at Westminster, slipping away afterwards to a village in the country, where he hid for nearly two months. Finally he was caught and brought back to the Tower of London, where the jury interrogated him. He testified that he was under the orders of Dr. William Horsey, chancellor to Bishop FitzJames. Around midnight on December 3, he said, Horsey, John Spalding the bell ringer of the cathedral, and he climbed up to Hunne's cell, where they found Hunne lying in his bed, and there they killed him.

Several witnesses testified that they had seen Charles Joseph leaving the precincts of the prison in the dim light of early morning on the day Hunne's body was found. It was known that Charles Joseph and Spalding had quarreled, but it was surmised that the quarrel had been feigned to make people doubt that the two of them could collaborate in murder. In the end Horsey was implicated solely by the testimony of a man in peril for his life. Were we writing the Hunne case today as a detective novel, we might easily imagine some twist in the plot that would have Charles Joseph slip into the Lollards' Tower and murder Hunne in an intricate revenge against Horsey for some slight or insult. But the coroner's jury was not in a mood to see elaboration of plot. It brought in an indictment for murder against Horsey, Spalding, and Charles Joseph. They were charged as "felons to our lord the king with force and arms against the peace and our sovereign lord the king and dignity of his crown."

What motive did these men have to kill Hunne? Here is the biggest problem in the case. More wrote later that Hunne's action in praemunire had failed and that he was driven to the desperation of suicide. The surviving records of the King's Bench tell a different story. The case was postponed for two years after Hunne brought it, and it was to be heard in the January term of the court in 1515—after Hunne was dead. The latest authority to write on the affair maintains that More was telling the truth, that the judges had made up their minds although they had not announced their verdict. The claim is that they must have privately conveyed their decision to the bishop, who otherwise would not have dared interrogate Hunne on December 2.

It is at least plausible to suppose that More was telling the truth, that in effect Hunne's case had already been decided by the Court of the King's Bench and that the hearing in January 1515 was to be only a formality in which the decision was announced. Still, More's word is all we have to prove that the case had failed by the time Hunne died. If More was wrong—or if he was converting the opinions of interested lawyers into something of greater substance when he told the story, or if he was simply lying—the men around the bishop, fearing that the praemunire might succeed and that the Hunne case might then become a trial of the place of the English church in English life, might well have been driven to seek a radical solution to a radical problem.

The indictment of Horsey, Spalding, and Charles Joseph came while London was still in an uproar over the affair. The worst seemed to have happened to the church, since the indictment posed the great constitutional question that would be settled for all time by the English Reformation: Who was supreme in England, the church or the secular authority? By ancient ecclesiastical practice, Horsey at least, and perhaps also his two fellows, should have been given over to the custody of the bishop and tried in the Bishop's Court, where they could not be condemned to death. No church court could hand down a death penalty, although one might announce officially that some people were not fit to live. In heresy cases, the church could decide that the accused was indeed guilty of heresy, but it then turned the convicted heretic over to the secular authority to be burned, since the church could not stain itself by shedding blood. Putting criminals to death gave the secular authority a reason for being. A clergyman guilty of murder was not a heretic, and the church jealously guarded its right to keep the so-called criminous clerk under its own jurisdiction. The battle had already been partly lost in England, for clerical privilege could not keep a priest from being tried and executed for treason, although such a condemned priest was always degraded from clerical status before he was put to death. Only a few months before Hunne died, the new pope, Leo X, had ruled once again that no layman had any rightful jurisdiction over a clergyman in any case whatsoever. The English government paid no attention.

In 1512 Parliament, in an anticlerical mood, had passed a brief law against the privileges of criminous clerks. In the Middle Ages, a "clerk" was not merely a priest ordained to administer the sacraments. A clerk was anyone certified by the church to fulfill some peculiarly religious vocation. Teachers and students in universities were clerks, and so were vergers who kept up church buildings, and characters like Charles Joseph and John Spalding, charged with menial duties around church property, were perhaps clerks, too. If a man wore the tonsure—his head shaved on top—and if he could read Latin, he could be considered a clerk, and if on trial for his life, he could literally save his neck by reading a text from the Latin Bible.

The act of 1512 moved against the swarm of "lower orders," as they were called—the unordained clerks—by making those of their number accused of committing murder in churches, in the homes of their victims, or on the king's highway subject to the jurisdiction of the common law. This quite reasonable piece of legislation subjected clerical felons to the same capital penalty for such acts that would be inflicted on common criminals. It specifically excluded ordained priests from its provisions. Nevertheless, the Parliament of 1512 felt the risk of antagonizing the English church and provided that the act should endure only until the next Parliament. Parliaments met only when they were summoned by the king, and so the act of 1512 might have gone without reconsideration for one or two decades had not a Parliament been called for 1515. Now that Parliament had to decide whether to renew, amend, or cancel the statute.

But before the Parliament could meet, the Hunne affair burst on the London scene. As Parliament sat, the uproar continued. Hall's account gives us to understand that old Bishop FitzJames was frantic. We may surmise from many things he said afterwards that More was anxious, too, and that he shared the fears of churchmen that the liberties of the Catholic Church in England were in danger.

For what could keep Parliament, under the duress of public opinion, from not only renewing the law of 1512 but strengthening it so it should bind not only the lower orders but the ordained priests and bishops of the church? What if Parliament acted to bring the English church entirely under the jurisdiction of king and common law, in effect abolishing the canon law in England and the liberties confirmed by Magna Carta? What if Parliament extended and defined the Statute of Praemunire to confiscate church property? These were matters of utmost urgency, and only two decades after the Hunne case agitated London, Henry's Reformation Parliament was to do the worst that conservative Catholics feared in 1515.

The difference between 1515 and 1534 was that in 1515 Henry VIII had no reason to antagonize the pope. He could not be sure how weak the church's hold on English public opinion might be, and he was not one to let public clamor drive him into anything. Thomas More's convictions may be divined from his *Utopia*, written in 1515, while the Hunne affair still raged. In his imaginary island commonwealth, an excommunication pronounced by the priests against a layman was immediately followed by arrest and punishment at the hands of the secular authorities. But the secular authorities let priests go free no matter what crimes they might have committed. "Neither do they think it right to touch with a mortal hand anyone—guilty of whatever horrible deed—who has been set aside as a gift to God in such a singular manner."

The Hunne case was finally resolved by royal intervention, brought about in part by Bishop FitzJames. At some time—probably February or March 1515 —the bishop wrote a frantic letter to Wolsey. In it he conceded an awesome point without seeming to realize what he was doing. He asked Wolsey to intercede with the king on behalf of Dr. Horsey. He did not try to shift blame onto Charles Joseph or to suggest that a man in danger of death might have tried to implicate Dr. Horsey out of spite. He simply said that Charles Joseph's confession had been wrung from him by "pain and durance." Although no evidence supports the bishop's claim, the phrase was legal terminology intended to persuade Henry to quash any indictment arising from the confession, since nothing wrung from a prisoner by torture could be used against him in an English court. The bishop wanted the king to have the matter taken up by impartial persons of the royal council who would hear testimony by all the parties. The king should quash the indictment returned by the coroner's jury so that Horsey might not come to trial. "For," said FitzJames, "assured am I that if my chancellor be tried by any twelve men in London, they be so maliciously set in favor of heretical depravity that they will cast and condemn my clerk though he be as innocent as Abel." The bishop's estimate of the strength of heresy in London contrasts sharply with Thomas More's later and

Tho: Moor L'Chancelour

THOMAS MORE. Portrait sketch by
Hans Holbein the Younger, sixteenth
century. The pricked dots reveal how
the sketch was transferred to the
canvas. Royal Library, Windsor.

Iudge More Sr Tho: Mores Father.

JOHN MORE, SENIOR, Thomas More's
father. Drawing by Hans Holbein.
Royal Library, Windsor.

MARGARET AND WILLIAM
ROPER, More's first and
favorite daughter and her
husband, More's first
biographer. Watercolor
miniatures by Hans Holbein.
Metropolitan Museum of
Art, New York.

Right: DAME ALICE MORE, Thomas More's second wife. Painting by Hans Holbein. *Below:* JOHN MORE, More's son. Drawing by Hans Holbein. Royal Library, Windsor.

Above: ELIZABETH DAUNCE (incorrectly identified as Lady Barkley), More's second daughter, married to William Daunce. *Right:* CECILY HERON, the youngest daughter, married to Giles Heron. Drawings by Hans Holbein. Royal Library, Windsor.

ERASMUS OF ROTTERDAM, leading
Renaissance scholar and friend to
Thomas More. After the original
diptych painted by Quentin Metsys
and sent as a gift to More. Galleria
Nazionale d'Arte Antica, Palazza
Corsini, Rome.

CARDINAL THOMAS WOLSEY as a
young man. He was Lord Chancellor
preceding Thomas More. Drawing
attributed to Jacques de Boucq of
Artois in the Arras Library.
Mansell Collection, London.

Sketch for a large portrait of the
entire More family. By Hans Holbein.
The painting was later destroyed by
fire. Mansell Collection, London.

repeated declarations that the vast majority of the English people stood true to the old faith. It is a remarkable confession by a bishop of the failure of the church among its people, and it helps to illuminate the yearning for a reformed priesthood that we find in the works of John Colet, Thomas More, and the later English Protestants.

A bishop with a better legal mind might have seen the danger of calling in a king to judge an ecclesiastical affair. Kings were laymen, and the church had battled for centuries to keep the bloody, greedy hands of laymen out of the church's spiritual business. FitzJames might have appealed to the pope, but under the circumstances such a legal act would most certainly have been widely interpreted as a violation of praemunire. Had the bishop steeled himself and appealed to Rome, the issues that created the English Reformation might very well have ended in the kind of compromise that the French worked out with the papacy in 1515 and in the Concordat of Bologna in 1516, a compromise that gave the French king such authority over the church in France that later French monarchs never found any advantage to embracing Protestantism. But, then, Horsey might have been hanged before the appeal got very far, and the bishop himself might have been imprisoned and his lands confiscated. As events would soon prove, the English episcopate lacked the gift of martyrdom.

Instead the bishop asked the king to stop the secular court's proceedings. He turned from canonical theories about the independence of the church to the urgent, practical need of the hour; he pleaded with Wolsey to intervene. "If you can help us blessed father in our troubles," he wrote, "we shall be obligated to you forever."

Wolsey was the right man to receive such an appeal, since he was in a strong position and took a strong view of ecclesiastical independence. Months later, FitzJames got his wish. Horsey stayed in prison until the anger of the London populace abated. Then he was arraigned before the Court of the King's Bench, where he was allowed to plead not guilty. Henry ordered his attorney general to accept the plea, and Horsey went free. Wolsey, by then a cardinal and legate of the pope in England, fined Horsey heavily and sent him to Exeter, where he was still alive in 1529 when More wrote that the former episcopal chancellor lived expecting reward "only of God for his long patience in his undeserved trouble." He apparently lived out his life in penury, and we are bound to wonder why Wolsey and the church treated the man so harshly if they truly believed he was innocent of any wrongdoing.

Years later when More presented his account of the case in *A Dialogue Concerning Heresies,* he twisted the issues almost beyond recognition. If we had only More's story of Richard Hunne, we would have almost no idea that strong evidence existed to indicate that Hunne had been murdered and that serious people were convinced by the evidence that murder had been done. More made it seem that all good men believed that Hunne had killed himself and that the only information to the contrary was foolish gossip. He did not give any of the evidence produced by the coroner's jury, and he spoke not a word of the depositions the jury heard from several of the principals. It is true that to publish a coroner's inquest was against English law at the time, and some have tried to defend More's silence about the jury's work by saying that he was only obeying the law. That is not the impression More himself gives.

If we were to accept the notion that More did not try to mislead his audience, we would have to ask why he brought the case up at all. He could have passed it over in silence. But obviously Richard Hunne's ghost was still stalking London, and More felt that he had to banish it if he could.

Almost inadvertently he recalls the clamor surrounding the case when he mentions that it was "many times in sundry places examined." He limits his account of these examinations to one held at Baynard's Castle, a hearing that had nothing to do with the inquest, since, by More's account, those in charge were various "great lords spiritual and temporal and other of the king's honorable council, sent thither by his highness for the nonys [express purpose] of his blessed zeal and princely desire borne to the searching of the truth." The coroner's inquest had been conducted by citizens of London, men of More's rank in society. What More describes was probably a hearing by members of the royal council like the one that FitzJames had requested in his frenzied letter to Wolsey, a council that would advise the king whether judicial proceedings should continue. After receiving their views, the king could decide whether to quash the indictment against Horsey and the others or to let the case continue in the royal courts, over which he was sovereign.

In his account of this council, More gives the impression that only ludicrous evidence was presented by foolish people. Someone had said he knew another who knew Hunne's killer. That man was questioned. But no, he said; there was a mistake. It was a neighbor who said he could tell the guilty party. The neighbor was brought in. But no. He, too, had been misunderstood. It was *his* neighbor. When this man was also brought forward, he also said no; he was not the one either. The person who could tell who killed Hunne was a Gypsy woman, now gone over the sea, a seer, a reader of palms, able to tell who had stolen things. "And therefore I think she could as well tell who killed Hunne as who stole a horse."

Then More recounted the tale of the man claiming to have seen Hunne as he was hanging and as the body was taken down. This man said he could tell that Hunne had not hanged himself. How could he tell? Why, said he, he had long served under two different almoners of the king, and in this job he had seen many men who had hanged themselves. From this experience he could tell whether a hanged man was a suicide or not, and Hunne, he said, was no suicide.

How many men had he seen hanged? asked the lord.

He could not tell.

A hundred?

No, not a hundred.

Four score and ten?

"Thereat a little he studied as one standing in a doubt who was reluctant to lie, and at last he said that he thought no, not fully four score and ten. Then was he asked whether he had seen twenty. And thereto without any sticking he answered nay, not twenty. Threat the lords laughed well to see that he was so sure that he had not seen twenty and was in doubt whether he had seen four score and ten." Finally the witness was made to admit that he had seen only one suicide by hanging and that that one was an Irishman named Cruikshank he had seen hanging in a barn.

The other testimony was from one who said that he had heard a high clergyman, a doctor of the English church, say that "if Hunne had not sued the praemunire, he should never have been accused of heresy." The great clergyman was asked to verify this startling bit of news. "Surely, my lords," said he, "I said not a thing so, but this I said indeed that if Hunne had not been accused of heresy, he would never have sued the praemunire." Then the accuser cried triumphantly, "Lo, my lords, I am glad you find me a true man. Will ye command me any more service?" The witness could not, wrote More, tell that the order of the words made any difference in what they meant. A lord told the witness, "For I have espied, good man, that as long as the words be the same, it makes no difference to you which way they stand, but all is one to you, a horse mill and a mill horse, drink before you go, and go before you drink."

Are these stories true? We have no way of knowing, but the last tale is especially dubious. In October 1515, in a letter to theologian Martin van Dorp of Louvain, More discussed the petty problems logicians set for themselves. One was the question of how meanings in sentences change when the order of words changes. Some Scholastic philosophers, More said, found important differences between the sentences "Twice have I drunk wine" and "Wine have I drunk twice." Common sense, he said, should prove that the two sentences meant the same thing. But one could change meanings by changing the order of the words; for, said More, there is a great deal of difference between the sentences "Drink before you go" and "Go before you drink."

Perhaps he was remembering the line from the recent Richard Hunne affair, just subsiding when he wrote to Dorp. But then again people who tell funny stories develop a sense for good lines, and they may repeat them again and again to different audiences. More thought the line about drinking and going was funny; he may have kept it through the years the way we store up such things in our heads, and with it he may have created a pious fiction for his *Dialogue Concerning Heresies.*

The *Dialogue Concerning Heresies* supposedly took place between More and a young man called "the messenger." Naturally, the messenger, a foil for More's wit, got the point as he must, since he was More's creature. He dismissed the Hunne case with the agreeable comment: "For here may a man see that misunderstanding means misreporting. And a tale that flies through many mouths catches many new feathers which when they be pulled away again leave him . . . as bare as a bird's arse." Yet it looks very much as if More buried the real substance of the Hunne affair under feather pillows of absurdity so that no one could see what lay beneath.

He hints that the examination in his account considered graver evidence than the three silly stories he tells: "But of truth many other things were there laid that upon the hearing seemed much more suspicious than these, which yet when they were answered always lost more than half their strength." Yet half is something, and More does not breathe a word as to what this more suspicious evidence might have been, thus depriving his readers of any opportunity to judge for themselves. Since the coroner's report was unpublished at the time, More could suppose that his subterfuge would work and that people would believe that the evidence for Hunne's death by murder was as frivolous as that which he here presents. Even dispassionate readers might well have wondered what the uproar over the Hunne case, and the years of fascination that it held for the English people, was all about.

More's rhetorical skill was exquisite, and with it he managed to turn one persistent rumor to good account. The rumor was that Horsey had begged the king for a pardon and that the king had granted it. More's foil asked a natural question: Did not the appeal for a pardon prove that Horsey was guilty?

"I have heard men say before this," says More, "that they will never refuse God's pardon nor the king's." He then passes into a flattering description of Henry as a king as merciful as any England ever had. Even so, he says, Henry would never have granted a pardon in such a heinous deed had Horsey been guilty. If Henry had granted a pardon, Horsey must be innocent.

Then, having belabored this rhetorical point, and having dragged the king into the narrative to be a witness to Horsey's innocence, More immediately turns to a circumspect rendering of what really happened. Horsey had not sued for a pardon; he had been indicted. He was arraigned before the Court of the King's Bench, and both he and his cohorts pleaded not guilty. Only then did the king, certain of their innocence, order his attorney general to accept their pleas. So there was no suit for a pardon; there was only a legal process that ended in acquittal.

Years afterwards More added his own testimony: "I never heard in my life (and yet have I heard all I think that well could be said) therein any thing that moved me, after the parties heard, to think that he [Horsey] should be guilty." He could bring Henry's action forward as evidence.

By the time More wrote, it was safe to assume that no one would step forward to announce that Henry had ordered Horsey's release for political reasons, regardless of the evidence. It is worth adding that More's firm judgment that Horsey had unjustly suffered by being banished from London came in *The Supplication of Souls*, published after Wolsey had fallen from power. Wolsey had been responsible for Horsey's exile. More would not have declared the exile a miscarriage of justice as long as Wolsey could defend himself; Wolsey might have ended More's public career. But in the latter part of 1529, Wolsey was gone, and it was safe to denounce one of his public acts.

We have already made reference to More's steady defamation of Hunne himself, whom he thought to be a heretic. More maintained that Hunne killed himself because his heresies had been found out, and in his *Dialogue* he has his foil say, "In good faith . . . knew I that he was an heretic indeed and in peril to be so proved, I would well think that in malice and despair he hanged himself." More even conjectures that Hunne hanged himself in such a way that suspicion would fall on Dr. Horsey and adds that it was unlikely that the bishop's chancellor would have committed murder when enough evidence had been assembled to bring Hunne "to shame and peradventure to shameful death also." It may be pointed out again that More's word is all the proof we have that the process against Hunne was strong enough to make the man despair. It is also worth noting that More seems to know that the situation of Hunne's body when found cast doubt on the story that Hunne had killed himself. Apparently More knew the evidence the coroner's inquest had considered.

More, giving an account of the trial in St. Paul's that declared Hunne a heretic, threw his moral support to Bishop FitzJames. "For I assure you the bishop was a very wise man, a virtuous and a cunning." FitzJames had, among other expressions of his conservatism, accused More's good friend John Colet of heresy for preaching against the wicked example clergymen gave the people. Nothing came of FitzJames's charges, and by 1529 Colet and the bishop were both long dead, so that More could refer to both of them in honorific terms and as if the Catholic Church had never known serious division before the Protestants came on the scene.

As a kind of postscript to his story, More added the tale of a carpenter in Essex "that used to make pumps" apprehended in a conspiracy to commit robbery. More participated in the interrogation of the carpenter along with "a great honorable estate of this realm"—probably a commission of the peace to preserve order in the countryside. The carpenter admitted not only conspiracy but heresy, saying that his brother had led both himself and his father astray and that the three of them used to attend midnight lectures with a conventicle of heretics in London. One of the heretics had been Richard Hunne; by More's account, the carpenter had been in the English army that Henry VIII had sent

to France in 1513, with which he served several years during the occupation
of Tournai. Only when he returned, the carpenter said, had he learned that
Richard Hunne "was hanged in the Lollards' Tower and his body burned for
an heretic."

Arthur Ogle in 1949 pointed out that the carpenter-soldier was a confessed
felon, apparently eager to accuse not only Richard Hunne of heresy but also
his own father and brother. The brother was arrested and thrown into the
Marshalsea Prison; the father was already dead. More is careful not to tell us
what happened to the brother, who, it seems almost certain, was eventually
released for lack of evidence. Otherwise More would have used his conviction
to support his argument. We may also wonder if a carpenter, member of a
profession considered barely honorable, would have consorted with a merchant
tailor of the social status of Richard Hunne, even in a conventicle of heretics.
Finally, the major question—which More manages to obfuscate—was not
whether Hunne was a heretic but whether he was murdered.

Even More's account of Hunne's supposed heresies is so vague that it can
scarcely bear examination. More claimed that Hunne sued the praemunire
after he was accused of heresy, but the modern consensus is that Hunne's suit
was filed before formal charges were lodged against him. That would make
plausible the popular belief that the bishop charged Hunne with heresy out of
revenge. It may well be that when Hunne refused to pay the mortuary ordered
by Cuthbert Tunstall after the hearing of May 13, 1512, Tunstall excommunicated him. Any excommunicated person might have been loosely styled a
"heretic" if he refused to take steps to have the ban lifted, and More—making
a case for the embattled Catholic Church in 1529 (and incidentally for his good
friend Tunstall)—might have used such loose talk to argue that Hunne sued
in praemunire in a bold effort to counter the charge of heresy. It might also
have been that Hunne was so anticlerical that he did read Wycliffe's books but
lacked the theological acumen to embrace heresy in any profoundly theological
way. His beliefs remain an enigma, and More did nothing to help us understand them. Later Protestants, including John Foxe, took him to have been one
of their own, but in spirit rather than because of any grand array of beliefs that
he might have held.

So it is clear that More's account of the Hunne affair is distorted and that,
perhaps of greater importance, he continually tried to throw dust in the eyes
of his readers, avoiding the major question of whether Hunne was murdered
and fastening his arguments on the lesser question of whether Hunne was a
heretic. In More's view, heretics were such demonic people that it was fair to
believe anything bad about them, no matter how outrageous. More presents
us with a Richard Hunne so depressed at being found out that he killed himself
and so depraved that he tried to make his suicide look like murder. It is at best
an unlikely combination of characteristics in one man.

To distort the reported evidence in an effort to protect the Catholic Church would have seemed to a man of More's devout temperament a necessity. His willingness to twist the evidence is a sign of his fear rather than any essential immorality, for he thought that if heresy conquered and the Catholic Church fell, the rational shape possessed by both history and the moment would fall into chaos. We may believe that telling the truth for truth's sake is the height of virtue, as it was in classical times, because we suppose that people lie only to serve themselves and we can scarcely understand commitment to an institution so absolute in its authority that it is worth a lie. We may say well enough that More would have received greater honor in history had he never been caught in willful distortion of evidence, just as we may say that some moderns who love him might have been deserving of greater respect if they had never tried to argue that he always told the exact truth. But it may be, too, that in our time—so different from More's—absolute truth and absolute honesty have become, like modern lying itself, expressions of the narcissism that afflicts us all. In his polemics for the Catholic Church, More was perhaps much like Machiavelli, whose science of the secular state made him believe that some ends were so important that any means to attain them could be justified.

More did not precisely lie about the Hunne case, but the most scholarly and dispassionate course is to admit freely that he did distort and to suppose that he did so deliberately—although like so many passionate debaters in dubious causes, he may have ended by convincing himself that everything he asserted was true.

9

CHURCH AND STATE
IN MORE'S CAREER

T HE HUNNE CASE provoked dissension between the clergy and
     the laity in England, but it was not enough to give the laity control of
English life as long as the king had reason to respect the ancient liberties of
the church. Henry chose to honor ecclesiastical liberties, but he astutely displayed various options, using many of the threatening tactics against the
church that he was to use at the beginning of his divorce proceedings a little
over a decade later. More's fate was tied up in all these maneuvers, and it seems
clear that More recognized the dangers as soon as they were raised, though
even he could not possibly see how great they were.

   Dr. Horsey was disposed of only after months of feverish maneuver and
debate while London seethed with anger at the clergy. Parliament, assembling
in February 1515, had to reconsider the act of 1512 that had put criminous
clerks under the jurisdiction of the king's courts. Should it be renewed, hard-
ened, or canceled? The sentiments of the most vocal part of the London
populace were clear: the clergy should be brought under secular law in criminal
acts. No one was yet suggesting that a secular authority should define church
doctrine. To take such a step would be to change the church itself and to
change also the perception of how God worked in the world. Others at the time
did not see these issues so clearly; Thomas More always saw them, and the
events of 1515 became links in a chain of events slowly reeling him to his death.

   The Convocation of the English clergy gathered at the same time as Parliament. The bishops and the abbots of the great monasteries sat in the House

of Lords along with the secular magnates. By the practice of centuries, these spiritual lords met occasionally on their own to transact business for the whole church of England while Parliament was in session.

On the Sunday before Parliament met in the winter of 1515, Richard Kidderminster, abbot of Winchcombe, opened the Convocation with a thundering sermon at Paul's Cross, the public pulpit by the cathedral, and declared that the parliamentary act of 1512 was "clean against the law of God and the liberties of Holy Church." Anyone party to the act, whether spiritual or temporal, "had incurred the censures of Holy Church." The abbot had no power to pronounce a formal excommunication; he was only declaring his high-flown opinion that anyone who helped put any sort of clergyman under the jurisdiction of the civil law could expect no welcome in heaven. Evidently he was stiffened in his opinion by the recent proclamation of Pope Leo X that all clergymen were immune to all secular laws for all crimes they had committed.

Kidderminster's sermon was a warning shot fired across the bows of Parliament when the English church should have been trying to break off the engagement. Henry VIII was not to be intimidated by a stubborn clergyman from the country, and the English were no longer in the devout mood to suppose that murderers wearing a tonsure and able to read deserved a leniency not granted to ordinary criminals.

The king, seeing Kidderminster's sermon as a provocation, summoned a special assembly at Blackfriars, the house of the Dominican order in London. Here the great lords of the realm and substantial persons from the House of Commons as well as some theologians and canon lawyers met to debate these momentous issues. More might have attended this meeting as a spectator; doubtless he sided with the clergy in the defense of their freedom from secular jurisdiction.

In the debate, the champion of secular authority turned out to be an unlikely character, a clergyman, Henry Standish, warden of the mendicant friars in London and later bishop of St. Asaph's, a passionate, ambitious, somewhat unpleasant man who happened to have his hands on the future. He hotly maintained that criminal clergymen should be tried by secular courts under the English common law. The English people, he argued, were not bound to accept anything they believed contrary to the public good, "which public good must be preferred to all the laws of the world." Although not calling it by that name, Standish had absorbed the Arthurian ideal of a Christian English empire, sovereign over its people and their religion.

Standish looked like a turncoat to the clergy, and they sternly summoned him to appear before the Convocation, where he risked being condemned as a heretic. He promptly appealed to the king for help, and he as promptly received it.

The prelates made their own appeal to the king, and it may be summarized in their sentiment that he should mind his own business. His coronation oath bound him to uphold the liberties of the church; Standish had opposed these liberties, and should the king uphold Standish, he might bring down on himself the unspecified "censures of Holy Church."

By now Parliament was angry and stirring. At the prompting of the Commons, the secular lords in the House of Lords reminded the king that his coronation oath also required him to hold temporal jurisdiction over his land. Dr. Standish was declared to be in "great danger against [on account of] the malice of the clergy."

In the end a second conference, rather in the nature of a hearing before the Court of the King's Bench, met at Blackfriars. "The Justices and the King's Counsel spiritual and temporal and also certain persons" of Parliament heard the case and ruled that clergymen proceeding against Dr. Standish would be guilty of praemunire. They also declared that "our lord the King might perfectly well hold his Parliament by himself and his temporal Lords and by his Commons quite without the spiritual Lords." It appeared that the English church was on the brink of losing both its property and its ancient liberties. Bishop FitzJames had reason for the panic we have already observed in him.

It was up to Wolsey to save what he could of the church's place in England. Pope Leo X made him a cardinal on September 10, and the news of his elevation would have reached London by the second hearing at Blackfriars, although the red hat did not arrive until November. He was now the highest-ranking clergyman in England as well as the closest counselor to the king. At Baynard's Castle on the Thames, before all the judges who had brought in the pronouncement against the clergy and clerical privilege, Wolsey went down on his knees to beg Henry for mercy. He said some humble words, but he courageously upheld the old order, claiming that to call clergymen before secular judges "seems contrary to the laws of God and the liberties of Holy Church," which he and all the prelates of the church were bound by an oath to maintain according to their power.

Henry stood by Standish and affirmed the right of English kings to judge criminous clerks under the common law and the crown. Yet after Horsey's release from prosecution by the secular court and with his subsequent exile by the church under Wolsey's command, the matter seemed to die away. Most probably Henry and Wolsey struck a bargain: Henry would not press the matter if Wolsey punished Horsey and if the clergy backed away from Standish. The Parliament did not renew the act of 1512 against the lower orders. The conflict between laity and clergy was not resolved; its resolution was only postponed.

In the acrimony of the Hunne affair and the Standish business immediately afterwards, the growing prestige of the monarchy was clear. Kings brought to their thrones an aura of holiness that seemed an alternative to the apparently false holiness of the priesthood. It was easy for the masses to go from passionate loyalty to the king of England to the further belief that he should charge himself with reforming the clergy and purifying the church. Kings now represented power, a power for good or evil, a power undreamed of in the Middle Ages, when kings lacked nearly all the instruments of authority available to them in the sixteenth century. Now kings had elaborate bureaucracies, primitive by our own bureaucratic standards but powerful by the standards of the sixteenth century. They had a rationalized legal system, subservient law courts and judges, and the power of cash money delivered to them by an obedient citizenry. They had also the emotional power of their office. And some men with a reforming bent, despairing of reform from within the church itself, yearning for a pure church so they might believe in a divine presence in the world, now were willing to turn to the secular order to cleanse the spiritual. A Hercules was needed to purge the Augean stables of the church; that Hercules seemed to many to be Christian monarchy.

Thomas More stood staunchly on the side of the clergy. He was always the devotee who had approached ordination but turned back, and he always exalted the clerical estate as if in so doing he might redeem himself from the guilt he had incurred by not joining it. He could only have been troubled by the turmoil of the Hunne affair and its aftermath. And we find evidence enough in his *History of King Richard III* of his own dark expectations for kings. Give a king like Richard both the power of the secular order and spiritual dominion over a subservient church, and what would happen to the revelation of God in the world? Here More shared the traditional view of the Western church that the secular order and the ecclesiastical institution must be separate if each was to perform its divinely ordained duties in the world.

Then, just as the Hunne affair and its consequences were hottest, he suddenly faced a threat to his own prospects. About September 1514, Erasmus was sent a grumbling letter by Martin van Dorp of the University of Louvain. In his letter, the twenty-nine-year-old Dorp, not yet a doctor although he was already lecturing on philosophy at the university, conveyed a mixture of humble respect and sharp criticism. He objected to two works, *The Praise of Folly* and the Greek New Testament that Erasmus had by now promised to the scholarly world in a printed edition. Whatever More's feelings toward Erasmus might have been, this ominous letter from Dorp brought him into an open struggle for the cause of good letters that would make him an ally of Erasmus for the next decade. More's entry into the controversy was stirred in part by a desire to defend his own good name.

Dorp reported that *The Praise of Folly* had been badly received among his colleagues. Theologians, said he, must retain the good will of ordinary people. Erasmus had attacked theologians indiscriminately, blaming every one of them for the sins of a few, and he had created much bitterness among the theologians of Louvain.

Here was a critical matter. After Paris, Louvain was the most eminent university in Europe. Should its faculty condemn Erasmus—as Dorp implied might happen—the effects could be disastrous for both Erasmus and More, whose name was indissolubly connected to the book.

Dorp had heard that Erasmus planned to publish notes on a thousand passages in the New Testament and to amend the Latin Vulgate by using the Greek original. But, Dorp asked, could the Vulgate, used for so many centuries, be in error? Could the great doctors and the councils have been led astray by the Vulgate? Would a discussion of the integrity of the scriptural text not cast doubts on the teachings of those texts?

Dorp represented a viewpoint that proved far more accurate than the confident expectations of Erasmus. Erasmus wrote continually about the sins and silliness of erring clergymen, but he believed implicitly in the strength of the church. He did not dream of the disasters that lay just over the hill. He thought —or said he thought—that the Christian world stood at the doorway to a golden age. He supposed himself to be one of the great artisans of renovation. His attacks on wickedness in the church were made in the spirit of one scouring the sides of a battleship, knowing that he must work hard and dig deep to scrape off the rust and barnacles but never once imagining that he could sink the ship with his tools.

Dorp assumed that Christian belief was precarious and that the church and its faith were in danger. His letter posed questions that would be posed more sharply later on by events. What should be the attitude of the learned toward the common people? At what point did criticism of Catholic customs become a menace to Catholic faith? Did scholars dare arouse the common people to greater disrespect for the church than was already prevalent in their ranks? The Hunne case, unfolding only a year after Dorp wrote his letter, showed how easily the common folk could be incited to dangerous rebellion against the church; Luther's Ninety-five Theses would, within another three years, show how abysmal the gulf between clergy and laity had become. Dorp's motives may have been mixed, but his questions were genuine and critical.

Erasmus did not see the letter written in September 1514 until the following March, when he stopped in Antwerp on his way to England to beg money from his patrons, especially from William Warham, the most generous of his English friends. Apparently it was circulating in manuscript, and anyone might suppose that it would soon be printed. Still pondering this unexpected attack, Erasmus arrived in London just when the city was feverish over the Hunne affair. More did not see the letter until later. He was a member of an embassy to be sent on a royal diplomatic mission to Bruges, and although he did not leave until May, Erasmus supposed he had already gone. Erasmus apparently did not think to go to the More house in Bucklersbury and look up More for himself, although the small size of London would have made such a journey only a short walk.

Erasmus had to be troubled by Dorp's letter, for it purported to represent the opinions of many theologians at Louvain. If the letter did presage an official condemnation of Erasmus by the faculty of an eminent university, the patronage he counted on from both England and Rome at this critical stage in his career might dry up. Bishop FitzJames could lash out dangerously against him, for the old bishop was ready to defame anyone who attacked the clergy. Perhaps Erasmus cut his English visit short because he was afraid of becoming an object of controversy. He had planned to stay until summer; he was back in Antwerp by the end of May.

Once returned to Antwerp, he made a careful reply to Dorp. He wanted to make Dorp a friend, and the tone of the letter is much in the style of cultivated friendship so popular with the humanists when they were not assailing one another. Erasmus continued to express his exasperation and contempt for Dorp in private, but this letter—usually printed with *The Praise of Folly* in its subsequent editions—is as mild as milk. He had not attacked all theologians in his book, he said; he had castigated only the bad ones. It was obvious that the Latin text of the New Testament was corrupt. Christians could not be bound to copying errors made "by scribes unskilled, drunken, or half asleep." Truth could never damage the church of Christ. Erasmus ended by sounding supercilious and condescending, as if only a fool could mistrust his orthodoxy and the purity of his purpose.

Dorp was not mollified; he felt mocked, and late in August 1515 he wrote an angry reply. It required little perception to see that Erasmus meant far more in *The Praise of Folly* than to attack only the bad theologians. Clearly Erasmus had attacked Scholastic theology itself and the Aristotelian methods used by Dorp's colleagues. Dorp wrote as a man demanding to be taken seriously, and his reply became a tirade, finally descending to crude mockery of the humanities Erasmus prized.

To Dorp, as to More (and to Martin Luther toiling anonymously then at his biblical lectures in Wittenberg and struggling to assure himself of the benevolence of God), every human value—including education—had to be subordinate to the eternal destiny of the soul. Dorp did not care about elegance of style or Greek grammar; he cared about the horrors of hell and the bliss of heaven. He cared for the certainty of salvation through the implicit faith one might have in the Catholic Church. Erasmus was a disciple of Origen, who so disbelieved in the reality of the physical that he could not accept the notion of actual fire in hell or the doctrine of eternal separation from God; he believed that eventually even Satan would return to his creator. Erasmus seems to have accepted much more of Origen, considered heretical by most Catholics, than he could safely admit, although Erasmus's language was so evasive that no one can tell at this remove exactly what he thought about final things. The least that can be said is that he did not write very much about them.

Dorp closed his letter with conventionally friendly expressions, although even these were disturbing. He had heard people speaking against Erasmus. His letter might be taken as a warning. He made no threats, but anyone reading his words with their angry tone might be forgiven for supposing that others at Louvain might be preparing to launch an official condemnation of *The Praise of Folly.*

At some time during the summer or fall of 1515, More and Erasmus met in Bruges, and Erasmus told him about Dorp. More must have felt uneasy, since his own advancement depended on Thomas Wolsey, and Wolsey was just then involved in defending the church against the anticlericals roused by the Hunne affair. By the autumn, the battle in England was at its peak, and since Wolsey remained in charge of diplomacy it would have seemed to his agents in More's embassy that his side would prevail.

So in October, More tried his own hand at placating Dorp, writing a letter that has always been praised as a great defense of the new learning in Christian thought. For whatever reason, Dorp drew back from attacking Erasmus, and the threat of censure against *The Praise of Folly* receded, at least for the moment. More never published the letter. Once Dorp backed away, More had no reason to put before Europe an argument that might rankle his sometime antagonist and start the troubles anew.

The letter to Dorp is one of only two More wrote against an adversary that do not seethe with insult and contempt. The other he wrote against a young heretic named John Frith years later. More's other controversial pieces, burning with passionate invective and tempestuous spirit, remind us that he was a saint of fire rather than of water, and that the two times he affected calm and benevolence, he had his reasons.

More's burden was to flatter Dorp, to win him over, and to persuade him not to be hostile to *The Praise of Folly* or to the coming Erasmian edition of the Greek New Testament. Like Erasmus, he argued that *The Praise of Folly* ridiculed only bad theologians, and he mocked the petty quibblings of the Scholastic logicians. Men who learn nothing but problems in logic are not truly educated, he said, echoing a common humanist sentiment. They do no good to the church or to the devout life.

What makes a good theologian? Here More was clear—and conservative. The best theology comes from the Bible *and* the ancient fathers of the church. More was never to deviate from this view, and we should note how far he was in 1515 from the slogan "scripture alone" that would soon be trumpeted by the Lutherans and the other "heretics" about to burst on the world. We may thus defend More against the charge of inconsistency which, from the beginning of Protestantism, has been lodged against him by some, who claim that the More who wrote before Luther was radically different from the More who wrote after Luther thundered onto the religious stage of Europe. More always believed that divine revelation came and was still coming to the whole Christian church; it was not locked in a book. The people in the church whose wisdom and piety most certified them to be trustworthy interpreters of revelation were the old holy doctors. In his letter to Dorp he lists some of them dearest to his heart, especially Augustine and Jerome.

Scripture is the "venerable queen of all letters," he writes, and he vigorously defends Erasmus's forthcoming edition of the Greek New Testament. Yet he thinks that scripture, to be useful, must be interpreted carefully and that the only valid interpretations take place within the ancient tradition sanctioned by the saintly doctors. The Greek New Testament should be studied because those closest to Christ in time were also nearest to him in spirit. The Latin copies of the Vulgate had been corrupted by nodding penmen. Greek itself was the key to the treasure chest of the liberal arts, whose incomparable wealth stood in sharp contrast to the poverty of Latin, a wealth that enriched not only the intelligence of men but also their characters.

His defense of the forthcoming Greek New Testament is combined with an extensive attack on the complexities of Scholastic theology with its addiction to trivia. The Scholastics, he writes, "have concocted about God some problems so ridiculous you would think they were joking, and some statements so blasphemous you would think they were jeering." They justified such debates by claiming that they made the faith clear to heretics. But, said More, heretics were either learned or unlearned. If they were unlearned—as most of them were, he thought—they could not be convinced by learned debate. But if heretics were learned, their skill was almost always in debate, so that they could go on and on without end. Theologians and heretics in such debates, said More, "are very much like two men fighting naked among piles of stones; each has plenty of weapons; neither has any defense."

More's argument—eloquently made—is that piety is better served by Greek studies that take Christians back to the devout works of venerable saints than it can possibly be by the quibbles of argumentative theologians. As usual, More tells some funny stories along the way to illustrate his point.

He recalls a dinner he attended at the home of an Italian merchant— probably Antonio Bonvisi, a fabulously wealthy trader in wool who lived in London and who, over the years, was probably Thomas More's best friend. There came a theologian from the Continent, in London for a scholarly disputation. The theologian was a fiercely argumentative man and, says More, "at table, no matter what statement was made by anybody, no matter how carefully and cautiously modified, or thought out, it had barely left the lips of the speaker when he would promptly tear it apart with a syllogism, even though the subject of the conversation had nothing to do with theology or philosophy, and was completely foreign to his whole profession."

The theologian boasted that he could argue either side of any question, and the merchant fell into the game, bringing up—among other matters—the topic of mistresses. The merchant maintained that a man keeping one mistress at home was less a sinner than one visiting ten whores elsewhere. The theologian rushed to the attack, defending the proposition that the ten whores made for less sin because of the difficulty of procuring them compared with the ease of keeping a mistress. The merchant, perceiving that the theologian did not know scripture, began making up scriptural texts to confound the theologian's arguments.

The theologian was undaunted; when the merchant flung a manufactured biblical text at him, the theologian simply reinterpreted it and made it fit his own argument by bending and wrenching. "And if the merchant would annoy him by insisting that was not the correct meaning of the passage which the theologian had given, the fellow would swear a sacred oath, making it credible to all, that such was the interpretation of the passage given by Nicholas of Lyra," the greatest biblical commentator of the Middle Ages. More mocked such theological foolishness and upheld the value of the ancient doctors and the Greek text of scripture. And he did so convincingly.

Yet there remains something vague about his effort. Although he stoutly maintains that the Greek text is better than the Latin, he does not point out any textual problems that the Greek can elucidate. His enthusiastic welcome of the forthcoming Greek text in print seems to be based on a general faith that Greek was the doorway to good things; nothing in the letter to Dorp offers a hint that More knew precisely what Erasmus was doing.

More expressed friendship and admiration for Dorp in his letter, but here and there we find some sharp words strung like thorns among the roses. More claims that Dorp has damaged himself by his attacks on Erasmus. People may flatter Dorp to his face, but, More says, "I wish you could view without being seen the facial expression of those reading this last letter of yours." If he should, More said, Dorp would discover that many important people are mocking him.

Very carefully More dissected various statements Dorp had made in his own writings, statements demonstrating how contemptuous of others and how self-serving Dorp had been. Many of Dorp's remarks taken up by More represent a heavy-handed humor; More delighted in dwelling on these sallies, showing how senseless they were, how witless, how vulgar. Why does Dorp think such things are funny? More offers a patronizing answer to this rhetorical question: "Every man is charmed by his own point of view," he says, "just as each person thinks his own fart smells sweet."

The letter is a fine rhetorical effort, and, as we have noted, it apparently accomplished its purpose. The threat from Louvain did not materialize, and More's own career was not placed in jeopardy because of guilt by association with an officially condemned book. At times the letter is disingenuous; some of the theological debates More condemned did have a serious purpose, although we may agree that a mind that troubled itself with them would not share tastes common to most of us. More assumes a patronizing tone to Dorp throughout—the wise friend admonishing a somewhat childish young man for that young man's own good. It skillfully managed a high moral tone without bogging down in specific details from either the forthcoming Greek New Testament or *The Praise of Folly*. We are left with a high-sounding vagueness typical of modern commencement addresses that clearly identify the speaker's commitment to the good and the true without hinting at how he will vote in the next election. The letter is written by Thomas More the lawyer, making a case—not an entirely likable man but one who appears again and again.

10

THE BUILDING
OF UTOPIA

MORE'S EMBASSY to Flanders brought him back in touch with Erasmus and marked the beginning of a warm and public phase of their friendship, punctuated by the exchange of several letters and by mutual aid. We may be sure that More's letter to Dorp, written during this embassy, came after many conversations between the two men. If More had been cool toward Erasmus—and the evidence is strong that he had been—he was not a man to fall into open quarrel with someone who had not attacked him, especially with someone who shared with him as many ideas and hopes for reform as Erasmus did. Erasmus always courted More assiduously with the mixture of cloying flattery, wheedling charm, and literate brilliance that made him for much of his career the companion of men in power. The evidence seems to show that on his embassy to Flanders, More succumbed to Erasmus's aggressive demand for friendship, especially as the two of them thought out ways of quieting Dorp and then as More developed the scheme for his *Utopia*.

More also enjoyed the conversation of a young man named Peter Gilles, introduced to him by Erasmus and destined to be a dear and lifelong friend to both of them. They must have talked of classical learning, and in the lengthening nights before smoky fires in the dank Netherlandish autumn, they must have belabored the miserable state of current society and compared it with the glories of the antique past that all of them loved through the lens of great books—including the New Testament—which magnified that past in their minds and hearts and made its denizens seem like giants on the earth. The negotiations of More's embassy languished. At some point he turned his attention to building a dream world he called Utopia, a world probably conjured up by the talk of good friends in a city that was otherwise for More a lonely place.

Erasmus tells us that More wrote the second part of the book first and at leisure, and the first part later on in greater haste. There is much to suggest that they discussed the work at length together. When he got his controlling idea, More must have turned to Erasmus for advice as do fledgling writers of today, asking counsel from those experienced in the arcane necessities of publication. When it was all done, Erasmus guided the work through the press of Thierry Martens at Louvain in 1516—sign enough that the faculty of theology at Louvain bore no animus against either Erasmus or More, although Erasmus in a letter to More of October 1516 referred to Dorp as "that stupid fool" and indicated that he was still making trouble.

The first edition of *Utopia* appeared about December 1516 in More's Latin. Four other Latin editions appeared by 1519, and the book was translated into German in 1524. Then interest in it seemed to flag; no other edition appeared in any language until well over a decade after More's death; the book was not translated into English until 1551. It enjoyed nothing like the tremendous popularity of any number of the works of Erasmus. *The Praise of Folly*, for example, went through thirty-seven Latin editions between its first publication in 1511 and 1536, the year Erasmus died. So we must probably revise the commonly held assumption that More became instantly famous because of *Utopia* and that the book had a large immediate influence.

About the middle of the sixteenth century, interest suddenly flared anew, and since then it has gone through edition after edition and translation after translation. Scholars have threatened to bury it under the prodigality of their studies; it has inspired dozens and perhaps hundreds of writers to set down their own utopian dreams, and—in a way—the very genre of science fiction derives from *Utopia*. Its title has become a common noun in our language, and the adjective "utopian" has taken on the pejorative connotation of a quality too good for human existence or possibility. For all its importance, the little book can easily be read in an evening; it may, however, require a lifetime to be understood.

Utopia remains mysterious and even perplexing. More wrote in a heavily ironic mode, and it is almost impossible to argue that here he must be serious and that there he must be joking. The tone is cast in the narrative realism typical of books written by voyagers returning from the New World to tell their stories to Europe. Since sailors are not customarily imaginative men, stories written by them have the same prosaic quality as those given us by the astronauts who in our own time have found new worlds. *Utopia* is a kind of literary masque, and More never removes the covering to let us see exactly what lies beneath.

The book is divided into two parts, or "books" as they are called. The first is a dialogue between More and a sunburned traveler named Raphael Hythlodaye, just returned from a voyage around the world when More meets him in Antwerp during the embassy of 1515. Raphael is a moralist, rather humorless, at pains to show how much worse Europe is than almost any other place in the great world that he has covered with his journeys. He and More discuss the European social order, and although Raphael does most of the talking, More has some good lines, and we even have a few words from Peter Gilles, who supposedly met Hythlodaye first and introduced him to More.

In the second part we have not dialogue but declamation, a monologue by Raphael that describes in a most orderly fashion the life and the institutions of an island commonwealth called Utopia lying somewhere off the mainland of the New World. The word "Utopia" is a coinage from Greek and can mean either "nowhere" or "good place." Since in his correspondence More calls his island "Nusquama," meaning "nowhere," it seems probable that he began by calling his book by the Latin title and later shifted to the Greek, liking both the double meaning of "Utopia" and the way this strange coinage would mask the imaginary quality of the book from those lesser souls who knew only Latin.

Utopia is profoundly devout and reformist. Every word is saturated with the values of the stoic Christian faith set forth by the ancient fathers of the church —values like community consensus over individual judgment, the physical life to be considered not as an end in itself but only as a vehicle for the much more important growth of the spirit, the notion that passion is an unmitigated enemy of virtue, devout simplicity, a hatred of idleness and frivolity. In the second part of the book, the declamation by Raphael, a long description of the religion of the Utopians comes at the end. This was in accord with the style of contemporary declamations in which the most important points were always reserved for last. The entire tone and import of *Utopia* remind us once again that no greater error about More can be imagined than to assume—as so many have done—that he began as a bold humanist reformer and for some reason lost his nerve when the Protestants raised their standard of revolt against corruption. Any careful reading of *Utopia* and all More's other works will show the same spirit at work early and late. *Utopia* came into print only a few months before Martin Luther wrote his Ninety-five Theses. The times did change, and More's spirit changed from a benign, almost dispassionate expression of his ideals to a furious declaration of his principles. But in *Utopia,* as later on, we find the Thomas More who saw the world as a wicked place and the human heart as a pit of darkness requiring the light of diligent public scrutiny if the monsters lurking there were not to crawl out and devour the person and the society.

More began *Utopia* in church. At least he tells us that he was coming from worship in the great church of Notre Dame in Antwerp when Gilles introduced him to Raphael. In More's tale, he, Raphael, and Gilles adjourn to the house where More was staying, and there, seated on a bench of sod in the garden, they fall into a long conversation. Not unnaturally for an age becoming accustomed to thinking of a new world, their talk involves comparisons between the new world and the old. Raphael believes that almost every place on earth manages its affairs better than Europe does, and he has brought home with him a thousand lessons in virtue taken from the examples of excellent people Europeans have never heard of.

Raphael's learning and wisdom so impress More that he supposes that this wandering wise man should settle down to become a councillor to a king. When More wrote this part of *Utopia,* back in England, some kind of invitation to join the royal council had probably already been tendered to him. He had in mind the well-known reluctance of Erasmus to tie himself to the service of any monarch—a reluctance that Erasmus himself had probably expressed at length in conversations with More during their time together in the Netherlands when they both had the leisure to talk and laugh together. Like Erasmus, Raphael refuses to enter royal service. He says he cares nothing for rank or possessions; he has already given away all he once owned to his relatives, and he feels he owes them nothing else; he wants only freedom. To be a courtier, he says, would be slavery itself.

Should he not think of the good he might do for the whole nation by entering royal service? No, says Raphael. Most kings prefer to make war rather than peace, and they are absorbed in the conquest of new lands rather than in governing well the lands they already possess. Foolish custom in Europe is too strong to be displaced by wisdom, and the habit of foolishness is everywhere in Christendom. A wise man involved in such business would soon be overwhelmed by the absurdities of the life of power.

Even in England absurdity is at home. Raphael has been there, visiting Cardinal Morton—who in fact had been dead since 1500. The John Morton of More's *History of King Richard III* is a complex and slightly ambivalent character; the Morton Raphael praises in *Utopia* is simply More's old patron and mentor, a man of immense civic virtue and sanctity, extolled here too much to be real.

To Morton's house while Raphael was there came an expert in the English law, boasting of the strict justice of his country. Hundreds were being executed for theft; yet thieves continued to steal, and the legal expert was puzzled. Raphael said such executions were unjust; he posed a novel idea: society itself is partly responsible for the crimes committed against it; therefore society should temper justice with mercy for those it helps plunge into theft and violence. In Raphael's voice More was proposing a sweeping application of equity to mitigate the harsh literalism of English law. Equity was the force of conscience that good men applied to cases when it was clear that the letter of the law might lead to injustice. The letter of the law required the death penalty for thieves who stole more than seven pence. But if they were forced to steal in order to live, should they be put to death? Raphael said no.

In England idle nobles paraded about with equally idle attendants, attendants turned loose to vagabondage and brigandage when the master died or when they themselves became sick, old, or infirm. Raphael spoke of wars that teach men nothing but violence and how soldiers come home from these wars with nothing to do, no profession save that of arms and blood, no prospects but crime or starvation. It was no surprise, he told those in Morton's house, that such men turned quickly to a violent life.

The most famous passage in this first "book" of *Utopia* condemns the enclosure movement. Nobles, gentry, and some of the huge rural monasteries like Glastonbury, holding great lands, were fencing off the old common pastures where peasants in the English villages had for centuries grazed their cattle and raised a few crops. With the growth of the wool trade these lords gave over their fields to the profitable raising of sheep, which, in Raphael's famous declaration, had grown "so greedy and wild that they devour human beings themselves and devastate and depopulate fields, houses, and towns." The image is striking, and any Christian European accustomed to seeing sheep as the symbol of the benevolent Lamb of God in Christian iconography must have been driven to ponder this new view of the sheep as the destroyer of the poor people Christ had come to save.

Yet the rise in the price of wool made some men rich, Raphael said. In the spirit of egalitarian and outraged orators through the centuries, he belabored the scandal of wealth squandered by the few on insidious pleasures like gambling, brothels, and drink while multitudes groaned in misery and in hunger. After such injustices, the law created a further outrage by putting to death those poor souls, driven off their land and forced to preserve themselves and their families by theft. Here Raphael produced a marvelous sentence that would not become fact in English (and American) law until centuries later: "In my opinion not all the goods that fortune can bestow on us can be set in the scales against a man's life."

It has usually gone unnoticed that More's embassy, on which he began writing *Utopia*, was intended to increase commerce, especially in wool, and that while he penned these immortal lines, he was working hard to add to the wealth of those classes in English society whom Raphael castigates for their heartless greed. Commentators on *Utopia* have also passed over in silence More's dear friend Antonio Bonvisi, who accumulated a fortune in the wool trade and apparently lived a luxurious life, though without the vices that Raphael here condemns. Whether More recognized these ironies himself is an unanswerable question, but at the least they reveal what we learn from a study of his other works, that when he wrote he built a world he could control and that, like most writers, he did not always take care to make that created world correspond entirely with the world where he had to make his way.

In the imaginary world of *Utopia*, his Raphael speaks for an ideal of justice that had no counterpart in reality. What penalty should be exacted for theft? Raphael, seeing every other society on earth as better than Christian Europe, cited the virtuous Polylerites, who, he said, lived in a secluded spot surrounded by mountains in Persia. Among them thieves were put to work and forced to make restitution to their victims rather than to pay a fine to the king. Provision was made for the wives and children of thieves; the whole family was not flung into the streets to starve when the head of the house had been convicted for wrongdoing that they had not shared in. When Raphael suggested during a discussion at Cardinal Morton's dinner table that such a scheme be tried in England, the English legal expert shook his head and muttered that the commonwealth would be upset.

The legal expert's was the old argument, tiresome to would-be reformers in every age, that because things had always been done one way, they could not possibly be changed. Morton thought that the king might experiment by suspending the death penalty for theft for a while, and was applauded by his guests. But the doubtful lawyer's skepticism was certainly the prevailing mood of most who pondered the scheme described by Raphael in *Utopia*.

In the end Raphael says again that he cannot possibly be councillor to a king. The dead weight of custom is too suffocating for him; kings are made by such customs, and they cannot be deterred from pursuing their customary follies. He poses a question: if he were councillor to the king of France, could he possibly keep France from trying to lay hold of Italy? "Suppose I argued that we should stay at home because the single kingdom of France by itself was almost too large to be governed well by a single man so that the king should not dream of adding other dominions under his sway?"

To illustrate wisdom in contrast to such Gallic folly, Raphael calls on yet another example from the superior world beyond Europe. The Anchorians living on the mainland near Utopia had a king who wanted to conquer another kingdom to which he had an old claim by marriage. His people realized that this projected foreign war would bring penury and rebellion at home as well as bloodshed and corruption for everyone who fought in it. So they put a choice to their king: he could not rule both kingdoms; he must decide which he would have.

All this could apply to France, since French kings had been fighting for Italy since 1494 and based their claims on an old marriage bond. But in spirit these remarks could also apply to England and to Henry's restless ambition to make good his title "king of England and France." Here, too, was a claim founded

on an old marriage alliance between England and France, one that had allowed
Edward III to claim to be the rightful king of France nearly two centuries
before More wrote *Utopia*. Would Henry or those around him have seen the
connection? Probably not. They would discern in it no more than an attack
on France the enemy, and so Raphael's bold words on the absurdity of princes
became nothing but a nationalistic attack on French foreign policy, an impression helped by the interpretative gloss in the margin: "Covertly the French are
urged not to seize Italy."

English affairs are touched on covertly indeed! Raphael protests against
those councillors who urge kings to dig up old and forgotten laws that everyone
has transgressed and by suddenly enforcing them, bring revenues into the
treasury by imposing fines. There are also councillors, he says, who urge kings
to collect taxes from their people under the pretense of making war. But when
the money is collected, these kings make peace and use the money for other
purposes. There are kings who seek to keep their people poor so that they will
have no spirit for rebellion.

People at the time knew that all these devices had been used by Henry VII
to wring money out of his subjects. More must have had Henry in mind when
he had Raphael make this general reproach against wicked kings. But the
criticism is so oblique that it was harmless, and harmless criticism could serve
only to let More show his educated friends that he could see the general
wickedness in the way things were. It is not a cry for reform but a bid for
supporting ironic smiles.

Once again, in this discussion, a foreign and unknown people becomes a
rebuke to Europeans. The Macarians, who live not far from the Utopians,
permit their king to have a treasury no greater than a thousand pounds.
Their aim is to restrain the powers of kings to do injustice and to leave
enough money in the hands of the people to allow business to go on. The
conclusion is obvious: avarice and absurdity rule the councils of kings, and
Raphael wants no part of such company. Unable to save a commonwealth,
he will save himself.

More protests. Such a view is perversely academic, he says. An idealist like
Raphael cuts himself off from the chance to do good. The true political
philosopher, More says, will "by the indirect approach . . . seek and strive by
the best of your power to handle matters tactfully. What you cannot turn to
good, you must make as little bad as you can. For it is impossible that all should
be well unless all men were good, a situation which I do not expect for a great
many years to come."

But Raphael is not to be dissuaded from his political isolation. In justification
of himself, he adds an explanation for the absurdity and injustice of the
European world: political evils come about because men hold private property.
So he prepares More and us for his description of Utopia, the ideal common-

wealth. There, he tells us, no private person owns anything, and there all the evils of European society are either muted or absent.

More disputes the wisdom of communism. Raphael promises to tell him of the marvelous island where communism is the rule of life, and so they go in to dine. Afterwards, when they have resumed their places on the grassy bench, Raphael prepares to begin his tale of Utopia, and so the first part of the book comes to an end.

Several things should be said about this much of More's great work. We have touched on one of them already. His point, at least for the fiction of the piece, is not merely that the island of Utopia is superior to Europe but that just about every other place in the world enjoys a better society than Europe has. Europe with its injustice and its cruelty is made to appear not the standard of value but the exception to all the standards. Things that Europeans accept because they do not think that they can be improved on are shown to be accidents of time and place that can be changed by reference to a great general consensus that rules other human societies.

In his later discussions of the authority of the Catholic Church, when he did battle against the Protestant heretics, More was always to make much of consensus. When England turned away from the grand old faith and went whoring after the novelty introduced by Henry VIII, More could retain his own confidence in the Catholic Church because he believed that the world beyond England's shores testified to a consensus that made the English schism petty and absurd. What he did with his legions of virtuous societies in the new world just opening to the European mind was to shape them into a kind of great secular church that by their serene devotion to reason condemned the eccentricities of European social customs, reducing them to the ridiculous— just as he was later to use the universal Christian church to condemn English heresy.

It has often been claimed that More's *Utopia* is part of the literature of the "noble savage" that we find in writing as diverse as the essays of Montaigne, the travels of Lemuel Gulliver, and the adolescent attacks on civilization by J. J. Rousseau. It is a little too simple to lump all these writers together. But it is true that they were each stirred by the amazing discovery that many societies did in fact lie out there beyond the great oceans and that they had not shared European civilization. Some Europeans, dismayed by the failures of their society, yearned for those other civilizations to be better than their own.

Deep in this yearning lay the conviction that Europeans knew much better than their practice might show. If all men *knew* better, some must *do* better or else the connection between knowledge and action assumed by all education seemed threatened to the core. So the hope for a better world existing some-where beyond the seas was a hope for the practical worth of the higher moral sense that was supposed to distinguish humankind from the savage beasts.

By 1516 these yearnings were fueled not only by the new discoveries but also by the pervasive conviction in men like More that something had gone terribly wrong with Europe. Gloomy Europeans wanted to believe that somewhere there must be places where the individual and society lived harmoniously together, places where ordinary citizens were relieved of the dread that eroded confidence everywhere in the old world.

Many, if not most, of these fears were economic, and money and property are frequent topics in nearly everything More wrote. Money was important to More for the same reason that it is important to most of us: it was the only guarantee of place in society. People who lost their wealth lost their station, and if a man of More's rank lost his money, his children might beg in the streets. Talent, virtue, and even birth meant nothing without money to preserve the place where such qualities might be seen and rewarded. The only solution More could see to the dreadful insecurity of a money economy was communism, and he probably hit on the idea for his Utopians because he worried so much himself about money.

When the second part of *Utopia* opens, Raphael is speaking of the island commonwealth, and he ruminates about how inferior Europe is by comparison. He describes Utopian geography, politics, city organization, customs, and religion, all in the understated tone of a man recounting things so real to him that he need not exclaim over them. He is an Argonaut, telling of wonders that have become commonplace in his experience.

To us Utopia seems unspeakably dreary, with a life so monotonous that it reminds us of some drab people's democracy. Everyone marches in lockstep. The peculiarities of individuals that make life interesting are thoroughly subjugated to communal needs. Nobody in Utopia except the long-vanished founder, King Utopus, is given a name in the book. In reading about Utopia's citizens, we can understand Raphael's oversight, for they seem like interchangeable parts in a great social machine, and the pleasure—if there is one —is to see the whole thing working, not to delight in the individuals who live there. A novelist in Utopia would have a hard time; an engineer would be at home.

Utopian civilization is founded on natural law, the law that Fortescue assumed when he wrote about English law in books More must have read. A few theorists of natural law have justified stratification in society. Thomas Aquinas thought that socially we are all created unequal. But More followed the tendency that was to become powerful in the constitutional history of the United States; natural law led him to posit radical equality when he imagined his Utopia. It is just this equality that seems so horrifying to us, because in More's work it translates into dreary conformity enforced by harsh penalties. Equality means that what is good for one is pretty much good for all, and here at least, it does not allow the kind of exceptional behavior that admits either great villainy or extraordinary genius.

Like More himself, the Utopians are urban people who take little pleasure in rural life, although all of them learn agriculture because they know that it is indispensable. They study agriculture from childhood, partly in school and partly on excursions to farms close to the city, where, like children in summer camp, they do some of the work. But as adults, no one is forced to endure the drudgery and isolation of the countryside longer than two years. Bands go from the cities to do their term on the land, raising crops and animals. The shifts are staggered; every new group that goes out finds another that has been in place for a year. The one-year veterans are expected to teach the newcomers all the secrets of farming in the year they will spend together—an assumption that must seem dubious to anyone who has spent much time wresting life out of the soil. Even with their supposedly lifelong study of the subject, the Utopians would surely have found a year's apprenticeship in agriculture to be inadequate.

More was ignorant both of agriculture and of the peasants who learned their skills on the land by the trials and errors of a lifetime. He knew only that farming was hard work; he probably also knew that after toiling all day in the fields, most farmers do not feel like discussing literature all night (as his Utopian farmers do), and he must have known also that, in some seasons at least, farming cannot be organized in six-hour workdays of the sort he gave to the rest of his Utopian work force.

Through Raphael's long declamation, More describes Utopian hatcheries that use incubators to hatch eggs. He counts it a small wonder that the newly hatched chicks follow the first moving thing they see when they peck their way into the light. They follow men or women, counting them as their mothers. More had not seen enough baby chickens to get over his surprise at this common behavior, and he had obviously not witnessed the consternation of a mother hen who has adopted ducklings when they take to the water for the first time in a most unchickenly style.

The Utopians have little sense of the beauties of nature that had permeated late medieval culture when poets and other artists delighted in the bucolic ideal. When a forest is in the way, the Utopians move the whole thing— heralds of the day when the awesome powers of nature would be tamed, shaped into whatever forms moderns find convenient.

More had classical city planning in mind when he designed Utopia. He gives his island fifty-four cities as much alike as geography would permit. Raphael describes the capital, Amaurote, which resembles London with its tidal basin and its fine stone bridge with great arches. The streets in each town are twenty feet wide—a size that would seem cramped to us. To a Londoner they would have been immense. They would also have seemed uncommonly straight, for

More described houses facing each other in rows. Italians like Leonardo da Vinci were designing such imaginary towns laid out in grids. But until modern times most cities grew according to the undulations of rivers and along streets formed by the meanderings of cattle, dogs, sheep, and pigs—paths never straight because animals refuse to move in straight lines. More, like others of his age, glimpsed an ideal city laid out in the grid that, in the age of giant machinery, has become familiar to us all, a pattern imposed on nature by the human mind and having little of nature itself in it.

The houses in Utopia are built of fireproof materials—another detail important to Londoners, whose city was perpetually threatened by fire and often burned. No Utopian house can be locked—something difficult to imagine in a medieval city where the rich barred their doors with enormous beams of wood and sometimes employed guards to fight off attackers. All the houses in Utopia are exchanged by lot every ten years. Since there is no private property, all wealth—including real estate—belongs to the community.

To us the most astonishing thing about Utopia is the relentless dedication of its citizens. They have been taught that the greatest good for the individual is to seek the good of all, and they have learned the lesson. So they not only own no property, but they all dress alike—leather clothes for work at their crafts, outer garments of unbleached and undyed linen or wool for public appearances. They must have seemed like a community of strict monks to readers at the time the book appeared.

For a man so well known as a father, More cared precious little for the family life of his Utopians. Families do not take their meals in private at home. They may if they wish, but few want to do so. In a society of awesome conformity, such an individual act as eating in private would be suspect. All the people on each street eat at a refectory where everybody can keep an eye on everybody else. No antisocial behavior has any chance to fester in secret. Raphael tells us with righteous satisfaction that in Utopia there is "nowhere any pretext to evade work—no wine shop, no alehouse, no brothel anywhere, no opportunity for corruption, no lurking hole, no secret meeting place." He also tells us that the Utopians are habitually merry. We wonder why.

Families live together in clans subject to the oldest man in the group unless he is senile. All the clans are kept at a uniform size, and if one group gets too large, some of its people are transferred to others that are smaller. The text is a little fuzzy here, but it seems clear that Raphael says that children are the ones shifted. We might suppose that a mother and father would be saddened to see their progeny taken from them in the interest of uniform size for the clans, but the assumption seems to be that even in this intimate and emotional matter they would understand that the good of the community is worth any sacrifice because it meant the good of all.

A general reason permeates the Utopian community, and although individuals may be flawed in this or that perception of the good, the community cannot err drastically if the whole group has a chance to make continual open and collective judgments. When communities can discuss things openly, reason and virtue will prevail. But if individuals crawl off to themselves to nourish their own desires and conceits, vice and absurdity will fester and make the whole body sick.

More, using Raphael's voice, is remarkably consistent in this perception of a general will working for the good and permeating all corporations. In the Utopian cities, rule comes down through a mayor and a council elected in republican fashion by the households of the town. A general parliament meets every year in Amaurote, but no king rules in Utopia. There once was a monarch —King Utopus, who conquered the island and gave it good laws. But he and his office had long since vanished when Raphael came on the scene. Raphael makes no resounding comments about this naked republicanism; he simply describes it. More, servant to a monarch with unbounded pretensions, could not allow Raphael to become imprudent on such a delicate subject. Only after some study and puzzlement do most readers discover that Utopia has no king. With citizens so virtuous, Utopia does not need a king to tell them what to do. They exist in the state of civic unselfishness that Machiavelli revered in the Roman Republic when he wrote his *Discourses*. And unlike the citizens of Machiavelli's Republic, More's Utopians have never lost their virtue; they are mature adults, quite capable of directing their own affairs without a prince who, as More and Machiavelli seemed to agree, can only conduct the business of state through guile and crime. The omission of a monarch is startling in *Utopia* once we realize it, and it is a signal preparing us for More's own later relations with his king.

The mechanism of political discussion in Utopia is the open assembly where the wisdom of the group is allowed free run in public debate. Not every citizen can share in such discussions; only the elected representatives are deemed worthy of such responsibility. People guilty of any private talks on matters of public interest are put to death—the only crime in Utopia besides adultery specifically mentioned by Raphael as worthy of capital punishment.

More's faith in the ability of assemblies to agree calls up a musical image he did not use. For any choir of singers, the harmonies are there somewhere, existing in an eternal state of mathematical precision. This voice or that may not be able to reach some notes, or it may not be able alone to develop the resonance required by the song. So by itself or even with another voice flawed in some other way, it can produce only a faint echo of the truth amid much discord. But a thousand voices singing together overwhelm the individual flaws and, with harmony matching harmony, swell to an ideal of impeccable glory and grace.

So do assemblies—like Parliament in England—provide a truth that individuals cannot reach on their own. And throughout More's life, he was always to trust the group over the individual. The corollary to such a view of group authority is the conformity that so many modern commentators on *Utopia* have deplored. When the choir sings the "Battle Hymn of the Republic," the tenor in the back row does not suddenly launch into "Dixie." The group defines the goals of society, and nothing is allowed to get in the way of progress toward the goals of simplicity, community, and discipline.

It is the usual thing to say that *The Praise of Folly* and *Utopia* are similar works. They both make heavy use of irony, and irony always assumes that the speaker or the writer says some things that are not true so that his audience can agree with him about some underlying point to his discourse. But *The Praise of Folly* and *Utopia* share little besides irony. They were written in different spirits.

The Praise of Folly mocks the way people choose goals for themselves, goals that do not make good sense, and the way profession contradicts performance. When Erasmus speaks of unworthy monks and ridiculous theologians, he is (as we have seen) harsh and bitter, his pen dipped in venom. But when he considers the rest of humankind, he is satirical rather than sardonic, and his view of the follies of humanity is humorous and sympathetic. Even Christ took part in the incalculable spontaneity of the universe, according to Folly, for what strained reason to a greater degree than the faith that God became man to save our souls? Erasmus did want reform in the church and in society, and the scorn he heaped on unworthy churchmen in *The Praise of Folly* was real. Otherwise he preferred to enjoy rather than to condemn, and he showed no great interest in changing the nature of human beings; he would laugh at scholars while he kept on being one himself. He certainly would not change the spontaneous grace of God toward humankind. Perhaps at heart he was cynical enough to avoid high expectations that the generality of humankind would inevitably disappoint.

In comparison, *Utopia* is heavy-handed and puritanical. We find none of the gentleness of Erasmus, none of his willingness to let human beings be frivolous. More is a rulesman in *Utopia*—just as he was a rulesman in life. He thought that a lot of the rules in European society ought to be changed because they were bad, but his solution was to impose others that were good. All the rules —in good Scholastic fashion—would point to a goal of complete harmony and conformity. If the Gothic cathedral represents the systematic ordering of diversity in stone much akin to the systematic ordering of philosophy and theology in Thomas Aquinas, More's *Utopia* represents that same orderly spirit in social planning.

His Utopian elders keep meals free of unworthy talk. Even when Utopians play games, they seek wisdom for life, molding their leisure to the goals set by the rules. How exciting for them to play at "Virtues and Vices" in the evenings

—one of their favorite amusements, so Raphael tells us. For here, he says, in a game much like chess, "is exhibited very cleverly to begin with, both the strife of the vices with one another and their concerted opposition to the virtues; then, what vices are opposed to what virtues, by what forces they assail them openly, by what stratagems they attack them indirectly, by what safeguards the virtues check the power of the vices, by what arts they frustrate their designs; and finally, by what means the one side gains the victory."

It is not hard to see in this passage the relentlessly self-regulated man who drove his first wife to tears of anguish because he was resolved not to let her pass her life in idleness or frivolity, the man who could not bear to waste time himself, the man who detested idle games. He would have been at home in his Utopian commonwealth where everything turned like one of the new mechanical clocks, and every human cog worked for the purposes of the virtuous machine and never for itself alone.

Nearly every commentator on *Utopia* has much to say about its communism and the origins of communism in the conviction of the Christian fathers that private property was a vice that entered the world with the fall of Adam and Eve from paradise. To the fathers of the church, private property was a necessary vice, allowed because men were sinful, but a vice nevertheless. (It was much the same view that Augustine and others had of sex.) More's Utopians lived by the natural law in the perfect communism that had been forsaken by the rest of the world. (They could not, of course, live without sex.)

What we often fail to see is the close relation in More's thought in *Utopia* between communism and his intense drive to see that everybody works, that nobody wastes time, that no one lives in idleness. He lived in an England where sturdy beggars held out their hands in the crowded city streets and vagabonds roamed the highways. There was nothing for these people to do because to put them to work required somebody with money to pay them, and the money was not to be had. It seemed to More that poverty was devouring the soft under-belly of society and that these miseries afflicted England because of an absurd reliance on gold and silver, metals far inferior to iron and providing no good essential to human life. In the midst of such absurdities, men who should work, men who *could* work, were idle. And idleness was not merely an economic problem; it was an opening to the worst vices of the human heart. A proverb of the time held, "When the fiend finds man idle, he puts in his heart foul thoughts of fleshly filth or other follies." Many other proverbs carry the same warning; and it is perhaps a key to More's own prodigious quest to be always busy to discover in the popular wisdom that such activity kept sexual tempta-tion at bay.

So More's vision of communism is not only a means of conquering the vices of private property but also the surest way to quell the vice of idleness and its attendant evils. His Utopians guide themselves by the principle that would be enunciated by Marxists centuries after More had died—from each according to his ability, to each according to his need. Everybody works; everybody has enough. In fact, the produce of such universal labor is so great that no one has to work over six hours a day. The needs of society can be met without drudgery, and time is left over for a creative leisure spent in a remorseless quest for self-improvement.

Such prodigious industry not only builds up abundance for the Utopians; it also provides an excess for export. They sell goods abroad, and since they do not need to import many things, they take payment in gold and silver. The result is a mercantilist's dream: they amass huge surpluses of these precious metals. Since bullion is of no use at all within the boundaries of Utopia, and since the Utopians in their stern addiction to simple virtues do not want to become corrupt by love of these metals, their practice is to store them at home in ways that do not provoke envy. They use gold and silver to make chamber pots and prisoners' chains, and they mark those guilty of disgraceful acts by making them wear "gold ornaments hanging from their ears, gold rings encircling their fingers, gold chains thrown around their necks, and, as a last touch, a gold crown binding their temples." (It is like More to make criminals look like kings—often criminals in More's own experience.)

The Utopians do occasionally use their gold and silver outside the country, lending money to other nations and rarely calling in these debts. Whenever possible they hire foreign mercenaries to fight their wars, choosing to spend their gold rather than their blood. War, Raphael says, is a thing fit only for beasts, and the Utopians hate it.

But war is inevitable, and it is reasonable to make war as humane as possible. Here humane impulses lead to suspect practices. The Utopians pay to have the kings of enemy nations assassinated, and they reward traitors from the other side. Such practices make wars shorter and therefore less bloody.

Yet when forced to fight for themselves, the Utopians are fierce warriors. Priests, women, and children follow their men into battle. The priests try to keep battle from falling into butchery, restraining their own troops from ferocity in victory and sometimes restraining the other side as well when the Utopians are being defeated. The presence of the women and children plucks up the valor of the Utopian soldiers.

The section on war illustrates the limits More placed on his conception of Utopia. He never held that the orderly and disciplined ways of the Utopians sufficed to win the world to their views or to banish sin from themselves. Neighboring peoples, virtuous though they were, did not take such inspiration from Utopian examples that they spontaneously imitated Utopian institutions. The generality of human beings could not be bent so far.

Even Utopia has crime, and it has slaves. Most slaves have been bought from other countries or else captured in war. Some have been Utopian citizens, reduced to servitude because they have violated Utopian law. Utopians occasionally commit adultery; if they do so twice and are caught, they are put to death. Sexual sins always stirred More's deepest wrath, and he had little patience with them. But he did not claim, even in the fiction of *Utopia,* that any society could be so nearly perfect that fornication and adultery might be unknown. To have made such a claim for his Utopians would have been to deny the Christian doctrine of original sin and to embrace the Pelagian heresy, vehemently attacked by Augustine because the Pelagians taught that the rigorous exercise of habitual good will could make human beings live above sin, without the requirement of supernatural grace from God.

More was to the marrow of his bones a medieval Christian, saturated with pessimism about a frail humankind weakened by original sin. His great vision was to see that society must assume large responsibility for the wicked things some individuals do, and for the purposes of his *Utopia* he was willing to grant that in a rigorously supervised society, the overwhelming majority could learn that it was better to help the community than to pursue private gain.

In some respects Utopia resembles a vast herd in which all the members move as one over a green and spacious pasture. But every herd has its occasional maverick; always sin lies at the door, ready to pounce, and even in Utopia some fall victim to its power. The relentless openness of the society, the resolute eagerness of the Utopians to spend time with each other and to check up on what everybody is doing, the loathing of idleness—all are part of More's recognition of sin's terrible power, a power he must have felt continually in himself. If the Utopians let down their guard for an instant, sin will rush in. In the midst of their paradise of reason and virtue, we are brought into the almost horrifying tension of More's awful view of human nature. Erasmus now and then said conventional things about the dangers of sin, but his view of human nature was fundamentally optimistic. Nowhere in his works do we find the intense, melancholy awareness of the inevitable power of sin in the best of humanity that we find habitually in More and that is assumed in the rigor of all Utopian customs and institutions.

Sin in Utopia is what Augustine called *superbia,* the overweening pride that is the mother of all vice, the narcissistic adoration of the self as the center of the universe. The predominant school of theology in More's time held that humility was the first step to salvation, that the individual must acknowledge his own worthlessness before God's grace could begin to save him. Individual humility is the way of life in Utopia, where personal self-seeking is rigorously controlled by ritual, order, conformity, and mutual observation. Those who say that Utopian society is the monastery extended to whole families are much closer to the mark than those who see it as a book of serious political theory.

There is also something monastic in the relations of the Utopians with their foreign neighbors. The original theory of the monastery was that it allowed heroic believers to live life at the limits while ordinary Christians remained in the world. St. Anthony, one of the first monks and one dear to More, went out to the Egyptian desert after the conversion of Constantine and did battle with the demons at a time when Christians no longer did battle with the Roman authorities. His struggles were the staple of monastic artists throughout the Middle Ages, culminating in the stunning Isenheim Altar of Grünewald, who completed his painting in More's lifetime. The monk was supposed to be as humble as clay before God. Humility was signified in a good monastery by precise ritual, rigorous abnegation, and individual poverty (accompanied often by communal wealth). At times, to our own self-indulgent age, these monkish exercises in meekness are so incongruous that they become the stuff of comedy.

But this excessive humility toward God almost inevitably led to a certain arrogance toward the miserable, grasping world beyond the cloistered walls. Anselm said that only a few would be saved and that most of them would be monks. The vision of the Apocalypse held that one hundred and forty-four thousand virgin males would stand before God on the final day in their robes of purest white; it must have seemed quite monkish to readers in the Middle Ages. And if one took literally the number of saints in the vision, one could come up with some alarming conclusions about the prospects for salvation even among monks. The people beyond the cloister had little chance at all, and Anselm could make his pronouncement with a certain divine confidence.

The curious result was that good monasteries guarded their own denizens and imposed strict penance on monks who fell to keep them from hell. And yet for centuries they regularly did business—good business—with the outside world, a world doomed to perdition. The world was simply that way, and because it was so unalterably set in its own being, the monks never imagined that they should do anything but accept it and make whatever profit they could from it.

Now here are the Utopians wearing their simple robes of unbleached wool and linen—just like Cistercian or Carthusian monks—and yet they manufacture dyes to sell abroad. Here are the Utopians who have plenty of cattle and sheep and eat enough meat to make the average European peasant sick if he changed to it suddenly from his meager diet of grain and wine or beer. But they have slaves to do the butchery, for, says Raphael, "they do not allow their citizens to accustom themselves to the butchering of animals, by the practice of which they think that mercy, the finest feeling of our human nature, is gradually killed off." We might expect a people as virtuous as the Utopians to become vegetarians so as not to inflict the harm of butchering on anyone. But the thought never occurred to them. We have noted their scorn of gold and their loathing of war, and yet their loathing did not make them true pacifists. They paid mercenaries, using their own citizens only in cases of mortal danger. Here again we see an assumption of casual superiority toward those not of their community, a superiority that seems to have been an indissoluble part of the monastic spirit.

The apparent ambiguity of the Utopians toward the outside world is especially well shown by their attitudes toward war and gold. Within their community, they are completely communistic. Yet they go to war with special dedication to defend their allies, especially when the property of friendly merchants is unjustly taken as booty by enemies. Says Raphael: "They are more grieved at their allies' pecuniary loss than their own because their friends' merchants suffer severely by the loss as it falls on their private property, but their own citizens lose nothing but what comes from the common stock and, as it were, superfluous at home—or else it would not have been exported. As a result the loss is not felt by any individual."

The Utopians own everything in common at home; yet they fight furiously to defend the private property of others! The vision is paradoxical only if we fail to recall all those monastic theologians dedicated by vows of poverty, chastity, and obedience who nevertheless spent studious hours worrying out theories of the just price for merchants and degrees of consanguinity in marriage for the great world beyond the cloister.

It is too much to ask that a book like *Utopia* be fully consistent, and we would all be well served if scholars admitted the inconsistencies and stopped trying to make *Utopia* walk on all fours like a bad metaphor. Some of its inconsistencies must have come from the circumstances of its composition. More did not have much leisure to spend on it. We shall never know, of course, but it is probably one of those works that appear in a flash of intuition to writers in every century, More seems to have given much care to his leading ideas and little to what Emerson called "foolish consistency." But almost unconsciously he would have had the model of a good community in his head, and it seems likely that it was the monastery that he had given up for marriage. Marriage kept him from becoming a monk, but it did not prevent him from living a fictional monastic life, complete with marriage, when he built his *Utopia*.

Behind his model was a pattern of thought that was utterly Christian and medieval. The world is the way it is. We do not know why, despite all we know of the creation and the fall. Pockets of goodness are possible, but even they have their flaws, and their goodness is not by itself enough to convert the world around. Such communities believe that it is better to protect what they have than it is to run the risk of losing all by trying to change the world outside.

The Utopians might have told the plundered merchants of their allies to give up private property, take to Utopian communism, and forget about lost private goods. But they said nothing of the sort. They fought the thieves and fought fiercely. From time to time they established colonies with Utopian institutions —just as great monastic houses sometimes sent monks out to establish sister houses in the wilderness. And they believed that vacant lands could be rightly taken away from nations that did not use them well. But there is no sign that the Utopians ever contemplated conquering all the hinterlands near them as King Utopus had once conquered their own island. They might have thought of imposing a similar virtuous order on all their neighbors. But they did not.

For all their zeal and virtue, the Utopians possessed a Christian sense of limitation. It was More's sense. He had a strong apocalyptic view; perfection for the world would come only when Christ came again. In the meantime we must take what goodness we can find without straining for the impossible. Every monk stood in a corrupt world that imposed boundaries even on what virtuous men could do; so did every Utopian.

11

UTOPIA'S RELIGION AND
THOMAS MORE'S FAITH

TOPIA'S RELIGION has often been seen as somehow contrary to the faith for which Thomas More died. But a close study of the religion of the Utopians shows us that More was much less changeable about the things important to him than are most men.

There are some obvious superficial differences between Utopian religion and Catholic faith. Utopians possess a natural religion since it comes from their own perceptions as virtuous human beings and not through some special, historical revelation such as the appearance of God to Moses or of Christ to the world; its dogmas are not found in a sacred book like the Bible. The Utopians are pagans, but pagans of a special sort. Their "natural" theology so resembles the ethical teaching of Christianity that it is no wonder that Raphael could report that many of them were being converted to Christ.

More knew his classical paganism well enough to give some of his Utopians over to the worship of the sun, the moon, and the planets or else to a hero of the past so glorious that a few took him to have been the supreme god. Was More speaking of heroes like Hercules? Or was he implying that the Utopians have some natural intuition of the Christian revelation of the incarnation? The latter supposition is probably the right one: it is in keeping with Christian belief that many ceremonies and literary works from Greek and Roman life were foreshadowings of Christ and doctrines of the church. Virgil's Fourth Eclogue with its promise of a child coming to rule was only one example.

But having nodded toward a restrained and decorous paganism—no bacchic

festivals, no orgiastic rites, no human sacrifice, no shedding of blood of any kind
—More turned inward to the heart of the best pagan religion and assumed like
Plato that behind the multitude of forms lay one grand and eternal reality. He
has Raphael say:

> But by far the majority, and those by far the wiser, believe . . . in a certain simple
> being, unknown, eternal, immense, inexplicable, far above the reach of the
> human mind, diffused throughout the universe not in mass but in power. Him
> they call father . . . All the other Utopians too, though varying in their beliefs,
> agree with them in this respect that they hold there is one supreme being to
> whom are due both the creation and the providential government of the world.

This variety—hardly variety at all—is beginning to be displaced, so Raphael
says, by the steady progress of all toward belief "in that one religion which
seems to surpass the rest in reasonableness," the religion Raphael described as
that already held by most Utopians.

That religion is harmonious with many of the teachings of Christianity
about God and the devotion owed Him by mortals. The view that pagans could
know much of God without special revelation was common among Christians.
Aquinas is only the best known of a multitude of theologians who thought that
any reasonable person of good will could know that God exists and is both
infinite and good.

But Christianity is a historical religion and not a religion deduced from first
principles. Christians have received revelation. That is, God has intervened in
history and told His people things that cannot be known by reason alone. The
doctrine of the Trinity, for example, could be neither discovered nor understood by philosophy; it came only through the revelation God made in Christ.
Still, although virtuous pagans could not know Christian doctrine, they could
win salvation if they lived up to what reason told them of God and the world.
Christian theology dealt much more harshly with those who heard the Christian proclamation and turned away; the Utopians were hearing and being
converted.

This progressive conversion to Christianity helps us understand the religious
toleration in Utopia detailed by Raphael. King Utopus found the Utopians at
war with each other over religion when he conquered the island. Indeed his
conquest was made possible because the Utopians had been weakened by
continual quarrels about religion. He was not himself sure what God wanted
in the way of worship. (He could not be sure since he did not know Christianity.) But he did not believe that anyone ought to be compelled to religion by
violence. So he laid down three articles of faith that every Utopian had to
accept. Everyone had to believe that the human soul was immortal and that
after death there is a state of rewards and punishments. Everyone must also

believe that the world is guided by divine Providence. People refusing to believe these articles were ostracized by other Utopians, but they were not beaten or put to death. They were forbidden to hold office or share in the civic life, and they were not allowed to argue their beliefs before the common people. Anyone arguing any religious position too vehemently was subject to exile or enslavement.

More could not imagine how anyone could live in civilized society without believing in the immortality of the soul. If we did not believe in punishment after death for sins committed in this life, we would all live like the devil. And if we all lived like the devil, civilization would fall apart. The argument has been common enough in the Western tradition. Voltaire accepted a form of it. So have many others.

The immortality of the soul was being debated in many places as More wrote his *Utopia*. The Fifth Lateran Council in 1513 condemned those who denied that the soul was naturally immortal, but the decree did not prevent Pietro Pomponazzi of Bologna from writing in 1516 that no one could prove by reason alone that the soul survived death. Pomponazzi was careful. He claimed that in fact he did believe that the soul was immortal because the church told him to believe and he trusted the church more than reason. It was a "neutral problem," he said, one that could be neither proved nor disproved. But he argued with great and scrupulous care that nothing we observe of human life compels us by reason to suppose that the soul can do without the body any more than the body can endure without the soul. Pomponazzi put reason and faith at odds with each other with the disclaimer that of course he was devoted to the faith. Reason became only a game, although anyone taking the trouble to read his *On the Immortality of the Soul* will see that it was a most important game. Literal-minded modern scholars tend to take Pomponazzi at his word, believing that he did indeed put faith above reason. This modern view seems naïve, and although Pomponazzi did not reveal his innermost feelings, it looks as if his tractate is a cry of naturalism against the prevailing supernaturalism of his day, a supernaturalism that Thomas More upheld all his life and died to vindicate.

To our ears Pomponazzi's argument sounds simple enough. He was being rigorously empirical, commenting not on his authorities but on his experience. In fact, he was much closer to the real teachings of Aristotle on the soul than medieval commentators like Aquinas, who had managed to work their way around Aristotle's dangerous surmises about the indissoluble connection between body and soul. Aquinas held that the natural desire of everyone for immortality proves that the soul is immortal, just as the innate desire of a child to eat proves that there is food. Pomponazzi merely observed that as far as reason could see, people left nothing of themselves behind.

Such a view was not necessarily impious. One could believe that the soul died at the death of the body and that God would resurrect the dead—soul and body—and that the power to live after death was a gift of God's grace, not a quality inherent in the soul. One could argue that the idea of resurrection in the New Testament contradicted the Platonic teaching that the soul was naturally immortal. In some of his more radical early pronouncements, Martin Luther seemed to take this view. William Tyndale, More's great Protestant foe in England, believed in "soul sleep," the unconsciousness of the soul between death and the day of doom. Thomas More, preoccupied with death throughout his life, could not stomach such a reversal of the way Catholics had regarded the soul for centuries.

His Utopians had a social justification for belief in the immortality of the soul. They asked how civilization could survive if people did not believe they would be punished in an afterlife for crimes committed in this world, even if no earthly tribunal convicted them. The Utopians thought society would fall apart without such a belief. They assumed that sin would rush in to overpower anyone left alone, so people had to be watched all the time. Society itself could not do all the watching—although in Utopia privacy was almost as rare as atheism and almost as much suspected. God had to do the watching when, despite the best efforts of the Utopians, citizens managed to be alone.

Pomponazzi held that virtue and vice were their own rewards. The virtuous person was happier than the vicious person, and people would seek happiness naturally if they had the chance. Epicurus and Lucretius in the Greek world had held much the same confidence in human nature; Erasmus seemed to agree. It is an optimism that strikes us as hopelessly romantic, and the minute regulation and implacable openness of Utopian society show that More never shared it.

The Utopians have often seemed optimistic because they favored a philosophy of pleasure called "Epicurean" by modern scholars. More did not mention Epicurus or Epicureanism in *Utopia,* and despite the resolute efforts of some recent writers to make More an Epicurean of the spirit, the idea that pleasure was the goal of human life was neither radical nor uncommon in the Middle Ages and the Renaissance. Fortescue in *De laudibus* had taken for granted that human beings desire pleasure. Like More in *Utopia,* he held that the highest pleasure always included virtue. Fortescue said that both Stoics and Epicureans were agreed on the point, and it would naturally follow that one should choose the higher pleasures over the lower. More always believed with his Utopians that without strict discipline, the ordinary lot of human beings would be deceived into mistaking lower pleasures for the greatest good. The Utopians have never heard of Adam and Eve; but they recognize original sin.

Raphael tells us that the Utopians support their doctrine of pleasure by reference to their religion. Since religion tells them of a future state of rewards and punishments, they know that the highest pleasure of all is the virtue that, however hard, will be rewarded after death. Without such a belief in immortality, Raphael confesses, the Utopians have no clear standard to tell them the difference between pleasures of the flesh and those of the mind and soul; in fact, they say that people would be foolish to deny themselves some of the pleasures open to the senses in this life if they did not believe in a life to come —a tacit confession of original sin by the Utopians, who have discovered that people have an inclination to do those very things that strict logic and religion forbid.

Utopians must believe in divine Providence; we have already encountered the doctrine in More's story of John Morton's opinions about the rise and fall of kings in *The History of King Richard III*. Christians had to believe in some form of Providence if they were to believe that God had some purpose for creation. Providence would be turned into predestination by Luther and his followers, and More would react vehemently to their teachings. But like most Christians who take God's omnipotence seriously, he was forced to embrace a form of predestination himself in the end. He does not talk about it much in *Utopia*—here Providence seems to mean nothing other than the customary Christian faith that no matter how chaotic the world may seem, God is still in charge. The calamities that seem meaningless—sudden death, illness, or fall from high position—are in fact part of the grand design of God, unfathomable to us but not to Him.

Beyond these three tenets—immortality, an afterlife with punishments and rewards, and Providence—Utopians can hold various religious beliefs without persecution from the authorities. Why did More introduce this element of toleration into his ideal commonwealth? He later became a furious exponent of the traditional Catholic view that heretics should be burned. Did he change his mind? No.

We have mentioned those Europeans who believed that the Catholic Church was in great danger even before Luther burst on the scene. They were mostly conservatives. Dorp was one, and old Bishop FitzJames was another. For others the church was so fixed in the life of Europe that they simply had no inkling of the chaos to come. More and Erasmus were different spirits, but in 1515 and 1516 they were united in their confidence that the Catholic Church would always endure, an unbroken vessel holding the culture and the hopes of Christian Europe. More could preach toleration in *Utopia* through Raphael's talkative mouth, and he could thereby call ironic attention to the intolerance of rival theologians, friars, and monastic orders screaming "heresy" at each other over any disagreement.

A certain strain of Neoplatonic romance might also have influenced More. As we have noted, we do not know much about his early admiration of Pico della Mirandola except that he did translate a short biography of the Italian humanist and mystic. He knew Pico's belief that all religions shared some doctrines—a commonplace of the Neoplatonists in Italy during the later fifteenth century. His friend Marsilio Ficino suggested that this diversity of religions might have been ordained by God. Pico toiled long, hard, dangerously, and unsuccessfully to reconcile the differences and won for his efforts the hostility of conservative theologians who accused him of heresy and the enmity of a pope who accused him of arrogance. More was never sympathetic to anyone who deviated from the teaching of the church, and in his translation of the biography of Pico, he added a note of his own about Pico's "high mind and proud purpose," which had got him into trouble. Still he must have recognized that many of the accusations lodged against Pico were unfair, and in his *Utopia* he might have resurrected toleration in religion as a rebuke to the intolerance of those who had harassed his ideal man.

But the most plausible reason for religious toleration in *Utopia* is also the simplest: The Utopians were virtuous pagans, living by reason alone and without the revelation that came to Christianity through historical events. They had deduced some general principles, but they did not know Christian doctrine. Had they been intolerant of any religious expression of others, they would have been intolerant of Christianity—and therefore unreasonable. The tour de force that More engineered required religious toleration. Far too much has been made of it.

All the Utopians, by Hythlodaye's account, are steadily advancing toward the high-flown and decorous monotheism most of them already profess. This progress would be more rapid were it not for the superstitious tendency, even among Utopians, to see any misfortune to anyone contemplating a change of religion as a divine punishment, a misinterpretation of coincidence for judgment by God.

But Raphael says that as soon as Christianity was preached to them, the Utopians began to be converted. They were being moved by the name of Christ, his teaching, his character, his miracles, the constancy of the holy martyrs, and the similarity of Christianity to the highest form of their own religion. The conversion was not proceeding without unpleasant incidents: one Utopian convert became so vehement in denouncing other religions that he was sentenced to exile—not because he became a Christian but because he violated the Utopian principle of religious toleration. Here surely we have an ironic reference to the squabbling theologians of Christian Europe.

The Utopian Christians do not yet have a priest to administer the sacraments. Converts could be baptized by members of Raphael's party since, in Catholic doctrine, any Christian (or even non-Christian) can baptize in the absence of a priest. But without a priest, the Utopians are deprived of the other sacraments. When Raphael left them, they were debating whether they might elect one of their number to the priesthood, although such a course would have violated the apostolic succession supposed to be passed on through the sacrament of ordination. New priests had hands laid on their heads by priests who had had hands laid on their heads in a succession going all the way back to the apostles and finally to Christ himself. More would later vehemently defend the apostolic succession, but in *Utopia* Raphael says only that the issue of whether to select a priest or to wait for one had not been resolved by the time he departed.

We may have here a relic of some dinner talk between More and Erasmus. Erasmus would likely have stood for the right of the Utopians to elect their priests and to have them consecrate the eucharist and administer the other sacraments without benefit of ordination. It is hard to imagine More with his reverence for tradition surrendering the orthodox understanding of the sacrament. But at table with friends when he was far from home, in a world where the church seemed secure, such a debate would have been harmless enough. The note that the Utopians had not made up their minds on the subject when Raphael saw them last may have been a witty reference to an argument still unresolved among happily disputatious dinner companions.

It seems clear enough that the Utopians would soon be Christians. In effect, Raphael's story of their conversion is an idealized account of the conversion of the Roman Empire. It is an old maxim of history that those who rule the present command our vision of the past, and the medieval church had a nearly unanimous opinion of how the Romans were converted. Cruel emperors and their cohorts, all inspired by Satan, tried to drown the church in the blood of martyrs. But the martyrs suffered heroically, miracles abounded, the masses were persuaded, and finally God's purpose could be withstood no longer. Not until the eighteenth century was there any general sense among the educated in Europe that the conversion of the Empire had been helped along by greed, violence, chicanery, political intrigue, and wild superstition.

The medieval view of how Rome met Christ could easily be encapsulated in Raphael's story of the conversion of the Utopians. The Romans heard the name of Christ, his teachings, his character, his miracles, and they witnessed the constancy of his many martyrs. The triumph of orthodoxy took a while—three hundred years, in fact. But Christianity won out in the end because it was the perfection of the best in classical civilization, and the wisest and the best Romans were open-minded enough to see the obvious. The mighty works of God done to confirm this faith were such that only the willfully wicked could fail to see that Christ was God's own being in the world.

During those early centuries while Rome was being brought to Christ, the fathers of the church—to More's mind the greatest saints after the apostles —lived and wrote. More could not suppose another incarnation for the benefit of his Utopians, and because they had the wisdom to be open-minded until the true faith came to them, the Utopians would make no martyrs of their first Christians. And More could let himself dream a while of a rebirth of pure

Christianity in a new world among people with all the classical virtues and none of the classical vices.

There was one profound difference between how Raphael announced Christianity to the Utopians and how the early fathers had interpreted Christianity to the Roman Empire. To the fathers, the indispensable text was scripture, but Raphael and his band took no Bible with them to Utopia. The omission is startling and not accidental. More knew the Bible well, and Raphael carried with him such a load of Greek books that the Utopians, soon mastering Greek, rapidly began to absorb the best of classical wisdom. But he did not have room in his trunk for a Bible.

Here we have a vision different from that of Erasmus. Erasmus longed for the Bible to become so common, translated into so many vernacular languages, that everyone could read it—weavers, travelers, plowboys, even Turks and whores. Such a hope was never More's; he thought Christians could have had their faith untarnished and sufficient even if the Bible had never been written. True Christian doctrine was passed along orally from generation to generation in the church, the product of a living community rather than a dead book. That is the spirit we find in *Utopia*.

Like medieval Christians, the Utopians made a distinction between religion and philosophy, but they also held that the two could not be set against one another. A Pietro Pomponazzi would have been greeted with mystification and hostility in Utopia. Raphael tells us that the Utopians never held a discussion about philosophy without using principles taken from religion. Religion could not be revelation in Utopia, but the inseparable joining of religion and reason provides a corollary to More's later argument that reason should always be a handmaid to faith and not faith's master. More never had any use for time-wasting games, and in his mind a Pomponazzi would have made a game of reason and all to no pious purpose.

His was the general opinion of the earlier Middle Ages. Anselm of Canterbury (born an Italian) expressed it when he spoke of the use of reason in religion as "faith seeking understanding." The Christian receives faith from the tradition of the church and through experience with the God revealed through the church. Only then does the believer discover that Christian doctrines hold together systematically. They are not absurd. The Christian does not acquire doctrine by reasoning up to it from logic alone. Logical deductions made in a study do not lift us up to the mysteries of God. Nor can reason abstracted from history lead us to the conclusion that Christ was incarnate in Palestine in the early years of the Roman Empire and that he was crucified outside Jerusalem for our sins and that he rose again from the dead so that we, too, can triumph over death.

The Catholic Church always held that deductive reason ("philosophy") was a category different from the revelation of God in history. No logician sitting in a corner without historical knowledge can deduce out of thin air that Caesar crossed the Rubicon or that Columbus discovered America. But once historical reality is known, it can be fitted into a context that allows us some systematic understanding. And once we know what God has done in history, we can see some of the reasons for His act. For example, if we know that Christ died for our sins, we must also see as reasonable the proposition that our depravity must have been far too great for any lesser sacrifice to accomplish our redemption. But such an inference does not begin with abstract reflections on human nature; it begins with the effort to understand a historical event.

More always held this traditional view, that the Christian must accept first what tradition tells about Christ and that only then can reason assemble propositions that make the faith plausible and systematic. And this is his assumption in Raphael's presentation of the relation of philosophy and religion in *Utopia*.

But reason may be defined in many different ways, and sometimes More's use of the word is blurred. He knows the reason that allows us to sort out the various articles of the Christian faith. And he knows also the reason that allows us to make sense of our own experience. That experience includes what we observe of the world, and the Utopians used reason to understand the natural sciences.

When More wrote of "philosophy" in *Utopia*, he seems to have had in mind the basic human faculty for knowing what we observe and for making inferences about it. I may observe a human footprint in the sand, and I may infer that somebody made it by walking there too recently for the print to have been obliterated by wind and rain. I cannot tell much of anything about the person who made the footprint—whether he (or she) was kind and generous or mean and greedy. I cannot tell anything about the person's ancestry or purposes. I can merely observe that a human being has passed by.

As we have seen, Aristotle and his disciples were continually seeking for some way of uniting all that we observe and all our inferences into a great system without contradictions. The Aristotelian is always establishing a truth not self-evident; he does so by means of general principles or observations supposedly clear to everyone, moving upward from discovery to discovery like someone climbing a ladder. Or else he is like a stonemason carefully setting one block of knowledge on top of another. The theory is that in time a perfectly harmonious building of knowledge will encompass all human learning.

Aristotle reasoned up to God—or to a god. But he was like someone studying a footprint on the beach; he could not deduce much about that god, and Aristotle's deity could just as well be a machine as a loving—and judging—creator. When Aristotle had empirical information, as in observations of natural phenomena, he tried to systematize it, and so he left to us works that tried to reduce physics, poetics, rhetoric, and a host of other subjects to systems that could be easily taught.

Religion in Utopia has a philosophical quality to it. Miracles happen in the commonwealth—though Raphael does not describe any of them. The miracles represent empirical reality; they must be fitted into the general system of knowledge that the Utopians share. What does one infer from miracles? To observe them without inferring the power of God causing them would be an impossible contradiction—at least to the Utopians. So in good Aristotelian fashion, they observe miracles and infer that God is their source. They are reasoning from effect back to cause.

But what kind of God is it? That question apparently gives Utopian "philosophy" the same difficulty that it gives anyone who tries to construct a natural religion by making a chain of inferences from observable phenomena. So More gives us a higher category, a "reason" that is superior to philosophy. We may call it "intuition," though in our day "intuition" has come to mean merely a "hunch" or something equally uncertain. In Plato's thought, intuition is the surest knowledge we can have; it is knowledge we possess directly because we are the beings we are.

All Utopians must believe three things—the immortality of the soul, a future state of rewards and punishments, and a guiding Providence of God. Hythlodaye tells us specifically that these are principles of religion and not of philosophy. That seems to mean that More takes these beliefs to be unmistakable human intuitions.

We may use an illustration that More did not use. If I say that "reason" tells me that the sky is blue and that trees in summer are green, I mean only that the human mind through the mysterious instrument of the eye perceives something that I call "color," which does not seem to be in the perceptions of dogs or cattle. Unless I am color-blind, color is an immediate part of any perception that I have of the physical world. I do not discover color by deductive logic. In fact, when I run into the color-blind person, I find it excruciatingly difficult to explain color at all. I may say that color can be proved because different colors emit different frequencies of light that can be measured. But such a statement is inadequate to demonstrate color to the person who cannot already see it. We can say only that this understanding of frequencies is in harmony with our direct perception, but it cannot replace the perception itself. Without the perception, we cannot give much meaning to statements about frequencies; color remains only a number, something outside ourselves, something fearfully abstract.

In the same way, More seems to be saying that a certain religious consciousness is an immediate perception of human nature and that unless we have it, we are not truly human. From it we can know that the soul is immortal, though we may not be able to explain immortality by "philosophy." It is rather a knowledge that arises from intuition, from our very being. Our natural religious consciousness may be heightened by miracles that provide additional evidence to our spontaneous perception. The God we know by intuition must be assumed to work in His world. But without the intuition that sets them in context, the miracles might be nothing more than frightening and utterly incomprehensible disruptions of the familiar order of nature. We cannot go by logic from miracles to intimate knowledge of God any more than we can pass easily from knowledge of frequencies to proving that colors exist. We must first have the perception; only then can we make sense of the numerical qualities that are a part of color, or the miracles that proceed from God.

"Philosophy" to More is this *outer* thing, a world not immediately open to perception but one we find rather through the block-building of Aristotle that begins with sense experience, then allows us to discover evidence and finally to make connections that assemble the evidence into a system. In moving from the known to the unknown, we use both induction and deduction—processes of the mind that move to conclusions not self-evident. But philosophy of this sort can work only if we trust the sensual perceptions that allow us to assemble the evidence in the first place. The good Aristotelian becomes incredulous, annoyed, even angry when you say to him, "But I don't trust the five senses." In effect, Thomas More—like Cicero—adds a religious sense to the five bodily senses. In his *Utopia*, philosophy based on objective analysis and careful logic can guide us in the quest for moral values only if the religious sense is taken into account. Our five bodily senses can be skewed if we drink too much wine or if we take dope or if we go for days without sleep. In Europe the religious sense was skewed by a grasping and proud society; in Utopia it was allowed full freedom of expression.

The distinction between discursive reasoning and religious intuition in *Utopia* helps us understand the shock that later struck More when he met Protestant heretics with their gloomy insistence on the total depravity of the human soul. The Protestants who denied the natural immortality of the soul seemed to More to be denying one of the fundamental modes by which men and women are able to see themselves as human beings with an eternal worth in the universe.

It was not merely the question of the soul that haunted him; of much profounder significance was the very religious consciousness called into question by the way Protestants approached religion. They claimed to take everything from the Bible, and declared that anything not validated by the express word of scripture could be abandoned. They claimed that the Holy Spirit was necessary to interpret scripture correctly. Still they always held that the book was sufficient to answer all answerable religious questions, and since they disagreed so quickly and so violently with one another, More could denounce them as impossible protagonists of a dead book whereas Catholics espoused a living faith imprinted on the hearts of true Christians. He would ask his foes again and again how they knew the Bible had any value if they rejected the Catholic Church that had given them the Bible in the first place. Turn to the book and reject the church, said he, and you will shortly have no religion at all.

He would write so passionately because to his mind Protestantism threatened not only the Holy Catholic Church but the understanding of human nature that made any religion possible. In his *Utopia* he could hold that we have a natural religious consciousness, and he could assume that the very presence of the consciousness proved that its object—God Himself—did have an objective existence. This is circular reasoning, to be sure, but it did not seem so to More.

As a Christian he held that the Catholic Church with its centuries of tradition and its hosts of saints was a natural development of the fundamental religious consciousness in all human beings. God had worked with special power in those before Christ whose observance of the natural law purified their lives so that their religious consciousness had the freedom to guide them. He had inspired the great common body of Christendom with proper religious truth, and the existence of the united Catholic Church in time and in space proved that human beings were capable of receiving the special grace of revelation and that they could respond to it with agreement—just as the generality of human beings can recognize colors and agree on the names that should be applied to them although they cannot precisely define them.

Protestantism brought savage and irreconcilable disagreement about religion and called in question humanity's capacity for religious consciousness. To believe that religious consciousness was general and validated by the observable consensus of Catholic history was to believe something about the means God chose to work with the world. God could have worked in other ways; More always admitted that. But in fact human nature and human experience testified to the ways God had chosen, and More thought it evident that God had chosen to work within the religious consciousness implanted in human beings with the image of God Himself at creation. However feeble might be their efforts, humans showed through their innate religious consciousness combined with good will and resolution a capacity to work harmoniously with God. The image of God had been devastated by sin but not destroyed, and all people—Catholics or Utopians—could by their very nature bring themselves into a place where God's grace could meet them and work with them for redemption. However pessimistic the Utopian view of human nature may have been, it fell far short of the total depravity proclaimed by Martin Luther, William Tyndale, Ulrich Zwingli, and the Protestants who came after them.

When Protestants rejected the Catholic Church and its teaching that a united tradition proved the Catholic view of God's working in the world, the worth and very existence of a religious consciousness itself—which, alas, is not as evident to most as light and color—was bound to be questioned. Catholics said, "The truth of the faith is proved by consensus, and consensus arises from the kind of beings we are—religious beings whose religious consciousness is a valid and natural way to God." Protestants said, "Human beings are totally depraved, and any 'natural' consciousness of God is perverted, so that the existence of a religious consciousness in itself tells us nothing at all about how we ought to serve God." Once questions began to be asked about the worth of religious consciousness, any intelligent, impartial person could see how hard, how nearly impossible they were to answer in any way that did not mean the collapse of religious belief sustained by rational argument. If this fundamental religious consciousness was only a figment, God might be so different from human beings as to be the "Wholly Other" of modern Protestant conservative theology, a being so different from ourselves that our only attitude must be a patient waiting for Him to speak and a willingness to obey absolutely whatever He tells us. But once the belief in a valid natural religious consciousness in human beings is destroyed, we can just as easily go in the other direction and claim that all religion is merely a figment and that God does not exist.

In *Utopia,* More gave his people a religious consciousness, an intuition that existed above reason but harmonized with it, and without making his Utopians Christians he nevertheless validated the intellectual suppositions about human nature that made belief in Catholic tradition possible. Human beings are like this, no matter where they may be found, he tells us. This kind of human being makes the Catholic Church the most plausible expression of God's incarnation in a single human being, Jesus of Nazareth, and His continued presence in creation through the sacraments of the church and the inspiration of His people.

12

UTOPIA:
CONCLUDING POSTSCRIPT

MORE'S DESCRIPTION of the priests of Utopia reflects both dissatisfaction with the corruption of Christian priests and yet an utter dedication to priesthood itself. In this respect, he is again different from Erasmus, who praised priests only when he had to and spent his life, it seems, wishing he could cease being one.

The first book of *Utopia* expresses the almost obligatory mockery of unworthy Christian clergymen, the mockery that we find in Erasmus and in innumerable other works of the time. But in the second book, we find the Utopian priests enjoying enormous respect and privilege. Twice More makes the point that the source of this esteem is that Utopian priests are chosen for their great holiness and are therefore few in number. The Utopian commonwealth did not know the disgrace of a Europe where shameless clergymen furrowed and teemed like lice in the fabric of society, where priesthood itself was scorned by many because of the laxity of those who bore their sacred status in vain.

The purity of the Utopian priests makes them effective guardians of public morals. Here More is one with John Colet's oft-expressed declaration that good priests make good people and bad priests infect the whole society. The Utopians who did commit sins and found themselves rebuked by the priests were not only disgraced in the eyes of their peers but also felt themselves disgraced. The priests could prevent anyone of bad morals from attending the religious ceremonies, and Raphael says, "There is almost no punishment that is more dreaded." So the priest who refused to let Richard Hunne come to mass would have found vigorous support among the Utopians. The judgment of priests in such ethical matters is so highly respected that excommunicates are punished by the secular government if they do not repent. The More who later urged the governing authorities to burn heretics condemned by the church surfaces in this account of Utopian customs described by Raphael Hythlodaye. Priests hold the powers of heaven and hell in their hands, and the Utopians believe in that power because the priests are so good that their goodness is their power's warrant.

The priests teach the young in Utopia—a reflection of the hold of the church on education in Europe. They also accompany the Utopian army but, like priests in Catholic Europe, carry no weapons and shed no blood. They go to war to mitigate slaughter, and an enemy can save himself from death if he cries to them for mercy; even his property is spared if he touches their robes. (Again we meet the surprising care More shows for legitimate private property in this book supposedly in praise of communism!) The Utopian priests are so holy that on those rare occasions when the fierce Utopian army must retreat, they can leap into the fray and persuade the enemy to have mercy, for even foreign soldiers revere the goodness of this extraordinary priesthood. And we have mentioned the immunity enjoyed by the rare priest who commits a crime, an immunity from any prosecution by the government.

Priesthood in Utopia is so sacrosanct that anyone who might dare do violence to a priest—even one guilty of crime—would be committing sacrilege. Clearly More confirms, through Hythlodaye's account, the clerical immunity from secular law so furiously disputed in the Hunne case, and if Cardinal Wolsey read *Utopia,* he would have been pleased at More's stand. Yet More implicitly condemns the miserable reputation of the English clergy that had caused Londoners to suspect that clergymen had murdered Hunne in his cell. Had the English clergy been as good as the clergy in Utopia, no one would have suspected any of them of murder. In Utopia priests are so few and so pure that society can tolerate the rare offense of an occasional apostate with less pain than it would inflict on itself by eroding the sacred institution of priesthood.

How seriously should we take *Utopia?* Disagreements abound. The irony of the work comes to us through profoundly serious issues, but we cannot tell where irony ends and literal recommendation begins.

The best we can do is to say that the details of *Utopia* raise problems but not necessarily solutions. When More said that Utopians were willing to kill themselves rather than to endure a slow, wasting death, he was not recommending that Europeans violate Christian morality by killing themselves in like situations. He was perhaps saying that the overwhelming terror before death that made his contemporaries shudder was undignified and unworthy of human beings who believed in the immortal soul.

The communism in *Utopia* was certainly a moral statement rather than a program for action, a statement directed partly against the greed of the rich in Christian Europe and partly against the enforced idleness that created beggars unable to find work unless they could be commanded by coin.

Later, when he was doing battle against the Protestants, More savagely attacked the communism of the Anabaptists, who tried to put into practice the apostolic sharing of the book of Acts. He must have agreed with the church fathers who supposed that communism was in keeping with the natural law and that in a good world ruled by reason all property would be held in common. He had doubtless read the report of Amerigo Vespucci, with whom Hythlodaye was supposed to have voyaged, that the natives in the New World held all things in common. But we cannot imagine that a man of his conservative temperament would have wanted to turn Europe upside down for the sake of a new economic order.

Besides, the world was sinful, and nobody expected the natural law to apply perfectly to a sinful society. Some things contrary to the natural law had to be tolerated as a condescension to the fallen creation. Capital punishment was but one example; the laws of men had to stoop to their object, and private property was necessary because sinful men were greedy. Though in his ideal society More had all men hold things in common, he never gave the slightest hint that he favored rejecting private property in the real world that he saw every day. As we have observed, a surprising number of citations from *Utopia* may be adduced to show a considerable preoccupation with private property, and in More's own life his aim seemed to be to acquire as much for himself and his family as he honestly could.

He does seem quite serious about letting prospective husbands and wives disrobe in the company of each other and a suitable chaperone before they are married so that each can be certain of acquiring a healthy and sexually attractive mate. This little detail from Raphael's description of Utopian customs has excited ribald giggles and puritanical horror from the time *Utopia* was published, and modern commentators have usually treated it as a joke. But there is nothing shocking about the idea when it is considered in the light of More's own combination of sensuality and abstemious religion. We know that his own sexual drive was intense, and we have noted that he gave up ordination because by his own confession he burned to marry. If a man who might have become a priest married a woman to relieve himself sexually and to beget children, and then discovered when she undressed that neither sex nor children were possible, he might be said to have robbed both God and himself.

More also seems quite serious in the grand declamation already noted about Raphael's plea that thieves should not be put to death. More places in the mouth of the venerable Cardinal Morton the truly radical suggestion that the king should test the validity of such thinking by suspending the death penalty for theft. By having the cardinal—safely dead for sixteen years when *Utopia* appeared—make this suggestion More was proposing something that could be done in the real world. "If success proved its usefulness," the cardinal says, "it would be right to make the system law." The proposal was not taken up by Henry VIII; Raphael had a justified skepticism about the capacity of kings to take good advice. But the advice, apparently, was seriously meant.

In recent times several worthy critics have been troubled by Raphael's vision of Utopia. They find his story full of contradictions and painful fantasy. The Utopians believe that if a country has unused land, another country has the right to take that land by force. The Utopians believe that in war they can morally hire assassins to kill the leaders on the other side. Utopian society is static; Utopians have lost all individualism. And the island commonwealth has many other undesirable features that were enough to prompt Max Beerbohm to write, "Utopia? Oh, pardon me. I thought it was hell." Consequently contemporary critics have argued that More meant his readers to rebuke Raphael rather than to praise him.

Raphael wants too much, these critics say, and he ends with nothing workable. In the first part of *Utopia*, Raphael argues that it is a waste of one's life to become a councillor to kings because kings never take good advice. The fictional More in the first part argues to the contrary. It is the duty, he says, of a wise man to do the best he can in a bad situation, and if not to perfect the rule of kings, at least to make it better. So the new critics argue that the vision of Utopia in the second part of the book is the corollary to the position Raphael takes in the first part—selfish, purist, and finally no good to human society, no good to social reform. They claim that More built it only to tear it down with his final remark, that it is better to wish for these things than it is to expect them. If human beings try to improve what they have they are better served than if they intoxicate themselves with grandiose dreams of a world that can never be. Such is the case against Raphael and against Utopia, and the critical reasoning that spawned the case seems to have been impregnated with the notion that Utopia is a bad place and that a good man like More could not have meant for us to think it represented his real vision of a good society.

These are elegant ideas, but it is not plausible to suppose that More's intentions were as elaborate as these modern critics have made it seem. They assume that he had a vast conception for his book; it seems much likelier that in the busy life of the embassy, broken by long stretches of tedium, he conceived the idea of *Utopia* as a latter-day Platonic *Republic* intended to show Europeans how much better reason was than the wicked habits into which they had fallen. As a Christian, More could not hold that reason was perfect, and his wit would lead him to throw in details to show how even reason could be silly. But reason was still a much better guide than passion, and a reasonable society that made Europeans better aware of the unreasonableness and the inhumanity of their own could at least be imagined.

More never gave the slightest hint in any of his correspondence about *Utopia* that he intended to play as elaborate a game as the new critics have imagined. Nor did anyone who wrote prefaces of praise for the book let slip the thought that the Utopian commonwealth was intended to be a bad place. With all charity and respect, a biographer of Thomas More must suppose that those who have decided that Utopia was intended to be a failed, hateful place have been moved by revulsion against the modern police state rather than by a serious study of *Utopia* within the context of its own time.

The fundamental quality of *Utopia* is conscience, the sense that something has gone terribly wrong with Christian Europe and that even a pagan might see the corruptions of Christian society. But with the conscience there is satire. And satire is always the weapon of the helpless, of those who have no weapons but their own amusement, who can laugh only because there is little chance of doing anything that will change society very much, and because it hurts too much to cry.

13

THOMAS MORE,
ROYAL COUNCILLOR

T HE YEARS 1516 and 1517 marked the beginning of More's fame
in England and his reputation in Europe at large. Together the incidents of these years added up to a major turning point that seems today like
one of the passages of life, especially like the change men often make somewhere around the age of forty when they cut themselves loose from youthful
aspirations that have proved to lie beyond their powers.

By 1516 More was thoroughly immersed in the law and in the public life.
His *Utopia* seems like a beginning to us—the beginning of his fame as a
humanist. But it is really more of an end, a concluding postscript to his early
hopes for a life of scholarship and a literary reputation. It came after he had
written some undistinguished verses as a very young man, a translation of a
biography of Pico that had attracted little attention, the translations of Lucian,
the unpublished *History of King Richard III,* and a scattering of epigrams as
yet unpublished. The epigrams came out in 1518 with the third edition of
Utopia, but had the Protestant Reformation not broken upon Europe, More
would very probably never have published another thing, and any biography
of him would have been nearly impossible.

His family was growing. He had three daughters, and though by 1516
Margaret, the eldest, was not yet as old as Juliet when she fell in love with
Romeo, a father still had to think of her marriage and of giving a respectable
dowry to her husband. The other girls would have to have their dowries soon

afterwards, and More would have to see to the education of his son John. All these things would cost money.

Dame Alice had a daughter, also named Alice, from her first marriage, and More was charged with the responsibility of providing for this girl. This task would have been made less onerous because Dame Alice brought with her the property of her deceased husband when she married Thomas More in 1511. More also had an adopted daughter, Margaret Giggs. We do not know how she came to live in the More household, but she was almost certainly a ward, an orphan with property, given to More, who was her legal guardian and looked after her estate. Such wardships were eagerly sought, often abused, and strictly regulated by law. More collected several wards during his public career, and the evidence is strong that he handled them all with complete integrity even while he profited from them according to the usages of the times. He treated both Margaret Giggs and Dame Alice's child with tender love, and they remained devoted to him until the end; Margaret Giggs was the only member of the family circle to see him die on the scaffold in 1535.

Altogether he had many obligations, and they required continual labor and energy. A literary career might be possible for a wealthy layman or for a priest like Erasmus with no responsibilities beyond himself. But More had less and less time for letters; he had to work hard, and he had to seek reward where he could find it.

The greatest rewards were to be had from royal service, and it seems likely that More had aspired to become a member of Henry's council for a long time. It was a reasonable aspiration for a man of his age and ability. But there were degrees of royal service, and some members of the council were much closer and of greater importance to the king than others. More had to be sure that Henry would pay him enough to make royal service worthwhile.

He had reason to doubt the king's generosity during the embassy to Flanders. In July 1515, he received a royal fee of only twenty pounds whereas his fellow emissaries Tunstall and Sampson got thirty apiece. In the same month, Sir Richard Wingfield, serving as ambassador to France, received three hundred thirty-three pounds, six shillings, and three pence. Undoubtedly Wingfield supported a large entourage with so much money; but still the disparity is notable. Why did More get so little? Perhaps Henry thought he was wealthy enough to give his service to the state. If so, More did not agree. In that same month of July, Tunstall wrote Wolsey saying, "Master More at this time, as being at a low ebb, desires by your grace to be set on float again." He had been promised thirteen shillings and four pence a day for expenses on the embassy, but apparently this per diem was not regularly paid.

In January 1516, More received sixty pounds for his "diets" in Flanders, probably an installment on his per diem; if it was the only installment paid, it was far less than he had been promised for an embassy that stretched out over six months, and it was paid much later than a man of his means could afford to wait. In February 1516, he wrote Erasmus saying that the embassy had ended happily enough but he had suffered financially from it. It was one thing, he said, for priests to be appointed to such duty, for they had only themselves to look after, but it was quite another to send a layman with a family at home. He said that the king had paid him enough to provision the servants who accompanied him to Flanders but he had not been able to persuade his family at home to go without food during his absence.

In this same letter he said he had been offered a pension from the king but he had thus far refused it and expected to refuse it in time to come. His position with the city would be compromised, he thought, if he should accept it. In handling affairs for his clients before the king, he might be suspected of insincerity should it be known that he was taking money from the king at the same time.

On the face of it, More's remark about the "pension" is difficult to interpret. It probably means only that he was offered a retainer to take a position on the fringes of the royal council, at that time an amorphous and sprawling body which G. R. Elton has called "large, mixed, and intermittent." The king and Wolsey, who became Lord Chancellor of the Realm replacing Archbishop Warham on Christmas Eve 1515, called on the members of the council for various services, including embassies abroad. Complaints to Wolsey abound throughout the correspondence from those in royal service that they were not being paid enough to meet their expenses. Apparently the government had difficulty in those years finding enough cash to pay for its day-to-day operations. So if More refused the king's pension early in 1516, the reason was almost certainly not that he lacked ambition but that he was not offered enough money. The pension was not sufficient to allow him to give up his business for the city, and, as he told Erasmus, he could not conduct that business with any credibility if he was taking money from the king.

Yet he continued to attract the attention of his superiors, and it seems that he worked hard to make them think of him. Ammonio wrote Erasmus in February that More had returned home from honorable service on the embassy and now frequently shared the palace fires. No one bade Wolsey "good morning" earlier than More, Ammonio said.

And there can be no doubt that a king wanting a good servant would be drawn to Thomas More. We have already noted the day at Eltham when Henry was a boy and More was a young man who came to dinner, and we have remarked on the epigrams that More wrote extolling the young king on his accession to the throne in 1509. *Utopia* appeared in December 1516 and earned its author a very modest international reputation, making More the only Englishman in recent years to publish a book read fairly widely on the Continent. Kings liked to have writers as ornaments to their courts, and with More,

Henry could think of himself in the company of the French kings, German emperors, and Italian princes who kept writers to apply a literary polish to the routine crudities of governance. More was an accomplished orator; we meet him in this capacity again and again, and such men were essential to royal courts.

More was also charming company for a king with some claim to learning and the wish to be appreciated by learned men. Roper says that when More did join the council the king had long private conversations with him about astronomy, geometry, divinity, and occasionally politics. Sometimes the king would lead him out onto the roof of the palace "to consider with him the diversities, courses, motions, and operations of the stars and the planets." More was so witty, Roper says, that the king and queen used to make him eat supper with them so they could delight in his conversation. These invitations became burdensome, he says, because More saw that he could not get home once a month to be with his wife and children, and he could not be absent from the court more than two days without being sent for again. Feeling "this restraint of his liberty," he began to be silent and to restrain his mirth, so that in the end he was not sent for so frequently.

More was also a lawyer, and a good one whose excellence was recognized by his peers in the profession, although he continually complained of how onerous his profession was to him. (He probably found his colleagues dull; among his early friends, not a lawyer can be found.) Kings leaned on their lawyers as blind men depended on their canes. Roper tells us that the immediate occasion of More's entry into the council was a confiscation of a ship belonging to the pope. The pope, being a prince as well as a pontiff, had a large merchant marine; perhaps the ship was carrying alum, used in the dyeing of cloth and one of the staples of papal commerce. Henry had some sort of financial claim against the pontiff, and in accordance with common maritime practice, his agents seized the ship as a forfeit when it docked at Southampton. The pope's ambassador asked for an English lawyer to represent his case in a court of admiralty; he got Thomas More.

By Roper's account More distinguished himself in three ways. He was a quick and adroit master at translating the proceedings into Latin so the papal ambassador could understand them. He was also able to relate English law to the Roman law, called "civilian" law, prevalent in the rest of Europe. And he argued so brilliantly that he won the case for the pope, obtaining the release of the ship. Roper says that More's handling of the case was so excellent that "for no entreaty would the King from thenceforth be induced any longer to forbear his service."

But probably the chief reason Henry wanted More in his council was the very one that made More first refuse the offer: More was a city man. By 1517 he was probably the best known and the most brilliant of London's public servants. Henry, who always courted London, wanted a man on the council who had the confidence of the city and who could represent the royal interests among the merchants and professionals who directed city affairs.

In the spring of 1517, More's importance in London was demonstrated in a dramatic way, when he played an influential role in trying to suppress the tumult and violence of Evil May Day. On that day, apprentices, sailors, idle clergymen, and others of a vulgar sort rioted for several hours against foreigners.

Like all medieval cities, London had its share of violence, but riots within the city walls had been almost unheard of for better than a century. In its way, the riot of Evil May Day was as significant as the Hunne case of two years before. The Hunne affair demonstrated the popular resentment against the Catholic clergy, a resentment that would be fanned into useful flame by Henry in his schism from Rome. Evil May Day showed how volatile the London mob could be and how much anger against foreigners, especially Frenchmen and Italians, lay just under the surface of society, there to be mined when a king might need it for his own purposes. It also demonstrates—at least as we read in the account by Edward Hall—how much Londoners loved their city and how jealous they were to guard its privileges.

Hall says that the troubles of the spring of 1517 were economic. Artisans from Genoa and France and other foreign parts had wormed their way into the favor of the king and swarmed in London, putting out of work the "poor English artificers." These foreigners flouted the laws of the city—presumably those regulating commerce, although Hall does not say so. They added insult to economic injury by mocking their English hosts.

Hall gives several anecdotes to show how hideous the foreigners were; none is believable. He was writing late in the reign of Henry VIII when hatred of foreigners had become England's national sport and passion, and Hall hated them as much as anybody. He tells of a Lombard who seduced the wife of an Englishman and persuaded her to bring her husband's silver plate to the Lombard's house and to remain with him. (People often kept their wealth in the form of plate that could be sold if the need arose.) The offended husband demanded his wife back; the Lombard would not give her up. The husband asked that at least he get his plate back; the Lombard refused that, too. Finally the Lombard had the poor husband arrested because the man would not pay his wife's board with her thieving host.

The Lombards—a name applied by the English to all Italians—kept businesses in Lombard Street and operated both as respectable bankers and as petty loan sharks. Some of the greater bankers among them offered credit to noblemen and the crown, but in general the Lombards were seen as men without conviction and without principle. More later told the tale of a Lombard who prayed to God for relief from the gout and, when God was silent, turned to praying to the devil, saying, "Any help is good." Lombards, like clergymen and nuns, were habitual targets for jokes, and people habitually mocked can easily become targets for violence.

So it was that in the last week of April 1517 general discontent erupted into skirmishes against foreigners, and a rumor spread that on May Day there would be a riot. Wolsey was disturbed. He summoned the mayor, John Rest, and warned him to take precautions. The mayor called the aldermen into session at the Guildhall, the place where the city of London's official business was transacted, on the evening of April 30 to see what should be done.

Thomas More took part in these discussions, probably as legal counsel to the city, although Hall tells us that he was already in the royal council. More and Richard Brook, a Serjeant-at-Law and recorder for the city, acted as liaison between the city and the royal council sitting at Greenwich; they brought in the order of the council to impose a curfew on the city until seven in the morning.

But by that time—nine in the evening—when the spring twilight would still have been pale in the narrow streets and the rolling fields beyond the walls, the order for curfew was too late. Young men had gathered on the open lands outside the city, where they seem to have heard sermons. Contemporary preachers nearly always got themselves involved in popular tumults; they were often from the lower classes, and there was enough in the Bible about the blessings owed to the poor to make for dangerous thoughts when such expressions were taken literally and preached passionately.

When officials ordered the crowds to disperse, someone cried "Prentices and clubs," the ancient "Hey rube" of the city's common laborers. Clubs and weapons came "out at every door," Hall says. By eleven o'clock nearly a thousand young men and a handful of women were pouring through the twisting streets, releasing prisoners from the jails and threatening public officials who came out to reason with them.

One of these was Thomas More, who seems to have been in a contingent of unarmed magistrates sent out to calm things down. Hall says that the mob ran through St. Nicholas's slaughterhouse beyond the walls and swarmed toward St. Martin's gate, where More and others met them and pleaded with them to disperse. It would have been quite dark by then; the crowds would have been carrying torches, and the waving brands, the noise, and the general excitement would have had a powerful effect on every heart. Thomas More, whose love for the poor masses was always outweighed by his loathing of the destructive mob, urged them to desist.

Hall says that More had almost got the crowd quieted down when the people living in the district joined the fray, throwing out bricks and stones and hot water apparently aimed at the rioters—although Hall is unclear on this point. Whatever the intent of the people throwing things, several "honest men" were injured. One was a sergeant at arms named Nicholas Downs, who was standing by More. Being injured, he cried out, "Down with them!" With this last pretense of reason dropped, the rioters swept on, spoiling houses and turning their wrath against foreigners.

More was not hurt. If he had been, Hall would have said so. But it may be that he never got over that moment, for there is little evidence that he ever again sided with the poor against authority as he had done in his *Utopia*. Any Tudor Englishman was likely to view tumult as a manifestation of Satan and to see disorders and riots as an outbreak of the cosmic forces always striving against the purposes of God.

Nearly everyone who has written about More has assumed that he was always the guardian of the poor against the voracious greed of the rich, and it has usually been supposed that he joined the royal council because Wolsey had a reputation for defending the poor and that More believed the two of them could accomplish something toward mitigating the suffering of the destitute in English society. It is certainly true that More's duties as councillor did include hearing complaints from the poor in an informal judicial body later known as the Court of Requests. But it is striking that More voices no special concern for them in anything that he wrote after *Utopia*—not in his letters, not in his theological works, not in his devotional treatises.

Analogies are always dangerous, but like most dangers they also have their attractions. When we look carefully at the whole body of More's work, we may recall the liberal pope Pius IX, who in the midst of the revolutions of 1848 was suddenly converted into one of the most conservative pontiffs of modern times. Did More pass through a similar conversion? The burden of proof must lie with those claiming that the passion for the downtrodden that is so rhetorically powerful in *Utopia* persisted throughout his life, that interest in alleviating the distress of the poor was something other than a job that he took, as he took other jobs during his royal service, because someone ordered him to take it. The evidence seems to show that his mind turned to order rather than to equity, and it is at least plausible that his experience quite literally in the middle of the Evil May Day riot was one cause for this change. His close encounter with tumult would have fueled his imagination when he heard of the outbreaks of violence and popular revolt in Germany in the course of the Protestant Reformation.

The riot burned itself out before dawn. It does not appear that anyone was killed or even seriously injured, unless we count Nicholas Downs, who was not hurt too badly to raise his furious voice. Hall's most precise detail about damages is that in one place the rioters broke into the house of a foreigner and threw "shoes and boots into the street." From this distance it all looks very much like the rites of spring. But Tudors could not take lightly rites that turned into riots. During the fray, Richard Cholmeley, Lieutenant of the Tower, "no great friend to the city," fired off several cannon in the general direction of the town center. The shots "did little harm," Hall says, "howbeit his good will appeared." The remark is sarcastic; the Lieutenant of the Tower was often in conflict with the city concerning jurisdiction over the Tower precincts, and it seems likely that Cholmeley regarded the whole city as an enemy and believed that a few shots fired indiscriminately into the middle of things would teach a lesson.

Early in the morning, consequences of greater seriousness ensued. London was put under military rule by the crown, and the Earl of Shrewsbury and the Earl of Surrey marched troops into the city. The Earl of Surrey in 1517 was the young Thomas Howard who, on the death of his father, would inherit the title Duke of Norfolk and later would be, as Roper called him, More's "singular dear friend." He was a hard, ruthless soldier with no great feeling for the city. Business came to a halt. Armed men patrolled the streets, insulting such citizens as dared show their faces. Husbands were ordered to keep their wives at home.

The rioters were charged with treason, the most serious offense after heresy in English law. The charge immediately took them out of the city's jurisdiction and brought them under the king's justice. If convicted, the guilty party could be hanged, cut down while still alive, and disemboweled, although most often the penalty was limited to hanging "by the neck till dead"—a form of mercy. Six pairs of gallows were set up in the city. The executions of those convicted in drumhead courts-martial were swiftly carried out; some of the victims were as young as fourteen. Londoners watched the bloody show in appalled anxiety, not knowing when the killings would stop or when they would get their city back again.

On May 7, John Lincoln, a petty tradesman, perhaps simply a peddler, was put to death. He had been one of the chiefs in the riot. But as three of his companions prepared to die after him, the ropes already around their necks, word arrived from the king to stop the executions. The crowds were ecstatic; the prisoners were locked up again, but the troops left the city. London praised the king for his mercy. Machiavelli in Italy had already written in *The Prince* that one way for a ruler to win the hearts of his people was to make a spectacular end to horrors he had caused to be inflicted on them himself.

The drama was not yet done. On May 11 the king held a solemn assembly at Greenwich, probably intended to put the royal foot on the city's neck one last time so that Londoners would remember who commanded the realm. The city recorder and several aldermen presented themselves dressed all in black to make a formal apology for the riot on behalf of the city and to beg the king's forgiveness. Henry kept a hard face and refused their plea; London had not groveled enough. He told them to take up their case with Cardinal Wolsey, a special humiliation since only a few months before in the Hunne case London had been vehemently asserting the superiority of English law over all clergy-men, and now a clergyman with a will to power made them bend their knees. Was More among these emissaries? Probably. But we do not know.

Thus the scene was set for the great pardon of May 22 at Westminster Hall. The mayor and the aldermen and all the great men of the city came to entreat the king for mercy. The great lords of the realm were also present—probably to awe the city people. Four hundred men and women were led in, bound with ropes and wearing nooses around their necks. According to Hall, Wolsey reproached the mayor and all the other officers for their negligence in letting the riot happen—a reproach that must have galled them and left in their hearts a hatred for the cardinal that would later help bring in the Reformation with its polemics against all proud prelates. In the end Henry pardoned the lot, and so amid much joy and relief the troubles caused by Evil May Day came to an end and the gallows came down.

A persistent tradition has held that More had much to do with the king's pardon. The source of the legend seems to be the Elizabethan play called *Sir Thomas More*, perhaps written partly by Shakespeare. R. W. Chambers, in his biography of More, offers the view that the play testifies to a general opinion about More in London and that it represented the truth. The theme of the play is that More was a champion of the poor, a friend to the outcasts of the city. The play is filled with fantasy and with historical howlers, and it is hard to imagine how it can be used to prove anything. When we pick our way through the older sources that tell of Evil May Day, we must call in question the entire tradition that finds More acting as spokesman for the poor and dismiss the much later and inaccurate play as a literary surmise of no historical value.

In his *Apology*, written in 1533, More briefly recalls Evil May Day and his own part in it. The glimpse he provides is tantalizing. He tells us only that he was appointed among others to a commission of inquiry to discover the causes of the riot. "And in good faith after great time taken and much diligence used therein, we perfectly tried out at last that all that business of any rising to be made for the matter, began only by the conspiracy of two young lads that were prentices in Cheap." He shows not a particle of sympathy for the rioters; on the contrary, he likens them to heretics who love to carry out their evil deeds in the night so that it will seem that their numbers are greater than they are. He does say that many of the rioters were hanged for treason under "an old statute made long before" that made a traitor of anyone who attacked a person who enjoyed the king's safe conduct—such as the foreigners against whom the rioters directed their anger. He offers no word of compassion for the victims of the king's justice, and when he likens the rioters to heretics, he is using one of the most derogatory similes in his vocabulary.

So he appears not as the friend of the rioters but as a voice of the city. The mob was not quelled by his speech but rather seemed to do most of its mischief afterwards. He did not take any part that we can see in winning pardon for the prisoners taken by the soldiers, though he would have lamented with his fellow citizens the military occupation of his beloved city and the affront that it gave to London's ancient liberties. He would have worked hard to appease the king lest the soldiers be ordered back into London.

Obviously he conducted himself circumspectly enough to continue in the king's favor and in the favor of Wolsey. Roper's description of the royal invitation to More to join the council makes it sound like a command. But if it was, it did not have to be spoken in a loud voice, and it must have come with assurances that More would be looked after financially, although it seems that he did take some temporary losses.

His first assignment was an embassy posted to Calais in the charge of Sir Richard Wingfield and William Knight, both experienced diplomats. The embassy entered into commercial negotiations with the French and had a slow, frustrating time. In October, More wrote to Erasmus at Louvain, complaining. "Nothing could be more hateful to me than this embassy," he grumbled. He said that he was set down in a little town by the sea, cursed by bad weather. At home, he said, although he hated litigation, he was at least paid for it. His lord (evidently Wolsey) had promised that he would be reimbursed for his expenses in Calais. "When I receive something," More wrote, "I will let you know."

The remark that he was paid for litigation when he was at home seems to show that despite his entry onto the royal council, More kept his private practice, at least for a time. It seems that at the beginning, his service to the king was an occasional affair and that his fee of a hundred pounds a year was a supplement to his income as lawyer and undersheriff and not a replacement for it.

He did not tell Erasmus of his appointment until 1518; it has often been held that More was reluctant to break the news to his friend because he knew Erasmus would disapprove. But it may be simply that More's early position was irregular, on the edges of power, and that he did not truly think of himself as a full-fledged councillor. Not until July 1518 did he give up his post as undersheriff of London, a job that had earlier led him to refuse the king's pension because of possible conflict of interest, and in the same year he discontinued his practice in the courts. Only in June 1518 did he receive his first annual councillor's fee, backdated to the late summer of the previous year, after having had to petition to get the fee paid. It seems that perhaps the king made some kind of commitment to More and then forgot about it until More reminded him, possibly when the king asked him for further service, although there may have been a simple reason—now lost to us—for what happened.

No evidence exists to show that More exercised any important influence over any policies undertaken by the government during all the years that he served on the council until 1529 when he became Lord Chancellor. Wolsey dominated royal affairs so completely that no room was left for anyone except possibly the king himself to have a voice.

More understood the realities, and he did his share of flattering Wolsey—much to the discomfiture of devout moderns who do not think it proper for a saint to have resorted to such tactics. But he did. About January 1517 he wrote someone at court (we don't know his correspondent) saying that he had intended to dedicate *Utopia* to Wolsey but that Peter Gilles robbed the work of its virginity by dedicating it to someone else. The book was inscribed to Jerome Busleyden, servant of Charles of Spain, who in 1519 became Emperor Charles V. Gilles and Erasmus prevailed upon Busleyden to contribute a prefatory letter of praise, so the dedication looks very much like a quid pro quo. More wrote him a letter cordially thanking him for his assistance. We may safely doubt that More ever had any real intention of dedicating *Utopia* to Wolsey.

Rather quickly More became a kind of personal secretary and companion to Henry. In this capacity he exchanged letters with Wolsey; twenty-one of these survive. There must have been dozens, perhaps hundreds, that have been lost. They show More dutifully reading Wolsey's letters aloud to the king and summarizing the king's replies and other wishes for Wolsey. (Henry hated to write letters in his own hand. That Anne Boleyn could later so captivate him that he penned his love letters to her is testimony to the vehemence of his passion.) More wrote in English with a flexible style and in circumspect phrases. He seldom expressed a thought of his own, and when he did, it was never in contradiction to what we know of Wolsey's or Henry's wishes. In *Utopia* we find Hythlodaye vigorously advocating the notion that councillors ought to speak out boldly when kings act foolishly. The More who speaks in *Utopia* objects to Hythlodaye's views as uncompromising and fruitless. Councillors should be more subtle, willing to bend their views to do what good they could. When he became a councillor himself, More followed his own advice. Until the royal divorce was bruited, we do not know what he said to his sovereign in private conversation beyond Roper's account of the amiable talks More and Henry had about inconsequential intellectual matters. The image we find in his letters is that of a go-between, a man so docile that he seems never to have opposed anything his masters wanted.

At times in these letters he played the courtly game according to the rules of the day, throwing in some of the flattery that Wolsey loved. In September 1523 he wrote to Wolsey about a letter Wolsey had written in Henry's name to Queen Margaret of Scotland, Henry's widowed sister. Henry and Queen Catherine were immensely pleased with the letter, More said. The king's liking for it was greater than anything More had seen in him before. The royal pleasure was, said More, "as help me God in my poor fantasy not causeless, for it is for the quantity one of the best made letters for words, matter, sentence, and couching that ever I read in my life."

Other letters gush with similar effusions. More knew that flattery was the oil that lubricated the machinery of court. Perhaps a little self-mockery stirred his mind even when he used that oil in copious spurts. Years later he recalled a moment when "a great man of the church" (Wolsey, Harpsfield tells us) made an oration and at dinner afterwards asked all his entourage what they thought of it. Everyone stopped eating and fell into a deep study "for the finding of some exquisite praise," for no one wanted to be thought common or vulgar in his flattery. Everyone did his best, and then came the turn of an ignorant priest who knew no Latin at all. But, said More in mock exasperation, "the wily fox had been so well accustomed in court with the craft of flattery that he went beyond me too far." Even this priest was surpassed by a high churchman, a doctor learned in the laws of the church. When his turn came, he "would speak never a word, but as he that were ravished unto heavenward, with the wonder of the wisdom and eloquence that my lord's grace had uttered in that oration, he sent a long sigh with an 'Oh' from the bottom of his breast, and held up both of his hands, and lifted up his head, and cast his eyes to the heavens and wept!"

Wolsey was won over; he trusted More, and he was always kind to those he trusted. His trust went only to the loyal and the malleable. He arranged for More to be speaker of the House of Commons in the Parliament called in 1523, and afterwards he wrote More a letter full of praise for his work—a letter Wolsey knew the king would see since after the Parliament More went back to his job as special secretary to the king. Henry did see the letter and was apparently impressed. More was grateful and wrote to Wolsey to express his thanks:

> And so liked your grace in one letter both [to] give me your thanks and get me his. I were, my good lord, very blind if I perceived not, very unkind if ever I forgot, of what gracious favor it proceedeth, which I can never otherwise repay than with my poor prayer which, during my life, shall never fail to pray to God for the preservation of your grace in honor and health.

From the early days of his royal service, More's friends assumed that he had influence over the king because the two were so frequently together. In April 1518, Erasmus wrote a friend that More was "completely given over to the court, always with the king, to whom he is secretary." Henry obviously did like to have More around, to enjoy his talk, and to employ his graceful tongue and pen in affairs that Henry could not or would not handle himself; the king has left no reputation for eloquence behind. G. R. Elton has called More Henry's "tame humanist," and although the remark may seem harsh, it has the smack of truth.

In June 1520, when Henry went to meet King Francis I of France at the Field of the Cloth of Gold on English territory just outside the walls of Calais, More went along in Henry's entourage of some four thousand men and women. The two kings met in all the efflorescent pageantry of gaudy chivalry and magnificent waste. They jousted—though not with each other—while their retainers fought with blunted swords. They shot at marks; they rode at rings with their lances. They drank much wine and toasted the women with the extravagant romance appropriate to the occasion. They even wrestled, with the result that Henry was thrown on his royal rear by his French rival—much to Henry's chagrin. It was altogether a magnificent spectacle.

More met William Budaeus, a learned French scholar and correspondent of Erasmus's. We have a couple of letters More wrote him afterwards. They fall into the conventions of humanist friendship. The two men had corresponded before, and Budaeus wanted to publish More's letters, but More denied permission until he might have the opportunity to go over them again to see if the Latin was pure and the remarks he had made not subject to the attacks of "captious critics."

Otherwise we have not one word about the Field of the Cloth of Gold from any surviving work More wrote. The reason for the silence is most probably that he had no major part in any of the negotiations that accompanied the glorious frivolity. He was a decoration for the event, of no greater consequence than the great tents and the masques that entertained the throng.

He realized how little influence he had and did not try to enlarge it. Early in his career as councillor, he wrote John Fisher, using a couple of apt comparisons:

> Much against my will did I come to Court (as everyone knows, and as the King himself in joke sometimes likes to reproach me). So far I keep my place there as precariously as an unaccustomed rider in the saddle. But the King (whose intimate favor I am far from enjoying) is so courteous and kindly to all that everyone who is in any way hopeful finds a ground for imagining that he is in the King's good graces, like the London wives who, as they pray before the image of the Virgin Mother of God which stands near the Tower, gaze on it so fixedly that they imagine it smiles upon them. But I am not so fortunate as to perceive such signs of favor, nor so despondent as to imagine them.

The humility was conventional; the comparison of himself to an uncertain horseman was true enough, as was the allusion to the aspirations of the hopeful. He probably did feel uncomfortable when he first went to court; he had come from being somebody in the city to being merely on the edge of importance in the council. He was a family man, unwilling to be away on embassies for months at a time, aware of the needs of his children, and worried about the future, which, he knew, depended on favor from above. He could only work hard, stay in the good graces of his superiors, and hope.

As it turned out, his hopes were not empty. In May 1521 he was knighted and appointed undertreasurer of the exchequer. The office had light duties and a high salary—£173 6s 8d a year. In this office More acted as an overseer to the officers responsible for collecting money and disbursing it and keeping accounts. His main responsibility seemed to be to certify the balance sheets presented to him four times a year. The appointment was a mark of special royal favor, and other perquisites quickly began falling into his lap.

In his splendid book on More's public career, J. A. Guy has enumerated such of these privileges as can be found in the surviving records. Most interesting for More's biography are two wardships, those of Giles Heron and Anne Cresacre. Heron's deceased father had accumulated a tidy fortune in the royal service; More became its administrator, collecting the normal fees for this executive service, and when young Heron came of age in 1525, succeeded in marrying him off to his daughter Cecily. Anne Cresacre lost her father when she was an infant, and was seized by a member of the country gentry and married to his bastard son before either child was six years old. In 1524 the young girl "was old enough to resolve that 'she would rather never have husband than to have John Rokeby,'" the boy to whom she had been wed. She was thereupon kidnapped by a rival family and forced to marry a young man who, in effect, raped her. Wolsey, furious at this outrage, took Anne away from this household and conferred her and her wardship on Thomas More—who married her to his son John in 1529. By 1525 More was bringing in between four hundred and five hundred pounds a year. If Roper says accurately that More's income as a private practitioner was four hundred pounds a year, he had not made a great profit by entering royal service, though he had been well paid. The trouble with such speculation is that we do not know if Roper's figure for More's early income is correct or not.

Although More did not exercise any influence over any great questions of state in these years, he did keep busy, and his work was not unimportant. As we have seen, he had a special talent for making Latin orations, and we find him often at this duty, both welcoming important dignitaries to England and speaking for his country on diplomatic missions abroad. His legal training was useful to the crown, and he became one of the councillors who helped judge various suits that came to the courts of Whitehall and Star Chamber. In the spring of 1520 he helped negotiate a treaty of commerce between England and Brabant and Flanders. In June 1520, just as the meeting on the Field of the Cloth of Gold was getting underway, More was given a commission with some others to settle disputes between England and the German

Hanse towns; he negotiated with the merchants of the Steelyard, the German enclave in London not far from London Bridge. More seems to have been high-handed in these negotiations, perhaps because the Hanse merchants early became a channel for the flow of the Lutheran heresy from Germany into England.

In 1521 he was one of the redactors of Henry VIII's blast against Luther, *The Assertion of the Seven Sacraments.* Henry must have appreciated the services of one of the few members of his council capable of making an extended theological argument, especially since the result of this labor was to win for Henry the title "Defender of the Faith" from the pope.

In April 1521, the leading noble of the realm, the Duke of Buckingham, was arrested for high treason. This Buckingham was the son of the Duke of Buckingham who rides darkly through the pages of More's *History of King Richard III.* When his father betrayed Richard and was caught and executed, the young son escaped almost miraculously from Richard's vengeance. It may be that this early deliverance, combined with the high honors he received under Henry VII and Henry VIII, persuaded him to think his destiny lay higher than a dukedom. From his father he had inherited not only an unstable temper but a bloodline that ran back to Edward III. Anyone who thought seriously about such things could see that his claim to the throne rivaled that of Henry VIII.

Buckingham was superstitious; he listened to at least one soothsayer's promise that he should have all. He hated Wolsey for his presumption, and Wolsey in turn spread rumors that Buckingham was speaking treason. Apparently the duke did say that if Henry died, he would seize the kingdom for himself. In April, Buckingham was summoned from his estates, arrested, and in May condemned to death. He was executed on May 17 by beheading on Tower Hill.

Buckingham was popular in London, and when he died—judicially murdered, so it seemed to many—the citizens grumbled dangerously. On July 5 More was the king's messenger to the mayor and the aldermen of the city, expressing Henry's displeasure with those murmuring against Buckingham's death. On July 9 he was back, this time ordering the city officials to prepare arms and munitions in various locations against the threat of riot.

More's superiors knew him to be loyal and circumspect. On July 25, 1521, as Wolsey was about to embark on a diplomatic mission to Calais, Henry had Richard Pace, another secretary, write Wolsey a letter that shows the king's confidence in More:

> The King signifieth Your Grace that whereas old men do now decay greatly within this his realm, his mind is to acquaint other young men with his great affairs, and therefore he desireth Your Grace to make Sir William Sands and Sir Thomas More privy to all such matters as Your Grace shall treat at Calais.

More accompanied Wolsey on the embassy that departed in August. He stayed until October, visited with Erasmus in Bruges, but does not appear to have been a major figure in the negotiations. Back in England when the embassy was finished, he fell again into habitual attendance on the king, acting as an aide and a secretary, being the intermediary between the king, who traveled on restless progresses through the realm, and Wolsey, who stayed close to Hampton Court, doing the executive work of the government.

Wolsey's policy was to make England a force to be reckoned with in European affairs, and in this pursuit he kept England wobbling back and forth between Francis I of France and Emperor Charles V. The almost unanimous view of modern students is that Wolsey's policies were a disaster for England, for the country never had the resources to bring off the game Wolsey tried to play in international politics. We may say in Wolsey's defense that at least he gave an impression of English vigor and strength abroad and that in a world of royal jackals ready to fall on the necks of the faltering, his energy made Europeans take England into account and be wary of adventuring against her.

Despite occasional flurries of peace with France, Henry's passion continued to be to make good the claim to the French throne that English kings had asserted for centuries. In retrospect Henry's ambitions seem preposterous. But for him France was what it had been for his predecessor Henry V, a dream to grant meaning to a life that would have seemed tiresome without it. Winning France was not an affair of resources and logistics; winning France was to be a campaign filled with moral victories and martial displays, a theater of battle on whose stage the king would prove, not that he could compel the entire French nation to submit to him, but that he was worthy to be king. Henry, like a monk yearning for the assurance of salvation, seemed certain that once he was deemed worthy of the French throne, he would somehow ascend it, and having done so, he would be greeted by the joyful acclamation of the French people. At times his self-deception seems wonderful. By 1522, despite the truce consummated on the Field of the Cloth of Gold, an English army under Thomas Howard, Earl of Surrey, marched across northwestern France, burning towns and making life and death as painful as possible for that part of the French people who got in the way of the English war machine. Surrey heard an absurd rumor from a French traitor that the royal council in Paris was about to send King Francis I to his estates and appoint a governor to rule in his stead. More wrote Wolsey that both king and queen "marvelously rejoiced in the good news" and hoped that Henry himself would be that governor to whom the French people would turn in their hour of need. Henry believed that such an arrangement might prepare the way for him to be king of France just as Richard III had prepared the way for Henry VII to become king of England. More, reporting these fantasies, sounded a note of skepticism. "I pray God if it prove good for his Grace or this realm then that it may prove so and else in the stead thereof I pray God send his Grace one honorable and profitable peace." More would have recalled that the fatal preoccupation of English kings with France had always harmed England, draining it of men and treasure, sending the English armies home with everything lost and nothing gained. But his careful prayer that Henry's ambition would "prove good for his Grace or this realm" was as close as he came to hinting that such an enterprise might not benefit England.

The senseless raids by English troops on French towns and villages cost money, and the ever energetic and resourceful Wolsey set out to raise it. He began in 1522 with an audacious move: he made a census of the whole realm to determine the wealth and military capacity of the English nation. The military goal of the survey was set forth publicly among the people, although taxed citizens might have suspected the other motives of the government easily enough. The larger, economic aim was quickly revealed when the government asked people with property worth twenty pounds a year or more to lend 10 percent of their wealth to the king. The clergy was expected to make a contribution of its own. The census was highly unpopular, and it did not achieve its goals. Wolsey got a forced loan, but it was not as much as he wanted, not sufficient to let him avoid calling a Parliament.

From what we already know of More, we might have expected him to resist Wolsey's maneuverings. We have seen his wrath toward Henry VII for that king's financial exactions, and we have noted in *Utopia* his apparent passion against the injustices committed by kings who taxed their subjects into poverty. But we have no evidence that More raised any objections at all. In the Parliament that Wolsey had to call in 1523, More won the gratitude of the king and the cardinal alike by helping get a tax bill through the Commons.

The Parliament of 1523 met in a mood of disgruntlement, and it accomplished almost nothing beyond the levying of a tax for the king. But it fixed several new men in the national view. One was Cuthbert Tunstall, More's old friend and fellow diplomat. Tunstall had been made bishop of London in 1522 when Bishop FitzJames died, and he delivered the sermon for the opening of Parliament in the presence of both houses, Wolsey, Archbishop William Warham, and the king himself. The sermon was a conventional lecture on the king as father of his people. He seems to have spiced all his admonitions with fulsome assurances that Henry VIII was the very model of a good ruler.

Thomas Cromwell, whom fate would make the agent of More's death, was also in the audience. The Parliament of 1523 seems to have been his first brush with high politics, and he was not happy with the outcome. In the course of these debates, he delivered a strikingly bold speech against the war policy that was draining English blood and English gold off to France, and when Parliament closed, he wrote an impatient letter to his friend John Creke expressing his annoyance with all the fatiguing deliberations that had led to so little of

consequence. Cromwell always liked to get things done as efficiently as possible, and he hated dead ends of the sort that the Parliament of 1523 seems to
have been.

Like Thomas More, Cromwell was an urban man whose business associates
were merchants and lawyers and whose friends were scholars. His energy and
intelligence helped him rise from relatively lowly origins to follow the law as
a career and to become a member of Gray's Inn. But it was his commercial
bent that made him wealthy. He had made at least one mercantile voyage to
Italy, and there he picked up some of the ideas long afloat in Italian cities,
including the conviction that the Christian prince, though a layman, had a
duty to reform the church in his dominions. Hardly any belief short of outright
rejection of Christianity had been more bitterly opposed by the medieval
papacy. Like most merchants and common lawyers, Cromwell disliked priests,
resented their privileges, and had no patience with their pretensions.

As we have mentioned, More became the speaker of the House of Commons
for the Parliament of 1523. The Commons represented the country gentry and
the cities, on whom taxation fell with special force, and More's popularity
among Londoners would have made him the ideal man for the job, for his
fellow citizens could certify his reputation to those from other towns who
might not know him. As More had had no parliamentary service that we know
of since the session of 1504, his name would not have been familiar among
gentry and burghers in the realm at large.

The speaker was the head who gave the body its life, since until the House
elected a speaker it had no legal existence. The "election" of the speaker was
a fiction, since the House at this time always accepted the candidate favored
by the monarch. Naturally the monarch wanted to nominate someone who
could be trusted to further the crown's point of view while at the same time
retaining the confidence of the House itself.

More is best remembered in this Parliament for his defense of the principle
of free debate in the Commons. In our time this freedom has been translated
into immunity for congressmen from any lawsuit that might be brought for
something they might say on the floor of the Congress. In More's day it was
a narrower immunity, meaning only that the king would not fine or imprison
anyone who, during the debates, said something against the king's interests.

Roper's account is the fullest we have of More's request for parliamentary
immunity. He has More say that just as men differ in wisdom, so do they differ
in their power to speak. And just as "much folly is uttered with painted,
polished speech, so many, boisterous and rude in language, see deep indeed and
give right substantial counsel." Sometimes people get so absorbed in making
a point that they speak in ways they later regret. So if the counsel of Parliament
is to mean anything, its members must be allowed immunity for what they say
as they toil toward their conclusions. The king should remember that both he

and the Parliament want the same things—the prosperity and the preservation of the king.

Henry apparently granted this request. Cromwell's speech against the war in France would seem to be a consequence of this freedom. More's statement on the matter is of a piece with his best earlier thought about the superiority of senates over the rule of a single man, and it has a nicely liberal ring to it: People do have a general reason despite their vices. Reason works toward concord; vice creates chaos. In a Parliament there may be many vicious men, but this one has one vice and that one another, and the vices cannot combine against the universal reason all men share. If I oppose this wise measure for some selfish partiality of my own, most people can see what I am doing, and they can speak against me. When any matter of general interest comes up, the safest course is to discuss it openly and freely in an assembly, for there truth has the best chance to prevail. So More had described the Utopians with their free assemblies, so he believed in the power of the Parliament, and so later he would believe in the superiority of the general council over the pope.

It is quite dubious that More deserves the credit for introducing the principle of free speech in Parliament, a credit many of his modern admirers have tried to give him. His own speech against the king's tax bill in 1504 and its aftermath—when Bishop Fox tried to persuade him to admit that such a speech was a fault—testify to considerable liberty in Parliament long before 1523. What More did, apparently, was to express the rationale for this freedom in language that people could remember—and so they did.

His principle was that assemblies were a better guarantee of truth than individual judgment by a monarch could be. On this principle, truth had a hard time in the Parliament of 1523. Wolsey demanded a whopping tax, making his request arrogantly in a speech to the House of Lords and claiming national security as justification for the imposition. The king of France had, he said, suborned the Scots to invade England. The Duke of Albany was scourging the borders; the country was in peril; Parliament must respond. Border skirmishes were a commonplace, but the Scots had not recovered from Flodden, and whether they had the power to launch a real attack on England was much doubted, especially by Londoners, for whom Scotland was much farther away in their imaginations than Spain and for whom the Scots people were almost as exotic as American Indians.

The day after Wolsey's speech, says Hall, "Sir Thomas More, being speaker, declared all the Cardinal's oration again to the Commons, and enforced his demand strongly saying that of duty [any] man ought not to deny to pay four shillings to the pound."

The Commons quite sensibly pointed out that there was not enough precious metal in the realm to pay such a tax. "The merchant that is rich of silk, wool, tin, cloth, and such merchandise hath not the fifth part in money. The husbandman is rich in corn and cattle, yet he lacketh of that sum. Likewise victualers and all other artificers be rich in household stuff and not in money. And then consequently, if all the money were brought to the king's hands, then men must barter cloth for victuals and bread for cheese, and so one thing for another . . ."

Even the author of *Utopia* could hardly view with equanimity a return to a barter economy. The impasse seemed complete. The Commons sent representatives to Wolsey to ask the king to take a smaller sum. More must have been among them. Wolsey was adamant. He declared that he would rather have his tongue ripped out with tongs than to move the king to take any less than four shillings to the pound. Wolsey, certainly the most hated man in England by 1523, could hardly have made a less compelling declaration, since few members of that Parliament would have long hesitated at a choice between relocating Wolsey's tongue and paying Henry's taxes. The debate dragged on; nothing was resolved. Wolsey insisted on coming to the Commons himself—a gesture so utterly out of keeping with the ancient privileges of that body that it must have provoked rage wherever the House of Commons was respected.

Roper gives a quite unbelievable account of More's words to the Commons concerning the appearance of the cardinal. The question arose whether Wolsey should be received with only a few of his men or with the entire gaudy retinue that made a mammoth parade of any journey he made through the streets. Obviously Wolsey wanted to come with all his servants, hoping thereby to overawe the Commons with the magnificence of his retinue. Roper holds that Wolsey was incensed because members of the Commons were gossiping about the debates in every tavern. So he has More say:

Masters, forasmuch as my Lord Cardinal lately, ye know well, laid to our charge the lightness of our tongues for things uttered out of this House, it shall not in my mind be amiss with all his pomp to receive him, with his maces, his pillars, his pole-axes, his crosses, his hat, and Great Seal, too—to the intent, if he find like fault with us hereafter, we may be the bolder from ourselves to lay the blame on those that his grace bringeth hither with him.

What is incredible is that More would have mocked Wolsey so openly in the House of Commons. More may have said something within his own family to this effect, showing his fatigue with Wolsey's pomposity or perhaps spinning out a fantasy of what he should have said. But for a man as careful and as politically minded as he was to voice such mockery anywhere it might have been heard and carried back to Wolsey is not to be believed. The end of the story is that More worked out an agreement that allowed Wolsey to appear in the Commons against all the customs of that body. Although Roper wished to convey the impression that More withstood the great cardinal, Roper's account really shows the opposite, for here—as in every issue that arose before Wolsey fell from power—More took Wolsey's side.

So Wolsey came with his great entourage to preside over the debate, ready, undoubtedly, to deliver a sharp answer to anyone who dared speak against royal policy in his commanding presence. The members of the House knew that the guarantee of free speech given by the king was worthless if the cardinal should be there to mark every word; so they remained silent. Wolsey fumed. He tried to force the members to speak, but to no avail. Roper has him grumble, "Here is without doubt a marvelous obstinate silence."

More replied on his knees, says Roper, and his speech was a mixture of flattery and true grit. The House was struck dumb by Wolsey's presence, More told the cardinal, because everyone knew that Wolsey could confound the wisest and best learned in the realm. More argued further that the cardinal's presence in the debate was "neither expedient nor agreeable with the ancient liberty of the House." Wolsey suddenly arose and left in a huff.

Hall speaks of Wolsey's highly irregular visit to the House of Commons, but he knows nothing of More's resistance. Rather he tells us that More slowly worked out a compromise through long and complicated negotiations between the knights of the shires and the representatives from the English cities. The knights and the townspeople held their wealth in different forms, and there was a natural conflict between them over any taxation. More's plan set the tax at twelve pence on the pound for Englishmen with estates of fifty pounds or larger.

So Henry and Wolsey got their tax; it was not as much as they had requested, but they probably aimed high on purpose. Even so Thomas Cromwell grumbled to his friend Creke, "We have in our parliament granted unto the king's highness a right large subsidy, the like whereof was never granted in this realm." More helped them work their will, although Roper does his best to give the impression that More strove against king and cardinal throughout. Roper has a nice scene between More and Wolsey after the Parliament. The two were walking in the gallery of Wolsey's palace at Whitehall.

"Would to God you had been at Rome, Master More, when I made you speaker," Wolsey said.

"Your grace not offended, so would I too, my lord," said More. And Roper says:

> And to wind such quarrels out of the Cardinal's head, he began to talk of that gallery and said, "I like this gallery of yours, my lord, much better than your gallery at Hampton Court." Wherewith so wisely brake he off the Cardinal's displeasant talk that the Cardinal at that present (as it seemed) knew not what more to say to him.

But, says Roper, Wolsey tried to get revenge in a terrible but subtle way; he proposed More as ambassador to Spain. More, hearing this suggestion from Henry himself, replied that to go to Spain would be his death. Roper evidently means that More could not bear the climate, which had indeed caused the death of many an Englishman within living memory.

Here again when we can check on Roper, we find him in error. We have a letter to Henry from Wolsey dated August 24. In it Wolsey says that the king knows of More's faithful diligence in the Parliament just closed. It is the custom, Wolsey says, to give the speaker one hundred pounds for his household in addition to the hundred pounds the speaker usually receives as his fee. Wolsey is prepared to pay the additional honorarium as soon as Henry authorizes it. "No man," says Wolsey, "could better deserve the same than he has done." He adds, "I am the rather moved to put your Highness in remembrance thereof because he is not the most ready to speak and solicit his own cause."

Henry made the authorization at once, and two days later More wrote saying that the king had agreed to Wolsey's request.

Nor is it likely that Wolsey would have considered it punishment to make More ambassador to Spain. In 1523, Emperor Charles V, who was also king of Spain, was England's ally, and More would have seemed the natural choice for such a major post, given his gift for friendship, his oratory, his Latin, and the skill he had in patient negotiation. He seems always to have been rather anti-French and pro-imperial, and when the emperor came to London in 1522, More greeted him with an oration.

More's family responsibilities and the love he bore his children would have made the embassy to Spain seem worse than a punishment to him. He also would have been far from London and the chance to pick up the fees that helped make him a prosperous man. He probably did make the excuse that Roper gives, that he knew Spain would not agree with him. Wingfield, the able and experienced diplomat who had served as More's superior on the embassy to Calais in 1517, did go to Spain on a mission in 1525 and promptly died there. Within his own family More may have joked about Wingfield's fate as proof of what would have happened to him had he gone in Wingfield's place, and Roper—ever humorless and literal-minded—devised the gloomy tale that we have.

The Parliament of 1523 gives us a case history of More's relations with Wolsey and Henry. He is the loyal servant, showing no sign of independence except in his efforts to find a better way than they could think of for getting a tax. He shows a diffidence to authority in keeping with the side of his personality that shows up in his religious works. He is also a practical man, something of a functionary, a go-between for the king and the House of Commons in their relations with one another. He does not originate policy;

he works at carrying out the policies of his superiors, and this he does faithfully and without question.

We know from his epigrams and his *Utopia,* as well as from his Lucian-like declamation on tyranny, that in principle More hated excessive taxation. But here he is, working for taxes that seemed quite excessive to most of his countrymen who had to pay them. Roper tells us that he lived in More's house for sixteen years and never saw him in a fume; yet when we read More's fierce polemical works, we find a fury that has been a continual embarrassment to modern admirers. They have usually tried to bury it under a blanket of silence.

It may be that we have here a personality of a sort not unknown to us in the pressure cooker of the modern world, a man keeping himself under tight control to do his job and hold his position, increasingly requiring some outlet for the collected fury silently and destructively building under the surface of his rigid restraint and outward calm. Roper says More chastised himself with whips. This was hardly normal behavior, even in the religious sixteenth century, and the detail may have larger psychological significance than it has been granted. The rigorously self-controlled in our own time who burn with an inner fury may require a release from tension in alcohol, sexual flings, physical exercise, passionate love affairs, violent abuse of their families, or in other aggressive ways. More may have found an outlet in his extreme religious devotions and in his equally extreme religious writing.

More's service as speaker, Wolsey's praise, and the king's reward would seem to show that his star was rising, but the English sky was clouding over, and the year 1525 began ten years of troubles that ended in his death. For More the entire decade was full of adversity, danger, and defeat.

The year seemed to begin auspiciously. On February 24—the twenty-fourth birthday of Charles V—imperial troops crushed a French army at Pavia near Milan. Francis I, fighting bravely and foolishly in the midst of his soldiers, was taken prisoner while his army was massacred, and he was carried off to Spain. Charles now seemed master of Italy, and the French throne seemed ready at last for an English king.

In England news of Pavia was greeted with rejoicing. A much later story that everyone tells has Henry VIII receiving the news while still in bed on March 9. He is said to have cried to the messenger, "My friend, you are like St. Gabriel who announced the Coming of Christ." Bonfires blazed over London that night, and churches rang with the triumphal *Te Deum,* and Henry and his court believed that the hour English kings had awaited for centuries was now at hand.

Henry expected Charles to help him invade France and take the French throne, but these hopes were quickly dashed. Charles was a victim of hubris, and in the end his overweening pride destroyed him and wreaked havoc on the

people he ruled. But in 1525 even he recognized that France could not become
an English colony and that the Hundred Years' War between the two could
not be undone. He knew that he had enough to do in Europe without seeking
to preside over the dissolution of the French nation. He was cruel to Francis,
but he did not want to kill him or even to keep him in captivity. He wanted
to treat with him, and he was perfectly willing to forget all his empty promises
to Henry VIII. So from the glory of Pavia, Henry was destined to tumble again
into humiliation on account of his wife's family.

Wolsey had already begun to retreat from the alliance with Charles. Perhaps
he was disappointed because, despite promise after promise, Charles failed
twice to use his influence to make Wolsey pope. Henry glumly went along with
his Lord Chancellor in a reshaping of English foreign policy, and on August
30, 1525, at one of Wolsey's country estates, a treaty of alliance was signed
between France and England. Thomas More was one of the English negotia-
tors; for his services, the French, desperate for English friendship, promised
him a yearly pension of thirty-five pounds. We do not know if it was ever paid.

More probably wanted England to withdraw from continental affairs altogether. In 1534, while he was in the Tower awaiting death, he recalled a debate
within the council when some said that the French king and the emperor were
likely to fall into war and that it was "wisdom that we should sit still and let
them alone." Then Wolsey told the fable of the wise men who heard that a
coming rain would drive anyone insane who was touched by it. So they hid
themselves in caves to keep dry and expected to come out after the storm and
rule the madmen. But when they emerged, the fools began to beat them.
Wolsey said that if England should be so wise as to sit still while the fools
fought, nothing would stop them in the end from ganging up on the English
nation. Said More, "This fable for his part did in his days help the King and
the realm to spend many a fair penny."

Wolsey's reputation dipped precipitously because his imperial policy had
failed, and the murmurings against him became a roar. He feared that enemies
close to the king might turn Henry against him, so he replied to this threat
by reshuffling the royal council and by removing some of his political foes from
Henry's Privy Chamber, the group most closely attendant on the king. Men
in Henry's entourage who might speak against Wolsey were assigned to other
duties. In these displacements, Thomas More lost his post as undertreasurer
with its handsome fees and became chancellor of the Duchy of Lancaster—
hardly a promotion since the position required hard work and paid nearly
eighty pounds less than that of undertreasurer. J. A. Guy does not believe that
More was removed for actively opposing Wolsey but rather that he was merely
a pawn in Wolsey's game. But if More was known as one favoring an early
version of England's Splendid Isolation, even in private conversation, Wolsey
might have found it expedient to get him away from daily attendance on the

king. Certain it is that within a few months of his appointment as chancellor of the duchy, More was no longer royal secretary.

The cessation of secretarial duties is hardly surprising, for as chancellor of the duchy, More had to preside over the business and judicial affairs of the vast estates scattered across England and Wales that were the personal property of the English kings and a major source of royal revenue, providing an income that kept Henry VIII, for all his wasteful military adventures, from sinking into the crawling penury that plagued the beggarly court of Charles V. It was an enormous responsibility that devoured time, but More seems to have thrown himself into it with his characteristic obedient energy, and the slender evidence that survives suggests that he carried out his duties with devotion and integrity. Along the way he managed to pick up various lucrative privileges—such as the right to export a thousand woolen cloths in 1526, a right he must have sold to a merchant in the cloth trade. But it is quite probable that the years between 1525 and 1529 found him in some financial straits, not in danger of poverty, but with resources stretched thin by all his obligations. It would have been natural for him to blame Wolsey for this turn of events, although he would have been far too circumspect to voice any complaints.

Meanwhile events at home and abroad kept on their fatal course. Even after the treaty with the French in 1525, Henry kept pressing Charles V to dismember France and to dethrone Francis I, who remained a prisoner in Madrid. Charles was deaf to the importunities of his avaricious English uncle. In 1526 he forced Francis to sign the Treaty of Madrid, took the two young sons of the French king as hostages, and let him go. Francis immediately renounced the treaty because it was signed under duress. The pope, fearing the emperor's designs on Italy, supported Francis. Charles treated the young French princes despicably, and the elder died as a result of the deprivations of this captivity, opening the way for the younger later to become king as Henry II. The Italian wars continued; now England was dragged along by French and papal policy. Henry felt himself betrayed by Charles, his wife's nephew, as he had once been betrayed by Ferdinand, his wife's father. It is not especially surprising that in these years he drifted further and further from his wife and that he became captivated by one of her ladies at court, Anne Boleyn.

Henry's fascination with Anne had probably begun as early as 1525. Catherine was growing old, and though her virtues were real enough, she seems to have had an uninteresting mind. She was devout and popular, but her slavish devotion to her husband's whims and welfare and her dutiful presence at dances, masquerades, and jousts were not sufficient to enable her to keep Henry's allegiance. He always craved drama and excitement, and Anne seems to have provided both in abundance.

Then there was the fatal book of Leviticus with its prohibition against the marriage of a brother to a dead brother's wife. "They shall be childless,"

Leviticus thundered. The rule arose in a clannish and nomadic society where brothers probably had to be kept from quarreling over women whose presence could not be entirely concealed in a world of tents and daily intimacy. Henry regarded it as the word of God, eternal and unbreakable, and he decided that Pope Julius II had erred in allowing his marriage to Catherine to take place at all. Serious doubts had been expressed at the time, and the young Henry seems to have shared them. Now the solution appeared simple: if one pope had erred, another could put the error right again. So in 1527, Henry began devoting all his energy to persuading the pope to do his will.

He thought he had a great advantage. In May 1527 the beggarly and vicious imperial army of Charles V in Italy, mutinous because it was unpaid, got out of hand. The Duke of Bourbon, regarded as a traitor by the French because he was a Frenchman in the service of the emperor, led the army against Rome, where the pope, Clement VII, had done all he could to oppose the joining of Italy to the empire of Charles. Early on the misty morning of May 6, the army stormed the walls of the Eternal City. Bourbon was shot dead in the first assault, and Spanish and German mercenaries—some of them German Lutherans—subjected Rome to the worst sack it has endured in all its history.

Cardinals trapped in the disaster sent out calls for help all over Europe. One was Lorenzo Campeggio, whose friendly relations with Wolsey had been long and constant. He wrote Wolsey begging for aid, and Wolsey did his best to help. So did Henry, and in doing so the king believed that he was building credit with the pope and that the pope must reward him by granting his request for a divorce.

There was not much that Henry or anyone else could do to help Rome. The pope was shut up in the Castel Sant' Angelo, powerless to stop the pillaging and the burning and the brutality. Once his troops were in the city, the emperor, who was in Spain, seemed content to leave them there to give the pope a lesson. They stayed for months, until the plague finally dispersed them. Pope Clement VII was a timorous man; he learned the lesson the emperor expected him to learn, that Charles was not a man to be taken lightly or offended needlessly.

Henry was driven into closer relations with the French, and in early July 1527, Wolsey set out for France with a thousand attendants. More either departed with Wolsey or else joined him soon afterwards. When they met Francis I early in August, Wolsey wrote home to his king that More and Francis had talked.

The mission to France was not merely to do something to help the pope; it was also to advance the king's "secret matter" and to win support for the divorce. Wolsey was eager and circumspect. He stopped for the night at Rochester on his way to Dover, and there he talked away the evening with John

Fisher. Fisher had had a message from the queen; he knew that talk of a divorce was in the air. He was judiciously noncommittal.

What did Thomas More know of Henry's marital problems? In 1534 he wrote to Thomas Cromwell saying that before he left for the Continent in the summer of 1527, he had heard rumors of Henry's preoccupation with Leviticus. When he returned from the embassy, he reported to Henry at Hampton Court. There, as they walked in a gallery together, Henry suddenly urged the case for divorce on More and asked his opinion. More told him what he thought, so he said to Cromwell—but he did not tell Cromwell what he said. Obviously More disapproved of the divorce though he never revealed the grounds for his disapproval. Henry was kind, More said. The king asked him to talk with Edward Fox, the royal almoner, who was deeply involved with Henry's negotiations with the pope. He also asked More to read a manuscript of a book being prepared on the matter. This was probably the work published in 1531 giving opinions from several European universities favorable to Henry's side, though in 1527 it probably would not have been more than an outline.

The effort to get the pope to grant Henry his divorce might have enjoyed an almost routine success a century earlier. But in 1527 and in the years that followed, there was no chance at all that Pope Clement VII could have granted Henry the desire of his heart.

One reason was the overpowering effect of the Sack of Rome on Italy. We know now that the enterprises of Charles V were too vast ever to be made good. But in the aftermath of the greatest devastation Rome had ever known, the pope, who had remained shut up like a caged bird for months, might be forgiven his conviction that Charles V was dangerous. And Charles stood firmly on the side of his aunt, Henry's lawful queen.

But there was another matter, apparently entirely overlooked by historians. It is simply that the prestige of the papal office, in a time when no one could foretell the future of the papacy, had to be guarded at all costs, even at the price of losing the English allegiance for a time—and surely no Cassandra at the papal court could have dreamed that England would be lost to the Catholic Church forever. By the end of the 1520s, when Henry's marital affairs came to the papal court, Luther and his minions were making the papacy the central issue of their revolution. They were talking about the Bible and about justification by faith and about a religion of spiritual meekness and simplicity that in fact they found beyond their grasp. The first years of the Reformation were a fairy tale striving to be born. But beyond all these matters was the conviction that the pope was the core of all wickedness, and both the pope and the papal office became the targets of furious heretical propaganda.

Henry came riding onto this battlefield like a messenger from another world with a simple request. He had found a biblical reason to end his marriage to a wife he no longer loved, a wife too decrepit to do his kingdom the good everyone saw as the chief duty of a queen. Henry was always a morbidly insecure man; with his upbringing he could hardly have been otherwise unless he had had the penchant for obscurity that lured some younger sons of kings into the clergy. He did not have that penchant, and like most of us, he imagined that he had some responsibility to keep his world going even after he no longer inhabited it. For this task he needed a son, and in the past popes had granted the sanctity of their opinion to requests of other kings that were not dissimilar.

Henry's desire had a fatal twist to it. He claimed that a previous pope—Julius II—had made an error in granting the dispensation that had allowed Henry to marry Catherine. Henry's view was that the dispensation contradicted the law of God and that neither Julius nor any other pope had such power. If Clement VII granted the divorce, Europe would have been treated to the spectacle of a pope admitting that a recent predecessor had erred, and erred in exactly the way that Luther and the rest were shrilling that popes had always erred—by subverting the law of God and substituting for that eternal law their own corrupt opinions. Such an admission in such a time would have seemed to a weak man like Pope Clement VII enough to wound the papacy mortally, and he could not do what Henry asked.

Clement could play for time, and that is what he did while Wolsey, whose only support was his king, struggled frantically and utterly in vain to get the pope to do the king's will. By 1529, all Wolsey's hopes were dashed, and he fell like Lucifer from his eminence.

In the summer of that year More and his friend Tunstall were the chief English delegates at the closing negotiations of the Peace of Cambrai between France and the Empire. They contributed little but their signatures, and their presence did nothing to mitigate the smashing defeat this treaty marked for Wolsey's foreign policy, which, after Pavia, had been directed against Charles V. Francis I gave up his claim to Italy, and Charles was left with hegemony over the divided peninsula. The pope's worst fears had come to pass.

As the treaty was being drawn up, Cardinal Campeggio, holding a joint hearing with Wolsey on the divorce in England, adjourned his court. The pope revoked the case to Rome, and for all practical purposes the struggle to win papal approval of Henry's divorce was over. Campeggio went home; his baggage was opened despite his diplomatic passport. Wolsey was left to be the scapegoat of Henry's wrath against Rome, and in early October he was stripped of his power and made to surrender the Great Seal of the Realm. For the first time since 1515, England would have a new Lord Chancellor.

14

HOUSEHOLD, FAMILY, AND
PRIVATE LIFE

HEN WE THINK we know a man or woman from sixteenth-century England, it is usually because that person has left a record of public deeds or a roll of literary titles that we can call with confidence. Although Thomas More was both a public and a literary figure, his public career and his literary remains have been largely unnoticed by the generality of educated people and unstudied by most scholars of the period. He has rather gained an enduring place in the popular imagination by what we know of his private and family life, and his name has come down to us gilded by the affection that he lavished on his children, especially his eldest and best-beloved child, Margaret.

Compared with More's private life, Shakespeare's is nearly opaque mystery laced with unbelievable or implausible legends. Even flamboyant royal figures like Henry VIII or his daughter Elizabeth I leave us feeling that for all the things we know of their lives and reigns, something is missing when we try to piece together the puzzle of what they were as personalities.

Both scholars and merely interested readers have assumed, on the contrary, that we perceive a depth in Thomas More that we do not see in many another because More's inner life leaped into public and permanent view in his loving relations with his children and in the details that we have of his family life. This perception is probably mostly wrong, since we have not understood much of what we know. Nevertheless, his private life remains the part of him we all like best.

Until his imprisonment in the Tower, it was a life lived out in a comfort that, by the standards of the period, bordered on luxury. About the time he married Jane Colt, he moved into a large house "builded of stone and timber," and called the Old Barge, in Bucklersbury Street. It was a large, rambling place that included several gardens. He must have lived in only a part of it for a while, for in 1513 he leased the whole complex. Apparently he held the controlling interest in the property until his death.

The house was splendid enough to be the official residence that a man of affairs was supposed to keep, and More's purchase of it shows an ambition to be known as somebody in the world of London, where recognition was everything. A five-minute walk would take him to the Guildhall, where the mayor and the aldermen administered the city, and his house was even closer to the headquarters of the Mercers' Company, London's oldest and most respected business fraternity, to which both Thomas More and his father, John, belonged. It was a house where an aspiring young man could see the great personages of the city and be seen by them in return.

Jane More presided at the Old Barge until her death in 1511. Dame Alice took over only a month after Jane was in her tomb and briskly carried out the large managerial responsibilities of the establishment. When the family moved out to the estate in Chelsea in 1524, these responsibilities increased, and Dame Alice handled them efficiently if not tolerantly. As we have already noted, during a grain shortage in 1528 that brought with it public unrest, More reported to the royal council that he was feeding a hundred people a day at his house. Dame Alice must have been in charge of this operation. In the fall of 1529, some barns burned on More's property, destroying not only stores of More's household grain but also some grain his neighbors were keeping in his buildings. He wrote Alice from Woodstock, where he was with the court, telling her to learn what his neighbors had lost in the fire, to let them know that he would make good their losses, and saying that he would not leave himself a spoon if by so doing he should allow a soul to lose anything by mischance in his house.

He concluded this letter by asking her to think of what they should now do with their land, how they should provide grain for their house, whether the fields should be kept or sold off, whether tenants should be kept or sent away. His tone is that of a man seeking good counsel from one in whom he had complete confidence.

Yet Dame Alice was, by all accounts, testy. It has always been assumed that she is the unnamed wife who crops up in anecdote after anecdote in More's later literary works. More wrote some of these stories as illustrations of female stupidity. One of the best known is the tale of the husband who was trying to explain to his wife some of the implications of a round earth. He said that if a hole were bored through the earth from one side to another, and if a millstone were thrown down that hole, "it should finally rest and remain in the very midst of the earth." His wife made no effort to understand what he was saying, "but as she was accustomed in all other things, studied all the while nothing else but what she might say to the contrary." And when he had done, she pointed to the spinning wheel that a servant girl was working and asked the girl to bring her the little flywheel used to regulate the speed of the spindle. Now here is the wheel, she said, "and it is round as the world is, and we shall not need to imagine a hole bored through, for it hath a hole bored through in deed. But yet because ye go by imaginations, I will imagine with you. Imagine me now that this wheel were ten mile thick on every side and this hole through it still, and so great that a millstone might well go through it. Now if the wheel stood on the one end and a millstone were thrown in above at the other end, it would go no farther than the middle, you think? By God, if someone threw in a stone no bigger than an egg, I think if you stood at the lower end of the hole five miles beneath the middle, it would give you a pat on the pate that would make you claw your head, and yet should you feel no itch at all." The husband in this story was trying to teach his wife something to improve her mind, something abstract and intellectual and beyond her, and she resisted. Everything in the story fits what we know of both Dame Alice and More; he could not let her mind rest but gave her daily tasks for self-improvement and demanded a reckoning from her when he got home in the evening. She found this tiresome and probably demeaning.

This anecdote mentions the wife's habitual impulse to argue against anything her husband said. More must have been an overpowering figure to his family, but Dame Alice—unlike Jane Colt—withstood his demands for complete dominance. In one of Harpsfield's anecdotes, More notes that he had never seen her ruled by anyone yet. She was obviously a strong woman with a sense of herself, but not well educated, lacking the words to refute her husband's sallies. So she made herself stubborn, the immemorial defense of those who feel themselves pushed to understand things beyond their grasp, and because of the stories told about her bad temper and her apparent foolishness, she comes down to us as an intellectual burden to her spouse and her main role in most accounts of More's life has been to demonstrate his meekness and goodness. Although in several of his letters he mentioned his pleasure in talking with her, More himself contributed these tales of Dame Alice's stubbornness and obtuseness. They should be seen as part of what Stephen Greenblatt has called More's "self-fashioning," his building for himself a public image both for his contemporaries and for the posterity that, he hoped, would remember him.

But if Dame Alice habitually resisted her husband and carped at his conversation, he must bear some of the responsibility. From what we have noted of how More reduced his first wife to tears with his remorseless demands that she better herself, we may suppose that he gave the impression of never being satisfied to both of the women he married. Of course, he was never satisfied with himself, but that fact could scarcely lessen the pain he inflicted by making his wives feel bad about themselves.

And there is the possibility—noted early in this book—that More never had sexual relations with Dame Alice. Harpsfield says that More did not marry her for "bodily pleasure," a statement that probably deserves to be taken literally. His domineering attitude would not then have been mitigated by the physical love which might have made her sympathetic to his wishes. If she was a woman with normal sexual needs, she would have viewed her husband with continual frustration and a bit of anger if he did not love her body with his. One wonders if they regularly slept together. In the Tower of London he wrote to Margaret of how he had been obsessed by the fear of pain and how he had "lain long restless and waking, while my wife had weened [thought] I had slept." He does not say he was in the same bed as his wife, and if he was restless—tossing to and fro beside her—one wonders how she could have supposed him to be asleep.

More's own father confessor in his later years, the priest John Bouge, wrote shortly after More's execution that More wore his "hard and rough shirt of hair" almost a year before Dame Alice knew about it. It seems improbable, though perhaps not impossible, that he could have done such a thing if they were as intimate as bedfellows. Stapleton tells us that More "even as a youth . . . wore a hair-shirt and slept on the ground or on bare boards with perhaps a log of wood as his pillow." He seems to imply that More continued this arduous practice into adulthood. If that is so, Dame Alice was hardly likely to have shared the planks. In A Dialogue of Comfort More tells a tale about a woman—usually taken to be Dame Alice—who, when she went to bed, "used on the inside to shut every night full securely her own chamber to her, both door and windows, too, and used not to open them of all the long night." In the story, More spoke of the husband, too, and it may be significant that he seemed to go out of his way to mention "her own chamber" rather than "their" chamber. His quest for a personal sexual purity may have imposed a toll on his wife that she charged to his account by her persistent, stubborn resistance to his will.

Holbein painted Dame Alice about 1527 or 1528. He gives us a large, imposing woman, richly dressed, wearing rings on her fingers and gold chains around her neck. Her nose is quite large, although it does not appear hooked as Ammonio suggested. (Holbein, who depended on selling his work, may have done a little discreet retouching.) Her forehead is broad in the style of ideal female beauty at the time. She holds an open book that she is supposed to be reading, but her eyes have wandered to her left, away from the page, indicating that something—perhaps a trifle out of place—has distracted her. The whole conveys the impression that reading is a chore, something she did not do easily or habitually, and the general effect of the book is to make her seem to be posing for the artist—probably using a pose her husband suggested. At the end of one of her neck chains hangs a heavy crucifix; a little higher and suspended from another chain is a medallion with a woman's profile—probably the Virgin Mary. Dame Alice appears as a woman of substance, somewhat self-conscious before the artist, but confident that someone as got up as she is must be making a very good impression. Her face has none of the sober intensity that we can see in Holbein's portrait of her husband, but it is not bland, and it is not unattractive.

Holbein gave us several drawings of the various members of More's household. They appear as wealthy middle-class people proudly sporting clothes in the latest fashion, hardly imitators of the stern puritans of Utopia, whose dress had been monochromic and painfully simple. But More was not living in Utopia; the members of his family, as Holbein painted them, lived well and innocently delighted in showing their place in the world to a realist painter who captured every line of their artless self-satisfaction.

More's care for his children reveals the same earnest, continual quest for their improvement that he had inflicted on his wives, although without, apparently, the rigor that made poor Jane Colt burst into tears—but then they were brought up in his house, and she was not, and he had a greater influence on their development. When he became a member of the royal council, he was often away from home, and he wrote frequently to his children. The topics of these early letters were nearly always related to education. More's household had the reputation of being a school and was often referred to as such by those who wrote about him. He educated not only his own children and his wards but eleven grandchildren as well.

His letters to his children are filled with love and wit, but there is also an insistence in them that cannot be taken lightly. He asks that they write him almost every day—he will take no excuses. He praises his son John for not trying to make any, and he tells the girls that if there is nothing to write about, they should write about that nothing at great length. Girls, being women and "loquacious by nature," should always have "a world to say about nothing at all."

When they write, they should always use great care. He tells them that they should write everything down in English first and later translate it into Latin. He assumes that they will write a draft, then make a fair copy so that if they have made any mistakes, they can catch them in time. By writing and rewriting, he says, the most trifling things can be made serious, "for while there is nothing so neat and witty that will not be made insipid by silly and inconsiderate loquacity, so there is nothing in itself so insipid that you cannot season it with grace and wit if you give a little thought to it."

When they wrote, he replied with a letter of his own, thanking them extravagantly, praising their efforts; he knew that young writers work harder and perform better under the lure of praise than against the prick of humiliation. His own letters were probably meant as models for them to emulate; when his children were young, he wrote them in Latin; when they were older, he wrote in English. (At least these early letters are preserved for us in Latin by Stapleton.)

Always he urged them on in their studies. Writing to Margaret, he spoke of his delight in receiving a letter from her and said, "Later letters will be even more delightful if they have told me of the studies you and your brother are engaged in, of your daily reading, your pleasant discussions, your essays, of the swift passage of the days made joyous by literary pursuits." He warned her against idleness. "For I assure you that, rather than allow my children to be idle and slothful, I would make a sacrifice of wealth, and bid adieu to other cares and business, to attend to my children and my family, amongst whom none is more dear to me than yourself, my beloved daughter." Here was the author of *Utopia*, admonishing his children against the wicked vice of sloth that opened the gates of the soul to the wiles of Satan.

Margaret was always his most beloved. Once when she wrote asking for money, he sent her exactly the amount she requested, but he chided her for not asking for a larger sum. Still he claimed to take pleasure in that not having much, she would write him more often, for, he said, "I like to be asked and coaxed by my daughter, especially by you, whom virtue and learning have made so dear to my heart."

In March 1521 he sent a letter to his children beginning, "Thomas More to his whole school, greeting." In his typical way he commended them for their studying, mentioning with a little joke their progress in astronomy: "I hear you are so far advanced in that science that you can not only point out the polar star or the dog star, or any of the ordinary stars, but are able also—which requires the skill of an absolute astronomer—among the special and principal heavenly bodies, to distinguish the sun from the moon!"

He carried letters from his children around with him. Once as he was conversing with the bishop of Exeter, he accidentally took a letter from Margaret out of his pocket; at least More said he did it accidentally. The bishop took it and looked at it and saw that it was written by a woman. After reading it, he declared he would not have believed it possible for a woman to write such a thing unless More himself had assured him that it was so. More, ever the doting father, thereupon produced a declamation and some poems that Margaret had written and that he just happened to be carrying around with him. The bishop read all these with exuberance and insisted on giving More a Portuguese gold coin to send to her. More tried to refuse the money; but in the end he had to accept it, and he sent it on to Margaret with a letter telling of the incident, saying, "This hindered me from showing him the letters of your sisters, for I feared that it would seem as though I had shown them to obtain for the others too a gift which it embarrassed me to have to accept for you." He closed with a piece of sage political advice: "Write him your thanks carefully in the nicest letter you can. You will one day be glad to have given pleasure to such a man."

The bishop of Exeter was surprised that a woman could be learned in Latin. More's views on the education of women were progressive, but they were not unique. The sixteenth century is the first after the classical age when we find fairly large numbers of educated women in all the European countries, in many respects a century of great queens and great female religious figures. In England alone the list of accomplished women is long enough to show that More's views were part of a stream of thought and not merely a drop in the desert of feminine servitude. He was driven to this position by his own lifelong devotion to the ideal of self-improvement for everyone and also by the accident that God had given him an unusual number of daughters and female wards to educate.

In 1518 More wrote a long letter on the subject of education to William Gonnell, tutor to the More household, a young man for whom More had deep affection. Apparently the two had been debating the place of praise in education, and Gonnell had written to argue that Margaret's lofty character should not be humbled. More made a loving reply, in part a conventional Christian exposition on the evils of pride, agreeing with Gonnell that Margaret should not be humiliated, but saying that she and the other children should always be taught the virtues of humility, the horrors of pride, and the foolishness of those who sought fame and tried to please everybody. His view was that pride was so horrible that we must begin rooting it out in childhood—an opinion not surprising from the author of *Utopia*.

Within this rather platitudinous recital, we find More's opinions about the education of women. Such education is new, he says, but he is convinced that if a woman learns even a little literature, she will be better for it than if she possessed the wealth of Croesus and the beauty of Helen. Women can learn; of that he is certain. They share human nature with men, he says, and so they are raised above the beasts and suited for studies that require reason. Even if a woman's brain is inferior to man's—as More clearly supposes—the remedy is not to leave her in ignorance. No, her tutors and her parents should labor so much the harder "that the flaw of nature might be corrected by industry." Both Jerome and Augustine had urged women to study, and women of that ancient time, says More, wrote letters so well that doctors of the sixteenth century could scarcely understand them. The moral is clear: women may be inferior, but education betters them, and so they should study and learn.

In 1521 Erasmus wrote William Budaeus in France of More's efforts to have his entire household share in literate society. More made his children write letters to Erasmus and sent them on without changing a syllable. Erasmus exclaimed over these epistles, finding the ideas by no means tedious or infantile. In More's household, gurgles Erasmus, "you never see a lazy girl, never a girl given over to feminine foolishness. Titus Livy is in their hands. For they are advanced enough to read such writers without a translation unless they find a word that would perhaps have stopped me—or someone like me."

Erasmus speaks of those foolish little wives who come home from church exclaiming that the preacher has delivered a marvelous sermon, able to describe the face of the man as if they were painters—but unable to say a sensible thing about what he has said. More's girls, Erasmus writes, "will recite almost the whole sermon in its correct order and with discrimination. And if the priest has babbled something foolish, something impious, or something otherwise improper for a preacher—which we see happening frequently nowadays—they know whether to laugh or to ignore it or to express their indignation. Now that's the way to hear a sermon!"

The education More gave his daughters is what we might expect from the man who imagined the young people of Utopia dutifully sustaining the oral examinations administered nightly by the elders at the supper table and amusing themselves with the parlor game of "Virtues and Vices." The image of young girls with Titus Livy in their hands is fetching in its way, but we wonder if they ever played with dolls.

More practiced what he preached to his children. He used every moment and let them know how well he was spending his time so that they might do the same. In a letter probably written in the fall of 1517 when he was on a diplomatic mission to Calais, we find him composing Latin verses in his head while he is riding on horseback through pouring rain and muddy bogs. It is a letter filled with affection and inspired with his belief that love, wit, and coaxing are better than slaps and beatings. It deserves to be quoted in full:

I hope that a letter to all of you may find my four children in good health and that your father's good wishes may keep you so. In the meantime, while I make a long journey, drenched by a soaking rain, and while my mount, too frequently, is bogged down in the mud, I compose these verses for you in the hope that, although unpolished, they may give you pleasure. From these verses you may gather an indication of your father's feelings for you—how much more than his own eyes he loves you; for the mud, the miserably stormy weather, and the necessity for driving a diminutive horse through deep waters have not been able to distract his thoughts from you or to prevent his proving that, wherever he is, he thinks of you. For instance, when—and it is often—his horse stumbles and threatens to fall, your father is not interrupted in the composition of his verses. Poetry often springs from a heart which has no feeling; these verses a father's

love provides—along with a father's natural anxiety. It is not so strange that I
love you with my whole heart, for being a father is not a tie which can be ignored.
Nature in her wisdom has attached the parent to the child and bound them
spiritually together with a Herculean knot. This tie is the source of my consideration for your immature minds, a consideration which causes me to take you often
into my arms. This tie is the reason why I regularly fed you cake and gave you
ripe apples and fancy pears. This tie is the reason why I used to dress you in silken
garments and why I never could endure to hear you cry. You know, for example,
how often I kissed you, how seldom I whipped you. My whip was invariably a
peacock's tail. Even this I wielded hesitantly and gently so that sorry welts might
not disfigure your tender seats. Brutal and unworthy to be called father is he who
does not himself weep at the tears of his child. How other fathers act I do not
know, but you know well how gentle and devoted is my manner toward you, for
I have always profoundly loved my own children and I have always been an
indulgent parent—as every father ought to be. But at this moment my love has
increased so much that it seems to me I used not to love you at all. This feeling
of mine is produced by your adult manners, adult despite your tender years; by
your instincts, trained in noble principles which must be learned; by your pleasant way of speaking, fashioned for clarity; and by your very careful weighing of
every word. These characteristics of yours so strangely tug at my heart, so closely
bind me to you, my children, that my being your father (the only reason for many
a father's love) is hardly a reason at all for my love of you. Therefore, most dearly
beloved children all, continue to endear yourselves to your father and, by those
same accomplishments which make me think that I had not loved you before,
make me think hereafter (for you can do it) that I do not love you now.

More published this letter in the second edition of his Latin epigrams, so
that it is, in part at least, one of the ways he fashioned an image of himself
before a public audience. The sincerity of his emotions is manifest, but so is
that practical side of him that offered love in return for the proper performance
of his children. They were to get an education and go forward in the world;
he would cherish them and be proud of them.

He did what he could to help them on their way. He took great care to marry
them well. We have already had much to say about William Roper, who
married Margaret in the summer of 1521 when he was about twenty-three or
twenty-five and she about sixteen. He was the son of a prosperous lawyer, John
Roper, who had served with More on several royal commissions. His mother
was the daughter of Sir John Fineux, chief justice of the Court of the King's
Bench at the time of the Hunne case. Young William came to live in the
household of Thomas More in 1518, probably boarding there while he pursued
his legal studies at Lincoln's Inn. His devotion to Margaret was great. She died
in 1544; he survived her by thirty-four years, but never married again. The little

biography that he wrote of his father-in-law abounds in quiet praise for his wife.

More's two other daughters were married on the same day—September 29, 1525. It happened to be the day More became chancellor of the Duchy of Lancaster. Elizabeth married William Daunce, son of Sir John Daunce, a member of the royal council, who had served with More on commissions Wolsey appointed to keep the peace of the countryside by speeding up the hearing of cases. Cecily married Giles Heron, one of More's wards, a resident in the More household after the death of his father in 1522. The two weddings, celebrated at the same time, were irregular in that they were not done in a parish church but rather in the private chapel of Giles Alington at Willesden, a suburb of London. Alington was the second husband of Dame Alice More's daughter Alice, and he had large estates. Cuthbert Tunstall, More's good friend and now bishop of London, had to issue a special license for the weddings to take place as they did. Evidently it was a great family occasion, and Tunstall was willing to do his part to see that it came off happily. More's son John married Anne Cresacre in 1529; she had been a ward in the household since 1524.

More also did very well by Margaret Giggs, another ward. About 1530 she married John Clement, who had years before been a tutor in More's house. Clement had studied medicine and had become one of the most prominent physicians of the realm. More loved both of them, and they reciprocated his affection.

But it is evident that he reserved his strongest love for Margaret, his eldest daughter, the most learned of his children, the most like him, the recipient of his most affectionate letters. Even after she was married, he continued to press her to continue her education, and it is clear that he was immensely proud of her for her accomplishments.

In one letter, More ruminated that Margaret's learning had its bad side. He had shown one of her letters to Reginald Pole—later to become an adamantine foe of Henry's divorce—and that young man had refused to believe that a woman could have written so well without the help of a teacher until he learned that at the time she wrote there was no teacher in the house. More reflected that Margaret was to be pitied because men would not believe that she could write so splendidly without the help of a man. Her reward should be all the greater, More said, since, though unable to hope for true reward for her labors, she continued in her "singular love of virtue" combined with "the pursuit of literature and art." Margaret was not, he said, one to demand the praise of the public; rather she regarded her husband and her father as audience enough for all she wrote.

Shortly before the birth of her first child in 1523, More wrote his daughter, "We pray most earnestly that all may go happily and successfully with you. May God and our Blessed Lady grant you happily and safely to increase your family by a little one like to his mother in everything except sex. Yet let it by all means be a girl, if only she will make up for the inferiority of her sex by her zeal to imitate her mother's virtue and learning. Such a girl I should prefer to three boys."

The child was a son, named Thomas for his grandfather. In his honor, Erasmus dedicated to Margaret his commentary on the hymns for Christmas and Epiphany written by Prudentius, a Spanish Christian poet contemporary with St. Augustine. He flattered Margaret and all her sisters for their learning and said that no one could doubt that these were daughters of Thomas More. If Roper were not her husband, Erasmus said, he could be taken for her true brother, meaning—presumably—that Roper showed the love of learning evident in all the More children. He also took the opportunity to praise Christian marriage such as that entered into by Roper and Margaret; their kind of marriage was painful, he said, to those who professed that virginity was a superior state—this to the daughter of Thomas More, who later said it was heresy to claim that marriage was better than virginity.

Harpsfield tells us that Margaret's learning was so great that she emended a Latin text from St. Cyprian to recapture the original meaning. Margaret is said to have written a meditation on death in friendly competition with her father, who wrote on the same subject. More's incomplete work survives as *The Four Last Things*. Margaret's does not. What has survived from her pen is a translation of the paraphrase of Erasmus on the Lord's Prayer, printed about 1526. It is an excellent, literal rendering that shows a fine sense of both Latin meaning and English rhythms.

Sometime after Roper married Margaret, she was struck down with the sweating sickness, the dread English plague that ravaged the country again and again in the sixteenth century, striking people dead who had been laughing and healthy only hours before. The doctors gave up on her when she went into a coma and could not be wakened; More retired to his private chapel and wept on his knees before God, pleading for Margaret's life. While he was praying, it came to him that she should have an enema. He announced this flash of insight to the physicians. Roper has this news fall on them as revelation. Yes, they said, she should indeed have an enema; it was the natural thing; they wondered why they had not thought of it themselves. They administered the enema quickly, causing her, so Roper says, to be "thoroughly awakened." And although God's marks—blotches on the skin that were supposedly a fatal sign of the plague—had appeared on her body, she recovered. Roper believed that More's sudden inspiration was a miracle.

More told Roper that had Margaret died, "he would never have meddled with worldly matters after." Presumably More meant that he would have withdrawn from all secular business and passed the rest of his life in meditation. Margaret probably came down with her affliction in 1528, a year when the sweating sickness struck virulently in May and ravaged the country on into the summer, afflicting many men close to the king and driving Henry himself into frantic movement from place to place to avoid the plague. It was the year before More became Lord Chancellor of the Realm, and we may speculate on how different his fate might have been had she died and he retired from secular life.

There can be no question that Margaret was the woman he most adored through all his life, and she as clearly adored him in return. She was an intelligent and loving woman who gave him all a perfect wife might give except the temptation to engage in sexual intercourse—the act that he believed threatened the salvation of his soul. Freed from that temptation by their kinship, he could lavish on her all the generosity and warmth he never gave his wives. It almost seems that teaching his wives new things was his substitute for sharing with them his most intimate thoughts. With Margaret the relation was otherwise.

More's move out to Chelsea in 1524 was as far as he went in the propensity of royal servants to acquire country estates considered more suitable for the king's men than houses in the crowded city. (He owned several manors but did not reside in them.) Chelsea lay not far to the west of Westminster. Then it was almost open country. Today Chelsea is part of the metropolis, swirling with traffic, thronged with pedestrians, suffocating with the fumes of motor exhausts. Only the serene and shady quiet of the green grounds of Christopher Wren's Royal Naval Hospital near the Thames offers a hint of what the place was like in More's time—a retreat remote from the stench, crowds, and noise, the mud and the dust of London, but still near enough to allow easy communication. One can easily walk from Chelsea to Westminster today in a half hour. More could have made the journey on horseback in only a few minutes, though even for such short distances the roads were so abysmal that travel over them was a tribulation. More usually went down the Thames to court in a boat rowed by servants.

We do not know what More paid for his estate in Chelsea or even how large it was. He seems to have built the house torn down in 1740 by Sir Hans Sloane, for whom nearby Sloane Square is named. We do not know what the house looked like when More lived in it, but it was grand enough to pass eventually into the hands of William Cecil, Lord Burghley, Elizabeth's great secretary and minister, and still later it came into the possession of George Villiers, Duke of Buckingham, friend to Charles I. Given the Tudor passion for knocking down buildings and putting them up again, we cannot be sure how long the house remained as More designed it, and we cannot even be certain that this was his house; at one point three different houses in Chelsea were claimed by residents to have been More's.

We have a sketch made of the More family by Hans Holbein for a large painting later destroyed by fire. The drawing, now in London, was made in 1527, about a year after Holbein came to England. The family is gathered in one of the rooms at Chelsea. We get an impression of high ceilings with the exposed beams typical of Tudor architecture. Large and expensive books stand neatly on a shelf of a heavy cupboard to the left, and on the cupboard are a silver pitcher and several other silver dishes testifying to the prosperity of the master of the house. Behind is a thick cloth hanging. To the extreme right another fine silver pitcher and a couple of books rest on the shelf made by a tall, narrow window. We can look through a doorway giving onto another room and see another bright window, recalling the comment by Raphael in *Utopia* that citizens in the island commonwealth used much glass in their windows to let in the light and to keep out the wind.

High against the wall in the middle we see a clock—a necessity for one so conscious of time as Thomas More. Its weights are visible at the bottom, and although the clock is elevated so that everybody can see it from any place in the room, we cannot tell what time it is. The clock is still in existence. Like all the clocks of its time, it had only an hour hand. We may assume that the only time the family might have been gathered like this would have been just before evening prayers or before a meal. They all look stiff and formal, and Holbein must have drawn them one by one whenever he could get them to pose.

More sits in the middle, looking very much as he does in the famous Holbein portrait in the Frick Gallery, but though he is a bit austere in the sketch, he does not wear the grim expression we see in the portrait. His knight's chain of heavy gold links made like the letter "S" lies over the thick fur collar of his robe.

His father, John, sits at the place of honor to More's right. John More did not live in Thomas's house, and it was extremely rare in England at that time for married men of the wealthier classes to live in the houses of their fathers. That More's own children and their spouses lived under his roof is an anomaly, testifying to his own patriarchal view of the family.

The rest of the household is grouped around the two oldest males. Everyone is dressed in heavy clothing, and everyone except More's son John wears a hat or a headpiece that covers the ears. We may assume that the place was cold and drafty—as all big Tudor houses were—at any distance from the enormous fireplaces of such homes. A candle in the right window shows a flame bent toward the room by the draft, and More himself sits with his hands folded in the left sleeve of his robe as though to keep them warm.

The dominant female in the room is Margaret, a large, stern woman sitting on a low seat set rather forward of the rest of the group and to More's left. She holds a prayer book on her lap and looks straight ahead as if absorbed in meditation. Dame Alice sits behind and at the extreme right of the scene, far to her husband's left, on a slightly higher level than Margaret, looking at a book she holds on a low reading desk covered with a pillow. Both her position in the drawing and her lowered eyes serve to isolate her from the rest of the family —perhaps an unwitting commentary on a gathering where none of the children was hers.

Dame Alice wears a heavy cross around her neck, and so does Margaret. More's daughter Cecily, seated just to Margaret's right and slightly behind her, has a rosary at her side. Otherwise we find no obvious religious symbols in the drawing—no cross on the wall, no paintings of saints—and the sketch encourages the belief that although More defended images in the piety of the common folk, he was not personally devoted to them. The drawing itself, though perhaps influenced by religious groupings painted by Italian artists, is thoroughly secular, showing no trace of the intense spirituality of the Netherlandish painters working at that time just across the Channel.

The only person looking directly at the artist is Henry Patterson, More's fool, who was feebleminded or mad. His staring eyes show an intense vacancy. Six of the ten figures of the family group hold books, and Margaret Giggs bends toward Judge John More in a futile effort to draw his attention to some absorbing thing she has just read in the volume in her hand. He is too busy looking like a judge to bother.

Beside Dame Alice is the faint sketch of a pet monkey mentioned by Erasmus and others as a denizen of the house. Erasmus told Hutten that More loved bizarre animals and kept a little menagerie in his home. A much later version of the scene painted by someone who followed Holbein's sketch shows a small dog curled at More's feet in the style of medieval effigies on tombs, where the dog represented loyalty. More did send a couple of greyhounds as a gift to Budaeus, who loved to hunt, but in *Utopia* More has Hythlodaye comment on the disgust wise men feel when they hear the barking and howling of hounds. (Luther felt a similar annoyance with dogs.) In the Holbein sketch there is no dog, and we may assume that had a dog entered the room we see here, More would have booted the beast out of the house.

There seems to be a rug on the floor, indicating a level of opulence known only to the rich. The poor covered their floors with rushes. We do not know if there was a latrine in the house, though we may suppose that one was probably set at some distance from the main dwelling. Europeans of those days were not fastidious about such things; Francis I, king of France, urinated into fireplaces, and the much later Château of Versailles lacked indoor facilities for anyone but the king. Henry VIII had an ornate potty chair, but lesser sorts had a jakes in the back yard. We may suppose with some confidence that More's house did not have a bath.

More built a little chapel set apart from the house; there he could withdraw for his private devotions. Roper said it was called the New Building—some evidence perhaps that More bought a house already in being and did not have it built himself. The New Building had a library and a gallery where More could walk, undoubtedly reading some work of devotion as monks often did when they strolled in their cloisters. Roper tells us that on Fridays More passed the day here, "spending his time only in devout prayers and spiritual exercises." These exercises included, no doubt, the self-flagellation with whips that Roper mentions elsewhere.

More also had a chapel in his house, and there in the evening when he was at home, he and all his household met to say their prayers. When More was absent, Dame Alice seems to have assembled the family, for More addressed her as the religious leader of the band when he was away.

At one corner of the estate was the little church near the Thames that still stands as Chelsea Old Church. To this sanctuary he brought the bones of his first wife, Jane Colt, and installed them in a new tomb. The epitaph that he intended for himself and for her is there to this day, having survived time, German bombs, and the even greater danger of architects who have renovated the building. He expected to lie there himself with Dame Alice and with Jane, and on his epitaph he said, "I cannot decide whether I did love the one or do love the other more. Oh, how happily we could have lived all three together if fate and morality permitted. Well, I pray, that the grave, that heaven, will bring us together. Thus death will give what life could not."

The house at Chelsea was distinguished enough for a king to visit even before More became Lord Chancellor of the Realm. Roper gives the impression that Henry came often, arriving at least once unexpected for dinner. Afterwards the king and his councillor walked in one of More's gardens, Henry holding his arm around More's neck. His surviving armor shows Henry to have been a huge man, and Erasmus comments that though More was not short, he was not tall either. If the general collections of armor from the period are any indication of the height of the average man, we may suppose that More would have seemed quite short to us, and there is something to give us pause in the spectacle of a big bear of a king walking about a garden with a heavy arm draped around a rather slight Thomas More's neck.

But Roper was delighted and deeply impressed. Once he had seen the king walk arm in arm with Cardinal Wolsey, but he had never seen him treat anyone else so familiarly. (Henry probably could not get his arm around Wolsey's neck because Wolsey was monumentally fat.) More reacted to this chumminess, so Roper says, with words that must be repeated by any biographer: "I thank my lord, son, I find his grace my very good lord indeed; and I believe he doth as singularly favor me as any subject in this realm. Howbeit, son Roper, I may tell thee I have no cause to be proud thereof, for if my head could win him a castle in France, it should not fail to go."

His house was partly a place for official business. When More became Lord

Chancellor and led the fight against heresy in England, he examined suspects there in the company of the bishop of London; he kept at least one heretic in the stocks at his house, and others were imprisoned there. Roper says that when he was Lord Chancellor he "used commonly every afternoon to sit in his open hall to the intent that, if any persons had any suit unto him, they might the more boldly come to his presence and there open their complaints before him." J. A. Guy has confirmed this story by noting More's initials and signature on many documents annotated by him at Chelsea.

But above all, his home was the place for his family and for those More adopted into his household. It was a strict and successful academy. Erasmus wrote that no one ever quarreled there and that More never let anyone leave in anger. No one had lived there, Erasmus said, without rising to better fortune, and no one had ever stained his reputation by being there.

In addition to evening prayers, the whole family went to church on Sundays and on holy days, and they were always on time so they could hear the whole service. At Christmas and Easter the family got out of bed to hear midnight mass, and on Good Fridays, More assembled everyone at the New Building and had the story of the passion of Christ read aloud, usually by his secretary, John Harris. At meals one of the daughters read from scripture, and after the reading, More conducted a friendly little colloquium on the meaning of the passage, during which everyone was required to speak. At the end of the meal, the feebleminded Henry Pattenson was allowed to talk, presumably to amuse the group.

To our age, laughter at the babblings of a feebleminded man would smack of cruelty, but Pattenson probably enjoyed the attention he received. More once took him along on an embassy to Flanders, and people struck by Pattenson's appearance threw things at him to provoke him. He gathered some rocks, hid them in his coat, and jumped up on a table and proclaimed—in English, of course—that everybody in the room who had not thrown anything at him should leave, for he was going to assume that everyone who remained had some part in tormenting him. No one understood what he was saying, and presently someone threw something else at him. Thereupon Pattenson unloaded a rock onto the head of a bystander and, More says, broke his pate so that the blood ran down his ears. Those acquainted with mental retardation can recognize such behavior; More enjoyed it, encouraged it, and reported it, and Pattenson was undoubtedly pleased at his modest celebrity.

By all accounts, More's pious instructions were relentless. Harpsfield tells us that Dame Alice pulled her hair back painfully under her headdress to give herself a broad forehead—one that shows plainly in Holbein's representations of her. She also pinched her waist with a corset to make it small. More watched these cosmetic agonies and commented, "Forsooth, Madam, if God give you not hell, he shall do you great wrong, for it must needs be your own of very right, for you buy it very dear, and take very great pain therefore." He meant that Dame Alice was expending much pain in quest of the deadly sin of pride and that it would be unfair if she did not receive the punishment for pride in consequence.

By Roper's account, More had confidence in the success of his teaching. To his children More said:

> It is now no achievement for you children to go to heaven, for everybody gives you good counsel, everybody gives you good example—you see virtue rewarded and vice punished so that you are carried up to heaven even by your chins. But if you live the time that no man will give you good counsel, nor no man will give you good example, when you shall see virtue punished and vice rewarded, if you will then stand fast and firmly stick to God, upon pain of my life, though you be but half good, God will allow you for whole good.

Roper repeats a number of these sermonettes with which More encouraged his family to virtue. This one embodies one of the theological precepts of the age. Those who want to be redeemed must do the best they can. Often that best is feeble, but God meets our efforts with His grace and counts our best as enough. Later, when More refused to compromise with Henry VIII and set his course toward death, his family did not follow his example but rather bowed to the king's will. They were but half good in those trying times, but More supposed that God would allow them credit for being wholly so. Even in their submission, they were doing the best they could, and More never expected as much from them as he did from himself.

He did want their love, and he received it. Margaret Giggs later told Stapleton that she would sometimes deliberately do some misdeed so "she might enjoy More's sweet and loving reproof." Roper says that when More departed from his house by the river to go into the city, his wife and children habitually came down to the boat, where he kissed them all goodbye and bade them farewell. And when he lay in the Tower, a prisoner for his refusal to swear Henry's oath, Dame Alice could find no greater temptation to lure him away than to recall his house, for she concluded her exhortation to submit to the king by saying, "And seeing you have at Chelsea a right fair house, your library, your books, your gallery, your garden, your orchard, and all other necessaries so handsome about you where you might in the company of me your wife, your children, and household be merry, I muse what in God's name you mean here still thus foolishly to tarry."

More replied that any house—including a prison—was as near heaven as his own, and he passed to a rumination on the vanity of earthly possessions, saying:

I see no great cause why I should much joy either of my gay house or of anything belonging there unto, when, if I should but seven years lie buried under the ground and then arise and come thither again, I should not fail to find some therein that would bid me get me out of doors and tell me it were none of mine. What cause have I then to like such an house as would so soon forget his master?

It is a response typical of the man, and in it we find the quiet resignation before God's will most sweetly and most long remembered by those who shared his household and carried their recollections of him into the exiles of time and place.

15

MORE, ERASMUS, AND THE
GREEN YEARS: 1516-21

I N 1 5 1 6 , Erasmus brought out his edition of the Greek New Testament in March and saw Thomas More's *Utopia* through the press in
December. The publication of the two works brought the two men together
in a common defense of humanist reform against attacks by conservative
Catholics fearing novelty and criticism. In the next five years they defended
each other vigorously against opponents of their work, and they enjoyed the
warmest days of their long acquaintance. To many they seemed to stand for
the same things, and only the coming of Martin Luther and the Protestant
Reformation made it clear how different More and Erasmus really were.

Their similarities were important, and in these years dominant. Both More
and Erasmus believed that a good education disciplined life and led to virtue.
Humanist reform aimed at spreading education to rulers of both the church
and the secular government in hopes that the good effects of sound learning
would trickle down to the rest of the society and purify the whole. It was an
authoritarian concept, suitable for an authoritarian age: make the people at the
top good, and they will force or cajole or inspire others to be good, too.

More and Erasmus, like most educated men in their day, feared the masses.
Both of them believed that the virtuous should rule and that the virtuous were
few, but to both even a bad prince was better than anarchy. In the abstract
both believed that a republic of virtue offered the best hope for society—a
republic expressed in general assemblies where wise and weighty men could
decide intelligently and dispassionately the affairs of church and society. Both

felt most at home in cities which enjoyed a fair amount of freedom from
interference by kings, where quasi-republican assemblies directed the affairs of
an urban corporation. Both were conciliarists in their view of church authority;
that is, they supported the idea that a sacrosanct gathering of bishops and other
great prelates had much greater authority than the dictates of a solitary pope
speaking from the isolated splendor of the papal office.

But both of them recognized the power of kings and popes, and both tried
as best they could to influence them to do good. Erasmus toadied to individual
popes with greater effusions than More ever used; More seldom had anything
at all to say about popes or the papacy. But the situations of the two men were
different. Erasmus was an international figure, needing the patronage and
protection of popes, and he flattered them to win them to his side. Both More
and Erasmus seemed to work on the principle that even flattery had a virtuous
goal—to make the object of praise live up to what was said about him.

Erasmus was much the greater educator, and although it is seldom studied
today, his Greek New Testament—which he called the *Novum Instrumentum*
—was at the time his greatest tool. He hoped it would lead scholars back to
the gospels and to the sacred letters of the early apostles. Study in the purified
scripture would lead to the purification of life—a reform that Scholastic philosophy with all its questions and dubious answers had been unable to bring about.
The Scholastics were learned, but in the wrong things—or so More and
Erasmus supposed. Erasmus, especially, believed that education in the right
things would bring about the renewal of morality that so many people thirsted
for.

The "right things" to Erasmus were the edifying stories of Jesus and his early
followers and the loving-kindness of God to His people and of His people to
one another. The primitive church knew giants on the earth; a reacquaintance
with that time might not lead to developing men of that same almighty stature,
but it could make Christians much better than they were in the sixteenth
century. If men were educated in the gospels, so Erasmus thought, they would
live like Christ and the Christians they studied in the sacred text; if they were
educated in the logical puzzles of the Scholastics, they would be fit for nothing
but logical puzzles—certainly not for the goodness and the grace that Erasmus
found in the Bible and in the early church.

Europeans could scarcely see the Bible as a book in itself. After the invention
of printing, printers with an eye for sales regularly cranked out Bibles in Latin
and in the vernacular, and by the time of Erasmus and More, Bibles had been
published in every major European language—except English. Latin Bibles
often appeared with commentaries that almost swallowed up the scriptural
text. Monumental among these was the great *Biblia Latina* published in six
huge volumes by John Froben in 1498, in which alongside the text of scripture
stood voluminous theological notes by medieval commentators, the notes in

small, cramped type with many abbreviations. More probably owned this edition, since he quotes extensively from the commentaries it includes, but people do not sit down to read through six large volumes. Such tomes may be used as reference, but few readers are intrepid enough to read them from cover to cover, and the extensive commentaries made it difficult indeed for a reader to separate actual scripture from what had been said about it. Educated people could take up Erasmus's *Novum Instrumentum,* a fairly large work in one volume, manageable on a desk, and they could enjoy the delicious feeling that it comprised much learning in a small space and that they could read it through if they set themselves to do it.

Erasmus was the first to edit and publish the Greek text of the New Testament in type. In parallel columns with the Greek, he presented his revision of the Latin Vulgate. More called it a "new translation," but in fact the changes were few. Yet the translation drew widespread attention to the Bible, or at least to the New Testament, as a *book,* as no other Bible had done since the invention of printing. People could read the gospels without the distractions of an elaborate commentary strung alongside scripture. The heretic Thomas Bilney, whose death by fire More later celebrated with unseemly glee, testified to the influence of the work. Writing to Cuthbert Tunstall in 1527, he said:

> At last I heard speak of Jesus, and even then when the New Testament was set forth by Erasmus; which I understood to be eloquently done by him, being allured rather by the Latin than by the word of God (for at the time I knew not what it meant), I bought it even by the Providence of God.

At the back of the book, tucked away so they would not interfere with the pleasures of reading scripture for itself, Erasmus appended textual notes by chapters. (Like all the Bibles at the time, the *Novum Instrumentum* was not divided into verses.) Here Erasmus used history as a tool for reform, bringing to the scriptures a critical spirit born of the great perception of Renaissance historians that the present is different from the past.

Once we recognize that past and present are different, we are driven inexorably to decide which is better, whether to see history as progress or decay. Erasmus, like most other humanists, had already decided that the past was far superior. So he used the past in the *Novum Instrumentum* to launch a quietly prodigious attack on the Catholic Church of his time, an attack couched partly in his Latin emendations to the Vulgate and partly lying like a dagger in velvet in the Latin textual notes at the back.

In several places his quiet radicalism is astonishing, and Thomas More, who greeted the advent of the book with rejoicing, would later reject with horror many of the positions taken in these notes, although he did so against the

Protestants and not against Erasmus himself. Erasmus suggested that marriage was not recognized as a sacrament in scripture and that the sacrament of penance was more properly an affair of the heart rather than an outward ritual that involved a priest. In some texts and notes he seemed to challenge the traditional Christian faith in the Trinity of the godhead, and he minimized the horrific old teaching that an eternally burning hell awaited the damned souls in the next world. He seemed also to suggest that the true church was not a hierarchical order but rather a simple gathering of believers.

Various heretics later laid hold of some of these readings, magnified them, stripped away the studied ambiguity that Erasmus had couched them in, and made them centerpieces of dogma. Conservative theologians, scorned by More and mocked by Erasmus, smelled danger when the *Novum Instrumentum* appeared. More seems to have sensed no danger, and it is doubtful that he took the trouble to read the notes carefully, at least when the work first appeared. He was busy, and now he and Erasmus were firm friends, regardless of whatever coolness had gone before. In 1515 when he was far from kith and kin, he and Erasmus had sat together in Flanders, speaking of Utopia and reform. By the time the *Novum Instrumentum* came out, More was absorbed in finishing his own book, and he knew that Erasmus was essential to its success. Erasmus had agreed to get a publisher for *Utopia* when More had done with it, and he had also agreed to make sure that the book found a welcome among continental scholars. More could easily have obtained an English printer, but then he would have made himself only an English reputation. Distribution counted in that day as it does now, and no books printed in England in these years—not even those published in Latin—exerted any great influence on the Continent.

Our first surviving letter from More to Erasmus dates from 1516. More was acting as an agent for Erasmus, expediting money from Archbishop Warham and other English patrons. He also worked hard, although apparently without success, to get Erasmus a good horse. The two men wrote back and forth, and the letters exude friendship, although they never radiate the gossipy intimacy we find in the letters exchanged by Erasmus and Ammonio.

In August, Erasmus came to England for a short visit and stayed at More's house in Bucklersbury. He hoped for some contributions from English friends, but he was disappointed. He failed to get a new horse, promised by the aging Christopher Urswick, because Urswick went off on a hunting trip and forgot about him. So Erasmus departed, "tired of Britain," he told Ammonio, and feeling that Dame Alice was tired of him.

When he left London, he stopped longer than he intended at the house of John Fisher in Rochester. Fisher wanted instruction in Greek. Learning that his friend was still in Rochester, More hurried down to see Erasmus again as if, Erasmus wrote Ammonio, afraid that it might be a long time before they saw each other again.

The reason for More's galloping visit to the departing Erasmus probably had something to do with *Utopia*. Erasmus wrote Ammonio on August 23. Shortly afterwards he went on to the Continent, and on September 3 More sent him the manuscript of *Utopia*, saying with conventional humility, "I send you my book on Nowhere, and you will find it nowhere well written." As J. H. Hexter has noted, the implication was clear that Erasmus expected the work and that More did not need to say anything else about it since the two men had already thoroughly discussed it.

Other letters followed. About September 20, More wrote to inquire if Erasmus had received the manuscript, "which I long to see published soon and well furnished, too, with glowing testimonials, if possible, not only from several literary men but also people well known for the part they have taken in public affairs." The mention of testimonials from men in public life is worth a thought; it may mean that More hoped *Utopia* would earn him a reputation as a political philosopher, one worthy of being invited to the court of Henry VIII. It is possible that *Utopia* was part of More's strategy for being invited to membership in the royal council.

On October 31, More wrote again, telling Erasmus that the only foes of the *Novum Instrumentum* in England were some drunken Franciscans. He reported further on his ever hopeful and ever unsuccessful efforts to get Erasmus a horse, and he closed with effusions of joy because Peter Gilles liked *Utopia*. More wanted to know what others thought of it, and he begged his friend to send the manuscript around. But, said More, even if others disdained the work, "your vote will be more than enough for my judgment. We are 'together you and I a crowd': that is my feeling, and I think I could live happily with you in any wilderness." The quotation is from Ovid; the sentiments are those of a novice writer grateful to a friend who was seeing his work into print.

Tunstall spent most of the year on the Continent in diplomatic service for Henry VIII and frequently saw Erasmus, who passed on the *Utopia* manuscript to him. Like a good friend, Tunstall wrote praising the work in November, and More replied with a rapturous letter of gratitude. He knew, he said, that Tunstall read only the classics; so More felt even more grateful to him for descending to read and to enjoy *Utopia*.

In early December, More wrote Erasmus again about the phantom horse and mentioned Tunstall's letter in praise of *Utopia*. More passed into a playful daydream, one that should sufficiently refute the bizarre modern argument that he meant his description of the Utopian commonwealth to be an ironic attack on the use of reason without faith:

So you can't think how I now fancy myself; I have grown taller, I hold my head higher, for I have continually before my eyes the perpetual office of prince which my Utopians are planning to confer on me. In fact I see myself already crowned with that distinguished diadem of corn-ears, a splendid sight in my Franciscan robe, bearing that venerable sceptre consisting of a sheaf of corn, and accompanied by a distinguished company of citizens of Amaurote. Thus equipped, at the head of a long procession, I greet the envoys and the rulers of other countries, who are greatly to be pitied compared with us, however much they may foolishly pride themselves on their childish finery and the women's ornaments with which they are bedizened, loaded with chains of contemptible gold and made to look absurd with purple and gems and other such airy nothings.

He continues the fantasy for a few lines, inviting Erasmus to make the "brief journey" to Utopia, and closes with the announcement that dawn is breaking, turning him out of his little realm and "recalling me to my treadmill in the market-place."

Erasmus did what he could, procuring a letter from Jerome Busleyden, burgher of Mechlen and councillor to Charles of Spain. More had visited in Busleyden's spacious home. Peter Gilles also contributed a letter in praise of the book, and Erasmus succeeded in procuring yet other testimonials for the edition of 1518. Yet it is astounding that Erasmus himself did not write a letter to support the 1516 edition. He seemed to want to put some distance between himself and More's work. In a letter to Gilles, written October 17, 1516, Erasmus said, "I am getting the Nowhere ready; mind you send me a preface, but addressed to someone other than me, Busleyden for choice. In everything else I will act as a friend should." It is a strange remark, perhaps susceptible of various interpretations, but it looks as if Erasmus meant that he would be a friend to More by getting the work in print but would not go so far as to endorse it. Even in his long letter in praise of More to Hutten in 1519, Erasmus seemed to stand back from *Utopia*, mentioning the book without special praise and with some quibbling about the unevenness of the style. More was not an accomplished Latin stylist; perhaps Erasmus was just a little ashamed of the book, or perhaps he sensed that More's defense of *The Praise of Folly* in his letter to Dorp had been less than wholehearted and felt piqued. We do not know.

Still, by the end of December 1516 the work was out, and More was delighted. He wrote Erasmus that month that he expected copies daily "with the feelings of a mother expecting her son's return from foreign parts."

By January the first copies had reached England, and More sent one to Archbishop Warham. He begged Warham to receive it though "it was written in undue haste." He had not intended to publish it at all, he said, but Peter Gilles "allowed his affection to outweigh his judgment, and without my knowledge had it printed."

Erasmus helped *Utopia* along, recommending it to friends. To William Budaeus, the French scholar, he suggested buying the book and taking the time to read it. To another friend he said that the book would make him laugh and that it would reveal the origins of all the evils in public affairs. But then in March 1517, he wrote in some annoyance to More that one Marliano was putting out the tale that Erasmus was the real author of the first part of the book. Erasmus was not amused; he had done what he could to squelch that tale.

Meanwhile More loyally supported the Greek New Testament. The work had no sooner appeared than Erasmus set about revising it and adding to it. More urged William Latimer, an English Greek scholar, to help out on the revision. Latimer begged off, citing his own ignorance of New Testament Greek, but he promised to send Erasmus any suggestions that might come to mind. We do not know what More thought needed emendation, but Latimer implies that More put much pressure on him to enlist his aid.

More helped Erasmus in other ways. Sometime before 1516, Erasmus wrote a funny little dialogue called *Julius Excluded* in which Pope Julius II, dead since 1513, appears at the gates of heaven, only to be turned away by St. Peter, who does not recognize him. The dialogue was not only an attack on the memory of Julius; it was partly an assault on papal pretensions in general. Erasmus wrote it anonymously and always refused to acknowledge that he was its author, although he also refused to deny it outright. In December 1516, More wrote that he had in his possession several manuscripts belonging to Erasmus "entirely in your own handwriting," among them the first draft of *Julius Excluded*. He wanted Erasmus to tell him what to do with them.

By the summer of 1517, Erasmus was uneasy about the popularity of the work, then circulating widely in manuscript, and he was trying to cast off the suspicion that he had written it. The following year *Julius Excluded* found its way into print, much to the dismay of the author, who for once was telling the truth when he disclaimed responsibility for publishing it. In 1519, More took the matter up in a long letter defending Erasmus from the slanders of a monk named John Batmanson. Like Erasmus himself, More equivocated, saying that nobody could prove that Erasmus had written *Julius Excluded*. But suppose he had written it, More said. "Suppose the man is opposed to wars and that he was angered at the troublesome times, and under the impulse of strong emotion he went further than he wished once peace was restored and emotions were calm." Having excused Erasmus, More blamed those who had put the work into print. He did not defend the maligned pope or rush to the judgment that Erasmus was really a devotee of the papacy and never could have penned an anti-papal book. Here, as he does so often, More shows himself a master of evasion when evasion is needed.

In March 1517, Erasmus asked More to send along revisions of *Utopia* as quickly as possible for the edition to be brought out by John Froben of Basel in 1518. Before that edition could appear, an unauthorized version of the little work was put out by the house of Giles Gourmont in Paris in 1517. Of this Paris edition we know surprisingly little. It is of a handy size but swarms with errors, and it was seen through the press by Thomas Lupset, an English student in Paris and a friend of More's, one of the learned young men More so successfully gathered around him in these years. We do not know why Lupset did this edition. Perhaps he intended it as homage to his friend.

Erasmus was now in the full flower of his fame, sought by rulers as an ornament to their courts but firmly resolved to keep his independence so he could devote himself to scholarly pursuits. In March 1517, in a letter to Ammonio, he lamented the preoccupation with business that had torn both Ammonio and More away from the muses that might have possessed all their genius.

Erasmus always feared that he might be ordered back to the confines of the monastery. He had, after all, taken vows that bound him to a monastic community for life, and many people—especially monks who found his fame onerous and his learning dangerous and his criticism of them in *The Praise of Folly* outrageous—thought it was high time for him to return. Ammonio labored to get him a dispensation from Pope Leo X that would permit him to live in peace in the secular world, following his scholarly pursuits. In January 1517, the dispensation was granted. Erasmus had to return to England to receive a formal absolution from his vows in a ceremony conducted by Ammonio in Westminster, probably at the great abbey church, on April 9. More and Erasmus saw each other at this time. It would be interesting to know if More attended the ceremony and of greater interest yet to know what he thought of his friend's decision to forsake the cloistered life that More always looked to with such aching nostalgia.

Erasmus stayed for a while with John Fisher at Rochester, urging on the bishop the continued study of Greek. He went back to the Continent on May 1 and wrote More at the end of the month, saying that Dorp was still causing trouble and referring to further correspondence between Dorp and More. Dorp was indeed wobbling in a way that makes the man seem, in retrospect, almost unstable. Following More's letter in 1515, Dorp had veered over to the side of Erasmus and the new learning and had praised Greek studies in a public lecture. Then he veered back again and began to attack Erasmus as before. Perhaps Dorp was responding to shifting sentiments in the theological faculty at Louvain. But he annoyed Erasmus and evidently brought More back into the conflict as a quiet peacemaker. By 1519 Dorp had swung back to supporting Erasmus, and More wrote him a flattering and grateful letter.

Throughout 1517 More and Erasmus exchanged letters filled with friendship and their common irritation at the obscurantists who stood against the new learning symbolized by the Greek New Testament. By July, Erasmus was installed at Louvain. He wrote Tunstall that Edward Lee was a student there, studying Greek. Lee was perhaps the brother of Joyce Lee, to whom More had dedicated his *Life of Pico* in 1505. Erasmus seemed to be corresponding with almost everyone engaged in classical studies, regarding such men as colleagues-in-discipline and comrades-in-arms for the renovation of church and society.

In London the sweating sickness attacked during the summer, and in August, More wrote Erasmus that Ammonio had succumbed to the disease. "He saw himself very well protected against the contagion by his modest manner of life, thinking it due to this, that though he rarely met anyone whose whole household had not suffered, the evil had so far attacked none of his own people. Of this he boasted to me himself and to many other men beside, not many hours before he himself was carried off. For this sweating sickness is fatal only on the first day." We hear a somber note of reproach in this report. Ammonio had boasted of his security against death. To More's mind, such presumption was to tempt God. His own family had not been touched, More wrote. He had heard that the disease was raging in Calais, where he was soon going on a diplomatic mission. "But what can one do? What one's lot brings must be endured. I have prepared my mind to face any outcome." The theology of humility is at work here; one publicly resigns oneself to the will of God, and behind the resignation is the hope that God will see the resignation and pass over those who bend their necks to His stroke.

Sometime in August 1518, Erasmus wrote Germanus Brixius, author of the long epic poem in praise of the French commander of the *Cordelière* in its fiery battle to the death against the English ship *Regent* in August 1512. We have noted More's mocking epigrams against this piece—epigrams that apparently circulated in manuscript up to a year before its 1518 publication. Erasmus had heard that Brixius was angry and that he was preparing a response. He begged the offended poet not to reply. More had written, not against Brixius personally, but against "some imaginary Frenchman, and he wrote in wartime." It was time to forget such things now that peace had been established between England and France. "It is expedient also for the cause of humane studies in general that their disciples like the ancient Cretans stand side by side, now that the enemies of literature are banding together so unpleasantly. And finally, I am reluctant to see two men at odds to both of whom I am devoted." Erasmus remembered Dorp's hostility to humane letters; and he knew of other enemies as well.

Despite all this placating talk, Erasmus was charged by More with having the epigrams printed along with the new Froben edition of *Utopia*, and Erasmus did nothing to dull these darts against Brixius, although he had his opportunities. Late in August 1517 he wrote Beatus Rhenanus, who helped Froben with the printing of Greek and Latin texts, urging Rhenanus to make sure that More's works were carefully printed, but he made no mention of editing out the epigrams. More himself had written as early as September 1516, asking Erasmus to "give some thought to the propriety of printing my remarks about Brixius, as some of them are rather caustic, although it might well seem that I had provocation from his insulting comments about my country." We have no evidence that Erasmus did anything of the sort. Perhaps Erasmus rather enjoyed the insults More dished out against Brixius; the Frenchman was a thoroughly modest talent, and once Erasmus had diverted opprobrium away from himself by making a perfunctory bid to Brixius to keep still, he may have enjoyed a superior writer's pleasure in seeing an inferior mocked.

In October, while he was in Calais, More received a diptych of Erasmus and Peter Gilles done by Quentin Metsys. He was delighted. He wrote Erasmus expressing his pleasure not only in the representations of his two friends but in the astonishing realism of the painter. "The spectator might well suppose them cast or carved rather than painted, so much do they seem to stand out and project with the proper relief of a man's body." The realism is indeed remarkable; Gilles holds a letter from More that duplicates More's own hand-writing. More wrote Peter asking for the return of the letter. "It will double the effect if it is kept hanging alongside the picture. If it has been lost, or if you have a use for it, I will see whether I in my turn can imitate the man who imitates my hand so well."

To Erasmus, More poured out his appreciation for the avowal of friendship that the portraits represented. "I am entirely free from vainglory," he wrote. "And yet, to tell the truth, this is the one itch in the way of ambition which I find it impossible to shake off, and which tickles me in a most agreeable manner, when it comes into my head that distant posterity will remember me for my friendship with Erasmus, attested in letters and books and pictures and every other way."

The friendship was about to be tested on both sides. By the autumn of 1517, opposition was consolidating against the *Novum Instrumentum,* and one of the work's most virulent foes was Edward Lee. There were many others. In March 1518, Froben brought out his fine edition of More's *Utopia* and included, within the same binding, epigrams from both More and Erasmus. Among these were the slings and arrows against Brixius. (Froben brought out another edition in November, so the book must have sold well.)

The Froben edition of *Utopia* included for the first time a prefatory letter from Erasmus; its praise is quite faint. "What would this wonderful, rich nature not have accomplished if his talent had been trained in Italy, if it were now totally devoted to the service of the muses, if it had ripened to its proper harvest and, as it were, its own autumnal plenty?" The letter is addressed to Froben. Erasmus says, "Such is the reputation of your press that, if it is known that a book has come from the house of Froben, that is enough to have it please the learned world." But Erasmus says not one word of his own in praise of *Utopia,* and those vaguely complimentary remarks that he makes of More himself are brief. It may be that the presence of some of his own epigrams in this large and handsome volume helped persuade Erasmus to write the preface he had earlier refrained from writing. But nothing, apparently, could persuade him to be uncompromisingly favorable to the work of his friend.

We have quoted several times from More's epigrams, which first saw print in 1518. Epigrams—short, pungent expressions intended to convey a witty or a solemn thought in a memorable way so that others will quote it—are always popular among learned souls who prize language and brood over death. Quotable epigrams offer a hope of quick immortality, at least of a sort. And as if to establish the connection between the immortal fame of brilliant utterance and a life everlasting, commemorative epigrams were often buried with the dead in the funerals of the Renaissance. More's epigrams are interesting but not brilliant, and their fame has not endured.

Erasmus said of More in his preface, "When a mere youth he amused himself with epigrams, most of them written when he was but a lad." Again we catch the faint note of reserve about More's writing; Erasmus seems to be telling the world not to expect too much from this collection.

More included the flattering coronation poems done in honor of Henry VIII's accession and probably presented in manuscript to the king at the event itself. He also made several Latin translations of Greek epigrams, sometimes acknowledging his sources and sometimes not. He mocked astrologers, women, and corrupt clergymen. He delivered himself of many conventional thoughts on the certainty of death and the vagaries of fortune. We have mentioned his congratulatory lines praising Henry's victory over the city of Tournai in the French war of 1513. In another epigram, on a man who affected French ways, More expressed common English prejudices without managing to rise above them:

> He pays [his] servant nothing—like a Frenchman;
> He clothes him in worn-out rags—in the French manner;
> He feeds him little and that little poor—as the French do;
> He works him hard—like the French;
> He strikes him often—like a Frenchman;
> At social gatherings, and on the street and in the market-place, and in public
>   he quarrels with him and abuses him always in the French fashion.

But the most biting of More's epigrams are reserved for Brixius, and Brixius was not one to turn the other cheek. Early in 1520 the French poet published a long, bitter poem called *Antimorus*, written with a Greek omega in the title, so that *Antimorus* meant not only "Against More" but also "Against the Fool." Some of his lines hit the mark:

You tell me I reek too much of the old poets;
Certainly no one could say as much of you.

Brixius made More an incompetent poetaster. He tacked an appendix in prose onto his poem, pointing out in detail the errors in More's versification and a multitude of errors in More's Latin diction. In many instances Brixius was correct.

Most serious of all was the attack he made on More's coronation poems. In flattering Henry VIII, Brixius said, More had slandered Henry VII. How could the son accept such servile praise when it was couched in base attacks on the father? When More wrote these epigrams, Henry gave no sign that they displeased him. But in 1520, almost on the eve of his sudden decision to bring the Duke of Buckingham to the block, Henry might have been looking for examples to demonstrate his power, and a man with his capricious temperament might well have considered some action against an author, especially one on his council, publicly accused in Europe at large of not treating his house with the proper respect. To send epigrams in manuscript to a new young king, joyful at his release from paternal captivity and at his accession to power and resentful of a shrewish father, was one thing; to publish these same epigrams when a king was now accustomed to power, without a son, and threatened by ominous murmurings about the insufficiency of his lineage, was quite another. The attack Brixius made was not only crudely insulting, accusing More rather effectively of ignorance in both Greek and Latin; it was also dangerous. Brixius suggested that a king who cared for his father and his house would exile such a poet, sending More to Utopia. Exile—or worse—was not beyond the possible.

Brixius did not stop with sarcastic and vehement attacks on More's epigrams; he dredged up every stylistic flaw he could find in *Utopia* and in More's translations of Lucian and blasted those as well. Brixius reeks of pedantry and bad temper, and *Antimorus* is an exercise in massive retaliation that quickly becomes tedious, but his detailed assault on More's Latin diction demonstrates that More's learning was something less than a professional scholar might appreciate, and it gives us a clue to Erasmus's reluctance to praise *Utopia*. We should hardly be surprised that More, busy as he was all his life, should lack the polish in language that he might have gained through a total devotion to letters. But like an author who today sustains a devastating and unanswerable review, More felt himself not only humiliated before Europe but crushed in that part of himself that had taken pride in his learning. So he made an almost hysterically vindictive response.

By the spring of 1520, he had a copy of *Antimorus,* and he delivered himself of a seething "letter" addressed to Brixius but really destined for the printer and the Latin reading public of Europe. He sent an equally burning tirade against Brixius to Erasmus, perhaps hoping that Erasmus would publish it and come clearly and publicly to his side in the quarrel. But Erasmus was only embarrassed; he saw to it that More's letter to him found no wider audience.

In his *Letter Against Brixius,* More flings insults at Brixius with the same vitriolic abandon that would later mark his attacks on Luther and other Protestants. The most interesting thing in the long epistle is his careful dance around the accusation that he had slandered Henry VII. More said that Henry VII had done many good things for England; he had been a prudent king, but in his old age, in bad health, he had listened to many wicked councillors who had brought calamities on the commonwealth.

More's blame of councillors for the misdeeds of Henry VII probably does reflect something of his real thought. It was standard practice to condemn royal councillors when a king did badly; the rhetoric of the rebellions of the time hardly ever condemned kings; rebels habitually declared that they took up arms against those who imprisoned kings with bad advice. More believed, as nearly everyone else did, that kings were greatly influenced by the councillors they chose—one reason, certainly, why he became a councillor himself, and we should not take his defense against the charges of Brixius to be hypocritical. We may doubt his full sincerity when he wrote that from the decay Henry VIII had found, the young king had lifted the nation, and that to the good deeds done by the father, the son had added others that were better. Henry VIII's record in bettering the national life up to this time was not as glowing as More made it, and surely More knew Henry's failures as well as anybody did.

Yet as always when he had the chance, More showered Henry VIII with praise, saying that to do so was to praise Henry VII, too, for to laud the son was to praise the parent who had given life to the child. All the greater glory was due to a son who corrected the errors of the father rather than imitated them. More praised Henry for doing nothing in the dark—high praise indeed from the maker of Utopia, where all governmental deliberations went on under intense public scrutiny. Henry consulted with the common people, with the nobility, with all ages, ranks, sexes—conduct that deserves to be praised to the skies, More said.

We are again at one of More's great themes, one visible everywhere in *Utopia.* Society works best with all its parts in harmony, a great system like the universe itself. Every part—large or small—has its necessary place. The king for More is like the Aristotelian principle of reason that keeps the order working and preserves the whole against chaos. What he does not spell out is his lifelong belief that a good king does not act against this order or try to act above it. The king is the force that preserves order, but the king is also a part of the order—just as intelligibility is part of the physical world. Reason in the Aristotelian universe could not be opposed to the sun or to the earth or to other parts of the cosmic order of things. These are my illustrations and not More's, but they accurately express his thought, and they help us understand better his expressions about kings, expressions that at times—as in this letter against Brixius—seem obsequious and contradictory.

Brixius had appended to his *Antimorus* Erasmus's short letter asking him not to publish the little book. The letter included typical Erasmian flattery for both Brixius and France. Brixius claimed it did not arrive in time to keep him from printing *Antimorus*, although it obviously did get to him in time to be included—a fact that galled More and made him wish with even greater fervor that Erasmus might come out clearly on his side.

Much to More's annoyance, Erasmus refused to take sides. Instead he wrote valiantly to both men urging calm. He addressed himself also to friends like William Budaeus, who had good relations with both More and Brixius. By the time the controversy flared into the public eye in early 1520, Erasmus was under attack by conservatives who condemned his Greek New Testament, and he wanted his friends to rally to him and to stop fighting each other.

On April 26, 1520, Erasmus wrote More begging for silence. He pretended that he had not seen More's *Letter Against Brixius*, and it is just possible that More's work with its covering letter had not arrived. But it is also true that all his life Erasmus claimed not to have read things when he could avoid trouble by pretending ignorance. He said he had written Brixius in vain to suppress *Antimorus*, but in the end, he said, Brixius had only hurt himself. If More replied, people would suppose More no better than his adversary. Brixius was a good man, Erasmus said, devoted to good letters. More's epigrams had wounded him. More should not be surprised if a young man of vehement temperament, thirsty for fame, imagined that the injury done him required retaliation. Yet in such a quarrel, good letters could only suffer from the "pertinacious conspiracy of the barbarians." Erasmus proposed a deal: Let More promise to cut the offending epigrams from future editions, and Brixius would suppress *Antimorus*. Deprived of fuel, the fire would slowly die.

More quickly composed a long and truculent reply. Clearly he believed Erasmus was only pretending ignorance of his *Letter Against Brixius* and its equally vehement covering letter. He continued to justify himself and to accuse Brixius of bad faith. He ridiculed Brixius's claim that he did not have time to suppress *Antimorus* as Erasmus requested. Even so, he declared himself willing to accept the peace that Erasmus proposed. His own reply to Brixius was already in print, he said, and he was sure that Erasmus had received a copy. Nevertheless, More declared himself willing to buy up all the outstanding copies and to burn them if Brixius would suppress *Antimorus*.

Yet despite More's promise, some copies of his tirade against Brixius did circulate. William Budaeus saw one when he and More met at the Field of the Cloth of Gold in the summer of 1520, and More forced Erasmus to read a copy when they met later at Calais. Erasmus afterwards wrote Budaeus that the letter was so harsh "that I who to some seem mordant appear absolutely toothless in comparison." When More brought out another edition of his epigrams later in 1520, he added four new ones against Brixius as insulting as any of the others. He probably did not think Brixius had lived up to the bargain Erasmus had supposedly struck. *Antimorus* still circulated; More did not have it in him to withdraw without having the last word.

Erasmus continued to work hard to calm both men. In June 1520 he wrote a stern letter to Brixius admonishing the young Frenchman that he was doing himself no credit by writing against More. "More provoked you, but he was himself provoked. His answer was more civil than yours by far—as Frenchmen do confess to you. And he wrote in wartime, you after years of the most peaceful relations." Erasmus praised More's intellect and integrity and re-proached Brixius for trying to make More look like a fool. "His intelligence is absolutely incomparable, his memory the best, his ability to speak the liveliest." But even here Erasmus did not praise More's Latin diction or his writings.

Brixius did not reply to More's later epigrams, and so the quarrel died away like a fire in a forest that has been burned to the ground. By August 1521, Erasmus wrote Budaeus thanking him for persuading Brixius to withdraw from the war, and he said More planned no further hostilities and did not even remember the little conflict. This was the letter in which Erasmus extolled the More household and the learned and virtuous conduct of More's daughters, who read Livy and knew how to listen to sermons.

Erasmus published this letter to Budaeus in praise of More as well as the stern admonition to Brixius in the collection of correspondence he called *Epistolae ad diversos,* which issued from the press of John Froben in Basel late in 1521. More must have felt himself at last vindicated in the eyes of the learned community of Europe, which viewed Erasmus as the center of their universe. He probably also saw the wisdom of Erasmus's plea that the quarrel between himself and Brixius harmed the cause of good letters, and as the days cooled his anger, he very probably saw as well how much damage he had done to the image of himself that he wanted to present to the world.

As it turned out, the quarrel was so petty that it had little influence on anything, and the only interest it holds today lies in the dark light it throws on More's character. On the eve of the Protestant Reformation, he demon-strated the unrestrained rhetorical fury that he would later show in his polemi-cal works against heresy. It was a common style for sixteenth-century contro-versy, and it may reveal the underlying tensions that pushed men to fight at the sign of any provocation. That these men in personal conversation might normally be restrained, courteous, and urbane did not prevent them from savage thrust and counterthrust when they saw the flash of steel in the hand of a foe. More, Erasmus, and many other humanists affected to disdain the chivalric code that compelled those with aristocratic pretensions to make so much of honor that they could stain the world with blood at the slightest hint that someone else thought less of them than they did of themselves. But in truth the humanists subscribed to much the same code; they merely chose a different set of weapons. More had this fury, and the Reformation would give him occasion to release it as violently as anyone else in the century.

16

THE GREEK
NEW TESTAMENT

ERASMUS WAS subject to the same tensions as More and many others of this anxious time. By 1518 his Greek New Testament was coming under loud and sustained attack in England and elsewhere as conservative theologians saw in it an outrageous assault on customary practices in the church. Erasmus reacted to criticism of his work with the same unbounded wrath that he had sought to pacify when it appeared in More and Brixius.

Like Erasmus himself, More first saw the issue of the Greek New Testament as a battle for the place of Greek studies in Christian education, a place More believed essential for the reform of society. When early in 1518 More heard a preacher down from Oxford deliver a ranting sermon in London against Erasmus and against literature in general, and also heard rumors that a party of students and dons at Oxford, calling themselves "Trojans," had banded together to oppose Greek and to mock anyone learning it, he wrote the university a sharp letter both as a royal councillor and as an alumnus. His tone reflected studious modesty, a little flattery, and a spirit of reconciliation.

He could not think, he said, that such idiocy represented anything but a faction. The learned doctors must know that, except for Cicero and Seneca, all worthwhile philosophy was found among the Greeks, to whom we owe the liberal arts. The New Testament was written in Greek, and the greatest of the Latin fathers had aspired to learn Greek. To know Greek was a need of the universal church, and no sensible Christian could oppose it. The faction at Oxford must be suppressed. If this proved difficult, More had some suggestions. The dons could seek the help of William Warham, Archbishop of Canterbury; Thomas Wolsey, "the most learned of the bishops"; and the king himself, whose love of the liberal arts, said More, was well known. Having fired off this heavy artillery, More closed benignly with hopes for peace.

The letter may be seen not only as a vigorous defense of both the new learning and Erasmus but also as an episode in More's alliance with Thomas Wolsey on the royal council. More wrote the letter from Abingdon, where he was with the court. Wolsey had by then become a strong advocate of Greek studies, and he planned to grant to Oxford a great benefaction and to supervise the reform of the curriculum. Within a year after More's letter, Wolsey had established a chair of Greek studies in the university—not the first time Greek had been taught there, but the first time it was solidly established. The university was eager to please Wolsey, and More's letter was written to an audience ready to comply and probably in deep chagrin—as universities sometimes are —over the loud antics of a minority of its faculty and students.

More got his reward eventually. In 1524 he became Lord High Steward of the university, charged with handling the business affairs and the lawsuits of the faculty. He accepted the appointment in a letter exuberant with joy and gratitude. Since by then Wolsey was Oxford's greatest patron, the appointment must have come at his suggestion.

Erasmus briefly described the affair of the "Trojans" to a continental friend, saying that through More and Richard Pace, another royal servant, the king had imposed silence on the dissidents. He also told a little tale of a disputation between More and "a certain theologian" in which the king himself took part. The king accused the theologian of pride and folly because the man had condemned Erasmus's Greek New Testament without having read it. In his general embarrassment, the theologian tried to make amends by saying that he was not entirely against Greek letters since they had been derived from Hebrew!

In his letter to Oxford of 1518, More pointed out that Greek studies at Cambridge were pursued with enthusiasm by students and teachers alike. More urged Oxonians to do likewise, and his favorable remarks about Cambridge must have burned in those who read his letter at Oxford.

Yet opposition to Erasmus's edition of the New Testament was firmly in the English church's tradition of skepticism about the value of the Bible in religious life. The Lollards had used Wycliffe's English translation of the Bible to preach heresy for many decades, leaving among conservative clerics an enduring suspicion of anyone making scripture a tool for reform. Undoubtedly this reserve provoked those who craved reform to a thoroughly romantic vision of what scripture could do if it were unleashed, a vision which in the England of 1518 had not yet been tarnished by the tumult and shouting of those who took scripture as an absolute standard, only to fall into prolonged vicious quarreling about what it meant. And although More could not know it when he wrote his admonishing letter to his old university, the students of Greek at Cambridge whom he praised—those young men poring over Erasmus's Greek New Testament in their quiet rooms near the Cam—were about to pose a greater danger to the old church than the most rabid "Trojan" reactionary at Oxford could have imagined.

The sides in the affair of the Greek New Testament were not neatly drawn. The English church—like the church all over Europe—was divided and subdivided by factions who fought each other on one issue and joined on another, only to split apart when some new controversy presented itself. The effect of these shifting alliances and internecine fights was to make the church incapable of uniting against the greatest threat to its traditional understanding of itself. That threat in the sixteenth century was not heresy but secular government.

In the great investiture controversy of the eleventh and twelfth centuries, the popes in Rome had commanded the allegiance of most of the German bishops in their battle against the German emperors, so that in the end the power of the emperors fell to ruin in the German lands. At the heart of the controversy had been the claim of emperors like Henry IV that they received their power directly from God and not through the pope. Seeing themselves as quasi-priests, the emperors had claimed the right not only to appoint the bishops in their territories but also to control elections to the papacy. And if a pope turned bad, the emperors believed, they, as the rulers of the Holy Roman Empire, had the right to depose him. The Germans had preserved the fiction that they were the true heirs of the Romans, that the Roman Empire had been divinely "translated" to them, and that their emperors had natural sovereignty over Rome and everything in it, including the papacy.

A succession of popes beginning with Gregory VII (1073–85) fought the emperors on theological grounds. The popes claimed the high superiority of the priestly estate over the secular realm. "Who in his last hour . . . has ever implored the aid of an earthly king for the salvation of his soul?" Gregory VII asked. "And what king or emperor is able, by reason of the office he holds, to rescue a Christian from the power of the devil through holy baptism, to number him among the sons of God, and to fortify him with the divine unction? Who of them can of his own words make the body and blood of our Lord—the greatest act in the Christian religion? Or who of them possesses the power of binding and loosing in heaven and on earth? From all of these considerations it is clear how greatly the priestly office excels in power."

In Gregory's view—one adopted wholeheartedly by succeeding popes—the church must be completely independent of lay government if either was to be what God intended. Clerical celibacy, imperfectly observed by priests before the investiture controversy, became one of the great issues in this fierce debate, since celibacy now was seen as a sign of the purity and high estate of the priesthood. Gregory VII came close to saying that the secular state was satanic. "Who does not know that kings and leaders are sprung from men who were ignorant of God, who by pride, robbery, perfidy, murders—in a word, by almost every crime at the prompting of the devil, who is the prince of this world— have striven with blind cupidity and intolerable presumption to dominate over their equals, that is, over mankind?" He stopped short of declaring the state evil by nature, but he did hold the Augustinian view that the secular state existed only because Satan had corrupted God's creation. The state was needed to bear the sword, to punish evildoers, to maintain order, and to ensure a stable society where the Catholic Church could administer the sacraments, propound good doctrine, and save souls for the life to come. Gregory and his successors were willing to go to war against any prince who disputed the church's claim to independence from lay authority.

By the sixteenth century, the Catholic Church had lost much of its moral authority, and the most binding loyalty most people felt was to the secular government that defended them against a threatening outside world and, in its kings, embodied an ideal of what people supposed was best in human life. Government became an object of hope for reformers who had given up on the power or the will of popes to bring order to Christian civilization. The Protestant Reformation accelerated the shift of loyalties from universal church to national governments, and by the end of the sixteenth century both Catholic and Protestant confessions everywhere in Europe had fallen under the dominion of secular authorities, who then unabashedly used religion for their own purposes and made the church within their borders part of the reason of state.

The internal divisions of the church show up sharply in the controversy over the Greek New Testament in England, and we see More picking his way through them. His position was not simple. On the one hand, he stood firmly by the old order, believing fervently in the necessary independence of the church from the secular government. On the other, he championed the new learning represented by Erasmus, emphasizing individual study, individual ethics, and criticism of the existing state of the church. This new learning was to contribute powerfully to the Reformation, although neither More nor Erasmus could have dreamed of such a consequence when they joined forces to promote that learning in England and in the rest of Christian Europe.

A virulent foe of the Erasmian New Testament was Henry Standish, who had made a name for himself in the Hunne affair by championing the right of English kings to take legal jurisdiction over the English clergy—at the time a radical position indeed, sharply contrary to the standard papal proclamations on ecclesiastical independence. But in his practical theology, Standish was conservative. He was emotional, and he had a flair for preaching. A second edition of the Greek New Testament appeared in 1519, and in July 1520, Erasmus wrote with disgust to a continental friend about a sermon Standish preached in St. Paul's churchyard against the book. Standish was so carried away by some of the word changes Erasmus had made in his Latin translation that he broke down and began to weep before his congregation.

After the sermon, Standish, recovered from his sobbing, had lunch at the court. Two friends of Erasmus sat down with him, one married and the other a "bachelor." From the description Erasmus gives of the married friend, commentators have usually assumed that it was More. (Perhaps Erasmus did not mention More by name because of the bad odor his name had acquired in learned circles on the Continent in the quarrel with Brixius.) The married friend began to question Standish and wounded him by a show of great theological knowledge, much greater in fact than Standish's own.

Standish, probably smarting from being so thoroughly humiliated by a layman, did not give up. After the meal, he pushed his way into a circle that included the king and the queen and melodramatically flung himself on his knees, calling on the royal couple to live up to their ancient duties of protecting the Catholic faith from heresy. The recent books of Erasmus, said he, were about to destroy the Christian religion. He lifted his face imploringly to his sovereign and rolled his eyes to heaven.

Erasmus's two friends pounced on him. They imitated his very gestures with a great show of earnestness, evidently to the vast amusement of everyone except Standish. The married friend asked Standish to name the heresies of Erasmus. Standish declared that Erasmus denied the resurrection, did not accept the sacrament of matrimony, and taught the wrong doctrine of the eucharist.

Standish was probably not so wide of the mark about Erasmus's real opinions as most scholars have taken him to be. But Erasmus was sufficiently vague to make it impossible to this day to know exactly what he thought about some of these doctrines. His friends were persistent with Standish. Did he object to the idea of translating scripture? If so, what did he make of Jerome, who translated the Vulgate? Standish replied that he did not object to the Vulgate because Jerome had translated the epistles of Paul from the original Hebrew! "Excuse me, Reverend Father," the bachelor said. "Would you mind repeating that? I was not paying attention." So Standish in a very loud voice repeated his idiocy. The queen picked at the king's sleeve and made him listen. And when Standish had made his point unmistakably, the bachelor said, "I would not have imagined, Reverend Father, that you could be so mad as to imagine that these epistles were written first in Hebrew when even boys know that they were written by Paul in Greek." It was the kind of show More would have loved, and he may very well have been, as many suppose, the married man who played a part. (The similarity of this story to Erasmus's earlier one about More and "a certain theologian" may mean that Erasmus conflated the two; if so, the "married man" was certainly More.)

Erasmus was enraged at such malicious and foolish opposition, but he was encountering much the same treatment from stubbornly ignorant clergymen on the Continent, though they were not usually in the entourage of kings. Standish was stupid and blundering, and in the end he did no great harm because Henry apparently did not take him seriously about Erasmus or anything else.

Edward Lee was another matter; he belonged to an important family of Kent, and his grandfather had been mayor of London. He belonged to a class that would normally have despised the ignorant Dr. Standish despite Standish's elevation to become bishop of St. Asaph in 1518, doubtless as a reward for his part in the Hunne affair. Lee had some knowledge of Greek, and he had studied at Louvain, where he had met Erasmus. Among those who cared deeply for him was Thomas More, who sent greetings to Lee in a letter to Erasmus of October 1517.

Lee was regarded as devout, but he had a streak of meanness in him. He wrote critical notes against the Erasmian New Testament of 1516. He circulated them, and someone sent a copy to Erasmus, who pronounced them worthless and declared that he had no time to reply to everyone who made cavils against his work. Lee persisted. Erasmus was goaded into greater insults. Now he called Lee a fraud, an impostor, both mad and stupid, ignorant and malicious, and, said Erasmus, he knew almost nothing of Greek. When the second edition of the Erasmian New Testament appeared in 1519, Lee enlarged his notes and spread them around.

More was inevitably drawn into the squabble. In May 1519 he wrote Lee a long letter and gently but firmly tried to dissuade him from publishing the hostile notes. He reproached Lee for circulating secret criticisms in an effort to win fame and said that Lee had often distorted what Erasmus had really said. More claimed not to have read all the notes, and he said that he wanted to write as short an answer as possible because he did not have time to reply at length. He implied that what Lee had said was not worth the effort of a long response.

More's tactics were similar to the ones he used in his 1515 letter to Dorp. Lee was only hurting himself with such attacks; he was being deceived by his friends. Most good and wise men of More's acquaintance thought that Lee was making a fool of himself, and if he persisted, he was going to bring calumny down not only on himself but on all Britain. The shoemaker should judge nothing but shoes, More said, admitting that he was no theologian. Even so, he could answer most of Lee's objections himself without any great difficulty. In fact More did not answer any of them, and again we find that bizarre vagueness we have noted in his defense of the Erasmian Greek New Testament.

He did argue for Erasmus's good character. "Erasmus," said More, "I confess I vehemently love, nor is there any good reason why he should not be embraced by all the Christian world." Erasmus had labored tirelessly in the cause of good letters, More said. No one for centuries had been his equal in learning in matters both sacred and profane. But in a tender way More also called to mind the old friendship between the More family and the Lees. He recalled kissing Lee when the boy was only ten, and he remembered how bright Lee was as a child, how full of promise. More still awaited the moment when all Britain would be celebrated for Lee's industry. But Lee would win only scorn if he persisted in his plans to publish against Erasmus. It was a magnificent rhetorical squelch of a sort that would have indeed been a stab in the heart to one who had recognized that his early promise had not been fulfilled.

About the same time, More took on a young monk who had rallied to Lee's side. He was John Batmanson of the Charterhouse, the monastery closest to More's heart. Batmanson wrote More a letter begging him to renounce his friendship with Erasmus, who was, he said, a pestilent source of contagion. Erasmus was a vagabond, a false theologian, a scoundrel, and the herald of Antichrist. We have only More's stinging reply and not the monk's letter itself, but from what More wrote we can see that Batmanson also attacked Erasmus for writing in an elegant style! Here was a man who came close to declaring that ignorance was bliss and that the best Christians were the crudest men. It was an arrogance and a challenge to the new learning that More could not let pass in silence, especially since the monk had made himself such an easy mark. It was always a part of More's polemical style to make it seem that his foes were fools, and here was a grand opportunity to suggest that anyone opposing Erasmus had no greater standing than this foolish monk.

More's reply is his usual mixture of benevolence and assault. Clearly More thought that the monk was young and silly, but just as clearly he believed that the man could be redeemed from his wrongheadedness. He called the monk's style turgid and ungrammatical and said that it showed the young man had never had any leisure for learning. The monk thought that the Septuagint included the New Testament, and More scornfully pointed out that the trans lators of the Septuagint, the Greek version of the Old Testament, had died two hundred years before Christ was born. The monk had raised quibbles about new words Erasmus had substituted for old ones in the Vulgate—such as the word for "net." More showed that these were foolish and ignorant questions.

He spent a longer time on a more serious issue and for once considered a genuine theological problem in the Erasmian text. Erasmus had substituted the Latin word *sermo* for the Vulgate's *verbum* in John 1:1 where the King James version would later translate, "In the beginning was the Word, and the Word was with God, and the Word was God." This verse took on importance because the word *verbum* had long been taken as a refutation of the Arians, those ancient heretics who claimed that Christ was not the equal of God.

When Erasmus translated the Greek word *logos* as *sermo*, many thought that he was trying to imply that Christ was inferior to God the father. More gave the young monk a lesson in Greek and in history, showing that *sermo* and *verbum* were used interchangeably in the scriptures and by the fathers of the church to translate *logos*.

He also touched on one of the great problems of the century. What was the relation of the old and the new in the church? The conservatives howled that Erasmus was introducing innovation. His translation differed from the Vulgate, sanctified by its use for so many centuries by so many generations of Christians. As we have repeatedly seen in this book, Catholics believed that the spirit of God dwelled continuously in the church and that the church could not follow any practice for long without divine sanction. Was not Erasmus implying that for all the centuries the church had used the Vulgate the people of God had been in error?

The question was not so baldly put, but it lay coiled among all the objections conservatives made to what Erasmus had done. More's position seemed to make sense to those who shared the humanists' views. Erasmus was not really doing something new; he was recovering the old. The Greek text was the oldest text of the New Testament, and in going back to the source, Erasmus was reaching to antiquity. The use of *sermo* and *verbum* to translate *logos* was an example. More mentioned several Latin fathers of the church who had used the words interchangeably. The fathers translated John 1:1 in many ways, none in contradiction to the faith of the church that Christ was equal to God.

More's citations on this point are awesome in their ease and comprehensiveness. They reflect years of reading and pondering, and they demonstrate the prodigious memory that made him the marvel of those who knew him. They convey the impression that his mind was saturated with patristic lore. It is probably safe to say that he was to a much greater degree than Erasmus immersed in the spirit of the fathers.

What More does not do in his letter to Batmanson is to make a cogent, linguistic argument for Erasmus's choice. If *sermo* and *verbum* were interchangeable in patristic literature, why did Erasmus not stick to the more traditional *verbum?* Why did he choose the more provocative *sermo?* More is silent on the point.

He does address the general problem of how readers should react when Erasmus contradicted some patristic belief. Suppose Erasmus did on occasion contradict this father or that? Though More revered the fathers and thought that after the apostles they were the best men who ever lived, he knew that they were only men after all. They could err, and they did err.

He unfolded a long list of doctrines that had been points of disagreement among different fathers of the church. Augustine thought that it was wrong for a man to marry again after he had put his wife away for adultery as long as the adulterous first wife still lived. Ambrose thought that such a man might marry again. Did neither err? Jerome thought that a man who had one wife before he was baptized might take another afterwards without committing bigamy. (The early church had been exercised over matrimonial problems that arose when one partner was Christian and the other pagan.) The church now judges, More said, that Jerome had erred. Augustine thought that children who died before they were baptized were subject to eternal torments. "But now how many believe such a thing," asked More, "unless Luther clinging tenaciously to the doctrine of Augustine wishes to restore this ancient opinion?" (It is the first mention of Luther in More's surviving works.) And who among the ancient fathers did not believe that the Virgin Mary was conceived in original sin—a belief that now almost all the Christian world rejects. (Despite More's claim for unanimity about the doctrine in his time, the immaculate conception of the Virgin Mary was not made formal dogma in the Catholic Church until 1854.)

More gave a picture of the patristic church that has some affinity with the sane, temperate religion of the Utopians, a devout and sincere society, seeking enlightenment, willing to accept correction, above all willing to bow to the consensus of the community when that consensus became clear. In time God worked everything out and revealed the truth to His people, but while the quest for truth went on, errors were made, and all books had their mistakes. The process of seeking truth was still going on, in More's view. And to accuse Erasmus of heresy for whatever errors he might have committed was to raise tumult and sedition among the common people, who had no discrimination to judge such charges.

More turned from Erasmus to the religious orders represented by the young monk himself. He did not condemn monks or the orders out of hand, but he did speak of the gross corruption in the monastic and religious life of Europe in general. He recalls one incident when the abbot of a monastery led a conspiracy to commit murder, parricide, and sacrilege, pausing beforehand to lead his fellows in a "Hail Mary" recited on their knees.

He wrote of his own acquaintance with a Franciscan friar at Coventry who told people that daily recitation of the Psalter of the Virgin Mary was sufficient to save anyone from hell. The local pastor objected to this crass version of salvation. The friar preached a furious sermon against him. About that time More went to Coventry to visit his sister. Immediately he was set upon by a crowd exercised over the question: Did recitation of the Psalter of the Virgin Mary guarantee salvation? More could only laugh.

But he could not shake off the issue. He was invited to dinner, and there was the friar—"cadaverous, stern, and gloomy." The argument began at once, the friar basing his conviction on miracles credited to the Virgin in response to human devotion to her. Even if the miracles were truly reported, said More, no one could be so presumptuous as to suppose Mary would assure the salvation of anyone who lived like the devil even while reciting her psalter every day. But no one listened to him; people wanted to believe the friar. And, says More, "the result of my labors was that he was lauded to the skies, and I was laughed at as a fool."

This is the kind of religion Erasmus condemns, said More. When Erasmus was dead and those who envied him were also gone from the earth, later generations would admire him with greater fervor. The monk could not have made his foolish charges against Erasmus without having a conviction of his own holiness, "which is the one most dangerous attitude in a religious; and, by my love for you, I want you to rid yourself of it completely. For it would help me and others in the same condition, tossed as we are on the waves of an unhappy world, to look up to you religious and to marvel at your orders as models of angelic life, so that, while we admire the virtue in others, our own way of life may seem all the more worthless."

No sentence More ever wrote expressed better his view of the ideal relation between clergy and laity. He sounds like Colet, who died in 1519, about the time this letter was written. Both Colet and More believed that the clergy had to redeem the battered hopes of sinful humanity by their pure lives; the secular world reeked of wickedness, and those who lived in it needed the clergy to provide both the sacraments and a model for goodness. Otherwise people would begin to think that all there was to life was a ruthless and ceaseless competition and carnality that was the death of all goodness. Such seems to have been the deep conviction embedded in More's admonition, and in it we see that his own longing for the religious life he had forsaken to pursue his career in the world was still strong.

More's letter to Batmanson may be the best controversial piece he ever wrote. It is sharp, learned, and sometimes sarcastic, but it is also benevolent. He did not want to shame the young man by revealing his name in print, so he addressed his letter simply "to a Monk." Only modern scrutiny of the letters of Erasmus has plucked out the name. To More the Christian religion was greater than outward observances alone; it was a matter of the head, the heart, and the senses. None of the three could be left out without corrupting the whole. It was pernicious to look for evil in the work of Erasmus, who was trying to do good. Above all, More was thoroughly committed to the old Christian ideal—never without its foes among Christians—which held that learning was a way to virtue.

The prattle of an ignorant monk posed no real threat to Erasmus, but it did enrage him, and he was alarmed and angry at Lee's persistence and bad will. He wrote Lee a scathing and threatening letter in July 1519—one that ought to be read by moderns who suppose that Erasmus was always as temperate, tolerant, and kind as the ideal Christian he extolled in his works. Erasmus's piety was always more a matter of art than life. He published this poisonous little piece in *Farrago*, a collection of his correspondence that appeared in the fall of 1519 and included both his first letter to Thomas More, done in 1499, and his flattering description of More to Ulrich von Hutten, written in July 1519. Clearly the intention behind the collection was to show Erasmus moving easily among the great and the learned of the earth so that Lee's attacks on him would seem all the more ridiculous and ignorant in comparison. In effect More was enlisted as a public soldier on the side of Erasmus whether More wanted to be or not.

Lee replied, bringing out his *Annotationes* against Erasmus in 1520. He would have published earlier, said he, had not Thomas More asked him to refrain. Erasmus soon issued his *Apology*, accusing Lee of raising "seditious clamors among the people." And Erasmus continued to write scurrilous letters condemning Lee to people all over Europe.

More wrote two letters to Lee after the *Annotationes* appeared. They were cordial, but they revealed More's disappointment. In the first he briefly reviewed the quarrel and recalled his earlier counsels of moderation. He rebuked Lee gently for the virulence of the *Annotationes*, a virulence that began with the frontispiece and continued throughout with slanders greater "than the ears of moderate men can bear." More took note of the threatening letter Erasmus had written, but he refused to condemn Erasmus himself, and he begged Lee to return grace for acerbity. The battle was unprofitable to everyone. Lee should come back to England. Would that he had not gone away to study at Louvain if his quarrel with Erasmus was the result! But no matter who was to blame for the quarrel, More looked forward to seeing Lee again.

More wrote on February 27, 1520. The next day a copy of the *Annotationes* with a letter from Lee arrived. Lee's letter was full of reproach for the one More had written him in May 1519. More was threatening him, Lee said, and Lee was angry. More replied on February 29, and here he was sharper about the *Annotationes*. As in his previous letters, More pointed out that the Greek New Testament had been approved by the pope. How could Lee write a book so thoroughly condemning Erasmus's work when that work had been twice approved by the Supreme Pontiff? As he had done before, More recalled the example of Dorp, who had attacked the work of Erasmus and then relented; he wanted Lee to do likewise. He closed with personal expressions of affection.

As Erasmus continued his campaign against Lee, More wrote him, too—a short note in April 1520, while More's fierce quarrel with Brixius was in full burn. Erasmus had urged moderation on both Brixius and More; now More had a chance to return the favor, and he did—surely with a certain irony. The quarrel between Lee and Erasmus was becoming a tragedy, he said. Nobody was persuading anyone; everyone was only agitating everyone else. More refused to be a judge; he wanted only peace. Erasmus had already rushed into print with the *Apology* against Lee. More said he wished the little book had been written with less bitterness. Erasmus should imitate Christ and exhibit "true Christian modesty." There was no better way to be like Christ than to return good words for bad and not only good words but good deeds. The imitation of Christ was at the heart of Erasmus's oft-proclaimed "philosophy of Christ," and More was gently giving his friend advice on how to follow his own teachings expressed in so many eloquent and popular books.

Lee and Erasmus patched together a truce in May, but it failed to hold, and before long Erasmus was writing vehemently against Lee again in public and in private. He could urge peace on More and Brixius because he thought they were both good and correctly educated men and that their foolish polemics over national honor had nothing to do with anything worthwhile. He viewed the quarrel between himself and Lee as a battle for the only important principle worth fighting for—good learning against bad. Erasmus had no profound sense of nationality, although in one of his nastier letters he did threaten Lee with the fierce wrath of his brothers, the savage Germans. (The Dutch were then considered Germans.) When he was not making rhetorical menaces of his own, Erasmus had no sympathy for the pugnacious nationality of others.

But pugnacious nationality was to be the look of the future, overwhelming both the educated and the uneducated of Europe. Thomas More—who would die for the old, international church—was throughout his life a loud voice in England for the national spirit that would wrench his land away from the common Christian communion of Europe, dividing Europeans into camps of pride and hatred that still endure.

Erasmus could scarcely see the import of these passionate nationalistic feelings. He thought that Lee exhibited simple arrogance and malice toward biblical study and classical wisdom, disciplines Erasmus believed were the hope for reform in the Christian world. Lee's knowledge of Greek made him a greater villain, for the ignorant obscurantists Erasmus had to battle continually could see in Lee a champion worthy of Erasmus himself. Erasmus responded by trying to demolish Lee's reputation since it was his reputation that made Lee so dangerous an enemy.

The strange new world of print played its role in the ferocity with which More and Brixius, Lee and Erasmus went at each other. The duplication of pages seemed to be a repetition of voices. All of them were men whose place in the world depended on reputation—not on aristocratic lineage or inherited wealth but on what other men thought of their talents and their characters. They probably saw their very existence threatened by the printed attacks of their adversaries. Neither More in his self-serving quarrel with Brixius, nor Erasmus in his equally self-serving battle with Lee, looks admirable, although they were both provoked by ungallant foes and all four of them lived in a tempestuous age that believed battles could be won by books and that foes might be smothered in pages.

It is worth noting, too, the role-playing that went on so often in print, a role-playing often at variance with what people were when their deeper fears and aspirations were touched. We have pointed out on several occasions More's desire to present a consistent image of himself to the public, an image that was in part good father, in part brilliant and humble writer, in part Christian stoic careless of the things of this world and diffident about his own place and reputation. Erasmus, too, had a dramatic mask to present to the world—the learned scholar, the wit, the devout imitator of Christ, the loyal and affectionate friend, the spokesman for reform, the voice for peace, the humble sufferer of many tribulations for the sake of the good he might do to Europe. Yet under pressure from those who refused to take them as they wanted themselves to be taken, More and Erasmus could fling down their masks and exhibit a primitive savagery that was the antithesis of everything they wanted others to believe about them.

The Greek New Testament served to release furies all over Europe. Erasmus evidently worried about its reception before he published it, but he just as evidently had no idea of how huge a controversy it would provoke, or how the intentions of many who used it would be so different from his own in editing it. This work, done in scholarly quiet (and in haste), provided a spark that ignited all the explosive tensions that had been accumulating for years and in the end became too much for the old order to contain.

17

LUTHER AND THE
PROTESTANT REFORMATION

IN LATE OCTOBER 1517, Martin Luther drew up ninety-five
theses or propositions for debate about the power of papal indulgences
to release souls from purgatory. Luther, like Erasmus, was an Augustinian
monk, but unlike Erasmus, he was darkly preoccupied with the salvation of his
soul and nearly crushed by the burden of his own sins. He was a professor of
theology at the obscure University of Wittenberg, founded only a few years
earlier by the Elector Frederick the Wise of Saxony in the ugly and remote
little town in east-central Germany that was the seat of his government.

We have several times had occasion to note similarities between More and
Luther. Both sprang from the same aspiring class; their fathers were city
dwellers with high ambitions for their brilliant sons, ambitions they hoped to
see fulfilled by putting those sons to the study of law. Luther gave up the law
and, much against his father's wishes, entered the monastery. More was powerfully drawn to a clerical career but decided to marry, and acquiesced to his
father's wishes and became a man of the law. Both More and Luther had
intense sexual drives that troubled their piety. Both felt their own sins as an
almost impossible weight of guilt, and both longed passionately for heaven and
feared the judgment of God.

In each of them burned an intensity that was often comic but could become
fury at the slightest provocation, and each did battle for principle against an
uncompromising and ruthless foe. Neither of them could believe that an
opponent was honest or free of malice; each assumed that enemies were

inspired by the most depraved wickedness. Each found it impossible to compromise doctrinal positions, and each disputed so passionately and at times so viciously for his own version of faith that in the cool detachment of our own religious nonchalance, we may wonder if each might have been driven by the horrifying suspicion that Christianity might be a myth.

The last point is an important one, usually evaded or simply denied by modern scholars who in a commendable desire to make distinctions between the mentalities of present and past argue that radical religious skepticism is a modern affliction and that atheists in the Renaissance were few or nonexistent. They see the Reformation of the sixteenth century as beginning in a reaction to the intolerable corruption of the Catholic Church, a reaction Luther shared with More and Erasmus and the great mass of Christian humanists.

But as we have said earlier in this book, corruption was probably no greater than it had ever been, and a good case can be made that the church in the fifteenth century was far purer and more lively than it had been a century before. The mind of Europe had changed, however, even if morals had remained nearly the same or had improved. Philosophers had discovered that the truths we learn by natural reason may not correspond to the truths revealed by God in the Bible and in the church's tradition. We have already noted Pietro Pomponazzi and his refusal to believe that natural reason could prove the immortality of the soul. In spite of this, he professed to believe in immortality, because the church taught it and he would believe the church regardless of what reason taught. But did he? The answer does not come easily. It does seem unlikely that the long-continued intense debate about the relation of reason and faith could have generated the energy it did if people had not supposed that reason might threaten faith.

Reason did pose a threat; that seems evident now. And More and others like him attempted to soften its impact by arguing always for the superiority of faith; even in Utopia philosophy held a distinctly subordinate place to religion. In Christian Europe, More held that God at times required His people to believe doctrines that contradicted reason, a kind of test to see if they were truly obedient to Him or not. So he himself accepted the primary philosophical thought that drove Pomponazzi—although he may never have heard of Pomponazzi himself—the opinion that reason and faith did not necessarily arrive at the same conclusion.

He also accepted the possibility of atheism. We have seen that in More's *Utopia* anyone participating in civic life had to profess belief in God—a requirement that would seem strange indeed if everyone believed in God spontaneously. The Utopians were also required to believe that God rewarded good deeds and punished evil in an afterlife—again a requirement that makes little sense if everyone took an afterlife for granted.

Luther's first great discovery was predestination, a doctrine he had taken from Augustine and Paul and one he had worked out for himself before he began the controversy over indulgences. The doctrine of predestination affirms that no matter how chaotic the world may seem, no matter how obscure and without purpose or how confusing an individual life may be, God is working out a plan that turns all the chaos into a grand design and fits the individual into a scheme of Providence where everything eventually works out as God planned it in the beginning. To our age with its romantic notions of fair play and freedom, predestination seems stern and gloomy and even reprehensible. But those who passionately embrace predestination are nearly always those overcome by the apparent meaninglessness of things and by the apparent inability of individuals to make a difference. To these bruised souls, predestination comes as sublime consolation, a liberation from the oppressive compulsion to succeed in or to be responsible for a world that moves in its own relentless way, beyond our control. "Whatever will be, will be," says a modern popular song, and the response of people to that lyrical sentiment is supposed to be relief. Were Luther alive, he would sing along, for such was his reaction to the doctrine he had formulated for himself as early as the summer of 1517. The doctrine of predestination does not tell us what our experience means, either in the happenings of daily life or in the greater vista of important events. But it does affirm that there is a meaning, that the world is not chaos, and that God has His own purposes that will eventually be victorious so that the night will shine as the day.

The doctrine defers the discovery of meaning and thereby announces that our reason is a frail tool since it cannot hope to penetrate to God's precise purposes in allowing this or that to happen. Predestination begins with experience, not with logic, and experience inevitably crushes the feeble shelters logic tries to build for freedom of the will.

But predestination was only Luther's first great principle; the second was justification by faith, a doctrine that he seems to have developed fully only in the refiner's fire of the enormous controversy stirred up by his theses against indulgences with their attack on the high-flown claims of the papacy to bind and to loose on earth and in the life to come. One may believe in predestination and believe that one is predestined to be damned, and indeed Luther held that we should be willing to resign ourselves to hell if such was the will of God. Yet such resignation was almost impossible for an intense spirit like himself, and he wrote that he had sometimes been tempted to hate God—sign enough that the benevolence of God if not His existence could be a lively question.

Justification by faith meant that the earnest seeker after salvation heard all the promises of Christ directed to him personally and trusted God as the loving father who would bring the believer safely home. It went beyond the teaching of general predestination to the confidence that the believer was among those predestined for salvation, and its power lay in the assurance it offered to scrupulous souls like Luther, haunted by their own unworthiness, desperately afraid of divine judgment, needing some word of affirmation to dissolve all the negation they felt in their own hearts.

The doctrine had several interrelated parts. One was the comfort of knowing that we do not relate to God through a rule book. God is not a great score-keeper, totaling up good and bad thoughts, good and bad deeds, doubts and affirmations, arriving at a final score that determines whether we win heaven or lose our souls. God comes to us already announcing that He has, through Christ, done all the necessary work in salvation, that He has redeemed us, and that our response should be an outpouring of grateful love that brings about a daily life spontaneously filled with devotion to God and doing good to all the world around. Justification by faith would relieve Christians of the compulsions of ritual piety and of the propensity to strike some bargain with God whereby one might win salvation in exchange for some action.

It also relieved some of the anxiety created by the standard Catholic teaching that one's future state depended on a constancy of daily effort beyond the power of most men and women. If a soul wavered on the deathbed and doubt stole into one's mind at the doorway to eternity, God might punish that doubt with purgatory or hell, regardless of whatever good deeds that person had done throughout life. Everything in a good life might be rendered nugatory by a bad end. Justification by faith took away that awesome responsibility and allowed Christians confidence beyond doubt, the assurance, even while doubting, that one's eternal fate was not affected by some intellectual or emotional inability to believe at every moment.

Handling doubt is a part of justification by faith sometimes not seen by those who interpret the doctrine only as liberation from what Luther (and Paul) called the "works of the law." Such doubt is twofold. First, there is doubt that we are indeed among the elect, that we have been justified. How can I know that I am among the elect, that I have not been damned by divine fiat from the foundation of the world? Luther's answer to this question seemed to be something like this: If I seek God and salvation with all my heart, that yearning is in itself proof enough that I am among the elect. The seeker oppressed by his sins will be the finder whose reward is guaranteed by his thirst for God. The damned have no such desire; they are satisfied with themselves and with the religion of outward forms and inner pride. Much of Luther's preaching through the years centered on this expression of comfort to those who feel uncomfortable in their faith. He never speaks as if one has an experience of justification and continues through life afterwards in unbroken peacefulness of soul. On the contrary, Luther's preaching reaffirms the need for justification by faith every day and does so because the Christian is continually yearning. We are always sinners; we are always justified. That was one of Luther's central paradoxes, and in the Christian life that paradox expressed itself through a continual proclamation that justification was indeed by faith.

But justification by faith was also a means of handling another doubt, if anything more serious than doubt about one's own salvation—namely, doubt about the validity of Christianity and the existence or nature of God Himself. A devout sixteenth-century man or woman must have been attacked by racking guilt in the wake of temptations to disbelieve in Christianity. The doctrine of justification by faith carried with it an assurance that God's grace could take care even of these doubts and that the Christian who wavered in his convictions was not by that wavering to be cast into hell. For that was another of the great paradoxes of the age—that those who disbelieved could seldom bring themselves to accept disbelief as a principle of life, that on the contrary they believed that disbelief might lead them to damnation, an ironic and eternal affirmation that the religion they had not been able intellectually to accept was in fact implacably true. There is a great deal of evidence that Luther fought this battle between belief and unbelief all his life and that Thomas More waged the same war. And it is possible to look at the entire sixteenth century as not merely a crisis over the means of interpreting the Christian religion but as a crisis of belief about that religion itself.

Luther hated the Jews. His modern apologists insist that his horrific attacks on the Jews late in his life were a consequence of old age, and they point to tracts he wrote earlier in which he extended his hand to the Jewish people. But when he was young he had expected the Jews to be converted; he never showed them any tolerance or approval if they intended to remain Jews. He would love them only if they accepted his gospel—which meant that they would cease being Jews. When he saw that they were not going to be converted, he turned on them with some of the most scurrilous works in the ugly tradition of Christian anti-Semitism.

The reason for this hatred is not difficult to find: the very existence of the Jews was a continuing testimony to Christians that the Christian religion was not the overpowering revelation they wanted to believe it was. Jews were able to live a religious life without demanding resurrection of the dead as a condition for their devotion. Surely Jewish vagueness or incredulity about a life after death must have presented Christian thinkers with an alternative that they had to take seriously. And it might be argued that the great waves of Jewish persecution throughout the Middle Ages came at just those moments when Christians were seeking some powerful affirmation of their own faith against great surges of doubt. It appears that one of these climaxes of belief occurred in the Renaissance, culminating in the Protestant Reformation of the sixteenth century.

Why such a climax should have taken place early in the sixteenth century is a question no one can answer completely. If corruption itself was no greater than it had ever been, the attention paid to it *was* much greater since the

printing press had made criticism of corruption popular. The occasional feverish outbreaks of violent religious enthusiasm like that associated with
Savonarola in Florence in the 1490s gave wide popular credence to the fearsome view that unless the church reformed, Antichrist would arrive to blud-
geon the world for its sins before God appeared in the thunderous judgment
of doomsday. More and Luther were both apocalyptic souls; they did not think
the day of reckoning could be far away.

The general uncertainty and pessimism of the fifteenth century made it
seem that some sort of great turning point lay hidden in the dark clouds on
the world's horizons. *Utopia* was finally a pessimistic book; readers perusing the
account of the marvelously ordered and rational society described by Hythlodaye could not imagine that anything like it could ever come to Europe.
More's final comment, that it was better to hope for such things than to expect
them, put the seal on the resignation the book was bound to call forth. In 1517,
Erasmus wrote his friend Wolfgang Capito that he supposed the world was
entering a new kind of golden age. He may have momentarily believed what
he said, though he was quickly disabused of such optimism. More never made
such a happy prediction. And the mood of both Erasmus and More was to
criticize existing society rather than to praise it.

When Luther came striding onto the European stage, most Christians in
the audience believed that he was playing an old part—the doomsday prophet
calling for a renewal of piety, denouncing the clergy for their sins. Luther was
deeply sincere, and he drew fascinated attention because he played the part
so well. He was probably the most brilliant wordsmith European civilization
produced between Dante and Shakespeare, and a few might name him the
superior of both the others. Neither More nor Erasmus ever wrote a line that
many people quoted, but when Luther spoke, people all over Europe repeated
what he said.

His learning was prodigious, his wit savage and hilarious, his powers of
expression stupendous, his brilliant mind fired by a furious energy, his warped,
narcissistic character cursed by contradictions worthy of the Mephistopheles
of Marlowe, with arrogance and despair locked inseparably and fatally together.
He spoke, and Christians waked up to a new voice crying like John the Baptist
to a slothful church. Still no one had any notion that he would change things
as much as he did.

In March 1518, Erasmus sent More a copy of Luther's *Ninety-five Theses*.
The little work was accompanied by a bantering letter filled with anti-papal
sentiments and sardonic complaints. The pope and some princes, Erasmus
wrote, were preaching a new crusade against the Turks. All husbands younger
than fifty and older than twenty-six were being summoned to battle; their wives
were ordered by the pope not to fall into unchastity during the absence of their
men. If business kept husbands at home, their wives were to act exactly like

those wives whose husbands went on crusade. Husband and wife were to sleep in the same bedroom but in different beds. They were not even to exchange a kiss until this terrible war for the sake of Christ was honorably and happily concluded. Many wives would have a hard time living up to such demands, Erasmus said. But he professed confidence that More's wife, because of her prudence and piety, would obey them to the letter. He added with tongue in cheek, "They write me from Cologne of some book just issued from the press concerning Julius disputing with Peter at the gates of paradise. They do not ascribe any name to the author."

The friendship between More and Erasmus was at its height. The letter presupposes conversations in which the two friends had both lamented and joked about the moral plight of a papacy to which neither felt large devotion. So there is every reason to think that Erasmus expected More to enjoy the *Ninety-five Theses*. And there is every reason to suppose that More did exactly that.

As the forces Luther had unleashed grew stronger, the distinctions among More, Erasmus, and Luther became manifest, but in the beginning no one could see clearly what was happening. Luther tapped a furnace of incandescent German nationalism, and in the exuberant enthusiasm gushing out for his cause throughout the German lands, many were blinded as to the essence of the cause itself. Luther and Erasmus corresponded. Erasmus wrote him on May 30, 1519, claiming ignorance of Luther's books, neither approving them nor disapproving them, and saying, "You have many in England who think the best of your writing, and among them are some great men."

Was Thomas More one of those great men who thought the best of Luther? The supposition is likely. More would have appreciated Luther's fire and wit as well as the attack on the crude, mercenary side of the indulgence traffic. As his "Letter to a Monk" written in 1519 shows, he saw Luther then not as a hateful heretic but only as an extreme Augustinian. In 1520 when he wrote Edward Lee defending the Erasmian Greek New Testament, More commented that those attacking the work, which was approved by the pope, disparaged the papacy and that, compared with them, Luther himself seemed devoted to the "sacrosanct Roman See." There is no heat about Luther in the letter. It looks as if in 1520 More still saw the German as only another critic of ecclesiastical corruption, not as a heretic.

On October 19, 1519, Erasmus wrote a long letter to Albrecht, archbishop of Mainz, about Luther. He was much harder on the theologians attacking Luther than he was on Luther himself. He expressed dismay over Luther's increasingly vehement tone but not over anything particular he had said. Indeed he declared that Luther had much right on his side. Luther had dared to doubt indulgences after others had exaggerated their value. He dared to deprecate the power of the pope after others had exalted that power too much.

He dared to question the pronouncements of Aquinas, but some preachers preferred Thomas to the gospels. Luther dared to reinterpret the sacrament of confession, but the monks extended confession without limit to trap the consciences of men. (Erasmus meant that friars and monks made trivial rules, then made Christians feel guilty for breaking them and hauled them into the confessional to fleece them with unjust fines disguised as penance.) In short, Luther wrote much more imprudently than he did impiously, and people were always around to shout "Heresy!" when there was no heresy, people ready to intimidate bishops or even the pope.

Erasmus—and More, too, at this time—probably saw Luther as another John Reuchlin, the great German scholar who, a few years earlier, had come under prolonged attack for his belief that the Hebrew language and Jewish literature offered a way into the mysteries of God. Reuchlin's foes opposed almost the entire humanist enterprise with its stress on Greek and Hebrew and its love of classical learning. Some of Luther's foes had been Reuchlin's, and Erasmus seemed to think that if these people won their battle against Luther, they might be emboldened to turn on him. Yet Erasmus did not want to mix his cause with Luther's. He did not want to be distracted from his own work, and he did not share Luther's vehement temper, at least not in the scholarly image Erasmus put before the world.

Although Erasmus was to become thoroughly exasperated with Luther, he was never to change the fundamental convictions expressed in his letter to Albrecht of Mainz. Luther would always be for him only one of the miseries of the church; Christians could not afford to devote all their energies to the battle against Luther, leaving ignorant monks and impious theologians unmolested and uncontrolled.

Thomas More, however, was soon to see Luther as a mortal threat to the church and perhaps as a threat to meaning in the universe. If he had not veered away from Luther already, his first reading of Luther's *Babylonian Captivity of the Church* was enough to drive him into fierce and uncompromising enmity toward the German reformer—now clearly in More's mind a heretic.

Luther wrote *The Babylonian Captivity* in Latin during the summer of 1520. Here he leveled a ferocious attack on the ancient sacramental system of the Catholic Church. Luther said that to be valid a sacrament must have been instituted by Christ himself and that it had to have a clear text of institution in the scriptures. He eliminated the sacramental status of extreme unction, marriage, confirmation, and ordination. He declared that only baptism, the mass, and penance could be called sacraments, and penance he interpreted as merely a confession of sin that any Christian could make to any other Christian, ending the mediating power of the priesthood, which More revered. In previous works Luther had claimed that all believers were priests and that no special order of priesthood should be kept in the church.

In the *Babylonica,* as it came to be called in England, Luther spoke out vehemently against the doctrine of transubstantiation—the belief that during the consecration of the eucharist, the bread and the wine were literally changed to the body and blood of Christ, so that nothing was left of the bread and wine except the miraculous illusion that they were unchanged. Here was the center-piece of Catholic ritual, a daily testimony given for centuries that God the Creator had not abandoned the physical world but regularly visited it, despite its corruptions, and made His presence known through sensual experience. All the sacraments, but especially the mass, helped preserve the Catholic Church from the ever-present temptation to fall into a body-soul dualism that would make the physical world of no account and turn salvation into an effort to escape the body at all costs, a view that would have rendered impossible any Christian attempt to make this world a better place.

The mass was also the centerpiece of Thomas More's own piety. He eventu-ally defended the veneration of images, the use of pilgrimages and relics, and the practice of prayer to the saints as well as other manifestations of popular piety, but there is no evidence that they were important to his own daily devotions or to his religious life. The mass was something else. Reverence for the mass permeates his own works and most of the testimony we have about him from his own century.

On the surface, the *Babylonica* is an assault on the sacramental understand-ing of the church, the notion that God always presents Himself both visibly and invisibly at once and that Christians by grasping the palpable can also somehow appropriate the invisible essence of God hidden in the visible thing. The devout could receive communion and share the spiritual power of God hidden in the physical elements; no one quite understood how this sharing was possible, especially in a corrupt world where physical things had become tools in the claws of Satan to push souls into everlasting perdition. But generations of pious and trusting men and women had experienced their private miracles in this ancient and public ceremony, and now Luther was saying that without the faith of the communicant, God was not in the sacraments at all, making it seem that they rested on some fallible human conviction rather than the promises and power of God.

There was also a more profound and troubling attack here, an assault on the confidence Catholics had in the sacred character of history. We have several times called attention to the essential importance of the Catholic belief that God's spirit animated the institution that Christ had established; the Catholic Church was a continuing incarnation, God's body in a world of sin and ignorance. Anything done for centuries in the church must have had God's approval or else God would have changed it. The church itself was a kind of grand sacrament, endowed with outward and visible forms, enlivened by the

Holy Spirit so that, as the mind moves the hands, God moved the church in everything it did.

Luther wanted personal salvation and with it a personal assurance that God lived in the world, which he thought could be achieved only through a starkly private connection between God and the individual Christian. He loved to make pronouncements such as his view that were Peter the apostle here among us, we would not know whether he was redeemed or not. In one sense he was uttering a theological commonplace, since any Catholic would believe that hypocrisy was always possible and that the person we take to be devout may in God's eyes be depraved. But the Catholic Church believed that consensus could reveal which of the dead were saints and which were not, and the sense of this faith was that the relations between God and the individual were never so hidden and private that the community lost all possibility of sound judgment about the state of a soul in its midst. The general Catholic sensibility was always to make salvation a communal affair in that the community existed before the individual soul in time, around it in life, and after it in death, and that the participation of the community in the drama of redemption helped decide how the individual soul would fare in time and eternity.

For Luther the world was so dark with mystery and the Catholic Church so corrupt that beyond the confines of Wittenberg, whence he seldom strayed after he became notorious as a heretic, no one could be sure of the salvation of anyone, no matter how great that person's piety or how renowned his reputation. Predestination taught him that everything had its purpose, but that purpose was hidden from humankind, and he could not understand why God had allowed the papacy, the Antichrist, to take charge of a church supposed to be holy. Luther's world swarmed with demons and witches, and in all this darkness the individual tended to be left alone with his faith in God.

Luther was not as radical as many who came after him, but still he had the heart of a revolutionary, willing to sweep away with a stroke the elaborate devices and patterns of compromise that had evolved through centuries of Catholic tradition, joining together disparate multitudes in a common community and allowing them varieties of religious expression under a common authority. Thomas More revered the church and its unbroken communion from the time of Christ, and found in his devotion to its ancient traditions his own peace with God and his hope for heaven. These traditions attained such a noble place in his own mind because of the testimony of a community beyond numbering, a community that had hoped and prayed and endured.

Erasmus never understood Luther's thirst for salvation, and he hated the passions that Luther's reformation vented in Europe. For him the Lutheran affair was not—as it was to More—primarily a menace to the eternal salvation of the souls of Christians; Luther's movement and the turmoil aroused by it were rather a danger to good letters, a point he makes again and again.

Erasmus was deeply offended and perhaps frightened by the accusation flung at him by many of his enemies that he had been the real cause of the Lutheran mess. He rebutted this charge again and again by dwelling on the ignorance and malice of those who made it. But he never tried to defend, as More did, all the practices in the church that Luther attacked. On August 31, 1523, Erasmus wrote Ulrich Zwingli, the reformer of Zurich, and made a startling admission: "For I think that I have taught everything that Luther teaches but not so atrociously since I abstained from certain enigmas and paradoxes so that I might choose more fruit to grow out at last." The statement may show how little Erasmus truly understood Luther, but even so, Thomas More would have been stunned to see it. (He did not see it, because the letter was not published.)

In the fall of 1520, Erasmus wrote a long letter to More about his tribulations at the hands of a preacher in Louvain named Nicholas Egmondanus. The next year he published it in his collection called *Epistolae ad diversos,* intended once again to remind the world of his wide acquaintance with distinguished men. So the letter to More was in fact a tract for the times. More had heard that Erasmus and Egmondanus had had an interview with the rector of the University of Louvain, Godescalc Rosemondt, and he had written Erasmus for information about the meeting. More's letter is lost. We cannot therefore know the spirit in which he wrote, but we have the long and self-serving account of the interview that Erasmus produced for More and Europe at large.

Egmondanus had preached sermons claiming that Erasmus changed shape according to circumstances, accusing him of duplicity, of twisting everything by the tail. He demanded that Erasmus write against Luther. Erasmus played verbal games and evaded the question, saying he was not fitted for controversy and that besides he had better things to do.

Erasmus wrote mocking Egmondanus, making out that the man was a fool. Ten years earlier, a letter from Erasmus about an ignorant preacher who accused him of duplicity might have provoked a smile from More. But More would have received this letter at about the same time that he read Luther's *Babylonian Captivity* with its thundering attack on the Catholic understanding of the sacraments and the sacredness of tradition. And he must have echoed the question Egmondanus posed so vociferously: Why did not Erasmus write against Luther when Luther so clearly represented a mortal danger to the church?

In the summer of 1521 when More went with Wolsey on a diplomatic mission to the Continent, Erasmus was at Bruges with the court of Emperor Charles V. There the English delegation came, and Erasmus wrote later on that he had seen not only More but Tunstall, Wolsey, and his former patron, William Mountjoy.

Apparently the visit between More and Erasmus was cordial. It was the summer of Buckingham's execution and of the murmuring in London against the king's justice that had brought the popular duke to the block, murmuring that (as we have seen) More was required to investigate and rebuke. After such tensions More must have found relief in his diplomatic journey to Flanders. And there was a comic interlude which he and Erasmus must have enjoyed.

At Bruges he had with him a servant, a German he calls only "Davy." David had lived for a while in England and had married an English woman. He claimed that his wife had died at Worcester while he had been on a trip to Germany, and to More he had often lamented her death, praising her virtues and telling of praying bitterly over her grave. Working with remarkable haste, he managed within two weeks of his arrival in Bruges to become engaged to an "honest widow's daughter." But on the very day that they were to be married, More received a letter from Dame Alice announcing that Davy's English wife was still alive and that she had come to the More house looking for her husband.

On hearing the letter read to him, Davy did his best to affect surprise and delight, for, as he said, "she is a good woman."

More said, "Yea, but why art thou such a naughty, wretched man, that thou wouldst here wed another? Didst not thou say she was dead?"

"Yea marry," said he. "Men of Worcester told me so."

"Why, you false beast," said More, "didst not thou tell me and all my house that thou were at her grave thyself?"

"Yea marry, master," said he. "So I was, but I could not look in, ye know well."

The episode with Davy must have been enough to fuel some good talks between More and Erasmus, and naturally they would have talked of other things as well, especially of Martin Luther. The imperial party had just come from the Diet of Worms, where Luther had appeared in April, where he had refused to recant his heresies, and where he had been pronounced a heretic by the emperor himself. Luther was in hiding, an outlaw of the Empire, rumored to be dead.

It may have seemed in this August of 1521 that the entire Lutheran madness had dissolved like storm clouds on a summer's day; then the supposition that Erasmus should write against Luther would have seemed vain.

In that moment, political affairs would have appeared much more important, and even these seemed under control. More and Erasmus would have parted in good spirits and in friendship. They never saw each other again.

18

THOMAS MORE, THEOLOGICAL COUNCILLOR

HENRY VIII may have been outraged at the publication of Luther's *Babylonian Captivity* in the summer of 1520, but he also saw an opportunity. He had long sought some special religious title from the pope, something equal to the "Most Christian King" awarded the king of France or to the "Catholico" bestowed by the pope on the king of Spain. Henry had no such title, and when he asked for one, pope and cardinals hesitated. But in the winter and spring of 1520–21, Henry wrote the *Assertion of the Seven Sacraments,* part of a general campaign against Luther's heresies, one that included the formal burning of Luther's books. In the fall of 1521, after Henry had sent a beautiful presentation copy to Pope Leo X, the papal consistory granted him his wish; he became "Defender of the Faith," a title that neither he nor his Protestant heirs have ever relinquished.

Nearly everyone who mentions the *Assertio* (a scholarly work, it was written in Latin) passes over it with a few platitudes, for almost no one has read it. It is said to have extolled the power of the pope, and modern scholars assume that it would have pleased the most ardent papalist in the Catholic Church. But this is not so.

Henry called the pope the Vicar of Christ. He praised Pope Leo X for his innocent life and begged the pope to correct anything in the *Assertio* that might be in error. He condemned Luther for attacking the pope in public. Luther, by withdrawing from the papal communion, had broken the commands of both love and obedience, for, Henry said, all the church recognized the Roman see as mother and primate. He argued that popes did indeed have power over purgatory—the issue that was central to Luther's theses against indulgences.

On the surface we have a lot of strong-sounding talk about papal power, but when we look closer at the *Assertio*, we find a haze of ambiguity that makes Henry's exact thoughts on the subject difficult to know. Important questions are not posed. How far does papal power extend? Can the pope err in doctrine? Is a pope supreme over a general council? Can a pope be deposed for any reason but heresy?

And how far should popes be obeyed? Should kings obey them in temporal matters? Certainly not, we can say with some assurance. England had already been called an empire in Thomas Malory's *Le Morte d'Arthur,* published by Caxton within a decade of More's birth. Empires did not take orders from any power on earth beyond themselves, not even from the pope. In the Hunne affair, the English government had ignored papal claims for clerical immunity from secular jurisdiction. And in Roper's story about the pope's great ship seized by the English at Southampton, we have Henry's government treating papal commerce as if it had been the commerce of a secular state.

What about the pope's spiritual role in defining Christian doctrine? Henry made some vague gestures in this direction, quoting Jerome, who said that even if his faith were not approved by others, it was enough for him to have it approved by the bishop of Rome. Henry did not make a clearer statement and seemed almost to evade the issue. "I shall not wrong the pope," he said, "by anxiously and carefully sitting as judge on his law as if it were a dubious thing."

Hundreds of tracts and books by theologians great and small that defended the power of the pope against Luther spewed from the presses of Catholic Europe in these years. Now they lie dusty and unread in the old libraries of Europe and America. It is rare to find among them an argument for papal power as mild and as ambiguous as the one Henry makes in his *Assertio.* If we look through the dull, heavy tomes of Bishop John Fisher of Rochester, we find thumping and unequivocal support for an extreme papalism, a support much stronger than anything Henry ever gave. Fisher believed that the pope had a unique role in defining doctrine, and he would have agreed heartily with the decree of the First Vatican Council in 1870 that when a pope speaks on faith and morals *ex cathedra,* his pronouncements are infallible.

So, though others eagerly asserted the pope's doctrinal role, Henry did not. Since the conversion of the world to Christianity, Henry says, all the churches among Christians have been obedient to the see of Rome. That vague statement is as far as the king goes. And even the power granted to Peter to bind and loose on earth and in heaven, the primary text of papal power, Henry interprets to mean that since any priest has the power to absolve men from their sins and free them from eternal punishment, surely the "prince of all priests" must have power over purgatory. It is a very unclear statement. Henry appears to have supposed that custom and tradition made essential doctrines clear to all Christians; the pope merely presided over that which was known to all, in much the way (to use a modern analogy) that Americans expect their President to guard a tradition held in common by all the people without imagining that that tradition is made or defined by the President alone. Such democratic views of papal authority abounded at the time among moderate Catholics. Erasmus held them; so did Thomas More. So, it seems, did Henry VIII.

Later, when he was fighting for his life, Thomas More recalled the *Assertio*, writing Thomas Cromwell in 1534 that when Henry was composing the book, the king wanted to assert the papal power vigorously. More advised caution, saying that kings and popes often fell into dispute and that if the king made too much of papal power in the *Assertio*, he might be embarrassed by his own words later on when some quarrel arose between Henry and some pope. But Henry, said More, "showed me a secret cause whereof I never had anything heard before." More does not say what this cause was, at least not to Cromwell. Roper tells us that Henry declared that it was from the pope that he had received his "crown imperial," but we do not know what this cryptic remark might mean. Perhaps Henry referred to papal recognition of the Tudor house on the morrow of Bosworth Field. The important thing is that More's statement to Cromwell has led modern scholars to agree that More lost his argument to persuade the king to mitigate his assertion of papal power.

In fact, the text of the *Assertio* itself proves that More won his point. Papal power is treated at length only in the matter of indulgences. The cloud of praises for Leo's person and the vitriolic denunciations of Luther's public disobedience obscure Henry's lack of precision in defining papal primacy. Any conciliar thinker, member of the diffuse party that believed in constitutional control of the papacy through regular meetings of a sovereign general council of bishops, could have read the *Assertio* with approval. Nothing in the work suggests that the pope is anything but the servant of the whole church; nothing grants him the sovereignty that popes were claiming for themselves and that their defenders against Luther were now claiming for them throughout Catholic Europe.

Other things in the *Assertio* are commonplaces that More himself would take up when he entered the literary battle against heresy. Of course he affirmed the sacred quality of tradition. The Catholic Church was founded by Christ, and Christ promised to be with the church until the end of time. The church could therefore not err in significant matters, for if it erred, Christ had broken his promise, and such a breach of faith could not be if God were God and Christ were His son.

How did Christians reconcile church practices not expressly sanctioned by scripture? Henry—and More after him—fell back on the old notion of an oral tradition, a theological truism among Catholics. The last verse of the Fourth Gospel declares that Christ did so many things that the world could not contain the books that might be written about them. The Aristotelian Middle Ages had the idea of a divine economy; nothing worthwhile could be lost. For centuries Catholics had assumed that everything Christ had said and done was preserved in the tradition of the church, even if it had not been written down while Christ was on earth. Henry declared in the *Assertio* that even the gestures used by priests in the mass had been taught by Christ and handed on through the centuries, and Thomas More was to repeat this fine bit of nonsense.

As we might expect from the title, Henry defended the divine institution of all the sacraments in the form that Catholics practiced them in the sixteenth century. He damned Luther for saying that faith alone could justify the Christian, and he denounced with special vehemence Luther's assertion in the *Babylonica* that no sin but unbelief could damn a soul. Henry took Luther to be saying that Christians might safely kill, steal, fornicate, and blaspheme and still reach heaven so long as they accepted the truth of the creeds of the church.

Henry imagined that Luther was defining faith as mere intellectual assent, in the way that I might be said to have a certain "faith" if I believe that Harvard College was founded by Puritans who wanted to train ministers of the gospel. I can believe this historical account without remotely being a Puritan myself. Henry thought—or said he thought—that Luther was teaching that anyone could believe in the fact of Christ and live like the devil and still be saved.

In all this, the *Assertio* was an occasion for royal mudslinging while Henry himself stood firmly on the ground of Catholic convention. He appears to have understood nothing whatsoever of the immense spiritual power in Luther's words or of the thrilling liberation thousands felt in reading them. But the *Assertio* was hardly written in a spirit of disinterested benevolence.

Thomas More quoted Henry's book again and again in his own polemical career, using the king's arguments when he did not use the king's words, though with a vehemence that is absent in the *Assertio*. Did More write the book? Though Luther heard rumors that Henry had not written it himself, More said later on that he had been only a redactor of the work, sorting things out and arranging parts. Certainly the Latin style is not his.

But we have good reason to suppose that More's counsel was important as the writing went along. Henry took several months to put it together. Since he never in his life otherwise showed the slightest talent for writing extended prose, we may assume that the book was done in committee. More was the only person of theological competence to have been with the king every day, and he was astute enough to frame arguments carefully and to allow Henry to believe that they sprang full-grown from the royal brain. He would not have been the first councillor to put his thoughts into a public document published in a ruler's name; in the quotations More later made from the book we probably have the key to those parts that originally involved him most.

Luther was not dead as the rumors had had it. He read the *Assertio* in the spring of 1522 at a time of extreme danger for himself and his movement. He had expected kings to rally to his cause; they had instead rejected him, and Henry's book probably seemed a culmination of disaster. Luther must have feared that his reformation would be doomed if other rulers, including the German princes, followed the lead of the English king. So he replied with all his vehemence. It is unlikely that any tract addressed to any king in Christian Europe had ever been as insulting, as vitriolic, as obscene as Luther's little book entitled *Against Henry, King of the English.*

Someone had to reply for the king, since Henry could not write an answer himself; to do so would have been to descend from the throne into the mire of controversy in a fashion unbecoming to a king. More had proved himself a spirited controversialist in his battle with Brixius and in his "Letter to a Monk," which had been published by Erasmus. Of greater importance would have been his close association with the king's book. If Henry recognized More as his chief theological councillor, More would have been the natural choice to defend the work on which he had expended so much effort. He was also the only person at court recognized as a popular writer in Latin. His *Utopia* had not made him famous, but it had been a modest success, and a king searching for a literary champion would spontaneously turn to a councillor with a literary reputation. For his part More would have taken up the task out of a passionate desire to defend the Catholic Church and perhaps out of a desire also to defend the arguments he had contributed to the *Assertio.* If he had been heavily involved in framing the king's book, Luther's virulent counter-attack would have struck him with a force like that of Brixius's *Antimorus,* driving More to protect his own creation.

He called his reply the *Responsio ad Lutherum,* the *Response Against Luther,* and he wrote under a pseudonym. In fact, the *Responsio* came out in two versions with two pseudonyms. A shorter volume came out first, supposedly written by a Spanish theologian named "Ferdinand Baravellus." Before this work could be released, More read Luther's angry attack on Ambrose Catharinus, a Catholic theologian who happened to be the source of the proverbial saying that the Reformation came because Erasmus planted, Luther watered, and Satan gave the increase—a parody of I Corinthians 3:6. (The epigram infuriated Erasmus, but More took no part in that quarrel.)

Catharinus had defended the Catholic Church as a hierarchical institution with the pope at the top and the bishops carrying authority into all the inhabited world. In *Utopia* More had portrayed a growing Christian community existing without hierarchy, indeed without much institutional form at all, since not only bishops but ordinary priests were absent. It would be unwise to make sweeping inferences from the skimpy treatment More gives the new Utopian Christians, but we may suppose that a man in 1515 and 1516 discouraged with the lack of learning and the corruption in high places in the church might have let himself dream awhile of a spontaneous Christian religion, arising out of a love for God through Christ and free of many of those exterior forms and institutional offices that so often harmed the church in Europe. But having read Luther and having digested the exchange between Luther and Catharinus, More saw anew the place for institutional authority in the Catholic Church and added a large section on that subject to his *Responsio*. The revised work appeared in July 1523 under a new pseudonym, that of "William Ross." Now there could be no doubt that the writer was English and that there were other defenders of the faith in England besides the king. We do not know why More used a pseudonym at all, although it may have been to avoid public association with a work of such vitriol so soon after his public fury against Brixius. The *Responsio* was so virulent that Erasmus said it could teach Luther himself something about vehemence.

Another possibility is also intriguing. Perhaps More did not want to associate his name with the defense of the *Assertio* because he feared some might leap to the conclusion that he had written the *Assertio* himself. If he had contributed a great deal to the king's book, he would have been sensitive to the fear that the news might get out. As it was, no one thought of him as a theologian because he had published nothing theological at the time the *Assertio* appeared. Henry's secret would have been safe both on account of More's circumspection and because the European public at large had no reason to suspect More's help. The pseudonymous *Responsio* would have then been a means of curtailing the suspicion that would have been rife had More published under his own name.

What we see at a glance in the *Responsio* is an almost unbearable hatred of Martin Luther and of anything else that might threaten the authority of the Catholic Church. Rage may lead to art, as in the *Modest Proposal* of Jonathan Swift; it led More only to crude vituperation that at times is almost hysterical. Punning on the rhetorical and logical distinctions between prior premise and posterior argument, he wrote of Luther: "Since he has written that he already has a prior right to bespatter and besmirch the royal crown with shit, will we not have the posterior right to proclaim the beshitted tongue of this practitioner of posterioristics most fit to lick with his anterior the very posterior of a pissing she-mule until he shall have learned more correctly to infer posterior conclusions from prior premises." That is one of the milder parts of this tedious work.

More calls Luther insane, a drunkard, vainglorious, and self-contradictory.

We need not go on, for More's plodding insults and witless vulgarity offer only a monotonous scatology as wearing as the talk of small boys in school wash-rooms. He expected his Utopians to rush into outrageous passion the moment they were allowed the dangerous freedom of an unsupervised private life; given the privacy afforded by his pseudonym, Thomas More did exactly what he anticipated of his fictional creations.

The method of the work is almost as bad as its spirit. More proceeded by quoting a few lines of Luther's book against the king, refuting them at length —often at very great length—quoting Luther again and refuting him again for page after dreary page. As has been mentioned, he often quoted Henry's *Assertio* to prove that the king had successfully shown Luther wrong on this point or that. It is the work of an orator (and More was much better known as an orator in his own day than he was as a writer), an orator imagining that he is speaking rather than writing, measuring the response of the crowd to every line, never thinking of the weariness of a reader confronted by a long, repetitive book.

More believed that anyone who saw Luther's text could see at once that it was wrong. But should readers not get the point, there was More's long refutation to help them see how Luther had erred. We may surmise that people who wanted to know what Luther was saying now had a text that would not endanger them if the authorities found it in their possession; they could read Luther without having to pay attention to More's comments at all, since Luther's words were set off from More's in block type.

Fundamental to More's argument was the authority of the church based on Christ's foundation and promise. Christ had established a church, a church embodied in a continuing institution that endured through history; he had not written a book. He had promised to be with his disciples to the end of the world, and he promised to send them the spirit of truth to lead them into a revelation of perfect Truth. By these promises, the universal church possessed the active spirit of God, and it could not err once it had a chance to test error.

Luther spoke in these years of an "invisible church," a church beyond and above the hierarchical, institutional church that Henry and now More defended. Luther believed that the true church, the true people of God, consisted of only the elect, the predestined to salvation. No one but God could know who was predestined and who was not. So to mortals living in the world of sense experience, the church was invisible. The notion fitted perfectly into Luther's terrific sense of paradox (akin to More's sense of irony). He was absorbed by how contradictory common experience—which he saw permeated with mystery—was to the belief that an almighty God ruled the universe and directed it to a good end.

In Luther's view, God did everything, but God wore many masks, and all things divine were dark to human sight except when God chose to give light through revelation. The pope who claims to speak for God really speaks for Satan; the sinner tormented by the fear of God is actually beloved by God. The nominal Christian who works hard at doing good is damned for the pride that makes him imagine he can earn salvation. The visible institution called the church, spread across Europe in the form of bishops, priests, monks, nuns, friars, buildings, rituals, traditions, and all the rest, claims to be the church of God, but it is really the congregation of Antichrist with the pope as almost the incarnation of Satan. The true church of the redeemed is hidden, to be known to all mortals only on the great day of doom.

In the *Responsio* More sees the church on earth as an institution that is a divinely inspired teacher, preserving true doctrine, certifying it, clarifying it, presenting mortals with a decision to make about what to do concerning the church's truth. Unless the church's doctrine was true, no one could know how to get to heaven. God had promised the gift of truth to the church, and He had promised that the church should endure until doomsday. Only one church had existed during all the centuries since that promise had been given. If the Catholic Church with all its institutions was not the church of the promise, the promise itself was bad and God was a liar. Luther's invisible church could not teach anything because no one could see it; only an institution, animated with the spirit of God but visible to the world, could carry out the divine mission set for the people of God.

Luther claimed to get his doctrine from scripture alone. More knew great chunks of the Bible from memory, but we have already noted how in his "Letter to a Monk" he thought the Bible must be joined to the tradition of the church if it was to serve Christians. He was never one to imagine that Christians, whether educated or uneducated, could get all necessary doctrine exclusively from the Bible. His Utopians managed to absorb Christianity without any scripture at all—now he could not tolerate Luther's teaching that the Bible was sufficient in itself to inform Christians what they should do and believe.

More pounced on Luther's advocacy of scripture alone and made several points. How did anyone know what was scripture and what was not? Luther said in his *Babylonica* that the church discerns the word of God from the word of men, apparently supposing that the predestined who made up his church had a divine gift that enabled them to know what was revelation and what was not. More repeated Luther's statement again and again, taking it as an admission that the Catholic Church had to certify scripture before anyone—including Luther—could know what was scripture. It was a strange perversion of Luther's meaning given More's unabating attack on Luther's interpretation of the word "church," but More chose to assert that by "church" Luther here meant the same Catholic Church that More was defending. Henry had made the same charge in the *Assertio*—probably because More had urged it on him.

For the rest of his polemical career, More berated Luther with this statement that the church discerned the true scripture from the false—not understanding or not caring that Luther had never meant it in the way More professedly took it.

Despite More's unfair use of Luther's statement, More's argument was a good one. Christ had not written a book; the canon of scripture developed over centuries. Books like Hebrews, II Peter, II Thessalonians, and the Gospel of John were quite late in being accepted as canonical, and the book of Revelation always occupied a precarious place. No one could make sense of it, though zealots appeared again and again to spread the intoxication of its prodigious fantasies. In the sixteenth century, the most ardent biblicists among the Protestants—including Luther and John Calvin—left it alone, as Erasmus had done in his notes to the *Novum Instrumentum*. More's point—a conventional one in Catholic thought—was that the church certified scripture and that to bring down the church was to bring down scripture itself.

He followed the logic of his own argument without hesitation and here sounds very different from the Thomas More who wrote the letter to Dorp in defense of the Greek New Testament of Erasmus. The church did not need scripture, for scripture was only a book, a lifeless thing, and the truth of God was living and active. The old law had been written on stones and on the dead skins of beasts; Christ had written his law in the hearts of the faithful, and as the faithful lived together in communion with God, the law of God—the revelation He intended for the world—lived through them. The church lived by the Spirit, and More—aware of the many errors copyists had made in transmitting scripture—would express with increasing vehemence his conviction that the church would endure even if scripture vanished utterly away.

Above all, he would turn again and again to the lack at clarity in scripture and the need for an authoritative interpretation. In More's view, all the heretics of history had depended on the Bible, but a Bible interpreted by their eccentric and perverted minds. The Arians, denying that God and Christ were equal and coeternal, took proof texts from scripture, and without an authoritative church to certify what reading was correct, who was to say that the Arians were wrong? The More who in the *Responsio* denigrates scripture in favor of church tradition is closely akin to the More who did not include a Bible in the literary baggage of Raphael Hythlodaye on that intrepid traveler's visit to Utopia—so much so that the More who supported so strongly and so vaguely the Greek New Testament of Erasmus against Dorp and a monk seems almost an aberration. But Luther's arguments had raised the specter of doubt throughout Europe, and a fearful More was now defending something that was to him infinitely greater than a scholarly book; he was defending the Catholic Church, the last bastion of meaning in time and eternity.

Just where was authority in the church? More always spoke of "common consent." He meant much the same thing that lawyers did when they spoke of precedent and the priestly nature of their discipline. He meant custom, a collection of habits agreed on by multitudes, which by long enduring had achieved authority and even divine sanction. Like Henry before him, More located the inspiration of custom in an oral tradition. Christ had spoken and done far more things than had been written down. The oral tradition about those words and deeds remained in the church, handed down from century to century, engendering customs that had authority merely because they were agreed upon. The authority of this oral tradition was best proved by its superiority over much that was written in scripture, and More delighted in making long lists of things agreed on by Lutherans and Catholics alike that either had no scriptural sanction or else flew in the face of the written word.

For example, all Christians worshipped on Sunday, though God had given the Sabbath, the seventh day of the week, to Abraham as an everlasting covenant; it turned out not to be everlasting, though no clear command in the New Testament ordered that the day be changed. Obviously, More supposed, Christ had given some oral direction on the subject, and the church followed it—against the text of scripture in the Mosaic law.

More was fond of bringing up the washing of feet. The Gospel of John recounts the story of Christ washing the feet of the disciples on the evening before he died. He commanded his followers to wash one another's feet, and he told Peter that the act was necessary for salvation. The church interpreted his command symbolically, not making the rite a sacrament, and Luther and his supporters did not observe it as one. Why not? Because Christ had made some oral interpretation as a gloss on what scripture recorded that he had said, making it clear that the washing of feet was not to have sacramental status.

Then, dealing with the book of Acts, the Council of Jerusalem, in an attempt to make a compromise between Jewish and gentile converts to the new faith, had forbidden certain foods to all Christians. Among them was anything made with blood—an ingredient of English pudding. How had these restrictions been lifted? By an oral tradition distinct from the written word of scripture. Christ had commanded his disciples to baptize in the name of the Father, the Son, and the Holy Spirit. But in the book of Acts, his disciples baptized in the name of Jesus alone. The church later returned to the Trinitarian formula. Why? The oral tradition, said More.

All Christians—including Martin Luther, Thomas More, and William Tyndale—believed that Mary had never had sexual intercourse, that she was a "perpetual virgin." More and Luther also believed in the assumption of the Virgin, that after her dormition her body was physically taken up into heaven. There is nothing of such doctrines in scripture. Where do they come from? More said the oral tradition.

More insisted that scripture was the servant of the church, not its master.

Scripture was incapable in itself of creating the communal belief and shared assumptions that he thought necessary to any society. The church, a body of living souls, guided by the Holy Spirit, could not err; scripture was only a tool that, without the church, remained lifeless and powerless.

Beginning with the *Responsio* and continuing in his later works, More would proceed with what is at times almost an attack on scripture. In a way, this relentless assault on the Lutheran teaching of "scripture alone" was a corollary to the arguments raised by philosophical theologians against the authority of reason. Both reason and scripture had to be put in a subordinate position so that the church might seem all the more exalted and God all the more powerful.

In time textual scholars would find in the pages of scripture different traditions, different documents, contradictory testimony, simple errors of fact, all thrown together by a historical evolution that increasingly seemed accidental. More believed that God mastered history and that everything in the church happened in consequence of a divine plan for His people. Scripture was what God intended it to be, a servant to the church, and "tradition"—which More saw as tending always toward agreement and consensus—was the way God sanctified history, making the centuries add up to something. Textual critics would gradually lose their interest in making history holy; they would start studying the Bible as they might any other ancient book, finding in it errors that neither More nor Erasmus ever dreamed of and undercutting the notion of any divine authority in the world of men.

Erasmus probably saw greater mysteries in scripture than More did, but Erasmus drew back rather than ask dangerous questions about them. As Montaigne would do later in the century, he would from time to time profess his faith in the church because of its antiquity and because of the lack of any alternative that seemed as good. But he would never defend the tradition of the church and the sacral quality of church history with the vehemence and the dogged insistence that More brought to the task. Erasmus believed that Christians should use the Bible to find Jesus, and having made that discovery —an ethical one with a minimum of doctrinal encumbrance—they should reform life and society.

Erasmus always felt the futility of trying to define doctrines too precisely and of trying to know too much about the mysteries of God. In 1523—the year More's *Responsio* appeared—he wrote an acquaintance: "Many problems are now postponed to the deliberations of a general council; it would be much better if we could put off such questions to that time when . . . we shall see God in the face." More always believed that if any doctrine or practice was accepted by the masses of Christians—a doctrine like the immaculate conception or the assumption of the Virgin Mary or the veneration of saints and relics or the practice of pilgrimages—it had to be accepted by all Christians since

God would not allow the masses to err in their consensus for long. So More, who had mocked superstitions, who always feared the mob and scorned the ignorant multitude, locked himself into the trap of making the common consensus an expression of divine revelation that must be defended to the death.

The *Responsio* marks not only More's work as theological councillor and defender of the church but also a widening of the differences that had always existed between him and Erasmus and the worlds of thought they represented. By 1523 all Europe was repeating the question Egmondanus posed in 1520: Why did Erasmus not take up his pen to defend the Catholic Church? Why did the prince of scholars not attack Martin Luther, the prince of darkness? In June, Cuthbert Tunstall, now bishop of London, wrote Erasmus an impassioned letter urging him to battle. Erasmus replied quickly, begging off and urging moderation. "In Luther's writings are some things that I hear reproved which, in sober debate among the learned and the honest, might strengthen the spiritual and evangelical life from which the world has surely fallen as much as it can."

Some substantial disagreements between More and Erasmus are already clear to anyone who looks closely at their works. The sacramental status of marriage became one of the great issues in the Reformation. Erasmus contributed to the Lutherans' weapons in his reading of Ephesians 5:32, where the Vulgate calls marriage a *sacramentum*. Erasmus pointed out that the Greek word is *mysterion*, the word we transliterate into English as "mystery." In his notes he argued that the sacramental status of marriage could not be proved from scripture and that many of the early fathers had not considered marriage a sacrament.

In the *Assertio*, Henry ignored Erasmus and used the Vulgate's reading of the text to prove that in Ephesians Paul had made marriage a sacrament— precisely what Erasmus denied. In the *Responsio* More followed his king (or his own advice to Henry earlier) without a glance toward the Erasmian note: "You will find, I think," he wrote against Luther, "no sacrament named by the term sacrament in scripture except this one which you now stupidly attack —matrimony." He continued to make the same argument as long as he wrote polemical works—and never once did he even hint that Erasmus had provided a cogent reason to suppose that the sacramental status of matrimony could not be derived from the Latin text of Ephesians.

Why did More remain silent about such an obvious problem? Luther had made an analysis of the text in both *The Babylonian Captivity* and in his savage attack on Henry, using Erasmus's insights without mentioning Erasmus by name. *Sacramentum*, he said, meant mystery, a holy thing, and the Bible often used the word "mystery" for things other than sacraments. More could have noted Erasmus's views since Erasmus never openly denied the sacramental status of marriage; indeed he professed to grant matrimony so much force that he feared that some theologians might accuse him of heresy if he persisted in such views. He probably referred to his exaltation of matrimony with respect to virginity—heresy as More himself would later define it. More could have argued that matrimony was a sacrament, not because scripture said it was, but because the church said it was—an argument in keeping with his standard position on the authority of tradition. Since he was silent about the problem, his readers could catch him in one of the worst errors a lawyer or a rhetorician can make, that of ignoring contrary evidence, leaving it to be exposed by his enemies or—worse—discovered by the well-meaning who wanted to believe in him as champion and guide.

It looks very much as if More could not make a concession in a real argument that meant so much to his view of himself and the world. He could banter with Raphael Hythlodaye in *Utopia* because those arguments were essentially academic; he had no overwhelming preoccupation with the plight of the poor or for the cruel justice meted out to convicted thieves. But he could not concede a point to Martin Luther lest his entire edifice of thought come tumbling down on his head.

It is just possible that he was ignorant of Erasmus's notes on Ephesians 5:32. Most scholars assume that More knew the Greek text edited by his friend and that he had studied all the notes. Yet we have no evidence that he ever read the work thoroughly. In the *Responsio* he makes a somewhat vague reference to a reading Erasmus had made from the Greek. Here the issue was whether bishops could bind all Christians with rules—an authority Luther denied. The text was John 21:15–17, where Christ commands Peter three times, "Feed my sheep." More said that Erasmus interpreted the Greek word behind "feed" to mean "rule." In fact, Erasmus wobbled on the issue, and More did not report everything Erasmus said. In his other polemical works he scarcely ever used the Greek text at all.

It may be that More did not want to open the way to further ills. To point out Erasmus's reading at Ephesians 5:32 would have been to fuel the efforts of conservatives like Catharinus, Lee, and others to tar Erasmus with Luther's brush. More could hardly have profited by such an event. He was by now well known as a defender of the Erasmian New Testament whether he knew the work well or not. Throughout England and the Continent, the names of More and Erasmus were inseparably joined in the minds of the educated because of *The Praise of Folly*, which, by the time More wrote his *Responsio*, had appeared in twenty-three editions, the latest in 1521. Erasmus's prefatory "letter" to More appeared in all of them. If More disagreed openly with the notes of a work he had so vigorously defended—probably without knowing exactly what was in it—many conservatives would have gleefully condemned him out of his own mouth, shouting a thunderous "I told you so" across

England and the Continent as well. Or so he must have thought. Always acutely sensitive to attack, he could not have been disposed to open the gate to reproaches against himself. Tyndale, vastly influenced by Erasmus, later argued that More had once been of the same mind as the heretical reformers but that he had been suborned by bribes to support the clergy against Luther. The accusation stung More to fury—even, if possible, to a greater fury than usual in his polemics.

So he rarely mentioned Erasmus at all. We have seen his fleeting reference to an Erasmian textual reading in the *Responsio.* He alluded to Erasmus without mentioning him by name in a later letter against John Bugenhagen, unpublished in More's lifetime. In only one other instance in all his polemical or devotional works did the name of Erasmus come up. That was in reply to the charge Tyndale made that More had not attacked *The Praise of Folly* but now assaulted those who wanted to remedy the ills it exposed. Tyndale called Erasmus More's "darling." More replied vigorously. When he wrote *The Praise of Folly,* Erasmus had no malicious intent, said he. And, he added ominously, "had I found with Erasmus my darling the wicked intent and purpose that I find in Tyndale, Erasmus my darling should be no more my darling. But I find in Erasmus my darling that he detesteth and abhorreth the errors and heresies that Tyndale plainly teacheth and abideth by, and therefore Erasmus my darling shall be my dear darling still."

He wrote these words in 1533, and in the same work he was still quoting Henry's *Assertio* with fervent and stubborn approval to prove that the king stood firmly by the old faith. It was the year that Anne Boleyn was crowned queen of England. Under those circumstances, the mention of More's "dear darling" seems more of a threat than a statement of friendship. He and Erasmus had been friends; they had shared many things. But if a choice had to be made between friendship and the Catholic Church, More had no hesitation in saying what his choice would be.

Unpleasant as it is, the *Responsio ad Lutherum* brings us as close to the real Thomas More as anything else he wrote until that time. Here he had the freedom to be himself, unfettered by the formal demands art made in his *History of King Richard III* or *Utopia.* Here was where he could pour out the deepest passions of his soul in the belief that those passions coincided exactly with the will of God. More the royal councillor was diffident, almost obsequious, never taking any initiative on his own that we know of, never contradicting the will of his superiors, never expounding in any form that has survived a set of ideas that might have been of practical use in making royal policy. But when he defended the Catholic Church, he was a tiger, roaring his truth at top voice, threatening to devour anyone who disagreed in the slightest with his narrow and multitudinous canons of orthodoxy.

However, though the forms of the earlier works and the *Responsio* are different, the works themselves demonstrate a quality of More's mind that was constant all his life. He wanted order. He wanted people kept in line, disciplined, communal, and busy. He believed that human society was a precarious business, that sinful human beings required all-encompassing authorities or else their world would degenerate into licentiousness and chaos. There could be no individualism in Utopia; there was no individualism possible in More's view of religious orthodoxy; and a royal council was not a place for independent ideas, since no matter how bad kings were, they served the divine purpose of giving order to a population which, lacking the high education and fervent communal solidarity of the Utopians, would sink into anarchy if kings lost their power.

Erasmus could compromise and count some doctrines of so little importance that honest men could disagree about them without endangering their own salvation or the religious life of the society. He seems to have supposed that anyone could be a Christian merely by accepting the Apostles' Creed! More's *Responsio* reveals an entirely different mind, for here every doctrine becomes as important as every other doctrine, since if one is proved wrong, the entire authority of the church falls to earth. Within only a few years More was pushed by his own terrible assumptions into arguing that if Christians had venerated a particular relic for a long time, that relic had to be genuine since God's promise to be with His people certified every church practice that endured for many years.

The tensions produced within More by such obstinate rigidity must have been excruciating, and had it not been for his sense of irony and soul-saving humor, they might have become unbearable. It may have been that such inflexibility toward the outside world was a consequence of his own self-knowledge, an expression of how rigidly the wildness of his own mind and body must be controlled if he were not to tumble headlong into hell.

There are two points to consider about More's polemical works, beginning with the *Responsio*. They have an intrinsic interest as an expression of Catholic theology at the end of the Middle Ages and in lethal confrontation with heresies produced both by Catholic excesses and by the tumultuous changes in the times. But for a biographer they have a greater importance; they open windows into Thomas More's soul, and they reveal an inner torment and tension that make even more imposing the stoic image of himself he presented so doggedly to the world, the man in control, the man master of himself and of the scene. In our own sad time, when seeming natural has become the studied goal of the multitude of celebrities who control our politics and rule our society and manipulate our minds, and when public sincerity has become the opiate of democracy, it is easy enough to judge More harshly for the disparity between his own inner fury and the outer role he assumed of the unperturbed wise man, always detached from the passions that swirled around him. He may seem dishonest in the fundamental way of those who refuse to acknowledge themselves. But it may be that here was a case of art disciplining life and that the role More assumed before the world, a role Roper and all the biographers dependent upon Roper have taken to be the real man, was in fact the way he held his inner self in check and made himself continue in the world.

19

THE FOUR LAST THINGS:
DEATH AND DYING

EUROPEANS at the end of the Middle Ages were obsessed with death. In part this morbid sensibility was provoked by a fairly sudden reaction against the traditional Christian teaching about the immortality of the soul. For centuries the culture of Europe had been informed by the incessant proclamation that this life was nothing in itself, that it was only a preparation for a life to come in heaven or in hell, and that every living moment should be charged with the realization that man's fate was to stand before God in judgment.

After the Black Death of 1348 and the myriad other swift changes of the fifteenth and early sixteenth centuries, the certainties of faith had become worn down by doubts, and death, which had been seen as a gateway to an afterlife, became a horrible end in itself. The sculptured and painted effigies of a solemn and invincible Christ in judgment faded in the popular mind before the leering triumph of death, now often personified as a skeletal master of life, leading a wild dance to the grave. Funerary monuments bristled with carved representations of rotting corpses eaten with worms and snakes, putrescent flesh collapsing into the bones.

The inevitable decay of the body became more vivid in the imagination than the fate of the soul, and both literature and the visual arts joined in a mournful chorus that at times threatened to drown the lighter notes of human culture in a solemn and unwavering anthem of despair. It was as if a society existing for centuries with one set of expectations now found them suddenly void and could not find an equilibrium that might allow it to go on. That God should condemn the world to the horrors of death made Him seem all the more terrible, and in one of those psychological transfers common in every religion, we can see in the sixteenth century the terror before death transmogrified into a terror before God, whose ways became darker and more mysterious than they had ever been.

The energy of More's life with its vehemence and its rigidity came in large measure from his preoccupation with death and the fear of what fate might await his soul afterwards. Perhaps to relieve his tension or maybe to strengthen his resolve, at some time after 1520 he wrote a little treatise commonly called *The Four Last Things*, a meditation on death, unfinished and unpublished in his lifetime. It was a fragment, probably preserved by the family until it was handed over to his nephew William Rastell to be printed in the folio edition of More's English works issued in 1557.

We have hundreds of such treatises left over from the later Middle Ages, some of them intended to comfort the afflicted, others aimed at afflicting the comfortable, frightening the living into virtue and away from sensual pleasure by forcing them to look death in the face.

In *A Dialogue of Comfort*, written during his imprisonment in the Tower before his trial and execution, we have an eloquent example of the literature of dying well, written by More to discipline his mind and to ease his own fear, to help him achieve the good death admired by the people of Utopia, where citizens were praised for dying cheerfully but buried in shame and silence if they expired in terror.

The Four Last Things belongs to the other class of morbid literary meditation, the sort that seeks to agitate rather than to comfort. The title comes from the apocryphal book of Ecclesiasticus 7:40: "In all your works remember your last things, and you will not sin against the eternal." Medieval commentators counted four "last things"—death, judgment, heaven, and hell. They thought that the greatest single source of sin was the failure to acknowledge these final realities by those who lived like pigs in a world of daily mud.

One way to help Christians resist sensuality in life was to vivify these final realities through various depictions. Paintings and drawings of hideous demons —almost comical to us—offered one path to this goal, as did stained-glass windows with their ethereal visions, and Gothic sculptures of a judging Christ with his right hand upraised, parting the sheep from the goats on the great day of doom, sending the blessed to dwell with the saints and the damned to be stuffed into the raging mouth of a fierce dragon representing hell. Dante's *Comedy* is a literary avenue to the same destination. The detailed reality of inferno, purgatory, and paradise was expected to raise the eyes of readers from the mundane to the sublime and make them purge themselves of carnal evil. Dante's tale ascended from moralism to supernal art; More's piece did not rise nearly so high, but it is well worth studying. Surprisingly enough, it is filled with vivid glimpses into the daily life of the period, and some of his phrases ring in the mind.

While Dante and others in the high Middle Ages gave death and dying scant attention and fixed their vision on judgment, heaven, and hell, More—like others of his time—wrote only of death and broke off his treatise before dealing with the three other last things.

His theme throughout is the dualism of body and soul, and as he had done in *Utopia*, he made pleasure the canon by which to judge the ultimate value of things. "And like as the soul excelleth the body, so doth the sweetness of spiritual pleasure far pass and excell the gross and filthy pleasure of all fleshly delight, which is of truth no very true pleasure, but a false contrary image of pleasure." But why then are men so devoted to bodily delights? Because they are ignorant of the pleasures of the soul. Those lacking appreciation of precious stones are as happy with beryl or crystal as they are with a diamond. "But he that by good use and experience hath in his eye the right mark and very true luster of the diamond rejecteth at once and listeth not to look upon the counterfeit be it never so well handled, never so craftily polished." (The metaphor is a sharp turnaround from *Utopia*, in which the wise citizens of the rational island commonwealth spurned those who set special value on real stones when counterfeit gems looked as fine. And we may get some insight here into More's feelings toward his first wife, who, according to the story Erasmus tells in *The Praise of Folly*, happily received fake jewels from her husband and treasured them lovingly because she supposed they were genuine.)

Yet More does not write from the eminence of one who has experienced the high spiritual pleasure of the soul and wishes to draw others into its bliss. *The Four Last Things* bears no resemblance to *The Cloud of Unknowing* or other works of mystical devotion that enriched the literature of late medieval England. These mystical books were done from the standpoint of those who had caught a vision of God and in their works summoned other mortals to share this vision that reduced to ashes every earthly pleasure. More writes as one who knows that such a heavenly vision exists but who has experienced it only from afar, rather as a longing than as any sort of consummation. So he turns to the other side of the soul-body dualism, to the body and its ephemeral pleasures. His aim is to show that these pleasures are all false, supposing that once their falsity permeates the consciousness of any mortal, that person will turn with greater earnestness to seek the spiritual pleasure that exists somewhere out there, rather like a Utopia of the soul.

The knowledge of death—the deep-down, detailed consciousness of our earthly fate—is the instrument with which More hopes to purge us of our body's propensity to seek its own pleasures. If people could only see death—

RICARDVS · III · · · ANG · REX ·

Above: RICHARD III. Painting by an unknown artist, sixteenth century. National Portrait Gallery, London.
Right: HENRY VII. Painted terracotta bust by Pietro Torrigiano, sixteenth century. Victoria and Albert Museum, London.

HENRY VIII. Painting by an
unknown artist, ca. 1520.
National Portrait Gallery, London.

Left: CATHERINE OF ARAGON, Henry VIII's first wife. Painting by an unknown artist, sixteenth century. National Portrait Gallery, London. *Below:* ANNE BOLEYN. Henry VIII's second wife. Painting by an unknown artist. National Portrait Gallery, London.

Death and the Miser. Painting on wood by Hieronymus Bosch, ca. 1490. This work visibly expresses the morbid sensibility of the early Renaissance that appears in More's *Four Last Things.* National Gallery, Washington, D.C.

Opposite: MARTIN LUTHER. Painting by Lucas Cranach the Elder, sixteenth century. National Museum, Nuremberg.

Right: MARGARET GIGGS CLEMENT, one of More's wards, married to John Clement, a former tutor in the More household. She was the only family member to see More die. Drawing by Hans Holbein. Royal Library, Windsor. *Below:* "The Martyrdom and Burning of William Tyndale," woodcut engraving from Foxe's *Acts and Monuments of the Martyrs,* 1653.

THOMAS CROMWELL, royal secretary
when Thomas More was put to
death. Painting by Hans Holbein.
Frick Museum, New York.

JOHN FISHER, conservative bishop of Rochester, who with More supported the Catholic Church against Henry VIII and died two weeks before him on Tyburn Hill. Painted terracotta bust by Pietro Torrigiano, sixteenth century. Metropolitan Museum of Art, New York.

A page from "De Tristitia Christi," More's last work, written while he was in the Tower of London, and the only work, aside from letters, still existing in his own hand. Original in the Royal College and Seminary of Corpus Christi, Valencia.

their own death stalking them and waiting for them—they would not sin in this life.

Like most people in his day, he believed that dying was an almost unbearable torment. He would not have any sympathy with the modern perception that most of us die fairly well and in reasonable peace when our time comes, that, as Montaigne said, the fear of death is greatest among those who are in good health, least among those who are on the threshold of death itself. More imagined the "dolor and pain" and "grievous pangs" and "intolerable torment" that all men feel "in the dissolution and severance of the soul from the body." The anguish of Christ on the cross at the moment of his death was proof enough to More that the parting of soul and body produced a pain unimaginable until we experience it. His description of the easiest death he could imagine is horrific:

> Thou seest I say thyself if thou die no worse death, yet at the leastwise lying in thy bed, thy head shooting, thy back aching, thy veins beating, thine heart panting, thy throat rattling, thy flesh trembling, thy mouth gaping, thy nose sharping, thy legs cooling, thy fingers fimbling, thy breath shorting, all thy strength fainting, thy life vanishing, and thy death drawing on.

Such a stark vision, kept ever in the imagination, was supposed to counter the folly of deadly sins. More considers pride, envy, coveting, and gluttony, and breaks off his work in the midst of a discussion of sloth. All the deadly sins arise because people imagine the pleasures of the body to be more important than the fate of the soul. But if they recall that the body is inevitably destroyed by death, they will see that the lust that leads to sin has its price and should be spurned.

The work contains no ruminations about heresy, but it does spell out an almost standard popular view of how we receive salvation—a view that Luther rebelled against with all his might—and in so doing, More managed to add another horror to the moment of our dying. He thought that we are all pilgrims in the world, faced at each instant with the choice of God or Satan. We must walk carefully, guarding against presumption on the one hand and despair on the other. Presumption is the confidence that we have somehow earned salvation by our own good works; despair is the conviction that we are so wicked that repentance is impossible and that we cannot please God. When we are dying, Satan works busily at our souls, tempting us with the sin that is most likely to deliver us into his hands. "For well he knoweth," says More of Satan, "that he either winneth a man forever, or forever loseth him" at the moment when that man lies dying. Satan tempts the presumptuous man to think of his good deeds and his good life and to imagine that he deserves heaven because he has done so well in his life. And so he thinks not to cry to God for mercy and passes from self-satisfaction to eternal damnation. To those who have lived badly all their lives, Satan brings despair so that they will not cry to God for mercy because they believe they have no hope. And so they, too, are damned.

The Christian must walk always and die finally between presumption and despair; such was the demand of late medieval piety, and such is the teaching of More in this piece. This kind of piety created a tension that kept the Christian continually striving to please God. Without it, More thought, the world would fall into savagery, for unless there was some effort to please God among humankind, sinful humanity would abandon all restraint in the pursuit of passion. Yet the strain was tremendous, for until the very last moment of life, the issue was in doubt, and the dying man, tormented by horrible pain and satanic temptation, must doggedly hold out until the end or be forever damned. Luther could not bear this terminal uncertainty, and he began his journey toward heresy by demanding to *know* if he was to be saved.

To assist the Christian pilgrim on his journey to God between presumption and despair, the church provided the sacraments, and the sacraments became a model for other aids to piety. As we have noted, the sacraments were both physical and spiritual, rituals apprehended by the senses but also permeated by a secret divine power that poured into Christians who partook of the rites. Images, relics, rosaries, holy water, and a myriad of other material aids to devotion also combined, supposedly, a physical thing and a spiritual power.

In a curious way, *The Four Last Things* represents the fatigue with visual images among many of the devout in the later Middle Ages. No period ever saw a greater multiplication of images, relics, and other tangible aids to religion. They crowded every church, the images gaudily painted, representing saints in wood, stone, glass, canvas, and clay. But as they multiplied, these objects provoked a strong reaction among those (like Erasmus) who thought they seduced Christians from inward devotion to God and from the spiritual mending of the soul. Eventually the Protestant Reformation virtually swept them away.

In *The Four Last Things*, More recognized an elemental psychological truth of human nature: Physical images of both bliss and horror are not as powerful as the inward imagining of such things. He saw that the horrific representations of death the late Middle Ages abounded in had lost their effect:

> But if we not only hear this word death, but also let sink into our hearts the very fantasy and deep imagination thereof, we shall perceive thereby that we were never so greatly moved by the beholding of the dance of death pictured in Paul's as we shall feel ourselves stirred and altered by the feeling of that imagination in our hearts. And no marvel. For those pictures express only the loathsome figure of our dead, bony bodies eaten away the flesh. Which though it be ugly to

behold, yet neither the sight thereof, nor the sight of all the dead heads in the charnel house, nor the apparition of a very ghost is half so grisly as the deep conceived fantasy of death in his nature by the lively imagination graven in thine own heart.

The dance of death in St. Paul's comprised macabre drawings showing death as a dancing skeleton leading away people from all walks of life. The charnel house was usually a long, open shed at the edge of a cemetery where the bones of the dead were piled indiscriminately when their flesh had rotted away in the grave. Cemetery space in crowded cities was limited; the bones of common folk could not be granted the luxury of eternal rest. When the flesh was gone and the danger of contamination had passed, the bones were dug up—as Yorick's were—to make room for fresh corpses that needed a place to rot in peace. More's observation that we become inured to such spectacles is borne out by Johan Huizinga's observation in his *The Waning of the Middle Ages* that it was the fashion of the people of Paris to have feasts in the charnel house attached to the cemetery of the Holy Innocents. As the effect of representations of death wore off, artisans and artists tried to recapture the emotional force of the macabre by multiplying images and by making them all the more grotesque.

In seeing that images were losing their power to excite either genuine horror or true piety, More was, to a degree, returning to a view long held by mystics that the most powerful images are not those we make with our hands but rather those we create in our hearts. Here his turn of mind recalls the sermons about hell in James Joyce's *Portrait of the Artist as a Young Man,* sermons with a greater power to horrify than any tableau of flames and demons done with brush and paint. More's own worst horror was very probably the mental dread that fell on him during insomniac nights when he thought of death and eternity alone in the dark. We have noted the lack of evidence for the usages of popular piety in his own private devotions. He never went on a pilgrimage that we know of. We find no images of saints in the two thoroughly secular portraits done of him by Holbein. And when we look at the remains of his tomb in Chelsea Old Church—the tomb where he was not destined to lie—we are struck by how much there is of epitaph and how little there is of iconography.

Indeed his treatise on the four last things might be called an essay on the imagination as much as on death. More is heir to centuries of Christian thinking about the power of the imagination both to cleanse and to corrupt. To imagine death is to purify our souls, although usually, in his view, the imagination becomes a vehicle for wickedness. The worst sins, he says, are pride, envy, wrath, and coveting—all of them dependent on the force of a perverse imagination. Our pride leads us to imagine that we are exalted over other people, when in fact we are all prisoners condemned to death in the same terrible prison of earthly life, and under death's dominion "young, old, poor, rich, merry, sad, prince, page, pope, and poor soul priest" are all equal.

Our wrath bursts out according to the estimate we have of ourselves in our own imagination, since the more highly we esteem ourselves, says More, the more angry we become when we are rebuked by an inferior. In Spain, he says, it is a greater offense to strike a blow with the naked fist than it is to draw blood from an enemy with a sword. Why do the Spaniards make such a distinction between the two? Because one who draws a sword against another considers his foe a man, and since the Spaniards "take themselves for so very manly men," they blaze with anger at a blow given by the bare hand because it means that the person who gives it considers his adversary such a boy "that he would not vouchsafe [deign] to draw any weapon at him."

As we might expect from More, he supposes that the worst sign of the depravity of our bodily life is our propensity to sexual sins, "the filthy pleasures of the flesh," but even here the imagination works as wickedly as the body itself.

> For when the eye immoderately delights in long looking at a beautiful face with the white neck and the round breasts and as long as it finds no barrier, the devil helps the heart to frame and to form in the fantasy by the foul imagination all that ever the clothes cover.

The imagination can lead us astray, making us fancy pleasures that are not pleasures at all, and leading us to destruction. Our mother Eve provides the archetype of the wicked imagination for the human race, for she saw the forbidden fruit and imagined the pleasure she would take from it,

> And so entered death at the windows of our own eyes, even into the house of our heart, and there burned up all the goodly building that God had wrought therein.

Why do we covet? Because our fancies conceive ridiculous pleasures. More tells of the thief who, at the bar of justice where he was condemned to be hanged on the morrow, managed to cut the purse of a bystander. "And when he was asked why he did so, knowing that he would die so shortly, the desperate wretch said that it did his heart good to be lord of that purse one night yet."

And even in the moment of death, when we should be bemoaning our sins and begging God for forgiveness, some presumptuous souls, supposing that they have lived well enough to have earned salvation on their own merits, succumb to the wiles of Satan, who twists their fancy:

And instead of sorrow for our sins and care of heaven, he puts us in mind of provision for some honorable burying—so many torches, so many tapers, so many black gowns, so many merry mourners laughing under black hoods, and a gay hearse, with the delight of goodly and honorable funerals in which the foolish sick man is sometimes occupied as though he thought that he should stand in a window and see how worshipfully he shall be brought to church.

In the end, the perverse imagination gives us only damning illusions, and the man who cannot see reality is like a knave proud of wearing the gown of a lord in a stage play, says More, and worthy of derision for that foolish pride since when the play is ended, he will walk again a knave in an old coat.

The aim of this treatise is to correct our imaginations, to dissolve our illusions and replace them with a vision that fixes itself on the ultimate reality —death. The topic is morbid enough and solemn enough. Yet More manages to touch it with a humor almost unknown in the lugubrious treatises on death and dying common to the later Middle Ages. He could never forsake his wit —not here in this rumination on death, not on the scaffold when he came to die himself. Like Chaucer—or like all great humorists, for that matter—he delights in throwing incongruous details together. Here he describes the last moments of a dying man:

> Think ye not now that it will be a gentle pleasure when we lie dying, all our body in pain, all our mind in trouble, our soul in sorrow, our heart all in dread, while our life walketh awayward, while our death draweth towards, while the devil is busy about us, while we lack stomach and strength to bear any one of so manifold heinous troubles, will it not be as I was about to say, a pleasant thing, to see before thine eyes, and hear at thine ear, a rabble of fleshly friends, or rather of fleshly flies, skipping about thy bed and thy sick body, like ravens about thy corpse now almost carrion, crying to thee on every side, "What shall I have? What shall I have?" then shall come thy children and cry for their parts. Then shall come thy sweet wife, and where in thine health haply she spake thee not one sweet word in five weeks, now shall she call thee sweet husband and weep with much work and ask thee what shall she have. Then shall thine executors ask for the keys, and ask what money is owing thee, ask what substance thou hast and ask where thy money lieth.

Yet it is a grim humor, and the message of the treatise is stern. Like Martin Luther, More saw the human mind as a dark forest where all sorts of beasts crouched, ready to spring on the soul. The worst sins derived from the impulses and the imagination, from the folly arising from fancy rather than reason.

Although he wrote *The Praise of Folly*, Erasmus believed that good education was the surest road to virtue because the disciplined mind could control not only knowledge but the passions. With More and with Luther we have a view that is both more pessimistic and more profound. To both, the perversions of the mind are boundless, beyond any cure that mere education can provide. With his continual stress on the power of the imagination, More stands near Ignatius Loyola and the Catholic mystical tradition that aimed at filling the mind with overpowering images which, like some blast of fire, would burn away the temptation to sin. More wanted to be a mystic, but lacked the gift; he did have mystical sensibilities. Erasmus often gave lip service to the mystical tradition, but he never truly belonged to it, and his way was a practical, unemotional piety that found in passionate fancy a danger to the stability of soul that he believed was the mark of the good man. Like Ralph Waldo Emerson, to whom in so many ways he was a spiritual ancestor, Erasmus lacked any powerful conception of sin, and so his definition of goodness was often banal. Thomas More saw sin rooted in the imagination, and he found the road to such virtue as might be possible beginning there, too.

Johan Huizinga made a pregnant remark about the literature of death piety in the later Middle Ages. He said that it knew only the two extremes— "lamentation about the briefness of all earthly glory, and jubilation over the salvation of the soul." And, says Huizinga, "all that lay between—pity, resignation, longing, consolation—remained unexpressed and was so to say absorbed by the too much accentuated and too vivid representation of Death hideous and threatening."

The humor of *The Four Last Things* keeps More's work from falling neatly into the category of unrelieved horror that Huizinga considers the theme of the late medieval vision of death. And More himself does not quite fit the description Huizinga gives us of writers and artists whose preoccupation with the misery of death ate away all the gentler emotions that death may evoke. Yet Huizinga's wisdom reaches toward More even if it does not entirely embrace him.

More mentions pity in *The Four Last Things* when he uses the fall of a great lord (evidently the Duke of Buckingham) as an example that should help us shun envy. How can we envy the great lord who vaunts himself over the world for a season, when in one day that lord may be hanged, drawn, and quartered, and our envy "suddenly change into pity?" There is a formal pity in the first part of *Utopia* when Hythlodaye, More's creation, takes the part of the poor in Europe condemned to death for stealing when if they did not steal they would starve. Yet it seems in retrospect a rhetorical pity rather than a real passion that continued throughout the rest of More's life, and what strikes us most about his other works is the singular absence of pity toward anyone who might have benefited from that emotion in him.

The other qualities—resignation, longing, and consolation—did appear in More when he drew near to his own death, when he tried to resign himself to the will of God, when he longed for peace through release either from the threat against his life or from the tribulations of death itself, and when he sought to console his family for his own departure out of this world. Yet he could never entirely give free play to emotions that might have allowed him to speak the language of the ages. He is no Hamlet, brooding over death not as physical torment nor as a gateway to judgment nor as an opportunity to give edifying lessons, seeing death as an ultimate reality with only the possibility of a dream behind it and that dream more disturbing than consoling. More was a Christian, of course, and Hamlet only marginally so, and therein lies a major difference. Yet it is a little disconcerting and more than a little disappointing that when More comes to speak of death, he draws up before the temptation to compassion and begins instead to preach sermons. It is almost as if an outbreak of sorrow for death would have released floods of other emotions that faith was now too fragile to bear.

20

THE REFORMATION
CONTINUES

MORE AND ERASMUS differed in how they saw the central danger of Lutheran reform—More as a threat to salvation, Erasmus as a menace to good letters—but they agreed in their fear that it would lead to sedition, although even here their fears took different shapes.

Erasmus always blamed both sides, Lutheran and Catholic. He disliked Luther's spirit, but he was dismayed when Catholics burned Luther's books. In his letter of 1520 to More about Egmondanus, he wrote that although Luther's books could be removed by force from libraries, they could not so easily be removed from the souls of men. He thought that opposing Luther with passion and hatred would only increase the fury abroad in Christendom. Better to write good books instead of bad, to seek pure learning, and to let the Lutheran affair wither away in a natural death.

Public spectacles like book burnings created hysteria in the crowds that witnessed them. Erasmus feared any release of passion in the mob, which he contemned. The masses should not meddle in matters they could not understand. Once the ignorant started to invade territory that should be the property of scholars alone, scholarship itself was in danger. A mob in tumult has no judgment.

Erasmus censured Luther for bringing abstract doctrines like predestination into public debate. The ignorant suddenly supposed themselves expert in matters that had humbled theologians for centuries. Erasmus was appalled. He wanted people to live like Jesus—a simple thing, he thought, but enough to occupy any ordinary Christian for a lifetime. Luther had unleashed a wild sectarian spirit that swept the mob into proud eccentricity. Erasmus wrote a friend in 1519, "Indeed I think that if someone now got up and taught that it was religious for men and women to jump around naked in the market, the sect would not be without its disciples and its patrons."

More saw wrongdoing only in the things Luther did and said. He never blamed Catholic authorities for any measures they took against heretics. On the contrary, he thought they should be more determined and even stricter. He defended book burning and believed completely that the living bodies of heretics ought to accompany their corrupt books to the pyre.

More was shocked by the vulgarity of Luther's reply to Henry. As we have repeatedly seen, he was no great lover of kings, and his *Utopia* is in its way a hymn of praise to rational republicanism. But we have also seen how authoritarian his republic was, and authoritarianism is the true measure of his temperament. He believed that the order of society was held together by thin cords of habit and force. Like most in high position in his time, he saw the multitude as a scarcely contained chaos, capable of bringing all civilization down in a moment, held barely in check by the restraints of the law with its threat of lethal retribution. To insult kings was to raise the devil and bring trouble to the earth.

He knew early on that some German princes were nodding toward Luther, though in 1523, when he wrote the *Responsio,* not even Luther's own ruler, Frederick the Wise, had declared himself for the Lutheran heresy. More could see the greed of princes for the profits to be made by taking sides against the old church. He made a grim prediction:

> For just as very many of the princes look not without pleasure on a degenerating clergy, undoubtedly because they pant for the possessions of those who defect and hope to seize them on the grounds of abandonment, and just as those princes rejoice that obedience is withdrawn from the Roman pontiff with the hope that they will be able to dispose and divide and squander it all for themselves at home, so too there is no reason for them to doubt that the people look to the time when they may shake off in turn the yoke of the princes and strip them of their possessions; once they have accomplished this, drunk with the blood of princes and reveling in the gore of the nobles, enduring not even common rule, with the laws trampled underfoot according to Luther's doctrine, rulerless, without restraint, wanton beyond reason, they will finally turn their hands against themselves and like those earthborn brethren, will run each other through.

Here was one of the great preoccupations of the age. Authority over the roiling masses of the ignorant and the destitute was a fragile thing. To break off a piece of it was to risk shattering it all.

While More was writing his *Responsio,* Henry VIII sent an angry letter about Luther to the Saxon princes, Duke George of Leipzig (a loyal Catholic) and the Elector Frederick the Wise, Luther's protector. More probably helped write the letter; indeed he may have written all of it, since both the style and the arguments are his.

As might be expected in a letter to rulers, "Henry's" epistle claims that Luther's heresies lead directly to sedition. If Luther had his way, the letter says, all religion would be smashed, all laws overwhelmed, good customs corrupted, governments ruined, all sacred things profaned, the sacraments of Christ trampled underfoot, the freedom of the will destroyed, and faith extolled in such a way that good works would become worthless and license granted to sin.

Here is the clangorous note against predestination that we can hear ringing in the *Responsio,* a warning that the doctrine as Luther preaches it will lead inevitably to the dissolution of society itself. Henry VIII had not mentioned predestination in the *Assertio* because it had not figured in *The Babylonian Captivity.* In the *Responsio,* More took up the argument that we see in this letter, an argument that he was to make again and again, that Luther's predestination created sedition and vice because the doctrine made God the source of evil and made human beings shun responsibility for their own acts.

In this letter, Lutheran reform is seen as a revolution not merely in religious doctrine or in the way Christians use the sacraments but in how Europeans understand themselves and live together in society. More thought that the human community could survive only if the individuals making it up believed that they would be held accountable for their choices and punished if they chose the bad. Luther's teaching removed human choice and made punishment and reward capricious, destroying—so More thought and this letter implied—the social utility of religion.

The letter makes no mention of Luther's attacks on the papacy. This eloquent silence, in addition to the style, is persuasive evidence for More's authorship of Henry's epistle. More always studiously avoided making precise definitions of papal power, and he preferred to avoid the subject altogether if he could. Henry obviously did not feel strongly enough about it to insist that some defense of the papacy be included in this letter sent out under his name. The omission adds weight to the argument that the treatment of papal primacy in the *Assertio* lacks the conviction of ardent papalists writing elsewhere in England and on the Continent.

While More was developing into a competent theologian by writing against Luther, Erasmus was finally prevailed upon to enter the fray. Much of the persuasion came from English friends. In September 1524 he reluctantly brought out a thin little work he called *A Lecture on the Freedom of the Will.* Here, in a dispassionate exercise more fitting for a university lecture hall than for the rude street of polemical debate, he seized the moral and social implications of the doctrine of predestination and advised Luther to stop talking about it.

More must have been disappointed. He believed that the fundamental issue raised by Luther was the authority of the Catholic Church. Erasmus scarcely mentioned the church at all. Like More, he feared the wicked might use the doctrine of predestination to justify their evil deeds. If they were predestined to be wicked, they could blame God for their crimes and go on committing them. The doctrine perplexed Erasmus, and he wished to remove it from public debate, where it could do only harm. He hated assertions, he said, and nothing he ever wrote better illustrates the character of his mind or better shows how different he was from Thomas More, who made assertions almost as readily as he breathed.

More held with all the passion of his soul that the sacred traditions of the church prove we have some choice to make about our salvation. Erasmus barely touched on tradition but turned rather to probable cause. Everywhere in the Bible, he wrote, people were assumed to be responsible for what they did. Both the Old and the New Testament were filled with commands and with the promises of rewards and punishments for the responses people made to them. If they were punished for disobedience, and if God caused their disobedience, the punishment was unjust. Such was the general consensus of the church, Erasmus said, making a slight, quick bow to tradition, and it seemed better to him to go with this consensus than to flout it. If Luther rejected the teaching of the church and wanted others to reject it, too, he would have to prove his authority. He and his followers might live supremely moral lives—but they did not. Or they could work miracles as Christ and the apostles had done. If Luther could heal only one lame horse, Erasmus said, we might listen to him.

Unable to see these signs and wonders and evidence of superior virtue in Luther, Erasmus declared himself willing to hold to the old ways. He sounds like Montaigne much later on in the century, feeling that he might as well stay with the church because nothing better had come along. He does not show the love and passion Thomas More felt for a church that was mother, father, and continuing incarnation of the living God, the community of the living and the dead, extending from creation through time and into eternity.

Neither Erasmus nor More held that freedom of the will is absolute. Grace is God's help to us in making the right choice. Grace is God's love that pursues us when we have sinned. Neither Erasmus nor More argued that we can ever do enough to merit salvation. Despite Luther's slanders to the contrary, the Catholic Church always considered such teaching heresy. The Catholic view, espoused by More and Erasmus and legions of their contemporaries, held that God always helps us do what we can never do without Him. Still, we can do *something*. If I were drowning, and someone threw me a rope, I would have to seize the rope and allow myself to be pulled to safety. (More himself used this illustration in a later polemical work.) Grace is the rope, and grace is also the Person willing to save me; free will is the faint strength I have to reach for the rope. I could by no means provide the rope for myself, but if I did not choose to grasp it, I would drown. Luther held that we are utterly passive in the work of salvation; God gives all, and we only receive. We are as passive, Luther once wrote, "as a woman in the act of intercourse." (He was still a bachelor when he wrote these words, untroubled by the reality of the experience of what he described.)

More would have agreed with almost everything Erasmus wrote in the treatise on free will. What is lacking in the work is More's stress on the exercise of free will within the sacramental system of the church. In More's view, the church provided the sacraments as periodic helps, strengthening the Christian life, making it always available for us to choose. The mass and penance were especially important in confirming faith. Freedom of the will for the Christian means the freedom to approach God through the sacraments and to be gracefully received. Erasmus's free will has little to do with the sacraments; in consequence, his view seems to mean the freedom to do good works in general, making free will seem abstract, disconnected from the sacramental practice that meant everything to More.

As a polemical work, Erasmus's piece is weak and inept. Luther was blazing away at the Catholic Church, its pope, its councils, its clergy, and, above all, its very conception of itself and how God works in the world. Catholics like More believed that if God inspired and guided tradition, He could be known through the tradition, just as we may know an author by studying his works. Luther's God could be known only through scripture as it was read by the predestined believer. That a practice or belief in the church had endured over many centuries meant nothing to Luther; his question was whether or not God was pleased with the doctrine on the form of piety. To answer it, Luther went to the Bible. The Bible tells us much about God's acts—some of it horrific. The Bible is not a philosophical or systematic work, and Luther's awful God, known only in the Bible, was cloaked in a mystery that makes the Catholic God seem radiantly clear in comparison. To Luther the existence of the Catholic Church over 1,500 years proved nothing about God's purposes. Look at the Moslems, Luther said. They, too, have existed for many centuries, but what does their existence prove about God? Nothing that we can say for certain. These were crashing statements about critical issues, and Erasmus evaded nearly all of them. In his polemics, More met them head on.

Yet More and Erasmus remained united in their fear that Luther's vehemence would lead to sedition. Soon they seemed to be prophets. In the German lands, the torrent of expectation loosed by Luther gained force. Emperor Charles V, preoccupied with his impossibly grandiose political dreams, could give only passing attention to the Lutheran matter. A pamphlet warfare raged among the competing religious warriors. Writers and printers discovered that they could throw off all restraint and lampoon their foes in language and cartoons that for sheer quantity and vulgarity were hitherto unknown in history, and such works would be bought by the hundreds, even by the thousands.

Luther's own rage charged the air with violence. In 1520 he wrote:

> If we punish thieves with the gallows and bandits with the sword and heretics with fire, why do we not so much the more attack with arms these masters of perdition, these cardinals, these popes, and all this sewer of this Sodom of Rome that endlessly corrupt the church of God, and why do we not wash our hands in their blood?

Multitudes of ordinary people, unaccustomed to vernacular fury in the printed word, were swept into passions that we may better understand if we consider the power of the modern press, radio, and television to excite people to hysteria, riot, and even war.

In the summer of 1525, peasants in the southern and western parts of Germany revolted against the lords who owned the land. They were incited by fiery biblical preachers who took literally the many declarations in scripture that the poor were the chosen people of God. The peasants were numerous, and many had seen combat service as mercenaries in the emperor's Italian wars. But they were badly led, and the nobles slaughtered them in battle and went on killing them like rabbits, almost for sport. Near Colmar in Alsace, a high mound of earth is said by today's peasants to have originated when the skulls of their ancestors were heaped up by their merciless conquerors.

Luther had no sympathy for peasants who tried to apply his teachings to correct secular wrongs, and once the revolt was underway, he wrote savagely and hysterically against them, crying that they should be killed like mad dogs. He was afraid for his own movement, although as it turned out, the princes and cities of Germany converted by Luther's doctrines finally began making their position known in 1525 and afterwards. The bloody vigor of good Lutherans in their ruthless massacre of the peasants, combined with Luther's fiery venom spewed out to encourage the slaughter, seemed to persuade many men of power that they could keep lands, offices, and authority, and embrace Luther, too; then they could do themselves even more spiritual good by confiscating the material possessions of the church.

In England, More and others learned of the Peasants' Revolt with shuddering horror. They saw it as a direct consequence of Luther's doctrines and a confirmation of their conviction that the advent of Lutheranism in England would bring violence and revolution. In a royal proclamation, Henry VIII declared that Martin Luther was the cause of all the slaughter.

While the revolution was in full burn, Luther married a runaway nun on June 13, 1525, making his reputation worse, if possible. The marriage was sudden, and it shocked even his intimate friends. The moment seemed utterly inopportune. But no moment would have suited to mitigate the horror and the ridicule that most Catholics felt at Luther's union.

The *Decameron* of Boccaccio, written in the middle of the fourteenth century, had long since demonstrated the pleasure Europeans took in tales of lecherous monks and their profligate women—often nuns. Chaucer's *Canterbury Tales* used the same themes, and enjoyed huge popularity. Now it seemed that one of those lecherous monks, butt of a thousand vulgar jokes, had stepped to the bar of history claiming to be, not a clown, but a prophet of God.

More was aghast. Under canon law, a monk who married a nun was guilty of incest. More repeated the charge with the ardor of a fire bell. In time the very frequency of his clangor dulls our ears to it, but his furious intensity must give us pause:

> But now the chieftains of these execrable heresies both teach and use more sensual and licentious living than ever did Mohammed. Which though he license men to have many wives, yet he never taught nor suffered his folk to break their chastity promised once and solemnly dedicate to God. Whereas Luther not only teacheth monks, friars, and nuns to marriage, but also being a friar, hath married a nun himself and with her liveth under the name of wedlock in open, incestuous lechery without care or shame.

This was a cry from the bowels of a man who had fought the battle with sexuality and lost, giving up priesthood to become a husband, now discovering "reformers" who told him that his battle had not even been worthwhile.

Luther's wife was a thoroughly grasping and unpleasant woman, a cast-off daughter of the petty nobility. Her people never fled a fight when they could make one, and Luther claimed that it was she who provoked him to write against Erasmus. Yet it seems hard to suppose that Luther had to be urged into a fight. He was the Robert E. Lee of theologians, a man of high moral principle given to headlong charge at the sight of his enemies' guns set along a line of battle.

Now Erasmus held the line to be taken, and in November 1525, Luther let loose against him the long tractate *On the Bondage of the Will.* Erasmus had wanted to suspend judgment on predestination and quit talking of it in public. Luther said of the doctrine:

> This is the one and supreme consolation of Christians, to know that in all things God does not lie but immutably does everything of His will and that this will cannot be resisted or changed or impeded.

As we have already said, the doctrine suited Luther's experience and his temperament. He lived in a world of the mind where nothing was clear to human reason. No one could understand how Satan had usurped the church that called itself Catholic and Christian. No one could tell how the Antichrist had been installed on the papal throne or how Christians could have been flung into catastrophic error for so many centuries that doctrine, liturgy, and popular piety had all gone miserably astray. Perhaps most important of all, Luther did not understand how he had been so mistaken as to plunge with all his soul into the legalistic trap of the monastery, there to toil in futility and sinful overestimation of the power of the human will, struggling to purge himself from guilt.

Predestination offered the only satisfying alternative to the terrifying suspicion that all this might have been without meaning, that life itself was only a succession of accidents coming from one void and going to another. If God was in charge, all this meant something; no mortal could know what it meant except that somehow God willed it and was working out a purpose for the world and every creature in it. Predestination seems to console most those who find themselves in chaos and yearn to believe in order.

More, of course, could see only the dangers of the doctrine, none of its consolations. Through the 1520s he was drawn increasingly into defending the church and to developing lines of communication with others who had assumed the same task. In 1525 he met John Eck, one of Luther's most dogged opponents, who came to England hoping, it seems, for appointment to a post in an English university. He arrived in August, bearing a heap of his books to be distributed in places where they might do the most good. He would have had his own story of the peasants' war to tell, and he would have found eager listeners in Thomas More and John Fisher during visits he made to them both. Eck was not alone in his pilgrimage to England. Several impecunious Germans who had written against Luther came in the expectation of some sort of award from Henry, author of the most celebrated polemic of all. More wrote to Wolsey in 1523 expressing a certain frustration about the advent of one of these uninvited guests. But Eck was of a higher species, and he seems to have received a cordial welcome.

More gave him a copy of his *Responsio,* and Eck took it home with him. Judging from the marginalia he made in the book, which still exists, we can say he even read part of it. The British Library possesses a worn copy of Eck's anti-Luther *Handbook of Commonplaces.* The frontispiece of this little work contains a flattering letter to More in Eck's own tiny hand, and it was long assumed that this was a presentation copy, given by Eck to More in England. But recent research shows that the book was a copy intended for a printer in Germany and that Eck planned to dedicate an edition of the work to More. It never appeared. Perhaps Eck saw that he had no hopes in England and thought it unprofitable to waste a dedication.

At least Eck had met and talked with the two most prominent anti-Lutherans besides the king in England. Fisher had written several books against Luther in Latin, publishing them under his own name. More had written the *Responsio* under a pseudonym, but it seems obvious that his authorship was now an open secret. Eck's copy includes a note in Eck's handwriting that the real author was More.

Of all More's continental correspondents, the most important was John Dobneck, who called himself Cochlaeus. He wrote a veritable library against Luther. At this distance he looks like one of those prolific second-rate thinkers who cluster around the central problems of every age. In his younger days he wrote aimlessly about music, about grammar, about the art of writing poetry, and about the fathers of the church.

Luther's actions gave him a passion for opposition and a reason for being. The titles of Cochlaeus's books run on for page after page in the British Library catalogue; the books themselves have rested almost undisturbed for centuries. Perhaps Cochlaeus deserves more. Although he was a humorless pedant, his patient and single-minded dedication to the Catholic Church was monumental. To him and to others who wrote less but still much, the Catholic Church owes, at least in part, its preservation as the church most German-speaking people still profess.

He and More did not begin to correspond until about 1527, although in August 1525 he published a strong attack on Martin Luther, blaming him for the peasants' rebellion. Luther had provoked the peasants to war, he said; then Luther had betrayed them with his murderous little book *Against the Thieving and Murdering Gangs of Peasants*.

Cochlaeus took the rhetorical stance of seeing the peasants as pitiable and deluded men. On the one hand, he could sympathize with the masses of honest but ignorant peasants who tilled the soil; on the other, he could castigate Luther as the beast who had caused calamity to fall on them and then betrayed them. The book was dedicated to John Fisher, and More seems to have used it in composing his own polemics against the heretics.

In the same year, Cochlaeus also got out two books on Martin Luther's German sermons. One was short; the other quite long, including excerpts from thirty-six sermons Luther had preached in German. Cochlaeus tediously refuted five hundred propositions he deemed heretical in these sermons.

I have elsewhere demonstrated that all More's citations from Luther's German works came from one or the other of these books by Cochlaeus. One was Luther's "Sermon on the Rich Man and Lazarus," done in 1523. Here he had put forward his suggestion that the souls of the dead might be unconscious between death and the general resurrection at the end of time. More quoted it again and again and always interpreted it as Cochlaeus did, as license to sin in this life because the fear of punishment was to be long deferred after death.

Neither Cochlaeus nor More considered the role of consciousness in time and the fact that if a man is not conscious of the passing of a million years, the time goes by in less than an instant.

In 1526, Cochlaeus published a vehement attack on the grandiloquent *Epistle to the English* written by John Bugenhagen, a Pomeranian doctor of theology and one of Luther's closest friends. Bugenhagen had imitated the epistolary style of the apostle Paul, beginning his letter with the greeting "To the Saints that are in England, grace to you and peace from God our Father and from our Lord Jesus Christ." He followed his high-flown beginning with a summary of Luther's theology and encouragement to the English Protestants to persevere.

More wrote an assault on Bugenhagen in 1526 or 1527, the first polemical writing in his own name against a heretic, although he never published it, and we do not know if he ever sent it to Bugenhagen. The book marks an important step in More's own development, since it shows him willing to take on a heretic without some prodding from his king and without a pseudonym.

We cannot be sure that More used the work of Cochlaeus against Bugenhagen. Obviously More was devouring works against Luther written on the Continent and building in his own mind a defense of the Catholic Church, a defense drawn from a great many sources.

This increasing contact with the leaders of the German Catholic offensive against Luther carried More even further from the spirit of compromise and reconciliation that Erasmus wanted to follow. Erasmus protested that Luther was often scandalously misinterpreted, but More followed the spirit and often the texts of those who made the worst of everything Luther said.

Perhaps it is only a luxury of modern scholars who no longer care deeply about heaven or hell to wish that More had given careful thought to Luther's works so that he might have responded to Luther at his best rather than to the empty evils conjured by ferociously unfair people like Eck and Cochlaeus and others. There is no evidence that More ever made any detailed study of a large cross section of Luther's works. We assume that he read *The Babylonian Captivity* carefully, as well as Luther's crashing reply to Henry VIII. But we can make such an assumption about no other major work that Luther wrote, not even the treatise *On the Bondage of the Will.* More saw Luther only through the eyes of those who hated him, and he appears to have read only those things that would confirm his hatred.

21

WILLIAM TYNDALE: THE COMING OF THE REFORMATION TO ENGLAND

IN 1 5 2 5 , William Tyndale published his first edition of the New Testament in English and laid the cornerstone for the edifice of English Protestantism, which would eventually be extended around the globe by the architects of the British Empire. Tyndale did not cause the English Reformation; the revolt against Rome was led by the king. But without Tyndale's Bible with its powerful language and dynamic cadences, the spirit of English Protestantism would have been something other than what we now know. Most of his work eventually was incorporated into the great Authorized Version of the Bible done in the reign of King James in 1611, surely the most important single book in the development of our taste for what is right and good, not only in language but also in life. From a cultural perspective, the year 1525 has a much better claim to mark the end of the Middle Ages than the traditional date of 1485 usually given in the textbooks.

But although 1525 is the great landmark year of the English Reformation, the quiet incursion of new ideas into England had begun much earlier, the way prepared by Lollardy and the general spirit of anticlericalism among the English people, and then by the fascination of young scholars with the Greek New Testament of Erasmus with its revised Latin translation and its provocative notes.

Among the young men at Cambridge University—praised by More in 1519 for its encouragement of Greek studies—were some with religious sentiments that would lead to English Puritanism. Of these, the most influential was

Thomas Bilney, whose death in 1531 by burning at the stake would give More much pleasure and—so More thought—serve as a vindication for the harshest possible punishment for heresy, since More said that Bilney had recanted his heresies before dying.

Bilney, born about 1495, possessed a great spiritual intensity. He hated swearing and could not bear to hear singing in church, or so John Foxe tells us, considering "dainty" music a mockery to God. At Cambridge, when he was a student, he would occasionally hear the delicate notes of a recorder drifting up from the room below, where Thomas Thirlby, later an Anglican bishop, frequently played. On those occasions, Bilney would say his prayers aloud as if to exorcise the demon of music. Perhaps like Ulrich Zwingli, who forbade instrumental music in his reformed church at Zurich, Bilney loved music and believed that anything he naturally loved he must, as a world-denying Christian, hate. It was a view of love and hate that found its way into the theology of William Tyndale too, and it may have had its roots at least partly in *The Enchiridion* of Erasmus with its plea to Christians to mortify the flesh and to simplify worship to make it more spiritual.

Certainly the influence of Erasmus on Bilney and others like him was immense. Bilney passed through a dark night of the soul, similar to the terrible assaults of despair that nearly destroyed Martin Luther, and after searching everywhere for relief, he found the consoling Jesus whom Erasmus set forth in the Greek New Testament.

From scripture—and undoubtedly aided by Erasmus's notes—he took a view of Christ as the divine model of devout simplicity that condemned the elaborate forms of a seemingly mechanical piety that did not reach the heart. Bilney took Christ as a practical example, seemingly accepting Erasmus's counsel in a literal way that Erasmus never took for himself.

Bilney ate only one meal a day and took the other to prison, where he fed and preached to those confined. He ministered to the sick, and he preached wherever he found an audience. He was apparently a great pulpiteer. Although he was both short of stature and slight of build, so that people called him "Little Bilney," he was remembered long after his death as a man of great personal power and as the kind of Christian Christ had intended his followers to be.

He moved many to follow him in a biblical evangelicalism that exalted the sufficiency of Christ and denigrated ceremony and wealth—views that were not Lutheran, although they could lead to it. He converted Hugh Latimer and Thomas Arthur and John Lambert—all to be martyrs for their faith. But perhaps his greatest accomplishment was to convert Robert Barnes, who would become, except for Tyndale himself, the foremost advocate of Luther's thought in England, making him—like Tyndale—one of the major adversaries of Thomas More.

Barnes was an Augustinian monk, about Bilney's age, who had entered the house of the Austin friars at Cambridge while still a child, perhaps placed there as a ward. He had a facile mind, and in 1517 his order sent him to Louvain to study theology. In 1521 he returned to Cambridge, where he became part of a large group of students and young dons, some of them, like Stephen Gardiner, very conservative, who met at the White Horse Tavern to discuss Martin Luther and the new theology coming out of Germany.

Bilney was in the group, and Barnes fell under his spell and was converted, probably to Bilney's intense personal commitment to Christ. Later on Barnes followed that commitment into Lutheranism.

Barnes was gregarious, witty, talkative, likable, and as shallow as a saucer. By 1523 he had won a doctorate, enabling him to publish books on theology. He was doomed to the shadows by his lack of genius until Tyndale and the English Reformation came along and, like all the great upheavals of our history, gave boldness, loudness, and persistency rewards that had previously been reserved for talent alone.

Another of the group that gathered at Cambridge during the early part of the decade was John Frith. He was somewhat younger than the others, having been born in 1503. Like most who became strong voices for Lutheranism or "Evangelicalism" in the English Reformation, Frith's origins were lowly without being base (his father was an innkeeper), and he rose in the world by the powers of his mind that others noticed early. He was witty and charming, and he had a remarkable gift for friendship. We do not know of any special closeness between Frith and Bilney during their association at Cambridge. But whether they were converted by Bilney or not, the young men who gathered at the wooden tables and ale pots of the White Horse Tavern were united by a yearning to make the old words of religious faith mean something strong and real. They shared the intensity that had driven Luther to search through the Bible for some respite from his own horrid sense of wickedness—and were for the most part scrupulous men looking for peace with God no matter what conflicts divine peace might cause them on earth.

All such people in England were not, of course, concentrated in the White Horse Tavern. Early in the decade, while the group at Cambridge remained in obscurity, Thomas More found heresy in his own household and heresy of a sort that anyone in the Cambridge group would have understood and cheered on. William Roper, Margaret's young husband, became enthusiastic about Luther's doctrine. Harpsfield tells the story. The account is a bit confusing, and Harpsfield's dedication of his work to Roper does not certify all the details. Harpsfield says Roper was a Lutheran when he married Margaret. This is hard to believe, since we cannot imagine that More would have allowed his beloved daughter to marry a heretic. Roper had lived in the More household for perhaps three years before the marriage took place; More would have known his opinions. When Roper fell into heresy, he was not one to keep it secret. Harpsfield says he took the bridle in his teeth and ran off into evil doctrines like a headstrong horse. Roper was ready to proclaim his new faith at Paul's Cross, and he even wanted to sacrifice a great part of his wealth to become a Lutheran preacher!

What probably happened is that Roper fell into his passion for Luther about the time he married Margaret, keeping his thoughts to himself, perhaps not quite knowing where they were leading him. Within a month after the wedding in July 1521, More went to the Continent on the diplomatic mission that was the occasion for his last visit with Erasmus. He was away for several months. As head of the house in his absence, Roper may have indulged himself in the liberty of reading and talking about subjects forbidden when More was present.

Harpsfield tells enough to show that Roper's conversion to Luther's views followed a familiar pattern. An excessively scrupulous soul wrestled mightily but in vain with the rules of piety and suddenly came to the conviction that the "law" could not lead to salvation, that only grace, given through God's predestining power, would suffice. Harpsfield says that Roper strove for salvation through fasting and ceaseless prayers and that he wore himself out in pious exertions and became convinced that he could not please God. In the theological parlance of the time, he fell into despair, which was a mortal sin. It may well be that his decision to marry was a critical event. We have observed often enough in this book that for many devout Catholics—including Thomas More —marriage was much inferior to sexual abstinence, just as the layman was inferior to the clergyman. Roper may have fought a losing battle with his sexual impulses, stimulated certainly by the presence of Margaret in the house with him and the knowledge that she was available as a wife. She died in 1544; Roper lived on until January 1578 and never married again—certainly a tribute to the love he bore his wife but perhaps also a reflection of a puritanical reluctance to marry when the sole reason might be to gratify the passions of the flesh. He might very well have been imitating his father-in-law, who married a second time but perhaps never had sexual intercourse with his second wife. For preternaturally scrupulous Catholics to give themselves up to marriage was to admit something about their natures that might seem to risk hell itself.

So when Roper married, he discovered Luther. Harpsfield tells us that the Lutheran works he most admired were *The Babylonian Captivity* and *The Liberty of a Christian Man*. Both pulsate with the conviction that no one can please God by making excruciating efforts to follow elaborate rules. Both meant to prove that the devout soul can count on salvation because God has promised it to those who seek Him in faith rather than in ritual works.

To overscrupulous souls vexed, perplexed, and wearied by their heavy, mel-

ancholy guilt, this was good news indeed, and Roper heard it gladly. Harpsfield
tells us that Roper began consorting with German merchants in the Steelyard.
These merchants had close connections with German Lutherans, drawn
thither as much by Luther's opposition to papal taxes as by his theology.
Through them, heretical books poured into England—among them a Lutheran
Bible that Harpsfield says Roper acquired. If Roper could read German—and
since he had connections among the German merchants, we may suppose he
could—he was probably reading Luther's New Testament that appeared in
Germany in September 1522. It sold so well that a second edition came out
in December of the same year, and copies must have reached some Germans
living in England.

The "Lutheran Bible" Harpsfield mentions could have been Tyndale's English New Testament—advancing Roper's flirtation with heresy to sometime
after 1525. But since Harpsfield otherwise mentions Tyndale's work by name,
it seems likely that Roper's Bible was Luther's.

Wolsey summoned Roper and the Steelyard merchants before him to examine them for heresy. The merchants were forced to renounce their heresies
publicly at Paul's Cross. But because of More's position, the cardinal let Roper
off with a friendly warning. We know that in January 1526 More himself
conducted a raid on the Steelyard and confiscated Lutheran books and caused
four merchants to be arrested. Could Roper have been netted in this raid? It
seems unlikely. Harpsfield loved a good yarn, and he would have told us if
Roper's own father-in-law had turned him in. The irony would have given
Harpsfield the occasion for the kind of moralizing he was fond of.

More did his best with Roper, all to no avail. Harpsfield has him say to
Margaret:

> Meg, I have borne a long time with thy husband, and I have reasoned and argued
> with him in those points of religion and still given to him my poor fatherly
> counsel. But I perceive none of this able to call him home. And therefore, Meg,
> I will no longer argue and dispute with him but clean give him over, and get me
> another while to God and pray for him.

This was a forbearance that More never showed in his later years, when heresy
was a clear and present danger to England. His attitude fits the early 1520s,
when the threat seemed remote, a perversion of the Continent offering only
a minor taint to English life.

Roper was redeemed in time; we do not know how. After More's death he
suffered prison and exile for the Catholic faith, and his loving memoir of his
father-in-law is in itself a testimony to his own loyalty to the cause for which
Thomas More died. Harpsfield gave the credit to More's prayers—as Roper
himself must have done.

After 1525 heresy became an obvious danger to the old ways, and the authorities could no longer look away when students and young dons gathered in taverns to discuss the new doctrines or when preachers became too vehement in their denunciations of abuses in the church. The principal religious reason for the change in the English mood was the English New Testament of William Tyndale, the excitement it caused, and the popularity it enjoyed in England.

Tyndale is something of a mystery to us—even an enigma. We lack a good modern edition of his works. His books are unread by all but a few specialists, and in the pounding throb of his monumental self-righteousness and viciousness, we are easily hypnotized into a trance of inattention. He seems to have been a humorless and thoroughly unpleasant man, seldom able to keep a friend for very long. But he was a genius with language, and he was brave, constant, and intelligent—so intelligent that he became Thomas More's most formidable intellectual adversary.

He was born near the borders of Wales and perhaps there absorbed the thrilling poetic cadences of language that even today can make unbelievers weep at the united voices of a Welsh choir singing old hymns in a thunder of feeling. Sometimes he called himself Hitchens and at others Tyndale. More was sure that there was something shameful about this name-changing, for he shared our view that a man with an alias carries with him the reek of dark deeds. In Tyndale's case, it was probably nothing more than a relic of rural parts, where for centuries the Christian name was the only name a man had and where surnames marked only the affectations of the gentry.

In 1512 he took his B.A. at Oxford; in 1515 he took an M.A. It was the year of the Hunne case, and even up at Oxford, Tyndale may have felt the heat from the explosion of anticlericalism in London. He was for a time a country chaplain and a tutor to a nobleman's children. Somehow he learned Greek.

He drank in Erasmus, and when Luther came on the scene, he, like so many others, turned from Erasmus to stronger fare. John Foxe is the chief source for Tyndale's life, and from his account we may see that even as a youth Tyndale was contentious, that he disliked the pomp and wealth of clergymen, that he found in the Bible the source of all religious knowledge, and that he ran into people—probably Lollards—who assured him that the pope was the Antichrist.

Tyndale was outspoken and got in trouble with the local authorities. They threatened to run him out of the area. He replied that he could live on ten pounds a year and be happy as long as he could preach and teach. Ten pounds was not much; the sum reveals his austere side. He wore no linen; that is, he wore neither a shirt nor underwear beneath his outer garments. He ate nothing but boiled meat, and he drank small beer. He lived with a simplicity that resembles that of Thomas More's imaginary Utopians.

Like most abstemious men, he felt horror toward sexual sins and perhaps horror toward sex itself. He said that priests in the country knew only the Latin of the service books and the book supposedly written by Albert the Great entitled, as Tyndale had it, *The Secrets of Women*. The book was, in fact, a kind of handbook of various kinds of knowledge and included a discussion of female anatomy, sexual intercourse, and giving birth. One of its chapters is entitled "How to Know When a Girl Has Lost Her Virginity, etc." Tyndale said that priests pored over it night and day.

While he was in the country, Tyndale translated *The Enchiridion* of Erasmus from Latin to English. Tyndale was as moved by this little book as by anything else he ever read except perhaps the Bible—which he read through the lens provided by the self-denying *Enchiridion*. He was enthralled by its appeal to a simplicity that stood in sharp contrast to the ritual complexity and wasteful ostentation of the prelates of the church, and he responded to its call to the devout and holy life. Tyndale waxed hot and furious in his denunciations of wickedness among priests. He circulated his translation of *The Enchiridion* and apparently used it as a text for his own vehemence. He was examined for heresy, threatened—insulted like a dog, he said later—and decided it was time to move on.

He went to London, arriving in the teeming city with an idea whose time had come: he wanted to translate the New Testament from Erasmus's Greek text into English. Needing a patron, he applied at the household of Cuthbert Tunstall, newly elevated to be bishop of London. Tunstall was known as a friend of Erasmus and as an advocate of reform in the church. He was also a friend to Thomas More, whom Tyndale believed to be a partisan of radical renovation in Christianity. It must have seemed to him that Tunstall would readily accept his offer to put the New Testament into the language of the English people. But Tyndale was bitterly disappointed. Tunstall had enough chaplains; he did not need another. There is no sign that he knew of Tyndale's earlier run-in with the authorities. Tyndale must have seemed no different from many another poor clerk begging at his door; there is no evidence that the two men ever saw each other face to face.

So Tyndale made his way to Germany, probably to Wittenberg and to Martin Luther—though we cannot know for sure. At any event, after many tribulations he finished his translation, and by the spring of 1526 or perhaps even earlier, German merchants were smuggling it into England and selling it to avid readers. Apparently it enjoyed a huge sale, although accounts differ as to how many copies were printed, and all the accounts are only guesses.

Tyndale's English has largely survived in the King James Version of the Bible. It is simple and direct in style, almost untainted by the contemporary effort to "augment" the language by adding polysyllabic Latin and French words. Luther had gone out among the common people to learn their words for common things. Tyndale, doing his work in exile, far from home, did not have this opportunity. But unlike Luther, he had not spent years of isolation from his native tongue in a monastery where only Latin was spoken. He had a fine ear and a passion like Luther's for simple renderings that anyone could understand. These qualities he combined with a cadence and power in language that, until he came along, was unknown to English prose. English had already developed a capacity for narrative, for vigor, and even for poetic beauty. William Tyndale gave it the sublime.

Tyndale was not content merely to translate. He wanted to direct readers into the right understanding of scripture. Though, like Luther, he was sure that scripture was its own best interpreter, he could not resist the temptation to spend pages and pages explaining the text just in case its supposed marvelous clarity might somehow be opaque to those who read it alone.

He appended a prologue to his work, hardly more than a translation of part of Luther's prologue to his German New Testament of 1522. Here Englishmen could read that scripture alone showed the way to salvation—a position implicitly condemned by the standard Catholic faith that the church was the custodian of salvation and that scripture was only one of the treasures the church possessed.

Even clearer was the distinction between law and gospel fundamental to Luther's thought. The law commands us to do what we cannot do. When we perceive our weakness, we see that we cannot help ourselves. Just when we are tempted to despair, we find the gospel, the good news that Christ has done for us what we could not possibly do on our own. This news liberates us from the curse of sin and from the blackness of despair. In Tyndale's English, it "maketh a man's heart glad and maketh him sing, dance, and leap for joy." So scripture provokes in us a recapitulation of salvation; it stirs a reaction in us much as a script will inspire an actor to create a play all over again as if it had never been done before. Tyndale always stressed feeling as a sign of salvation; here his tone differed from Luther's. Luther was suspicious of intense emotional outbursts in religion because he thought they might lead to bizarre enthusiasms and wrong doctrine.

Tyndale stayed with Luther's early view that salvation is a private matter between God and the Christian, a drama played from the Bible that, as far as the individual Christian was concerned, was unrelated to the drama played last year or last century or a thousand years ago. Tyndale never had much to say about heroes of the faith who lived after biblical times. He tended to scorn tradition, and he could not see the purpose of the Catholic argument that he ridiculed in his prologue: "Such holy persons did thus and thus, and they were holy men; therefore, if you do so likewise ye shall please God."

Tyndale also provided marginal glosses to help the reader interpret the scriptural text. Both glosses and prologue exalt predestination. The elect are awakened to salvation by hearing the gospel preached. More believed that predestination would be taken as a license to sin, but Tyndale taught that the predestined love the law of God and that although the true believer might on occasion slip into sin, he would never abandon himself to evil with the excuse that God had predestined him to be lustful. Why does Christ give commands if we have no freedom to obey or disobey? (The question was Erasmus's.) Tyndale says that the commands are the agency God uses to cause obedience in the elect. What is the role of good works? The performance of good works by the elect shows the world that they are among the blessed. Christians do not earn salvation by the good they do; they do the good because they are already saved.

So Tyndale's New Testament brings us again to the great divide in the Reformation. On one side were Luther and Tyndale and a host of others speaking to souls tormented by the fear that they could not please God. The spokesmen had experienced that torment as a lonely, hopeless struggle against the holiness of God and the filthy fragility of their own nature. The prologue speaks of those who deceive themselves by thinking that they observe the law because they abstain from what the law forbids and perform the acts that the law requires. What they fail to see is that the law also requires that we love God and our neighbor with all our heart.

We are again at the psychological self-examination that made so many in the later Middle Ages scrutinize their own hearts, test their own emotions, crawl dismally on all fours through the dark sewers of their hidden selves, where they wallowed in melancholy at the wickedness they found there. Their question was always something like the following: Can I say I love God only for Himself? Or is my love inspired by the selfish fear that if I do not love God, He will punish me with everlasting hell? Are any of the emotions I have selfless? Or is all my motivation in some way related to pride and greed? Any of us exploring our most selfless acts will probably find buried in our hearts some selfish desire—if only the desire to be praised for our goodness. The introspective and tormented people who were unable to free themselves from such condemnation were those to whom the Lutheran gospel was addressed. It was the gospel of Tyndale's prologue.

We know enough about Thomas More—the self-flagellation, the hair shirt, the brooding over death—to suppose that he endured torments of his own about salvation. He assuaged these fears by devotion to the sacraments and to the traditions of the church certified by the saints and the promises of Christ. But in addition to providing a way of salvation, the Catholic Church took seriously its task of providing a civic religion—one that offered a morality capable of holding the human community together on earth. Tyndale would hold that since most people were not predestined to be Christians, the king would have to enforce Christian ways on all. Like many another Protestant, he passed quickly from a denunciation of the Catholic Church to high praise for secular government. The Catholic Church was compelled by its own sense of civilizing mission to give everyone a chance for reward who did those things that made a decent human society possible. People had to take responsibility for themselves. The Catholic notion of grace, fairly represented in both Erasmus and More, is that everybody can receive it by making some effort, which God will meet.

By limiting the Christian gospel to the elect, Luther and Tyndale were in effect cutting off the moral rudder by which the Catholic Church had guided Western civilization. They were obliged to turn to the secular state to do the job of civilizing. People were not rewarded in heaven or punished in hell because they gave alms or committed murder in the earthly life; they went to bliss or damnation because God sent them there, and they lived lives in this world appropriate to their predestination to heaven or hell.

The secular state had a responsibility to preserve order in the world. Christian rulers had an obligation to impose Christian morals on everyone, regardless of religion. And secular rulers would also protect their people from the pope and his minions. Rulers were appointed by God; it made sense to Protestants to believe that they were ministers of God's will and that the truly Christian monarch would do all he could to ensure that his people lived in outward conformity to Christian law.

But anyone like Thomas More who helped govern a secular state in the sixteenth century knew how fragile order in society was. More subscribed to the view that no state was strong enough to restrain by outward force alone the evils of the human heart. Some inner compulsion had to exist in us all to make us do good, and the best compulsion was the religious hope for reward or dread of punishment. It is no wonder that some people of that time, unacquainted with the modern, liberal notion that society can best hold together under the collective force of individual selfishness and unable to imagine the immense power of the modern state, believed that the way of Tyndale and Luther spelled doom for civilization.

Tyndale's translation was a true reflection of the prologue. He probably relied both on Luther's German and on the third edition of Erasmus's Greek New Testament, published in 1522. It is clear that he took many Erasmian readings. He translated the command in Luke 13:3,5 as "repent" rather than "do penance." In Ephesians 5:32, Tyndale said of matrimony, "This is a great secret," the word "secret" standing for the Vulgate's *sacramentum.*

Of greater importance was Tyndale's use of the word "congregation" for "church." He followed Erasmus, who had used the Latin *congregatio* instead of the word *ecclesia.* Both men were striving to get away from the sense of the church as a hierarchical institution; both wanted to emphasize the spontaneous gathering together of like-minded Christians. But Tyndale pushed his view into heresy by sharply denying any validity to the hierarchical church, and Erasmus was neither so bold nor so vehement.

Tyndale also translated the common Greek word *agape* as "love." The usual translation in the Vulgate was *caritas,* and "charity" was the word used by English preachers and writers. It is in fact the better word to express the giving and selfless qualities implied by the Greek original, the kind of love that Jonathan Edwards described as "disinterested benevolence." The King James Version of 1611 came back to "charity," and centuries of us have since learned the rolling declaration of Paul to the Corinthians: "If I speak with the tongues of men and of angels and have not charity, I am become as sounding brass or a tinkling cymbal."

Tyndale used "love" because the word better fitted his own conviction that passionate feeling was a sign of salvation. It was the word commonly used in the great English mystical tradition represented by books like *The Cloud of Unknowing.* It seems likely that this tradition is the source of Tyndale's own passionate teaching that true Christians feel their faith.

In many places Tyndale substituted the word "favor" where Catholics normally used "grace." His aim was to wean readers away from the many complicated definitions of grace in Catholic theology. Grace was for Catholics available in all the sacraments. Tyndale wanted to express the Lutheran conviction that grace was God's free act by which He chose some for eternal salvation without any merit or will or choice on their part.

Tyndale, like Luther, wanted to get rid of the Catholic dogma that there had been a special Christian priesthood in the early church. He regularly translated the Greek word *presbyter* as "elder" or "senior," a usage actually in keeping with the Vulgate and with the Greek text as well, although the Catholic Church had long taught that every disciple and nearly every other Christian man mentioned in the New Testament had been a priest. Luther, and Tyndale after him, read the New Testament as a book about lay people who had come out of the priest-ridden religion of the Jews and inaugurated or re-established a faith built on the joyful and spontaneous religious experience of ordinary men and women.

We may say in passing that some of Tyndale's changes caught on and some did not. He himself seemed to have reservations about "favor" in place of "grace" and quickly went back to the latter word in his own theological works. "Congregation" never succeeded in displacing "church," although among the English and American Puritans—Tyndale's truest heirs—the word experienced a modest revival and survives in the name of the Congregational Church in New England.

"Love" has displaced "charity" only in modern translations, but the word "charity" still possesses a sense that the word "love" cannot convey, especially in our society, where love can mean so many things. But "repent" did replace "do penance," and the King James Version solved the problem of *mysterion* in Ephesians 5:32 and elsewhere simply by transliterating it as "mystery." "Mystery" is much closer to Tyndale's "secret" than it is to the Vulgate's *sacramentum.*

Tyndale's work was popular and dangerous, and the authorities reacted vigorously to it. Thomas More was apparently charged by the royal council to take the lead in the attack on heretical books. We have mentioned his raid on the Steelyard of January 26, 1526. The German merchants had been bringing in Lutheran books for years. More's descent on them at this time was probably prompted by Cochlaeus, who had got wind of an effort to print Tyndale's New Testament in Cologne, a Catholic city, and succeeded in putting the authorities onto Tyndale, who had to flee upriver to Worms to finish the job. Cochlaeus wrote to the English officials. His letter is lost. Doubtless he told them of the plan to smuggle the New Testament into England among goods shipped down the Rhine and across the Narrow Seas. More's January raid was too early; Tyndale's translation did not emerge whole from the printer in Worms until March. But it is likely that More, not knowing the schedule, moved as soon as he heard from Cochlaeus.

The tide could not be easily rolled back. More's raid led to a few inconsequential arrests, but it apparently did nothing to stop the Germans from selling heretical books. Cuthbert Tunstall tried to stop the spread of Tyndale's English Bible by buying up every copy his agents could find. Duke George of Saxony had tried the same tactic against Luther's New Testament in 1522, and Tunstall's scheme may have worked, though More is said to have advised against it. Copies of the first edition of Tyndale's work are so rare that only two are known to exist, and both are badly mutilated.

Yet the book must have got around. Englishmen were starved for a translation because the authorities had not provided one and the Lollards had built up a tremendous expectation for what the Bible could accomplish. In the end the Englishmen who had counted on the Bible for so much were disappointed; they had wanted a new world, but all they got was a new religion. Still, when the book first appeared, literate Englishmen among the merchant classes and even some among the nobility greeted it with hope and joy.

In October 1526 another holocaust of books was set at Paul's Cross. Tunstall, never inspiring, preached the sermon calling for the destruction of Tyndale's books. The crowd was not convinced. Many believed that the clergy burned the New Testament because the gospel contradicted what the clergy taught and the way they lived.

Before this onslaught, Thomas More became increasingly alarmed and probably frustrated. Heresy was pouring into England through books. Books must be met with books, although no clergyman in the country—not even John Fisher of Rochester—had the power or the will or the eloquence to address the English-speaking audience that Tyndale and other heretics were summoning to revolution. More had already written against the new doctrines, though never in print under his own name. It was inevitable that his friends should beg him to write more and just as inevitable that he should feel a compulsion in himself to defend the faith on which both civilization and his own salvation depended.

22

PUBLIC DEFENDER
OF THE FAITH

SOMETIME in the late summer of 1525, Luther and his friends in
Wittenberg heard a rumor that Henry VIII was leaning toward evangelical doctrine and that Wolsey was about to fall from power. The source of
the rumor is a mystery, but people around Luther welcomed the news.

They needed supporters. The Peasants' Revolt was coming to a bloody end,
and Luther was being loudly blamed for it. It was not yet clear how many
German princes and imperial cities would agree that Luther was responsible
for the carnage and the terror that had swept through the South German lands,
but his situation was precarious. With much difficulty he was persuaded to
write a letter of apology to Henry VIII. After several false starts, Luther got
off a proper letter in September. It seems to have taken until the following
spring to arrive in England.

Tact was not one of Luther's gifts. His approach to Henry was not of a sort
to soften the hard, blunt edge of Henry's wrath. He began by declaring that
he had not previously understood that Henry was not the true author of the
Assertio, but now that he knew the king's real sentiments, he was willing to
do his part in a reconciliation. There followed several rhetorically self-effacing
remarks accompanied by a little fulsome praise for Henry's majesty. But in
effect what Luther offered was friendship on his own terms, and one of those
terms was that Henry admit previous error and convert to Luther's gospel.

Henry—or somebody delegated to write in his name—replied with a broad-
side against Luther intended to show that the royal mind was as unchanging

as granite and that Luther had been, was now, and ever would be a heretical dog.

It looks very much as if Thomas More wrote this letter. In July 1526, William Knight wrote to Wolsey, mentioning in passing that "the King told me that the copy of the letter of Luther is in More's hands." At the end of September, Wolsey wrote More that it would be a good idea to send Henry's reply not only to Luther but to the German princes as well, and to include Luther's letter to make the king's response understandable.

We feel More's style in "Henry's" reply. Luther is pounded for marrying a nun, and the letter calls the marriage "incest." "Henry" makes other points that resemble More's in his *Responsio* and in his later polemics as well. Most interesting is an enumeration of Luther's heresies in the form of a list—a tactic More had used before and would use again. The list includes More's familiar catalogue of Luther's errors—writing against the sacraments, condemning chastity in priests, denying holy orders, disbelief in transubstantiation, taking away from all men the benefit of the mass, making women confessors and ministers of all sacraments and allowing them to consecrate the body of Christ, claiming that there was little difference between the Virgin Mary and the nun Luther had made his whore, blaspheming the holy cross, and teaching that there is no purgatory but rather that all the souls of the dead sleep until the day of doom. No mention is made of Luther's attacks on the papacy—a telltale sign of More's influence if not his authorship.

It was perhaps this experience of writing yet another theological tractate in the king's name that prompted More to write the letter to Bugenhagen which we have already noted. The "letter" is really a little book, rarely read and rarely commented upon. Yet it marks a great divide in More's life. He was now engaging in polemics on his own and not as an adjunct to his king.

He wrote it sometime before the spring of 1527 in Latin, although it was not published until 1568. The tone and the arguments are familiar. More used the Peasants' Revolt to prove that his earlier predictions had been correct, that Luther's doctrines inevitably led to tumult, massacre, and rapine. Luther had incited the laity against the clergy, armed citizens against the magistrates, and stirred common people against princes. Was it the gospel, More asked, to destroy the sacraments of Christ, to spurn the saints, blaspheme the mother of Christ, contemn the cross of Christ, scorn vows made to Christ, pollute virginity consecrated to Christ, teaching monks and nuns to marry each other, making them perpetual whores?

More advanced the standard arguments for the infallibility of the Catholic Church, although utterly missing in this "letter" too is any defense of the papacy. The papacy is mentioned only once and that in passing. Somewhere in the church the papacy must have a place; popes had ruled from the beginning, and the papal office was part of the tradition More defended. But what authority did popes have? The man who was to be England's greatest Catholic martyr never clearly expressed himself on that question.

By the time he wrote against Bugenhagen, More knew that the heretical movement had split into warring camps that hated each other as much as they all hated the Catholic Church. Luther was firing salvos against Ulrich Zwingli, the reformer of Zurich, and Zwingli was not meekly turning the other cheek. The peasants had been driven to revolt by radical preachers whom Luther detested. Zwingli had approved the drowning of Anabaptists—fit punishment, he thought, for their teaching that only believers should be baptized and that children unable to profess their faith should not receive the sacrament. The Reformation had quickly deteriorated into the brawl among sects that would become familiar in all countries where Protestantism was strong.

In his letter, More mocked these bitter divisions. In his view, the Catholic Church had always held a consensus on the major points of faith, and it had endured since the time of Christ while innumerable heresies had risen and fallen utterly away, leaving no trace.

The Protestants claimed that they took all their doctrines from scripture. Against Bugenhagen, More commented sharply on the unreliability of scripture and repeated a thought he had expressed in the *Responsio:* the church could not stand on a book written on paper; it must abide with the gospel written in the hearts of the faithful. It is in the letter against Bugenhagen that More begins to sound the strong note that would ring again and again in his other polemical works, that miracles authenticate the Catholic Church and that heretics never produce any—this from a humanist scholar who had earlier scorned the credulity of the masses in their acceptance of false miracles and foolish wonders.

His flourishes against Bugenhagen are devastating. Nowhere else in his writing do we find such conscious use of rhetoric. The Protestants claimed that the Catholic Church was corrupt. Where then was the true church? Everyone agreed that there had to have been true Christians continually living in the world from the time of Christ or else Christ would have broken his promise to keep the church safely in being until the day of judgment. But if the Catholic Church was not a community that included true Christians, where were they? More uses repetitive parallelism in a long periodic sentence to hammer at Bugenhagen's view that true Christians had always existed but had nearly always been unknown to the world at large:

> But if you contend that there were always some, though so few that they were
> unknown in the world, so dispersed that they never got together, so illiterate that
> they never wrote, so infantile that they never spoke, and that despite this
> dispersion they were the true church, you must also confess that against your

church the fathers, whom the church of Christ always venerated as saints, wrote perpetually.

Bugenhagen had expressed the early desire of the Lutherans to make doctrine as simple as possible. To the English he wrote that Christians should have only one confession: "Christ is our righteousness." He was trying to get away from the elaboration of doctrines built up as the Catholic Church had waged its various wars over dogma through the centuries. He was assuming that Christians could be united through their loving experience with Christ because divine election would make them hold together in a community even as God held them to Himself.

More made capital of Bugenhagen's simplistic simplicity. Under that creed, he said, anyone, including women, could hear confession and consecrate the body of Christ, and all Christians could deny purgatory, renounce the freedom of the will, and refuse to submit to human laws. He was still harking back— as he would again and again—to the things he found most horrifying in the *Babylonica.* He wanted to show that the heretics taught a simple confession to spare themselves the revelation of what rascals they actually were. He thought that their beliefs were so monstrous that to state them clearly was to refute them utterly in the eyes of good people—and one of the most monstrous was the early view of some Protestants that women deserved equal status with men in the ministerial offices of the church. It was a view that nearly all Protestants quickly abandoned. Throughout the letter against Bugenhagen we see More's conviction that human beings have a certain religious sense that lets them know intuitively when some things are right and others wrong. And More supposed that any sensible person could see the error in giving women equal status with men in the church of God.

The issue of predestination is treated more thoroughly in the letter against Bugenhagen than in anything More had written earlier. The Lutherans accused the Catholics of the old Pelagian heresy, the belief that human nature was good enough without special grace to earn salvation on its own if people would only choose to do the right thing. More correctly replied that the Catholic Church was not Pelagian at all since the church made nature and grace different things. Nature was corrupt and weak because of sin. Grace, which was help from God freely given, was always present, always strong, always available for the sinful mortal who showed any desire at all to reach for it.

The letter against Bugenhagen also spells out More's own view of salvation, a view common among Catholics at the time: God was free to do anything He wished with His creation. But because He was just, God revealed to humankind what He wanted, and He did not play games whose rules were hidden. One rule was that people must do good works. These works were not in themselves enough to merit our salvation, for all our good is mixed with some evil. But when we do the best we can, God accepts our best as enough. He does not need our good works, so He can put any value He wants on them. We might say that God's evaluation of our good deeds is like that of a wealthy man who does not need the pencils sold by a beggar yet still buys them and pays handsomely out of compassion for a helpless man doing what he can to make a living. So works have a place in the divine economy even though these works are imperfect because of our fallen human nature. They are signs of charity, and without works, as James wrote in his letter in the New Testament, faith is dead.

Against Bugenhagen, More made one of his most telling assaults on the Lutheran teaching of predestination. Trumpet the doctrine as they might, the Lutherans nevertheless exhorted, pleaded, and sometimes threatened, all in a way that implied that their hearers had some choice about an eternal destiny. More wondered why. If people were predestined to be what they were and what they ever would be, was it not fatuous to speak to them as if they had responsibility? Were they not merely a part of nature, incapable of responding to any appeal that they choose a destiny on their own?

> Who exhorts the stone to form itself into a statue? Who exhorts the air to rain or the earth that it bear seed? If fate is the cause of all things and neither is there any freedom whatsoever among men, as Luther so mordantly holds, there is absolutely no reason left to you that you should move anyone to virtue or castigate evil.

The Lutherans would reply in the spirit of Tyndale's glosses on the Sermon on the Mount. God does not predestine the elect in isolation from the general human economy of cause and effect. Election does not come out of a void. The elect hear preaching and exhortation, and with these divine instruments they are moved to know their eternal state. God ordains the preaching and the exhortation, just as He ordains the election itself.

But the practice of preaching predestination never quite measured up to the doctrine. Preachers charged wth exhorting come to believe that something depends on how they exhort, and people listening to a sermon come to believe that they have some real power to respond, either by doing what the preacher exhorts them to do or by rejecting his demands. If they believe the preacher, they assume that they will be held accountable for what they decide. All mainline Protestant denominations have drifted away from predestination. The growth among Protestants of evangelical fundamentalism with its vigorous declaration of free will offers proof enough that predestination does not do well in the pulpit.

So More had a good issue here. When Lutherans taught predestination but made exhortations from the pulpit, they contradicted themselves. Had he been able to read German, he would have found Luther threatening congregations with the loss of their salvation if they surrendered copies of his German New Testament to Catholic authorities. If salvation is predestined from the foundation of the world, how does anyone "lose" it?

It is surprising that More did not do something with this contradiction later on. Instead he came back again and again to what infuriated him most about predestination: it put the blame for sin on God.

Much of his argument is like that of Erasmus in his *Lecture on the Freedom of the Will*. The obvious meaning of the New Testament text in many places is that people are commanded to do some things and to abstain from doing other things. Rewards are offered for obedience and punishment threatened for disobedience. None of these commands makes sense if people have no power to keep them. Both More and Erasmus are at pains to show that the Bible must be taken at its word in such texts or else the most fundamental ethical teachings of Christianity become an insoluble puzzle.

More mentions Erasmus in this piece against Bugenhagen—though he does not call him by name. He speaks only of the work called *A Lecture on the Freedom of the Will* by "the most erudite of men and one deserving much merit from the church of Christ." The praise is similar in wording to the commendation More offered Erasmus in the *Responsio,* although there he had used his name. He does not dwell on Erasmus's treatise; he is, rather, preoccupied with the intemperate and uncompromising statement of predestination in Luther's answer to it, *On the Bondage of the Will.*

Why did More never publish this book? It is a splendid piece of polemic, in many ways the best theological work he ever wrote. All the elements of his theology, presented so verbosely in the *Responsio,* are here in a concise summary, and anyone wishing to know the shape of his religious thought can do no better than to begin with this little book. Yet it lay among his papers unpublished until 1568, when it appeared on the Continent among English Catholic exiles.

It is unlikely that More ever sent the letter to Bugenhagen. It was not a private missive but rather an open letter intended for publication. We may offer a plausible guess as to the reason he did not have it printed.

More very likely would have shown this piece to someone whose theological acumen he trusted. Cuthbert Tunstall was a friend, but no theologian. The most logical and most learned theologian in the realm was John Fisher. But Fisher, a voluminous writer against Luther in Latin, was an ardent papalist. In everything he wrote, papal power was sovereign, the cornerstone of the visible church on earth. Had he read More's letter against Bugenhagen, he must have been struck—perhaps thunderstruck—at the absence of any defense of the power of popes. He naturally would have objected, and More might have chosen not to press for such a discussion in public at a time when Catholics had to forget their internal disagreements and present a united front against Luther. So he put the work away, perhaps intending to go back to it.

More's arguments for the sacred traditions of the Catholic Church as he marshaled them in this letter might be invincible on the assumptions he made. But the world was not to be won by invincible logic set down systematically in books. The religious future of Christian Europe lay in the hands of young men of passionate temperament who yearned with all their hearts for a direct relation with God, unmediated by hierarchies or sacraments, and in the hands of monarchs who, whatever their temperament, looked for greater authority and saw in the religious upheaval an irresistible opportunity for worldly advantage.

Thomas More was so far from understanding the experience of the young men and so far from sympathizing with royal ambitions that history in England pushed him quickly aside. Tyndale's English New Testament was only the first gush of a flood of heretical books that now poured into England. That flood stirred Thomas More to build a wall of pages against it—pages now seldom read and often embarrassing to those who love More and want to keep his name alive. We must recall that his ponderous books and their furious rhetoric are emblems of his helplessness before events. He wrote because he could do nothing else.

Even as he wrote against Bugenhagen and pondered further literary involvement on his own, he was working hard to persuade Erasmus to do something more to defend the Catholic Church. The two men corresponded regularly in these years, but few of their letters to each other have survived. In those that do remain, More continually urged on his famous friend the necessity of defending the Catholic Church, and just as continually, Erasmus begged off. Stapleton wrote long afterwards that as heresy increased, More's love for Erasmus "decreased and grew cool." Stapleton was evidently correct, although More and Erasmus never came to a formal break. As Erasmus had written in 1519, formal breaks were not More's way in ridding himself of friends he did not want any longer. Besides, the names of the two men were inextricably linked in the minds of Europeans educated enough to care about such things, and More was on record as having praised Erasmus and having defended his work. To engage now in an open quarrel would be to make an admission of error that More—always defensive about such things—was probably incapable of making.

Yet he could only have been vexed at the continued publication by Erasmus of successive editions of his *Familiar Colloquies,* originally little dialogues intended to help students learn useful Latin phrases—much like any phrase book of today is meant to help tourists be cheerful in a foreign language.

In the edition of March 1522, Erasmus began to use the colloquies as a vehicle for his ideal of simple, lay piety and also for his continued attack on some of the same abuses in the church that Luther was condemning at the top of his voice. To More the colloquies would have seemed maddeningly ambiguous—as they appear today. One could hardly condemn the ideals of piety that Erasmus espoused or defend the abuses that he exposed. But in these tumultuous times their spirit remained detached from the torrid issues believed by men like More and Tunstall to be critical. One could hardly tell whether the author of the colloquies was Lutheran or Catholic. Many were later translated into English, some to be used as propaganda by Henry VIII as he destroyed the monasteries in England. They are among the few things Erasmus wrote that still seem witty, and we can applaud their nonpartisan common sense and sometimes bawdy humor. But to Catholics like More who believed that Luther and his epigoni threatened the household of faith, the order of civilization, and the road to salvation, the colloquies must have sounded like jokes at a funeral.

In "The Godly Feast" of 1522 married laymen sit around a dinner table in a country villa, reading scripture and discussing the Christian life without reference to priests, vows, or sacraments. No speaker condemns priests, but they seem hardly necessary. The colloquy called "The Whole Duty of Youth" praises John Colet, dead since 1519. But the piety of the piece is so simple, so free of doctrinal definition, that it manages to avoid touching on any of the issues that aroused the greatest passions in the fight against Luther. In his letter against Bugenhagen, More stormed against Bugenhagen's view that the only necessary creed for a Christian was the confession "Christ is our righteousness." He might well have condemned Erasmus for the same offense in the colloquies; certainly these Erasmian characters speak as if they believe that nothing else is necessary.

In "The Whole Duty of Youth" Erasmus attacks unworthy priests who babbled the secrets of the confessional to anyone who would listen—an offense also loudly condemned by the Protestants. He strikes hard at unworthy monks and manages to convey the impression that the ideal of piety built on monasticism was bound to produce hypocrisy. Monks were absurd to isolate themselves in the monastery and to believe that their adherence to uncomfortable habits granted them a greater certainty of salvation than the ordinary Christian who helped society with its secular business.

In the edition of 1526, two colloquies outraged his critics. One, called "Eating Fish," mocked Catholic fast days on which the devout were required to eat fish rather than beef or pork. It expressed vigorously Erasmus's glum conviction that the Catholic Church had fallen into the hands of legalists who made religion a rule to be kept rather than a life to be lived—a conviction helped along by Erasmus's dislike of fish, a food that made his stomach heave when he ate it.

The other offending colloquy, "A Pilgrimage for the Sake of Religion," mocked two English shrines, the tomb of St. Thomas Becket at Canterbury and the shrine of Our Lady of Walsingham. One of the pilgrims seems to be John Colet, who, safely dead, could not object to what Erasmus was doing to his reputation. At Canterbury the keepers of the saint's relics—greedy for offerings—haul out old bones to be kissed, some with rotting flesh still clinging to them, and produce old handkerchiefs still dirty where the saint blew his nose. Small wonder that Henry's men used this colloquy to help justify the royal confiscation of the splendid old shrine!

Yet More persisted in his patient efforts to push Erasmus into further controversy as a defender of the Catholic Church. In 1526 Erasmus published the first part of his *Hyperaspistes (A Weighty Consideration),* a long, tedious reply to Luther's vehement attack on him of the year before. Much of the work wallows in self-pity; Erasmus accuses Luther of cruelty and protests that he has never assaulted Luther's character—a disclaimer that could hardly have pleased More, who smote Luther hip and thigh. As in *A Lecture on the Freedom of the Will,* Erasmus never gets around to defining the church in any coherent, historical way, so that we are left in the dark about what he means by the word. Whenever he touches some of the burning issues of the controversy with Luther, he jumps quickly away.

His English friends kept after him to do something else. In December 1526, More wrote in diplomatic urgency. He began by touching on the matter always dearest to Erasmus's heart—the state of Erasmus's health. He and Tunstall were troubled not only for Erasmus, More said, but for all Christendom lest "this illness interrupt the brilliant works you have been writing to promote Christian piety." Piety was the great word for Erasmus. He made a distinction between piety and polemic; More did not. The work of piety More desired most to see concluded was the last part of the *Hyperaspistes,* promised by Erasmus in the first half. Said More, "You could have no other work in mind that would be more profitable for others, more satisfying to your friends, and more notable or more urgent for yourself." He also mentioned that Queen Catherine of Aragon was most happy with the work Erasmus called *The Institution of Christian Marriage,* which he had finished and dedicated to her in August 1526. The implication was that favor with the great would be the reward for further writing about these important matters.

More urged the completion of the work against Luther. Had Erasmus lost courage? More hoped not. "You have endured, dearest Erasmus, many, many struggles and perils and Herculean labors; you have spent all the best years of your life in exhausting work, through sleepless nights, for the profit of all the world; and God forbid that now you should so unhappily become enamored of your declining years as to be willing to abandon the cause of God rather than lose a decision."

The letter is long and friendly, though without the blazing affection of the letters More wrote a decade earlier as Erasmus was guiding *Utopia* through the press. It is throughout a carefully construed attempt to coax Erasmus into the battle that More thought had to be waged against Luther. He knew that Erasmus had to be cajoled, not driven, and he was fully aware of the enormous reputation Erasmus enjoyed in the European world. He was aware also that the reputation was deserved, and the recollection of their happy days together never left him.

Erasmus replied on March 30, 1527. He considered More's request and again begged off. He wrote that More and Tunstall imagined that it would be a great thing if he gave himself over completely to the fight against Luther. But this, he was convinced, would be like throwing stones at hornets. Words could not cure the evil; they could only stir the world into tumult and increase the insolence of the monks and the fury of the theologians. Erasmus held doggedly to his conviction—onerous for More—that the monks and the theologians were greater foes to true piety than were the Lutherans.

He made excuses. The contagion could more easily be suppressed in England than on the Continent. He was living in Basel now, and things were precarious there. Heresy was strong. Oecolampadius, the heretical reformer of Basel, had written secretly against Erasmus's treatise on free will. (Erasmus felt betrayed, for Oecolampadius had helped him produce the first edition of the *Novum Instrumentum*—yet another example of the propensity of young Greek scholars to espouse heretical thinking.) Tumult was likely if the matter was pressed, Erasmus said. He did not wish to offend magistrates who desired peace and silence—and, he might have mentioned, magistrates already committed to heresy. Why did he not leave Basel? His health made it impossible to live anywhere else; he said he would not live three days if he moved.

Besides, he did not want to be a leader of faction, he said—and how More must have smarted to read that defenders of the Catholic Church should now be called "leaders of faction." He had neither the talent nor the spirit nor the experience to do battle. Nothing horrified him so much as conflict. It did no good to cite scripture against Luther, he said, because Luther interpreted scripture to suit himself—as if More had asked him to convert Luther rather than to defend the church against Luther.

Erasmus refused to agree that polemics made piety. He cited the work he had to do—another edition of the New Testament, an edition of the *Adages*, a refutation of the calumnies of Noel Beda, a dogged theologian of the University of Paris who had led a campaign against Erasmus there. (Erasmus might not have time to defend the church, but he always had plenty of time to defend himself.) He said he must continue his paraphrases of the New Testament, and he wanted to get out a new edition of Seneca.

So he had neither time nor strength to enter the fray. If he wrote anything to console the monks and the theologians who granted too much efficacy to human works and merit, he said, he would offend his own conscience. In a private letter like this one, Erasmus would admit that both Paul and Augustine —especially the latter, whom More revered—seemed to stand firmly against free will. Erasmus confessed again his difficulty here and wrestled briefly with it to no certain conclusion: if people accepted predestination, what could motivate them to do good? He had no answer. The insanity of the times could not be stopped, he said, except by the authority of princes or by the departure of the warring principals from the scene. His deepest opinion remained that the Protestant schism would fade away like all the other schisms in the history of the church; time would heal all things. We may wonder what he would have thought had he known that the warring principals would leave warring children to carry on the conflict for longer than four centuries and probably to the end of Christian history.

Many complained that Luther had taken much from him, Erasmus said. But Luther had also taken things from scripture, twisting holy writ to suit himself. Erasmus commented wryly enough that he could not be blamed if Luther did to him what the German had also done to the Bible, wrenching things that Erasmus had written in innocence. "I do nothing but warn," he wrote bleakly, unconsciously admitting his futile role as Cassandra to Europe, refusing to acknowledge that he had done anything to upset the religious order, claiming never to have introduced new rites or doctrines, never to have written in anything but a temperate style. He implied, in short, that he had always been ineffectual in bringing about reform as he had wanted it to come—by friendly persuasion.

Erasmus fell easily into black moods of self-pity and paranoia in these years, and this long letter is as black as any. People everywhere attack him, he says, giving tedious and mournful details. Some Catholics show greater vehemence toward him than toward Luther. Louvain and Paris conspire against him, and in Paris, Louis de Berquin, who had translated some of Erasmus into French, was in prison. (Erasmus probably did not know that Berquin had set out to prove that Luther should not be condemned outright since many things that he said had also been said by Erasmus. In his muddled way Berquin had incited Noel Beda against Erasmus, and in 1529 Berquin would be burned at the stake. In 1532 More would crow in print over Berquin's execution by fire.)

Now Erasmus lamented that no intelligent theologians were left in Paris and that no one understood him. Yet in Rome, seat of the papacy, no one dared publish a word against him. "What a fate is mine!" he cries. "At the summit of the world, I am revered by the mighty. But by the lowest sort of men, I am spat upon, shit upon, and pissed upon."

He would conclude the *Hyperaspistes,* he told More, but clearly he had neither hope for the work nor much interest in it. The last part of the book did appear in the summer of 1527, as Erasmus promised. It is one of the few things he wrote that has never appeared in any language except the Latin in which he wrote it. The silence is well deserved.

He closed on the same sour note he had sounded throughout his letter. There were those, he said, who supposed that all would be wonderfully well with the church if things could only be restored to how they had been before Luther. Erasmus thought such people were foolish.

It is an old man's letter, bristling with the querulous liberty of the old who, having put up with the importunities of life for years, now demand to have their own way no matter who wants them to bend in another direction. Nothing in it could have pleased More. It was not published as long as either man lived, for neither cared to give it to the world. Had More seen another letter that Erasmus wrote the same day, to John Maldonatus, a Spanish theologian, he would have been even less pleased. Here, as clearly and as forcefully as he ever did, Erasmus presented the main issue of the Reformation as a war of good letters against ignorance, and he saw both Catholics and Lutherans fueling ignorance with all their might. The only salvation that interested him, according to the letter to Maldonatus, was education, and he saw the cause as hopelessly lost. If anything, his rage burned with more heat against Catholic monks and Catholic theologians than against Lutheran heretics. He must have thought that these were the people who had ruined his life's work.

So More's efforts to bring Erasmus to the front in the war against Luther failed, and in the meantime heresy grew in England, demanding an English response. Tyndale remained in exile. By 1526 the leader of the so-called new men in England was Robert Barnes. On Christmas Eve, 1525, he preached a crashingly Lutheran sermon at Cambridge, and in a wink he was accused of heresy.

Wolsey needed a convincing demonstration against heresy just at that moment, believing that strong measures would deter the spread of the contagion. He needed a heretic to punish, and Barnes was available. The garrulous Lutheran was soon taken to London under arrest to stand trial before the cardinal.

Wolsey seems to have treated the matter lightly—much to More's annoyance. The cardinal never distinguished himself as a theologian, and he probably could see nothing in Barnes beyond standard English anticlericalism. Wolsey had no streak of religious fanaticism in him; neither was he cruel, although he could be vindictive to those who thwarted his political and personal ambitions. He probably could not understand the passions that drove a man like Barnes. Wolsey's world was a comfortable place in 1526, and he had a hard time seeing why any intelligent person would willingly choose discomfort.

Barnes boldly attacked the pomp of the clergy, including the silver pillars and poleaxes that Wolsey had carried before him on processions as symbols as his authority. Wolsey's reply was what we might expect of a secular statesman, preoccupied with the symbols of office and with their power over the emotions of the ignorant and impressionable masses.

> How think you? Were it better for me, being in the honor and dignity that I am, to make coins of my pillars and poleaxes and to give the money to five or six beggars than to maintain the commonwealth as I do?

Barnes described this conversation years later, when Wolsey was dead and unable to reply, and he claimed that he had told the cardinal that the commonwealth had existed before Wolsey lived and that it would remain after he died and that to dispense with the finery of office would do greater honor to God and greater good for his soul.

He may have told the truth, or he may have been trying to make himself look brave to his audience after it had become fashionable to execrate Wolsey's memory. In his account he makes Wolsey seem amused, and this part rings true, for haughty amusement is often a defense of experienced and powerful politicians when they meet simple, high-minded people sure that everything could be ideal if the politicians would only demonstrate good will by making some grand gesture.

Barnes went to trial. During the process, More made the raid on the Steelyard in which he had some German merchants arrested for selling heretical books. On Sunday, February 11, Barnes and the merchants carried faggots in St. Paul's in token of their confession that though they deserved to be burned, they had revoked their heresies and professed their loyalty to the Catholic Church. Wolsey was in attendance. John Fisher preached a sermon. A great pile of heretical books was burned outside the church, and Barnes and the Steelyard merchants marched penitently around the pyre. Barnes was sentenced to remain in custody for two years afterwards.

His custody was not strict, and within six months after the fiery humiliation at St. Paul's, he was quietly trading in Tyndale's New Testament. Several months passed before Tunstall learned of this illegal activity. Discovering it in the spring of 1528, he became so furious that he was ready to have Barnes burned as a relapsed heretic. But Barnes escaped his fate for the second time by faking suicide, leaving a note on a table and a pile of his clothing with another note on the banks of the Thames, urging the mayor to drag for his body, promising that it would have on it yet another note, sealed in wax. While the authorities were preoccupied with the dragging operation, he got himself over to Antwerp and on to Wittenberg, where his wit made him a great favorite of Martin Luther.

More's hatred of heresy and heretics was, of course, much stronger than Wolsey's. Scrupulous himself about the rules of piety, believing firmly in rules for others, and outraged by duplicity as only the scrupulous can be, he drew lessons from Robert Barnes that he tried to teach the English people.

He saw Barnes as a boastful heretic who loved to vaunt himself at the expense of the clergy. Yet when charged with heresy, Barnes fell into evasions and chose to deceive his foes to save his skin rather than to confess his faith bravely. Barnes's hypocrisy was indisputably proved by his dealings in Tyndale's Bible while he was pleading with both Tunstall and Wolsey to be released from confinement on the grounds that he was no heretic. Moreover, the lenient treatment he received from the authorities failed to save his soul or to keep others from the poison with which he was infecting English life. His conduct provided Thomas More with a tableau of heresy and heretics in keeping with More's fundamental assumption that heresy was from Satan and heretics were abominable.

Yet the heretics continued to draw support from the masses. Thomas Bilney of Cambridge impressed people by his ascetic ways and by his hard preaching against pilgrimages and the veneration of saints. Late in 1527 he was hauled before Wolsey and Tunstall, charged with heresy, and browbeaten into a recantation. Many murmured that he had been abused by the clergy only because he had condemned the corrupt living of priests. His recantation was a public humiliation, and it occasioned a great anticlerical outburst by a population that had not forgotten the Hunne affair. Bilney became a sort of martyr.

Having failed with Erasmus and facing the heresy now couching at the door of English life, More had only two tactics left. His first was to do all he could as a royal councillor to bring the power of both church and government to bear against the heretics, to crush them and their beliefs, and if need be to burn heresy out of England with fire. His second was to write against heresy, to write in English, not with the Erasmian desire to win the heretics over, but rather to strengthen the faith in those innocents whom the heretics were seducing into hell and to rally public opinion to support the uncompromising harshness he wanted from the government.

In March 1528, Cuthbert Tunstall commissioned More to carry out one part of this policy—the writing, granting More official permission to read heretical books, asking him, "a Demosthenes in both English and Latin," to refute those books by writing in the vernacular. The commission must have come after long discussions between the two friends, and it is probable that More asked for it. He had badgered Erasmus to write against heresy; Erasmus had refused. Now More would do it himself, put business aside, and rob himself of time and sleep to defend the most essential thing in his life—the Catholic Church.

The immediate result of Tunstall's commission was the great *Dialogue Concerning Heresies,* which appeared in June 1529. The larger consequence was a parade of English polemical works from More's pen that for all their ferocity and dreary dullness still offer the most significant literary monument we have to his mind and heart. It is to these works, rather than to the reasonable *Utopia,* that we must go to find a More of flesh and blood.

A Dialogue Concerning Heresies is the best of the lot. It has often been called *A Dialogue Concerning Tyndale* because More devoted so much of the book to attacking Tyndale's New Testament and two other works that Tyndale brought out in 1528, *The Parable of the Wicked Mammon* and *The Obedience of the Christian Man.* Both these works are fierce, and More thought them dangerous. The former exalted justification by faith and held the standard Lutheran position that good works were sinful if they were done with a view to reward. The latter called on Christian princes to reform the church. (A later story has it that Anne Boleyn gave a copy of *The Obedience of the Christian Man* to Henry VIII and that the king read it for a while with gusto, then tucked it away to read at leisure.)

More assaulted all of Tyndale's positions in his *Dialogue,* mentioning Tyndale with greater frequency than any other heretic, although castigating others as well. He reviewed the Thomas Bilney affair, laboring mightily to prove that Bilney had been fairly and mercifully treated and that it was slander to hold otherwise—proof enough that the English audience to whom More directed the book was still grumbling that Bilney had been unjustly abused. And it was here that he considered the Richard Hunne case in the detail that we have already noted, a review obviously necessitated by the lively prowling of Hunne's ghost through anticlerical and heretical circles in London and the rest of the country.

A Dialogue Concerning Heresies is often witty. Yet it continually reveals the cast-iron rules-maker we find in *Utopia* and in the Latin polemical works that we mentioned earlier. Beneath the wit, beneath the studied efforts to seem fair-minded, beneath the apparent friendliness in tone, there lies an icy inflexibility and an unyielding resolve to make the worst of his opponents, to twist the evidence to make it mean what More insists it must mean, and to prove that anyone who opposes the church is totally wrong and malicious, even insane. One may defend the book as a lawyer's work, one that makes the best possible case for a jury, aiming not so much at establishing the truth as at winning a victory. Still, the work is disappointing, especially as the work of a saint. We have already seen how he distorted the Hunne case to make it seem that only fools imagined that clergymen had had any part in Hunne's death. He carried the same spirit into everything else he wrote in the *Dialogue,* so that what we have in the end is not discussion but diatribe.

Much in the *Dialogue* sounds like a refutation of views expressed in the *Familiar Colloquies* of Erasmus, although Erasmus is not mentioned by name. Even the form is reminiscent of the colloquies, those sprightly little dialogues usually between two people, although in some of them several speakers hold forth. But while Erasmus used the colloquies to call attention to abuses in the church, More used his *Dialogue* to maintain that the abuses were scarcely significant before its glory.

In the *Dialogue*, More is approached by a young student, sent by one of More's friends because the friend thinks More can answer the theological questions the student is asking about new doctrines stirring through England. The young man, called the "messenger" and otherwise unnamed, has an apt tongue, and he and More argue in a jovial way about nearly everything at issue in the Reformation except the place of the papacy, which, as usual with More, is passed over in as much silence as he can muster.

The young man gets in some good licks against corruption in the church; he tells some merry tales, and More tells some, too. They laugh a lot. More is patient, witty, anecdotal—and invincible. In the end he has answered all the young man's questions and sent him away with Catholic faith confirmed and youthful spirit at ease. The tone is lively and friendly.

The "messenger" is usually taken to represent William Roper during his heretical phase, but that supposition is hardly credible. As Harpsfield testifies, Roper was far deeper in heresy than the "messenger," who in More's *Dialogue* is a questioner and not a convert to the new doctrines. Harpsfield also shows that More viewed Roper's tumble into heresy with an anguish and ambivalence entirely lacking in the arguments of the More in the *Dialogue*. It is probably better to see the young man in this piece as an Erasmian thinking of becoming a Lutheran.

The light touch of the *Dialogue* is reminiscent of the *Familiar Colloquies*, but the aims of the two works are entirely different. More loved a good story, and the *Dialogue* shows him at his bawdy best, a spiritual descendant of Chaucer, whose works he knew well and apparently loved. He gives us some belly laughs, showing flaws in the life of the church so gross that they are somehow minor in the face of the enormous authority of the whole. Erasmus's wit after Luther came on the scene was by comparison darker, more pessimistic, directed not so much toward obvious flaws that everybody could recognize as toward the general confusion in the church about what was good and what evil. More points to the occasional stain on the hard, strong surface of the church, and in his work we can see that the stain can be wiped away without doing any permanent damage to the structure itself; Erasmus gives us a structure rotting and perhaps doomed to fall, to be saved only by knowledge, and he is skeptical that knowledge is going to come.

Erasmus attacked some of the common forms of popular piety without leaving much room for good in them; pilgrimages, the veneration of saints, virginity, prayers to the Virgin Mary, the piety that made relics talismans, the repetition of masses, all find little support in his *Familiar Colloquies*. More admitted some crudities but in the *Dialogue* defended popular piety with zeal.

One of the tales More puts into the mouth of his "messenger" (who does most of the criticizing) reminds us of the Erasmian colloquy "A Pilgrimage for the Sake of Religion." Erasmus makes fun of two English shrines; typically, More mocks a shrine in France. He may have visited St. Valéry's in Picardy on one of his continental journeys, though he could have been relying on hearsay. At any rate, the tale is from the Thomas More whose preoccupation with the nether parts and the waste products of the human body shows in much of his own work and in many stories told about him.

At St. Valéry's, so the messenger tells us, the pilgrim could find the walls hung with wax models of male and female genitalia in testimony to the miraculous cures the saint had effected on those parts of the human anatomy. (The shrine was obviously like Epidauros in Greece and many another throughout the world to which people with ailments in these parts resorted in the long centuries before modern medicine.) On the altar were two silver rings, one larger than the other, and there men, choosing the ring that made the better fit, inserted their "male gear," as the messenger called it.

A monk stood by with threads of "Venice gold," and he instructed each man how to tie a knot around the penis, presumably while it was thrust through the appropriate ring, to protect against kidney stones—one of the great horrors of the time, often blocking the urination of middle-aged men for days and causing, when passed through the urinary tract, the most excruciating pain known to the age. The knotting was accompanied by ritual prayers.

One of the men in the party "that was a married man and yet a merry fellow" thanked the monk for the thread but "desired him to teach him how he should knit it about his wife's gear which, unless the monk had some special craft in knitting, he thought would be troublesome because her gear was somewhat short." The monk rattled his keys and sulked away.

Later this merry visitor was approached by a wise woman who told him that she had the sure preventative against the stone. She would mold a candle in the shape of his penis and burn it and so burn away the possibility of the disease. The man, despite his mocking wit, was truly afraid of the stone, and he took the matter up with his wife. What should he do? The wife was irate and protested vehemently. This was witchcraft, she said. As the candle burned, so would her husband's sexual potency, and then where would she be?

The messenger also told the story of St. Wilgefort, or St. Uncumber, as women called her; she rid women of their husbands in exchange for an offering of oats. He spoke of St. Elizabeth of Leominster in the days of Henry VII, a woman who posed as a creature so ethereal that she lived only on the host that rose miraculously from the altar to her perch in a cage above. In truth, the host rose on a thread arranged to deceive the gullible, and at night she came down from her roost and slept with the priest. She was discovered when she was shut up in a cage and craved food and defecated besides—something that, in the popular imagination and apparently in More's as well, saints were not supposed to do. She ended her days as a whore in Calais, telling the tale to all who would listen.

So it went with these and other merry tales, and to the superficial observer, it might seem that More and Erasmus were strumming on the same lyre, still in harmony in their desire for reform in the church. But in fact Erasmus ends by attacking popular piety and More by defending it, and the roles of the funny story in the *Familiar Colloquies* and the *Dialogue* are at opposite poles of intention. Erasmus tells the stories only to condemn; More tells them according to the ancient rhetorical principle of *concessio,* a concession that parries a blow and robs an attack of its force. Always he admitted an abuse only to launch an ardent defense of the underlying practice. He could laugh at the shrine to St. Valéry and leave it to the investigation of the University of Paris, as he told the messenger, but then he moved quickly to the general principle he defended:

> To all these matters is one evident easy answer, that they nothing touch the effect of our matter, which stands in this whether the thing that we speak of as praying to saints, going in pilgrimage, and worshipping relics and images may be done well, not whether it may be done evil. For if it may be well done, then though many would misuse it, yet doth all that nothing diminish the goodness of the thing itself. For if we should for the misuse of a good thing and for the evils that grow sometimes in the abuse thereof not amend the misuse but utterly put the whole use away, we should then make marvelous changes in the world.

At times More's defense of popular piety reaches toward the absurd. If a relic has been venerated for many years in the church, he says, it must be genuine or else God would not have permitted the veneration to continue. So he had to claim that all the churches in Europe said to possess the head of John the Baptist did indeed have at least a part of it. In his discussion of saints, he gives us a great catalogue of names from *The Golden Legend* and other sources, some no longer venerated by the Catholic Church because they are regarded as mythological. But More defended them all.

As if in response to Erasmus's claim that Christians should not pray to saints for any but spiritual benefits, More made a fine distinction. He thought it unworthy to pray to saints for anything we can do for ourselves or for some unnecessary thing. We should not pray to St. Dorothy for flowers despite her constant association in iconography with a basket of flowers. But we can ask saints to grant us benefits we cannot win for ourselves. It is acceptable to pray to St. Appoline when we have a toothache because part of her martyrdom was to have her teeth yanked out by pagans. We can pray to St. Roke and St.

Sebastian for deliverance from plague, for certainly we cannot deliver ourselves. It is perhaps all right, More says, to pray to St. Loy, who had been a blacksmith, when we worry about our horse on a journey.

He defends images, at least for the simple. We should venerate them and through them the reality they represent; no one in his right mind confuses an image of the Virgin Mary with the Virgin herself—a questionable assumption and one the Protestants vigorously disputed. We should go on pilgrimages. Why? Because God is pleased when we do. God is everywhere present, but through the centuries He has worked miracles at shrines. He goes on working them, and the miracles show that He blesses the pilgrimages to the shrines where miracles take place.

In the first book of *A Dialogue Concerning Heresies*, fourteen chapters are given over to a defense of miracles. Luther, unable to disbelieve entirely that something wonderful did take place at shrines, held that Catholic miracles were works of Satan to delude Christians into believing a lie, and Tyndale agreed. The messenger repeats their opinions and elevates them to a somewhat more sophisticated level—sounding a little like some David Hume born out of his time, showing that More had pondered the issue at some length.

The messenger says that both reason and nature are against miracles. More replies that miracles are not against nature but so far above nature that we cannot understand them. But then, he says, we cannot understand many things. We cannot understand the birth of children, and who would have believed in former times that ships could sail around the world and not fall off the bottom? (Evidently the writer of *Utopia* had kept up with the news of the voyage undertaken by Magellan and finished by Sebastián del Cano.) God's ways are above our ways. What is undoubted is that good men have regularly testified that God has done miracles in the church; no one can suppose that so many witnesses were always wrong. It is almost identical to the argument in our own time that so many sightings of UFOs must prove the existence of visitors from outer space, and it assumes that a consensus among great numbers of people must always be right.

The miraculous has intruded itself often in this biography, illustrating ambiguity in More's thoughts, a double-mindedness typical of the man, rending to him, and characteristic of the age itself. More's *History of King Richard III* seems thoroughly modern in its view that history is human action, secretly and mysteriously controlled by Providence but not broken by miraculous intrusions, although some things—like Richard's teeth, which grew before he was born, and his unnatural birth—presage wickedness to come. Now in the *Dialogue*, when More defends miracles so staunchly, we might expect him to tell of some to provide evidence for his assertions. And he does—although all but one of them come from the distant past. He tells us about St. Erkenwald and the beam at Barking Abbey that the saint miraculously stretched to fit. He recounts several New Testament miracles that seem to justify pilgrimages. In the Gospel of John, people were cured if they could be first into the pool of Bethsaida after it was agitated by an angel. God could have healed the sick without the pool, but He chose that method of effecting cures, and so He does with pilgrimages.

Some complain, says More, that miracles are done for slight causes. But the first miracle Christ worked was for a slight cause: the host of a wedding in Cana in Galilee ran out of wine. Miracles have validated relics, says More. Here he goes to the fantasy-filled *Golden Legend* with a disturbing alacrity. When the true cross was found, a corpse was restored to life by its touch, certifying its authenticity. The head of John the Baptist and the body of St. Stephen were discovered by miracles. He buys whole the old tale that King Agbar of Edessa sent an artist to paint the portrait of Jesus. The artist could not catch the image; Jesus pressed the artist's cloth to his face, leaving a holy image imprinted. (A garbled version of this tale became the legend of St. Veronica.)

But what of recent miracles? More says they go on daily in the church. But can he locate one? He says that there had been at Rhodes a miraculous thorn that burst into bloom every Good Friday until the Turks seized the island. Presumably the thorn was no more.

What of miracles in his own experience? We have no proof that he ever went on a pilgrimage or to a shrine himself. But he recalls that the daughter of Sir Roger Wentworth was healed from demonic possession by a miracle. Wentworth was a friend of More's and occasionally accompanied him on diplomatic missions, and More must have known the girl and her affliction. The cure took place in consequence of a pilgrimage to Ipswich, where there was a famous image of the Virgin. Later the girl became a nun. Such seizures and their "cures" have probably been common enough through the ages to provoke both wonder at the occasion and a broader, more general acceptance of hysterical behavior that now and then overtakes people.

It is the best More can do. He did not have friends who told him convincing miracle stories. His own skepticism did not allow him to multiply tales when he could not name the names and know the places.

It was a striking and doubtless painful schism in him. He was reaching back in his piety to the God of the Bible, the living God, the God who parted the Red Sea and made an axhead float on the surface of a pool and turned back the shadow on a sundial and raised Christ from the dead. Luther and Tyndale are popularly called "biblical" because they made so much of "scripture alone" as the source of faith. But the Bible is many contradictory things. More's God, breaking continually into ordinary life in unmistakable manifestations of His power, made More as biblical as anyone else in the sixteenth century, even though he could not locate the miraculous in his own time. Obviously he wished that he could, but the skepticism engendered by his exposure to classical science and philosophy and to classical wags like Lucian who ridiculed superstition prevented Thomas More from easy belief in miracles that happened to people and in places he knew.

However, he does not seem the least ambiguous in *A Dialogue Concerning Heresies* or in any other of his polemics. Throughout he castigates heretics as wicked men and argues in painful detail that everything they believed would lead to the overthrow of civilization, the end of religious belief, and the triumph of hell on earth. He writes of predestination as if the doctrine had been held only by heretics, although we know from his own "Letter to a Monk" in 1519 and from Erasmus's letter to him in 1527 that he knew Augustine had held a view of predestination much like Luther's. And of course More knew huge chunks of Augustine's works almost by heart, quoting him continually with easy familiarity when it suited him to do so. But here More becomes the lawyer, unwilling to admit any evidence—beyond a few peccadillos of the clergy—into the testimony that might weaken his case before the all-important jury he was seeking to convince, the English people.

It may be that this rigid affirmation of unshakable certainty was nothing but a rhetorical stance. But it is also possible that it was an expression of a trait we know well enough in our own time from the clinical observation of people under stress—an unwillingness to admit doubt to oneself, a resolute effort to turn back a silent inner voice of skepticism with a ringing shout of affirmation. Such people may doggedly state and restate these affirmations, or they may surrender them in a rush, often discovering that life as they have meticulously built it up dissolves to nothing.

Luther was married to his nun by the time More wrote *A Dialogue Concerning Heresies*, so More could indulge himself in the most tiresome part of his polemics—lampooning the monk Luther for incestuous relations with the nun Kate. The cacophony of More's furious tirade is remorseless: how could anyone give hearing, he asks, "to a fond friar, to an apostate, to an open incestuous lecher, a plain limb of the devil, and a manifest messenger of hell?" More marveled at things people would accept if novelty was gradually thrust upon them. Look at Luther, he says. "If he should in the beginning have said all that he hath said since, who could have suffered him? If he should in the beginning have married a nun, would not the people have burned him?" So it goes, an acid rain of bitter contempt for Luther's marriage and supposed lechery drenching the page whenever Luther's name appears.

To More, Luther's worst sins besides heresy itself were his teachings about marriage and his doctrine of predestination. He could never grasp the powerful moral compulsion in Luther's version of predestination. His own countrymen who would become Puritans in his century would lead the most austerely moral lives ever known to large numbers of laymen in Christendom. They would do so under the driving force of predestination, for they would be eaten alive by the compulsion to prove to themselves that they were indeed among the elect, a proof they attained by doing those good works taken to be the consequence and sign of their election.

More's recitation of the horrors of heresy in the *Dialogue*—witty and telling though it may have been to a reader already devoutly committed to the old faith—could not hold the teetering doubter, wondering if satisfaction for a genuine religious hunger might be found in the new doctrines. More tried to represent such people in the person of his messenger, and he persuaded his own creation easily enough. The messenger has some good lines, and as in a bad novel, we can see the shape of the character More wanted him to be—sincere, naïve, and earnest with a little dash of humor to salt his dullness. But despite all this, he is finally only a foil, a two-dimensional character cut out by More like a paper doll to be dressed and manipulated as his creator wished. No real person torn between heaven and hell, the flesh and the devil, in the turmoil of religious revolution, could recognize himself in the meek, docile, and colorless creature that More made.

A few other details in the *Dialogue* deserve comment. One is the way More presents himself as a busy and important man with important friends, a man willing out of Christian charity to take some precious hours out of two days to talk with a young inquirer about the faith.

We might argue that part of this self-portrait was intended to show that serious men of affairs accepted the old faith without qualm and that only the young and the unestablished were tempted to wander into dangerous novelty. But he probably also enjoyed giving this portrait of himself to the world—a respected man whose life was the royal court, whose judgments were trusted by both weak and strong. It was part of his self-fashioning, akin to the image he presents of himself in *Utopia* and the later *Dialogue of Comfort Against Tribulation,* the image he gave to Roper and that Roper passed on to posterity.

The account More gives of Thomas Bilney is also worth a note. He does not mention Bilney by name—perhaps supposing that the name might arouse passions better left dormant until he had gotten into his argument and it became obvious it was Bilney he was talking about. He says that Bilney was a heretic: he attacked images, veneration of saints, and pilgrimages. More, defending everything the church did and taught, could not tolerate such beliefs. Yet we can easily make the case that Bilney was merely a Christian who took Erasmus literally and sought to exemplify the Erasmian "philosophy of Christ." He held none of the identifiable Protestant doctrines.

Did Bilney read this patronizing account of himself written by More? From John Foxe we know that by the time *A Dialogue Concerning Heresies* appeared, he was already suffering black depression and perhaps suicidal guilt because he had recanted. More's triumphal recounting of Bilney's career and renunciation of his heretical beliefs could only have deepened the melancholy of a sensitive man who had started on the way, taking friends with him, but then pulled back, leaving them to go on without him.

The savage side of More's character emerges at the end of the *Dialogue*, where he argues vehemently for the burning of heretics. One chapter heading summarizes all: "The author showeth his opinion concerning the burning of heretics and that it is lawful, necessary, and well done." Some of this vehemence might have been an admonition to Cardinal Wolsey, who, distracted by Henry's quest for a divorce, was doing little to pursue heretics in England.

More's modern admirers have always dwelled on one surprising passage in the *Dialogue*—his advocacy of an English translation of the Bible. We have already observed his adamantine conviction that the church with its oral tradition could quite happily continue without the Bible and that in any case the church granted the Bible its authority. In the *Dialogue* as in his other polemical works, More regularly repeated an assertion of Augustine, who said that he would not have received the scriptures had they not been certified by the Catholic Church. And his general mood was always to denigrate the use of scripture in favor of the common consent of the church. But here—for the only time in his religious works—he comes down hard in favor of an English translation of the Bible.

He has just discussed the Hunne case when he takes up the matter of the translation. Hunne was guilty of reading a Wycliffe Bible, More says. But why do the only Bibles in English have to be heretical? Why does England not have a sound version of the scripture in the vernacular? The messenger presses the embarrassing questions, and More replies somewhat lamely that he has seen many old English Bibles that were not heretical. He could not have argued that he had seen any such Bibles in print, for, as we have seen, England before Tyndale was the only country in Europe lacking its vernacular printing of scripture.

But in principle, More holds, the idea of an English Bible is splendid. Some have said that the English language is too barbaric for holy writ. More rejects this argument and sings a hymn of praise to English common speech. Some say the Bible should not be translated because it is dangerous to the common folk. More points out that Greek, Hebrew, and Latin were languages of the common people at one time or another, and if the Bible came in these languages, it should also be available in English.

He worries about the propensity of the common people to dispute things they have little knowledge of. He thinks that they should read the sacred pages only for devotion. Hardly any passage is so difficult that it will give no reward to the reader who pursues it honestly, he says. But simple Christians should avoid getting in over their heads. Scripture is tricky: a fly can wade in it, he says, but an elephant can drown. Despite the dangers, several scholars should get together and make a translation that could be approved by the proper authorities and then printed.

Once this Bible is printed, More says, it is not to be sold to anyone who happens to have the price. The Bibles should go to the bishop, and each bishop should decide who had the right to read it. Presumably the bishop, through some kind of examination, could determine who might be trusted and who not. Then he could pass out copies for nothing. Perhaps More smarted at the profits made by the German Steelyard merchants who sold Tyndale's translation—profits easily confused with piety by those of a mercenary bent making the most of a good thing.

What are we to make of all this? Standard wisdom holds that we should take it as we see it, assuming that More wanted an English Bible and that he stands on the side of modernity. It is worth pointing out, however, that More could make arguments for positions he did not entirely agree with and that much of his life is hard to interpret because we do not know when to take him seriously and when not.

He knew scripture almost by heart, and he seems to have quoted it frequently from memory when he wrote—reason for the slight errors we occasionally find in his readings. When he translated scripture into English himself, as he did in his English works, he did it well. We have noted that his style was much like Tyndale's—simple rather than "augmented," cadenced, and direct. Though he had no Hebrew, he did know Greek, and he may have been the only Catholic scholar in England both utterly committed to the old faith and capable of giving his countrymen an orthodox translation of the New Testament to rival Tyndale's heretical version.

He did not so choose. He was so busy that we can hardly expect him to have devoted himself to the all-consuming task of translating scripture. He might have pushed others to do it. We have a tantalizing reference in a letter from Miles Coverdale to Thomas Cromwell about 1527. Coverdale, who later made the first royally authorized translation of the Bible into English (plagiarizing Tyndale outrageously), speaks of the "godly communication" he and Cromwell had "in Master More's house on Easter eve." Was the "Master More" Sir Thomas? And if so, were the three men discussing an English translation of the Bible? The questions are unanswerable. We can only know that after *A Dialogue Concerning Heresies* More was to amplify his conviction that scripture, though valuable, was not essential to the faith.

Then why would More have made this argument for a translation so at odds with his general and oft-expressed thoughts on the Bible? It is possible that he may have argued for an English translation when he wrote the *Dialogue* in the skillful rhetorical way he had Hythlodaye argue for communism in *Utopia;*

having decided to make the argument, he brought his best talents to it, although it might not have represented his most profound feelings on the matter.

There is another possibility. On May 25, 1530, in Star Chamber, Tyndale's New Testament was again formally condemned. Hall tells us that on the same day, Henry ordered the bishops to prepare a new translation of the Bible. By June 22 he seems to have backed off. On that date he issued a proclamation announcing that after much consultation with his bishops, he had decided that an English version of scripture was not essential, especially in these times when translating the Bible might result in an increase of errors rather than in any benefit for souls. But he intended, he declared, at a convenient time "to provide that the Holy Scripture shall by great, learned, and Catholic persons [be] translated into the English tongue."

A close reading of this proclamation indicates that Henry wanted a translation but the bishops had talked him out of it—for the time being. He was willing for the moment to take their advice, but he reserved the right to encourage such a translation later on.

All this came after A Dialogue Concerning Heresies was in print. But Henry had probably been attracted to the idea of translating the Bible because he based his case for a divorce on Leviticus. He may have supposed that since he was making so much of the Bible, it would be a good idea to put a copy into the hands of every literate Englishman. Such discussions might have been going on as early as 1527 or even before when the conjunction of Tyndale's Bible and Henry's infatuation with Anne Boleyn made an authorized translation attractive for several reasons. Henry probably imagined that with an English Bible readily available, everybody in the realm could see the justice of his case, giving himself the support of public opinion he needed. More would have shared in these discussions in his role as theological councillor, and in A Dialogue Concerning Heresies, perhaps for the moment convincing himself, he might have presented the king's point of view.

The Dialogue is worth reading, and apparently it was read. A second edition appeared in 1530. It was by far the best thing in English that defended the old faith on the eve of schism from Rome. In it More assumed the confident tone of an important and learned man, sure that heresy was a passing show and that soon the true church would triumph again over its despicable enemies just as it had always triumphed before.

Yet if he was as confident as the fictional More of his piece, why did he write so much and at such length? And why was he so inflexible as to take the extreme positions we have noted—believing, for example, that long veneration of a relic authenticated it? Why did he repeat such notably weak miracle stories from The Golden Legend as the one about St. Erkenwald, who stretched the timber of Barking Abbey to fit? Did he really believe them? Perhaps he wanted

to, but he did not think them sufficiently credible to use again in the voluminous polemical works he was yet to write. And there is his distortion of the
Hunne case, noted at length earlier in this book, where he makes it seem that
no serious evidence was ever adduced against the clergymen accused of
Hunne's murder. Whatever it may be, such twisting of the facts is not a mark
of confidence.

It may be that *A Dialogue Concerning Heresies* was much like More himself. It tries very hard to present a calm, confident, and superior face to the
world, but underneath there lies a terrible intensity that is anything but calm
and confident. The work seems to be part of the long tradition in Western
literature in which art becomes a device to tame life, presenting life not as it
is but as the author very much wishes it were, and mightily fueled by the almost
unbearable tension between ideal and reality.

23

ELEVATION TO
LORD CHANCELLOR

N O M A T T E R what More and others did, heresy increased in England. Hardly had the first edition of *A Dialogue Concerning Heresies* appeared when a lawyer named Simon Fish, a "gentleman of Gray's Inn," so John Foxe said, someone More must have known in the legal fraternity of the city of London, attacked the clergy.

Fish was not so much a heretic as he was an anticlerical, and the threat he posed was all the greater because of his general orthodoxy. His ringing bitterness against priests suited the mood of many literate Londoners, who along with great numbers of Englishmen everywhere believed that priests, monks, friars, nuns, and all the supporting ranks who enjoyed clerical status defiled English life and corrupted the English law.

As we have noted, anticlericalism was not new in England. Chaucer had laughed at the clergy, depicting many of them and their hangers-on as guilty of malice, lust, greed, or some other corruption. Only the "poor parson of a town" is saintly, and he is dull.

Perhaps the worst offense of Chaucer's easygoing clergymen is their thorough secularism. They are at home in the world, content to soak up its rewards, eager always for more than they have, showing little interest in the afterlife except as it gives them opportunity to gull the common people into pouring money into their pouches and doing them other favors.

In *A Dialogue Concerning Heresies*, More laughs as Chaucer did at the antics of those clergymen whose stock in trade is deceit. Yet, as we have seen, in More's polemics these tales were merely a rhetorical concession, and he turned quickly from them to a defense of the clergy as a whole:

> If a lewd priest do a lewd deed then we say, "Lo, see what example the clergy gives us," as though that priest were the clergy. But then forget we to look what good men be therein and what good counsel they give us and what good example they show us. But we fare as do the ravens and the carrion crows and never meddle with any lively flesh. But where they may find a dead dog in a ditch, thereto they flee and thereon they feed apace. So where we see a good man and hear or see a good thing, there we take little heed. But when we see once an evil deed, thereon we gape, thereof we talk and feed ourself all day with the filthy delight of evil communication. Let a good man preach, a short tale shall serve us thereof, and we shall neither much regard his exhortation nor his good example. But let a lewd friar be taken with a wench, we will jest and rail upon the whole order all the year after and say, "Lo what [an] example they give us."

Finally, even More acknowledged the general reputation of the clergy in the sentiment expressed in his *Dialogue Concerning Heresies* that the state of the clergy would be better if fewer men were ordained—a view he had voiced as early as the *Utopia* years. And nothing he could write could dam the torrent of anticlerical feeling in the country at large. Wycliffe's influence was probably kept alive by anticlericalism as much as by anything else in his doctrines. In the end, the general alacrity with which England renounced allegiance to the old forms once Henry VIII and his minions showed them a new way was probably a consequence of this pervasive anticlericalism rather than of any thirst for heretical doctrine.

Anticlericalism was built partly on disappointment that the church had not lived up to the high moral standards that clergymen were supposed to exemplify. And as we have frequently noted, the age was beset by turbulence of many kinds. In England the destitute tramped the highways looking for some way to survive, the sweating sickness struck again and again, the vagaries of economics sent fortune's wheel spinning, and new currents of thought undermined old certainties, putting fear into the core of life.

Scholars were as afraid as anybody and, as the Protestant Reformation proves, as much in need of reassurance. In the Renaissance view of history, the present was radically different from the past, and scholars in the sixteenth century must have seen their age as cut off from the antiquity that offered an ideal security. We should probably understand the humanist quest for the original sources as the search for some ground that would make the world intimate again and God seem near. When clergymen in the tense and frightened sixteenth century lived as if God did not exist, the rest of the society could only compare them with the suffering saints of *The Golden Legend* and despise them, not merely for living a lie themselves but for living as though the gospel itself were a lie, creating in ordinary folk the black and terrifying suspicion that perhaps it was. Chaucer's summoner, a minor ecclesiastical figure, tells a tale about the farting of friars; an age saturated with the stories of saints knew, as More did, that saints were associated with good smells and flowers but that friars were something else.

Late in 1528 or early in 1529, Simon Fish gained notoriety by publishing a vitriolic little tract against the clergy called *A Supplication for the Beggars*. This polemic owed much to Tyndale's *Obedience of the Christian Man* with its view that it was up to the king to reform the church since that task was impossible for a wicked clergy. In some ways *A Supplication for the Beggars* also showed the influence of More's own *Utopia*. Fish made an appeal on behalf of the throng of beggars that infested England. Why were they beggars? Because the clergy drew off so much money that not enough was left in England to pay people to work. Like the More who wrote *Utopia*, Fish conceived a vision of a powerful nation built by the energy of its united inhabitants, performing useful labor and growing in virtue. He said that the five orders of begging friars collected an amount greater than forty-three thousand pounds a year from the English people. His calculation is specious, but he made it with such aggressive confidence that laymen grumbling about the exactions of the clergy now had a statistic; Fish had, it would seem, discovered the power of statistics to support lies.

We should recall that in *Utopia* More has a character in Bishop Morton's house say to a friar, "For the Cardinal made excellent provision for you when he decided that vagrants should be locked up and put to work. For you are the biggest vagrants of all." Fish went far beyond More. He claimed that the clergy owned one-third of the property of England. Like Tyndale, he charged them with perpetual disobedience to the crown. The Romans and the Turks could not possibly have been so strong had they had a similar crowd of locusts within their societies, devouring their substance, Fish said.

Not content with counting the money the clergy drained out of the realm, Fish counted the women the clergy had turned into whores. One hundred thousand, he declared with unabashed certainty. Such assertions are always appealing to those who want to believe the polemicist. Clergymen were carriers of disease, he said, conveying syphilis and leprosy from woman to woman. Some priests boast, said he, that they had meddled with a hundred women. And who would work for three pence a day when she could sleep an hour with a friar, a monk, or a priest and make twenty pence? The bastards of the clergy flooded the realm. No honest husband could tell if his wife's children had been fathered by him or not. There was only one remedy—the sword of the prince. Henry should assert himself and smite.

Fish denied the existence of purgatory, probably revealing a heretical bias.

But this was as far into doctrine as he ventured. It was an effective sally. Like Luther and Tyndale, he said that the doctrine of purgatory had been concocted as a device to milk Christians willing to pay for the relief of loved ones supposed to be suffering the pangs of their purgation. But though it seems clear that Fish's sentiments lay with Luther, Tyndale, and others like them, he was a publicist rather than a thinker, and he probably found theology too difficult to understand.

His tract was dangerous not only because it exploited a popular and powerful prejudice but also because it was read in high places. John Foxe later reported that Anne Boleyn put it into the hands of the king, just as she is supposed to have done with Tyndale's *Obedience of the Christian Man.* By Foxe's account, Henry was equally enthusiastic about both works. Fish fled across the seas, but when More was Lord Chancellor, he returned in secret and hid in London. If Foxe's information is correct, Henry sought him out about 1530—showing how little More's influence counted with the king by this time. Fish was invited to Henry's chambers, and Henry even took him on a hunt! Foxe also says that the king ordered More to leave Fish alone—and that More promptly had Fish's wife detained, for Henry had not placed her under royal protection.

All this came later. More's immediate response to *A Supplication for the Beggars* was to publish a long reply to Fish called *The Supplication of Souls,* and in it he took the part of the souls in purgatory whose suffering was prolonged because of the skepticism about purgatory promoted by Simon Fish and others like him.

At least that is what he started out to do. *The Supplication of Souls* is cast in the form of a pleading letter from the burning souls in purgatory, a letter addressed to the living who might be taken in by Fish's work. But More lacked the artistic energy to sustain his device, or perhaps in the press of events he was simply writing too fast. At any rate, the careful image he formed for himself in *A Dialogue Concerning Heresies*—superior, calm, secure—came apart in *The Supplication of Souls,* and he descended into bad-tempered polemic and name-calling. He devotes much space to proving from scripture and tradition that purgatory exists, although it seems unlikely that souls burning in the "dark fire" of purgatory, in heat hotter than all the fires that ever burned on earth, as More has them say, should feel compelled to prove that there is such a place. The book is painfully long, and it rambles. Like all More's polemical works after the *Dialogue,* his *Supplication* tries to smother the fire of opposition by burying it under a stack of pages.

Still, the work is witty here and there, and it raises some interesting questions about More. It reflects his lifelong preoccupation with the intimate relation between the visible and the invisible worlds, the living and the dead. Purgatory, he says, has been proved in every country—presumably even non-Christian ones—by "apparitions." He does not claim to have seen such an apparition himself, and he does not speak of any in detail. He recognizes that some people doubt that such things have occurred, but he makes the same case that he did for miracles—the witness of so many good men cannot be false. And again we see his uneasiness, a certain tension between what he wanted with all his heart to believe and the vague and uncertain quality of the evidence he felt comfortable in adducing.

He recognizes popular hostility to the clergy in terms that remind us of old Bishop FitzJames's squawk at the time of the Hunne affair—which More treats yet again in *The Supplication of Souls.* Fish has said that the clergy foment sedition against the king. More replies that the charge is ridiculous, that the clergy require and support the king's peace, for in any popular tumult they know that they would "be the first that should fall into peril." Fish has said that the clergy rule Parliament. More speaks of how the laity control both Lords and Commons, and he says of Fish, "And surely if he had been in the Common House as some of us have been, he should have seen the spirituality not gladly spoken for."

To counter Fish's charge that the clergy provoked sedition, More wrote at length about the long subservience of the English church to English kings. He detailed the powers of command that kings had exercised over the church in England, and he argued that convocations had never denied the king what he wanted. Henry did not have to read More to see his own way into the future, but in More's comments, we can find reasons why an English king might undertake a revolution in at least some confidence that his clergy would support him.

More believed that anticlericalism, heresy, and sedition always went hand in hand. In his *Supplication* he went back to Wycliffe's days and to Lollardy after Wycliffe to prove that insurrection and heresy had afflicted England together. We may wonder if such a tack was wise even though we realize that More's prejudices made it inevitable. The English people were so anticlerical that they finally did say, in effect, "If this be heresy, make the most of it." More's position might have been stronger if he had been discriminating, if he had vented a little rage against unworthy priests and monks. Then some readers might have been persuaded that one could be perfectly orthodox and yet furious at the clergy. But in his *Supplication* More drifted further into his habit of defending the clergy by claiming that the unworthy made up only a tiny part of the whole. He made it seem that anyone who attacked them gave proof of heresy. In the *Supplication* we again find a long list of Luther's heresies, and More's message is plain: if Fish denies purgatory and attacks the clergy, he must be guilty of all these other heresies as well.

We can discern in the *Supplication* the apocalyptic note that was to become so loud and insistent in More as he saw the battle going against him. It is the part of him that reminds us of Savonarola or a thousand lesser prophets who predicted the end of the world and saw signs of cosmic doom everywhere. Unlike Erasmus but like Luther, More brooded over the prophesied moment when God would withdraw His grace from a wicked world and allow creation to dip into hell until Christ himself returned to judge the quick and the dead. The tradition was ancient; its horrors thud in the book of Revelation and elsewhere in the Bible. They enjoyed a flourishing life in the later Middle Ages.

Fish has argued that if the clergy be put to work, England would be a better place. But More replies:

> But he should have said, after that the clergy is thus destroyed and cast out then shall Luther's gospel come in, then shall Tyndale's testament be taken up, then shall false heresies be preached, then shall the sacraments be set at nought, then shall fasting and prayer be neglected, then shall holy saints be blasphemed, then shall Almighty God be displeased, then shall he withdraw his grace and let all run to ruin, then shall all virtue be had in derision, then shall all vice reign and run forth unbridled, then shall youth leave labor and all occupation, then shall folk wax idle and fall to unthriftiness, then shall whores and thieves, beggars and bawds increase, then shall unthrifts flock together and swarm about and each bear him hold of other, then shall all laws be laughed to scorn, then shall the servant be set nought by their masters and unruly people rebel against their rulers, then will rise up rifling and robbery, murder and mischief, and plain insurrection, whereof what would be the end or when you should see it, only God knoweth.

It is almost a classic description of the utter depravity that is to fall on the earth just before the great day of doom. Such visions have always inspired dread rather than hope among the faithful, probably because those who have the visions are consumed with doubts about their own power to prevail against the hideous evil that is to overcome the world before the return of Christ.

It is in the *Supplication* that More seems to grant the power of the pope to issue indulgences to release souls from purgatory. The passage is brief and ambivalent, and not much should be made of it. Throughout we find the same uneasiness in treating the papacy that we see in all More's comments on the subject.

As always, More's prose is most lively when he speaks of death and of the way we are soon forgotten. He has the souls in purgatory say, "What a sorrow hath it been to some of us when the devils hath in despiteful mocking cast in our teeth our old love borne to our money and then showed us our executors as busily rifling and ransacking our houses as though they were men of war that had taken a town by force."

More probably wrote *The Supplication of Souls* hastily in the summer of 1529, just after he completed work on the first edition of *A Dialogue Concern-*

ing Heresies and as Wolsey was falling from power. His *Supplication* went through two editions very quickly; so it must have been read, and its uncompromising defense of the clergy in England and the special status of priesthood would have endeared him to conservatives in the realm. But conservatives now did not have the ear of the king and the tide was running higher and higher against More's opinions even as *The Supplication of Souls* appeared, which must have deepened his conviction—expressed in both these works—that heresy could only be extirpated from England by a resolute, fiery campaign by the government itself. Just such a campaign seemed possible when he got his chance to become Lord Chancellor of the Realm shortly after he finished his work on his *Supplication.*

In the summer of 1529, More and his friend Tunstall were the chief English delegates at the closing negotiations of the Peace of Cambrai between France and the Empire. Following the crushing defeat of the French at Pavia in 1525 and the subsequent imprisonment of the French king by Emperor Charles V, Wolsey had shifted the English alliance from the unfaithful emperor to the needy but equally unfaithful French king. One of the English aims was possibly to maintain the independence of Italy and the papacy against the threat of imperial domination. Emperor Charles, powerful nephew of Queen Catherine, was devoted to his family and especially to his aunt; a pope under his control could not possibly grant Henry a divorce. But the sack of Rome by imperial troops in the spring of 1527 and the final, humiliating defeat of a French army at Landriano in June 1529 handed both Italy and the pope over to Charles, and Henry VIII must now fear lest the emperor turn against England. Fortunately for Henry at least, the Lutheran princes in Germany and the renewed threat of a Turkish invasion of Austria from the Balkans kept Charles occupied, and he was as eager for peace with England as England was eager for peace with him.

Such was the treaty signed at Cambrai in August 1529, and it represented the disastrous end of Wolsey's foreign policy. Francis I gave up the French claim to Italy. And because Charles V was left with hegemony over the great and divided land south of the Alps, the pope could not grant Henry a divorce. More mentions his service at Cambrai in his epitaph. He had always been hostile to the French, and the imperial ambassador Eustace Chapuys, who arrived in England later that year, always counted him as a friend to Emperor Charles. More would have been pleased at the results of Cambrai because they seemed to presage a period of peace between England and a reliable Catholic monarch. He would also have been blind indeed had he not seen the obstacle Cambrai now put in the way of Henry's projected divorce.

Henry, however, kept doggedly on in his matrimonial purposes. From the time he had decided to put Catherine away, he had always wanted his "great matter" decided in England by pliable English bishops; Catherine insisted on appealing directly to the papacy so that the case would be decided in Rome. The king and Wolsey had prevailed on the pope to send an Italian cardinal, Lorenzo Campeggio, to London to hear the case with Wolsey. Henry and Wolsey hoped that Campeggio might agree to the divorce and grant it under the pope's authority. Campeggio seemed an excellent choice from the perspective of the English government. He was titular bishop of Salisbury, collecting the income from the see without the inconvenience of residing there. He had been one of the Italian high clergymen who during the sack of Rome and its occupation by imperial troops in the spring of 1527 had sent plea after plea to Wolsey and to England for help—help that was apparently granted. It was doubtless supposed that he would repay these English debts by agreeing to an English solution for the king's problem.

On June 21, Henry and Catherine both appeared before the two cardinals. The cardinals announced that they would not allow Catherine's appeal to Rome. Henry, sitting under a canopy of cloth of gold, spoke at length about the matter he said was dearest to his soul—the state of his own conscience. Catherine protested that his conscience had taken a very long time to awaken. Henry answered that this had been so because he had loved her so much and that now he desired nothing greater than for this court to declare that his marriage was valid. Still, he told the judges, it was thoroughly unreasonable to allow Catherine's case to be taken out of England to Rome because Charles V now had so much power there.

It was too much for Catherine to bear, and she forsook the decorum of the court to throw herself on her knees at her husband's feet, calling on him to remember her honor and the honor of their daughter, for if Catherine were not his true wife then she was no better than a mistress and their daughter Mary only a bastard. He should not be displeased because she defended the honor of his household, she told him, and then she swept out of the room, refusing the cry of the officers of the court to come back. She did not appear before them again.

Catherine was immensely popular in the city of London, and she had allies. One was John Fisher, who waged open war, bringing to bear both books and sermons against the plan of the king to put Catherine away. On June 28 he appeared at the cardinals' court. Henry had claimed that his only desire was to see justice done, Fisher said. The king had required everyone who might shed light on the royal marriage to do so. Therefore, Fisher said, burning his ships on the beach behind him, he would be unfaithful to his sovereign and he would risk the damnation of his own soul if he did not come forward in public with what he had learned after studying the matter. The king's marriage, he said, could be dissolved by no power on earth or in heaven, and he declared himself ready to lay down his life in its defense. John the Baptist, he said, had been willing to die for the sake of marriage. It was a bold allusion to one of the most celebrated tales of biblical villainy and heroism. John had been imprisoned by Herod Antipas for protesting Herod's marriage to Herodias, who had been taken from Herod's brother Philip. Herod divorced his own wife to receive her. Herodias insisted that John the Baptist be imprisoned for his impertinence, and later when her daughter Salome danced—presumably lasciviously—before Herod, he promised any reward the girl might desire. Coached by her mother, she asked for the head of John the Baptist on a platter —an event illustrated time and again in the iconography of the Middle Ages and the Renaissance. To an age saturated with saintly lore, Fisher would seem to be likening Henry to Herod—whose villainy was compounded by his role in the trial of Jesus. Fisher declared that marriage was not so sacred in the time of Herod and John the Baptist as it became after Christ shed his blood— meaning, presumably, that the crucifixion validated all the sacraments, of which marriage was one. Fisher declared himself ready to suffer any penalty that his stand might require. It was a fierce speech, completely unexpected, and in case the papal legates had not got the message, Fisher presented them with a book he had written on the subject.

It was an audacious and striking gesture, and it contrasts sharply with the diffident silence that More always maintained concerning the king's "great matter." Of course, More had a family to support and a career to advance and all the worldly ambitions that bound him to the king. Then, too, he could never shake off the reverence for authority that had begun with his reverence for his father, an attribute that is one of the trail markers along the labyrinthine corridors of his personality. To oppose openly the king of an ignorant, tumultuous, and largely vicious populace was to open the way to disorders that, in the Augustinian political tradition that More (and Martin Luther) shared, were far worse than the king's evil. He seems to have maintained until nearly the last the hope that Henry might see the wrong himself and move to repent and to right his errors.

If such was More's hope, it found no fulfillment in the aftermath of Fisher's speech. Henry was angry, and probably from that moment on Fisher was marked for death whenever the king might feel safe enough to bring the daring old man to the block. At the time Fisher was the spokesman for a large and dangerous public opinion. The queen commanded wide support; she had refused to return to the court being held by the two cardinals, and they could not make her reappear. Campeggio stood firm against the beseechings of the English and refused to grant any kind of decree. The process dragged on through the month of July in a summer that was unusually cold and dank. On July 23, Campeggio announced that the court would adjourn in honor of the summer holidays in Rome! He insisted on consulting with the pope before any decision was reached. With that, the Duke of Suffolk, a fierce anticlerical, roared, "It was never merry in England whilst we had cardinals among us."

When a great silence fell on the hall, he repeated the words "in great despite." Wolsey courageously rebuked him and stingingly recalled Suffolk's pleas to him when Suffolk had married Henry's sister without permission. But Wolsey's favors had been given long ago, and Suffolk felt no gratitude that could be the coin of patience now.

Even before Campeggio had adjourned the court, Clement VII had revoked the case to Rome, although the news took several weeks to reach England. It was what Charles V wanted, and Clement wanted no more of the emperor's displeasure. When the messengers bearing the papal revocation arrived in London in August, Wolsey's efforts to win a divorce through the papacy were in total collapse.

Campeggio went home. His baggage was opened despite his diplomatic status. Wolsey was left to be the scapegoat of the king's fierce anger against the pope. Anne Boleyn wanted his head. Her uncle, the Duke of Norfolk, also wanted Wolsey out of the way. In September, the king saw his chief minister for the last time. And in October, Suffolk and Norfolk, fellows in engineering the cardinal's fall, came to Wolsey's house at Westminster to collect the Great Seal of the Realm. Wolsey resisted; he had received the Great Seal at the king's own hand, he said. He would not let it go without seeing the request from that same royal hand. Suffolk and Norfolk went back and got a letter from the king. When they reappeared, Wolsey could do nothing but let the emblem of his office go.

The choice of More to be Wolsey's successor was a serious and far from simple affair. The office of Lord Chancellor was what the king permitted it to be; Henry had let Wolsey be virtually the assistant monarch. The main formal duty of the Lord Chancellor was to preside over the court that heard cases appealed from the common-law courts to the king. Wolsey had enlarged the responsibilities of that court, drawing cases away from the Court of the King's Bench. However, his main preoccupation was not the law but rather the king's executive business, and he had presided over both foreign and domestic policy.

Wolsey's gargantuan unpopularity had added a great swell to the sea of anticlericalism rolling against the English church. Henry and his inner circle, including Norfolk and Suffolk, seemed to have decided early that the next chancellor should be a layman. Laymen had been chancellors before, but not in the living memory of anyone in the realm. It was unclear whether the new man should be a noble or a commoner.

The debate seems to have been intense, and it finally settled on More. As a steadfast defender of the clergy, he would have been acceptable to the conservative bishops and to conservative noblemen like Norfolk. He had proved himself docile and obedient to the king through many years of service. He was a foe of heresy, a splendid common lawyer, a fine speaker, and a friend to the city of London. Perhaps his greatest advantage was that he had had long experience in government without managing to offend any powerful persons or groups.

His legal background must have been of particular importance. In hearing appeals from the common-law courts, the Lord Chancellor was supposed to administer "equity" or "conscience." That is, he was to make sure that the administration of the law followed the spirit and intentions of those who had made it. Equity was an old idea, going back at least to Aristotle. It was always an issue in cases where it seemed that strict observance of the law might create injustice rather than justice.

John Fisher gave an example of equity in a sermon preached long before More became Lord Chancellor. Suppose, he said, that a town has made a law that anyone who enters after curfew will be put to death. Then suppose that a friend of the town gets word of a surprise attack to be made at dawn by the town's enemies, and that he climbs over the wall in the middle of the night to carry his message of warning. According to the strict wording of the law, the man should be put to death. But equity or conscience recognizes that such a law was not intended to punish such a man. The Lord Chancellor, then, was to apply conscience to those cases, most of them involving land rights and commerce, where strict construction of the law might bring injustice. In a time when strong men in the countryside were always looking to seize land on the basis of some faint legal claim, the equity process allowed the Lord Chancellor to keep the peace by using his conscience, his sense of fair play, and, we might add, his simple common sense to assure some claimants possession and to deny it to others. The Lord Chancellor and his officers had to pick their way swiftly through the jungle of false deeds, real deeds, lost papers, claims of debts, wills, and all the rest to establish and keep tranquillity in the realm. And the Lord Chancellor's office, backed by the royal power, could become a critical rival of the common law itself with its long, ponderous, and almost sacrosanct tradition of writs and orders. A respected and sensible common lawyer like More might be hoped to win the confidence of the English legal fraternity and at the same time preserve the justice without which domestic tranquillity is impossible short of the imposition of a force no government in the sixteenth century could bring to bear.

More was also Henry's friend of long standing, and we may go back—as perhaps Henry's mind did—to that day and perhaps others like it long ago when young Thomas More came to call on child Henry at Eltham. The old friendship between sovereign and subject must have overcome the most formidable obstacle to More's nomination—his opposition to the divorce, an opposition not vehement and public like Fisher's, but just as unyielding.

Some moderns have assumed that More became Lord Chancellor only because Henry promised that he would not have to involve himself in the divorce. But by the accounts of both More and Roper, Henry continued to urge his "great matter" on More after he became Lord Chancellor, although the king always assured him that he should follow his own conscience. It was, given Henry's temperament, a lethal condition; the king was so sure of his righteousness and the rightness of his views that he supposed any good conscience must follow his own. And More did not help matters by tendering his opinions on the divorce to the king whenever Henry asked for them, something More always claimed he did.

Still, we do not know exactly what those opinions were, for More never put his thoughts to paper, and he was so discreet that he never shared them with anyone except the king and possibly with Dr. Nicholas Wilson, a friend with whom he studied the issue of divorce in the writings of the fathers of the church and in the Bible. He evidently expressed his opinions tactfully and mildly to the king at the moment when he was elevated to the post of Lord Chancellor, and he must have made it clear that although he could not speak for the divorce, neither would he speak against it. He refused to read books supporting the queen. He probably consoled himself with the long view that Henry's dispute with the pope was only another in an almost traditional series of quarrels between kings and popes about royal marriages. In the past these storms had always blown over. More could hope that he might shelter himself in silence until this one, too, had passed.

The grounds of his opposition were complex. John Fisher stood simply and boldly on the pronouncements of popes. Pope Julius II had granted the dispensation allowing the marriage to take place; popes could not err in such things, and that settled the issue for Fisher. But never in his entire life—not even when faced with inevitable death—did Thomas More write a line to suggest that all the power of deciding right and wrong in such a case lay with the papacy.

It seems most plausible to see More's opposition as part of his intense antipathy toward sexual sins. In Utopia, men and women guilty of adultery were condemned to slavery, and if they fell into the sin a second time, they were put to death. More provided for divorce in Utopia, but only by the common consent of both parties and only after investigation by the council. Here, as in so much of his work, we can only guess at the intent behind this surprising liberality. Divorce was common in the Roman world; perhaps he allowed a controlled system of divorce for Utopia because he was following the example of classical Rome. And perhaps his marriage to stormy Dame Alice provoked him in 1515 to suppose that something might be said for divorce. At least it might be said in a book like Utopia, in which society proceeded according to reason rather than revelation.

But his uncompromising hostility expressed so monotonously against heretical priests who married is sign enough of his horror of adultery among supposed Christians in his own time. Anne Boleyn seems to have resisted Henry's sexual advances for a season, perhaps until shortly before their marriage. But by the summer and fall of 1529, Henry to all appearances was living openly with her. She went on the hunt with him and kept state like a queen. More could hardly have been expected to become an advocate of the king's divorce when he knew it would open the way to legal union between Henry and his mistress—a union that would be a sign to all the world that crime does pay.

More's conscience would have led him to take Queen Catherine's part out of his sense of equity. True, Catherine had slept with Arthur for five months and had appeared in public as his wife, and many were ready to testify to Arthur's boasting about his sexual exploits with her. But she had lived with Henry for years as his unquestioned wife long after Arthur had turned to dust. She had borne him one surviving child and several who died; although she had no issue from Arthur, she became pregnant in her marriage to Henry with a regularity that suggests no early difficulty in conception despite her tragic inability to bring children to healthy birth. Had she had intercourse with Arthur regularly, five months would have been long enough for her to become pregnant, and she did not. Moreover, she claimed to be a virgin when she married Henry, and she claimed also in public and in private that Henry knew she was a virgin—a claim Henry met with a certain noticeable confusion. No matter what the technical wording of the Bible and the canon law might be —and More did not believe that either was entirely binding on Christians— More must have supposed that conscience and equity must validate the marriage.

And it may have been that More, the obedient royal councillor for so many years, the secretary, the servant, ever diffident toward his monarch and toward Wolsey, ever eager to please his superiors and to advance, now found himself pushed to make yet another submission, and found himself with only one bastion left to defend against his bearlike king—the sovereignty of his own conscience, that private, even secret part of himself where all that remained of his manhood lay.

He surely felt the contradictions of his life that we have frequently noted in this book. He was a humanist who had absorbed all the classical ideals of individual virtue and heroism. But he was no hero, no true leader. And he was a devout Christian, revering the cross and the succession of martyrdoms in testimony to the glorious independence before God that the revelation of Christ was supposed to give those who left all to follow him. Yet he had exercised no independence, and he was far from being a martyr.

He had bowed humbly to his king, he had flattered Wolsey, and he had made his way cautiously along the slippery precipice of royal favor until finally Henry tried to push him into yet another act of docile obedience, one that More could not do and still feel himself a man. We cannot know, of course, but it may have been that More's reflections on his own surrenders through so many years now steeled him to resist this last demand that he allow Henry to treat his conscience like a blank sheet on which secretary More might take the king's dictation.

Why did he agree to become Lord Chancellor? Personal ambition undoubtedly played a part. Here was a promotion he could hardly turn down, a remarkable and unforeseen culmination to all those years as an obedient royal servant, shifted here and there in the apparatus of government as his superiors found him useful. Given Wolsey's enormous power in the office, More must have supposed that his own authority would also be great, and he enjoyed authority, an important place in the world.

But apart from mere personal ambition, More must have seen the office as a commanding height from which to protect the church from its many enemies, a divine commission to do what he could to save a bad situation, perhaps even a divine call. He believed in the living God of the Bible and of Christian tradition; that God spoke in the daily life, not only with miracles but also with opportunities, and as More's discussion of God and kingship placed in Bishop Morton's mouth in *The History of King Richard III* shows, the opportunities presented to high men of state came with a divine seal stamped upon them.

He took the office on October 25, 1529. Three days later he wrote a brief letter to Erasmus commenting on his reasons. The letter is friendly, but not intimate, a public rather than a private missive, surely intended for publication. (In fact, Erasmus did not publish it, and it did not appear in print until 1933!)

More made his usual disclaimers. He had been longing for leisure, he said, when he was suddenly plunged into affairs of the greatest importance. He promised to do the best he could with such little talent as he had. He praised Henry as the best of kings and expressed delight and gratitude for royal favor. He hoped that he could make good the hopes that had been placed in him, and he promised hard work, loyalty, and good will. In closing he wished Erasmus success in all his endeavors and commented that all Christendom depended on the work that Erasmus was doing. Perhaps this was subtle encouragement to Erasmus to shoulder his responsibilities in the battle against heretics.

The burden of the letter seems to be its protestation of loyalty to Henry VIII. More must have felt uneasy at taking his high position when he opposed the king's will in the divorce. He must have known that no matter what Henry said about respecting his conscience, the king expected him to be convinced that the divorce was right and good. By writing to Erasmus, More was probably considering his audience in Europe at large, but to a greater extent, he was addressing the king and the court where he must now serve. In the long retrospect that we now enjoy, it seems obvious that More was saying something like this: "I am loyal to my king, as loyal to him as anyone on earth can be. My inability to approve of his divorce and to argue for it in public in no way detracts from the essential loyalty I feel for him, a loyalty that will keep me from ever saying a public word in opposition to him." But Henry believed that real loyalty meant that More would consider the evidence impartially and come over to Henry's side. So More began his office under the shadow of a tragic miscalculation by both the king and himself.

As Wolsey was sliding to his fall, Henry summoned a Parliament—the traditional act of English kings when things were not going well. It opened on November 3, 1529, and it was adjourned several times. Before it went home for good in 1536, it had broken the English communion with Rome, installed Henry in the place of the pope, rallied the realm around its monarch, and so had become perhaps the most significant Parliament in English history.

The king himself was present on opening day, and so was Edward Hall, the great chronicler to whom we all remain indebted. Thomas More, standing at the king's right hand, delivered an oration that might have come from the first book of *Utopia*. The good shepherd protected his sheep and foresaw things to come. Henry, England's own good shepherd, considered how laws made before this time were by long continuance and change made insufficient for these days. By the frail conditions of man, many new enormities had come up among the people, and no existing law was adequate to deal with them. By "new enormities," More probably meant heresy, and his comment must have reflected his hope that the Parliament would harden laws against heresy in England.

More then passed into a reflection on authority—one that Henry in the ceremonial pomp of the moment may have failed to grasp. What makes a prince? If he counts on wealth, More said, he is only a rich man. If he counts on honor, he is only an honorable man. But a prince is a prince because of the multitude of his people and the number of his flock, "so that his people make him a prince."

The thought may seem commonplace at first hearing, and Henry probably took it so. But it is consistent with all we know of More's opinions about princes and popes and others who hold authority. The corporation—government or church or commonwealth of Utopia—possesses in its members its essential life, its supreme legality, and its fullness of power. The body may choose to entrust that power to a head—a king or a pope—to carry out the general will that may be expressed by one man more effectively than by a multitude of clamoring voices. Yet the head has no just power except when he is expressing the common consent. What to do about an unjust head is a somewhat different matter. But the justice of king or pope is for More justice only when it expresses this common consent. Without common consent, tyranny enters at the door. This view of common consent was at the base of the conciliar movement in the Catholic Church, still alive during the Reformation, although it had suffered a century of opposition by popes. And ironically enough, it was just this view that informed Luther's comment in *The Babylonian Captivity* that Christians could not be bound to any law without their consent—although as he so often did, Luther expressed an old idea so baldly that it sounded like nonsense, and More, misinterpreting him, attacked him for it again and again, not realizing or not wishing to admit that this cherished idea of Luther's was one that More cherished himself.

More followed his remarks on the nature of kingship with an assault on Wolsey that has always troubled More's admirers because it was so vehement and so cruel. The king must always purge his flock of those who are rotten and faulty. More called Wolsey a great "wether which is of late fallen." A "wether" was a castrated ram or a eunuch, and it may be that More was making a savage joke about Wolsey's clerical state, which, by the law of the church, allowed him no outlet for sexuality. It was well known that Wolsey had not kept his vows of chastity and that he had fathered at least one bastard—a son whom he seemed to love dearly named Thomas Winter. So More's term "wether" may have been ironic.

More attacked Wolsey for deceiving the king. But "his grace's sight was so quick and penetrable that he saw him, yea and saw through him both within and without." Wolsey's punishment was gentle, More said, for the king was merciful. No one should suppose that a similar offender would be let off so easily.

The speech was not More's only blow against Wolsey. The cardinal had fallen; now he must be broken. He was given a choice of trial before the King's Bench—where sat old Judge John More—or attainder by Parliament. In either court the charge against him was that he had violated the Statute of Praemunire, that he had applied law contrary to the law of England. He chose the King's Bench; had he asked to have his case heard by Parliament, the resulting bill of attainder could have punished him with death. The King's Bench could take away his property and put him in prison—but it could not take his life.

Even so, More and the Lords drew up a bill of particulars against Wolsey in forty-four articles. More's name leads all the signatures on the bill, although we do not know exactly what part he played in putting it together. The articles comprise a merciless indictment of the cardinal's policies and his person, stooping to the accusation that by his own disgraceful diseases, he imperiled the king's life through contagion, for he knew that he had "the foul and contagious disease of the great pox broken out upon him in divers places of his body," and still "came daily to your grace whispering in your ear and blowing on your most noble grace with his perilous and infective breath."

Historians always note those articles that accused Wolsey of usurping Henry's authority, for using the expressions "the King and I" and "I would ye should do thus," for making ambassadors report to him before they went to the king, for concluding agreements in the king's name of which the king was ignorant, for keeping information from the king, and many other offenses.

But equally important was a long series of reproaches for crimes the cardinal had committed against the English church—for making unjust exactions against religious houses, for removing from monasteries the right to elect their own abbots, for robbing bishops and archdeacons of their rightful jurisdictions, for slandering the clergy of England by writing to Rome that they were all reprobates, for lying about the number of monks in religious houses so he could suppress some of them and take their property, for taking the property of bishops when they died, and so on. We see the hand of Thomas More in some of these charges, most of which would have enraged the new Lord Chancellor.

His motives in these attacks on Wolsey were surely twofold. He could not have become Lord Chancellor without the support or at least the acquiescence of Suffolk and Norfolk, and these men were committed to keeping Wolsey out of power and to crushing him once and for all. Both Anne Boleyn and Norfolk, her uncle, were afraid that if Wolsey could get to the king, he might win again the old favor that Henry had always shown him. Norfolk seems to have been terrified that Wolsey would return to power, and his terror seems justified. Cavendish gives us a stirring account of how Lord John Russell rode with a small party through a drenching rain to Hampton Court in the middle of the night on All Saints' Day, November 1, 1529, to bring a gold ring set with turquoise from Henry and the message that the king loved his former minister as much as he ever did. Noble messenger and fallen minister spoke in secret for a long time, and Russell rode away while it was still dark so that he might be back at Greenwich by daybreak. More's speech a couple of days later may then have been partly an effort to set Henry's mind irrevocably on the course the monarch had already taken, to throw Wolsey over and to leave him no chance of returning to power. Certainly his strong speech against the cardinal put More squarely in the political camp of the Duke of Norfolk and provides some reason for Roper to have called Norfolk More's "singular dear friend."

But just as clearly as these political motives influenced More, religious impulses also played their part in this speech. Wolsey had been a blight on the English church, responsible for much evil, the cause of a dangerous increase in anticlericalism, a sluggard in the pursuit of heresy, and in sum, a menace almost as great as heresy itself to the tranquillity of the faith in England. More had a furious quality to his character, as his polemical works show, and he had every reason to vent some of this fury against Wolsey. Also, by attacking the old regime, More prepared for a new one, and in his speech he was doing his part to establish a new order, one that might bring about a Catholic reformation in the realm.

Yet as Lord Chancellor, More was able to do almost nothing to advance the cause that he declared in this ringing parliamentary inaugural. He probably never had much chance to do anything other than what he did. Throughout history strong leaders have usually been followed by weak ones, and Wolsey had been far too strong to make anyone comfortable with the prospect of another administrative tyrant. Besides, Henry himself now resolved to take charge of policy.

A few weeks before More assumed the office of Lord Chancellor, a new imperial ambassador took up residence in London. He was Eustace Chapuys, mentioned earlier, and he had come to look after Catherine's affairs and to report on England to his master, Emperor Charles V. He was energetic and hardworking and intensely loyal. He wrote dozens and dozens of long letters to Charles during the next years. Sometimes he was misinformed, and we can catch his errors. Yet in this correspondence the times come alive as they do in scarcely any other papers surviving from the reign of Henry VIII. His tone was nearly always detached and professional. Sometimes he was too optimistic, and sometimes he fell into passions of sympathy for the queen and her daughter, the abused Princess Mary, that stir us across the centuries. He badgered Henry and the English government with a view to making Catherine's treatment as good as it could be, and he was an aggressive watchdog for the interests of Princess Mary, perhaps being finally responsible for the preservation of her very life. Yet his greatest contribution to history is the legacy of rich letters to his sovereign, and not the least of their virtues is the conviction they carry that here was a devoted servant and a good man.

At one time or another Chapuys talked to everyone of importance in the English government. On October 21, a few days before More took the Great Seal and the oath of office, the Duke of Norfolk told Chapuys that the government was not now in the hands of a single person but was to be directed by the privy council. In the same letter he told the emperor that Norfolk and Suffolk were now closest to the king and that it would be a good idea for Charles to write them both. Since they were both on the council, they could not be mastered by any authority short of the king himself.

Chapuys wrote on the day More received the Great Seal from Norfolk who had taken it from Wolsey. "Everyone rejoices at his promotion," said Chapuys of More, "for besides the esteem in which he is generally held for his uprightness of character, he is considered the most learned man in the kingdom, and has always shown himself a good servant of the Queen." But Chapuys did not advise the emperor to write More, and it was obvious that the new ambassador could see that the new Lord Chancellor was not to have great influence with the king.

More could not enjoy the full confidence of his king as long as he refused to support the divorce. Henry, sure that all people of good will must eventually agree with him, used More as a respectable front. In the meantime the king carried on through other servants an intense diplomacy to obtain a papal dissolution of his marriage. The king's dangers and frustrations grew, and

More's own position itself steadily became more dangerous and frustrating.

As soon as the new Parliament began meeting, popular anticlericalism erupted in the House of Commons. The angry complaints of the members were directed toward the same general offense that had provoked Luther to post his theses against indulgences—the greed of the clergy in using spiritual office and privilege to extract money from its flock. The clergy, so the Commons declared, demanded too much money for the proving of wills. The ghost of the Richard Hunne affair came stalking into the chamber in the form of a protest against excessive mortuary fees required by priests to bury the dead. Priests did not reside in the parishes that supported them; many priests collected the income from several parishes and supplied spiritual benefits to none —sins that infuriated the reformers. The clergy engaged in business; the Mercers' Company of London—to which More and his father both belonged —pressed the charges against excessive clerical fees and against the participation of the clergy in worldly trade, perhaps because the enterprises of priests and monks rivaled those of laymen.

These complaints in the Commons were turned into bills against the clergy that were debated in both Commons and Lords during the few weeks that Parliament remained in session before Christmas. John Fisher carried the banner stoutly for the old ways, maintaining that passage of the bills would deliver the clergy into slavery. He came close to accusing the members of Parliament of heresy—an accusation that provoked the Commons to such wrath that Speaker Thomas Audeley was sent to complain about Fisher to the king.

Fisher's defense of the old liberties of the church was based on traditions that went back for centuries. In joint committees of the two houses that considered his remarks, someone—probably Edward Hall—gave a retort similar to Luther's response when the argument of tradition was flung at him. For many years thieves had regularly robbed people at a place called Shooter's Hill outside of London; was such robbery then lawful because it was traditional?

In the end the anticlerical attack subsided somewhat. Some legislation against excessive fees got by, but the other bills did not make their way into law. Still, the prospects for the future were chilling. The English secular authority, through Parliament, was moving with implacable resolution to make reforms in the church and to end the liberties granted to the church of England under Magna Carta. We have already seen that the church's conception of its divine mission was intimately tied up with its independence from secular authority. A church prisoner to kings or parliaments could not receive the free flow of divine revelation granted only to a church ruled by priests ordained in the apostolic succession that ran back to Christ. Without such a channel of divine grace, the world would fall into an apocalyptic epoch of horror, such as the one described by Thomas More in his tirade against Simon Fish.

As customary, Parliament adjourned before Christmas. Henry planned to call it back into session around Easter of 1530. He had sent his arguments for the divorce to the University of Paris. Its theological authority was second in Europe only to that of the pope himself. Henry hoped for a favorable verdict to lay before Parliament, calling on it to ratify what Paris had decreed, to declare his marriage null, and to permit him to marry Anne Boleyn with or without the approval of the pope. The king believed with some justice that the pope was prisoner to the emperor. Naturally the imperial hand laid on the papal throne would, to a right-thinking Catholic, void the pope's authority as long as that hand was there. But the verdict of Paris was delayed. It at last arrived in July 1530, but it was ambiguous. The plague had struck London again by summer, and the recall of Parliament was again postponed. It did not meet again until 1531. In the meantime, the fight for orthodoxy in England entered a critical phase, and More's wrestlings with his duties became increasingly a battle for his church that would shortly be transformed into a battle for his own life.

24

LORD CHANCELLOR
AND KING

EARLY IN 1530, Henry made several moves that seemed directed toward restoring Wolsey to royal favor—moves that could only have created deep anxiety in More, Norfolk, and others who had put themselves irrevocably in open opposition to the cardinal. Henry restored Wolsey's property, allowed him to continue as archbishop of York, and gave him three thousand pounds "in ready money"—a prodigious sum.

Wolsey was supposed to return to York and to assume actively his ecclesiastical duties in the diocese. Thomas Cromwell, once Wolsey's servant, now steadily rising in the king's service, continued to befriend his old master. Norfolk was angry and afraid. He told Cromwell, "Sir, me thinketh that the Cardinal your master maketh no haste northward. Show him that if he go not away shortly, I will, rather than he should tarry still, tear him with my teeth."

The prospect of being bitten by Norfolk, while not agreeable, was not sufficiently frightening to drive Wolsey on his way. Only after receiving still more money from the royal council and, by Cavendish's account, a promise of yet more from the king himself, did Wolsey move slowly up to Southwell in Nottinghamshire, where he settled down to spend the summer, keeping court in the country town almost as in days of old and looking for all the world like a confident man expecting a recall to power. The effect of his presence just beyond easy communication with London must have added to his mystery and consequently to his menace in the minds of policy makers on the royal council who must now wait to see what the king would do with his old minister.

More must have been particularly anxious. Wolsey remained the most eminent clergyman in the realm, committed heart and soul to obtaining the king's divorce. The advantage the fallen cardinal held over the newly risen Lord Chancellor became strikingly evident in June when royal officers arrived at Southwell in the middle of the night with an urgent request to make of Wolsey. Cavendish woke Wolsey up, and he received the messengers in his bedchamber, where they talked a long time. The messengers had brought a strong letter addressed to the pope, demanding favorable action on the divorce. They wanted Wolsey's signature, and in the surviving document—now in the Vatican Archives—Wolsey's signature leads all the rest. William Warham's is there, and the list of spiritual and secular leaders whose seals and signatures appear after theirs reads like a who's who of power in England. The document has been described as "physically perhaps the most impressive piece uttered by Tudor England—a large, finely-executed sheet, from which hangs centipede-like a thicket of seals of two archbishops, four bishops, twenty-five abbots, two dukes, forty other lay peers, and a dozen lesser folks." But Thomas More's name is not there. Neither is that of Cuthbert Tunstall nor that of John Fisher.

Chapuys explained why to the emperor. Henry had summoned all the prelates and high officers of the realm to court, commanding them to bring their seals of office for the purpose of addressing this document to the pope. Said Chapuys, "Not one of the prelates known to be favourable to the Queen received a summons, nor the Chancellor either, whom they suspect." Although he was Lord Chancellor, More was already scarcely other than a figurehead, and policy was going around him rather than through him. In September, Chapuys wrote the emperor that More had been speaking so much in the queen's favor that he had come close to being dismissed from office. With such a Lord Chancellor now in his service, Henry must have looked back with longing to his former great servant who had always strained himself to do the royal will.

In the end fate ran against Thomas Wolsey, and the threat to More's life and career from that mountainous enigma of ego and service was ended. Had Wolsey returned to power, More would undoubtedly have lost both position and property and perhaps his life as well. But Wolsey was not to be restored.

Norfolk's bitter animus against the cardinal persisted; Suffolk hated him, and so did Anne Boleyn and all her family, who had Protestant leanings and who saw Wolsey's policy of obtaining a divorce through the papacy as a dead end. Catherine of Aragon had blamed him for Henry's first doubts about their marriage, and although near the end she began to mitigate her hostility toward him in their common detestation of the Lady Anne, she was of no use to him in his present circumstances. The French king ignored him, and Chapuys greeted Wolsey's secret overtures with wary suspicion. Only Thomas Cromwell remained loyal—a fact that should give pause to those, among them many friends of Thomas More, who impugn Cromwell's character and see in him only an opportunist with no loyalties and no convictions. Except for Cromwell, the cardinal was left without help, alone to face the hatreds that now rolled over him and swept him away.

Moving slowly northward, hoping continually to be called back to service and glory, Wolsey planned a spectacular coronation of himself as archbishop of York on November 7, 1530. He was old and sick and so fat that he could scarcely ride his mule, a man perhaps kept alive by the energy of his hopes. In October he arrived at Cawood Castle, only seven miles from York. With him were six hundred horsemen—not enough to raise the country but more than plenty to raise a storm of recrimination from his enemies, who sedulously put out the rumor that he was about to lead a revolt against the king.

With his coronation Wolsey planned to open a convocation of the northern clergy—a great assembly for which he had not secured royal permission. Rumors flew that at long last the pope was about to bestir himself, order Henry and Anne to stop cohabiting, and threaten the king with excommunication—which would mean a papal grant to rebellion—if he did not obey. Should Wolsey publish such an edict in York, Henry might be faced with insurrection among the northern lords, always ready to throw down the gauntlet to London.

So royal messengers were sent galloping north, and on Friday, November 4, Wolsey was arrested at dinner in Cawood, and on what was to have been the eve of his stupendous coronation, he was moved, a prisoner, to Pontefract and thence slowly southward to face charges of treason. Now his hopes were all gone, and his life quickly followed them. He died in bed in Leicester on November 29 and so escaped the final humiliation. He was buried in the same abbey church where the battered corpse of Richard III had been interred after Bosworth, and shortly afterwards people were calling the church "the tomb of the tyrants."

His trial would have been a show had it occurred. In it Henry would have sought more than a judgment against a man. It would have been an act of vengeance against the papacy and the papal church that Wolsey represented. It almost surely would have speeded up the course of Henry's revolution against Rome.

More and Wolsey had maintained some communication during that year, although it is difficult to make much of it. In March the cardinal wrote to Cromwell saying that, as Cromwell had suggested, he had written to both More and Norfolk. The subject seems to have been something about Wolsey's property. As Lord Chancellor, More would naturally have been the person to approach concerning a deed or a title in dispute because of something done by the king or the Parliament. More also took part in a complicated piece of arbitration between Wolsey and one Thomas Strangeways, who claimed that the cardinal owed him seven hundred pounds.

In October, Wolsey's agents tried to get More to intervene to save a grammar school that Wolsey had established in his natal town of Ipswich. More received the agents courteously at Chelsea but told them that he could do nothing against the express word of the royal council.

One ugly note sounds in these relations. In June, Wolsey wrote in some chagrin and helplessness to Cromwell that he had indeed granted More's request to let William Daunce, More's son-in-law, have the use of Wolsey's house at Battersea. But, said the cardinal, he had never intended that his servant John Oxynherde, married to one of Wolsey's relatives, should be expelled. The two, husband and wife, were to be allowed to live there. Now Oxynherde's wife had appeared at Southwell to tell Wolsey that she had been ordered to move and that she had no place for herself and her children to go. Wolsey was surprised; Daunce, he said, had promised that they should not be disturbed. The cardinal asked Cromwell to see to it.

Daunce was apparently an unpleasant and grasping man. Roper tells us that when More became Lord Chancellor, Daunce, the husband of More's daughter Elizabeth, "said merrily unto him: 'When Cardinal Wolsey was Lord Chancellor, not only divers of his privy chamber, but such also as were his doorkeepers got great gain.'" Daunce expected, Roper says, to have some gain himself, especially since he gave More constant attendance, apparently, Roper gives us to believe, serving on More's staff.

Daunce, dreaming of the profits he might rake in from influence peddling, spoke of all those men willing to pay him if he provided special access to his father-in-law. But he knew he would be doing them wrong to take their money, he said (we may imagine that he spoke petulantly), because they could do as much good for themselves as Daunce could do for them. "Which condition," Roper reports, "although he thought in Sir Thomas More very commendable, yet to him, said he, being his son, he found it nothing profitable."

More answered in heavy irony, taking Daunce's grumpy observation as a statement of conscience. "You say well, son," More said. "I do not mislike that you are of conscience so scrupulous, but many other ways be there, son, that I may both do yourself good and pleasure your friend also. For sometime may I by my word stand your friend in stead, and sometime may I by my letter help him; or if he have a cause pending before me, at your request I may hear him before another. Or if his cause be not all the best, yet may I move the parties to fall to some reasonable end by arbitrement. Howbeit this one thing, son, I assure thee on my faith, that if the parties will at my hands call for justice, then all were it my father stood on the one side and the devil on the other, his cause being good, the devil should have right." It is not surprising that grasping Daunce expelled one of Wolsey's servants so he could enjoy Wolsey's property in Battersea all to himself.

None of these relations between More and Wolsey were anything but official, and there is nothing in them to suggest that, had the cardinal returned to power, More could have expected anything but toil and trouble. Wolsey's death must have been a great relief to the incumbent Lord Chancellor.

More wrote about Wolsey rarely in the works that appeared after the cardinal's ignominious death, and always the stories More told show Wolsey in a bad light, whether courting obsequious flattery or pursuing a bloody, expensive, and fatal foreign policy. More was hardly in a position to say much about Wolsey, since he could not defend him, and if he attacked the cardinal's memory, he would be making a concession to the heretics, who used Wolsey constantly as proof of the decay of the Catholic Church. More was capable of making rhetorical concessions, but he was never one to give aid and comfort to his enemies by granting that they were right in anything so important as Wolsey's career had been. However, it is hard to imagine that he did not rejoice in Wolsey's final collapse and timely death.

The Lord Chancellor had little else to cheer him during that painful year. His old friend Tunstall was translated from the see of London to become bishop of Durham and President of the Council of the North in June. Tunstall's departure to Durham would have distressed More; the two men had been friends and colleagues for many years, both of them devout, both conservative, both accustomed to dealing with each other on the king's business.

John Stokesley, who replaced Tunstall as bishop of London, had been one of the ambassadors Henry had sent to Rome to urge the pope to grant him a divorce. Now Stokesley undertook to instruct More, hoping to change the Lord Chancellor's mind about the king's marriage to Catherine. More listened politely, but after Stokesley had had his say, More "saw nothing of such force to change his opinion therein."

In December 1530, John More, Thomas's father, died. He was almost unbelievably old for the sixteenth century—close to eighty. His fourth wife was still alive, and she would survive his famous son. Thomas More had mentioned the old man again and again in *A Dialogue Concerning Heresies,* repeating his funny stories. As we know, More went down on his knees to receive his father's blessing whenever they met in going to and fro between the courts of Chancery and the King's Bench, and Roper tells us that when they happened to be at lectures in Lincoln's Inn, he would offer his father the chance to speak first, though the old judge, recognizing his son's higher office, refused to take it. When the old man lay dying, Thomas visited frequently to comfort him, and at the moment the father passed out of this world, the son held him in his arms and wept and kissed him and commended his soul to God.

It has been said by some psychologists that a father who lives a long time creates by his death a peculiar dread in the hearts of his children, especially his sons. They are able to pretend that they are immortal as long as he lives, but when he dies, they find that they are next, and they feel death at their throats. The consequence of the passing of such an aged parent may be the blackest depression. Thomas More hinted at such a reaction to his father's death when he composed the epitaph for his own tomb in the little church at Chelsea. Having praised his father warmly in the carved words visible to this day, he had written, "The son, all through his father's lifetime, had been compared with him and was commonly known as the young More, and so he considered himself to be; but now he felt the loss of his father, and as he looked upon the four children he had reared and his eleven grandchildren, he began, in his own mind, to grow old."

Throughout 1530, Bishop John Fisher passed into increasingly vehement and public opposition to the divorce. Old Archbishop Warham tried to dissuade him, but to no avail. (Catherine of Aragon complained bitterly that all Warham could say to her was, "The wrath of the king is death"—a quotation from the book of Proverbs.) In time Fisher's efforts were to become treasonable. He kept in close touch with Chapuys, who arranged to have a book against the divorce printed on the Continent. In the end the old bishop advocated a Spanish invasion to keep England in the old faith.

More could not support such daring, and he could not make himself the willing agent of treason. His alienation from Fisher in these days must have been pronounced, his own isolation made more profound by the differences he felt between himself and those who supposedly shared his views. One wonders if the two men were ever truly close. The forced rhetoric of friendship in the Renaissance was so common and so prolix that true feelings are almost impossible to know at this distance. We have little evidence of contact between them until they were both imprisoned in the Tower. No doubt More admired Fisher with all his heart, and Fisher might have been a confidant in time of peril had not the old bishop been so public in his views and so radical in his advocacy of imperial force as a way to right the wrongs of England.

We know that More was busy during 1530, but since his papers have been lost, we know little of what he was doing. He worked on a revised edition of A Dialogue Concerning Heresies. In the surviving records we find him doing occasional routine business for the king. But here, too, we see a striking contrast between his service as Lord Chancellor and that of Wolsey. Wolsey's name was on nearly everything; More's was not. After Thomas Cromwell officially entered the king's service and rapidly became Henry's chief adviser, More was not only unable to lead; he seems to have been unable to share much in the daily life of the government. Foreign diplomats like Chapuys respected him, but they knew he was not truly in command of the ship of state, and they mentioned him seldom in their reports.

He did devote himself to the legal business of the Court of Chancery. Roper tells of how he granted injunctions against some of the rigorous penalties imposed by judges in the common law and how the judges protested. The relief by injunction was one of the functions of equity inherent in the Lord Chancellor's office. Common-law judges were likely to protest that the Lord Chancellor's meddling in their affairs tended to substitute his conscience for the tried and true old usages of the common law. Yet these very usages often led to injustice when false claimants forged old deeds or concocted legal action against people of property and used the slow, heavy grip of common-law procedures to milk an opponent dry and to work what mischief they could. Or honest landholders might find someone squatting on their property and have to resort to those same slow procedures to rid themselves of a dangerous and voracious human pest. In an age before the central recording of deeds, land titles were always subject to dispute, often for frivolous causes, and J. A. Guy has correctly observed that "men of property lived in daily fear that they might be compelled to ride to Westminster and defend themselves expensively against unjust charges filed by false accusers." It was up to the Lord Chancellor to find some rough-and-ready way to stop false suits, and we may suppose that More did as Wolsey had done before him—followed his own intuitions as he examined both parties, working out an injunction to put in legal form what he felt in his heart. Roper says that More sat in his house at Chelsea every afternoon and heard anyone who came to him with a complaint. Professor Guy has discovered that many documents do indeed have More's signature and the notation that it was made at Chelsea. At least once More was fooled. On Friday afternoon, August 19, 1530, he granted four injunctions to one litigant, stopping actions relating to an estate in Essex. But it turned out that the case was not what the litigant represented it to be, and his foes were permitted to proceed with their action in common law the next November.

More was probably fooled other times as well. The common-law judges were naturally irritated by such procedures, which they were bound to think high-handed and idiosyncratic. More made an effort to deal with the judges. By Roper's account, he had them to dinner in the Star Chamber room at Westminster and proved his injunctions one by one, forcing them—so Roper says —to agree that in every case he had done exactly the right thing. But, try as he might, he could not get them to use greater discretion in applying the letter of the law to cases. He wanted them to join law and equity, to use their consciences when they interpreted the law and to refuse to be bound to the words of statutes and precedents when the words created manifest injustice. Christopher St. German, the greatest English legal mind in the early sixteenth century and a thinker who would shortly come into conflict with More, agreed.

"It is not possible," he said, "to make any general rule of the law but that it shall fail in some case." The English judges would not agree. More told Roper in private that they would not apply conscience to their administration of the law because they did not want to take responsibility on themselves. The natural cowardice of bureaucrats, we would call it, and that was, in effect, what More called it, too.

More tried hard to study complaints that came into Chancery as well as to the Court of the Royal Council, which met in Star Chamber. He was trying to eliminate frivolous actions that devoured the courts' time and the money of those property holders whose titles were frivolously attacked. But the job was too much for any one man, and Professor Guy has ascertained that "only a tenth of the extant fiats for process carry More's approbatory scrawl." Roper, of course, claims that More examined every one.

A later legend held that he cleared the slow-moving Court of Chancery of all its business, catching the dockets up to date for the first time in anyone's memory. The legend must have grown because More did spend more time on legal business than Wolsey and probably did things much faster. He also enforced the writs of the courts with greater rigor, and he imprisoned those who ignored his decrees. His own son-in-law Giles Heron proceeded with a suit when More had issued a decree against him, and More at once slapped him under a bond of 666 pounds to appear in Star Chamber for what must have been a memorable hearing.

But one man could not work a revolution in the pachydermatous pace of many processes of the English law. The age had its legal cases of chthonian darkness similar to the *Jarndyce* vs. *Jarndyce* memorialized by Dickens in *Bleak House*, and they continued their plodding course through the law courts for all More's term and long after his life had ended.

More's fate was tied to Henry's divorce, and as the king's anger with the pope steadily grew, More's position became less and less tenable. By August 1530, Henry was claiming that England had never been legally subject to the papacy, and he was muttering threats about withdrawing from the Roman communion if the pope did not listen to reason. To withdraw from the Roman communion meant that Henry would take the church in England into his own hands, a step that More could not tolerate.

In 1531, Henry began his great campaign to break the clergy to his will. When Parliament reassembled at last in January, the Convocation of the Clergy sat at the same time, and old Archbishop Warham, perhaps wishing to give some tangible sign of the clergy's loyalty to the king, moved the sessions over to Westminster, where Parliament sat.

Almost at once Henry began a campaign of blackmail. His negotiations with the pope had been enormously expensive, he said. The pope had been obstinate; the English clergy should take responsibility for the costs the king had needlessly incurred. Henry asked for a hundred thousand pounds! After only two days of debate, the clergy agreed to this exorbitant sum, to be paid in five years. Chapuys thought the English church would have to sell the chalices and shrines in their sanctuaries to raise the money.

In exchange the clergy begged for two concessions. They wanted a reaffirmation of the old liberties of the English church recognized under Magna Carta. This would have allowed the clergy to retain their autonomy, making the church what it had been in theory throughout the Middle Ages, a separate state within the realm. It would have meant that clergymen accused of crimes could continue to face trial in the ecclesiastical courts rather than in the courts of common law. It would have preserved the right of sanctuary that had for so long been a matter of acrimonious dispute between spiritual and lay authority. Above all, it would have kept the king from interfering in ecclesiastical affairs.

To be sure that the king did keep his distance, the clergy also requested a general pardon so Henry could not come to them again claiming damages for their past sins. And they wanted some definition and limitation of the Statute of Praemunire, by which all clergymen were threatened with the confiscation of their property and imprisonment of their persons. Praemunire was of special importance. Chapuys wrote Charles V that no one in England could understand praemunire because it was a law that the king interpreted in his own head and he made it apply to any case he chose. To have it defined at last would lessen the terror that it inspired.

Had Henry granted these concessions, Thomas More might have been freed from the net now dragging him to his death, because the independence of the church and its sacramental power in English life would have been assured. But the king was willing to grant only one of these requests—the general pardon. He did not immediately move against clerical privilege. But he made an additional demand that was devastating to the autonomy the clergy yearned to have and believed it must have if the church was to fulfill its mission, an autonomy that was the soul of Thomas More's definition of how the church worked in the world. On February 11, Henry bullied Convocation into naming him "Supreme Head" of the church in England. Cromwell or one of his agents added the phrase "in so far as the law of Christ allows." The saving words have usually been incorrectly ascribed to John Fisher. But their insertion seems to have been an effort by the government to soften the blow and to make Henry's new title acceptable to clergymen with sensitive consciences. Chapuys wrote the emperor that the reservation was of no consequence to the king; no one would argue with Henry over its meaning, and he could interpret it to suit himself. Chapuys wrote on February 21 that More was so dismayed at the king's new title that he wished to resign his office as soon as possible.

Henry soon had a semi-public opportunity to demonstrate his own interpretation of the title. A Lutheran preacher was hauled before the authorities for heresy, and by appealing to the king ended by engaging in disputation with several bishops in the king's presence. The preacher's heresies were listed on a parchment roll; when the king picked it up, he saw that the first article of "heresy" was the claim that the pope was not sovereign over the Christian church. Chapuys heard that the king immediately declared aloud, "This proposition cannot be counted as heretical, for it is both true and certain." Then the king let the preacher go free—a minor thing, perhaps, but an act in violation of the strict autonomy of the church in the determination of heresy. Now the king was saying what was heresy and what was not. Chapuys supposed that the preacher was released through the influence of Anne Boleyn and her father, "who are more Lutherans than Luther himself."

Meanwhile Thomas Cromwell and a cluster of similar-minded men around him had risen to supremacy within the royal council, shoving More aside and leaving him scarcely any authority at all. These men labored to give their king dominion over the church in England as a means of uniting the English people in allegiance to one sovereign. Their rational vision of unity was remarkably similar to that held by Thomas More, by Simon Fish, by William Tyndale, a vision expressed in various competing ways but having at its heart one grand ideal—an island commonwealth united in national strength and national purity, rationally ordering all its resources in one great corporation, eliminating moral, material, and human waste, eliminating poverty, putting the sturdy beggars to work and giving all its citizens purpose and dignity, unlocking the wealth that everyone knew England possessed, that somehow had never been equitably distributed.

Among these men was Christopher St. German, an elderly man, born perhaps as early as 1460, skilled in the common law, a nationalist, possessing perhaps the best political mind in the country, a man who but for his age at the time of Henry's schism and for the stubborn infelicities of his tortuous style might be recalled today as one of the founders of modern political theory, less witty than Machiavelli but much more practical and profound.

At some time early in 1531, St. German helped draw up a comprehensive plan for the reform of both church and nation. The draft proposal called for Parliament to appoint a "great standing council" to be charged with investigating such diverse matters as the value of an English translation of the Bible, the control of prices, and the detection of heresy. The powers of the clergy were to be sharply curtailed, and priests were to be limited to carrying out their traditional liturgical practices. Their other spiritual duties, such as conducting last rites, funerals, and the probation of wills, were to be performed without fee. The religious shrines that had been the target of protests by both Erasmus and Tyndale were to be strictly regulated. The common people were to get sermons with their relics, and no miracle was to receive publicity until it was investigated. Clergymen were not to speak ill of the people, and the people were to return the favor by speaking no ill of them. The government was to organize a huge public works program, financing it by taxes on households and on church property. Every town was to have its common chest to give aid to the poor, but the poor were expected to work when they had opportunity; otherwise they were to be punished, perhaps with death.

The great standing council was to have power to call tradesmen before it to investigate ways in which inflation—the curse of the time—might be controlled. It was, as Professor Guy has shown, a program quite similar to that advanced in 1532 by St. German in his *Treatise Concerning the Division Between the Spirituality and the Temporality,* "which More unreservedly abominated."

The reasons for More's abomination are not far to seek. Like this proposal, his *Utopia* had blazed with the ideal of a united, harmonious commonwealth. But there the secular authority and the religious institutions existed together like body and soul. Nobody in Utopia forced the clergy to be good; they were good by the nature of things, by the power of their religion, by their devotion to it. Somehow only the best people became priests, and somehow nearly all of them remained good during their tenure of office. When the rare bad priest did surface, he was left alone, exposed to the shame of the community, which was far greater than any punishment the state could impose on him by the power of secular justice.

But in St. German's program, the English Parliament was to take hold of the Catholic Church in England and force it to be good. But who was to make Parliament good? God's spirit inspired the holy Catholic Church, leading it (as More said repeatedly, quoting the promise of Christ) into all truth. No wicked priest was ever told by the church that his wickedness was goodness. But no divine promise granted a similar infallibility to the moral dictates of the secular government. Kings could be evil and indeed usually were. Governments bent by wicked kings became the tools of Satan, pursuing some dark purpose of God since God controlled even the devil, but certainly they were not capable of bearing divine revelation about Christian doctrine.

By placing Parliament in control of the church, St. German was proposing to overturn the divine order of things that supposed the supremacy of priesthood. More could foresee that the task of reforming the church by secular government was bound to fall into the hands of those who cared nothing for divine inspiration and everything for political expediency. St. German was conservative, anticlerical, but not heretical in religious doctrines—just as Henry assumed himself to be. Still, More could see well enough that "reform" for such people meant bullying the church under the pretext of purifying it. Their church would end by being an arm of the state.

Nothing came of this draft proposal for reform, but it was alarming that someone in high authority—probably Cromwell but perhaps Henry himself—

had put St. German to work on it. The draft was a signal from the English government of its intention, a sign of a coming storm that might very well shatter the old order and bring on the apocalyptic descent into depravity that More had described in his *Supplication* against Simon Fish.

More was sick at heart at the prospect. He clearly had no influence at all on policy now, and although he worked hard at the legal affairs of his job and battled heresy with what power he could muster, he could not control events. Worse, he was a respectable figurehead, kept by the government to lend it whatever authority his reputation gave him, serving by his very presence in the post of Lord Chancellor a cause which was to him abominable. It is not surprising that Chapuys learned that he wanted to resign his office. Yet he could not resign, for to do so would have been to run the risk of making his opposition to the king public. Those opposed to royal policy were looking for a standard to rally around, and a Lord Chancellor who resigned over a matter of such urgent principle would become that standard whether he wanted to do so or not. Such a bold appearance of opposition to the king might require the expenditure of a life, especially if the opponent was a layman like More, unable to claim whatever was left of clerical immunity against secular prosecution.

Even clerics were in danger. Chapuys wrote that John Fisher was sick and that he and his followers had been threatened with death by being thrown into the Thames if they persisted in their public opposition to the king. So they had been forced into silence. The threat of being thrown into the Thames was not merely a metaphor; it was a warning of judicial assassination of a sort that England had known frequently in the previous century.

Yet Henry's innate caution held him from any irrevocable step and probably gave More hope that the king might yet be deterred from his course. Late in February somebody tried to kill Fisher by poisoning the soup prepared in the bishop's kitchen. Two members of the household died, and some beggars seeking charity at the bishop's kitchen also perished when they ate the deadly broth. Fisher ate none and was spared. The cook was arrested and confessed to having put some powder in the soup given him by someone who told him that it would only make his fellow servants sick. The cook may have been planning a practical joke, but Henry had to be worried that popular suspicion might fall on him for such an obvious attempt on the bishop's life. Besides, he was himself inordinately afraid of being poisoned. So the offending cook was punished by being boiled alive in a great iron pot at Smithfield, as Hall says, "to the terrible example of all."

Chapuys wrote the emperor that More was one of those most solicitous for Queen Catherine and her friends "and certainly shows such sympathy and affection for all that concerns you that he is justly called the father and protector of Your Majesty's subjects." More was also exceedingly helpful to all the secretaries attached to the imperial embassy, and for those benefits the ambassador suggested that the emperor might mention More in some letters that could be shown to him as encouragement. Chapuys also mentioned that More was one of the few Englishmen strongly in favor of sending help to the imperial forces facing the Turks on the Hungarian plain. One of the secretaries in the imperial embassy had gently probed More to see if England might be planning some action against the emperor while he was diverted by the renewal of the Turkish menace at Buda. More replied that the English were making no such preparations and had no such power. It was an important revelation by the Lord Chancellor, especially since Henry did little to disguise his own pleasure at the renewal of the Turkish threat, telling Chapuys that the Turks were the affair of the pope and the emperor and not his own, and even observing that the Great Turk himself, Suleiman II, scourge of Christians in the Balkans and mortal danger to Vienna, "was a man of honor and good faith."

Charles wrote the letters in praise of More that Chapuys requested. But on April 2, Chapuys informed the emperor that More had begged him for the honor of God to leave him alone. He had, More said, given proof enough of his loyalty to Henry that he ought not to come under suspicion no matter who came to visit him, but considering the times, he thought that he should abstain from anything that might provoke doubt. If people did begin to suspect him, he might lose the liberty that he had always enjoyed when speaking to Henry about both the queen and the emperor. More told Chapuys to keep the letter until a better time, for if he received it, he would have to let the king know what it said. Obviously he did not believe that Henry would be pleased with what the letter contained.

In the same dispatch Chapuys gave an account of some of the things that More had done to prove his loyalty to Henry VIII. Late in March, Henry had commanded him to make a speech in the House of Lords against those who said that the king was pursuing this divorce out of love for some lady and not out of any scruple of conscience. It was a cruel ploy on Henry's part and a terrible humilation for More. But the Lord Chancellor did his duty, affirmed the troubles Henry had with his conscience, and to show that there was indeed a case to be made for the king, he adduced the seals of various universities that had ruled in Henry's favor.

Bishops belonged to the House of Lords, and a debate sprang up among some of them. Norfolk worried that things might get out of hand. He arose and declared that the king had not sent the seals down for debate but only for the purposes given by the Lord Chancellor. Then someone—Chapuys does not say who—asked More his own opinion. More replied circumspectly that he had given that opinion many times to the king; he would not give it to anyone else, and he remained silent.

Afterwards, More, Norfolk, Suffolk, the bishops of London and Lincoln, and several other high personages went down to the House of Commons, so Chapuys says, and repeated the performance. More made it clear that the members of the Commons were not to debate the matter or to challenge the authority of the universities that had ruled in the king's favor. Rather the MPs should go home and inform their neighbors that Henry was troubled in his conscience and that a case was to be made for the king's position according to scripture and canon law. More did not give his own opinion, but even a fool could infer it. John Stokesley took it on himself to justify the king; his bold pronouncements must have made the stiff silence of the Lord Chancellor all the more conspicuous to the assembly and, by extension, to every citizen who gathered with his fellows in an alehouse and heard the story at second or third hand. A man with the fixity of conviction that we find in Thomas More could scarcely have felt content with his performance. Henry was treating him as a puppet, and More had to feel demeaned by what he was forced to do.

The king's pardon to the clergy was conveyed by an act of Parliament. It is a long document. It is clear that the pardon was granted solely in exchange for the hundred thousand pounds the clergy had promised to pay. A part of the act includes a list of offenses not pardoned by the statute. Among them are high treason, murder, robbery of churches, the burning of houses, and the ravishing of women. The list reads like an indictment. As one reads felony after felony not covered by the king's pardon, one images that the ordinary readers supposed that these were indeed offenses regularly committed by clergymen and that the king was the great protector of the good common folk against scurvy priests and vicious prelates.

More had written in his *Dialogue Concerning Heresies* that most clergymen were sincere and devout and only a few bad priests gave a bad name to all, but people would always prefer to believe the evil than to speak of the good in their priests. Nevertheless, fierce anticlericalism remained the mood of the moment, especially of those around Henry. The wording of the statute granting the pardon to the clergy was a sign of the tack the government would take from now on. Under the pope, so the government indicated, the clergy had been allowed to sink into abominable corruption. But under the supreme headship of a pious king, the clergy was to be purified, their office dignified, and the nation they served sanctified.

A battered clergy was not helped by the vacillations of a pope who still refused to make any final pronouncement about the divorce. The queen and her allies were bitter and angry at the pope's delays, but they could not get the weak-spirited man to move. Henry was anxious. He commented contemptuously on the power of the pope's excommunication, but Chapuys reported that both Henry and Anne had trouble sleeping because they worried about what the pope might do. The reliability of information possessed by the imperial ambassador about what went on in Henry's bedchamber may be doubted. Yet Henry's unrelenting efforts to get the pope to decide in his favor show plainly enough that the king still feared the pope's authority and the credence in that authority that might still endure among the English people.

The king's fuming pronouncements about English independence from the papacy smell of bold radicalism at this distance and in view of Henry's later schism from Rome. But we should recall that the king was deeply conservative and that English royal fulminations against Italian popes belonged to a tradition that a conservative king might employ without meaning or wanting to give substance to his brave words. Had Clement moved boldly to affirm the marriage in 1529, the king might well have dropped the matter. But as 1531 came and passed away, Henry's rhetoric, fueled by his frustration and encouraged by councillors much more radical than he, became hotter and hotter, melting the constraints of tradition. The clergy, seeing his growing audacity, feeling popular hostility, and lacking strong leadership, began to melt, too, ready to be molded in the shape the king might later command.

Thomas More was caught in the flow of events, a Lord Chancellor increasingly alienated from his king, kept as a figurehead, used as a puppet, and reduced to impotence. It is striking to note how frequently Chapuys wrote of long conversations with the Duke of Norfolk, how seldom he wrote of anything that More had said to him. Norfolk had the king's ear; More had only the Great Seal, and that symbol of high office was cold comfort indeed to a man like himself with no power over policy.

25

THOMAS MORE
AND THE HERETICS

MORE DID HAVE legal powers of office that could be brought to bear against heretics, and these he used to wage unrelenting war against the enemies of the faith. But as his term of office dragged on, he lost the support of the king—the Defender of the Faith—even in this task, for Henry, in his ceaseless search for support, began flirting with some of the very heretics More was seeking to destroy.

When More wrote his *Dialogue Concerning Heresies*, he assumed—for public consumption, at least—the pose of a man worried that heresy might endanger some individuals although sure that the realm as a whole was safe from a general infection. But by 1529, the year the *Dialogue* appeared, Henry's anger against the pope was cooking, and it was only a matter of time before his rising wrath would converge with the anti-papalism of the heretics. Anne Boleyn and her father seem early on to have recognized the good to be had from the teaching of Luther that the godly prince had a divine commission to reform the church in his territories whether the pope approved of his reformation or not, that indeed it was the duty of the prince to resist papal demands and to protect his people from the wickedness of the bishop of Rome. Naturally, if the king should take charge of the church, the pope would have no authority to meddle in matters like divorce. Many councillors around Henry in 1529 were already pushing him to repudiate the papacy and to confiscate the property of the English church. Queen Catherine reported to Chapuys that Henry had told her that should the pope refuse to declare their marriage null, he would denounce the pope as a heretic and marry "whom he pleased." In the same dispatch Chapuys wrote that in a recent conversation Henry had said that Luther had spoken truly in many things, and that if Luther had limited himself to attacks on the wickedness of the clergy, Henry himself would have written in his defense.

Yet though he might bluster in private, Henry was still unwilling to provoke a complete break with Rome, dreading any move that might upset the tranquillity of his realm. It is evident from what Chapuys reported that Henry feared an invasion led by the emperor, an invasion that might easily have become a formal crusade. Bosworth Field was recent enough for Henry to recall how fickle the English people could be toward their kings, and he knew that although the English were anticlerical, they were not yet heretical. So he continued his strong diplomatic efforts to get his case decided in his favor under papal auspices, and throughout 1530 he steadily maintained a vigorous public antipathy toward heresy and heretics.

We have already noted his proclamation of June 22, 1530, in which he spoke favorably of eventually providing his people with an English Bible. In the same proclamation he declared several books heretical and forbade Englishmen to possess them. Three of the banned books were by William Tyndale—the translation of the New Testament, *The Parable of the Wicked Mammon*, about justification by faith, and *The Obedience of a Christian Man*, a hodgepodge arguing the Lutheran view that the Christian prince should reform the church. Included in the condemnation was a tract against the pope called *The Revelation of Antichrist*, scarcely more than a translation of a piece by Martin Luther. The translator was young John Frith, Tyndale's associate, now, like Tyndale himself, an exile on the Continent. More probably helped draft this proclamation. He was present when it was issued, and it must have pleased him immensely since it demonstrated that Henry was still on the side of the old faith.

Yet as the pope delayed and his own frustration grew, Henry restlessly turned to whatever help he might find for his "great matter." Sometime in 1530 he began his first tentative flirtation with heretics. His first object was William Tyndale, and his first agent was a man More himself had used as a spy, one Stephen Vaughan, a commercial agent posted to Antwerp by Thomas Cromwell.

In the summer of 1529, More and Tunstall had hired Vaughan to sniff out heresy among the many English merchants doing business in Antwerp. Vaughan promptly got into trouble with James Hutton, a kind of English consular official, who pressed charges against him and demanded that More and Tunstall post bail for their employee! If the bail were not posted, Hutton warned, he would throw Vaughan into jail. Vaughan wrote Cromwell that Hutton had hired the worst whore in Antwerp to accuse him. Why a whore's word should be good against Vaughan may be left to the imagination. Evidently Cromwell's friendship got him off, but More by then had lost confidence in him and Vaughan himself never tired afterwards of slandering More's character.

In the fall or early winter of 1530, Vaughan began trying to reach Tyndale on behalf of Henry. He managed to get a letter to Tyndale and to receive one in reply. Rumor had it that Tyndale was preparing an answer to More's *Dialogue*. Vaughan had not been able to get a copy of the reply, and he was not sure that it had been published.

Vaughan was entranced by Tyndale—confirmation enough, it seems, of More's suspicion of Vaughan's orthodoxy. He sent Cromwell a copy of Tyndale's letter to Henry (it has not survived) and added a few notes. Tyndale will not come to England because he is afraid, Vaughan says. And he is much more knowledgeable than the king thinks—perhaps an oblique reference to Henry's notion that Tyndale could easily be made into a royal propagandist. "Would God he were in England," Vaughan says.

In late March, Vaughan wrote again to Cromwell. He had by then obtained part of Tyndale's *Answer to Thomas More's Dialogue* in manuscript, and he had a copy made for the king. Vaughan was not sure how Henry would receive it, although he said that Tyndale claimed never to have written anything "with so gentle a style." Tyndale said he would not print the book until he knew how the king might take it. If Henry was pleased with it, he would probably come to England.

In the meantime, however, Henry had read Tyndale's *Practice of Prelates*, and his flirtation with William Tyndale had ended in a storm of wrath. The book had been published sometime during the second half of 1530; it may well be that More's zealous watch against heretical volumes kept it from coming into the king's hands for several months. There is irony in this supposition, for if Henry had seen the work shortly after it was published, he would never have begun his efforts to bring Tyndale to England.

The book is a dazzling attempt to interpret English history as an almighty fight to the death between the virtuous English kings on one side and the wicked popes and English bishops on the other. Cardinal Wolsey embodies the culmination of centuries of conspiracy, and Tyndale's hatred of Wolsey is so nearly boundless that it seems pathological. This hatred blinded him to events.

He was sure that Wolsey had planted the doubts in Henry's mind about his marriage—a view More shared, if Roper is a trustworthy witness. Tyndale was an imperialist, favoring Charles V, knowing that the Holy Roman Emperors had routinely done battle with popes over the centuries. Wolsey's efforts to obtain a divorce for Henry, he maintained, were part of the cardinal's plot to ally England with the French, whom Tyndale detested.

He seemed to believe that when he had explained all these matters to Henry and satisfactorily interpreted Leviticus, the king would see the light, take Catherine back, and suppress the disobedient clergy. He does not mention Anne Boleyn by name, but he does castigate Henry for having inveighed against the marriage of Martin Luther. He advised Henry to fear lest God, avenging Henry's willful blindness, "tangle his grace with matrimony (beside the destruction of the realm that is like to follow) much more dishonorable than his grace thinketh Martin's shameful." Throughout *The Practice of Prelates* he takes Henry at his public word, believing that the king was genuinely troubled by scruples of conscience and by nothing else. But Henry was as impassioned for Anne as a boar in rut, and he was just as dangerous. After looking through *The Practice of Prelates*, Henry wanted only one thing of William Tyndale, and that was to see him dead.

Communications were slow, and Vaughan managed to have two interviews with Tyndale and to send on part of the manuscript of Tyndale's *Answer* to More's *Dialogue* before he got word from Cromwell and the king to break off negotiations with him. Thomas More must have known of these overtures to the heretic he hated most. They were not so secret that Chapuys failed to hear of them, and on December 17, 1530, he apprised the emperor of Tyndale's work against the divorce. Henry, said Chapuys, "being afraid that the said priest will write still more boldly against him and hoping to make him retract what he has already said in this matter, has offered him several good appointments and a seat in his Council if he will come over."

More, always refusing to oppose his king by overt word or deed, could do little about these humiliating negotiations while they were in progress. But the king's wrath at *The Practice of Prelates* offered at least the opportunity for a renewed offensive against Tyndale and his works. The Venetian ambassador reported on December 16 that some three thousand copies of *The Practice of Prelates* were in circulation and that in response the government had "posted in all the most conspicuous places" an edict condemning it. Chapuys reported to the emperor in his letter of the next day that the edict had drawn the people into a public discussion of the divorce, something that had not happened before, and that its chief effect was only to whet the appetite of the people to read the book itself. The Venetian ambassador reported that Tyndale's brother and others—among them Steelyard merchants—who had circulated *The Practice of Prelates*, had been lately paraded through the city "with pasteboard mitres on their heads, bearing an inscription, thus, *Peccasse contra mandata Regis* ["We have sinned against the command of the King"], and the book suspended from their necks; and having completed the circuit of the thoroughfares, they were ordered to cast the pamphlet into the fire prepared for that purpose." Chapuys reported on the same spectacle and commented grumpily, "I cannot see what good is to result from all this, since it now appears that for one who spoke about these matters before, there are now a hundred who discourse of them freely and without fear." We can see the hand of More in the arrests—and perhaps the hand of the king and council in the mildness of the punishment; Henry had no intention of jeopardizing German trade by burning German merchants for heresy.

But as Henry's enthusiasm for Tyndale waned, it waxed hot for another heretic. John Frith, a collaborator with Tyndale on the New Testament and the translator of the tract by Luther into English that Henry had banned in his proclamation, had been an exile from England since 1528. His chief distinction in 1531 was that he had attacked the doctrine of purgatory. But in the murky religious atmosphere of those days his attack might be interpreted as simple anticlericalism rather than as outright heresy. At least his views on purgatory did not create an unbridgeable gulf between him and the king, although we can never be certain of what Henry really knew of the beliefs of any of the heretics he courted. In early 1531 the king—or at least his agents —believed that the young man could be won over, made to give up his radical beliefs, and persuaded to take the king's side in the divorce.

Sometime during Lent of 1531, Frith returned secretly to England. It has been speculated that More's warfare against heretics and heretical books had so demoralized the community of evangelicals in England that Frith came back to encourage them and to reorganize them. Frith made his way to Reading, where he was arrested. Foxe tells a confusing story about the incident, reporting that Frith was arrested as a vagabond, put in the stocks, and released when he spoke to the local schoolmaster in Latin and in Greek. By then, Foxe says, More had learned of Frith's presence in England and begun to scour the country for him. It seems quite likely that More learned of Frith's whereabouts through spies and successfully took him into custody.

On March 22, 1531—a date that fell in Lent that year and would thus place Frith in England—Chapuys wrote to the emperor about a conversation he had had shortly before with the Duke of Norfolk. Norfolk had mentioned that on the previous day "the finest and most learned preacher" among the Lutherans in England "had been arrested and was in danger of being publicly burnt alive." The duke was quite sorry at this prospect, "for he said the King had no fitter or better qualified man to send abroad on an embassy to a great prince."

Chapuys reported that the Lutheran preacher was brought before old Archbishop Warham and refused to answer questions unless lay members of the Privy Council were in attendance. Accordingly, Norfolk, Thomas Boleyn, Earl of Wiltshire, and other noblemen were assigned to the case, and before them, said Chapuys, "the said priest proceeded to make his declaration and propounded heresy enough." Two days later the man appealed to the king and was conducted into the royal presence. Then occurred the incident mentioned earlier when the king picked up the parchment roll containing a list of the priest's heresies and saw the claim that the pope was not the sovereign chief of the Christian church. And Chapuys passed along what Henry said: "This proposition cannot be counted as heretical, for it is both true and certain." Afterwards Henry sent the priest "back to his own dwelling on condition of preaching one of these days a sermon, and retracting some of his doctrines which the King does not consider as thoroughly orthodox."

This priest—hitherto unidentified—must have been Frith. Everything about the story fits with what we know of the young and brilliant preacher, by all accounts the most attractive of the early English heretics. The interview with the king and the subsequent liberation of the man square with what we know of Henry's desire to win Frith over to his side during 1531. The incident would have been a crushing humiliation for More and reason enough for him to have ignored it in his later writing about Frith. It was also highly alarming, for now Henry showed himself willing to quash any indictment against a heretic who might prove useful, regardless of what the man believed about doctrines More considered essential to Catholic faith.

The king was not content to woo English heretics alone. In June 1531, Chapuys wrote to Charles V that a German doctor, Simon Grinaeus, had recently been in London looking for old manuscript books to take back to Basel to be printed. Grinaeus was a friend of Erasmus, but he was also a disciple of Ulrich Zwingli of Zurich—in More's eyes a far worse heretic even than Luther. While Grinaeus was in London, Henry called him in and talked to him about the divorce. It cannot be doubted that Grinaeus traveled under the king's safe-conduct and that Henry viewed him and his city—heretical Basel—as possible allies. There is something faintly ridiculous in the spectacle of a frustrated king snatching up any available scholar who might be wrenched over to the royal side in a case that was becoming increasingly scandalous. In all these negotiations we see Henry's awful uncertainty, his fear of being alone, his yearning for some authority—any authority—that would confirm him in the course he had chosen.

A thesis of this biography of Thomas More is that he was, until his imprisonment at the last, a cruelly divided man, torn between the necessity of making his way in the secular world and the devout longing to simplify life and to prepare his soul for the eternal world to come. Henry VIII was also divided. He comes down to us as the worst tyrant ever to sit on an English throne. Yet he was all his life torn between his grandiose vision of a chivalric self and the inner reality, which was somewhat pathetic—the enduring, frightened child always longing for a firm hand that might lead his steps aright.

Grinaeus was not persuaded by the king's arguments, but he agreed to think them over in the company of his learned friends when he got back to Basel. Henry tried to oil the processes of this thinking by paying his expenses.

While Grinaeus was in London, Thomas More himself became his guide and guardian. Much later on Grinaeus wrote warmly to John More, Thomas's youngest child, about the help he had received from his father. More's modern biographers have argued that the incident proves More to have been gentle to heretics in person even while he was raging at them in print, for here was Grinaeus, a notorious heretic, remembering More with pleasure. The implication seems to be that More was somehow not serious in his polemical works.

But it is hard to see what else More could have done with Grinaeus, and the encounter with Grinaeus probably reveals rather the pain and humiliation he was made to suffer than his essential gentleness. Grinaeus was in London on what quickly became the king's business. More was necessarily circumspect. He could hardly have arrested Grinaeus, put him on trial, and burned him at the stake while the man traveled under the king's safe-conduct! Grinaeus wrote young John More that Thomas never left him without a guide. We may assume that the "guide" was More's means of keeping a heretic under surveillance even while extending the king's official courtesy. But what a painful business it must have been for More to force himself to be courteous to a notorious heretic and for the two of them, though continually together while Grinaeus was in England, never to touch on the subject of heresy and orthodoxy in any way that revealed More's deepest and truest feelings. It was an act of prodigious self-control on More's part, dictated by the anomaly of his position as the king's chief servant, but surely tormenting to a man of his conviction. Here indeed is the calm, stoic Christian of Roper's biography, but the calm must have cost him dearly. If the modern biographers have a valid point at all in contrasting More's courtesy to Grinaeus with More's fury in his polemical works, it may be only to make us wonder if the fury of the works was all the hotter because More the person was forced by circumstances to assume a role in radical contradiction to his inner self.

He did express something of that fury in the battle he waged against heresy, perhaps the most effective policy More pursued while he was Lord Chancellor. The policy must have annoyed Henry, since it was directed against many of the same people he was seeking to win over to his position on the divorce. But the king could hardly have made public pronouncements against More's efforts without dangerously alienating English public opinion, which was not in the slightest sympathetic to the king in his "great matter." If the king did indeed see to it that Frith went free after he had been ensnared in More's net, that act was sign enough of the royal power and a signal to More himself that the king would intervene against More's efforts anytime he chose. So More's policy continued in force only as a way of cleaning out those heretics who were of no obvious use to Henry. Now and then it profited by Henry's propensity to discard people and to take vengeance on those who disappointed him.

Even at its fiercest, More's struggle against heresy must have seemed lonely and uncertain. The clergy in London, demoralized by Henry's attack on them and the pope, could scarcely summon up either courage or energy to do prolonged battle, especially while Henry's flirtations with various notorious heretics were becoming increasingly public and bold. Clergymen in outlying areas where the influence of the capital was diluted proceeded in the old ways against the occasional outspoken heretic, but even here the ambiguity of the royal court and the uncertainty of the London clergy about heresy made itself increasingly felt. Thomas Cranmer, captivated by Lutheran doctrine, was in the king's inner circle by 1531. Others like Cranmer were making their way to the king's side, and from the governing center outward heretical opinions found an audience less and less inclined to traditional orthodoxy.

In November 1531, Stephen Vaughan sent Cromwell a copy of Robert Barnes's *Supplication*, a work published earlier in that same year. Here Barnes shamelessly flattered the king. He also presented the standard Lutheran view that the true universal or catholic church was not a visible institution but rather the community of the elect in time and eternity, invisible to the world, known only to God.

The doctrine of the "invisible church" offered dazzling rhetorical possibilities, and Barnes seized as many of them as he could. In a dreary moral atmosphere in which many Christians were so tormented by the corruptions of the Catholic Church that they wondered if God remained in the world at all, Barnes could declare that a church of limpid purity and perfect beauty really did exist. Since it was invisible, he was spared the necessity of proving its supposed perfection. And since he spoke of it so hotly and at such length, some might think it really existed.

As we have seen, Vaughan was a man of enthusiasms. He was in raptures over Barnes's book. He thought that it would sweep the common people into accepting it and, we may assume, once they had done so, Henry's sovereignty over the English church might be accepted too. If the true church was invisible, untouchable by any mortal hand, nothing should keep a king from becoming head of the visible and inferior institution called the church in the king's own country.

The obsequiousness of Barnes toward Henry indicated a pliable (and certainly ambitious) man who might be used to royal advantage. Barnes consulted Luther himself about the king's divorce; Luther counseled bigamy, saying that Queen Catherine should permit the king to marry a second queen according to the example of the patriarchs but she herself should not agree to be excluded from the royal matrimony or from the title "Queen of England." It was not exactly the advice Henry wanted, and we do not know if Barnes conveyed it.

We do know that, in December 1531, Barnes arrived in England under the king's safe-conduct. To More the visit was yet another humiliation, although he did his best to put a good face on it. Writing a few months later, he said that Henry was generous, that he wanted only to see if some spark of grace might yet be found in Barnes so that the heretic might be converted and his soul saved. But the real purpose of Barnes's visit was clearly to discuss the divorce and to see if some accommodation might be reached between England and the German Lutherans. It seems almost certain that Barnes and Henry talked, although we have no record of their conversation. Chapuys saw Barnes at court dressed in secular garb and noted that he came at the insistence of the king himself. To these discussions More was only a spectator, nearly impotent.

He did keep Barnes under surveillance. Later he delighted in publishing a circumstantial account of his comings and goings, as if to show Barnes how closely he was watched. He knew that Barnes had grown a beard and dressed like a merchant rather than a priest and wore a red Italian beret and in every possible way tried to disguise his clerical status. More also knew that he frequented a tavern at the sign of the bottle on Botolph's Wharf near the Steelyard and the bridge. While Barnes remained in the country, More argued that he had violated his safe-conduct by staying too long and that he could be arrested—if the king would permit it. Henry did not grant that permission, and Barnes departed from England sometime in the first half of 1532. By mentioning Barnes at all and alluding to the king's interest in him, More was showing considerable audacity, drawing attention to the royal flirtation with heresy, calling on the king to do his duty to squelch evil doctrines and to destroy those who propagated them, working as best he could to stir up public opinion against what Henry was doing—all the while declaiming that Henry's heart was in the right place and, in effect, seeking to push the king into living up to the declarations More was making on his behalf. It was another cause for division between Henry and his Lord Chancellor, and we may suppose that as More continued to write against heresy, bringing in the king's name whenever he could, Henry's irritation continued to grow until, in February 1534, More hinted at a promise he had made to Cromwell and the king to stop writing.

Barnes returned to England in 1534 and remained an important fixture in the country for the rest of the decade, instrumental in getting his former colleague John Lambert (who had been in the group at the White Horse Tavern at Cambridge) burned at the stake in a dispute over the mass. Finally Barnes was himself burned at the stake in 1540 when he ran afoul of Henry in the murky circumstances of Cromwell's fall. The importance of Barnes to this biography lies in how his presence revealed to More and to anyone else who cared to look that Henry VIII was so single-minded about his divorce that he was willing to consort with even the most unsavory heretics if they offered him support. Under those circumstances, attacking heresy was dangerous business for anyone who undertook it independently of the king.

Yet More remained dogged and undaunted in his war against heretics. It is the part of his career that is most dubious and most embarrassing to his modern admirers; yet paradoxically nothing better proves the mettle of the man, for his moves against heretics required a courage that has seldom been recognized, since even Roman Catholics today will scarcely praise his motives.

He had examined heretics at his house in Chelsea even before he became Lord Chancellor, usually in the company of Tunstall. As a member of the royal council, he would have used the license of the statutes against Lollardy that gave political officers who were not priests the authority to help conduct interrogations of heretics in the company of clergymen. Since he was the only lay member of the council to have performed such tasks, we may see both his interest in the matter and the regard shown him by high clergymen who included him in these examinations. When Tunstall departed to be bishop of Durham in 1530, More continued the interrogations with Stokesley and others, making a much stronger effort than Wolsey had ever done to ferret out heresy, and apparently putting large numbers of suspects under arrest, again by the authority of the anti-Lollard statutes.

His methods were not gentle. In 1533, when More was no longer in power, one John Feild petitioned Lord Chancellor Thomas Audeley and the royal council for a pardon from actions begun against him by Thomas More, which had brought Feild much grief. Early in January 1530, More had brought Feild and others to Chelsea and had confined him for eighteen days, taking bonds for his appearance in Star Chamber a week later. After that appearance he was sent to the Fleet prison and kept in solitary confinement for two years, frequently searched and once robbed of ten shillings that had been sent him "for necessaries." After two years he was transferred to the Marshalsea prison, not allowed to take even his bedding with him, and there kept until he became so ill that he was released, carried out by four men. By that time More was no longer Lord Chancellor, but he still had influence enough to have Feild committed to Marshalsea again, where he stayed until October 1532. Having been faithful under bond for a year, Feild applied to Audeley and the council for relief.

If his methods were harsh, so were his words about the sufferings of heretics. In February 1530, one Thomas Hytton was burned for heresy at Maidstone in Kent. In his *Dialogue Concerning Heresies*, More had boasted that he had never heard of a heretic willing to die for heresy if he could escape death by perjuring himself. In his *Answer* to More's *Dialogue*, published about July 1531, Tyndale recalled More's boast and presented Hytton as an authentic martyr. More learned that some heretics were venerating Hytton as a kind of saint, placing his name in the calendar of a heretical prayer book. More—chagrined and angry—later described Hytton's heresies as if to name them was to show how horrible they were. They included a renunciation of the mass and oral confession, a denial of purgatory and the efficacy of prayers for the dead, the wish that images of Christ and the saints be thrown out of churches, and the surprising opinion that no crime merited capital punishment—a belief at least akin to More's description of Utopian justice in which no one was put to death for theft! More called all these beliefs "abominable" and called Hytton himself "the devil's stinking martyr." He seems to have contributed nothing to the burning itself but his enthusiastic—almost savage—approval after the fact.

By far the most controversial heresy case involving More was another in which he took no active role himself in bringing the heretic to the stake. What is still controversial is More's account of what happened, and his own dedication to the fight against heresy is demonstrated by the irregular inquiry that he made into the case to obtain the information that he dispensed in writing about it.

On August 17, 1531, Thomas Bilney was burned in Norwich. When Bilney abjured his heresies the first time, he went into such black depression that, Hugh Latimer said later on, his friends were afraid to leave him alone. The implication is that he was ready to kill himself. Foxe tells us that one night in 1531 Bilney left Trinity College in Cambridge and announced that he would go to Jerusalem—speaking the words of Christ, for whom going to Jerusalem meant going to the cross. He preached to small groups in Norfolk and afterwards went to the fields to preach to the crowds that came out to hear him. He distributed Tyndale's New Testament and *The Obedience of a Christian Man*—works banned by royal proclamation. Obviously he was courting a martyr's death, for once a heretic had abjured his heresy, been forgiven, and fallen into heresy again, he was sure to burn if caught. Once the church had been smitten on one cheek, it had only one other to turn, and smitten there, could strike back with the fury of God against the damned.

Bilney made no effort to escape; he seemed rather to bask in the prospect of public immolation in witness to his vigorous though vague faith. This craving for violent death before a large audience ran through the tales of early Christian martyrs, and in an age such as our own which worships irrationality, it is easy enough to believe though impossible to understand. It is easy, too, to suppose that at times the death was of greater importance than the reason for dying. Death was renunciation, purgation, the final triumph of the soul over the body, of hope over the momentary but tyrannical demands of the present. Bilney got his wish. He was condemned by the clergy and turned over to the secular authority to be burned in keeping with ancient tradition.

We have heard so often of people burned at the stake that our familiarity with the words of the stories leads us to believe, erroneously, that we are familiar with the deed. Early woodcuts show heaps of wood piled up around the victim. The process of setting the fire and making the last formal admonitions to the one who would die took some little time. A condemned person —even one as resolved to die as Bilney had been—might reflect, with growing terror and perhaps with a wakening of impossible regret, on the prospect of his immediate, inescapable, and horrifying end.

Bilney was popular. He exemplified the austere and godly ideal that was part of English anticlericalism, an ideal against which the performance of ordinary priests and monks was measured and found wanting. Norwich was as anticlerical as any English city, and fierce debate broke out over the legality of the fire that burned Bilney. If Henry VIII was now "Supreme Head" of the church of God in England, did a sheriff in a town have the right to burn a heretic merely because the clergy declared the man worthy of burning?

And what did Bilney say at the last? Did he remain firm to the end, or did he recant his heresies and die in the Catholic Church? John Foxe, the martyrologist, maintained adamantly that Bilney remained true to the convictions that got him burned—though Foxe had as much trouble as anyone in describing exactly what Bilney believed. Thomas More maintained that Bilney had recanted and died a true Catholic and that his death proved the efficacy of burning.

The dispute over what Bilney said originated in Norwich itself among the people who saw him die. More, hearing of the outcry, instituted a Star Chamber inquiry to find out what had happened. Professor Guy, an expert in Star Chamber proceedings, holds that the inquiry was irregular since More made it on his own initiative, without waiting for a bill of complaint or for information filed in the proper form. Obviously More was intensely interested in the case, and his fierce hatred of heresy made him willing to jettison procedures that got in his way. Just as clearly, he wanted to be able to trumpet to the world that the most prominent martyr among the heretics had returned to the Catholic faith at the end and had not remained obstinate. On his side More had just as much trouble as Foxe later did in reasoning out how people could follow false doctrine to the death.

In the late fall of 1531, More called witnesses down to London and took depositions. One was Edward Reed, mayor of Norwich; another was James Curatt, an alderman of the city; a third was Thomas Pelles, the bishop of Norwich's chancellor. Pelles was the most important source for More's account of what Bilney had said at the end. From these depositions, an important and complicated story emerges.

Reed obviously stood on the side of those who believed Bilney did not recant. Just as obviously the Lord Chancellor intimidated him, so that the mayor from the provinces found it safer to say he could not remember some things rather than to commit perjury or to say things that might get him into trouble.

What is strikingly clear is that at his trial Bilney appealed beyond his ecclesiastical judge to the king as Supreme Head of the church in England. People in the audience then cried out that it was the duty of the mayor to take charge of the prisoner since the appeal to the king effectively removed Bilney from ecclesiastical jurisdiction. Reed seemed willing to do just that. But what did the new title mean? Nobody knew, and Reed asked Pelles for an explanation. Pelles apparently said that whatever the title meant, it did not mean that someone accused of heresy should be removed from the traditional jurisdiction of the ecclesiastical authorities. So the trial proceeded. Bilney was judged a contumacious heretic and turned over to the secular authority to be burned.

On the morning of the execution Pelles showed up with a formal list of errors that Bilney was to read at the stake along with the appropriate recantations that he was to make. Alderman Curatt told More that he had accompanied Bilney to the stake and stood very close to him, so that he heard every word Bilney read. But, Curatt said, he had not got the last of it because he had to step away and tie his shoe! What he did report was hardly the extensive list that the church authorities wanted.

In early October, Reed had called the aldermen together and told them that he would be going down to the next session of Parliament, where he expected an inquiry into Bilney's death. He was obviously worried. He wanted to get the story right, get it in writing, and get it stamped with the town's seal. (Tudor Englishmen had an imposing and touching faith in the power of seals to make things correct.) Curatt, in his deposition to More, said that he approved everything Reed read from his written account except that no mention was made of Bilney's revocation of the list provided by Dr. Pelles. After Curatt raised the point, Reed (so Curatt claimed) thereupon called him a liar and told him he was a false man not worthy to be in honest company.

As it turned out, Reed on that same evening dispatched a book Bilney had written; it went to the Duke of Norfolk. Just after mass on the morning he died, Bilney had given the book to Dr. Pelles. But Reed seized it from Pelles, claiming that since it had been written while Bilney was in the custody of the secular authorities, it should go to the mayor and not to the bishop's men. It looks very much as if Reed did not trust Pelles the ecclesiastic and wanted to make some use of the book—perhaps to prove that it contained no errors in faith and that Bilney had been burned at the demand of vicious clergymen when he should have been heard by the king, the Supreme Head of the church in England. Fearing for his own future and worried about his role in the execution, Reed was probably trying to shift blame to the clergy.

The covering letter that Reed sent to Norfolk makes no mention of any formal recantation by Bilney. It does contain the interesting remark, supposedly made by Bilney, that the pope's formal excommunication was only an outward curse and not the same as God's judgment—a position taken by all the heretics and, increasingly in these months, by Henry VIII, in contradiction to the traditional papal teaching that the power to bind and loosen on earth and in heaven meant that the pronouncement of excommunication by the pope was the expression of God's will. Bilney urged obedience to the church and asserted that he believed in the *Ecclesiam Catholicam,* so Reed said. Bilney would also leave the marriage of priests to be disputed by others after his death, and he said that he had always taught that virginity and chastity were greatly meritorious. He denied that he had disapproved of fasting and, in a telling blow, he said he wished that prelates would follow Christ's example and do it more frequently. If this was heresy, it was a mild version.

But Bilney had died as a heretic, and under no circumstances could Thomas More be persuaded that the clergy he was defending with uncompromising thunderbolts of rhetoric had burned an innocent or at least a scarcely guilty man. Reed was summoned before More on December 1 and again on December 5 to make depositions. He managed to give the impression that Pelles was hovering vulture-like over Bilney in the last days before the execution, wanting to know the exact date of the burning so that he might wring a revocation out of him—an enterprise that must have promised success to a clergyman like Pelles who knew of Bilney's passionate and unstable character. Under hard questioning by More, which we may imagine was threatening in the extreme, Reed admitted that Pelles had indeed given Bilney a paper to read at the stake but that Bilney read it either silently or so softly that no one could hear what he said! Bilney did kneel down and ask for absolution, and Reed thought that he submitted himself to the church, but he could not truly remember. Neither could he recall whether Bilney had revoked his errors or whether he exhorted the people to obey God, the ministers of the church, or the law. More scorned Reed, and in obtaining the depositions he very probably threatened the unfortunate mayor with the same fire that had consumed the subject of the investigation. The position of Curatt throughout looks thoroughly confused and ambiguous, and Professor Guy has pointed out that he had long and close connections with Thomas Cromwell.

Everyone finally seemed to agree that Pelles had given Bilney a piece of paper with something on it that Bilney read, either in silence or aloud. But what was on the paper? That was the sticking point. Pelles brought around a copy after the execution, wishing to have Reed notarize it with the town seal. But Reed evidently smelled a rat, and when he presented it for scrutiny to several aldermen and citizens, they said it was not the same paper Bilney had in his possession at the burning. It is plausible to suppose that Pelles, willing to paint the lily in the bright colors wanted by the ecclesiastical authorities, had made Bilney's heresies much more explicit and extravagant than they in fact were. If people could be made to believe that Bilney had recanted such a list, they would also believe that he was the outrageous heretic the church claimed he was, that the priests so under attack from every direction had been correct in declaring him guilty and that Bilney was well burned.

More wanted to believe all this himself, and he wanted with all his heart for others to do likewise. When he published his own account of the Bilney case shortly before he left office in 1532, More followed Pelles's version and gave no hint of the complicated controversy that had surrounded the case. Here and there he goes far beyond the plausible.

In More's account, presented in 1532 in the first part of his *Confutation of Tyndale's Answer*, Bilney's second recantation of heresy began at his trial, where, at the end, he got down on his knees before Dr. Pelles, begged him for absolution from the sentence of excommunication, and confessed to all that he deserved to suffer death. Nothing in this part of the story is confirmed in any surviving evidence not from More's pen.

On the morning he was burned, Bilney, says More, begged to receive the sacrament in the form of bread—the traditional Catholic way, quite in opposition to Luther's view that the laity should receive the sacrament in both kinds, the bread and the wine. Dr. Pelles objected, not trusting the sincerity of Bilney's new conversion, says More. But "finally perceiving him to be of a true, perfect faith, and his desire to proceed of a fervent mind," Pelles granted the request and administered the sacrament. But why, if Bilney had made the confession at the trial that More reports, did Pelles go on doubting the man's sincerity to the point of almost refusing him the sacrament? More gives us no answer.

He does tell us how reverently Bilney took the sacrament, reciting the collect *Domine Iesu Christe,* and beating his breast at the words "peace and concord to thy church," which by More's account he repeated several times, then crying to God for mercy in that he had so grievously erred "in that point." But what point? Was Bilney admitting that he had broken the peace and concord of the church? It is unlikely that he was confessing some offense against the eucharist, since he never rejected the traditional Catholic understanding of that sacrament, causing John Foxe to make nervous excuses for him on that score.

Then More says that Bilney confessed that he had for a time followed Luther and Tyndale off on their trail of the invisible church, denying that the visible church was the true church of God—a heresy that, in More's version, Bilney now fully recanted. But did he? Did he have anything to recant? As we have noted earlier, More makes the entire tale much clearer, even starker, than the evidence seems to allow, and recalling his shiftiness with the facts in the Richard Hunne affair, we have reason to mistrust his account of Bilney's last moments. Whatever he himself believed, Bilney was acting as colporteur for Tyndale's books, and that was enough to make More sure of his guilt, regardless of what happened at the trial. We cannot get closer to the truth because the evidence is lacking—as it was to More's readers. Was Bilney truly a heretic? He seems to have thought he was, and he courted death. He was probably a thoroughly good man with some heretical views and slightly crazy. Such people make difficult cases for both lawyers and historians.

Besides his defense of the clergy who had condemned Bilney, More had two other logs to saw. He trumpeted Bilney's recantation because it was a triumph for the Catholic Church and for his own view of how to deal with heretics. The most attractive and influential person among the dissidents had at the last been brought back to the true church, and the agency of his blessed redemption had been the sure, swift punishment by death that More thought should be inflicted on everyone who stubbornly deviated from the faith. Bilney was the shining example of the efficacy of fire, not only in purging away the poison that might corrupt the innocent who heard heretical preaching but in saving the soul of the heretic himself. More was so carried away with his vision of Bilney's salvation by fire that he claimed the flames had made the man a saint! Bilney suffered his purgatory in that fire, More said, and Christ "hath forthwith from the fire taken his blessed soul to heaven where he now prayeth incessantly for the repentance and the amendment of all such as have been by his means while he lived, into any such errors induced or confirmed. And I firmly trust that God's grace to the effect will work, and so I pray God it may." More was one of the greatest masters of irony in his age, but here he simply outdoes himself. He gives us St. Bilney praying in heaven for those whom he had led astray, men who denied the existence of saints altogether. It is hardly any wonder that first William Tyndale and much later John Foxe were driven to indignation by More's account. And it is worth reflecting a moment on the seriousness of More's vision, how violent death could be the doorway to heaven to those who died with their minds composed and their hearts committed to the old church.

More also had a hidden agenda. There was that matter of the appeal to the king as Supreme Head that Bilney had made at his trial. By showing Bilney's willingness to die and his complete recantation of his heresies, More was also proving that the traditional way of dealing with heretics was the right way. Reed and his secular cohorts who had wanted to take the case entirely into their hands could not have obtained the dramatic result that the ecclesiastical authorities had won. Though More was far too circumspect to spell this issue out, it is clear that to him Thomas Bilney stood as an example of the righteousness of the old ways when an independent church carried out the judgments of God in determining heresy, and the secular authority, acting in proper subordination and obedience, executed the judgment by burning the heretic. It was a position that he had defended at great length in his *Dialogue Concerning Heresies,* and in 1532 the very report of Bilney's death confirmed centuries of church practice and secular conformity to the church's just judgments.

As we have noted, More did not wait passively for the church to do its duty.

Throughout his term of office he fought hard against heretical books and those
who peddled them. J. A. Guy lays on his shoulders the responsibility for the
use of Star Chamber proceedings in carrying out this policy—proceedings that
later became so infamous that "Star Chamber" became a synonym for repression. Professor Guy has also discovered in his scrutiny of the archives instances
when book dealers seized by More for possessing forbidden works were forced
to ride horseback through the city, turned around so that they faced the horse's
rear, their clothing pinned all over with pages from the heretical books, while
they were pelted with rotten fruit.

It is not surprising that More was accused of cruelty to heretics and that
these charges should be a matter of concern to his modern admirers. He laid
himself open to the charges by his policy of examining heretics at his home,
albeit in the company of clergymen. Some heretics were even imprisoned there
—a reflection of the tradition, noted earlier, that a man's house was both his
home and a mark of his official place in the world. The procedure probably also
says something about public opinion in London or at least More's sense of it.
Enough people in the city might have sided with heresy to make the examination of heretics within the walls a risky business, one that could provoke uproar
and riot.

Londoners were as volatile as ever in these years, and in his capacity as Lord
Chancellor, More did what he could to impose order. At times he was hard
pressed. On August 30, 1531, priests and laymen rioted against John Stokesley,
the new bishop, because he was trying to collect money from his clergy to pay
his share of the fine imposed earlier on the Convocation of the Clergy by the
king. The mob attacked the bishop's palace at St. Paul's for an hour and half
and afterwards assaulted the chapter house. More must have been outraged at
this uproar by clergymen just when he was trying to brand the heretics with
charges of sedition and hold the church up as the bastion of order. He sent
out warrants for the arrest of fifteen priests and five laymen who were responsible for the riot. Hall tells us that some were sent to the Tower, some to the
Fleet, and some to other prisons, "where they remained long after." More says
nothing of any of this in his own works. But we may surmise that he wished
to avoid any further provocations to the London populace and that he thought
it much safer to examine heretics out in Chelsea than in the vicinity of St.
Paul's.

One of the heretics More imprisoned was a renegade priest named George
Constantine who trafficked in heretical books. Constantine and his friend
Stephen Vaughan, whom we have met before, seem to have been responsible
for most of the charges that More was savage to heretics in his possession.
Constantine, who had already been in trouble with the authorities, was apprehended and imprisoned at Chelsea by More in the fall of 1531 and interrogated by him. Constantine gave information that More used to arrest another

colporteur, a former Benedictine monk named Richard Bayfield. Bayfield had been condemned for heresy before and had abjured, but, More said, "like a dog returning to his vomit," he fled to the Continent and fell into heresy again. More said that Bayfield's heresies were well known "and his holy life well declareth them, when being both a priest and a monk, he went about two wives, one in Brabant, another in England. What he meant, I cannot make you sure, whether he would be sure of the one if the other should hap refuse him or that he would have them both, the one here, the other there, or else both in one place, the one because he was priest, the other because he was monk."

Bayfield, More said, would gladly have saved his skin by recanting again if that had been possible. But since the penalty for a second conviction of heresy was always death, Bayfield had to die, and so he did, much to More's grim pleasure. But George Constantine escaped, after informing on several other heretics, and made his way to Antwerp to take refuge with Stephen Vaughan.

In the meantime More had got wind of Vaughan's activities and had begun to see him as devious and dangerous. Vaughan knew of More's enmity and was afraid. Cromwell had written him in late November that George Constantine had been arrested and that More was interrogating him.

Vaughan replied in a heated, whining six-page letter. More was always trying to pin some evil on him, he said. The Lord Chancellor tortured heretics to get them to implicate others. So it was with Constantine. A man with his legs shackled with cold iron like a beast could be counted on to accuse his own father and mother if by so doing he might escape torture. The king should banish such punishments from the realm and lovingly reform the clergy like a father, Vaughan said. Then troubles would calm down. Vaughan explained what it was to be a secret agent. Among Christians he was a Christian, among Jews a Jew, among Lutherans a Lutheran. Unless he acted so, he could not do anything in Antwerp. At the end, almost as an afterthought, Vaughan adds the information that George Constantine had arrived in town after escaping from More.

It seems likely that Vaughan began writing in reply to Cromwell's anxiety and anger, feeling considerable anxiety on his own. Near the end he discovered that Constantine was in Antwerp and put the information in his letter just before closing. For us the important point is that Vaughan defended himself by accusing More of such cruelty that anyone subjected to it would confess anything. More thought Vaughan was a heretic. Vaughan, afraid, wanted Cromwell to know that he was only doing the king's business. By implication he was calling on the king for help against the Lord Chancellor.

More held both Vaughan and Constantine in contempt. Constantine, at least, seems worthy of the scorn More heaped on him. In the first part of *The Confutation at Tyndale's Answer*, More delights in telling how Constantine had feigned repentance from heresy to save himself, a repentance that Constantine sought to prove by informing on Bayfield and other heretics, one of whom—a bookseller named Robert Necton—More had thrown into the Newgate prison. After Constantine escaped, More evidently heard that he got to Vaughan in Antwerp; the Lord Chancellor wrote, "I will advise all good Christian folk and especially the king's subjects, to forbear and eschew his company." And in a declaration seemingly aimed at Vaughan, he said, "For that Englishman which shall be found to be familiar with him there, before his conversion here known and proved, may thereby bring himself in suspicion of heresy, and haply hear thereof at his returning hither."

Constantine showed remarkable talent for betraying people even in that devious age, and he went on informing on friends for various misdeeds and survived happily enough into the reign of Elizabeth. In 1532 he accused Stephen Vaughan of heresy.

Quite clearly such a man had to justify himself once he had escaped from More, and he did so by spreading tales about More's cruelty. Vaughan obviously found such stories to his own liking, and as we have already noted in his reply to Cromwell's letter about More's enmity, he was ready to pass on what Constantine told him. In time these rumors of cruelty became a flame of slander rippling over More's character. Cromwell undoubtedly fanned it because it would have undermined such standing as More had among the people, reducing his effectiveness as a spokesman for the old church. More himself was stung by these charges, and he felt driven to defend himself in his *Apology* published in 1533, months after he had resigned his office.

He was accused of beating heretics. He had ordered corporal punishment for only two, he said. One was a child, a servant in the household, who had been in bad company and had learned some heresy against the eucharist. The child repeated these heresies in More's house. More had a servant cane him in front of the family, as was the custom in punishing children.

By More's account, the only other person he had whipped was a feebleminded man in the habit of sneaking up behind women at prayer, and throwing their skirts over their heads. No one else, said More, had ever had so much as a tap on the forehead while being examined under his charge.

How were heretics imprisoned in More's house? More answers this question almost incidentally in recounting the escape of Constantine. Constantine was set in the stocks but broke them and climbed over a wall and fled. (More said he was not even angry when he learned that Constantine had fled; he merely told his porter to mend the stocks and lock them up lest the prisoner try to steal in again!) In making his excuses in Antwerp for betraying his friends, Constantine might protest that he had been treated like an animal. But the stocks were often used to hold petty criminals, and they were hardly considered cruel or unusual punishment.

More smarted under the charges as he always did when under attack. He wrote contemptuously of a bookseller named Segar from Cambridge, detained in More's house four or five days and there examined for heresy. Segar had neither bodily harm done him nor foul word spoken to him, wrote More. But later he claimed that More had wrapped cords around his head until he swooned and that More had tied him to a tree and beaten him. Tyndale added the detail that More had even stolen Segar's purse.

John Foxe lugubriously repeated all these tales, which he probably got by reading More's account of them, and refused to believe More's denials and satiric rebuttal. Foxe accused More of cruelty to every heretic entrusted to his care. But even Foxe had trouble with the yarn that More had stolen a purse; in the later editions of the *Acts and Monuments*, the story disappears. Still, More's reputation as a merciless torturer of heretics committed to his care lingered for centuries in the English consciousness.

Modern scholars have taken More solidly at his word. Yet in their zeal to absolve him of these old canards, they have forgotten that he must have been a terrifying antagonist to helpless men submitted to an inquisition before him, since he had the power to send them to the stake.

In December 1531, a leather seller named John Tewksbury was tried before Stokesley and More in Chelsea, condemned by Stokesley of heresy, and turned over to the secular authority represented by More to be burned. More reported that Tewksbury advised another heretic imprisoned with him, one "James," "Save yourself and abjure." Such a course was impossible for Tewksbury since he had been condemned for heresy and recanted before, and so he died. Tyndale claimed him as a hero. More replied with bitter sarcasm, "I can see no very great cause why unless he reckon it for a great glory that the man did abide still by the stake when he was fast bounden to it." Of Tewksbury's death itself More said, "There was never a wretch I ween better worthy."

About the same time that Tewksbury died, James Bainham, a lawyer, was a prisoner in More's house, where he was interrogated by More and Stokesley. After Simon Fish died, Bainham had married his widow. Foxe wrote later that More had Bainham tied to a tree in the courtyard at Chelsea and whipped, then sent to the Tower to be stretched on the rack while More stood by, commanding him to reveal the names of other lawyers infected with heresy. Presented with the choice between recanting his heresies and burning, he formally abjured in February 1532.

Then, like Bilney before him, he was devoured by guilt. He begged forgiveness before a conclave of evangelicals meeting in a London warehouse and soon after fell again into the hands of the authorities and was burned alive not three weeks before More resigned as Lord Chancellor. The Venetian ambassador, Carlo Capello, reported that the greater part of the population came out to see him die and that he perished with the greatest fortitude, showing no pain, talking all the time, and praying aloud. The story Foxe told of Bainham's whipping and racking at More's hands is universally doubted today, but More did rejoice in Bainham's death. The man was only a chatterer, he said, and in speaking of the process of detecting and burning heretics, More mentioned Bainham along with others who had died at the stake, and we can feel the thud of vindictive triumph in his sentence upon them:

> And for heretics as they be, the clergy both denounce them. And as they be well worthy, the temporalty doth burn them. And after the fire of Smithfield, hell doth receive them where the wretches burn forever.

To stand before a man at an inquisition, knowing that he will rejoice when we die, knowing that he will commit us to the stake and its horrors without a moment's hesitation or remorse if we do not satisfy him, is not an experience much less cruel because our inquisitor does not whip us or rack us or shout at us.

Yet More's labors were finally in vain. He himself testified to the general futility of his efforts against heresy when he wrote his *Apology* in 1533. He was then answering the charge that the clergy carried on a campaign of merciless persecution of dissenters. Except in London and Lincoln, he wrote, no one would find four heretics punished in any way in five years in any diocese in England. In some regions one would not find so many punished in fifteen years, and there were many places in England where no heretic was burned for twenty years.

In Lincoln about ten years earlier, he said, twelve or fourteen heretics were made to abjure, much to the delight of all good Catholics in the region. In London greater numbers of heretics were discovered because they were so numerous in the city. Even here only two or three times as many were punished as in the rest of the realm. But in the same work, More—by then out of office —exhorted the bishops not to falter in their zeal to suppress heretics by any measures at their command.

His own labor was utterly single-minded and not mitigated by any flash of mercy or tolerance. Heretics were enemies of God, servants of Satan, minions of hell, and beyond all that, they were usually lower-class, people without roots resolved to root out the grand old faith which was the only guarantee of meaning in the universe. More believed that they should be exterminated, and while he was in office he did everything in his power to bring that extermination to pass. That he did not succeed in becoming England's Torquemada was a consequence of the king's quarrel with the pope and not a result of any quality of mercy that stirred through More's own heart.

26

DEFEAT
AND DEPARTURE

ARLIAMENT MET after a long adjournment on January 13, 1532.
Cuthbert Tunstall was not called down from Durham and John Fisher
was not summoned from nearby Rochester because, said Chapuys, neither of
them favored the divorce. Fisher came to town anyway, prepared to do battle.
Henry—ever the pious hypocrite—sent for him and made a great show of
being delighted to see him and said that of course he would be happy to have
Fisher attend the deliberations in the House of Lords.

Increasingly, as Henry drifted from the Roman communion, Emperor
Charles V became the champion of English Catholics, and Chapuys, his
ambassador, became the agent around whom Catholic plans and plots re-
volved. Fisher remained in close contact with Chapuys, although he begged
the ambassador not to recognize him in public. Charles V, acknowledging
Fisher's dogged loyalty, sent him regular communications, which Chapuys
passed on through intermediaries. It is easy to suppose that Henry played a
game of smiles with his bishop while his mind seethed with knowledge of what
Fisher was doing. For the moment the bishop had little effect, since he got
sick and had to go home despite his best intentions.

The prelates summoned to the Parliament did not intend to be servile; they
seemed to sense that the lines were being drawn for a decisive battle, and they
were ready to fight. The country bishops must have believed that the population stood with them, since preachers were cheered in their pulpits for con-

demning the divorce while those who spoke in favor of it were hissed out of churches and sometimes threatened with violence.

But Henry's minions were better organized than the opposition, and they took a hard line. A bill was introduced to cut off annates to Rome. Annates were fees collected by the pope when a new bishop was consecrated. The payments took money out of England and stirred the economic anticlericalism expressed by Simon Fish, the conviction of merchants and others that England was being sucked dry of gold and silver by a rapacious papacy and that if payments abroad could be stopped, the economy at home would soar. The economic miseries of the time thunder through the records we have, and the combination of inflation and unemployment made some groups restless and perhaps revolutionary. No one could quite predict how far such people might go in their frustration.

Henry had trouble getting his bill against annates through Parliament. He was at the same time looking for ways of collecting more revenues from the estates of his feudal nobility, and his agents ran into a a general resistance to new taxes, a resistance that now helped the clergy. The bill as it was first presented breathed fire against the pope and threatened to withdraw the realm from the see of Rome. Henry seemed ready to leap into schism, and poised on the brink with him, feeling the rapacious hot breath of the government which suddenly seemed even more threatening than the greed of clergymen, the House of Lords drew back.

Henry got Cromwell to add a clause saying that the government would not immediately enforce the provisions against the papacy if the act against annates should be passed, offering hope that negotiation might still be possible. He was trying to threaten the pope and at the same time reassure the worried citizens of his nervous realm that he intended to do what he could to preserve the old ways. True, the English people continually displayed an almost ritual anticlericalism, but they also preserved within their historical consciousness the terrible papal interdict imposed on England during the reign of King John when priests could not administer the sacraments or comfort the dying or bury the dead. Every pilgrim's visit to the great shrine of St. Thomas Becket at Canterbury brought back to life a thousand legends of the bloodiness of England when Henry II had tried to impose his dominion over the clergy in much the same way that Henry VIII was seeking to do now—by taxing the church, forbidding appeals to Rome, and bringing cases involving priests into the royal courts.

History was only beginning to have depth for ordinary people at this time; if they knew that something had happened in the past, especially something bloody and terrible, it seemed to them to have occurred only a few years before. The accretions of myth layered over the original events made history more ominous, more likely (so it seemed) to repeat itself and plunge the land into darkness. So Parliament hesitated one last time, and for the moment the hesitation was enough to frustrate Henry's will—but only for a moment.

The king himself went three times to the House of Lords to argue for his bill. Finally he got it through with the help of the secular nobility. Not content with appearing before the Lords, Henry took the highly unusual step of going into the House of Commons and forcing a division, making the members who supported the bill sit on one side and the opponents sit on the other. With such bullying and pleading, he managed to get a favorable vote. (We can only imagine what More, who had argued so cogently for the freedom of the Commons in the Parliament of 1523, must have thought of this royal intervention in debates.)

Henry must have worried about these difficulties. He was always morbidly insecure about his place in the realm. Queen Catherine was threatening him with the military power of the emperor—a power which he ruminated about in public many times and which he seemed genuinely to fear. He must have heard the news of how preachers in the countryside were treated when they tried to take up his cause in public. The Venetian ambassador heard it and reported it to his city. Henry suffered the indignity of risking a sermon against the divorce whenever he attended preaching himself, and although he occasionally jailed courageous preachers, the angry chill of the undercurrent of opposition in which he found himself afloat must have frightened him. Henry frightened was a doubly dangerous man.

In their stubborn mood, the Commons refused to grant him more money. He claimed danger from the Scots and sent Thomas More down to the House to beat this old horse. Two members were brave enough to declare openly that the best defense of the realm was to remain friendly with the emperor. Thomas Temse, a member from Westbury, went further, urging the king in a speech to take back his lawful queen. Finally the grumbling Commons granted their monarch a small tax, much less than he had requested.

But the most important act of this session was an indictment against the clergy called *The Supplication Against the Ordinaries*. This was most likely engineered by Cromwell as part of the government's campaign against the church, although some think that it was a spontaneous complaint from the House itself. At any rate, it drew large support, and on March 18 a delegation handed it over to the king.

The substance was the usual thing. The Commons accused the clergy of greed, and the echo of the Hunne affair could be heard in the complaint that priests demanded exorbitant fees to bury the dead.

The parts of the *Supplication* that condemned the ecclesiastical courts were by far the most important. Here were courts, the Commons said, that imposed law on the English people without their consent. The laws were published in Latin, and their penalties were harsh. Henry had an "imperial jurisdiction" over England, the Commons said. As previously mentioned, in the legal folk-lore of the time, an "empire" was sovereign and owed no higher allegiance except to God alone. The church courts divided the English people and robbed the king of his due; they harmed the king's loyal subjects because they were rigged entirely in favor of the clergy. It took a rich man to fight a case in the church courts, and poor suitors, so the Commons said, had no chance at all for justice.

The *Supplication* took dead aim on the church's procedures against heresy. Here we see not merely a conflict between England's common law and the canon law of the church but also evidence of the enduring nationalism and self-satisfaction of the English people. Sir John Fortescue had only given voice to common opinion when he held that the English were better than other people, their laws better than other laws. To the Commons it seemed that to subject Englishmen to alien laws was to rob them of their dignity and of justice. To those who had read their Fortescue, such subjugation must have seemed like sacrilege against the way God had ordained His world, especially His sacred realm of England.

More had already placed himself firmly against the opinions now advanced by the Commons. In his *Dialogue Concerning Heresies,* he had had his "messenger" raise questions that might well have come from this unruly session of Parliament. The canon law of the church, said the young foil in More's piece, requires only two witnesses in cases of heresy, and it "careth not how bad they be, not though they be heretics themselves." In civil matters involving only a little money, the common law of the realm would not receive any witness who lacked an honest reputation. But the church made judgments that could lead to the utter destruction of a man in body and goods, carrying a sentence of death as painful as any that could be devised, and in support of its case it would admit and receive an infamous witness and believe one who had previously proved false.

More argued in rebuttal that heresy, theft, murder, and treason were not crimes people committed in the presence of an honest notary. So the church courts took such witnesses as were available. He was confident that the judges in such cases were astute enough and honest enough to tell when a witness was lying. He was also convinced that heresy was so horrible and so dangerous that church and society had the right to take the strongest measures against it. Seldom did he admit that the innocent might suffer in such proceedings. Never did he speculate that the damage inflicted on society by the suffering of the innocent might be worse than the harm that might come from letting a few of the guilty go free. He made no place in heresy cases, as he had for theft in *Utopia,* for the generous spirit of Fortescue, who wrote, "I would rather wish twenty evil doers to escape death through pity than one man be unjustly condemned."

The mood of *A Dialogue Concerning Heresies* was very far removed from the spirit of the Commons in this parliamentary session of 1532. More had glossed over the difference between common-law procedures against murder, theft, and treason and the canon-law actions against heresy; the House of Commons in its angry *Supplication* noted this crucial difference with a vengeance.

In cases of heresy, the Commons said, the accused might never know the names of witnesses against him. Even if the witnesses were vile, the accused might be brought into the church courts and presented with the oath *ex officio* that required him to testify against himself if he was guilty. He could not use the process of purgation available in the common-law courts whereby his honest neighbors could testify to his good living, releasing him from further inquiry when there was no concrete evidence against him—a rudimentary form of *habeas corpus*. No, in the church courts the accused on barest suspicion might be presented with a long list of heresies and required to swear that he did not believe any of them—opening himself to gossip and speculation: if he was quizzed on these matters, there must be some probable cause to suppose that he was guilty, no matter what he said. If he should admit to belief in any heretical view, he would be treated as if he were guilty of all. And he was not allowed to remain silent under questioning. Here was a matter of deep concern to English common lawyers, already persuaded that the accused might remain silent and that his silence should not be taken as self-incrimination.

More would later stand and fall on his own silence before his judges, claiming the civil right later fully recognized in the laws of England and the United States that the accused did not have to testify and that no one could be convicted on silence alone. In his public utterances on the *Supplication*, however, written a year after the document issued from the Commons, More stood firmly on the side of the canon law and the *ex officio* process that required the accused to answer all questions in interrogations about heresy. He would have explained himself easily enough with his conviction that heresy was so heinous and founded on such malice that scarcely any law could be too rigorous if it succeeded in cleansing the realm of heretical poison, for souls were more important than the civil law.

The reply of the bishops to the *Supplication* came early in May, and as Philip Hughes wrote, "The tone is extremely tough." Hughes also says More helped draft it. Though he gives no evidence to support this contention, many things in the reply do indeed sound like More.

The bishops denied that the clergy had provoked any division between themselves and the laity. On the contrary, they asserted the continual hostility of the laity toward clergymen. Priests were sometimes thrown down and assaulted in the streets, they said, but no one ever heard that priests assaulted lay people in that fashion. Some bad clergymen might be found, but most were good, and the Commons had brought only gossip to the bar.

The most important part of *The Answer of the Ordinaries* considered the relation between the laws of England and the laws of the church and Henry's part in making those laws. The laws of the church were founded on scripture and the determination of the church, said the bishops, and so they were the measure to which all other laws should conform. The kings of England had always recognized such laws. The bishops were still obliged to keep them. Henry could not interfere. "We," they said, "your most humble subjects, may not submit the execution of our charges and duty, certainly prescribed by God, to your highness's assent."

If Henry wanted, they said, he could make suggestions, and if God inspired the bishops to take them up, these suggestions would be translated into church law. But it was clear that the bishops would not grant Henry the right of making laws involving the church either by his own will or by the authority of Parliament. The bishops condemned in the strongest terms the recent Act in Restraint of Annates. It was contrary to the spiritual jurisdiction exercised by the English church for centuries. Even the pope could not take such jurisdiction away, and no parliament could remove it, even if it could be proved that the clergy had greatly offended.

As this book has pointed out again and again, here was the heart of the matter, the issue of spiritual independence—a much more comprehensible issue to loyal Catholics of More's own time than it may be today. The question was this: how does God communicate His truth to humankind? Where is the source of divine inspiration on which we can depend for purity and not poison? The bishops stood for a church independent of lay authority, able to absorb inspiration and to express it without the hindrance of the bloody hand of secular government.

Implicit in the bishops' view was the assumption that laymen were inferior to priests, that kings ordained to keep order in the world and thus worthy of high respect were nevertheless unworthy and incapable of making spiritual pronouncements. Kings and their secular servants—lords, judges, warriors, etc. —were granted the power by God to shed blood. The world had fallen into such depravity that someone had to have a divine authority to kill others, to extinguish the life that only God could give. But in the exercise of that authority, despite its divine source, kings defiled themselves. (It was a position not unlike that taken by the church with respect to marriage.) The toughness of *The Answer of the Ordinaries* lay in the bishops' conviction that as things had always been, so should they always be. In these hard pronouncements sandwiched between obsequious passages of ritual flattery to Henry, we find the best explanation for Thomas More's death.

Henry was angry. Putting on a different face for every need, he had apparently managed to convince many of the bishops that he was their true friend. The bishops had taken the king at his word, believing that he wished to be an impartial judge in the dispute between Commons and church. He shortly demonstrated that not merely the Commons but he himself was ready to punish the clergy for their impertinence.

Henry called their *Answer* "slender," "sophistical," and evasive. He made it clear that he would now push the Parliament to tighten the screws. He summoned Speaker Thomas Audeley and other dignitaries and announced that he had discovered that the clergy of the realm were but half his subjects and perhaps not his subjects at all. All prelates, he said as if he had never heard of such a thing before, took an oath of loyalty to the pope utterly contrary to the oath they took to the king, so that, Henry said, "they seem to be his subjects and not ours."

Audeley dutifully brought to the House a copy of the oath sworn to the pope by high clergymen and had it read to great effect. He also read, as Henry required, an oath to be sworn directly to the king repudiating any other oath the clergy might take. By Hall's account, at least, no action was immediately taken in the Parliament in response. But clearly Henry was sweeping toward a declaration that the clergy were outlaws. Just what would have happened if the English clergy had been removed from the protection of the law is anybody's guess. Could Henry have possibly carried through such a threat? Nobody knows. But the feeling against the clergy boiling in the Commons and in London made the bishops anxious. And the king—cruel, vindictive, self-righteous, and frightened—was in an uncontrollable rage.

The onslaught moved Thomas More into an increasingly open and increasingly dangerous opposition to Henry's policy. As Hughes suggests, he may have given some help to Stephen Gardiner, bishop of Winchester, the author of most of *The Answer of the Ordinaries.* He seems also to have been working behind the scenes to muster support for the old church in Parliament.

After More's death Cromwell wrote one Gregory Di Cassales about More's activity at this time. Cromwell was justifying what had been done, and his account must be taken with a grain of salt. Still, his story is circumstantial and plausible.

Cromwell said that More and Fisher conveyed news about the deliberations in Parliament to foes on the outside who used the information to stir up opposition to the divorce and to Henry's moves against the church. The public support of Catherine was strong, and as we have seen, popular opposition to the divorce was vocal. Tudor minds ran quickly to theories of conspiracy to explain popular unrest. Sir George Throckmorton, a member of this Parliament, later recalled to Cromwell a conversation with More that Cromwell cited as proof of More's bad will. Throckmorton had opposed the divorce and the steps against the clergy, although, like many another, later in the decade he swung over to the winning side. He thought it good to confess his past to Henry, and as part of his confession, he spoke with due contrition about a private interview he had had with More.

More told him, as best Throckmorton could recall, "I am very glad to have the good report that goeth of you and that you be so good a catholic man as ye be; if ye do continue in the same way that you began and be not afraid to say your conscience, you shall deserve great reward of God and thanks of the King's grace at length, and much worship to yourself." From Throckmorton's account, it appears that this interview took place soon after the opening of Parliament in January 1532.

It does look as if More, though circumspect, had now entered into a higher degree of opposition to the king. Rumors were flying about Anne Boleyn's fierce temper, her greed, her vindictiveness, her bullying of the king himself as well as everyone else around her. Chapuys reported much of this gossip to his own master, and it must have been common knowledge in the court circles in which More moved. More could easily suppose that the king would tire of his strumpet and return to his lawful queen and to sound Catholic doctrine.

Henry did tire of Anne, but opposition always made him bull-headed, and he must have known of More's. Aided by Thomas Cromwell, he moved boldly to squelch his foes. Late in April some of Cromwell's henchmen went up to Durham and ransacked the papers of Cuthbert Tunstall to see if they could find incriminating evidence that the bishop was working against the divorce. They found little and suspected that Tunstall had already cleaned out his files. Since More's papers have vanished, we may surmise that at some point— probably after he left office—his files were removed to some place where they might be thoroughly studied and that they were never returned. We may hope that they will turn up yet.

On May 13, Chapuys wrote to Charles V that Parliament was considering the abolition of all the ecclesiastical ordinances that governed the English church. The church would be forbidden to have any convocations without the express consent of the king, reducing the clergy, so Chapuys wrote, "to a lower condition than the shoemakers who have the power of assembling and framing their own statutes." The bishops were to be deprived of their right to detain suspected heretics, since bodies were under the authority of the secular authorities and the bishops could speak only to the soul. Chapuys reported that More and the bishops opposed the king as much as they could and that Henry was exceedingly angry, especially against More and Stephen Gardiner. The letter, sent off in cipher, concluded with the grim prayer that God might send down a remedy as required by the intensity of the evil.

But nothing in England could withstand the king in his rage. The English bishops were political men, and political men are rarely made of the stuff of martyrs. Their hold on the intellectual framework of the Catholic Church was slight; only John Fisher among them had been able to write cogently against heresy. They were isolated from the populace, and now they were bullied not only by the king but by great lords like Suffolk and lesser lords like the Earl of Wiltshire, Anne Boleyn's father. Even more dangerous and incomprehensible to them was the clever bureaucratic inventiveness of Thomas Cromwell and his band of resolute, impatient administrative innovators rapidly rooting out the worn old traditions of inefficient royal governance and replacing them with the steely and impersonal power of the modern state. The bishops were frightened both for their property and for their persons. They scarcely knew what was happening, and faced with the king's wrath, they took the ancient refuge of weak men, burrowing into the hope that this too would pass and that no one should resist the future before experiencing it.

On May 15, 1532, the English bishops humbly offered their submission to the king. It is a date as good as any to mark the transition of England from the Middle Ages to modernity. The ancient liberties of the church—liberties that traditionalists claimed came as the gift of Christ himself—were stripped away. The *Submission of the Clergy* is a short document that makes three large concessions: the clergy would never again put forward any law in Convocation without royal consent; Convocation would not meet unless Henry first gave his permission; all the laws of the church were to be reviewed by a joint commission of clergy and laymen. Sixteen of these commissioners were to be from Parliament; sixteen were to be priests; all thirty-two were to be appointed by the king. To More and others, Henry now seemed to have assumed a tyranny over the English church much like that endured by the Greek church under the Eastern Roman Empire in medieval Constantinople. The Greek church was now in bondage to the fierce and bloodthirsty Turks, a punishment Roman Catholics thought fitting for those who had allowed their spiritual affairs to be governed by a lay monarch.

On the day after the clergy submitted, Thomas More met the king in the garden of York Place near Westminster Hall about three in the afternoon and delivered up the Great Seal. A few days later Chapuys sent the news of More's resignation to Charles V.

It is a long letter, dealing with many subjects, and Chapuys mentions More's resignation only near the end. The imperial ambassador appears to have lost interest in the Lord Chancellor after More had so stoutly refused to look at correspondence with the emperor; during the last months of his tenure of office, More appears scarcely at all in the incessant and almost interminable dispatches that Chapuys sent off to his sovereign, minutely reporting on English affairs. Now he says that More, "perceiving the bad turn affairs are taking, that there is no chance of improvement, and that if he remains in office he will be obliged to act against his conscience, or incur the King's anger—as he already has done through his refusing to take part against the clergy—has now resigned and sent in the seals of his office on the plea that his salary is too small and the work excessive." The last remark suggests that Henry had been punishing his recalcitrant Lord Chancellor by pinching his purse. However that may have been, More's public career was at an end, his tenure as Lord Chancellor was done, his causes all defeated, and he retired to an uncertain private life in Chelsea.

It has been generally assumed that it was More's choice to resign on the morrow of the submission of the clergy. But he could hardly have arranged things so quickly, and it was never in the power of a servant of Henry VIII to choose so cavalierly the moment to depart from office.

True, he had wanted to resign for a long time. As Roper says, he saw that the king was resolved to marry Anne Boleyn. He did the best he could as a loyal servant to carry out the will of his sovereign, even going to the Commons to recite the favorable opinions from the various universities that supported the divorce, always keeping silent to everyone but the king about his own thoughts on the matter. Yet he feared increasingly that he might be forced to do something contrary to his conscience. So, Roper says, he begged his friend the Duke of Norfolk to intervene with the king so that he might depart from his office of Lord Chancellor in peace. Roper gives the impression that this expression of his desire to resign went on for a long time.

And undoubtedly Henry wanted him to leave as much as More wanted to resign. Chapuys's remark that Henry was furious with both More and Gardiner had come two days before the submission of the clergy, and it had been clear for months that king and Lord Chancellor were hopelessly alienated from one another. As though to prove how far this alienation had gone, Henry delayed in appointing a successor once More was safely out of the way. On May 20 he handed the Great Seal over to Thomas Audeley, giving Audeley authority to use it when it was required. But Audeley did not officially become Lord Chancellor until many months had passed. In the interim he was called Keeper of the Great Seal. And never again in Henry's reign was the office of Lord Chancellor of any great importance.

The indispensable man was now Thomas Cromwell, and he was more preoccupied with power than with titles. He was simply Henry's first secretary, running the administration with quiet efficiency and swiftly leading the way to a legal revolution in England. Henry evidently decided to be his own Lord Chancellor for a time. In his mood of outraged and aggrieved self-righteousness, he probably lamented the failures of his last two Lord Chancellors and decided that it was not worth the risk of opposition to put a strong man in the office. More had been impotent, but at the last, he was no toady. When in 1533 Henry finally did officially appoint Audeley to the office, it was only after Audeley had proved himself an obsequious nonentity.

The moment to let More depart had to be propitious for royal policy. A man of More's stature could not be allowed to resign in obvious opposition to the king while delicate matters were still under debate. If More left office before the king had obtained the *Submission of the Clergy*, he might have been a force to stiffen the spines of some of the wavering bishops. But with the *Submission* in his hand and with the fundamental confusion and cowardice of most of his bishops thoroughly established, Henry could breathe easier and afford to let More go.

So the timing of the resignation was Henry's and not More's, and Roper reveals as much. Norfolk, he says, "by importunate suit had at length of the King obtained for Sir Thomas More a clear discharge of his office" and "then *at a time convenient by his highness's appointment* repaired he [More] to his grace to yield up unto him the Great Seal." Carlo Capello, the Venetian ambassador, wrote his government on the very day of More's resignation that the king had deprived the Lord Chancellor of his office.

It seems clear that on the morrow of the *Submission*, the day when the document itself was placed in Henry's eager hands, he summoned More at last to bring the Great Seal and to surrender it as More had long wished to do. He could even play a royal charade, praising More during the ceremony of resignation and wishing him well. But these words of praise, like Henry's warm welcome to Fisher at the Parliament in January, were only window dressing. He could afford a few verbal gratuities since now he felt himself strong enough to master both kingdom and church no matter what More and others like him might do or think. He had crushed the old ecclesiastical order with the ease of a man stepping on a worm. It would have been surprising indeed if a man of Henry's fierce and vengeful temperament had not smirked when his Lord Chancellor, the best and perhaps the most dangerous of all his adversaries, admitted defeat and handed over the emblem of his office.

27

LAST MONTHS
OF FREEDOM

ORD IMMEDIATELY SPREAD that More's resignation had been a disgrace, and if Henry did choose the time and the circumstances, the event was indeed a humiliation. In October, Erasmus wrote a friend that the Lutherans were cheering at More's fall and that forty suspected heretics had now been released from prison in England.

The Lutherans had reason to rejoice; More was the last important advocate in the government for the eradication of heresy by fire. He had done all he could to stir the church into the prosecution of heresy and to see to it that the secular government lent its power to this spiritual enterprise. He had pursued heretics with all the power at his disposal, locking them up until their trials, constantly holding over them the threat of fire. After More's resignation, the general campaign against heresy expired. The government burned a notorious heretic now and then, but the victims were men Henry had tried to use and found intractable to his desires and offensive to his own tastes in doctrines. In these cases a pliable church could be made to prosecute the victim, and the government could as piously do its duty by burning him. Heretics favoring the king's cause could now find a haven in England as long as they remained properly obsequious to the authorities and preached their novelties with circumspection.

More felt a need for both vindication and security. On June 14 he wrote a long letter to Erasmus explaining his retirement. It is a public document rather than an intimate communication, and More expected Erasmus to publish it. He explained himself to Europe and, we may suppose, to his own sovereign. He was withdrawing from the world; he would be no threat to anyone. He vigorously declared his loyalty to his king, but now, he said, he was only concerned to prepare to meet death. Throughout he seems to have been suggesting to Henry that if left alone, he would make no trouble, he would be the center of no conspiracy; he simply wanted to die in peace.

His health was bad, he said. He complained of a persistent pain in his chest, indicating, as we have said, a bad heart—an ailment not surprising in a man as driven as he was. He said that he had most humbly begged Henry to let him resign. At last, out of generosity, the king took pity on him and let him go. He spoke glowingly of the many favors the king had granted him in the past. He clearly sought to convey the impression that the king had been reluctant to let him resign, that his departure was no disgrace, and that nothing but the precarious state of his own health could have induced him to seek relief from his office.

Judiciously he flattered Erasmus—perhaps to persuade him to publish the letter. He knew how reluctant Erasmus was to meddle in any affair that might draw him into a quarrel with princes. Obviously, too, More wanted to make one other statement to Europe at large about his own view of Erasmus, whose name, since *The Praise of Folly*, was inseparably joined to his own.

Erasmus was a marvel, More said; he went on publishing while his critics howled. Most of these critics were unworthy of attention, More said. But then ever so slightly he changed his tone. Did it matter, he asked, if even some good and learned men thought that Erasmus had handled this or that point with too little restraint? (He must have been thinking of Tunstall and himself among others.) All writers are guilty of such things from time to time, and, More said, Erasmus had confessed his lack of restraint and said that had he foreseen the rise of these pestiferous enemies of the faith, he would have made his criticisms with greater delicacy.

We have no record of this remarkable confession that More attributes to Erasmus unless More was referring to a forgery put out under Erasmus's name in which Erasmus was made to accuse himself. Indeed More's flattering letter ignores the timing of the sharpest attacks Erasmus made against the practices of the old church, those contained in the *Colloquies* published in edition after edition while the Protestant assault on the church was white-hot. But More was spinning a careful rhetorical web, saying for Erasmus what Erasmus had not quite said for himself. He did pick a thought out of the letter Erasmus had written him in 1527: heretics, More said, have twisted for their own purposes the words of the fathers, the apostles, evangelists, and Christ himself; it was to be expected, More said, that they might similarly distort the words of Erasmus.

But, More said, though Erasmus had ignored his malicious critics, he should make some accommodation for the pious who might be upset by what Erasmus wrote. It was a gentle criticism, meant not to alienate Erasmus but to change him and intended, too, to show that More's own Erasmianism was thoroughly Catholic and that he was on the side of those who believed Erasmus should attend to his obligation to the faith in hard times.

He closed the body of his letter on a note that takes on a tone of heavy irony in view of what was happening in England. The heretics were persistent and insidious, and their books were pouring into England from the Low Countries, he said. But the bishops and the king stood firmly against heresy, and thanks to them, the contagion was under control. More said he had written replies to some of these works, not because he worried about their effect on reasonable men but because shallow souls liked to flirt with new and dangerous doctrines.

It was a rhetorical tactic that he was to use repeatedly afterwards; he would declare that all England and England's king stood firmly on the side of the old faith. In so doing he seemed to be exercising an almost primitive belief that if we say something often enough and firmly enough, it must be true—a sympathetic magic with prose, creating on paper a world that somehow will become real. Maybe More did suppose that if Henry read these pronouncements about his own steadfastness to the faith, he would take them to heart and become steadfast.

Henry surely never bothered to read these sentiments from More's pen. If he had, he would have been stirred to the same fierce anger that arose in him when Queen Catherine insisted that she loved him.

On the same day that More wrote Erasmus, he also wrote John Cochlaeus, the doughty and prolix adversary of Luther in Germany. Again he explained his resignation as a consequence of bodily infirmity. By the by he rejoiced in the deaths of Zwingli and Oecolampadius, the one in battle and the other from illness. His main purpose, however, was to tell yet another continental correspondent that he resigned not on a matter of principle or in disgrace but for the sake of his health.

His resignation left him in straitened circumstances but not in poverty. We mentioned early in this book the family council that Roper describes at which More, after giving up the Great Seal, spoke of how they would slowly reduce their standard of living if necessary, descending first to the level of scholars at Lincoln's Inn, then to the level of the New Inn, then to "Oxford fare," and finally to begging in the streets.

The sentiments are noble, and the scene charming. But though More did have to reduce expenses, there is no sign that he and his family sank into poverty. He still had a pension of a hundred pounds a year and kept it until he entered the Tower as a prisoner. Dame Alice had an income of another hundred a year, and though he did not own vast estates, he did have some land, which yielded an income. He turned his official barge with its eight oarsmen over to Audeley, Roper says. But Roper also indicates that More kept a barge of his own. He kept enough property to make it worthwhile for him to set up for his family what we would call a trust fund—which Henry got Parliament to void after More's death, an act Roper bitterly recalls.

None of this betokens penury, and since a man out of public affairs would be relieved of many formidable expenses, we may suppose that More's retirement was comfortable enough. His situation could change with any change in the king's mind, and More and his family knew by now how changeable and dangerous that mind could be.

The clergy's formal submission did not end the confusion in England, and the populace awaited developments in a state of deep disquiet. Late in the spring two small whales were caught in the Thames—a bad omen, Londoners said—and someone counted fourteen people who had killed themselves by hanging or by drowning themselves in the river in the previous few days. Henry began rebuilding the fortifications of the Tower of London, a task requiring the labor of a thousand men a day, so the Venetian ambassador reported. The only immediate enemies that Henry could have had in mind were his own people. On July 5, a priest was hanged for clipping the king's coin. He was first drawn through the town at a horse's tail. Thirty women begged the king for the man's pardon, but Henry refused. The priest was hanged without being first degraded from his clerical status, and the Venetian ambassador remarked that it was a thing never done in England since the country embraced Christianity. Henry was showing the church how far he was prepared to go in asserting his power over clergymen, whose status since Becket's time had been sacrosanct.

Opposition to Henry's invasion of the church went on, and its leader was a surprise. He was Archbishop William Warham, primate of England, now tottering toward the grave. In March he had the temerity to speak in Parliament against the king, provoking Henry to fury. If Warham were not so old, Henry said, he would make him repent. In May, after some resistance, the archbishop bowed with the rest and signed the *Submission*. Then his courage came back as his life ran out. Sometime during the summer Warham produced a draft of a speech that he apparently intended to deliver in the House of Lords. But Parliament having adjourned in May, Warham had no chance to address the body before he died on August 23.

The draft of the speech is an important document because it reveals how men of conservative temperament saw the issues. Lacking any detailed statement from More himself as to why he chose to die, we can turn to Warham's paper and find opinions that More must have shared, and these will confirm one of the principal themes of this book, that More died as a martyr to an ideal in which the papacy had little importance.

Certainly we find in Warham no great exaltation of papal power, no hymn of praise to the papal office, no defense of the papal succession from St. Peter through the centuries as we find in John Fisher or in any number of continental theologians. Instead Warham defines what the liberties of the English church meant to an English prelate and presents his dark view of what would happen if they were taken away.

Warham recognized the right of the king always to grant or to withhold the "temporalities," the lands and revenues attached to the episcopal office, a right that had resulted from the great investiture controversy of the high Middle Ages. But popes confirmed the spiritual authority of bishops, and Warham said that in England archbishops had always moved to the consecration of bishops as soon as permission arrived from Rome. If archbishops lacked the freedom to confirm a bishop's spiritual authority until the king granted the temporalities, the spiritual power of the archbishops would depend on the power of a layman, the king, and such was against the law of God. If the king by withholding the landed estates that went with a bishopric might keep the bishop from office, the church might end by having no bishops at all, and since bishops ordained priests, there would be no priests and then no sacraments.

Warham was imagining the worst case: a church with no sacraments, no burial of the dead, no consolation, no religious service at all; the land in chaos, and the people in darkness. He could not have dreamed that his nation could go on happily for better than four centuries after his death in a religious life that contented most Englishmen simply because it asserted with great authority that nothing essential in the English church had changed. And it would have been beyond his worst nightmares to suppose that in time most Englishmen would not miss the sacraments because they found religion itself a matter of complete indifference and that their government would go on functioning quite well.

As befitted an Archbishop of Canterbury, he recalled English history, especially the heroic tale of his great predecessor, Thomas Becket, murdered in the cathedral at Canterbury in 1170 by Henry II's henchmen. Warham observed bravely enough and with reason that what Henry VIII now wanted was the same political power over the spiritual institution of the church that Henry II had sought in his day, and that to oppose that demand, Becket had given his life. His audience, recalling Henry II's demand that "criminous clerks" be tried in royal courts, would certainly have seen the similarity between that policy and Henry VIII's reach for supremacy in spiritual affairs. Warham named other kings—Edward III, Richard II, and Henry IV—who had all met misfortune for opposing the liberties of the church. He, for one, said he would rather be cut in pieces than to confess that he had violated praemunire if he upheld the old liberties of the church for which Becket had died.

He closed with a threat. He would not give bond to Henry, as the king had demanded, for he had no intention of leaving the realm. Archbishops of

Canterbury, he said, cannot be seized by the secular authority; whoever lays violent hands on a bishop or puts him in prison is damned, and only the pope can pardon him unless he confesses as he lies dying. Any place where a bishop is in prison is under interdict—that is, valid sacraments cannot be administered in that land.

Warham's death opened the way for Henry to nominate a more pliable Archbishop of Canterbury, and one of the most pliable men in the realm was available. He was Thomas Cranmer, another product of Cambridge University and the circle that met at the White Horse Tavern. He had come to Henry's attention by suggesting the universities as a court of appeal where the king might receive a favorable hearing on his "great matter." He hated the papacy as much as a fundamentally kind man could hate anything. He had literary gifts greater than those of any other Englishman at the time except perhaps William Tyndale. And for reasons that somehow get lost in the jungle of details we know about him, Henry VIII loved him as much as he ever loved any man. He was away on an embassy to Emperor Charles when Henry sent for him on October 1, probably at Thomas Cromwell's instigation. The English ambassadors with the pope were still trying to get the divorce case called back to England, and if that should happen, the Archbishop of Canterbury, in the absence of any English cardinal or legate, would be the cleric in charge.

Warham's opposition was only a token of the larger antagonism in the realm over how things were going and how uncertain the conclusion might be. But Henry moved anyway. On September 1 he had Anne Boleyn created Marchioness of Pembroke and granted her a revenue of a thousand pounds a year. The Venetian ambassador noted that she was covered with jewels and that her hair fell long over her shoulders.

The occasion was also marked by a solemn renewal of the alliance between France and England, supposedly against the Turks, although many, including the imperial ambassador, suspected that the common enemy of the two kings was closer to home. In October, Henry went over to Calais, taking with him the flower of English chivalry, including all the great lords of the realm, and a party of about two thousand. Anne went with him, invited by King Francis I, although the French king's outraged sister, so rumor went, refused to accompany him, as he wished, to this meeting with a royal strumpet. Instead, he took with him Madame Vendôme, annoying the English, for she had the reputation of being nothing better than a courtesan. Henry threw gifts around with the typical largesse of guilt, and Francis embraced him as an ally against both pope and emperor. Anne Boleyn danced with the French king, and they talked together awhile. It was a great, gaudy, breathtaking show, and Anne may have been quite swept away by the pageantry of kings. Until then she may have resisted Henry's clamoring for her slim white body, but either then or soon afterwards she surrendered. By mid-December, she was pregnant.

More's position in this surge of events was extremely difficult, and from our perspective it seems also ambiguous. He was retired to Chelsea now, isolated, having no constituency that we can discern within the royal council, plainly desirous of living out his days in peace, cognizant of the danger to his beloved family should he enter into open opposition to the royal will, but just as plainly troubled by the way things were going and frustrated at his inability to do anything about them. He had chosen the pathway of silence about the king's divorce, probably assuming that his silence would speak clearly enough to all who wanted to consider it—as it certainly did. But it must have been agonizing for a person of his temperament—loquacious, argumentative, and righteous— to keep still while his world seemed to be going speedily to hell.

What he did was write books—bitter, ugly, almost unreadable books— against heresy. In them he kept his silence about the king's divorce and the love affair with Anne Boleyn. But his silence was like a closed valve, making the pressure build to the bursting point in another part of his psyche, and the outlet for the explosion was his rage against the new religious doctrines and the men propagating them among the English people.

The largest thing he ever wrote was his gargantuan *Confutation of Tyndale's Answer.* He began this enormous work while he was still Lord Chancellor, and the first hefty part of it appeared in one volume about the time of his resignation. A second part appeared in another large volume in 1533, and although in its modern printed version the *Confutation* is over twice as long as this biography, the book was never formally completed. More abandoned it to do other things.

The *Confutation* is thoroughly unpleasant, and despite its enormous size, we find little truly new in it. More sings his familiar litany—the infallibility of a church that has existed since Christ founded it, a church that like Noah's Ark included both clean and unclean members, to be eternally separated only at the day of judgment. Anyone could criticize the immoral lives of some clergymen, but no one could honor God and contest the traditional teachings and customs of the church.

His wrath against heretics is greater than it was in *A Dialogue Concerning Heresies,* and we have already noted how More scorned their lives, mocked their lowly origins, and jeered at their deaths. All the lightheartedness of the *Dialogue* is gone. More's wit is as heavy as the *Confutation* itself, and it is all directed against the heretics. We find no playful sallies against superstition and corruption in the Catholic Church, no shrine of St. Valéry in Picardy, no woman posing as a saint in the day and sleeping with a priest at night, no King Agbar getting a portrait of Jesus himself, no St. Erkenwald stretching a beam to fit, no relics restoring the dead to life. All these little touches brightened the *Dialogue* and made it a landscape in which streams and hills and gentle surprises mitigated the stark, rocky outcroppings that appear here and there.

The *Confutation* is an interminable desert, stretching to a hellish horizon under the untempered sun, and we find burning on every page a monotonous fury that deadens the soul.

More widens the gap between faith and reason in the *Confutation.* In the *Dialogue* he had expressed confidence in the harmony between the two much as he had done in *Utopia,* in which the denizens of that happy isle had discovered many things by reason that Christians knew by revelation. But Tyndale's mocking contempt for Catholic practices pushed him into a more extreme position. Why should we fast? Why should we go on pilgrimages? Why should we imagine that the physical elements of ceremony, including the sacraments, could have any effect on the immaterial soul? How can we believe in transubstantiation when the doctrine is not clearly spelled out in the Bible?

More's answer was that we must obey orders. Christians do what God commands, not because they understand the command, but because the commands are divine. He had touched on this point in the *Dialogue* with respect to saints and to pilgrimages, but in the *Confutation* he dwelled on it at much greater length. He never held that reason, properly understood, was an enemy to the faith. But in the *Confutation* his emphasis was the Augustinian one that faith went far beyond reason, almost to the point of making reason as dangerous as Luther found it, and he castigated Tyndale for making "arguments grounded upon philosophy and metaphysical reasons." No matter what reason seemed to show William Tyndale, More believed that Christians were obligated to follow the faith whether they understood the reasons behind it or not.

It is the nightmare that stirred the age. In the hard, practical world of iron, blood, and earth, reason was making one conquest after another. To many, reason seemed to be conquering faith, causing serious men to renounce reason at least in regard to religion, to seek with passionate energy some authority that could prevail against the implacable force threatening to destroy trust in God and extinguish hope against death.

Luther made faith a surrender, a cessation of the struggle to understand anything in religion but the text of the Bible, a yielding that took the form of single-minded trust in Christ. Luther lived to contemn Copernicus with the same ridicule that Augustine lavished on those who claimed that people might live on the bottom of a round earth. Tyndale found his succor in powerful emotion that could dissolve doubt by immediate experience. And Thomas More, as troubled as any of them, found his confidence in an infallible church that by its triumphant and ceaseless enduring since Christ stood as the one hope of absolute and benign clarity in a world of shadows and foes. Like light, the clarity of the church was of mysterious origin; again and again in the *Confutation* More used the word "secret" to describe the inspiration that permeated the church from the lowest to the highest. How God kept the church faithful to His will was a mystery no one could fathom. But anyone could see the unity of the church and witness its broad track through the centuries, paved with an unbroken tradition, cemented with the blood of the martyrs, illuminated by thousands of miracles. All that was enough to prove that God had sustained the Catholic Church and would sustain it to the end of the world, no matter what philosophical reason might say to the contrary.

The *Confutation* rings with the clangor of More's own repressed sexuality. Luther is a lecher almost every time he is mentioned, and More took the view that all the turmoil that came from Luther's movement was nothing other than the lust of bad priests to break their vows and marry, and to make whores out of nuns. He berated Tyndale for suggesting that women could hear confession and for saying that in emergencies women might preach and consecrate the mass. Tyndale had imagined a Christian woman driven ashore on an island among people to whom Christ had never been taught. Could she not do anything that a proper minister of religion could do? Could she not preach? Could she not say the mass? We are reminded at once of the ruminations about unordained priests in *Utopia*, but More refused to admit such a possibility outside of books. The Providence of God makes certain that not a sparrow falls to earth "without our father that is in heaven," he says. So "there shall no woman fall a-land in any so far an island where He will have His name preached and His sacraments ministered but that God can and will well enough provide a man or two to come to land with her."

His most savage remarks in the *Confutation* were directed against the incest and sacrilege of priestly marriage, and surely even in the sixteenth century readers must have noted how often he came back to this subject, as though he simply could not believe that people so filthy and so corrupt were truly gaining influence in England.

We find always the lawyer's drive to win the case rather than to arrive at a dispassionate view of the issues. His method in the *Confutation* was what it had been in the *Responsio ad Lutherum*, to quote his antagonists line by line and thus to refute them for page after dreary page, so that, as a More scholar early in this century has said, if More had done battle with a centipede, he would not have left him a leg to stand on.

But of course he wrote because he could do nothing else, and the vehemence of the *Confutation* is a cry of frustration and helplessness. As he piled up his pages on the desk beside him, he must have believed that he was doing something, in the same way that a chantry priest singing in his lonely chapel for the soul of someone long dead had to think that the simple repetition of his prayers must account for something in a world directed by a God whose economy did not permit any honest effort for His cause to fall useless to earth. The *Confutation* is in its tedious and interminable way such an incantation, although we cannot see that it accomplished much except to relieve its author of frustrations that must have threatened to tear him apart.

An ideal Henry VIII, Defender of the Faith and loyal Catholic monarch, the creature of More's longing imagination, appears again and again. In regard to Henry's proclamation of March 6, 1530, against heretical books, More writes, "For I well know that the king's highness, which as he for his most faithful mind to God, nothing more effectually desireth than the maintenance of the true catholic faith, whereof he is by his no more honorable than well deserved title Defender, so nothing more detesteth than these pestilent books that Tyndale and such other send into the realm, to set forth here their abominable heresies withall." Nowhere is there mention of Henry's other title, "Supreme Head of the English Church and Clergy." More chooses to cite rather the king's "most erudite, famous book against Luther." That book is quoted both to testify to the value of the oral tradition and to support the standard Catholic contention that we know true scripture only because the church long ago made the distinction between the true and the false.

In his *Answer* to More's *Dialogue Concerning Heresies*, Tyndale had said that More had started out on the road to reformation and then had turned back because he had been suborned by the bribes of the clergy. Why had More contended with him but not Erasmus, who had forsaken the traditional word for the church, *ecclesia*, and instead had made it *congregatio*—which Tyndale, in his translation of the New Testament, had rendered "congregation"? More replied that Erasmus had had no malicious intent in his change but Tyndale was using the word to promote heresy.

He dwelled on Erasmus long enough to discuss *The Praise of Folly*, which Tyndale took as proof of More's former penchant for true reform. More said he had never in his life had it in his mind "to have holy saints' images or their holy relics out of reverence." And if there had been such an opinion in *The Praise of Folly*, no one could attribute it to More himself, since the book had been made by another man. Yet, he said, *The Praise of Folly* ridiculed the abuses of such things in the manner of a jester in a play, the way More's own "messenger" had done in *A Dialogue Concerning Heresies*. But to ridicule the abuses was not at all the same as condemning the proper uses.

More lamented that the onslaught of heresy had now changed everything, that it had made even good and innocent works too dangerous to be allowed among the people. The king, he said, "and not without the counsel and advice not of his nobles only, with his other counsellors attending on His Grace's person, but also of the right vertuous and special well learned men of either university and other parts of the realm specially called thereto, hath after diligent and long consideration had therein, been fain for the while to prohibit the scripture of God to be suffered in English tongue among the people's hands, lest evil folk by false drawing of every good thing they read in to the color and maintenance of their own fond fantasies, and turning all honey into poison might both deadly do hurt unto themself and spread also that infection farther abroad." This remark was disingenuous, for the king had expressed his desire for a translation but had yielded to the importunities of his council for the time being. Gone from the *Confutation* was the desire for a vernacular Bible More had professed in *A Dialogue Concerning Heresies*—it might stir up disputation rather than piety among the common people. Now, said More, if someone were to translate into English *The Praise of Folly* or anything More had written himself, he would rather burn those works with his own hands than to allow anyone to take harm from them, although no harm had been meant in the writing.

In July 1532, John Frith again returned to England to rally his comrades in faith. In October he was arrested and confined in the Tower. He quickly impressed Edmund Walsyngham, Lieutenant of the Tower, who wrote Cromwell that it would be a great pity to lose such a man as Frith if he could be reconciled. Cromwell himself visited Frith shortly afterwards, doubtless to win the young man over.

Frith's imprisonment was not hard—at least not for a time. According to one tale, he was allowed out of the Tower at night to visit the faithful. But this was surely not true. He was able to write, although furtively, and one work he produced was a little pamphlet on the eucharist called "A Christian Sentence." Here he attacked both the Catholic doctrine of transubstantiation and the Lutheran doctrine of the real presence of Christ in the bread and wine of the eucharist.

The subject divided Protestants. Luther rejected transubstantiation, but he tried to compromise. He taught that the physical body and blood of Christ were added to the bread and the wine, so that both bread and body, both wine and blood were taken at communion. His explanations tended to grow murkier as he wrote about the sacrament through the years, but he laced his doctrine with diatribes against his foes, so that as usual in Luther, the eloquence and power of his expression tended to hide the confusion of his thought, at least among his followers.

Frith was more radical, more attuned to the rising modern temper that removed God further and further away from daily life and the physical world, a temper that translated miracle into metaphor and strove against the tenacious desire of the common herd to muddy the pure laws of nature with the specious wonders of demons, ghosts, saints, angels, fairies, and the presence of God in physical things. He was a disciple of Zwingli and Oecolampadius, both of whom taught that Christ was not physically present in the mass in any way. Frith said that since Christ's body was in heaven and no physical body could be in two places at once, let alone on a thousand altars, Christ could not be physically present in the mass.

Frith, like all Protestants, considered transubstantiation "idolatry" because it involved worshipping a physical object instead of the invisible God. But to

Catholics the eucharist was and is a steadfast affirmation that God never forsakes His creation. To More, whose personal piety had little to do with saints, relics, pilgrimages, and the other common devotions, the mass was the center of religious practice.

Frith passed the manuscript of his little work to a friend, and the friend was persuaded by a tailor, one William Holt, to lend him the work. Holt took it directly to More. It appears that even after he stepped down from his office as Lord Chancellor More maintained an extensive network of spies who regularly reported to him about heretics. William Holt was one of these, and Fox claims that two others also got copies of the little work to More.

By December More had written a reply to Frith's work. It took the form of a "Letter" to a third party, and it is surprisingly gentle. We find none of the grinding invective against foes that marks his other polemical works. More rather took the line that Frith was a young man led astray by a vainglorious trust in his own wit. And though More would reprove him, he would not assault him.

Why did More treat Frith so kindly? The usual answer is that Frith was beloved by everyone and that like others, More fell under his spell. Frith's personal qualities did impress people, as we have already seen, and rightly so. He never descended into the pit of internecine strife where England's earliest Protestants belabored each other with as much fierce zeal as they condemned the pope. Frith is the only man of record able to retain the devoted friendship of quarrelsome William Tyndale for any length of time—although they had their disagreements. He was brave and brilliant, and he wrote voluminously and well. More may have seen in him some of the qualities he had perceived in William Roper when Roper sank for a time into heresy.

Yet the most probable explanation for More's gentleness is his deference to the hope that Henry VIII and Cromwell entertained that Frith might be won over to the royal side in the matter of the divorce. Frith first saw More's "Letter" against him in the London home of Stephen Gardiner, his old teacher, now bishop of Winchester. It was the day after Christmas, and Gardiner must have removed Frith from the Tower for the holidays. In his *Apology,* published in April 1533, More put the best face he could on Gardiner's kindness. The bishop was only tendering a "fatherly favor" to one who had once waited on him and been his student. But even here More mentions "other causes" to explain why Gardiner took an interest in Frith.

Chief among these "other causes" was the divorce. Gardiner was conservative about priesthood and the liberties of the church, but he favored the divorce. He and others advising Henry on religious matters wanted Frith's brilliance on their side, and Frith had never made any pronouncement against Henry's marital ambitions. Frith was a scholar, and he might have made some effort to fit both the royal supremacy and the divorce into an argument based on the church fathers, whose views on both marriage and the papacy were nebulous and contradictory.

Sometime while Frith was the target of royal persuasion Tyndale wrote him, warning against the argument that only by abjuring could he help the cause of the gospel in England. Gardiner and later on Thomas Cranmer, the new Archbishop of Canterbury, strove to get Frith to moderate his view on the eucharist so he could be useful in other ways.

More faced the same dilemma he had encountered with Grinaeus. He felt that he had to refute a heretic, but the heretic was of interest to Henry VIII. It was not politic to attack such a man with the usual invective. Yet More knew that Frith held views on the mass that Henry detested. Henry believed in transubstantiation until he died, and he had a special hatred for the Zwinglians, whose view of the mass as mere sign and symbol came to be called "sacramentarian." It is just possible that Henry's closest religious advisers had hidden from him the extent of Frith's heresies. In the *Apology*, published when Henry's flirtation with Frith was over, More wrote that Frith did not want the "brotherhood" to know what he thought about the mass.

There was truth to More's charge. Frith said that no one would be saved or damned for his beliefs about the mass. Tyndale always tried to keep discussion about the mass subdued lest such talk divide Evangelicals further and show their divisions to the world. It is quite unlikely that Henry—never a great reader—had read any of Frith's books or even suspected how radical the man was. More's tactic would have been to inform his sovereign, in a mild and somewhat indirect way, about the man his advisers were trying to bring over to his side.

Whether Henry read More's pamphlet or not we cannot know. But he did become enraged at Frith's views when he understood them, and in the summer of 1533 the young man was burned at the stake because he would not recant them. Like so many of the martyrs of the time, he seemed eager to die and refused to take an opportunity offered him to escape. In his *Apology*, published in April, Frith was no longer, in More's words, "the young man" but a "proud, unlearned fool," possessed of a "solemn pride . . . which not only speaketh lies against honest men, but also writeth false lies and heresies against the blessed sacrament of the altar." With Frith out of favor with the king and on his way to the fire, More could safely vilify him as he had vilified all other heretics.

Frith perished at Smithfield on July 4, 1533, the first important Evangelical writer to suffer death for heresy. Foxe says that the wind blew the fire away from him, so that his dying was prolonged, but he showed no sign of pain.

These months must have been the worst in More's life so far. By January 1533, Henry knew that Anne Boleyn was pregnant, and all the efforts to obtain a divorce approved by the pope now had to be thrown aside in the haste required to make the coming heir to the throne legitimate. On January 25, the king married her in a private ceremony kept secret from the nation at large. In the meantime couriers were sent speeding to Rome to win the pope's approval of Cranmer for the post of Archbishop of Canterbury. Chapuys, who smelled a rat, begged the emperor to see to it that the pope did not grant his approval before making a declaration about the king's marriage—a step the timid pope steadfastly refused to take despite the incessant, angry pleas of Queen Catherine, the exasperation of Chapuys, and the annoyance of the emperor himself. Chapuys reported Cranmer's reputation of "belonging heart and soul to the Lutheran sect" and hoped that the pope would take warning.

He also reported that the papal nuncio was frequently and publicly invited to court, where he was entertained with great courtesy. Chapuys supposed, in his astute and cynical way, that the king displayed the nuncio to lead the people to believe that all was well between Henry and the pope. No trace of suspicion appears in the dispatches of January and early February that Anne and Henry were already married. Then, on February 23, Chapuys wrote that Cranmer not only had pledged to follow the king's will in the divorce but had already performed the marriage in the presence of Anne's father, mother, brother, two of her intimate female friends, and a priest from the diocese of Canterbury. Rumors flew, Chapuys wrote, that the king waited only for the papal bulls confirming Cranmer's elevation before confirming the marriage openly.

Yet astonishingly enough, the pope did not delay in confirming Cranmer to the ancient see of Canterbury. Therein lies one of the most important facts of the English Reformation and one of the most profound mysteries of papal diplomacy. Perhaps it was simply that the pope yearned to please Henry in something and since the pope was already dying, he may not have been able to assess the warnings about Cranmer's orthodoxy.

While the couriers seeking the pope's approval of Cranmer's elevation were hurrying to Rome, the Parliament, called back once more by Henry's government, passed the great Act in Restraint of Appeals in February 1533. It began by reporting that "divers sundry old authentic histories and chronicles," probably meaning the tales of Geoffrey of Monmouth and the story of Arthur and the knights of the Round Table, had "manifestly declared and expressed that this realm of England is an empire." An empire owed no earthly allegiance to any power under God, and the statute was obviously aimed at the pope.

The preamble of the act declared that the king in England had supreme judicial power. The English church was said to be "for knowledge, integrity, and sufficiency of number . . . sufficient and meet of itself, without the intermeddling of any exterior person or persons, to declare and determine all such doubts, and to administer all such offices and duties, as to their rooms spiritual doth appertain." The king's duty in England had always been to protect both the secular and spiritual estates of the realm from "the annoyance as well of the see of Rome as from the authority of other foreign potentates."

Still, the preamble declared, suits had been made to Rome, and they had been long delayed. Among suits mentioned were those about wills and cases concerning "matrimony and divorces" and others "to the great inquietation, vexation, trouble, cost and charges of the king's highness and many of his subjects and residents in this his realm." In consequence, the act ordained that all these cases must be "from henceforth heard, examined, discussed, clearly, finally, and definitively adjudged and determined within the king's jurisdiction and authority, and not elsewhere."

In effect, the act ended the papal jurisdiction in England, although clearly Henry would accept that jurisdiction if the pope would only rule in favor of his divorce. The ecclesiastical theory behind the act was that the church was inspired in the whole body by the Holy Spirit and that the pope was unnecessary to the unity of Catholic doctrine, that indeed he was an obstacle to the inspiration that made the church of one mind in all places where Christians might dwell.

In the second part of his *Confutation*, which appeared sometime in 1533, More took oblique notice of the act and argued that no matter what one did with the pope, the church was still the church and that people like Tyndale and Barnes were still heretics. What he said is worth a long quotation since in his remarks we see plainly his reluctance to extol papal authority together with a reluctance to approve the Act in Restraint of Appeals and its underlying theology. More was responding to Tyndale's question "Whether the pope and his sect be Christ's church or not." Said More:

> I call the church of Christ the catholic known of all Christian nations, neither gone out nor cut off [from the whole body]. And all be it that all these nations now do and long have done, recognized, and acknowledged the pope not as the Bishop of Rome but as the successor of St. Peter, to be their chief spiritual governor under God and Christ's vicar in earth and so do not only we call him but Tyndale's own fellow friar Barnes, too. Yet did I never put the pope for part of the definition of the church, defining the church to be the common, known congregation of all Christian nations under one head the pope.
>
> Thus did I never define the church, but purposely declined therefrom because I would not intrick and entangle the matter with two questions at once. For I knew very well that the church being proved this common known catholic congregation of all Christian nations, abiding together in one faith, neither fallen off nor cut off, there might be peradventure made a second question after that, whither over all that catholic church the pope must needs be head and chief governor or chief spiritual shepherd or ells that the union of faith standing among them all, every province might have their own chief spiritual governor over itself, without any recourse unto the pope, or any superiority recognized to any other outward person.

And then if the pope were or not pope, but as I say provincial patriarchs, archbishops, or metropolitans, or by what name so ever the thing were called, what authority and power either he or they should have among the people, these things well I knew would raise among many men many more questions than one. For the avoiding of all intrickation whereof, I purposely forbare to put in the pope as part of the definition of the church, as a thing that needed not, since if he be the necessary head, he is included in the name of the whole body. And whether he be or not, if it be brought in question, were a matter to be treated and disputed beside.

It is a striking passage, revealing the ambivalence toward the papacy of England's most dauntless defender of the church in the language of the people, and with such ambivalence on More's part, it is easy enough to see why Henry had a much easier time than even he supposed he would in getting his anti-papal measures through the Parliament.

More might accept the pope as an administrative head of the church, necessary to its efficient functioning. Even the radical conciliarists of the previous century had done as much. But such acceptance did not mean that More ever gave up his view that any institutional body functions best when it is directed by a community of the wise and the weighty. He had experience enough to know that any kind of unconditional monarchy, whether spiritual or secular, could lead more easily to tyranny than to wisdom.

The Act in Restraint of Appeals constituted a revolution. The way was now cleared by statute for an Archbishop of Canterbury with the proper credentials to declare the marriage between Catherine and Henry null and to leave the mournful queen no appeal to a higher earthly authority. Within weeks after the act had passed, the pope had played into Henry's hands by officially granting to Thomas Cranmer the see of Canterbury and primacy over the English church.

By late March, the official papal documents certifying Rome's approval of Cranmer's elevation arrived in England. Before he took his public oath to the pope, Cranmer took a secret oath that he would not be bound by any oath he might swear that would be in contradiction to the laws of England. In effect, Cranmer was swearing to keep his fingers crossed while he took the oath that would in the eyes of the English people validate both his office and anything that he might do in it. It was a strange moral position for the new primate of the English church in an age when perjury was considered a damnable sin. And having been installed as primate of England and direct spiritual descendant of those missionaries sent to convert England by Pope Gregory I, he moved swiftly to become the instrument for the extirpation of the last relics of papal authority in the land that the pope had placed under his care.

By April 5, the Convocation of the Clergy under his leadership ruled on its

own that no pope could set aside the divine law that forbade a brother to marry
his brother's wife. John Fisher opposed the ruling to the last, and shortly
afterwards he was placed under house arrest. More, isolated in Chelsea and
powerless to influence events except by means of his books, turned himself into
a writing machine. Yet the way to schism in England was now open, and
More's pen became a thin bar across it, unable to stop his countrymen from
plunging through.

It was in that month of April, so filled with the building threat of storm,
that More published his *Apology of Sir Thomas More Knight*. The book was
intended both to defend himself from various charges and to defend the clergy
from the devastating assault by Christopher St. German, who had anonymously published *A Treatise Concerning the Division Between the Spirituality
and the Temporality* late in 1532. It seems clear that St. German was one of
the quasi-official publicists gathered by Cromwell to defend the king's cause.
It also seems clear that More knew who he was. But since he did not put his
name to the piece, More could attack him, calling him "the Pacifier" and
other, more insulting epithets, without being obviously guilty of attacking one
of the king's men by name.

St. German's *Treatise* enraged More the lawyer precisely because it was a
lawyer's book, using a lawyer's shrewd tricks just as More had done a few
years before in his own account of the Richard Hunne affair. The tone of the
Treatise is studiously calm and benign, and its theology is thoroughly orthodox underneath a studied acid surface of anticlericalism. His only intent, St.
German says, is to heal the division between the clergy and the laity and to
bring peace to the realm. But throughout the book, he describes only clerical
sins and these with vague generalities, making it seem that the clergy are
nearly all wicked and that they alone are responsible for the divisions within
English life.

He includes the standard compendium of complaints. Priests charge huge
fees for their spiritual services. They will not bury the dead unless they are paid.
Monks live in too much comfort. Clergymen quarrel endlessly, and they serve
in menial posts in the homes of great men, dressing like liveried servants rather
than as priests. They are greedy. They induce people to go on pilgrimages and
to buy indulgences and to make wills that favor the church, and their only
motive is profit. They lack good order and discretion. They are inflamed with
pride and with a desire for dominance, and they make no effort to reform
themselves.

From time to time St. German made some rhetorical exceptions, admitting
that there were some good priests around. But the general impression given
in the *Treatise* is that any fair-minded observer would conclude that the
English clergy were a scurvy lot. More fumed that the Pacifier's claim to
impartiality was like that of a man who tries to stop a fight by jumping between

the foes, striking one in the face while only pushing the other away, and claiming loudly to be fair to both.

The steady mildness of its tone and the solid orthodoxy of its opinions made the *Treatise* all the more dangerous. St. German did not object to images; he did object to plating them with gold and silver. He did not deny purgatory, but he expressed tolerance toward those who did deny it because the clergy used the doctrine in so many ways to make money. He did not come out in favor of heresy, but he condemned the way the clergy used heresy laws to oppress the laity and to put down opposition to ecclesiastical tyranny.

Above all, the *Treatise* represents the ideal of warm-hearted piety essential to the philosophy of Christ that Erasmus taught. Like Erasmus, like Colet, like More himself, St. German yearned for priests to live up to their professions so that the laity would be inspired by their example. Over a century earlier Chaucer had put that desire into the mouth of his poor town parson who said of priesthood and priests, "For if the gold rust, what shall the iron do?" And More himself had written, "For undoubtedly if the clergy be nothing, we must be worse as I heard once Master Colet, the good dean of Paul's preach. For he said it can be none other but that we must ever be one degree under them." St. German said, "And therefore it followeth, that if priesthood be whole, all the church flourishes. And if it be corrupt, the faith and virtue of the people fadeth also and falleth away, as if thou see a tree that hath withered leaves, thou knowest thereby that there is a defect in the root. So when thou seest the people live out of good order, know it for certain that their priesthood is not whole nor sound."

Like More and Erasmus, St. German had a profound conviction that the clergy had once been better than it was in the sixteenth century. The supposition may be doubted. But the notion that the past was golden was one of the great fictions of the Renaissance, and it held enormous power over the mind of the age. St. German, like More in *Utopia*, wanted the church to have authority not by mere law but by the irresistible moral power of its priests. The division between clergy and laity would never be reformed, he said, until people come to the point where they greatly fear and dread to run into the least censure of the church. "And that will never be, till the heads spiritual reform themselves and show a fatherly love unto the people, and not extend the sentences of the church upon so light causes and upon such partiality as they have done in times past."

These sentiments are in complete harmony with the ideal More had posed in *Utopia* of a priesthood so pure that ordinary citizens revered priests in spontaneous respect. But in his *Apology* More objected vehemently that the accusations of the Pacifier were hearsay evidence, a slanderous collection of "some says," repeated again and again to make it seem that all the clergy were afflicted by the vices of a few. St. German, of course, did not claim that all clergymen were wicked, although he did dwell on the bad. So had Erasmus in *The Praise of Folly,* and young Martin van Dorp at Louvain—long dead in 1532—had said the same things about Erasmus that More now said about St. German. But all that was in another time and almost in another world.

St. German's mild little treatise also resembles More's *Utopia* in its hatred of idleness—in St. German's work, the idleness of the clergy. He would not have protested, he said, had the clergy been active in prayers and in saintly deeds; but he did protest the wasteful leisure of those priests and monks who cared nothing for God and took money out of the pockets of hardworking laymen whose fundamental orderliness and reliability created the bones and muscles of the state. In St. German's view, the slack and sometimes wanton priests had become a band of parasites, and only a Christian government dedicated to practical reform could whip them—perhaps literally—into shape again and restore their usefulness to society. In part it is an old song, for like More in 1515 and 1516, St. German views with frustration the contradictory spectacle of a nation in need and a huge part of its population sturdy but idle and requiring to be put to work.

St. German's legal questions were as important as anything else in this little book. Like Fortescue decades before him, he did not want the innocent to suffer—quite in contrast to Thomas More, who, at least in heresy cases, did not want the guilty to escape. He detested the canon law of the church with its provision that the accused might be condemned without knowing the witnesses against him. Here he made the most radical suggestion in his treatise: he thought the clergy should be deprived of their right to be the sole judges of heresy.

He thought clergymen used heresy laws for selfish reasons against the innocent, and he hated the provision that allowed ecclesiastical officials to jail those suspected of unsound doctrine. He did not have to mention Richard Hunne to recall to his readers that apparently honest merchants might be hauled into the bishops' prisons and never be seen alive again. St. German wanted investigations of heresy to be a joint affair of the civil and religious authority. But real joint authority would require a single law, and St. German made it clear that the law he preferred was the English common law with its superior protection for the accused.

Good lawyer that he was, he pointed out that English civil authorities, such as justices of the peace, were already engaged in the investigation of heresy, investigations that, under the Lollard statutes, they carried on with the help of ecclesiastical officials. He could have said that Lord Chancellors of the Realm did the same with bishops, even when—as in the case of Thomas More —the Lord Chancellor happened to be a layman. All this despite the claim of the church that heresy was entirely a matter for the spiritual authority until the heretic was condemned and turned over to the secular government to be burned.

Here St. German must have been extremely vexing to More. He was arguing the quite modern view that law is made by observing what is happening and then by trying to compose written rules that grant some formal order to current practice. If justices of the peace—or Lord Chancellors—were already helping clergymen investigate heresy, the formal distinction between spiritual and secular authority in cases of heresy had already broken down, and good English law might as well acknowledge the fact.

Using the same procedure, St. German attacked the right of clergymen to be tried by spiritual courts when they were accused of crimes. He pointed out that clergymen were not excused from ordinary civil trial when they were accused of treason and that treason now included the counterfeiting of money. He had argued that priests were inferior in virtue to the laity or at best not superior; now he passed to the natural conclusion that clergy and laity should be tried in the same courts—the straightforward, honest courts of English common law. The punishment of a bad priest injures no good priest, he said. And if the secular authority punishes, it serves a worthy purpose—no matter what such practice might mean to the tradition of the church.

More replied ineffectually. He found himself in the impossible position of defending the old while novelty was sweeping the minds of his most literate and influential countrymen. He defended the virtues of the clergy when every alehouse rocked with mirth at their vices and every poetaster composed satirical verses against them. He tried to tar St. German with the brush of heresy, but any reader was likelier to see in St. German the lament of a thoroughly orthodox man for the plight of his church, and it appears that St. German did have a genuine distaste for heresy.

More claimed that only harsh measures against the heretics could keep the realm from being overwhelmed by them. It is in the *Apology* that his authoritarianism shows most clearly: his belief in a strong central power was so great that he always tended to think that people accused of crimes were guilty, and no argument to protect the innocent carried as much weight with him as the necessity to preserve society. Yet most Englishmen could not take seriously his dire predictions of calamity should king and populace tolerate heresy. They had little experience in internal chaos. Englishmen were far less bloody-minded when they were fighting each other in England than when they did battle with the French across the Narrow Seas, and nothing in English history of the Middle Ages quite measures up in horror to the Jacquerie in France or the Peasants' Revolt in Germany or the sack of Rome. Englishmen simply could not believe More when he painted the lurid effects of heresy because his picture was beyond their experience, fantastic and unreal. Besides, the most heretical voices in England and among Englishmen on the Continent were raised in favor of law and order and a strong secular government.

More used his flamboyant wit against the Pacifier, turning aside the complaints against the Catholic clergy with assaults on Luther and the other heretics, and he gets off one magnificently obscene pun. Says he, "Yet if religious Lutherans may proceed and prosper that cast off their [religious] habits and walk out and wed nuns and preach against purgatory, and make mocks of the mass, many men shall care little for obitis [masses for the dead] within awhile and set no more by a trentall than a ruffian in Rome setteth by a *trent une.*" A trentall was a set of thirty requiem masses for the soul of a dead person, all said on the same day; the *trent une* was an Italian punishment for a whore, giving her over to a gang of ruffians who raped her thirty-one times.

His defense of the clergy and the canon law was to no avail, and the most effective passages in the *Apology* are those where More defends himself. He shows how vulnerable he was to criticism, how jealously he guarded his reputation even while he espoused the extirpation of heresy from England by blood and fire. The rest of the book is a failure, and More must have known as much almost as soon as it appeared.

On May 23, Archbishop Cranmer declared Henry's marriage null from the beginning, and on June 1, Anne Boleyn was crowned queen of England and rode with her consort through the crowded and wondering streets of London. She was slightly more than three months away from giving birth to her first child.

Thomas More had done his best to withdraw from the dangerous public scene, but he kept at his books, and an age that feared books could not take lightly a man like him. Neither Henry nor the bishops who had capitulated to Henry's desires could let a former Lord Chancellor rest in peace. Cuthbert Tunstall, More's old and dear friend, came down from Durham for the coronation. Tunstall joined Stephen Gardiner, bishop of Winchester, and John Clerk, bishop of Bath and Welles, in sending More twenty pounds to buy a new gown so that he might attend the coronation in style. More took the money and bought the gown but stayed at home while Anne and her husband paraded through the streets.

Afterwards the three bishops came to reason with him. All three were stalwart conservatives, and Clerk and Gardiner had valiantly defended the liberties of the English church. Gardiner was the chief author of the *Answer of the Ordinaries* to the *Supplication* of the Commons, a reply whose tone had angered Henry VIII. He was always to be a foe of the Protestant leanings of Thomas Cranmer. When Convocation under Cranmer's leadership had voted on whether Catherine's marriage to Arthur had been proved consummated, Clerk was one of only six bishops to stand by their conviction that the consummation had not been proved at all.

But Gardiner had been Henry's chief ambassador in Rome to press for the divorce, and Anne Boleyn herself had written him thanking him for his efforts. He had a well-deserved reputation for duplicity, and at this moment he was exceptionally close to the king. During the coronation he and Stokesley had held the corners of Anne's royal robe. Anything said to him would find its way quickly to the king's ear.

All three of these bishops had ambiguous feelings about the papacy—like Thomas More himself. They might have argued that for conservatives to desert the king in his withdrawal from Rome would open the doors of England to heretics. We know that all three of them took a hard line toward heresy. If men such as they could bow to the royal will, why should Thomas More not do the same?

More told them that he was happy to honor their first request and buy himself a gown with their money. He was not rich, he said, and he could use a new robe. But the request that he attend the coronation reminded him of the tale of an emperor who had made a law that anyone guilty of a certain crime should be put to death, provided that the offender was not a virgin. The first person who committed the crime was a virgin, but the emperor nevertheless wanted her killed. What was to be done? The matter was resolved by a member of the royal council who declared, "Why make you so much ado, my lords, about so small a matter? Let her first be deflowered and then after may she be devoured."

The story is More's adaptation of a tale by Tacitus which tells of how the daughter of Sejanus was put to death with the rest of her family during the reign of Tiberius. Roper has More make his meaning clear in case anyone has missed it. Virginity was his symbol of purity. In Roper's account, More says to his friends, "And so though your lordships have in the matter of the matrimony hitherto kept yourselves pure virgins, yet take good heed, my lords, that you keep your virginity still. But some there be that by procuring your lordships first at the coronation to be present, and next to preach for the setting forth of it, and finally to write books to all the world in defense thereof, are desirous to deflower you; and when they have deflowered you, then will they not fail soon after to devour you. Now, my lords," he said, "it lieth not in my power but that they may devour me. But God, being my good Lord, I will provide that they shall never deflower me."

As Roper tells it, the story seems almost foolhardy. Tunstall was a good friend, but Gardiner had already spoken and written in favor of the divorce. More's reproach was bitter and insulting. These men had, in his view, already gone over to the enemy camp and did not know or willed not to know what they had done. There is no evidence that he ever saw Tunstall again.

Gardiner would have reported the scene immediately to the king, and it is hard to see how such a good story could fail to be repeated. By his absence from the coronation and by such bitter talk, More was making it clear to everyone who cared to notice that he stood in uncompromising opposition to the king's new marriage and to the new queen and that he thought the supporters of change were impure. Staying home from a coronation was hardly treason. Neither was it treason to say to one's close friends that in attending the coronation themselves, they were running the risk of losing their spiritual virginity. At least it was not treason yet. But both acts were enough to let resisters suppose that Thomas More might be a rallying point should the partisans of the old church have their day and rise against the king and his ministers.

To some that day seemed near and desirable. In February the Act in Restraint of Appeals had formally declared England an empire; the effect was to make the church in England by parliamentary statute independent of the jurisdiction of the pope; English citizens were forbidden to appeal any case from the English courts, spiritual or secular, to any foreign potentate. Cromwell drafted the legislation; Parliament passed it without change.

Despite the strong support for the act, resistance was strong, too. Many Catholics perceived that Henry was on his way to an open break with Rome, and they could not see the difference Henry saw between schism and heresy. On April 10, Chapuys wrote his own frank opinion to Charles V. The emperor must make war on England, for Anne would now take vengeance on Queen Catherine and Princess Mary. Said he, "An undertaking against this country would be in the opinion of many people here the easiest thing in the world just now, for this king has neither cavalry nor well trained infantry, besides which the affection of his subjects is entirely on Your Majesty's side, not only that of the common people but of the nobility in general with the single exception of the duke of Norfolk and two or three more." Both Catherine and Princess Mary, he said, were urging invasion. A few days later he wrote again, suggesting his own recall, since by remaining in London as the emperor's ambassador, he said, he was taken by the common people as a sign of the emperor's continuing friendship with Henry. Chapuys was always an optimist about popular support for Catherine in England; his was the mentality that would bring the Spanish Armada to disaster in 1588. But 1588 was much more than a generation away, and in 1533 it was quite clear that Henry, Cromwell, and their cohorts knew they were riding a tiger who must be tamed lest he devour them.

In July 1533, Clement VII, goaded at long last into action by events and by the emperor, declared that Henry's marriage to Anne was null and void, and he excommunicated both the king and Thomas Cranmer. Even now this timorous, tearful man refused to publish the decree of excommunication immediately. He finally released it on September 7—the day Anne Boleyn to the great disappointment and danger to herself and the realm, gave birth to a baby girl christened Elizabeth. By November the decree was published in the Netherlands.

As late as November 24, Chapuys was writing the emperor of Queen Catherine's conviction that if the pope would only rule in the case, the king and the country would return to the right path and that no invasion of England would be necessary. Chapuys thought that no one else in the kingdom agreed with her and told the emperor that the most effective way of dealing with Henry was to shut off trade between England and the emperor's domain in the Netherlands. On December 9 he wrote that the king and council were frightened at the possible effect of the decree of excommunication published in Flanders and that the English people "all to a man have rejoiced and trusted that since Your Majesty has begun the game you will go on with it, and put an end to the annoyances this king is causing you and them."

Henry looked to his fleet, so Chapuys said, and Norfolk had told the king that the fleet would be all but worthless against the imperial navy and that the best policy was to fortify the coast. It was, in the eyes of the English government, a perilous time, and no one who had followed the king this far could look to the future without anxiety. Sometimes that anxiety looked like terror.

More always protested his loyalty and obedience to the king, and, as far as we know, he never did a thing to encourage rebellion. In this regard his circumspection was greater than that of John Fisher, whose exchanges with Chapuys were certainly treasonable. But it is simple-minded to assume that More would have opposed a Spanish invasion or a Catholic rebellion that succeeded. Although he was not naturally a leader of men or movements, he could not have failed to adapt himself to a movement of any kind that toppled Henry in the name of the old faith. Despite his long years of submissive flattery to Wolsey, he turned sharply on the great cardinal when Wolsey fell; he had almost as sharply assaulted the rule of Henry VII when that king was safely dead. And we cannot assume that his flattery of Henry VIII would have long continued had that king, too, been displaced by events.

We have already noted several times More's account of how Bishop John Morton viewed the rise and fall of kings in *The History of King Richard III*. God makes kings and unmakes them, and when the son of Henry VI was killed, Morton's view, as More had him express it to the Duke of Buckingham, was succinct: "I purpose not to spurn against a prick, nor labor to set up that God pulleth down." God might use the instruments of intrigue and battle and even murder in the night. God decides if rebellions will succeed or fail. Morton, whom More loved, had changed allegiances several times and died in glory and honor. More was always unmistakable in his belief that Parliament could, in effect, declare anyone king. Later, when he was in the Tower, Richard Riche posed this case: "Admit there were, sir, an act of Parliament that all the realm should take me for king. Would you not, Master More, take me for king?"

More's answer was unequivocal: "Yes, sir, that would I." And it was to be expected that had Henry VIII been overthrown, some sort of parliament would quickly have been summoned to approve the deed and to certify another king —as parliaments had done frequently enough since Richard II had been toppled from the throne by Bolingbroke.

Englishmen knew their history, and to any historical-minded person Thomas More represented a clear and present danger to the revolution Henry was making, a mortal threat to Henry's throne and to Henry's life. By refusing to attend the coronation and by making a rebuke of a semi-public kind to three bishops who did attend, Thomas More was quietly raising a flag. It did not require much imagination to see it fluttering softly in its place on a hill apart, waiting for other men like himself to rally around it.

Yet the impression More conveyed in his works was that of a loyal and harmless citizen, a man yearning only to be left in peace to die. He was doubtless sincere, given the conditions of the country at the time. Yet he also had a role to play, and he must have known that such a public presentation of himself on the stage of current events would make any moves by the king against him seem especially bloodthirsty and cruel. He shrank from martyr-dom, but if martyrdom should come, his church would have the benefit of his example, heightened by meek innocence, which would make the character of the tyrant all the more stark and terrible.

This was the view of himself he presented in his last surviving letter to Erasmus, written about June 1533. He mentioned that he had received two letters from Erasmus. Neither has come down to us, but from More's letter we can guess what Erasmus said. Erasmus had not published More's letter of the previous year, and he tried to explain himself to More. Rumors were flying that More was in disgrace. If Erasmus published the letter, he might get himself into trouble with the English government and with Thomas Cranmer, who was sending him a pension. Erasmus had also reproached More somewhat about More's hatred of heretics.

So More wrote to reassure him and, above all, to prod him into publishing this and the previous letter, giving a public and harmless explanation of his departure from office. It was true, More said, that some loose tongues had been spreading the rumor that he had been asked to resign. He had answered these critics, he said, by making his epitaph public. In it he declared that he had resigned his office because of his health; no one had stepped forward to contradict him. His enemies, unable to refute his claim, had changed their tack and now declared that the epitaph was boastful. More, assuming his familiar role as the superior man unconcerned for the opinions of the vulgar multitude, said he cared not for the judgment of men as long as he had the approval of God.

But he wanted Erasmus to know that the king had approved. More reported that on the elevation of Audeley to the post of Lord Chancellor, the Duke of Norfolk had proclaimed in public that the king had unwillingly received More's resignation. In addition, More said, Audeley himself, addressing both houses of Parliament, had made the same pronouncement at the king's command.

It is worth noting that Henry authorized such pronouncements because he recognized that More had influence in the realm, and he wanted to convey the impression that he and his former Lord Chancellor were still on good terms. These declarations are reminiscent of Henry's public courting of the papal nuncio, noted by Chapuys a year earlier, when he felt it necessary to assure a grumbling populace that all was well between him and the pope.

If Henry was anything, he was master of the public face, and no one who reads the long and detailed dispatches Chapuys sent to the emperor can suppose that the king's public face, flashing with its studied radiance, revealed the dark soul of the private man. Still, More clutched at such straws as he could find, and the public face of the king was something to hold up before Erasmus to inspire that timorous soul into publishing More's letters of self-vindication.

Evidently Erasmus had expressed some doubts about More's attacks on heretics. Since Erasmus did not read English, so far as we know, he must have received his information from those who were familiar with the situation in England. No pen in that country was as fierce as More's, and More's defense of his works in the *Apology* proves that many Englishmen thought he went too far in vituperation. Erasmus, getting wind of that sentiment, must have expressed in some way his agreement with it.

In this 1533 letter to Erasmus, More enclosed his epitaph with its remark that he was a pain to thieves, murderers, and heretics. Erasmus could see, he said, that he did not give them much attention in this final statement about his life. Yet, he said, speaking of the remark, "I did that ostentatiously. I hate that sort of men so utterly that, unless they repent, I want to be as hateful to them as anyone can be since as I contend with them more and more, I vehemently fear what the world will suffer from them."

The epitaph itself shows easily enough why some of More's foes thought he was boasting. It is much longer than most epitaphs from that or any other time, and it recounts More's own history so that anyone reading it might know that he had been an important man. It flatters Henry VIII, of course, and details More's long career in his service. In the end it makes the proper and no doubt sincere expressions of piety before the coming of death and the life to come. It is a long statement by a man given to making long declarations about himself, an epitaph befitting the man who carefully set forth his own importance in his *Utopia* and, later on, in his *Dialogue Concerning Heresies*, the epitaph of the boy who had stepped in among the players during the Christmas pageants and made himself a part and driven ever afterwards to make an audience appreciate his role upon a public stage. Now the great play was nearly done, and More wanted to be sure that some memory was preserved of the part he had made for himself in life.

Naturally, the epitaph, included with the letter, conveyed the impression of a man folding up all his earthly cares, prepared to meet his maker, unwilling to harm anyone except the wicked heretics who must be harmed if society were to be preserved. More must have hoped that Henry and the council would read it and leave him alone.

This is the last letter from More to Erasmus that has survived. A few months earlier Erasmus had written to John Faber, bishop of Vienna, denying the rumors that More was in disgrace, yet cautiously declaring that he had not written any private letters to More since he had become Lord Chancellor— a statement that was probably not true. The letter to Faber has a public tone, and it provides another laudatory biography of More. Erasmus describes the More household where the liberal arts and piety were always joined and where neither disputes nor idleness found any place. He provides the interesting information that Cardinal Wolsey had thought no one more capable than More of taking on the onerous duties of the office of Lord Chancellor, and he says that Wolsey held this opinion not out of some special benevolence toward More, whom he feared rather than loved. He concedes More's wrath toward heretics and his resolve to keep them from sedition, but gives the misinformation that no one suffered death for heresy under More's administration. The letter looks very much like an apology for More before a European audience, one that More himself might have longed to have. But Erasmus must have had second thoughts about publishing it, and it did not appear in his lifetime.

He recognized his need for continuing patronage from England, and he took pains to see to it that this part of his income was not cut off. He was in touch with Anne Boleyn's father, Thomas Boleyn, Earl of Wiltshire. In March 1533, he dedicated to Boleyn his little book on the Apostles' Creed. It was so neutral toward many of the fighting issues in the Protestant Reformation that it became enormously popular in England and was used extensively during the Protestant regime of King Edward VI, Henry VIII's son and successor by his third wife, Jane Seymour.

In January 1534, Erasmus finally published More's last two letters to him. They appeared in an appendix to a book called *On Preparation for Death*. It, too, was dedicated to Thomas Boleyn. By that time Boleyn was accusing Thomas More of taking bribes during his service as Lord Chancellor. Erasmus could not have known of these accusations so soon, and had he known of them, we may be sure that he would not have published these last two letters at all. In February 1535, he wrote to his banker, Erasmus Shets, about his English pension. He had not written anything that could possibly offend the English authorities, he said. "I did not write anything to More or to Fisher after I heard that they were in prison." On August 31, 1535, when More had been dead for nearly two months, Erasmus wrote to Peter Tomiczki, bishop of Cracow, "In More I seem to have become extinguished myself, seeing that, as Pythagorus said, the two of us shared one soul." The comment comes near the end of a long letter in which Erasmus recounted all the tribulations he had endured, and it is rather a sign of the prevailing self-pity that darkened his later life than it is of compassion for More. By then Erasmus was old, with only a few months of life left, and in the way of old men, he found that the distant and beloved past and the acute sense of the loss of all things came strongly back with the news of the death of one with whom he had shared time.

When the pope's decree of excommunication became known in England, the immediate consequence for Thomas More was the end of his polemical writing against heresy. By now the government was clearly hostile to the continual flow of vituperation from his pen. He had remained scrupulously aloof from writing about the king's marital affairs. Still, there could be no doubt as to where he stood, and as long as he wrote, he remained a public figure whose very name called up in the public mind the thought of opposition to the king. In October 1533, More had brought out his *Debellacion of Salem and Bizance*, another attack on St. German, who had replied anonymously to More's *Apology*. St. German had called his answer *Salem and Bizance*. The "debellacion" of More's reply means "destruction." It is a long, painful book, an uncompromising restatement of his fundamental positions. He remarks at the beginning that he heard that some were angry because of his *Apology*. He cannot understand, he says, "for I had but spoken for myself and for good folk and for the Catholic faith." It is probable that the people most angry were those around Henry VIII who by this time wanted no one in England writing in favor of the old church.

His last polemic was *The Answer to a Poisoned Book*, done in reply to a Zwinglian view of the eucharist published anonymously by an English heretic and called *The Supper of the Lord*.

Sometime after the first of the year, William Rastell was summoned before Cromwell and charged with publishing a book of More's attacking a work put out by the king's council accusing Pope Clement VII of bastardy, heresy, and other things that would have made him no true pope. On February 1, More wrote Cromwell denying that he had ever written against any book put out by the king and his "honorable council." He knew his bounden duty as a subject, he told Cromwell; he would not ever write such a volume, especially since he had not studied the book in question and since he was ignorant both in the law and in the facts set forth by the book. In the course of this letter he mentioned that he had not published anything after his reply to *The Supper of the Lord*. That answer of his had appeared before Christmas in 1533 but by accident had been misdated 1534. Obviously, dangerous enemies were going to scrutinize anything More wrote and published now. It may be that sometime late in 1533, he had been ordered by the government to desist. For whatever reason, he published nothing else while he lived.

But his enemies were not done with him. Sometime in the summer of 1533, when England was filled with the turmoil surrounding Henry's divorce, More became involved in the business of the "Nun of Kent," Elizabeth Barton. In consequence, a frightened government made its first official threat to his life.

Elizabeth Barton was a visionary, a girl who in adolescence fell dangerously ill and, on recovery, went into trances and made oracular pronouncements. She became celebrated in the countryside where she lived, and in 1525 Archbishop Warham took her under his protection, installing her at Canterbury. Throngs flocked to see her, and from time to time important people sought her out, among them John Fisher. From about 1528 she seems to have been used as a tool by those opposed to Henry's divorce. She was coached in theology and spoke out against the divorce and the heretics infiltrating the country. She praised images, pilgrimages, relics, and saints. Fisher is said to have wept when he heard her, believing—as people then did about oracles—that he was hearing the words of God in a human voice.

More did not mention the Nun of Kent in anything he published while she lived. But he may have had her in mind when he told the story of Anne, the daughter of Sir Roger Wentworth, a girl cured of demon possession. Superficially, at least, he told the story in his *Dialogue Concerning Heresies* to prove that God still worked miracles at shrines; it so happens that her cure is the only miracle for which he ever claimed firsthand knowledge.

Like Elizabeth Barton, Anne Wentworth fell into trances, but unlike the Nun of Kent, she blasphemed God and raved against "all hallowed things." The family took her on pilgrimage to the shrine of Our Lady of Ipswich, and on the way "she prophesied and told many things done and said at the same time in other places which were proved true, and many things said lying in her trance of such wisdom and learning that right cunning men highly marveled to hear of so young and unlearned maiden when she herself knew not what she said, such things uttered and spoken as well learned men might have missed with long study."

More attributed her gifts not to God but to the devil, and when at last she was "brought and laid before the image of our blessed lady, was there in the sight of many worshipful people so grievously tormented and in face, eyes, looks, and countenance so grisly changed with her mouth drawn aside and her eyes laid out on her cheeks that it was a terrible sight to behold." But then, More said, God restored her to health, to a sound mind, and she was "in the presence of all the company restored to their good state perfectly cured and suddenly."

When More published these words, Elizabeth Barton was going into similar trances. Thomas Cranmer later described her original seizure in words so strikingly similar to More's description of Anne Wentworth that either they are a plagiarism or else they represent a stylized account of hysteria suffered by female oracles: "And when she was brought thither and laid before the image of Our Lady, her face was wonderfully disfigured, her tongue hanging out, and her eyes being in a manner plucked out and laid on her cheeks and so greatly disordered."

William Tyndale knew the Nun of Kent's story well enough to compare it with the account More gave of the cure of Anne Wentworth. More believed Anne Wentworth was possessed of the devil, Tyndale says in his *Answer to Thomas More's Dialogue*. But the same stories are told of the Nun of Kent, and the Nun is said to be inspired by God. If we believe in such things, Tyndale says—and he obviously does not—how can we tell the difference between divine inspiration and demon possession? That question may have been exactly More's point. By telling the tale of Anne Wentworth, More may have been sending a signal to his many beloved friends caught up in enthusiasm for the Nun.

The Nun became bolder and bolder, forcing herself into the presence of the king himself, prophesying that if he married Anne Boleyn he would not survive on the throne a month and that within six months the realm would fall victim to a great plague. But More could not, for whatever reasons, declare himself openly against her. His hesitation may reveal much about his own feelings both concerning the Nun herself and of how he thought God worked—or might work—in the world.

The tumult of Anne's coronation had scarcely died away when the government moved hard against the Nun and her noisy circle. Thomas Cranmer and Thomas Cromwell interrogated her throughout the summer in London, apparently working a good-policeman, bad-policeman routine on her to break her will. Cranmer listened to her patiently as if he believed every word she said. Cromwell did the intimidating. By August she was confessing to Cranmer "many mad follies." By September her closest accomplices were being arrested, including her confessor, Edward Bocking, who had been not only her confessor but also coach, confidant, and (so the government said) companion of her nighttime couch. In November the Nun and her cohorts broke completely. They were put on public display at Paul's Cross and forced to read abject confessions of the fraud they had perpetrated against the king and his people.

The truth of these confessions is still doubted. Cromwell was not above suggesting torture when he wanted important information out of people. Whatever the truth may have been, Cromwell and his agents now moved swiftly to destroy the Nun and her friends. But because the law of treason as then written could not be made to apply to hysterical women claiming to converse with angels, fly through the air, become invisible, and make prophecies about the death of kings, she was prosecuted by a bill of attainder passed when Parliament came back into session in January after an adjournment of several months. In effect, the bill of attainder became a law declaring her and her accomplices guilty of treason. The legal difficulties of the case made Cromwell turn his magisterial hand to revising the treason law, and in a short while that revision would ensnare Thomas More.

Many people associated with the Nun, including some of her closest friends, had resorted to Thomas More with tales of her powers—proof enough that the enemies of the king thought More was a friend. So he became one of the targets in the government's offensive against her. In the bill of attainder introduced in the Parliament on February 21, 1534, More's name was included with others mixed up in the affair whom the government now prosecuted for treasonable conspiracy. Cromwell wrote a stinging letter to Fisher accusing the old bishop of malice and duplicity and threatening him with the wrath of the king. He appears not to have written such a letter to More, but More needed no harsh letter to recognize his extreme danger.

He wrote both to Cromwell and to Henry protesting his innocence. We find an urgency and a pleading in these letters that we may understand well enough when we consider the barbarous penalties awaiting the Nun and her cohorts. In April she and her associates would be hanged at Tyburn, cut down while still alive, their abdomens cut open, their entrails drawn out, their bodies at last cut into quarters and posted in different places in the city. In More's letter to Henry, the Nun had become the "wicked woman of Canterbury," and to Cromwell he wrote a long account of what he knew of her to prove his circumspection and his guiltlessness.

Yet it is precisely this letter from More himself that shows clearly enough why a frightened government tried to implicate him in her case and why the king became even more determined that More should make some public affirmation supporting the revolution that Henry and Cromwell were making in England.

More recalled that some nine years earlier, Archbishop Warham had sent the king some of the Nun's sayings uttered in a trance—probably a collection gathered and circulated in manuscript all around the country while the Nun was addressing the crowds that came to see her. Henry asked More to review them. More said he found nothing in them worthy of attention. Some were written in rude rhyme, and as far as he could see, there was nothing in them that a simple woman might not speak well enough out of her own wit—without divine inspiration. Because it was continually reported that God was working miracles with her, More told the king that he would not be bold to judge the matter. Henry, More said, did not take the woman or her utterances seriously.

Still, people swarmed around her. More had heard that both Wolsey and the king had voluntarily spoken with her. Cranmer, writing in December 1533, confirmed that the Nun had seen Wolsey and that her fulminations had much delayed action on the divorce. But, More said, he did not know what passed between the Nun and Henry or Wolsey.

Later, one of the Nun's close adherents, Richard Risby, a Franciscan who would die with her, came to spend some of the Christmas holidays in More's house and fell to talking after supper one night about the Nun, praising her virtues. More said he was glad to hear of them, but when Risby began speaking of her visions, trying to tell More about the prophecies concerning the king and his divorce, More shut him up. "And therewithall I said unto him that any revelation of the King's matters I would not hear of, [that] I doubtc[d] not but the goodness of God should direct his highness with His grace and wisdom, that the thing should take such end as God should be pleased with, to the King's honor and surety of the realm." Risby fell back to other revelations she had made about the cardinal. These were safe since Wolsey was disgraced and dead, and More listened. Risby left the next morning. More claimed not to have seen him again until the friar, the Nun, and several other of her friends were forced to make public confession of their crimes at St. Paul's in November 1533, when More stood in the audience and heard them read prepared statements that everything about the Nun had been a lie.

Later on another Franciscan, Hugh Rich of the Friars Observant at Richmond, visited at More's house and, like Risby before him, tried to tell what the Nun had said about the king. Again More refused to listen. Afterwards More saw Rich twice, once in his own home and once in the garden of the Franciscan house. At neither time did they talk about any revelations the Nun had proclaimed about the king. Rich, who would also make public confession in November, did not tell More any of the fantastic miracle stories circulating about the Nun. Had he done so, More wrote, "I would [have] liked him and her the worse." More could not recall where he had heard the stories, but he said he thought at the time that they must have been dreams the Nun had had and had reported to her entourage, only to have them spread abroad as fact.

Still later, More was at the monastery of Sion, speaking at the iron grate where monks could speak to denizens of the outside world, and the monks told him that she had been there. Some disliked her; many wished More could see her and give them an opinion.

So back he went when she came there again, and the two of them sat talking alone in a little chapel. There he told her that he was not interested in her revelations but that he was attracted by the stories of her virtues and wished her to pray for him and his family. She replied with commendable humility and told More that she would indeed pray for him, "whereof I heartily thanked her."

One part of this interview is especially interesting. More told her that a certain "Helen" who had gone into trances and in them spoken "revelations" had been to see him recently. Helen told him that she had been advised by the Nun that her revelations were not from God but were rather delusions of the devil. Helen believed the Nun; the trances and the revelations departed, leaving her in peace.

After hearing More out, the Nun entered upon a humble discussion of how people should test the spirits to see if they were of God. More was pleased with the care and reverence of her words. She told him of a satanic visitation in the form of a bird that she herself had experienced. He did not say that he doubted her. They did not discuss the king. More gave her a double ducat, a gold coin from Venice, a handsome though not extravagant gift, and then went home.

Later he heard that many "right worshipful folks," both men and women, were gathering around her, and he wrote her a careful letter to be sure they were agreed on what had passed between them. He included a copy in his letter to Cromwell. In it he granted that God had done some wonderful things in the Nun, although he did not say what they were. He thought that God did sometimes visit people to bestow special revelations, but he recalled pointedly that he and she had never spoken of the king's affairs. He gave her a gentle warning: the late Duke of Buckingham had been led to his doom by the supposed revelations of one reported to have been a "holy monk." More advised her to recall that grim example and not to speak of the affairs of princes. Rather she should talk only of those common things profitable to the souls of great and small.

She had thanked More's servant for the letter. Afterwards, two Charter-house monks came to see More and spent a long time praising her virtues. But, More wrote Cromwell, they did not speak of her revelations. Still later, one of these monks returned to tell More how the Nun had saved a despairing man from suicide. At another time when he again visited the monastery of Sion, the monks asked him what he thought of her. He praised her virtues cautiously, saying he would speak no ill of her unless she were proved wicked.

His argument to Cromwell was that he had played the part of a circumspect Christian man willing to believe good about people until they should be proved evil. He made the point several times that others besides himself had been taken in by her pretensions to virtue. When he had heard her confession at St. Paul's Cross, More sent a servant to inform the proctor of the Charterhouse monastery that she was now proved a hypocrite. The proctor at first refused to believe it, and for More this incredulity had important implications. More could scarcely imagine anyone of greater holiness than the proctor of the Charterhouse, and if that man had been deceived by the Nun, how much likelier it was that others would also be deluded. But Cromwell and the others investigating the case carried no brief for proctors of any monastery, and the affair of the Nun of Kent became one of the stepping-stones toward the suppression of the monasteries that began in the year after More's death.

Most striking is More's great interest in the Nun throughout—we might even call it fascination. He knew the miraculous stories told about her. He visited monks on several occasions to speak about her. He entertained her friends in his house and listened to at least one of them talk the night away. He spoke to her privately. He gave her money. He wrote her a reverent though cautionary letter. He always admitted that he had been genuinely impressed with her piety until her public confession made faith in her impossible.

Always he was too circumspect to let her or her friends talk with him about any revelations concerning the king. But he must have known their general shape. He was probably trying to decide if they might be true. He was cautious. He told Father Rich that the miracle stories told about the Nun were not something good Christians had to believe merely because the stories were told. More said he had advised Father Rich not to wed himself to belief in the Nun's miracles, for if afterwards they were proved false, the friar's reputation as a preacher might be diminished, "whereof might flow great loss."

There is a seeming contradiction here. More said that Rich had not related any of the Nun's miracle stories to him and that if Rich had done so, More would have thought less of them both. Yet we have advice given to Rich as if More was aware that indeed the friar knew and believed the stories and told other people about them. A great skepticism about the Nun's miracles pervaded More's remarks to Rich in his account of their talk, and More wants Cromwell to know that that skepticism was always there.

Still, More believed that God lived in the world and continually worked miracles. That had been one of the major contentions in his polemical works against the Protestants. The account of the Nun's deceits gathered by one of Cromwell's agents reads like a tale from *The Golden Legend* or a catalogue description of the panels in a stained-glass window from the high Middle Ages. We can almost see the stylized Gothic scenes with stiff human figures bent in ritual attentiveness to a divine drama. An angel commanded the Nun to warn Wolsey of his impending fall. When he died, she saw devils contending for his soul. She brought him at last from purgatory to paradise by the strength of her penance on his behalf. Two renegade monks were on their way to join William Tyndale, but she kept their ship in harbor by the power of her prayers. And so it goes. A devout man, hearing these tales before they became evidence in a treason case, might easily wonder if the world of legend and stained glass might have come to reality in the present as it had so often in a marvelous past that still inspired the present with devotion. A man might yearn that it might be so.

More always believed that only the virtuous could claim divine inspiration. The fathers of the church and the saints certified their doctrines by the goodness of their lives, and when they told miracle stories, their sanctity was proof of their word. The corollary to this view was that heretics were always wicked, but the view itself is the heart of the matter—that goodness alone verifies the instance of the supernatural. It may very well have been that More took such an interest in the Nun's virtues because if he could believe in her saintliness, he would then have no trouble believing in her inspiration. But he could never quite manage to trust her that far.

There is irony and pathos in all this. Here is a man who ardently professed his faith in miracles done every day in the Catholic Church, a man who declared his faith in apparitions sent from God, a man who retold the ancient, magical tales of the saints and their wonders, now hearing reports of a miracle worker, revered by good and great men like John Fisher, saying things that Thomas More wanted to believe. It was a terrible time for him and his church, and in terrible times God had always spoken to pluck up the faith of his people. The activity of God in the midst of persecution and other tribulations was the central message of *The Golden Legend,* the theme of all the medieval accounts of church history compiled by reverent chroniclers, known almost by heart by Thomas More.

He did his best to prove to his own satisfaction that the Nun was what she claimed to be—and turned away. Something in her gave him pause, and he could not make himself believe her. Modernity was encroaching even here on the resisting but inevitably yielding heart of a medieval man who had absorbed too much of the skepticism of classical culture to believe easily in the miracles he wanted to believe in. He could never summon the credulity that permitted Fisher to accept her and led monks to treat her with awe and hope.

Cromwell had gathered a great deal of evidence implicating More in the affair of the Nun. Cromwell took depositions from the Nun herself and from all those associated with her. The Nun, Friar Rich, and Friar Risby all claimed to have reported revelations to Thomas More. Rich and Risby specifically said that More had listened to prophecies about the king and his reign. Yet another copy of the depositions contains the sentence, seemingly about Rich, "He confesseth that he hath showed other revelations to Sir Thos. More, but none concerning the King, for he would not hear them." It looks very much as if Cromwell did not think he had a case that would stick. His witnesses were undoubtedly frightened out of their minds and willing to confess anything he wanted, but in going over the case again and again with them, he could not find room for More's guilty connivance. One of Cromwell's agents sent in a report of the letter More had written the Nun, this before More sent a copy to Cromwell. The agent could find no harm in it. More's own long letter of explanation agreed with the facts Cromwell had at his disposal.

Yet it was also clear that the Nun and her associates had considered More an important man for their cause, and no one could doubt that if a rebellion did come, the rebels would consider More one of their own whether he wished them to do so or not. He was prominent enough in the realm to require the government to win him over or to break and destroy him.

Already by the summer of 1533 while the Nun was entering upon her travail, various charges had been made against More for supposedly taking bribes during his term of office. Could such bribes be proved, his name among the people would be blackened. Roper tells us that the charges were pressed by Anne Boleyn's father, the Earl of Wiltshire, "for hatred of his religion." More was called before the king's council to answer them, and he acquitted himself handily.

The Nun's case was of far greater consequence than trumped-up charges of bribery, but in Roper's view it was all to the same purpose, to cow More into submission, for "when the King saw that he could by no manner of benefits win him to his side, then, lo, went he about by terrors and threats to drive him thereunto." So More's name was included in the bill of attainder against the Nun, said Roper, "the King presupposing of likelihood that this bill would be to Sir Thomas More so troublous and terrible that it would force him to relent and condescend to his request—wherein his grace was much deceived."

More wanted to defend himself in a face-to-face interview with the king, but Henry refused to grant it. Instead he appeared before members of the royal council in an interrogation that took place a few days before March 7, 1534, when Chapuys mentioned it in a letter to the emperor.

By Roper's account, Thomas Cranmer, Thomas Audeley, Thomas Cromwell, and Thomas Howard, Duke of Norfolk, met with Thomas More. Roper accompanied his father-in-law to this convocation of Thomases, three of them destined for violent judicial death for one reason or another. (Norfolk would escape the scaffold only because Henry died the night before the duke was to be beheaded in 1547.) Roper did not attend the hearing itself, but he received his account of it from More. It was clear that the burden of the examination was not so much the Nun of Kent as More's refusal to approve publicly of the king's divorce and remarriage.

The councillors asked him to sit with them; he said he would stand. They recounted the benefits the king had showered on him, and they recalled all the high authorities that had consented to the divorce, including the Parliament itself. More expressed his gratitude to the king, but he said he had given Henry his opinion on the divorce many times when the king had asked for it and that he had never seen anything to make him change his mind. The arguments went on; More was mild but unyielding.

Someone accused him of provoking the king to write *The Assertion of the Seven Sacraments*, causing Henry "to his dishonor throughout all Christendom to put a sword in the Pope's hands to fight against himself." And they tried to frighten him, probably painting a lurid picture of the death awaiting the Nun of Kent and all those condemned to rope and knife with her. More remained calm. "My lords," he said, "these terrors be arguments for children and not for me." He claimed only to be "a sorter-out and placer of the principal matters" contained in the *Assertio*. Others had urged the king to make much of the pope's power. But More told him, "I must put your highness in remembrance of one thing and that is this: the pope, as your grace knoweth, is a prince as you are, and in league with all other Christian princes. It may hereafter so fall out that your grace and he may vary upon some points of the league, whereupon may grow breach of amity and war between you both. I think it best, therefore, that that place be amended and his authority more slenderly touched." But Henry was adamant, More said, insisting on asserting the pope's power to the uttermost. More reminded him of the Statute of Praemunire, "whereby a good part of the pope's pastoral cure here was pared away." The king shook off this objection too, saying, "Whatsoever impediment be to the contrary, we will set forth that authority to the uttermost. For we received from that See [of Rome] our crown imperial."

The irony here is delicious, and if More spoke as Roper reports, his inquisitors must have sweated. Above all they must have been startled at More's recollection that the king himself had once claimed that he owed his imperial status to the pope—a status which had now become the heart of Henry's claim that since England was an empire, its imperial head owed no allegiance to any other power on earth, including the pope. If a pope had given Henry his crown, the pope could as easily take the crown away, and the excommunication which by then had been published against the king would receive validity from the king's own mouth. Chapuys reported that after this interview the king cut off More's pension; it is easy enough to see why.

Afterwards More and Roper went back upstream to Chelsea, and on the way More was merry. Roper thought the reason for his happiness was that he had got his name removed from the bill of attainder. But when they walked into the garden at home together, Roper asked, "Are you then put out of the Parliament bill?"

More replied, "By my troth, son Roper, I never remembered it."

Roper was astounded. Then why was he merry? "In good faith, I rejoiced, son," More said, "that I had given the devil a foul fall; and that with those lords I had gone so far as without great shame I had never go back again." It is a revealing comment; to More the battle to be fought was not against the king and his councillors; it was rather against his own flesh and his fear of death. He had managed to conquer himself during that interview and to give himself an inner weapon for the war yet to be waged. He could now retreat only at the cost of humiliating himself before these wordly men against whom he had made a valiant stand. It is easy to see in this story the More mentioned so often in this book, the man who played a role on a stage of his own making, always putting himself in a superior position, controlling the passions that usually controlled others. Here he spoke rightly, for a man as conscious of his public image as Thomas More was throughout his life could not now retreat from the role he had cast for himself without marring the play.

That quiet, ironic superiority he felt toward his opponents is illustrated in another story Roper tells with loving rhetorical care. After the interrogation the Duke of Norfolk and More talked about things, and the duke tried to get his old friend to see reason. Said Norfolk, "By the mass, Master More, it is perilous striving with princes. And therefore I would wish you somewhat to incline to the King's pleasure. For by God's body, Master More, the wrath of the Prince is death."

More replied with one of the great lines that Roper gives him: "Is that all, my lord? Then in good faith is there no more difference between your grace and me, but that I shall die today and you tomorrow."

By Roper's account, Henry demanded that More's name be included in the bill. But the Lords resisted through three readings of the bill in their house. His councillors advised the king to concede, Roper says; for if More's name continued in the bill, the Lords might not pass it at all. Henry said he would go to the upper house himself to see the bill through. According to Roper, the councillors threw themselves on their knees and begged the king to do no such thing. If the Lords defeated the bill in his presence, he would be shamed throughout his own land and through all Christendom. So Henry grudgingly relented, and Cromwell, probably relieved, ran into Roper in the Parliament House and told him that More's name was out of the bill. Roper was dining that day in London; fear of his father-in-law's attainder had not paralyzed the routines of his life, and the good news did not cause him to break his appointment. He sent his servant to his wife, Margaret, at Chelsea to carry the word. More's response was sober and resigned: "What is put off is not cast off."

Such is Roper's story, written over two decades after the events he describes, when More's sacrificial sanctity was taken for granted by Catholic Englishmen who could scarcely find any room for terror or misery in their saints. But Roper's jewel of a tale does not quite match the tone of the grateful letter More sent to Cromwell on March 5, probably the very day that he learned that his name had been removed from the bill of attainder. More thanked Cromwell for relieving him from "this woeful heaviness in which mine heart standeth."

This letter also shows just how far More was willing to go to follow Norfolk's advice and to accommodate himself to the king's new marriage. And that was very far indeed.

Here he rehearsed the history of his knowledge of the king's "great matter" from the time in 1527 when Henry first broached it to him as they walked in the gallery at Hampton Court. More said he had given his opinion to the king when the king had sought it—certainly the opinion that Henry's marriage with Catherine was valid. But then More qualified his position:

I never have had against his Grace's marriage any manner demeanor whereby his Highness might have any manner cause or occasion of displeasure toward me, for likewise as I am not he which either can, or whom it could become, to take upon him the determination or decision of such a weighty matter, nor boldly to affirm this thing or that therein, whereof diverse points a great way pass my learning, so am I he that among other his Grace's faithful subjects, his Highness being in possession of his marriage and this noble woman royally anointed Queen, neither murmur at it nor dispute upon it, nor never did nor will, but without any other manner meddling of the matter among his other faithful subjects faithfully pray to God for his Grace and hers both, long to live and well and their noble issue too, in such wise as may be to the pleasure of God, honor and surety to themself, rest, peace, wealth, and profit unto this noble realm.

It is a remarkable concession, given More's known aversion to the divorce. But it is much like the philosophy of allegiance expressed by Cardinal Morton to the Duke of Buckingham in More's *History of King Richard III.* In the rise and fall of princes, God was in charge, although He did some things inscrutable to mortals. Anne had been anointed queen; Henry was "in possession of his marriage" in much the same way that a new king might be said to be in possession of the throne. In those circumstances More could only hope for the best—the best being that king and new queen might live long and well and that their "noble issue," the Princess Elizabeth and any other children God might give them, should do the same. What is lacking is any suggestion that More believed that the marriage to Anne had been just and righteous, or, as one of Cromwell's agents called it, "laudable." As long as that admission was not made, More was in the position of the neutral observer who would simply go on observing if someone attacked Henry's marriage as illegitimate and sought to pull down Henry's throne on account of it. The moralizing of the age was prodigious even if the age itself was less moral than most. Henry and his council had just issued a book denying that Pope Clement VII was a legitimate pontiff because of his bastardy and the numerous sins that he was supposed to have committed—taking the position, in short, that gross immorality robbed a man of his right to office. The natural corollary was that gross immorality in a king was a signal that his throne was for the taking—exactly the justification More assumed in his *History of King Richard III,* a justification that underlay the Tudor claim to the English throne. So Henry and Cromwell were resolved to use any means they could to make him bow.

After his long discussion of the king's "great matter" in this letter of March 5, More went on to a larger theological consideration of the place of the pope in the church. Here we find a steady, clear statement of just how far More would go in appeasing Henry and at what point he would resist.

More could rarely resist an ironic thrust, and he made one at Henry—though in the most respectful and superficially flattering way. He said that at one time he had not been convinced that the papal primacy was instituted by God. But then he read what Henry had written in the *Assertio,* and after arguing with his sovereign against it, he came over to the king's view. After his earlier discussion with the king, he said, he had studied the matter in the fathers of the church, and he concluded that his conscience could not rest should he deny the divine foundation of papal primacy. He could not, in short, accept the reduction of the pope to the status of a mere foreign prince.

Yet we must be careful to avoid reading this utterance in the spirit of modern Catholic students of More who have labored stubbornly under the constraints of the First Vatican Council with its proclamation of papal infallibility—a doctrine to which More never even remotely subscribed. Primacy in the sixteenth century was not absolute sovereignty, and it had nothing to do with infallibility. To say that the papacy was a human invention was to say that the papal office was designed by human minds for the convenience of the church and that those same minds might design some other form of governance that might serve just as well. Cathedrals were sacred places, but the architecture of a cathedral was a human invention, convenient for divine services. God did not decree that His people might worship Him only under Gothic arches, and when other forms proved more convenient, Christians could adopt them on their own without special inspiration.

More claimed that he had once believed in the human origins of the papacy. But given his strong sense of the divinity of tradition, he could scarcely have maintained that belief in harmony with his other thoughts about the Catholic Church. If the papacy had endured as long as it had, God must have set the office in the church, and Christians could not change it on whim; they required some clear, divine instruction. This is vastly different from saying that if the papal office has a divine source, popes themselves can never err; More held that priesthood had a divine source, but he never claimed that priests were always good.

In his polemics against the Protestants, More always held that a living God could change doctrines and practices among His people as He wanted. He had altered the command that His people be circumcised. He had changed the dietary provisions laid down by the Council of Jerusalem recorded in the 15th chapter of the book of Acts. He had modified the formula of baptism. But when God did change things, He used some unmistakable agency to let Christians know that God, not Satan, stood behind the innovation. In his letter to Cromwell, More brought up one of the ways in which Christians had often ascertained true inspiration—convening a general council.

He did not see how it was possible, he told Cromwell, for one part of the church to depart from the whole. Yet a general council might permit such a thing. People all over Europe were clamoring for one. The emperor was urging the pope to summon a general council, and the dispatches of Chapuys and other Spanish diplomats hum with projects for an assembly of the bishops that would settle religious differences by the traditional means the church had used to unify itself in times of great unrest.

So More was writing against a background of intense European discussion, and he said what others were saying—that a general council could make some final and authoritative decision about the place of the pope in the church. In his polemical works, More had steadily maintained that a general council could not err—a claim he never once made for the papacy. A conciliar agreement would give Christians certainty.

He noted that Henry had appealed from the pope to the future general council everybody was talking about. He did not say that such appeals as Henry's had been pronounced anathema by the popes who could not tolerate the notion that any power in the church could be superior to themselves. When Edmund Bonner, Henry's special ambassador, met with the pope when Clement came to Marseilles in November 1533, Bonner announced the appeal, and Clement immediately denounced it as contrary to a decree issued by Pope Pius II in the previous century. But More obviously did not take these papal fulminations as an obstacle to Henry's action. In the general council, he said, this pope might be deposed, and another chosen in his place. He was recalling the Council of Constance early in the fifteenth century, which had deposed three contending popes and elected its own man.

Again it is apparent that to More the papacy was not the major issue; the issue was the unity of the church and how the church heard the voice of God. A fragment of the Catholic Church, splitting itself away from the whole body, could not hear that voice, for a fragment was not party to the revelations of the whole any more than a severed arm shares in the life of the body it has left behind. More said that he had never set forth among the king's subjects any great advancement of the pope's authority, that indeed when he had written about the pope in *The Confutation of Tyndale's Answer* he had suppressed the passage. So Henry had nothing to fear from him and no cause to blame him.

He closed by begging Cromwell to continue to urge the king to be merciful to him. His words were properly humble, and they expressed solemn loyalty. But they also quietly set the limits of More's willingness to please his king: "I nothing have of mine own in all this world, except only my soul, but that I will with better [gladly] forego it than abide of his highness one heavy, displeasant look."

Now came the onslaught that More could not survive. On March 23, 1534, Parliament passed the Act of Succession. It declared Henry's marriage to Catherine null from the beginning and his marriage to Anne lawful matrimony, and it had much to say about marriage in general.

More could see in the wording of the act the civil power usurping dominion over a sacred realm, the sacramental power of the church here represented by matrimony. The intent of the act was clear; the English church was now independent from Rome, subject to absolute rule by Parliament, to the dominion of a secular assembly composed of men who married and handled female genitalia and did worldly business for worldly gain and killed other men in war and made treaties and broke them and lived under the shadow of the prince of this secular world, the devil.

The act expanded the definition of treason to include any attacks on the marriage of Henry and Anne. Mere speaking against the act itself was to be considered only misprision of treason, an offense insufficient to require capital punishment but one that could result in the loss of all possessions and imprisonment at the king's pleasure.

Citizens were to take an oath—not prescribed in the act itself—that they would bear faithful obedience to Henry's heirs by his "most dear and entirely beloved lawful wife Queen Anne" without consideration of any "foreign authority, prince, or potentate," renouncing all oaths previously taken in contradiction to this one. In addition everyone had to swear that "to your cunning, wit, and uttermost of your power, without guile, fraud or other undue means, ye shall observe, keep, maintain, and defend this Act and all the whole contents and effects thereof, and all other Acts and Statutes made since the beginning of this present parliament."

The mere acceptance of the marriage as an accomplished fact, an acceptance More had offered Cromwell early in the month, was now declared legally unacceptable. Englishmen were required to love the marriage with all their hearts and souls and to defend it with their lives and to seal their affection with an oath. Anyone swearing the oath also pronounced himself in wholehearted agreement not only with the sentiments of the act but also with all the other acts of Parliament passed since 1529, including the recognition of Henry as Supreme Head of the church in England as declared in the Acts of Appeals and Dispensations. More was left no legal hiding place.

Almost immediately the English people were subjected to a swarm of commissioners buzzing through the country to administer the oath to everyone they could find. Stephen Gardiner took a census that recorded every male over the age of fourteen in his diocese. He wrote Henry asking if women should be sworn, too. Apparently women were spared for the most part. But on April 22 Chapuys wrote of one of Princess Mary's chambermaids who was shut up in a room of the house and compelled to swear. The ambassadors from Scotland, Chapuys wrote, "laugh at the king, and not without reason, for his presuming that oaths violently obtained from his people can make his quarrel good and ensure obedience; whereas on the contrary, it only proves that laws and ordinances that require being sworn to are no good at all. This is the way in which people talk privately among themselves of the king's measures."

Nevertheless, the swearings went on. Important men were called in by special appointment to take the oath, and on Sunday evening, April 12, More's turn came. He was at his old home in Bucklersbury, visiting John Clement, by now the most celebrated physician in the realm, and Clement's wife, Margaret Giggs, whom More treated like a daughter. An officer of the court served notice on him that he was summoned to take the oath the next day at Lambeth Palace.

More went home to spend the last night he would ever pass in Chelsea. As he did before any important matter, Roper says, he went to the little church and confessed his sins and heard the mass and took communion. Early in the morning he did the same again. Always before, Roper says, when More was going away, he brought his wife and children down to the boat to kiss them all and to bid them farewell.

On this morning he left them behind at the house and closed the gate on them and with Roper took the boat toward the city. He sat gloomily for a time as the river slipped by, and then abruptly he whispered in Roper's ear, "Son Roper, I thank our Lord the field is won." Roper did not know what he meant, and so he said, "Sir, I am thereof very glad." Later, Roper says, "as I conjectured afterwards, it was for that the love he had to God wrought in him so effectually that it conquered all his carnal affections utterly." At Lambeth, where the commissioners were waiting, Roper left his father-in-law. They never spoke to each other again.

28

MORE IN PRISON

M ORE WAS the only layman called to Lambeth that day; the others were priests. Later he wrote from the Tower an account of what had happened and sent it to Margaret.

While he waited, several others were summoned into the room where the commissioners sat. Presiding was Audeley, now officially Lord Chancellor. At last More's turn came, and he was asked if he would swear the oath. He asked to see it; the commissioners showed it to him, sealed with the Great Seal of the Realm, which he could not fail to recognize. He asked to see the Act of Succession; they gave him a printed copy, and he read it in silence. When he was done, he told them that he would not impugn the conscience of anyone who had made the act or of anyone who might swear the oath, but his own conscience would not let him swear.

He declared himself ready at once to swear to the succession itself as the act decreed it; a succession was only a temporal matter, and time and again Parliament had ordered this or that succession according to its will. But the government had decided to require everyone in the realm to swear to the same form of the oath. Audeley expressed sorrow at More's answer and tried to change his mind. More was the very first who had refused the oath, Audeley said; the king was bound to be angry. More was unyielding but courteous. In a little while he was commanded to go down into the garden.

More did not go all the way down, "on account of the heat"—a surprising comment for early April in London. Perhaps his real reason for not descending was that the garden below swarmed with men who had sworn the oath, and More did not want to be in their company. He stayed instead "in the old burned chamber that looketh in to the garden" and there watched what went on below.

He saw Hugh Latimer come in with several chaplains who served Cranmer. Latimer, a vehement preacher, a supporter of the divorce, and a great favorite with the king, before whom he regularly spoke, had already been forced to recant some Lutheran views. He would shortly return wholeheartedly to heresy, and under Queen Mary he would burn, as would Cranmer and many another brought high by fortune in the time when More was being brought low. On that Monday morning as More watched, Latimer was laughing with the chaplains and embraced one or two around the neck so warmly that, says More, "if they had been women, I would have thought he had waxen wanton." Dr. Nicholas Wilson was led through on his way to the Tower. Wilson was a dear friend of More's, and he had been both chaplain and confessor to the king. He refused the oath and remained in the Tower until 1537, when he surrendered under the burdens of long imprisonment and the importunities of victorious authority and made his peace with the new order. His relative obscurity protected him—just as More's high visibility in the realm exposed him to lethal danger.

Later that day More heard that John Fisher had been brought before the commissioners, but he did not know what had happened to him. (Fisher had escaped imprisonment during the affair of the Nun of Kent only by paying a fine of three hundred pounds.) More was left, apparently for some little time, watching the raucous good fellowship of those below him until they had "played out their pageant," as he called it, implying that it was something done for his benefit. They departed like players leaving a stage, and he was called in again.

Again he refused the oath. The commissioners accused him of obstinance. Why did he not swear? He would not say. Under steady questioning he said that if the king would grant him immunity from prosecution, he would put his reasons in writing. The immunity was denied. More made the legal point that was finally to be written into the Fifth Amendment of the United States Constitution: "If I may not declare the causes without peril, then to leave them undeclared is no obstinancy."

Cranmer thought he saw a handle. If More would not swear the oath but would not condemn those who did, he must admit that the matter was dubious and uncertain. In such circumstances, Cranmer said, taking the line to be so exquisitely developed by modern dictatorships, More must submit his conscience to the king and let the king decide. More expressed his amazement to Margaret that such an argument could come from anyone reputed so wise, and he treated it with heavy, ironic contempt. If we took Cranmer's way, he said, "then have we a ready way to avoid all perplexities. For in whatsoever matters the doctors stand in great doubt, the king's commandment given on whither side he list solves all the doubts."

William Benson, abbot of Westminster, suggested another approach. More must surely think himself in error when he saw Parliament, the great council of the realm, take a side different from his own. More replied that if indeed he had been utterly alone, he would have been afraid to lean on his own mind against so many. But he was not alone, he said, for he had on his side "as great a council and greater to, . . . the general council of Christendom." He meant that he stood in the venerable and unbroken tradition of the Catholic Church and that Parliament could not command him against that sacrosanct council.

Cromwell was exasperated. He swore a great oath and said he would rather have his own son lose his head than that More should refuse the oath. Now the king would surely suppose that More had incited the Nun of Kent—whose fiendish execution would take place in little over a week. More remained calm —and firm. The interview closed with him again stating his willingness to swear to the succession but not to the entire act as it had been framed by Parliament. He was willing to leave every man to his own conscience, he said. "And me thinketh in good faith, that so were it good reason that every man should leave me to mine."

When Dr. Nicholas Wilson refused the oath, he was hurried directly to imprisonment in the Tower—perhaps as an example to More, who watched him being led through the garden a prisoner. But apparently the government did not feel secure enough to be so peremptory with a former Lord Chancellor —especially one with More's standing among the people. For four days he was left in the custody of the abbot of Westminster while the council pondered what to do next.

Cranmer was on the side of compromise. He did not know, he said, why both More and Fisher refused to swear the oath. It was either because the oath diminished the authority of the pope or because it approved the divorce. But he noted that both of them were willing to swear to the succession if they did not have to accept the "preamble" to the act—the long introduction that declared Henry's marriage to Catherine null and against the laws of God, his marriage to Anne sacred, and marriage itself subject to the laws of the secular order. Cranmer thought that if More and Fisher would swear to uphold the succession against all foreign potentates much good would come. The emperor's mouth would be stopped; Catherine and her daughter Mary would be satisfied that they would not damn their souls by abandoning their former status. For such men as Thomas More to admit that the succession "is good and according to God's laws" would quiet the realm. If the king chose, he could keep secret the form of the oath that More and Fisher took. Presumably Cranmer supposed that people might then think that Fisher and More had sworn to the whole act. It is what we might expect of the archbishop who had become primate of England by swearing a secret oath that his public oath would not bind his conscience.

It is hard to think that More would have allowed such secrecy. But he had no chance to decide. Cranmer sent his opinions on to Cromwell; Cromwell showed them to Henry, and Henry refused any compromise. If More and Fisher swore to the act and not the preamble, this might be taken by the people as confirmation of the authority of the pope, and that Henry and Cromwell could not allow. Roper says that the king and council might have accepted More's offer to swear to the succession alone except that "Queen Anne by her importunate clamor" insisted that the entire oath be administered to the man she now regarded as an enemy.

So on April 17, More was committed to the Tower. Roper says that More was wearing a chain of gold around his neck—probably the same one we see in the Holbein portrait, since (contrary to common opinion) that chain was not an official symbol of office. Sir Richard Cromwell, Thomas's nephew, was charged with conveying More to prison. In the thrifty way of the Cromwells, he advised More to send the chain home to his wife and children. But the More of stage and drama was still alive and well. "Nay, sir," he said, "that I will not; for if I were taken in the field by my enemies, I would they should somewhat fare the better by me." Here was the knight of chivalry—that More usually professed to despise—going forth in full armor to surrender to his foes, showing the world that though he might be captured, he was not yet conquered.

At the landing to the Tower itself, More's courage slackened; at least he made an uncharacteristically feeble joke. The porter demanded his "upper garment" as a fee—a commonplace in a day when the world turned on fees and when condemned men on the scaffold gave their executioners a tip for their services. More took off his cap as his "upper garment" and offered it, saying, "I am very sorry that it is no better for you." The porter was not amused. "No, sir," said this humorless and grasping functionary. "I must have your gown."

His confinement was not solitary. His servant, John a Wood, an illiterate, was allowed to stay with him. Wood had to swear to the Lieutenant of the Tower that he would report any treasonable utterance More might make. More had his books and writing materials; his spirits seem to have risen.

Roper tells us that after about a month, Margaret was allowed to visit her father. The two of them said the seven penitential Psalms together and chanted the litany, and after these ritual devotions, they talked. Margaret commiserated with her father for his woes, but he was in no mood to be pitied. "I believe, Meg, that they that have put me here think they have done me a high displeasure. But I assure thee on my faith, my own good daughter, if it had not been for my wife and you that be my children, whom I account the chief part of my charge, I would not have failed long before this to have closed myself in as strait a room and straiter, too."

The sentiment goes a long way toward explaining the resignation and fundamental peace of mind we find in More during his confinement. Here was the deeply devout but divided man who had wrestled with the choice between priesthood and matrimony, the man of hair shirt and flagellation and with the lifelong thirst for the monastic life, now given the desire of his heart by a government that sought to punish him and ended by blessing him. He was dedicated to his responsibilities; the care of wife and children was a penalty God exacted from men who chose matrimony; his reflections now, as Roper reports them, are full of relief and almost of religious ecstasy. He had had to leave his family through no fault of his own; God will surely "supply my lack among you," he said. So he found himself in a blissful state, telling Margaret, "For me thinketh God maketh me a pet and setteth me in his lap and caresses me." The man driven by time now had time enough; the man perplexed by multitudes of choices now had no choices left.

Sometime after More was in the Tower, Margaret wrote him urging him to take the oath. Her letter has not survived; it was not something that would be preserved by the family of a saint, a family that wanted to be worthy of his sanctity. The editors of the 1557 edition of More's English works preserved More's reply, and they appended a preface to it, explaining that Margaret did not really mean to persuade her father to swear the oath but that she wrote only to gain the confidence of Thomas Cromwell, who would naturally have read all letters going in and out of the cell of so important a prisoner. We cannot know if the devout Catholic editors of this edition of 1557 truly represented Margaret's motives. She did swear the oath, as did all the rest of More's family, including Roper. She adored her father; she most certainly wanted him to live; she probably would have been relieved for many reasons had he followed her example.

More replied with a letter that seems written for the eyes of Cromwell, the council, and the king. He steadfastly declined to give his reasons for refusing the oath—even to his most beloved child. He asserted his loyalty to the king. And he uttered a cry from the heart. He did not fear his own death, he said; the fear of death was assuaged in him increasingly by the fear of hell, the hope of heaven, and the passion of Christ. His worst fear was that by refusing the oath, he placed "my own good son your husband, and you my good daughter, and my good wife, and mine other good children and innocent friends, in great displeasure and danger of great harm thereby." But he could do nothing other than to commit them all to God and to the king's mercy.

Margaret's reply made no mention of the king; she spoke tenderly of her father's good life and of the life to come and of her fervent hope that all of them would meet together "in the bliss of heaven." The letter is sincerely loving and devout, but it is also an effort to show Henry and the council that More would, if left alone, devote himself entirely to saving his own soul and that he would take no part in worldly affairs, especially not in the affair of his prince's marriage. This was the strategy adopted by More in his own letters from prison and in his earlier letters to Erasmus—including the one that contained his epitaph. Margaret fell into this strategy naturally and pursued it until the last.

But the government was unyielding. In March 1534, Clement VII had finally ruled that Henry's marriage to Catherine was valid. Among the cardinals who argued the queen's case was Lorenzo Campeggio. The news arrived in London a few days before More was summoned to swear the oath; it may have been a reason for the timing of the summons itself, since Henry often lashed out when he received bad news. A few days later Henry launched his formal appeal to a higher authority than the pope—to a general council, an appeal unofficially announced months earlier. He alleged that scripture gave no greater jurisdiction to the bishop of Rome than to other bishops and that the Roman primacy had been sustained by the ignorant people and by the blindness of princes. The people should be taught that they should no longer see the pope as an idol but only as a man and a wicked man at that—a man who exemplified Christ neither in his life nor in his learning and who besides was a bastard who had bought the papal office. The document was inscribed by Cuthbert Tunstall, in London for the Parliament. Chapuys got word to Princess Mary of the pope's decree and reported that she had written that "she had received more pleasure at the news than if I had presented her with a million of gold."

Henry put on a good front when he got the news, Chapuys reported, but the ambassador wrote also, "He is very far from being pleased and seems agitated and thoughtful." The king had ordered the preachers of the realm "to pour down on the pope as many invectives as they possibly could" in their Easter sermons of Sunday, April 5. They had done so, "pouring forth the most strange and horrible abominations that could be imagined." Yet the queen was jubilant, and Chapuys awaited her thoughts on how the papal command for Henry to take back his lawful wife might be executed. Obviously Henry was not in a mood to be lenient with any of Catherine's English supporters whom he had in his grasp.

In August, Thomas Audeley went hunting on the estate of Sir Gyles Alington. Sir Gyles's wife, Alice, was the daughter of Alice Middleton More by her first marriage, and she loyally considered More her father. The day after Audeley killed his deer, he sent for young Dame Alice; she begged him to be, as he had been in the past, "still good lord unto my father."

Audeley told her that he had been willing to help More during the affair of the Nun of Kent but now he could only marvel that More was so obstinate in his own opinion, an opinion, Audeley said, that was shared only by Fisher, "the blind bishop." Audeley gloried in his own ignorance that kept him from putting his opinion above that of his prince. "I am very glad that I have no learning but in a few of Aesop's fables," he said, and then he told the one that we mentioned earlier. It was the story—not truly from Aesop—of the wise men who learned that a rain would fall that would make mad anyone that it wet. The men took refuge in a cave, thinking to become rulers of the madmen when the rain had passed. But the fools would not be ruled, and when they saw their own futility, the wise men wished that they had been wet along with the rest. It was a morally cynical, thoroughly Tudor attitude: the world was moving; it made no sense to argue whether the movement was good or bad; the best anyone could do was to move with it.

Audeley was so pleased with this fable that he told another, this one intended to illustrate the futility of a scrupulous conscience like More's in a world where the conscience of most bent to the needs of the moment. (It happened to be a tale later picked up by La Fontaine, who told it much better than Audeley did—as we might expect.)

A lion, an ass, and a wolf went to confession. The lion confessed that he ate every beast he could; the confessor forthwith granted him absolution because the lion was a king and also because it was his nature to eat all the other beasts. The poor ass confessed that he was so hungry he ate some straw out of his master's shoe and made his master take cold. This great sin the confessor could not forgive and he sent the ass to the bishop for punishment. The wolf confessed his gluttony, and as penance the confessor forbade him to eat any meal worth more than six pence. But this diet was not enough. One day the hungry wolf saw a cow and her calf, but he recalled that he was bound by his spiritual father. Still, he said, he would follow his conscience; thereupon he valued the cow at four pence and the calf at two and ate them both.

The fables needed no interpretation as far as More was concerned. Alice Alington wrote a sorrowing account of her interview with Audeley and sent it to Margaret More Roper. If Margaret's earlier letter asking her father to take the oath had been intended to win Cromwell's confidence, it may have done the trick. For whatever reason, she was allowed to see More, and she showed him Alice's letter. Afterwards she replied to it with a long letter in her own name that bears all the marks of a joint effort, something that she and her father carefully worked out together.

She spoke of her father's bad health—pain in the chest and cramps in his legs at night, symptoms that tend to confirm the supposition that More had a bad heart and the bad circulation that goes with some forms of heart disease. She also said that he suffered from the stone—though she does not tell us if he prayed to St. Valéry for relief.

But most of the letter is a dialogue, worthy of Plato, between Margaret and her father on the great issue in More's case, the authority of conscience. When should a man follow conscience to the death? When should he yield his conscience to a higher authority, and what should that authority be? Behind the wit, the anecdotes, the elegance, and the sober resolution of this letter looms the driving necessity some people felt in a confusing time to find an unimpeachable authority that would lead their steps aright in the dark.

Margaret took the side of Audeley and the government. How could More set his private opinion against the great majority of Englishmen who had sworn the oath? Did he not endanger his soul by his obstinacy before such general testimony? (By espousing the government's side, at least for the purposes of this letter, Margaret may have been ensuring her own safety—at her father's instigation.)

More's answer was studied and careful despite its occasional banter and humorous digressions. He refused again to tell anybody why he would not swear the oath; only the king knew his reasons, and he would not tell them to anyone else unless the king commanded him to do so. He offered only the tantalizing information that his refusal was "for more causes than one." He jokingly called Margaret "Mistress Eve" for trying to tempt him to renounce his conscience. And he steadfastly refused to condemn anyone who had sworn the oath claiming that their consciences made them swear. He could not think that these people had bent their opinions only to keep the prince's pleasure and avoid his wrath or out of fear of losing their worldly possessions or because they feared the discomfort of their kindred and their friends, he said. He would not imagine such things, he said with an irony as heavy as concrete, for "I have better hope of their goodness than to think of them so."

In the end we are all to be judged by how well we follow our own conscience. If a man swears to something he does not believe merely because other men in perfectly good conscience have sworn that thing, they may go to heaven for following their consciences, and he may go to hell for not truly following his own.

Many things through the ages have been subject to honest dispute. He recalled the long debate in the church over the conception of the Virgin Mary. Was she conceived in original sin or not? St. Bernard, who otherwise adored the Virgin, said she was born in sin like the rest of us; St. Anselm held the opposite view, that she was born without taint of human guilt. And yet both Bernard and Anselm were saints in heaven.

Such disputes were possible only until a general council made a ruling on the issue. After the council spoke, Christians were bound to make their consciences conform to its decrees or else be eternally damned. Nor could a man stand on his own conscience against "a general faith grown by the working of God universally through all Christian nations." Here we have his habitual devotion to the "common consent" that he had extolled through all his polemical works, the faith inspired in the church by the secret and mysterious but unmistakable working of God.

The "law of the land" was not the same as a conciliar decision by the church; secular law was not infallible, though people living under it were bound to keep it lest they incur some temporal and perhaps some divine punishment. Still, no one was bound to swear that every law is well made and no one was bound to observe any part of the law of the land that was against the law of God. As for Margaret's argument that so many good men had sworn the oath that More should swear it, too, he replied that he was quite sure that a far greater number of Christians living and dead favored his own position than its opposite, and he implied, too, that a far greater number of people in England agreed with him than disagreed—an opinion fully shared by Eustace Chapuys—even among those who had sworn the oath.

We do not know who read this letter beyond More's immediate family, though we may suppose that he would not have written anything himself or have allowed his daughter to write anything that he did not expect Cromwell and the rest of the council to see. For all its humility of language and praise of the king, the letter vibrates with an iron resolution and a protest. More might be silent with respect to his precise reasons for refusing the oath, but it was clear enough that he thought Henry was tearing the seamless garment of Christ and that the wrong being done by the king and his henchmen was obvious enough for any true Christian to recognize. As in everything More did in these times, the government could not fail to see in this letter a resistance that must be crushed if the new regime were to be secure.

Some things are touching. It is here that More mentions that he has often lain awake at night while his wife slept and supposed that he slept, too, thinking of all the harm that might come to him for refusing to follow his king. Nothing could be done to him, he said, that was as bad as what he had imagined, and so he was sure that he could bear the worst. We are face to face again with More's imagination and sense of exquisite detail that here fixed on the possibilities of pain. Those gifted or cursed with similar imaginations today may well imagine the horror of darkness that crouched over him during his long and insomniac nights. Yet having freely confessed his fear as though to exorcise it, he says also that fear would never be a sufficient reason to make him change his mind when his conscience dictated the course he must take.

Margaret tried one last tactic to get him to come over. Since, she said, the example of so many wise men did not move him, she would offer a reason that Master Henry Patenson had given. She had run into him and he had inquired after his former master; he had been angered to learn that More was in the Tower for not swearing the oath. "Why, what ails him that he will not swear?" Patenson said. "Why should he stick at swearing? I have sworn the oath myself." Margaret said she could do no other than to say the same to her father, "for I have sworn myself." She does not say what readers in the family would have known, that Henry Patenson had been her father's imbecile fool.

More's reply was in keeping with his conviction that women were inferior to men and that not so much was required of them. Laughing, he said, "That word was like Eve, too, for she offered Adam no worse fruit than she had eaten herself."

But was not Eve damned because she ate? We may explain many things about More's martyrdom, what it was and what it was not. Yet a certain insoluble mystery hangs over it, a mystery that baffled his contemporaries and confuses moderns, a mystery that rises from this long letter. What kind of martyr is it who will not make a strong, clear statement of the reasons for his martyrdom? His entire family swore the oath that he would not swear because he thought it would damn his soul. He did not reproach anyone in his family for what they all did. In his view of the world, fathers were supposed to be instructors in virtue to their households. Yet More refused to instruct his family about the oath. We may take his own statements at face value, of course— that he feared the harm that might come to them because of his refusal—and we may extrapolate from that love for them an unwillingness to see them suffer in any way, and perhaps infer a sentiment much like that of medieval monks who imagined that they helped redeem all society by their own solitary pains and penance; he may have hoped that he was redeeming all his family by his own steadfast resolution unto death.

He spoke much of conscience, refusing to condemn anyone who claimed good conscience as a rationale for action. Yet we have noted in this letter the biting irony with which he discusses the "conscience" of all those who found good reasons to bow to the king's will. He would not, of course, suppose that his own family circle had sworn the oath simply out of fear. We may conjecture that one reason for his silence was to spare the consciences of his dearly beloved. If they swore the oath in genuine ignorance of its true meaning, they could be saved in heaven; if he told them why the oath was damnable and why he refused to swear it, they would be informed, no longer saved by what Catholics would later call "invincible ignorance," and not able to claim a clear conscience before God. So his silence might, in his mind, have kept his children and his wife and all the rest of his household from hell. He may also have remained silent in the hope that Henry VIII might yet relent and spare his life if he did not go so far in offending the king that no mercy would be possible.

But even if we take all these rationalizations together, they somehow do not quite add up to a sufficient explanation for More's martyrdom. We have throughout this book explored More's conception of the church and joined it with the traditional Catholic conviction that the church must be independent if it was to be inspired. Refusing the oath, standing in the shadow of death, confronting martyrdom, More might be expected to be clear and uncompromising about these essential assumptions and to announce that they were the reasons he did what he did. Yet he did not. John Fisher believed in an infallible papacy that was the essence of the church, and he spelled out his doctrines whenever he had the opportunity. More did not share these views, and although he had other views about ecclesiastical liberty that we have discussed often, he did not express them when they might have done the most good, giving to the English people a rationale for his ordeal.

It is perhaps not too much to speculate that once he had refused the oath and been confined to the Tower, More became locked in an inner world of his own, a world where he atoned for his early decision to marry and to forsake priesthood, a world where he endured on earth part of the purgatory that a secular man like himself must expect after death, a world where private struggle so filled his being that he had no room for the struggle and fate of others who now, he thought, in the intense psychic freedom from care given him by his captivity, could be left to God.

Though More remained in prison, he did not stop writing. (Of course, it was no longer possible to publish.) Before he was shut in the Tower he had begun a work commonly called the *Treatise on the Passion*, and he may have finished it before he was locked up. Still, it is usually included in what are called the "Tower works."

The passion of Christ was a familiar theme of mystics who, in telling of the sufferings of Christ, were brought into an emotional unity with God. To More, for whom mystical ecstasy was an alien or at least an uncommon experience, a recital of the agony of the Savior brought God into human life and gave meaning to the suffering and death of moral men whose earthly existence Christ had assumed so that he might take them up to himself. The repetition of this sacred and familiar story of the passion was a kind of liturgy that created a reverent spirit and a willingness to forsake the earthly world in favor of the bliss of eternity, Christ's dwelling and one worth sacrificing everything to obtain.

The *Treatise on the Passion* is formally incomplete since it ends with the institution of the mass and does not pass on to describe the events of the day Christ died. The mass was to More, as to most Catholics, the heart of worship. In describing how it was begun by Christ, he could not resist attacking the heretics who persistently and—to his mind—maliciously assaulted the orthodox teaching of transubstantiation. He became so exercised on the sacrament of the altar that he wrote a short work commonly called *A Treatise to Receive the Blessed Body of Our Lord* and appended it to the *Treatise on the Passion*. Here he tried to show the proper spirit Christians should have when they took communion.

By far the greatest of More's Tower works and, to some, the finest thing he

ever wrote was *A Dialogue of Comfort Against Tribulation*. Like many of
More's other works, the *Dialogue of Comfort* turns on a fiction, that of two
men in Hungary about a year after Suleiman the Magnificent and his grand
army of Turks had ridden down and massacred a Hungarian army at Mohács
on the Danubian plain near Buda. Antony is an old man, sick, perhaps soon
to be a prisoner of the Turks, facing death or at least long exile and imprisonment—the choices More seemed to have when he wrote. Vincent is his young
cousin who comes to visit him in prison.

Most of the *Dialogue of Comfort* was probably written in 1534, and
throughout that year More and his family were doing their utmost to seek his
release from the Tower. The tone of Antony's utterances, however, is that of
a man preparing to die. There is a customary manner of "unchristian comforting," he says early in the book, that encourages the sick man to seek to get
better and to have life again. But real comfort is to urge all people, the sick
and the well, to ponder the four last things—death, judgment, heaven, and
hell. Then men will seek God and heaven and will be prepared to give this life
up in preference for the life to come.

The *Dialogue of Comfort* rambles gently from topic to topic like a boat
afloat on a placid sea and moved by soft waves. Throughout it manifests the
spirit of calm resignation that marks its opening pages. A week after More was
put in the Tower, the Nun of Kent and her cohorts were methodically butchered at Tyburn, and the authorities must have hastened to inform him of her
bloody fate. Were he to be convicted of treason, he might be subjected to the
same horrors, and much in the *Dialogue of Comfort* deals with the conquest
of fear. Yet we find no panic; rather we find serenity and composure, and the
Dialogue of Comfort is throughout the work of a man bringing the end of his
life into an unwavering harmony with the rest of it.

It may seem ironic that so much of More's consolation lies in his serene
confidence that God has His own purposes and that Christians must yield
themselves to those purposes in trust and hope. Such was the heart of Luther's
gospel, of "predestination," which More relentlessly damned in all his polemical works. But in the midst of his own tribulation he found peace in the faith
that God was directing all things to some end, a peace much like that Luther
found in the same confidence. For the Christian, God's purposes are always
good, though they may not seem so when we must suffer to fulfill them. We
may pray to God to do some things for us, Antony said. We may pray for food
and health, for deliverance from evil and for the salvation of our souls. But in
all mundane things we must leave everything to His "high wisdom" that better
sees what is best for us than we can see for ourselves. No one should commit
sin with the expectation that God will forgive, Antony said, "for grace comes
but at God's will," and those who sin presumptuously may discover that grace
is not offered to them in their hour of need. It all sounds very much like

Luther's pronouncements about predestination, although Luther's tone was much more strident and his declarations more paradoxical. But at heart both More and Luther found comfort in the same faith: the world is dark and confused, and the righteous suffer; there has to be a reason for these tribulations; that reason is to be found in the grand design that God is working out for the world. The doctrine of predestination does not tell us what the design is or how we fit into it; but it affirms that a design is there and that what we perceive as meaningless is really full of purpose, that the darkness we see is really light to God.

More describes some of the many tribulations that afflict humankind, and here he shows again a penchant for concrete detail and psychological insight, a talent so vivid in *The History of King Richard III* and so absent from *Utopia*. He describes the terrors of the imagination that torment some dying men who despair when they think of hell or worry about what will happen to their worldly goods when they are dead. Antony says, "Some have I seen even in their last sickness, sit up in their deathbed underpropped with pillows, take their playfellows to them, and comfort themselves with cards. And this they said did ease them well to put fantasies out of their head." To More, with his hatred of idle games, such conduct at the gateway to eternity was appalling. Antony says that he had seen such men play until death took them away. "And what game they came to, that God knows and not I. I pray God it were good. But I fear it very sore."

Among the worst tribulations is the temptation to suicide, treated here by More at some length. Antony spins out some chilling yarns, perhaps drawn from More's experience as an officer of the law. We hear of the shrewish wife of a carpenter, a woman who sought to anger her husband out of pure malice, hoping that he would kill her and be hanged for murder. She nagged him unmercifully. He bore it patiently until one day when he was flattening the side of a timber with his hatchet she reviled him until she indeed made him angry at her. His anger fueled her own. In a frenzy she laid her head on the timber and called him "whoreson" and dared him to chop off her head. So he did it —with a single stroke. (Antony relates that people nearby said they heard her tongue babble "whoreson! whoreson!" twice after the head was severed from the body.) Antony says the king recognized how much the man had been provoked and pardoned him.

The aim of this and other stories is to show that Satan is the source of suicidal thoughts and that the fundamental human motives for suicide are either malice or cowardice.

We wonder if More included this long rumination on suicide because he thought of suicide himself. The streak of melancholy that we have observed throughout in his character would have been an easy vehicle for such thoughts. Suicide was common in the classical world, and to many then as now to kill oneself in some circumstances was an honorable deed. In his *Utopia* More imagined a society where suicide was considered the praiseworthy way out of incurable illness, and those who killed themselves to avoid painful suffering and to free their neighbors from caring for them were highly esteemed. More's preoccupation with the supposed suicide of Richard Hunne and his certainty that Hunne had indeed killed himself may also give us pause. By the time he wrote his *Supplication of Souls* More had no doubt at all that a man in Hunne's hopeless state would hang himself.

In the *Dialogue of Comfort* he set his discussion of suicide within a consideration of one of the great, troublesome issues of the age: how do we tell the difference between divine revelation and demonic delusion? It was the central religious issue of the Nun of Kent affair. In some of More's anecdotes about suicide, people profess to believe that they are being led thither by God Himself. After some wrestling, More came back to the traditional Christian view, that suicide was a mortal sin and that suggestions to the contrary were Satan's wiles.

But even if More could shake off the temptation to hang himself or to leap to his death from a Tower wall, the matter was not simple for him. How do we judge those people who espouse a good cause knowing that it will mean their death? In some sense they can be called suicides, too, since they have a choice between life and death and choose voluntarily the way to death. Does God approve of such deaths or not? Samson came to mind at once in Antony's discussion. He pushed down the pillars of the Philistine temple and made the building collapse on both the Philistines and himself. Did he do good or evil? Was he saved or damned? Antony comments that all men are not certain that Samson was saved, although Antony reasons that he was, since he took his strength from God, and God seemed to inspire the temple's fall. Samson's story allowed Antony to bring up the notion of special revelation—again, one of the issues in the affair of the Nun of Kent. Special revelation could include God's occasional permission for His people to do something usually forbidden. Such revelation was not for everyone, but now and then under extraordinary circumstances, it could come. It was not then to be taken as an abiding rule by other Christians.

An example was the suicide of those virgins mentioned by Augustine who drowned themselves rather than be raped during persecutions. Augustine did not think it lawful for other virgins to follow their example. He did think that these might have been inspired by a special revelation of God.

Mention of those virgins who killed themselves rather than be raped brings us back to Roper's story of More's words to the three bishops who bought him the gown so he could attend Anne Boleyn's coronation. He could be devoured, More said, explaining why he did not go, but he would never be deflowered. Now, in the Tower, he was following a quiet course that would lead him to death, a death he might avoid by the simple expedient of swearing an oath that nearly everyone else of importance in the realm had sworn. Was it legitimate to court death in such a way?

He did not discuss these questions openly, and his long treatment of suicide breaks off somewhat abruptly. But the questions that bear on what he should do are implicit in his circumstances, and it is easy enough to see his dilemma. On the one hand, he could not swear the oath; on the other, he was bound by conscience to do everything possible to save his life short of damning his soul. He never claimed to have a special revelation to be a martyr. Part of the enduring spell More has cast on succeeding generations lies in the human wrestlings he had with death—the hesitations, the terrors, the ruminations about his choice, the final sense of confusion we have observed about just what it was that made him die. He made his choice to lay down his life, not with the bold, unthinking, and superhuman heroism common to legends and epics, but rather with the ordinary doubts and terrors that would afflict most of us in his situation. He is closest to us here, in these feelings of fearsome ambivalence that we all share in dire moments of the human condition.

One of the most attractive features of the *Dialogue of Comfort* is the return of More's lighthearted humor. In his polemical works written after the *Dialogue Concerning Heresies,* his wit became hard, cruel, and sardonic. Prison and the resigned serenity that confinement brought restored that part of him which, next to his courage and human compassion for his family, all of us like best.

Much of the wit in the *Dialogue of Comfort* was directed at Dame Alice, at least by the report of Nicholas Harpsfield, who preserved much of the More family tradition. Dame Alice could never understand why her husband chose a course so fateful to his life and so damaging to her comfort. She becomes in this work the voice of this world calling More back to physical comfort while he was seeking the comfort of Christ for his soul.

One tale that all biographers must repeat is Antony's story of the woman who came to visit a poor prisoner whose cell was small but comfortable enough. The prisoner had put mats of straw on the floor and around the walls, and she was pleased with his arrangements. But she could not bear the thought that at night the jailer shut and locked the heavy door of the cell. "For by my truth," she exclaimed, "if the door should be shut on me, I would think that it would stop up my breath."

"At that word of hers, the prisoner laughed in his mind, but he dared not laugh aloud or say anything to her, for somewhat in dread he stood in awe of her. . . . But he could not but laugh inwardly, for he knew well enough that she used, on the inside, to shut every night full surely her own chamber . . . both door and windows too, and used not to open them all the long night."

We have noted this passage earlier when we ruminated over the question of whether More slept in the same bed as his wife. Here it is worth pointing out again that More would not be More if he did not display the image of himself that he wanted the public to have of him. In this story he appears as the meekly suffering, superior man, humorously abashed by a carping wife. A bad man might have beaten such a woman; More wanted people to know that despite his superiority, he withdrew before her.

Much the same may be said for his story of the woman who berated her husband because he had no ambition. The man would neither labor to win high office nor accept one when it was offered him. It is the humble image More always wanted people to have of him. The wife was not impressed; she raged at her husband: "What will you do, that you care not to put forth yourself as other folk do? Will you sit still by the fire and make goslings in the ashes with a stick as children do? Would God I were a man, and look what I would do."

"Why, wife," her husband said, "what would you do?"

"What? By God, go forward with the best, for as my mother used to say (God have mercy on her soul), it is ever more better to rule than be ruled. And therefore by God I would not, I warrant you, be so foolish to be ruled where I might rule."

"By my truth, wife," said her husband, "in this I dare say you say truth, for I never found you willing to be ruled yet."

More is here the novelist, altering sometimes a little, sometimes much, the events of his life to conform to the images of his fiction. Perhaps there is a yearning. He probably very much wanted to be just the unambitious man of his many professions and stories, and yet he was introspective enough to know that he could never quite live up to his own ideal for himself. For most people of any profundity, such a recognition may be gloomy and frustrating. Writers have other lives besides the one they live in the world, and when they have the chance to build dreams for themselves in fiction, they usually do it. Dame Alice may indeed have said something like this when More was pondering the invitation from Wolsey and the king to join the royal council so long ago. Or perhaps she berated her husband when he began trying to resign the office of Lord Chancellor. And More may have wished to believe that she had pushed him along the way that now led to his imprisonment and would lead to his death.

It is usually said that, in the Tower, More's serenity about his own fate made him forget his bitter war against heresy and dissolved the hatred of heretics manifest in his works and memorialized in his epitaph. The *Dialogue of Comfort* is proof enough that this easy assertion is not true. In the *Treatise on the Passion* he denounced heretical interpretations of the mass so vigorously that the work became not merely a devotional recitation of the events of Maundy Thursday but also a rigid defense of the mass against its heretical foes.

He also took time to whip some of his familiar beasts, among them the Lutheran teaching that faith alone justifies sinners before God.

In the *Dialogue of Comfort* we do not find so many explicit declarations about heretics, although Luther's marriage is condemned. However, the entire work is a tour de force in which the Turks become an allegory for the Protestants who threaten to destroy Christian civilization. It is hazardous indeed to suppose that because these Tower works breathe a spirit of personal resignation and tranquillity in the face of death, they represent a softening of hostility toward the heretics. In all of them he speaks not one word of regret for what he has said about heresy, and not one particle of evidence exists to suggest that he mitigated his views.

Perhaps the most arresting image in the *Dialogue of Comfort* is that of God the jailer. The prison where God incarcerates us is the earthly life, "so sure and so subtly builded that albeit that it lieth open on every side without any wall in the world, yet wander we never so far about therein, the way to get out at shall we never find." "Upon our prison we build our prison; we garnish it with gold and make it glorious. In this prison they buy and sell. In this prison they brawl and chide; in this they run together and fight; in this they dice; in this they card. In this they pipe and revel. In this they sing and dance. And in this prison many a man reputed right honest ceases not for his pleasure in the dark privately to play the knave." (It is typical of More that sin breeds in privacy.)

God is angry with what He sees "where we forget with our folly both ourselves and our jail and our underjailers angels and devils both, and our chief jailer God, too, God that forgetteth not us, but seeth us all the while well enough, and being sore discontent too to see such wicked rule kept in the jail, . . . he sendeth the hangman Death to put to execution here and there sometime by the thousands at once."

He means that people like himself, locked in a cell in a prison made by men, are in no worse condition than those who think themselves free in the world, and he goes on to say that indeed prisoners like himself are blessed. For with the opportunity for meditation, such prisoners have time to think of the bondage of sin, and they have the freedom to reconcile themselves to the loss of all worldly goods—which were part of their bondage anyway—and to seek the treasures of the life to come in the bliss of heaven.

And that is finally the message of the *Dialogue of Comfort*, that loss of freedom, reputation, worldly goods, ease, family, friends, and all the rest are but the prelude to heaven. To be comfortable in the world is to court the eternal torments of hell, mentioned by More over and over in this work. To be persecuted in this world is to bar the gates to hell and to open the way into heaven.

Throughout the book, More brooded about physical pain. Could he endure without breaking if he were subjected to the tortures that the government could inflict on his weak body? He was not sure: no man can ever be certain of the answer to such a question. To a priest known to us only as "Master Leder," More wrote that if he should ever accept the oath, "(which I trust our Lord shall never suffer me), ye may reckon sure that it were expressed and extorted by duresse and hard handling," and to Margaret he wrote of how he had pondered the peril that could come by the refusing of the oath. And said he, "I found myself (I cry God mercy) very sensual and my flesh much more shrinking from pain from death than methought it the part of a faithful Christian man." But in the *Dialogue of Comfort* More came back time and again to the sentiments and sometimes the words of one of his favorite scriptural texts, I Corinthians 10:13, which he rendered, "God is faithful which suffereth you not to be tempted above that you may bear but giveth also with the temptation a way out." To Margaret, More continued his thought, speaking of the conflict between the wish to save his body and the fear of losing his soul, saying, "yet I thank our Lord, that in that conflict the Spirit had in conclusion the mastery, and reason with help of faith finally concluded that for to be put to death wrongfully for doing well (as I am very sure I do, in refusing to swear against mine own conscience, being such as I am not upon peril of my soul bounden to change whether my death should come without law, or by color of a law) it is a case in which a man may lose his head and yet have none harm, but instead of harm inestimable good at the hand of God."

One of the great themes of the *Dialogue of Comfort* and of the stoic Christianity that More always embraced is that all men die soon enough and that anyone who tries to save his life at the cost of his soul is playing with a fatal fantasy. Some of his sentiments about death recall his treatise on the four last things. Even a natural death is often terrible. Antony, in one of his speeches, seems to show More looking forward to the ax and contemplating the choices one might have. "As far as I can perceive, those folk that commonly depart of their natural death have ever one disease and sickness or another whereof if the pain of that whole week or twain in which they lie pining in their bed were gathered together into so short a time as a man hath his pain that dies a violent death, it would I think make double the pain that that is so that he that naturally dies, more often suffers more pain than less though he suffers it a longer time. And then would many a man be more unwilling to suffer so long lingering in pain than with a sharper to be sooner rid [of it]."

During these months More seemed convinced that he would die soon no matter what the government did. In his long letter to Cromwell about the Nun of Kent, written before he was imprisoned, he apologized for not writing with his own hand. "For verily I am compelled to forebear writing for a while by reason of this disease of mine, whereof the chief occasion is grown, as it is thought, by the stooping and leaning on my breast, that I have been accustomed to do in writing." To Dr. Nicholas Wilson, his fellow prisoner in the Tower, he wrote that he did not expect to live much longer. "I have since I came in the Tower looked once or twice to have given up my ghost before this and in good faith mine heart waxed the lighter with hope thereof."

The *Dialogue of Comfort* gives several hints about his life in prison. We have noted the visit of the woman who was probably Dame Alice. She found her prisoner warm and comfortable enough, with straw mats on the floor and around the walls to keep out the cold and the damp. Antony spoke of the terrors that haunt men in the night, and we may surmise that More's serenity was not so complete that it kept him from insomnia—the same insomnia that he had suffered before his imprisonment. But Antony takes an afternoon nap, and More probably did the same. For a man with heart disease, it was an almost ideal regime. In the first months of his confinement, More had his books and his writing materials, and he might very well have passed away what was left to him of his natural life in a monastic contentment that he had always yearned to have.

But a fearful and insecure government was not willing to let him die in peace. In the summer of 1534, Thomas Fitzgerald, son of the Earl of Kildare, led an Irish revolt that to Chapuys, at least, seemed successful. The imperial ambassador reported that in consequence Henry was in much worse humor than he had been in for a long time. In the same dispatch Chapuys reported a dinner conversation with the Scots ambassador, who proposed an alliance between his country and the emperor—an alliance that could put Henry's regime in mortal danger. In November, Chapuys reported that the Admiral of France, Philippe Chabot, had arrived in London, full of contempt for the English and for Queen Anne Boleyn. Chapuys remarked that the admiral's visit had been the occasion for much dancing and playing at tennis, in which the king took part, leaving us to marvel at Henry's energy. A suit of armor made for the king in 1515 had a waist of thirty-four inches; another suit made for him in 1535 required a waist of fifty-four inches. He had swollen to an obese hulk, but still he danced and played and hunted like a boy. The general impression was that the meeting with the French had been unsatisfactory and that a projected marriage between Princess Mary and the French Dauphin would not go through. So Henry's government faced a dangerous diplomatic isolation combined with smoldering tempers at home.

More was held in prison without trial in the hope that confinement might break his will. He was presumed guilty of misprision of treason because he had not sworn the oath; "misprision" meant criminal resistance to the government short of conspiracy or rebellion. Anyone who knew that someone was plotting treason and did not report it could be guilty of misprision. By applying the charge to those who did not swear the oath, the government seemed to be saying that the refusers must be sheltering some treasonable thoughts. Under the penalties of misprision, guilty parties lost their property, and even without trial More might have had his goods confiscated by the king. But for several months Henry allowed the More family to enjoy their possessions undisturbed.

In November, Parliament met again, and Cromwell and the king pushed through further legislation to consolidate the new order. A short act of momentous consequence granted parliamentary authority to the title the king had wrested from the clergy, "Supreme Head of the Church of England." Now there was no saving clause, "so far as the law of Christ allows." The statute gave to the king and to his successors authority to reform the church and to judge errors and heresies. It was much in the spirit of the plea for royal control over the church that William Tyndale made in his *Obedience of a Christian Man*, and it represented the statutory end of the liberties of the English church guaranteed by Magna Carta.

Another act ratified the oath to uphold the Act of Succession that subjects were required to swear. By an oversight, it seems, the wording of the oath had not been included in the original act. So technically, at least, More and Fisher were in the Tower because they refused to swear words drawn up at the whim of Cromwell and the council. Roper reports that More thought the oath he was given went beyond the statute. That defense died as the oath was written into the statute books, and the English were required by the law of the realm to swear to "keep, maintain, and defend the . . . Act of Succession, and all the whole effects and contents thereof," and not only it but "all other acts and statutes made in confirmation or for the execution of the same or of anything therein contained." Anyone now taking the oath was issuing a blank check drawn on his own conscience to any act the Parliament had passed or any that Parliament might pass with the stated purpose of upholding the Act of Succession. Whatever the oath before this statute, More could certainly not swear it now.

The statute that proved fatal to More was the Act of Treasons passed by this session. Though the records of the backstage maneuvering for this act are slim, it seems clear enough that it had to climb a mountain of opposition. Treason now was extended to cover words spoken or written against the king, the queen, or their heirs. Anyone saying that the king was "heretic, schismatic, tyrant, infidel, or usurper of the crown" was, on conviction, guilty of high treason—pretty good evidence that a fair number of people were tossing those epithets around. Englishmen recoiled before the dreadful expedient of making treason out of words alone. Apparently the government coaxed the bill through by putting great stress on the importance of the word "maliciously" in the text. No one was to be charged with treason merely for speaking ill of the king; some proof had to be adduced that the accused intended his words as part of some treasonable activity that the act did not specify. But a government with the executioner's ax in its hand was left to determine for itself what "maliciously" meant, and it was soon clear that anyone speaking against the king was assumed , guilty of the malice required by the statute to make him liable to death for high treason. Note that words had to be spoken or written against the king; even this government was not able to cow Parliament into equating silence with treason, and as long as More continued to say nothing, he might have been safe.

But the government was resolved to break his will. A bill of attainder was pushed through against him, declaring him guilty of misprison of treason for refusing to swear the oath and removing all property that the king had given him and requiring the forfeiture of all his goods. As G. R. Elton has written, the act smacks of Henry's wrath against his old friend and councillor, for it speaks of the way More "hath unkindly and ingrately served our sovereign lord by divers and sundry ways." Fisher and others were attainted during the same session of Parliament but by another act, one that does not include this formula. The date on which More's treasonous obstinacy is said to have begun —May 1, 1534—is somewhat mysterious. But there was nothing mysterious about the government's resolution now to break him or kill him. More had been allowed to have visits from his family, and he had had liberty to walk in the Tower garden. Now these privileges were taken away.

Sometime in the fall, about the time of the convening of Parliament, he wrote Margaret two letters that have survived. As we have seen, he gave echo to some thoughts expressed in his *Dialogue of Comfort*—probably because he was working on it at the time. If anything, the resignation he expressed throughout his long ordeal became more solemn and heavy. He wrote that he had committed everything "to the goodness of God, and that so fully, that I assure you Margaret on my faith, I never have prayed God to bring me hence nor deliver me from death, but referring all things whole unto his only pleasure as to him that seeth better what is best for me than [I] myself do. Nor never longed I since I came hither to set my foot in mine own house for any desire of or pleasure of my house, but gladly would I sometime somewhat talk with my friends and especially my wife and you that pertain to my charge. But since that God otherwise disposeth, I commit all wholely to his goodness and take daily great comfort in that I perceive that you live together so charitably and so quietly: I beseech our Lord continue it."

His wish to talk with Dame Alice suggests that there was greater warmth to their relations than the conventional image of her suggests—a thought to ponder, since that image was largely propagated by himself, perhaps another instance of the way his fictions about his life nudged reality aside and even dissolved it. He wrote Dame Alice that he was sure the king would be too kind to take anything from her. But around Christmas 1534, she wrote a piteous letter to the king, begging him not to impoverish her family and especially not to allow her poor son "to be cast away and undone in this world also." In May 1535, she wrote humbly to Cromwell, begging his help in her "great and extreme necessity." She was having to take care of her household and, in addition, pay fifteen shillings a week to feed her husband and his servant in the Tower. (More was eating well; he was able to send John Fisher apples and oranges after a snow that fell that winter.) To meet these expenses, Dame Alice had to sell off some of her clothes. She asked for an audience with the king. We do not know if she got it, but she was eventually granted a pension of twenty pounds a year and apparently lived on in Chelsea after More's great house was confiscated. Both William Roper and Gyles Alington suffered the suspicion of the government, and Roper was imprisoned for a while. But apparently both of them were able to give her some help, though as we have seen, her necessity did not stop Roper from bringing a legal action against her after More's death.

Meanwhile the government seemed content to leave both More and Fisher alone. The authorities must have been perplexed. The historical recollection of Thomas Becket and all the trouble his murder cost his king must have made the government hesitate to kill a bishop. More's silence was impossible to proceed against in any legal way. Cromwell's government had an almost compulsive desire in these years to preserve the form of the legalities, as if meticulous attention to the processes of the law would cast a spell over the actuality that might ensure the survival of the new order. Whatever their motives, their instincts were sound, for nothing could fuel rebellion so readily in England as a king's reputation for acting against the law. The trick was to get what the government wanted while preserving the legalities.

Undoubtedly many grumbled about the imprisonment of the two men, but there was no public outcry. The English were accustomed to seeing former royal servants go to the Tower and thence to the block; in Tudor England, governance was always a hazardous occupation. Henry's expedient of sending commissioners all over the country to make every English citizen swear the oath may have seemed ludicrous to Chapuys and to the Scots ambassador, but it probably had an effect. Those who had sworn the oath found it painless enough. If we judge by what his daughter Margaret and others said to More, many must have supposed that he was obstinate to refuse to follow the example of so many wise men who had said the words and signed their names. Those who might have felt guilty for what they had done probably felt a greater eagerness to see More and Fisher swear and thereby grant certification to their own oaths and reassure them in their own consciences. The hero is always grand in retrospect, but while he is being heroic about a nebulous principle most people do not understand, he is likely to make his contemporaries uncomfortable and even hostile. So the government could afford to let nature take its course and to leave More and Fisher to molder in prison and be forgotten.

Such things happened often enough in the Renaissance, and England had a long tradition of keeping people in prison for years on end.

More continued to live in reasonable comfort. His servant remained with him, and he still had his books and paper for writing. Sometime in these final months of his life he turned to the writing of his last great work, *De tristitia Christi (On the Sadness of Christ).*

It is a remarkable work not only for its content but also because it is the only one of More's long pieces of writing that has survived in manuscript in his own hand to the present. Somehow it was smuggled out of the Tower and eventually taken to Spain, where it was deposited in the reliquary closet of the Chapel of Relics of the Royal College of Corpus Christi in Valencia. There it remained shut up until, almost miraculously, it came to light in 1963. The modern discovery of the manuscript was not the first knowledge we had of the work itself. Mary Basset, More's granddaughter by Margaret, had made an English translation of it during the reign of Mary, and several Latin copies also circulated. But the manuscript with its pages of More's own careful hand—including his write-overs and revisions—brings us in a remarkably vivid way to his last days.

The work takes up the story of the passion of Christ at about the place where More's *Treatise on the Passion* breaks off. The mass has been instituted, the Last Supper is done, Judas has departed, and having sung a hymn, Jesus and his remaining disciples go out to the Mount of Olives. More follows the scriptural texts from the gospels, and like a careful medieval university lecturer, he comments on them, sometimes explaining, sometimes relating a little history, sometimes making a guess or two, but mostly drawing devotional lessons from the example of Christ.

Above all, these devotions deal with fear and how to overcome it by meditating on the sufferings and the love of Jesus. Like the *Dialogue of Comfort, De tristitia Christi* is art brought to the service of life, a literary discipline to strengthen his mind against the horrors of his imagination. Taken as a whole, the amazing variety of the work offers a stunning display of More's calm spirit at a time when he was both terribly afraid and indomitably resolute.

There is something, too, in this work of the need for an explanation that will make the biblical account believable. To offer any real comfort, the story of what Christ suffered had to be true. Yet many perplexing problems lay embedded in the gospel accounts, and part of More's almost unconscious intent seems to have been to work these problems out, to explain them, to resolve them, so that what happened to Jesus could be more surely brought into the world where we all live and suffer. *De tristitia Christi* is a rationale of faith for the world of agonizing doubt that was the Christian Renaissance; so the commentary, which often sounds like idle digression, is in fact an enormous part of the devotional purpose of the book. How did the gospel writers know that Christ had sweated great drops of blood when he prayed in the garden? The disciples were asleep, and Christ was alone; so no one could have seen him. More explains that Christ must have told Mary and the disciples about this bloody sweat after he was resurrected from the dead. It never occurs to his painfully rational mind to suggest a medieval explanation, one blithely adopted by the biblical fundamentalists of our own day, that the gospel writers were directly inspired and did not require a secondary source for what they recorded. The man who defended the principle of the miraculous so ardently could only go so far with miracle.

Other questions are handled with the same patient care. Why was it that no one was able to recognize Christ in the garden or immediately after his resurrection? Why was Christ afraid though he was divine? Why did he pretend to be deceived by Judas? And we have the detail that it must have been a cold night, for the passion came only shortly after the vernal equinox and the Bible tells us that servants were warming themselves around charcoal fires in the courtyard of the high priest when morning came. In all his own writing More treated concrete and illuminating details with loving care, and his literary eye turned to such things in the ancient texts.

Sometimes More turns the details into allegories, using allegory in this work with greater frequency than he does in anything else from his pen. Allegory always goes from the concrete detail to its spiritual meaning, and perhaps unconsciously More, the prisoner of iron and stone and unjust law, let his mind rove and float now in the liberty of a higher realm where thoughts were free. It should also be said that allegory is always an expression of faith in a universal reason or purpose permeating all reality, breaking out here and there in events that confirm the wisdom of God in creation. To recognize the allegorical significance of a seemingly unimportant act is to fit the particular into the general, to be brought emotionally and intellectually into union with divine wisdom. Allegory was to the Middle Ages what mathematics is to the present, a unifying set of symbols that made the apparently bewildering diversity of the phenomenal world spiritually coherent and open to the human mind. Allegory satisfied the constant human need for some reason to believe confidently that an orderly universe does exist behind the chaos we see—just as that need is satisfied in the modern age by mathematical laws. In both allegory and mathematics, events that an uninstructed observer may think have no meaning are seen by the knowing mind to fit into a great, embracing whole whose existence cannot be seen; allegory or mathematics (depending on the time and taste of the observer) allows that fundamental harmony of things to be inferred with confidence or at least with hope. So it was altogether natural that a man confronted by horrible death when he knew himself to be guiltless of having violated the traditions of the church or the traditional laws of his own land should turn to allegory in his last great literary work.

More notes that the brook Cedron that Christ had to cross to reach Gethsemane means "sadness" and that Gethsemane means "most fertile valley" or "valley of olives." He draws from these names the allegory that we must cross over the "stream of sadness whose waves can wash away the blackness and filth of our sins" before we can come to the everlasting joy of heaven.

He spends a great deal of time puzzling over the identity of the young man who followed Jesus and, being recognized by the mob, was seized and then wriggled free, leaving his cloak in their hands, and ran away naked. From this tale and from the account of the general flight of the apostles, More draws the conclusion that people who doubt that they can endure pain should flee if God gives them a way of escape. No one should desert his post if God has commanded him to stay. "But when flight entails no offense against God, certainly the safer plan is to make haste to escape rather than to delay so long as to be captured and thus fall into the danger of committing a terrible sin."

The theme of pain is everywhere in the book. More relates with calm tenderness the suffering of Christ praying in Gethsemane. He assumed that on that dark night Christ could foresee "the treacherous betrayer, the bitter enemies, binding ropes, false accusations, slanders, blows, thorns, nails, the cross, and horrible tortures stretched out over many hours." Here More must have felt close to his master, and we recall his letter to Margaret about the way his flesh cringed from the thought of pain.

He took comfort in the sorrow and fear Christ felt before death, noting that although Christ commands us to obey him to the end, he does not require us to be fearless when that end is hard. "The brave man bears up under the blows which beset him," More writes. "The senseless man simply does not feel them when they strike." Christ wants us to be brave and not senseless, and it is in respect of our frail nature that he allows us to flee punishment when we can do so without injury to his cause. Some brave souls in times of persecution have publicly professed their faith when no one was requiring them to do so, and some have freely exposed themselves to death when no one demanded it. But everyone is not so brave, and God does not demand of all of us what he requires of some. "And so if anyone is brought to the point where he must either suffer torment or deny God, he need not doubt that it was God's will for him to be brought to this crisis. Therefore he has very good reason to hope for the best, for God will either extricate him from the struggle or else aid him in the fight and make him conquer so that He may crown him with the conqueror's wreath." The conquest More had in mind was victory over fear and pain; the conqueror's wreath was the martyr's crown.

These passages give us a window into More's troubled thoughts. We have noted that there remains a certain mystery about his martyrdom, a mystery troubling to a biographer who stands before that gulf of ignorance that history always presents to us and that we cannot reach over. But here we must accept

Thomas More for what he was, not a loud martyr, not one of those shrill saints from *The Golden Legend* who expected a miracle to confirm them and their choice. He was rather a man with a profound and frightening sense of his own weakness, and with his awareness of audience, he could never have made loud and vehement declarations that, with torture and unbearable pain, he might have been forced to recant. We may wish that he had been more explicit, that he had been bolder in his assertions—as Fisher was bold. But More was not Fisher. He was himself, and his faith was strong enough to believe that all God's purposes, even in England, did not depend on him alone. More would do what his nature allowed him, taking life day by day and one step at a time. God would do the rest.

De tristitia Christi is filled with love for Christ, but it also blazes up here and there with hatred for the heretics who had wrought such devastation in the church. More condemned those who sinned against the traditions of the church by allowing lay people to commune in both the body and blood of Christ. He denounced the Zwinglians who taught that the bread and wine in the mass remained only bread and wine and that they were only symbols of the body and blood—Frith's view. Judas, who betrayed Christ with a kiss, is like the heretics who claim love for Christ while they commit treachery against him. So are the soldiers who hailed Christ as king of the Jews, not meaning what they said. The heretics protest love for Christ but really hate him. More mocked them for their principle that scripture alone was authority enough for Christians and for their lack of agreement not only with the old holy fathers of the church but among themselves.

He says that Judas, symbol of all heretics, could have repented up to the moment he betrayed Christ and that even afterwards God would have welcomed him back if Judas had shown any desire to return. Even so, the heretics —the "new men," as he calls them—can repent if they only will, and More prays that they will come home to God. But it is clear that he has as little expectation that they will repent as one might have had for the return of Judas to the circle of the disciples. Judas finally perished like a wretch, and More relates his doom with merciless satisfaction and grim admonition. "The air longs to blow noxious vapors against the wicked man. The sea longs to overwhelm him in its waves, the mountains to fall upon him, the valleys to rise up against him, the earth to split open beneath him, hell to swallow him up after his headlong fall, the demons to plunge him into gulfs of ever-burning flames."

There is much else against heresy in *De tristitia Christi*, and More's fury against heretics even at this point should not surprise us. We could hardly expect a passionate man like himself to have learned benevolence toward those whose revolution had led his king and his country into schism, plunged his family into penury, and given him so many long, sleepless nights of fear and helplessness. Had he suddenly discovered benevolence or even indifference to these people he had hated so long, or had he resigned himself to tolerating them, all the things he was doing that placed his life in danger, things that led him finally to the block, would have made no sense to him or to us.

More's treatise breaks off with the seizure of Jesus by the soldiers sent along with Judas to take him. At the end Mary Bassett's translation, William Rastel wrote: "Sir Thomas More wrote no more of this work. But when he had written this far, he was in prison kept so straight that all his books and pen and ink and paper was taken from him, and soon after was he put to death."

An argument can of course be made that More intended to end the book here and that we have a rhetorical whole.

The closing sentence does have a sense of summing up and conclusion. It is quite long: "After Christ had thrown down the cohort merely by speaking to him, after the ear of the high priest's servant had been cut off and restored, after the other apostles had been forbidden to fight and Peter (who had already begun to fight) had been rebuked, after Christ had once more addressed the Jewish magistrates who were present at that time and had announced that they now had permission to do what they had not been able to do before—to take Him captive—after all the apostles had escaped by running away, after the young man who had been seized but could not be held had saved himself by his active and eager acceptance of nakedness, only then, after all these events, did they lay hands on Jesus."

This sounds very much like a real ending and not an unexpected fracture. It had an obvious personal meaning to More. Like Jesus, he was about to be seized by his foes and carried to his death.

Around this time, More wrote a prayer of his own in the margins of a Latin Book of Hours with him in the Tower. The book, now preserved in Yale's Beinecke Rare Book Library, is bound with a Latin Psalter which also contains notes from More's pen. But it is the prayer which radiates More's own struggle with himself throughout his life and the solitude that he must now endure in prison. Nothing else that he ever wrote reveals the man with such economy and grace:

> Give me thy grace, good Lord
> To set the world at nought;
>
> To set my mind fast upon thee,
> And not to hang upon the blast of men's
>   mouths;
>
> To be content to be solitary;
> Not to long for worldly company;

Little and little utterly to cast off the world,
And rid my mind of all the business therof;

Not to long to hear of any worldly things,
But that the hearing of worldly phantasies may be to me
   displeasant;

Gladly to be thinking of God,
Piteously to call for his help;

To lean unto the comfort of God,
Busily to labor to love him;

To know my own vility [vileness] and wretchedness
To humble and meeken myself under the mighty hand of God;

To bewail my sins passed;
For the purging of them patiently to suffer adversity;

Gladly to bear my purgatory here;
To be joyful of tribulations;

To walk the narrow way that leadeth to life,
To bear the cross with Christ;

To have the last thing in remembrance,
To have ever afore mine eye my death that is ever at hand;

To make death no stranger to me,
To foresee and consider the everlasting fire of hell;

To pray for pardon before the judge come,
To have continually in mind the passion that Christ suffered for me;

Forhis benefits uncessantly to give him thanks,
To buy the time again that I before have lost;

To abstain from vain confabulations,
To eschew light foolish mirth and gladness;

Recreations not necessary—to cut off;
Of Worldly substance, friends, liberty, life and all, to set the loss
   at right nought for the winning of Christ;

To think my most enemies my best friends;
For the brethren of Joseph could never have done him so much
   good with their love and favor as they did him with their malice and hatred,

These minds [thoughts] are more to be desired of every man
   than all the treasure of all the princes and kings, christian and heathen, were it
   gathered and laid together all upon one heap.

It is the prayer of a man who had loved so much of life and so many of the delights he here renounces, and now begs Christ to release him from the bondage of such pleasures together all upon one heap.

29

THE LAST DAYS

I N APRIL 1535, the government's campaign against dissenters came to life again. Cromwell moved first against the Carthusians, the strongest and the purest of the monastic orders left in England. Their London prior, John Houghton, rejected the royal supremacy for what then seemed the obvious reason. Houghton asked Cromwell, "How could the king, a layman, be Head of the Church of England?" He was put in the Tower along with two other Carthusians, priors who had journeyed to London to get his advice. Richard Reynolds of the Brigittine monastery of Sion also denied the supremacy and was arrested. Reynolds had been interested in the Nun of Kent, and he had talked to More about her. Since these men had all spoken against the supremacy, they could be condemned under the new Act of Treasons. On April 29, the four of them were sentenced to suffer the full horrors of a traitor's death. They argued that their denial of the supremacy was not malicious and that they could not be condemned under the statute. But the judges ruled that anyone who denied the supremacy did so maliciously, and that was that.

Cromwell's tactics against More during these months included psychological subtlety of a sort often used to break the will of those in prison, alternations of good news and bad news, relaxation and rigor, benevolence and assault, that leave the prisoner uncertain of his own perceptions and drive him to find in his tormentor a protector and a confidant.

On May 4, Margaret was allowed to visit her father. On that morning the Carthusian priors and Richard Reynolds were led out on parade to their

monstrous executions at Tyburn. The council must have intended for More
and his beloved daughter to be together so that when he saw the men walking
to the punishment that might be his later on, her pleas for him to swear the
oath might have some effect. But More remained steadfast. He stood with
Margaret at a window and watched the poor victims on their way to slaughter,
and, by Roper's account, he said:

> Lo, dost thou not see, Meg, that these blessed fathers be now as cheerfully going
> to their deaths as bridegrooms to their marriage? Wherefore thereby mayst thou
> see, mine own good daughter, what a great difference there is between such as
> have in effect spent all their days in a strait, hard, penitential, and painful life
> religiously, and such as have in the world, like worldly wretches, as thy poor father
> hath done, consumed all their time in pleasure and ease licentiously. For God,
> continuing their long-continued life in most sore and grievous penance, will no
> longer suffer them to remain here in this vale of misery and iniquity, but speedily
> hence taketh them to the fruition of his everlasting deity. Whereas thy silly
> father, Meg, that like a most wicked wretch, hath passed forth the whole course
> of his miserable life most sinfully, God thinking him not worthy so soon to come
> to that eternal felicity, leaveth him here yet still in the world, further to be
> plunged and turmoiled with misery.

Roper is always a questionable witness, but here is one of More's most vivid
utterances, given while he was standing in the very shadow of death and
longing for the monastic life that he had forsaken so long ago to make a
different life in the world, and in lieu of that vanished opportunity now wishing
for God to take him home.

The monks More saw depart for Tyburn were butchered with the most
savage barbarism before a great crowd. Chapuys reported that they were not
degraded from the priesthood before they died and that the Duke of Norfolk
attended along with the Duke of Richmond (Henry's bastard son) and Thomas
and George Boleyn, and that forty horsemen of the king's bodyguard attended
also. The courtiers wore masks, and the king himself had expressed a desire to
attend. Chapuys wrote that it was generally believed that More and Fisher
would die soon and that the king, becoming accustomed to such cruelties,
might then turn on Queen Catherine and Princess Mary. Anne Boleyn,
Chapuys said, was "fiercer and haughtier than ever she was, and has been bold
enough to tell the King, as I hear, that he is as much indebted to her as ever
man was to woman, for she has been the cause of his being cleansed from the
sin in which he was living." Roper reports that about this time Margaret told
More that "Queen Anne" had never been in better condition. And More is
supposed to have replied, "Alas, Meg, alas! It pitieth me to remember into
what misery, poor soul, she shall shortly come."

Soon after the execution of the monks, Roper says, Cromwell came to see More, looked after his comfort, and assured him of the king's good will. From henceforth, Cromwell said, Henry had no more wish to trouble More's scruples of conscience. More was not taken in by this sudden show of kindness. He wrote a few lines of verse to fortune that ended, "Ever after thy calm, look I for a storm."

The storm did not long delay. On May 7, Cromwell came back. He brought with him an entourage of toadies who swarmed in the corridors of the Tower as More was led from his cell to a chamber where sat Cromwell and an undistinguished group comprising Sir Christopher Hales, Attorney General; Thomas Bedyll, Clerk of the Privy Council; Sir John Tregonwell, a judge; and Sir Richard Riche, a mediocrity sliding ever deeper into middle age with most of his high ambitions still unachieved, recently appointed Solicitor General. More was invited to sit with them. As he had done the previous April, he chose to stand.

Cromwell asked if he had heard of the statutes passed by the recent session of Parliament. More replied that someone had given him a book with the statutes in it but he had returned it, deciding that he was in no position to spend time on such matters. Had he read the first statute, Cromwell asked, the one making the king supreme over the church? Yes, More said, he had read it. What did he think of it? Both king and council wanted to know, Cromwell said. More expressed his surprise that he was being troubled again about his conscience. He had reason for his surprise if indeed Cromwell had assured him after the executions of the monks three days before that he would be left alone.

Apparently in the interval Cromwell and the king had picked up a strong rumor that Charles was about to invade England. At the moment Charles was actually planning a strike at Moslem power in Tunis. News of these military preparations had come to England, and it was natural that someone should suggest that talk of a Tunisian expedition was only a mask to hide plans directed against Henry. On May 8, Cromwell came to see Chapuys about these rumors, saying that such an invasion would be much harder and more expensive than people thought and that, said Chapuys to the emperor, "even if Your Majesty were to conquer this country, it would not redound to your honor so to have treated such a true and old friend" as Henry had been. "The emperor, moreover, could not," said Cromwell, "after his death bequeath the kingdom to his heirs; nevertheless the infamy of such an act would attach to his name forever." It sounds very much like a counsel of desperation, and since Cromwell alluded in the talk to the supposed welcome some Englishmen would give such an invasion, it is understandable that the government should exert itself at this point to force More to bend his knee.

But More gave no answer to the questions Cromwell put to him except to say that he had rid his mind of all such matters and would dispute the titles of neither kings nor popes, but would remain the king's true, faithful subject, praying for him daily. Cromwell replied that this answer was not sufficient and that the king would not be satisfied with it. He held out a bright hope. Henry was "a prince not of rigor but of mercy and pity," and if More would only submit, he would soon be in the world again among other men as he had been before. For a man of More's gregarious social temper, this was a powerful temptation.

Still he remained constant. He would occupy himself with nothing else in this world, he said. He would think only of the "passion of Christ and mine own passage out of this world." It was probably a reference to the writing of *De tristitia Christi.*

The group decided to consult, and More was sent out. When he was led back in, Cromwell told him that being a prisoner did not relieve him of his obedience to the king—something More did not deny. Cromwell also made a revealing comment: More's resistance to the Act of Supremacy had led others to resist it. He may have been smarting over the trial of Reynolds and the Carthusians only a few days before. Richard Reynolds, More's old acquaintance, had justified his refusal to accept the royal supremacy in words that instantly recall More's, although of course More was careful to speak in general terms about statutes and not about this statute. Reynolds was asked how he could persist in opposing a statute that so many lords and bishops in Parliament and the whole realm had decreed? He replied, "I say that if we propose to maintain opinions by proofs, testimony, or reasons, mine will be far stronger than yours, because I have all the rest of Christendom in my favor—I dare say all this kingdom, although the smaller part holds with you, for I am sure the larger part is at heart of our opinion, although outwardly, partly from fear and partly from hope, they profess to be of yours." In time, Reynolds said, when the king knew the truth, he would resent those who had given him bad counsel. If Cromwell remembered the letter from Margaret More Roper to Alice Alington, he would have been struck by the similarity of views, and the evidence is that Cromwell remembered everything.

The government doubtless felt the sullen displeasure of multitudes of silent people against the policies of the king despite the lack of any public and general protest. People like Cromwell could not lay hands on everyone in the realm who was part of this silent multitude, but he could rack More, and More probably became for him—as for the king—as much symbol as man.

More replied that he gave no advice to any man one way or another. And he made one of the great pronouncements of his ordeal:

I am the king's true, faithful subject and daily bedesman and pray for his Highness and all his and all the realm. I do nobody harm; I say none harm; I think none harm, but wish everybody good. And if this be not enough to keep a man alive, in good faith, I long not to live. And I am dying already, and have since I came here, been several times in the case that I thought to die within one hour, and I thank our Lord I was never sorry for it but rather sorry when I saw the pang past. And therefore my poor body is at the King's pleasure; would God my death might do him good.

Cromwell persisted. "Well, you find no fault in that statute; find you any in any of the other statutes after?" The statement and the question sound as if Cromwell is trying to give More a decent way out, but according to the preamble of the Act of Succession and the recent Act of Treasons, it was just as much a capital crime to speak against the statutes that supported the Act of Succession as it was to speak against that statute itself. Cromwell was subtly working at entrapment. More would not be beguiled. He refused to speak further of the statutes at all. So he was put back into his cell, and for the moment the matter rested.

Cromwell had to be perplexed by his problems. Anne Boleyn and the king were pushing him hard to break More down, and his conversation with Chapuys the day after this frustrating interview reveals an unquiet desperation. From this remove he looks like a man casting about frantically to bring order to a situation that threatened to dissolve momentarily into chaos, carrying the nation and himself with it. He was, like More, an emotional man who was required to suppress his passions often in the interest of efficiency.

Cromwell was supposedly the ally of Anne Boleyn. But already by 1535 she felt her hold on the king slipping. Chapuys reported in September 1534 that Anne and Henry had had a tiff about Henry's amorous interest in a "very handsome young lady of this court" and that in consequence of Henry's attentions, Anne had tried to "dismiss the damsel from her service." Henry had replied to her efforts with an angry letter, reminding her of her origins and saying that if he had it all to do over again, he would not do so much for her. In December 1534, Chapuys noted that Anne's jealousy of the woman—probably Jane Seymour, Henry's next and most beloved wife—still persisted. In January, Anne began to laugh loudly and for no apparent reason in the company of the Admiral of France, and that worthy felt himself grossly insulted. She had reason for her hysteria; she had failed to give Henry a son, and she would fail again. Rumors flew at home and abroad that Henry was tired of her.

Henry, fearing invasion, was eager for any accommodation with the emperor. Seeing the king's mood dangerously shifting like clouds on a stormy day, Cromwell had to think quickly and move subtly to keep things under control. He was regarded as Anne Boleyn's right-hand man, and yet he kept in close touch with Chapuys, engaging the ambassador in long, sometimes indiscreet conversations. In early June, Cromwell said that Anne Boleyn had told him she would like to see his head cut off, and he complained to the imperial ambassador that the king had become so fond of hoarding money that all the gold and silver of England would eventually fall into his hands, much to the detriment of private persons who needed the coin for commerce. Cromwell claimed that he and other privy councillors were searching for some means of checking the king's greed and persuading him to spend his money for the good of the nation.

Chapuys did not know what to make of Cromwell's loquacious confidences and suspected him of lying. It is hard to see what Cromwell had in mind. There may have been some clever diplomatic purpose behind these revelations; we may wonder if Cromwell, fearing the government might fall to insurrection sponsored by the emperor, was preparing an escape for himself by propagating the idea that he was being dragged along in the king's train. Still, it is easier than it once was to say that diplomats and political figures like Cromwell have always been rather less clever than we think, even in the age of Machiavelli —who was himself, after all, not clever enough to do much good for himself or for his state. All these reports about Cromwell from Chapuys give us a plausible portrait of an anxious and exasperated man, almost in spite of himself pouring out his worries to Chapuys, who was such a good listener.

The More family tradition, preserved in the sixteenth-century biographies, was dispassionate about Cromwell. It is probably best if we see the unfolding tragedy of the executions of both More and Fisher as Henry's play rather than one penned by his chief minister, who only scampered about, moving the props according to his monarch's fitful direction. After the fruitless interrogation of May 7, Cromwell seemed content to leave More alone.

Then Pope Paul III, who had succeeded to the papal throne on the death of Clement VII the previous September, made John Fisher a cardinal. Paul III was a man of reforming temper, despite his preoccupation with the fortunes of his bastard children, and he seems to have wanted simply the best clergyman in England to represent that country in the coming general council that he intended to call. He claimed that he thought Henry would be pleased with his choice!

But when the news reached London late in May, Henry went into one of his famous rages. Chapuys wrote on June 16 that the king had promised to give Fisher another and better hat, "for he would send the Bishop's head to Rome for that purpose." The king had commanded the members of the Privy Council to interrogate More and Fisher once again and compel them to swear the oath, and he had promised to have them both executed before St. John's Day; that is, June 24. In the meantime Henry had ordered sermons to be preached against the two men in nearly all the churches of London—precisely the kind of secular interference in the life of the sacred church that More was willing to give his life to prevent. Chapuys reported a new fervor on the king's part to convict both More and Fisher of "some misprision of treason," since to Henry's evident indignation there seemed to be "no sufficient cause to sentence them to death." Still, Henry's anger was full. Lady Anne had given him a banquet to divert him from the annoyance and, said Chapuys, "the king loves his concubine now more than ever he did—a fact which has considerably increased the Princess' fears, especially seeing how long the remedy is in coming." Was the "remedy" Princess Mary desired an imperial invasion? Chapuys does not say.

The interrogation Chapuys spoke of took place on June 3. This time More faced the king's heavy artillery and not a squad of cadets. Besides Cromwell, the delegation included Cranmer, Audeley, the Duke of Suffolk, and Thomas Boleyn. Again More wrote an account of the interview for Margaret, seeming to want to get his own version to the outside so that he would not be misrepresented by those who had reason to twist his words.

He wrote that he could see little difference between this visit and the last. The king and the council wanted him to make a clear declaration about the Act of Supremacy, and he refused to do it. But as Elton has noted, not only the delegation but the tone was different. Cromwell told More that the king was in no way content with his answer and thought that he had been the occasion of much resentment and harm in the realm, that he had an obstinate mind and an evil intent toward him, and that now, in the king's name, More was ordered to confess that Henry should be Supreme Head of the Church of England or else to speak his malice out plainly. The command, directly from the king, was as threatening as anything could be under the circumstances.

More remained calm. In fact, Cromwell's harsh words probably steeled his resolve, for they would have given him confidence that his resistance, isolated as it was in the Tower of London, was known among the people and that good Catholic Englishmen were strengthened thereby. We have to wonder if More, with his lifelong sense of drama, might have intended to present himself as innocent and as harmless as possible so that Henry's wickedness might seem all the greater, creating in life the dramatic contrast between goodness and villainy that became the staple of English Renaissance plays.

He told Cromwell that he was sorry that the king took offense at him. People had told the king many things that were untrue, he said, and Henry had believed them. In his account to his daughter More managed to inject a note of subtle warning. The time would come, he said, when God would show More's truth to the king "before him and all the world." And although that ultimate vindication might seem small comfort seeing that he might take harm in the meanwhile, "I thanked God that my case was such in this matter through the clearness of mine own conscience that though I might have pain I could not have harm, for a man may in such case lose his head and have no harm." In effect More was reminding his sovereign that both of them someday would have to stand before God and be judged for their consciences, and he was declaring that he was certain of his. Clearly he thought that Henry could not say the same.

Cromwell persisted, aided by Audeley, whose chief virtue in speaking seemed always to be to repeat the thoughts of others. The king might by law compel More to speak about the statutes one way or the other.

More posed a hypothetical case that would come back to haunt him at his trial. If his conscience did oppose any statutes, he said—carefully pointing out that he was only supposing a case, since he did nothing nor said anything against the act—it would be a hard thing to speak with the statute against his conscience to the death of his soul or with his conscience against the statute to the destruction of his body. Later he was reported to have said that the statute was a two-edged sword, that to deny it with the conscience would kill his body and that to affirm it against his conscience would kill his soul. Whether he mentioned the metaphor of the sword or not, More made it clear that he would not speak, and by inference he also made it clear what his real feeling was.

Then Cromwell brought up a touchy point. He praised More for having rigorously examined heretics. He said that in those examinations, heretics were required to make a precise answer as to whether they took the pope to be head of the church. It was a reference to the *ex officio* process of the canon law that did not allow an accused heretic to stand silent before his judges, a process More had vehemently defended in his *Apology*. Why then should not the king require his subjects to say precisely whether they took him to be the head of the church since such was now the law of England?

Again More refused to contend about the English statutes and tried to put the matter on a hypothetical ground. There was, he said, a difference between the two cases. The pope's power was recognized as an undoubted thing throughout the Christian world; it was not something agreed to in this realm and taken to be untrue anywhere else. He had said the same sort of thing several times before, and it meant this: the laws of the church were universally binding, but the laws of any separate nation within Christendom were not.

Cromwell replied with the impatience of a harassed man worn out with theory. "They were as well burned for the denying of that as they be beheaded for the denying of this." Death was death, and the penalty equalized the laws that brought it about. More replied with his familiar calm and his familiar argument. The laws of the whole body of Christendom were binding over any local laws to the contrary. The reasonableness or the unreasonableness of forcing a man to give a precise answer to those questions stood not in the difference between "heading or burning but because of the difference in charge of conscience, the difference standeth between heading and hell."

The members of the council argued with More but to no avail. They offered him another oath, one that would require him "to make true answer to such things as should be asked me on the King's behalf, concerning the King's own person," he said. He refused this oath, too, saying he would never take another "book oath" as long as he lived. Cromwell charged him with obstinacy, saying that people swore such oaths every day in judicial proceedings. More must have smiled as he replied that he had no doubt as to what sort of questions would follow after he had sworn such an oath—probably one to *tell* the truth, the whole truth, and nothing but the truth—and that he would as soon remain silent now as later. Audeley admitted that More had guessed their plan and thereupon showed More the two questions that the council wished to put to him: Had he seen the statute, and did he believe "that it were a lawful made interrogatory or not"? Apparently this was a question as to whether he believed the statute could justly require an oath in its support. Here was a subtle trick indeed, for if More had commented on the injustice of the oath, he would have spoken against the statute, and he would have been instantly guilty of treason under the recent act that made words a capital crime. He would not be gulled. He had already admitted that he had read the statute, he said, and he refused to answer the second question.

During the interrogation someone remarked that it was a marvel how much More stuck to his conscience while, as he reported to Margaret, "at the uttermost I was not sure therein." The remark had implied that conscience by its very nature was untrustworthy since no one could be entirely sure if his private conscience told him the truth. It was a problem More had often ruminated about in his polemical works when he pondered what might happen to the distinctions between right and wrong if the clear, infallible authority of the church should be destroyed. Then everyone would do that which was right in his own eyes, and society would fall apart. The single person, he always maintained, should measure his conscience against the requirements of God made clear in the teachings and the practices of the holy church.

Now his reply was firm: "Whereto I said that I was very sure that mine own conscience so informed as it is by such diligence as I have so long taken therein may stand with mine own salvation." He meant that his conscience agreed with the consensus of the church. He did not meddle with the consciences of others, he said, and he quoted Romans 14:4. "Every man stands or falls before his own lord."

In exasperation one of the council asked why, if he was willing to die as he claimed, did he not speak plainly against the statute and get it over with. More replied in the spirit of the ruminations about pain in his last works. He had not been a man of such holy living, he said, to be bold enough to offer himself to death lest God for his presumption allow him to fall. "Therefore I put not myself forward but draw back. Howbeit, if God draw me to it himself, then trust I in his great mercy, that he shall not fail to give me grace and strength.

His position was consistent throughout: conscience required him to refuse the oath to the Act of Succession and to refuse to grant the validity of the Act of Supremacy; but conscience also required him to save his life if he could, for life was a gift of God, and no one could decide to throw his life away with a good conscience if he could possibly save it.

The meeting broke up with Cromwell angry or perhaps merely frightened because he could not deliver More's soul on a platter to the king. Cromwell said he liked More much less on this day than he had liked him the last time they had talked, for then he pitied him, but now he thought More meant not well. It was a less than covert notice that Cromwell suspected More of malice. Malice, according to the Act of Treasons, could bring More to death. So Cromwell went away, and More wrote his account to Margaret.

It is all pure More, and we see him holding grimly on the dangerous course he had chosen with scarcely a glance at the blackening sky. But we do wonder what would have happened if he had been truly silent, simply mute, before his foes. In his own story of his interview with Cromwell and the rest, he shows himself going very far toward speaking his mind. Certainly no one of even modest intelligence—and Cromwell was far more than that—could fail to get a clear idea of his general grounds for refusing the oath, despite all his careful statements about hypothetical cases. The statute contradicted the laws of the church and stood in opposition to the laws of God.

It seems that he could not break a lifelong habit of self-defense under attack, of argument, of simple gregariousness. He could not refrain from falling into the habitual practice of legal rebuttal that had engaged his fancy since childhood. Roper mentions that when More visited universities at home and abroad, he took part in the disputations that were a regular part of academic life. Always when someone spoke a provocative line, More had to reply, to make a part for himself, and to win the audience over. Here we could wish that he had remained mute, for eventually he said enough to talk himself to the scaffold.

Yet it is hard to fault him, for his courage and his constancy were magnificent. Henry's fury was pathological. Not content with the barbarous execution of the Carthusian priors and Richard Reynolds, the government turned on three other monks of the London Charterhouse who would not bow to their king's pretensions. One was Sebastian Newdigate, a former courtier in the service of the king, who in that epoch of vast swings of temperament had taken up the monastic life. Acquaintance with the king won him no mercy; on the contrary, he was made to suffer as a trusted friend who had betrayed the king's love. With his two companions he was taken to the Marshalsea, a prison for common felons. According to a later story, the three were fitted with iron collars, bound by their necks to upright posts, and left in that condition for seventeen days. Iron fetters were bolted to their legs. "They could neither lie

nor sit nor otherwise ease themselves" or do anything "but stand upright, and
in all that space were they never loosed for any natural necessity." A much later
and probably unreliable story holds that Margaret Giggs, More's ward and now
the wife of John Clement, slipped into the prison in disguise and fed the
prisoners and washed them. They were finally executed at Tyburn on June 19
in the same barbarous fashion as their prior before them. Doubtless More was
kept well informed of all these events, for the government would have used
every possible fear to break his will.

The government increased the pressure on both Fisher and More now. On
June 11, John a Wood was interrogated. He testified that More and Fisher had
exchanged letters. Fisher's servant confirmed Wood's testimony and said that
Fisher had burned his part of the correspondence.

On June 12, Fisher was interrogated again. The authorities wanted to know
what he and More had written to each other. At first he said he did not
remember the contents of the letters. But on further consideration he said that
More's first letter had asked what answer he had given to the council on the
matter for which he was committed to the Tower. He had sent a reply; he did
not say what it was. Fisher also said that he had seen the letter More had
written to Margaret in which he said he would not dispute the king's title.
Since the letter was passed on to Fisher by the servant of the Lieutenant of
the Tower, the government must have taken it to signify an important concession by More, one that might move Fisher to do the same. Fisher wrote More
for a precise explanation and received it—but claimed not to remember More's
reply! More had written that he supposed the answers he and Fisher gave the
council would be much alike and suggested that they should avoid the suspicion
of having influenced one another. Throughout this interrogation Fisher was
obviously trying to avoid putting any weapon into the government's hand that
might be used against More, and at the same time he was trying to avoid
perjury—a damnable sin. He said, too, that if the cardinal's hat were laid at
his feet, he would not stoop to pick it up.

On the same day More received a fateful visit from Sir Richard Riche. Riche
came with a couple of henchmen to take away the last of More's books, some
having already been removed. The government was now resolved to make
More's confinement as miserable and lonely as possible. While the two henchmen bound the books up and put them in a sack, Riche engaged More in
conversation.

More was heartsick to see his books go. Stapleton tells us that after this day
More pulled the blinds down and sat in the dark. When the jailer asked him
why, he said, "Now that the goods and the implements are taken away, the
shop must be closed." It is a story that reveals how profound and black More's
mood became, and those who have experienced such assaults of depression

even for a time may find in this story of More sitting alone in the dark the most poignant detail we have about his ordeal. So he may have let his guard down as Riche prattled at him. Exactly what was said has been a matter of great debate, not only in More's time but in recent years among scholars. But what Riche claimed More said was enough to send him to his death.

We have three versions of the conversation. The most dramatic and the one nearly everyone cites—including Robert Bolt in his play *A Man for All Seasons* —is Roper's, who told the story in his account of More's trial on July 1. But we also have a badly mutilated memorandum from Riche himself, apparently written shortly after the conversation. In addition, we have a version of Riche's memo that became part of the indictment formally lodged against More. From these records we can construct a general view of what happened, but some of the pieces will always be missing.

Riche said that in a spirit of charity he spoke to More about the supremacy, telling him beforehand that he had neither special commission nor command to do so—probably an effort to lower More's guard by giving the impression that this was only a private and informal conversation between lawyers, a conversation that quickly became a moot. More's first statement was, "Your conscience will save you, and my conscience will save me." But Riche persisted, flattering More by saying that to give a man of such experience advice was like pouring water into the Thames. Then, as such people do, Riche gave his advice anyway. More should submit. In lawyerly fashion he put a case to support his view: "Admit there were, sir," said he, "an act of Parliament that all the realm should take me for King. Would not you, Master More, take me for King?"

"Yes, sir," More said, "that would I."

Roper says that Riche went on to suppose that there was an act of Parliament that all the realm should take Riche to be pope. What would More say then? The question is nonsense, and it was surely not asked. Roper, writing in the reign of Mary over two decades after More's death when all Catholics had rallied around papal sovereignty and the conciliar movement was utterly dead, wanted to portray More as papal as anybody and always tried to work the pope into the story. But the comment is recorded neither in Riche's memo nor in the indictment.

More replied rather to the case Riche posed about the power of Parliament to make a king. It was a light case, he said. He would pose a higher one. Suppose Parliament made an act that God was not God. What would Riche say then? Riche must have been a little annoyed at this translation of the interview from the theoretical to the impossible. But he was a lawyer, and he took what he could get. He said that God was not God by statute but that More's was indeed a high case. Riche would choose a middle case between the high and the low. "You know that our Lord King has been constituted Supreme Head of the Church in the English Land," he said. "Why should you not, Master More, affirm and accept him to be so in just the way that you would be obligated to take me and affirm me as king?"

Then More made his lethal slip—at least according to the indictment and to what Riche said and Roper reported. "The cases are not alike," More said, "for a king can be made by Parliament and by Parliament can be deprived, and to such an act any subject owes his assent as though being in the Parliament; but to the case of primacy, the subject cannot be obligated to give his consent to such a thing in Parliament. And though the king is so accepted in England, most foreign lands do not accept the same."

More did not here flatly reject the Act of Supremacy, but he said, according to Riche and the indictment, that the Parliament could not make such a law because it went against the universal law of Christendom. The two things—outright rejection of the statute and the declaration that Parliament could not make such a statute—amounted to the same thing. More had made a similar comment to Cromwell in his interrogation of June 3 when he said, "A man is not by a law of one realm so bound in his conscience, where there is a law of the whole corps of Christendom to the contrary in a matter touching belief."

It looks very much as if More had intended to silence Riche by reducing the argument about the power of Parliament to the absurd. Could Parliament make Riche king? That idea was absurd enough in More's mind, and he quickly snapped back with an absurdity that even Riche could recognize: Could Parliament decree that God was not God? That should have been the end of it. But Riche, unwilling to snap the conversation off with the joke, persisted. And More, tired and utterly depressed at the removal of his books, fell into the trap. Or so it seems.

Riche was too dense to realize that More had said something new. He went off saying, "Well, Sir, God comfort you, for I see your mind will not change which I fear will be very dangerous to you for I suppose your concealment to the question that hath been asked of you is as high offense as [any]." It would seem that Riche was still assuming that More had refused to answer the question in any significant way. Although Riche must have written his memo soon afterwards, perhaps because Cromwell told him to, the government did not think much of it, for on June 14 More was interrogated again.

This time the questioning was about More's relations with Fisher, who was to go to trial in three days. What had they said in the letters they had exchanged? More was careful, but he was candid—more so than Fisher had been in answering similar questions. Perhaps he realized that Fisher was going to die anyway and that he would soon follow him. By the account he gave to his questioners, he had said much the same thing to Fisher that he had said to everyone else. More wished the letters had been preserved, he said, but the Lieutenant of the Tower's servant, George, who had carried them back and forth, always said there was no better keeper than the fire, and he had burned them. More recalled that Fisher had hoped that since the word "maliciously" was set in the Act of Treasons, no one might be condemned who spoke without malice; More had replied sensibly enough that he doubted that such an interpretation would hold. After his last interrogation, he said, he sent Fisher word that the Solicitor General, Richard Riche, had told him that to be silent was the same thing as to speak out against the statute and that on that issue all the learned men of England would agree. The remark shows that despite Riche's declaration that he had no special commission to ask questions, More regarded the interview as a formal examination.

He added a note of explanation about his letters to Margaret. He had written to comfort her because he feared she might flee. Since he thought that she might be with child, he was afraid that she could take harm. He had written his letters after the examinations to calm her so she would take patiently whatever might come.

Yet the letters More wrote to his daughter do not seem to be letters of comfort; they seem rather like efforts to get his own view of these conversations before the world—or at least before his family circle—as clearly as he could, and we may suppose that they were copied and passed around in a sort of sixteenth-century *samizdat*. But he was eager to protect his daughter, who would have helped circulate the letter, and he commented that she had written him several times begging him to accommodate himself to the king's will; especially had she urged such a course on him in her last letter. To the familiar and persistent questions about the royal supremacy and the king's marriage to Anne, More made his persistent and familiar replies: he would say nothing about them. His questioners must have been greatly fatigued with asking them.

Fisher was brought to trial on June 17. His case was plain, and he was quickly condemned to be butchered at Tyburn with all the barbarities prescribed for convicted traitors. It required strong people to endure such executions up to the final horrors that the law demanded. The Carthusian priors and Richard Reynolds had still been conscious when they were cut down smothering from the hangman's noose and when their bowels were torn out and burned in a fire blazing by their bodies. By some accounts they had remained conscious to the very moment that the executioner cut into their chests to pull out their hearts. Fisher was already nearly dead of illness, and so his sentence was commuted to simple beheading on Tower Hill. He was executed on June 22, the first bishop since Thomas Becket to be put to death in England and the first in English history to die after a formal judicial process.

His body was so frail and emaciated that people remarked that he looked like a skeleton. He died in calm and good humor. When the Lieutenant of the Tower woke him at five in the morning to tell him that this was the day of his death, Fisher asked when the execution would be. On learning that it would be at ten, he asked that he might sleep another hour or so since illness had kept him from sleeping in the night. When the lieutenant came to fetch him at nine, the old bishop asked for his furred stole. When the lieutenant protested that it was ridiculous to take such care of his health when he would be dead in half an hour, Fisher replied that he was willing enough to die, "yet will I not hinder my health in the mean time not a minute of an hour." It was More's spirit if not More's statement.

When he had climbed the scaffold unaided, he stood for a moment to say his last words to the crowd. "Hitherto I have not feared death," he said. "Yet I know that I am flesh and that St. Peter from fear of death three times denied his Lord. Wherefore help me, with your prayers, that at the very instant of my death's stroke, I faint not in any point of the catholic faith for any fear." It was the theology of the age; if a man let his faith waver in the hour of his death, he would be lost for eternity. As a tree falls, so shall it lie, More said frequently, quoting the apocryphal book of Ecclesiasticus. Fisher was not so presumptuous even in the moment of his death to doubt that he needed the grace of God to lie true. When his head was cut off, spectators marveled that so much blood could pour from so lean a corpse.

Afterwards it was More's turn.

His trial is what we know best about him, and yet J. Duncan M. Derrett's brilliant analysis of the event made less than two decades ago shows us anew how much there is to be gleaned from a studious consideration of the familiar.

More was brought up to Westminster Hall by boat from the Tower and led in to face a commission of oyer and terminer, a court empowered to hear all the evidence and to make a final ruling that could be appealed to no higher authority other than the king himself. He faced eighteen judges including Cromwell, Audeley, the Duke of Norfolk, Thomas Boleyn, Anne's father, and George Boleyn, her brother. Charles Brandon also sat there—he was Duke of Suffolk, Henry's great friend, implacable foe of the clergy, fierce and resolute enemy of anyone supporting the old order, grandfather to Lady Jane Grey.

It was July 1. Fisher had been dead less than a week, and rain was falling in floods across the South of England. When More saw his judges, he must have known that he had no hope of evading death. But whoever the judges might have been, he would have had scarcely any chance at all, simply because the government in that time never brought a man of high standing to trial for treason if it was not certain of a guilty verdict. Still, this was an English court under English law, and More knew that law as well as anyone.

As Derrett has shown, More defended himself in a spirited way although he was so weak that he had to sit. His beard was long and gray, and he must have been wan and dirty from being shut up for so long. As the practice of the time required, the judges acted as both prosecutors and advisers of the accused. More had no counsel but his own wit and experience in the law—

counsel as good as any he could have found in the realm. Derrett takes More's trial as a real trial that could have gone either way, but this cannot be so. The government was rather producing a legal spectacle so that it could justify to England and to the world what the king had already resolved to do. More, knowing that he was doomed, strove to witness to the injustice of the proceedings and to the truth of the Holy Catholic Church and to set a precedent that men would remember when Henry was gone and passions had cooled and the law had resumed its grand march across English life toward ideal justice. More's attitude was that everyone connected with this trial, including the king, would eventually die. He was thinking of the unborn generations who would find in the trial a drama not dissimilar to the legends of the martyrs who perished in the Roman persecutions. He also used the trial as a stage from which he might appeal to the English people beyond the walls of the Parliament House, a sign to them that the good old faith still lived in their darkened land.

The stage was a court, and both More and his prosecutors played out the piece according to the legal rituals of generations. In effect More was charged with four counts of treason—that he had in the interrogation of May 7 refused to accept the royal supremacy over the church of England, that he had had treasonable correspondence with John Fisher while they were both prisoners in the Tower, and that on June 3 he described the Act of Supremacy as a two-edged sword, so that by accepting it one saved the body and killed the soul and that by rejecting it one saved the soul but killed the body. In the fourth count he was accused of a treasonable conversation with Richard Riche on June 12, when, according to the indictment, More "falsely, traitorously, and maliciously" spoke against the statute.

More answered the charges of the first three counts at length, and the court seemed to recognize at once that it had no case on them. On May 7 he had been silent, and silence was not treason. More got in a good stroke when he pointed out that by the general precepts of the English common law, the silent man was seen as giving his consent to the proceedings. Consequently the judges could not change the law to make silence into opposition. He and Fisher had exchanged letters; More said he had written about eight letters to the bishop, but they had been burned, and nothing Fisher had said about their contents could be construed as treason. The matter of the two-edged sword turns up again and again in the records, although More did not use this image when he described the conversation to Margaret; he probably overlooked it in his haste to write, for it does sound like him, and he did not deny that he had said it. But he had been careful to speak hypothetically. The judges had an abstract that seemed to show otherwise, but eventually they seemed to concede More's point without much debate.

So the government's case came down to Riche's testimony, and it was on that testimony that More was condemned. Roper claims that More charged Riche flatly with perjury:

> If I were a man, my lords, that did not regard an oath, I needed not, as it is well known, in this place at this time nor in this case, to stand here as an accused person. And if this oath of yours, Master Riche, be true, then pray I that I never see God in the face, which I would not say, were it otherwise, to win the whole world.

What was More's version of the conversation with Riche? We do not know. Roper says that he gave one but does not tell us what it was. Afterwards, according to Roper, More turned to a vigorous assault on Riche's character to impugn the witness and to convince the audience that Riche was a notorious liar. He and Riche had lived in the same parish, and More knew his reputation, he said, and no one ever took Riche to be a man worthy of confidence in anything important. Riche had a light tongue, and he was guilty of a sin More peculiarly abhorred—gambling with dice. All this rings true; More was always likely to respond to opposition with a stinging attack on his foe's character. In the polemical works he had used such attacks often to divert attention from parts of the argument over the church—like the papacy—that he did not want to pursue. The attack on Riche may have been a similar diversion.

Roper has him conclude his attack by an appeal to the good sense of the judges:

> Can it therefore seem likely unto your honorable lordships that I would, in so weighty a cause, so unadvisedly overshoot myself as to trust Master Riche, a man of me always reputed for one of so little truth as your lordships have heard, so far above my sovereign lord the King or any of his noble counsellors, that I would unto him utter the secrets of my conscience touching the King's Supremacy— the special point and only mark at my hands so long sought for? A thing which I never did, nor never would, after the statute thereof made, reveal either to the King's highness himself or to any of his honorable counsellors, as it is not unknown to your honors, at sundry several times sent from his grace's own person unto the Tower unto me for none other purpose. Can this, in your judgments, my lords, seem likely to be true?

Did More really make this ringing speech? We cannot know. Roper was not at the trial, and he admits to having his information at second hand from people favorable to his father-in-law. It is also true that it is dangerous to trust a historian like Roper who writes well, for at dramatic moments in their narrative, such historians are likely to write speeches appropriate to the occasion despite the important inconvenience that the principals involved did not think to make those speeches themselves.

The problem is this: We do not have a reliable account of everything that happened at the trial. We have Roper. Derrett has relied heavily on an account preserved and surely altered by Reginald Pole, an exile during this time, a man who would return to England under the reign of Mary Tudor, become Archbishop of Canterbury, succeeding Cranmer and seeing to it that Cranmer was burned, a man dedicated to bringing England back to papal Christianity, often not to be trusted in what he said happened during the reign of Henry VIII. And Roper is maddening because he admits, with a fatigue that all writers know, that many other things were said that he could not remember or that he had not written down.

Riche gave an oral account of what had been said on June 12. It was his chance to make a show before important men who could help him get on in the world, and he probably made the most of it. He may have gone beyond both his own memo of the conversation and the indictment itself. His embellishments could have been sufficient to provoke More to his famous outburst, an outburst that would be remembered by everyone who heard it.

The most likely place where Roper blurs things is in his record of what More said after he had flatly denied Riche's testimony:

> And yet if I had so done indeed, my lords, as Master Riche hath sworn, seeing it was spoken but in familiar secret talk, nothing affirming, and only in putting of cases without other displeasant circumstances, it cannot justly be taken to be spoken "maliciously."

If Riche had told a blatant and lethal lie, one that had driven More into such an eloquent denial as we have seen, More would hardly then have turned immediately to the proposition that even if what Riche said was true, it was all spoken hypothetically and without malice. What More probably said was that the account of the conversation in the indictment showed his comments to be hypothetical and without assertion about the Act of Supremacy. Such hypothetical arguments could not be construed as malicious.

Now he fell back on a common argument of lawyers in that time and this: What was the intent of the law? He declared that he could not believe that "so many worthy bishops, so many honorable personages, and so many other worshipful, virtuous, wise, and well-learned men as at the making of that law were in the Parliament assembled, ever meant to have any man punished by death in whom there could be found no malice." The word "maliciously" in the statute had the same controlling authority, he said, as the word "forcible" in the Statute of Forcible Entries. For if a man in a dispute enters the house of his adversary peaceably, he does not offend under the statute and cannot be charged for violating it. More then recited his history of loyal service to Henry to show that he could not be guilty of malice toward one whom he had served so well.

Roper gives the quite baffling detail that Riche attempted to confirm his story by appealing to the witness of the two men who had been packing up More's books while he and Riche talked and that both men said that they had paid no attention to what Riche and More were saying and could not testify about it. No lawyer worth his craft will ever put a supporting witness on the stand without knowing what he is going to say. Roper is the only source we have for this bizarre tale of speechless witnesses. Obviously he wanted us to believe that they knew Riche was lying and would not perjure themselves, and in fact they may have been startled to hear Riche go beyond the wording of the indictment in his oral account of what happened, so startled that they fell into the saving expedient of forgetfulness when they were asked to risk their souls by swearing a lie. In such an eventuality, the prosecution's preparation of them as witnesses may unexpectedly have run aground on the shoals of their consciences. We do not know, and Elton has good reason to be skeptical about the story.

None of More's efforts made any impression on the jury although it seems that he attacked the indictment and Riche's testimony in much greater detail. "All of which notwithstanding," Roper says, "the jury found him guilty." The jury's deliberations required only fifteen minutes.

The verdict has often been attacked on the grounds that More was convicted on the testimony of only one witness and the feeling was growing in England that two witnesses were necessary to condemn a man in a capital case. But the requirement of two witnesses was not laid down by statute until 1547, during the reign of Edward VI, and the common law had always been willing to accept only one witness if the judges deemed him to be of good character and if no other witnesses could be found. More himself had earlier discussed the difficulty of finding credible witnesses in capital crimes like heresy and treason, a problem being, he said, that people guilty of these offenses do not customarily bring notaries with them to record the deed.

As quickly as the jury pronounced its verdict, Audeley arose to pass sentence. More interrupted him. "My Lord, when I was toward the law, the manner in such case was to ask the prisoner before judgment, why judgment should not be given against him."

Audeley stopped, perhaps in some confusion but knowing that More was right. And so More spoke. Derrett has wisely shown us that what More did, in effect, was to make a motion in arrest of judgment, to argue that sentence should not be passed because the statute by which he had been judged was not valid.

As best we can tell, More began with the fundamental supposition that was clear in all Catholic discussions about the royal supremacy. A layman could not be head of the church. Roper has More say that the indictment was "grounded upon an act of Parliament directly repugnant to the laws of God and His Holy Church, the supreme government of which, or any part whereof, may no temporal prince presume by any law to take upon him, as rightfully belonging to the See of Rome, a spiritual pre-eminence by the mouth of our Savior himself, personally present upon the earth, only to Saint Peter and his successors, Bishops of the same See, by special prerogative granted; it is therefore in law, amongst Christian men, insufficient to charge any Christian man."

We may wonder if More really took the occasion to extol the papacy—a matter that he had never been comfortable about, even before his king became embroiled with popes. Still, he never doubted that the pope was head of the church, although he was never willing to define what that headship might mean. But the main line of his thought was clear: the Act of Supremacy contradicted a higher law, the law of the Catholic Church, the law of God. In such a conflict, the act of Parliament must give way.

Audeley responded with the familiar argument of the government. The bishops, the universities, and the most learned men of the realm had agreed to the act. How could More stand alone in such company and vehemently stick to his solitary opinion?

More replied that for every bishop that stood with the government, a hundred stood with him. And not only bishops, but the great majority of the living and the dead, many of them holy saints in heaven, stood with him also. And all the general councils for a thousand years stood against the statutes, as did the nations of Christendom. Here, among others, he mentioned the French. Derrett thinks that this remark was tactless, considering the recent unsuccessful efforts of the Duke of Norfolk to persuade Francis I to follow Henry's example and form an independent national church. At any rate, Norfolk spoke up here, saying, "Now, More, you show the plain, obstinate malice of your soul." Derrett supposes that Norfolk accused More of malice not toward the Act of Supremacy but toward the king's foreign policy.

More claimed that he wished only to obey his conscience. Derrett thinks that he meant that conscience required him to do all he could to overturn the act and to save his life; such an interpretation is possible, but surely More could have entertained no real hope that these judges would overturn the statute. It seems much likelier to suppose that he was using the motion in arrest of judgment as an occasion to make a speech and to let his audience know unmistakably the reasons for his death. The context of More's statement was a judicial court and the tradition of the capital trial. But the spirit of his utterance was that of the Christian martyrs who had died in the arena, confessing their creeds to the multitudes.

More called up the memory of Magna Carta and the liberties it granted to the church in England. The statute was contrary to that great bulwark of English law. It was contrary to the coronation oath the king had sworn to defend the church. Roper has More say that England could no more refuse obedience to the see of Rome than might the child refuse obedience to his own natural father. England could no more make a law against the general law of Christ's universal Catholic Church than the city of London could make a law against the Parliament of the whole realm.

Roper makes it seem that More's great speech put the judges into uncertainty. Audeley looked over to Sir John Fitz-James, Lord Chief Justice of the King's Bench, and asked him whether the indictment was sufficient. Roper says that Fitz-James answered "like a wise man": "My Lords all, by Saint Julian (That was ever his oath), I must needs confess that if the act of Parliament be not unlawful, then is not the indictment in my conscience insufficient."

Pole's later story, which Derrett very much wants to believe, held that an embarrassing pause followed this ambiguous pronouncement. Derrett says, "The hedging reply, a veiled question to the other judges, elicited no response." But the declaration by Fitz-James sounds not so much like a veiled question as the abrupt wisdom of a practical judge, a bit weary with the long proceedings, eager to get things over with and to arrive at the place where everyone in the chamber knew the trial was going.

Audeley said, in the same spirit, "Lo, my lords, lo, you have heard what my Lord Chief Justice saith." He then swiftly passed judgment. Was More, like Fisher, sentenced at first to the full barbarities of the laws of treason and his sentence later commuted to beheading? Or did Audeley immediately grant him the mercy of the ax? We cannot tell.

More was allowed to make one final speech, a speech that in the rituals of trials was usually an occasion for the condemned prisoner to beg for mercy. More took a different and resigned course.

More have I not to say, my lords, but like as the blessed apostle Saint Paul, as we read in the Acts of the Apostles, was present and consented to the death of Saint Stephen, and kept their clothes that stoned him to death, and yet be they now both twain holy saints in heaven, and shall continue there friends forever, so I verily trust, and shall therefore right heartily pray, that though your lordships have now here in earth been judges to my condemnation, we may yet hereafter in heaven merrily all meet together, to our everlasting salvation.

When Paul consented to the death of Stephen, Paul was a savage enemy of the Christian church, and Stephen was innocent of any malice. Later on Paul was converted and accepted Stephen's faith. More was here brilliantly using his knowledge of the Bible to tell the judges that they were enemies of God and that unless they changed, they would be in hell while he enjoyed the bliss of heaven, but that if they came over to his side, they would share in his salvation.

So it was over, and More was led out to the Thames and into the boat that would take him downriver to the Tower again. Roper says he was taken in charge by Sir William Kingston, a gallant warrior then Constable of the Tower. When he put More ashore by the Tower, he burst into tears, and More comforted him: "Good Master Kingston, trouble not yourself but be of good cheer; for I will pray for you, and my good Lady, your wife, that we may meet in heaven together, where we shall be merry for ever and ever."

Later Kingston told Roper, "In good faith, Master Roper, I was ashamed of myself that, at my departing from your father, I found my heart so feeble, and his so strong, that he was fain to comfort me which should rather have comforted him."

Margaret was waiting for her father at Tower Wharf, "where she knew he should pass by before he could enter into the Tower—there tarrying for his coming home." When she saw him, she pushed through the crowd, through the encircling guard with its pikes and halberds, and threw her arms around his neck and kissed him. He gave her his blessing and comforted her, and they parted. But Margaret could not let him go, and she pushed her way back again and again and embraced him and kissed him, "and at last with a full heavy heart was fain to depart from him." Stapleton says that at Margaret's second embrace More said nothing because his voice was choked with tears. He also says that Margaret Giggs Clement and More's son John kissed their father as well.

Executions followed swiftly on judgments in those days. More lived five nights after his trial. The trial was held on Thursday; on Monday, More wrote to Margaret the last letter of his life. With it he sent the hair shirt that he had worn for so long. The letter itself is a little masterpiece, filled with affection for those he loved best. He does not mention Dame Alice; perhaps her hostility to his stand and her anguish over her poverty had worn away their love at last.

Our Lord bless you good daughter and your good husband and your little boy and all yours and all my children and all my godchildren and all our friends. Recommend me when you may to my good daughter Cicily whom I beseech our

Lord to comfort, and I send her my blessing and to all her children and pray her to pray for me. I send her a handkerchief, and God comfort my good son her husband. . . . I cumber you good Margaret much, but I would be sorry if it should be any longer than tomorrow, for it is Saint Thomas Eve and the Utas of Saint Peter, and therefore tomorrow long I to go to God; it were a day very meet and convenient for me. I never liked your manner towards me better than when you kissed me last for I love when daughterly love and dear charity hath no leisure to look for worldly courtesy. Farewell, my dear child, and pray for me, and I shall for you and all your friends that we may merrily meet in heaven. I thank you for your great costs . . . I pray you at time convenient recommend me to my good son John More. I liked well his natural fashion. Our Lord bless him and his good wife my loving daughter to whom I pray him be good, as he hath great cause . . .

St. Thomas was the doubting apostle who did not believe until he saw the wounds of his resurrected Lord. More mentioned him often in his works. Because he might escape purgatory with the purification of martyrdom, More might hope to rise directly to the bliss of heaven. And he would have felt it bliss indeed to stand with that apostle and to see the wounds of Christ as Thomas had seen them and to say, with all doubts cast away forever, "My Lord and my God." The sending of a handkerchief to his daughter Cecily is reminiscent of those handkerchiefs people took away from Paul at Ephesus so they could touch the sick with them—one of the great proof texts for the validity of relics. Perhaps Cecily had asked him for such a token, and he sent it to her.

Early in the morning on Tuesday, July 6, 1535, Sir Thomas Pope, one of More's friends, came from the king and the council to announce that he would die before nine o'clock. It is hard to tell if More's reply is ironic or not; the man preserved his mysteries to the end, and his spirit of irony daunted many of his contemporaries as it daunts us today.

"Master Pope," he said, "for your good tidings I most heartily thank you. I have been always much bounded to the king's highness for the benefits and honors that he hath still from time to time most bountifully heaped upon me. And yet more bound am I to his grace for putting me into this place, where I have had convenient time and space to have remembrance of my end. And so help me God, most of all, Master Pope, am I bound to his highness that it pleaseth him so shortly to rid me out of the miseries of this wretched world. And therefore will I not fail earnestly to pray for his grace, both here and also in another world."

"The king's pleasure is further," Pope said, "that at your execution you shall not use many words."

"Master Pope," More said, "you do well to give me warning of his grace's pleasure, for otherwise I had purposed at that time somewhat to have spoken, but of no matter wherewith his grace, or any other, should have had cause to be offended. Nevertheless, whatsoever I intended, I am ready obediently to conform myself to his grace's commandments. And I beseech you, good Master Pope, to be a mean unto his highness that my daughter Margaret may be at my burial."

"The king is content already," Pope said, "that your wife, children, and your other friends shall have liberty to be present."

The interview shows Henry wary of More's oratorical powers, even on the scaffold. The Carthusians and Richard Reynolds had preached as long as they had breath while they were being put to death, and More was doubtless a much better orator than they. His gift for public speaking was what made him best known to the citizens of London and the court; it is the part of him that we cannot recover.

When Pope had taken his departure in tears, More dressed himself in the finest clothes he had. He was, as always, ready to be at his best before an audience. The Lieutenant of the Tower was scandalized. As part of his fee, the headsman received the clothes of his victim, and the lieutenant said that the man was a rogue. Finally the argument of the lieutenant prevailed—probably because More did not wish to give anything of high value to one who might use it for immoral purposes. More changed into a rough gray cloak that belonged to his servant John a Wood, but he did send the executioner a gold coin called an angel.

So he was led out to the scaffold on Tower Hill. It was to be his last stage. Richard Empson and Edmund Dudley, Henry VII's hated financial officers, had died there in 1510, and More had witnessed their beheading. Buckingham had perished there in 1521, and More had probably seen him die, too. Fisher had been executed on the same scaffold two weeks before. More walked to his death carrying a small red cross, symbol of the blood of Christ and symbol, too, of those ancient and almost mythological crusaders who had gone to the Holy Land to fight the infidel. We have a legion of stories about his progress up the hill through the pressing throng who had come to see him die. All are agreed on one thing: he kept his wit and his composure to the very end.

Hall tells of the woman who pushed through the crowd and beseeched him to release some evidence about a case of hers, evidence that she could not obtain after his arrest. He said, "Good woman, have patience for a little while, for the king is good unto me that even within this half-hour he will discharge me of all business and help thee himself."

The scaffold was old and tottering, and unlike Fisher, who ascended unaided, More needed a helping hand to mount its steps. He said to the Lieutenant of the Tower, "I pray you, Master Lieutenant, see me safe up, and for my coming down, let me shift for myself."

As tradition demanded, the executioner kneeled and asked More's forgiveness for what he was about to do. As tradition also demanded, More embraced and kissed him and gave him his blessing.

He was brief in asking all the people to pray for him. Roper says that he told them to bear witness with him that he should "now there suffer death in and for the faith of the Holy Catholic Church." A pamphlet called the *Paris News Letter* carried the report of the trial and execution to the Continent; it adds the eloquent detail that More said he died the king's good servant but God's first.

By the customs of executions of this sort, More would, after his speech, have taken off most of his clothes to give them as a fee to the headsman. Roper says that More told the executioner not to be afraid to do his work. His neck was short, More said; if the executioner cared for his reputation as a headsman, he should not strike awry. Fifty years afterward Stapleton wrote that More bound his own eyes with a linen band; he got the story from Margaret Giggs Clement, More's adopted daughter, who was the only member of the family to see More die.

The block on the scaffold was low and small. More, like Fisher before him, would have had to lie on his stomach to put his neck across it. He moved his tangled gray beard carefully out of the way; some remembered that he said it should not be cut in two because it had done no treason.

When he had arranged himself, he waited, doubtless reciting in his mind one of the ancient prayers of his beloved church.

EPILOGUE

S O THOMAS MORE DIED, and this long book must come to an end. He died for an ancient and noble hope, not merely that God had spoken to the Catholic Church but that a God as mysterious and as terrifying as a God of this strange world must be had spoken at all to frail and faltering humankind, erring creatures blinded by their perversity and stumbling miserably in the dark they had made for themselves. Into this darkness that deserved only wrath, God had sent His blessed light, and in that light the world took on an order, and human life took on a cosmic purpose that neither could have on its own.

Faith in the Catholic Church was a confidence that history does mean something despite its apparent chaos; human beings could not be precisely sure what every event might mean, but they knew that all things were moving in an unseen harmony with the grand design of God and that in the midst of tribulation and perplexity, the Catholic Church endured and prevailed. By its venerable traditions, by its holy saints ever present invisibly among men, by its daily miracles, by its stupendous and sacred unity, it showed mortals the way to God and made the great bridge of grace over which God continually moved from eternity into time. For Thomas More the church was itself a continuing miracle, and his vision of a united people of God, extending like a divine radiance through centuries of time and millions of souls, included the living and the dead, robbed death of its victory, and granted a splendor to life.

More was one of those men, frequent enough in our history, who were haunted all their lives by death even as they gave themselves with busy devotion to the life of a secular world. The Catholic Church was his only assurance against hell, or worse—non-being. More's church had to be at liberty to receive the continuing revelation and power of God, for he believed that God had yet great, good things to reveal to His people. God's church had to retain the original purity conferred on it by Christ. The dissidents wanted a pure church, but they demanded an impossible moral purity of the people in the church, or else they spoke as Luther did of a purity that God gave by imputation to all Christians, although the Christians themselves might be sodden with wickedness. The heretics were finally reduced to speaking of an invisible church that possessed the purity lacking in the church they could see in the world, and More thought this was nonsense.

He always said that the church was like Noah's Ark; it contained the clean and the unclean. The purity he wanted was sacramental purity, the correct continuation of what God had ordained, and a purity of doctrine that, like the sacraments, was necessary if men were to be saved. This purity depended on the sanctity of priesthood. Only priests had the special and wonderful authority to administer the sacraments, those holy acts that brought God daily and powerfully into human experience in ways that could be grasped by the bodily senses. True priests were made by God alone, acting through a church that stood at liberty from kings.

Here the tradition was old and complex, so well known in Catholic Europe that people did not necessarily think of everything the tradition included when they talked about it, just as we do not recall at once every source and part of the tradition of constitutional government or equality of citizens under the law.

It is the part of a legal mind like More's to consider the whole of the tradition. And he knew that in its origins and development the separation of church and government had been founded in the conviction that there was something impure, something wicked, perhaps even something satanic about the rulers of secular governments. If these people were to be redeemed in heaven, they had to make up for the personal guilt they had incurred in their bloody deeds of kingship by preserving the church and keeping priesthood alive and by humbling themselves to priests to confess their sins and to partake of the soul-saving sacraments.

A church in the clutches of a government that no longer protected it but rather ruled it was in the hands of the enemy, perhaps in the hands of Satan himself. Thomas Aquinas and many another could proclaim the divine origin of the secular authority, but it was like proclaiming the divine origin of hangmen. In the dualistic confusion always lurking just under the surface of the loudly declared monotheism of medieval theology, it was sometimes quite impossible to tell whether God or the devil held dominion over the mechanisms of government. But Catholics like Thomas More knew that a church ruled by a king was in bondage, unable to serve as the continuing incarnation of God in the world, for the words that a bound church spoke might not be God's words at all but the words of vainglorious and wicked men. The church to be the church had to be ordered by priests possessing a sacral character unique to their ordination.

This sacral character, which More always held in awe, is difficult for us to understand or even to see as we pore over the records of the church in the Middle Ages; most of our lives have been robbed of any sense of the sacred, and when we search for it, we are like color-blind people looking for green. Undoubtedly many notions were bound up in a confusing way with priesthood. The Christian priesthood was probably originally seen as superior to the laity not only because priests administered the sacraments but because priests also did not handle female genitalia, and the special horror that More felt for the thought that women might hear confession or that married men could consecrate the eucharist was partly related to his conviction that the sexual life was fundamentally impure, only barely redeemed by the sacrament of matrimony.

Princes were laymen. The popes of the eleventh century had demanded that priests have no sexual intercourse, and they had gone to war to make princes keep hands off the church. The two demands were part of the same vision of the sacramental church, a vision that suffused More's life, and it is not hard to imagine the revulsion he felt that a man like Henry VIII should crawl out of the bed of Anne Boleyn in the morning to put his corrupt hands on the Catholic Church and its blessed sacraments, to pour his polluted stream into its clear waters, and to make it speak with his wicked voice rather than to bow to its saving majesty.

So More died for the sacral church. He thought that the pope was the head of that church, but the papacy was merely one office among many in the priestly order, and it is a critical error to say that he died for the authority of the pope in England and to leave it at that, not explaining that he held none of the high-flown doctrines of papal infallibility that have spread their black wings over the skies of Catholic modernity.

Only twenty years after his death, the issue of his martyrdom was blurred, and Reginald Pole was spreading the word that the central doctrine for More was the papacy, ignoring More's unwillingness throughout all his works to commit himself to any notion of papal sovereignty. Had he lived, and had the heretics of his time passed away as he supposed they would, he would have been on the side of conciliar reform and constitutional limitation of the papal power. But such reforms had to be matters that a priestly church decided for itself, continually informed by God's continuing revelation; they would not be dictated by kings.

Still, we are left with the most puzzling question of all: what kind of man chooses to die for his faith? Martyrdom is an exceptional talent; that is why we make so much of it. And people like Thomas More, refusing to save his life by speaking a few words, remain as mysterious to us as suicides are to those who love life and hate the thought of giving it up. It is all well and good to spell out, as I have done, the intellectual reasons behind More's supreme act, but somehow they do not get to the heart. A generation before More climbed the scaffold on that July morning in 1535, his convictions about the necessary distinction between the spiritual and the secular orders were commonplaces of European civilization, as seemingly impregnable as representative government and the control of the military by the civilian authority in Great Britain and the United States today. Yet only a few Englishmen were willing to die for them, and Thomas More was the only layman whose death might be called martyrdom during the reign of Henry VIII. Confronted by such mysteries, social historians quote statistics, historians of theology cite doctrines, and biographers recoil before the task of sorting out the conflicting strands in the weave of character that add up to such an end.

More's inner conflicts and fundamental mystery loom darker than most of his modern admirers care to admit. The contradictions are stark and numerous, and at times they make him a disappointing hero. He felt a lifelong sensibility and repugnance to physical pain; yet he sent heretics to a flaming death with alacrity, and afterwards he mocked their torments. He had a stunning imagination, and in his various dialogues he gives us a human comedy of diverse characters, moved by diverse whims and purposes. But he never came close to imagining the profound religious appeal of Luther's doctrines to scrupulous souls in agony for the guilt of their sins, and he refused to suppose that even those heretics who died in witness to their hope could possibly be sincere.

For a busy man, his literary production was enormous, but some of his best works were not published during his lifetime, and he wasted himself in bitter controversies that weary and even embarrass us with their unmitigated fury. He could love with devotion and hate with passion. He was a calculator. He was almost obsequious to Wolsey as long as Wolsey was in power, but when Wolsey fell, More turned on him like a hawk diving to prey.

His ironic spirit made good literature, but it also makes him difficult to fathom, and sometimes it must have been bad company. We recall how poor Jane Colt wept at her husband's demands that she improve herself and how to make friends laugh he reported her delight over a necklace of false jewels that he had told her were real. We may also recall Edward Hall's comment, noted early in this book, "I cannot tell whether I should call him a foolish wise man or a wise foolish man, for undoubtedly he beside his learning had a great wit, but it was so mingled with taunting and mocking that it seemed to them that best knew him, that he thought nothing to be well spoken except he had ministered some mock in the communication."

He felt himself always on stage, and we weary of the self-serving of his image making, even when we recognize in it the habitual style of many Renaissance men unfamiliar with the artful subtleties and deceits of modern public relations. More looks proud of his humility. And we do not believe him when he tells us that he had not really intended to publish this work or that, that he was forced to take high office against his will, that he cared nothing for the opinion of others, and that he wanted only the simple life. We do not believe him because his acts prove entirely otherwise. Even the public spectacle he made of his real love for his family seems at times overmuch, part of the pageant he performed for an audience.

Yet there he stands in our history, an indomitable symbol, and few have known him well without feeling a heart lift up to what he was. His stern face looks out across my study from a cheap print of the Holbein portrait, a look of intensity and rigid self-control and perhaps a manly beauty equaled in few Renaissance portraits, and a look, too, of unfathomable mystery. Those of us who have labored on the Yale edition of his complete works and written about him and talked about him for well over two decades find him exasperating, annoying, loving, hateful, obtuse, brilliant, witty, demanding—and somehow very much an indispensable ideal we cherish for ourselves.

He died magnificently, but his death was not the headlong rush of a fanatical zealot into oblivion; it was the fearful, considered decision of a man of great self-knowledge, doing what he had to do and wishing almost until the end that he did not have to do it. No one can sit, as I have done at times, in the New England twilight looking at that strong, sad face and believe that Thomas More will ever be anything but a stranger to those who study him—this divided man who believed in miracles as long as they happened in the remote past, who wore a rough hair shirt next to his skin and made his way steadily in a world of ermine and velvet, a man who flagellated himself with whips and made charming talk at dinner, a man who extolled virginity and married twice, who longed for the monastery and became Lord Chancellor, a man who laughed much in public and nursed a private melancholy, a man who died for an ethereal vision of the sacred that has faded quite away in the electric glow of our modernity.

But then in his writings we stumble on the familiar and the universal—a way of catching scenes of life and characters that we know in our world of the here and now, a Dickensian sense that makes us laugh even yet not only at the comic procession he parades before us but at the absurdities he makes us find in ourselves, so that there are lines in his prose that bring this strange man out of the remoteness of the past and drop him down by our reading desk in the late evening hours.

Like ourselves in the autumn of the twentieth century, he often took the imagination to be more real than the world of sense, and he lived out his life in an inconclusive struggle to bring his outer world into some kind of harmony with his inner being, discovering with the years that his victories were not quite triumphs but that his defeats were never devastations. A man can lose his head and come to no harm, he said at the last, and perhaps that wry resignation before the inevitable appeals to us most, for he finally found a way to stand before death and the dark with his dignity undefiled.

Erasmus a long time ago called him a man for all seasons, and so he has been, and so he will remain. Some will reproach me for not giving in this book a saint from *The Golden Legend*, immaculate and invincible, one of those epicene creations of sterile and impossible virtue who so tantalized and corrupted the desperately romantic Middle Ages.

But Thomas More belongs to no company of icons to be set glittering in the inaccessible reaches of our imaginations as in the gold mosaic of a wall. He was nearer to us, flesh and blood, and in him the good and the bad were always at war. Calculation dueled with spontaneity, humility with pride, love with hate. These conflicts went tumultuously on almost to the very end beneath the calm exterior that he kept toward the world, and an honest biographer cannot truly say that More's virtues were always stronger than his vices or that his vices were insignificant, or that his goodness as he himself might have defined it was always admirable.

Yet biographers have always felt themselves compelled to draw lessons from his life. Perhaps for us the habitual waging of such a hard, inner warfare in Thomas More is lesson enough for our season. For it may be that only those who patiently struggle without victory in such lifelong conflicts within themselves are worthy to be called saints.

BIBLIOGRAPHY

Les Admirables Secrets d'Albert le Grand, trans. Patrick Brehal. Paris, 1965.
Aquinas, Thomas. *Summa theologiae*. Many editions.
Augustine. *Against Julian*, trans. Matthew A. Schumacher. New York, 1957.
————. *On the City of God*. Many editions.

Bainton, Roland H. *Erasmus of Christendom*. New York, 1969.

Calendar of Letters, Despatches, and State Papers Relating to the Negotiations between England and Spain, Preserved in the Archives at Vienna, Simancas, Besançon and Brussels, ed. Pascual de Gayangos et al. London, 1867–1954.
Calendar of State Papers and Manuscripts Relating to English Affairs, Existing in the Archives and Collections of Venice, and in Other Libraries of Northern Italy, ed. Rawdon Brown and Allen B. Hinds. London, 1864–1947.
Campbell, William Edward. *Erasmus, Tyndale, and More*. London, 1949.
Chambers, R. W. *Thomas More*. London, 1938 (first published, 1935).
Chrimes, S. B. *Henry VII*. London, 1972.
Clebsch, William A. *England's Earliest Protestants*. New Haven, 1964.
Cranmer, Thomas. *Miscellaneous Writings and Letters*, ed. J. E. Cox. Cambridge, Eng., 1846.
Cross, Claire. *Church and People, 1450–1660*. New York, 1976.

Davis, John F. "The Trials of Thomas Bylney and the English Reformation." *The Historical Journal*, 1981, pp. 775–90.
Derrett, J. Duncan M. "The Affairs of Richard Hunne and Friar Standish." CW 9 (see More, Thomas, below), pp. 215–46.

————. "The 'New' Document on Thomas More's Trial." *Moreana* 3, pp. 5–22.

————. "The Trial of Sir Thomas More." EA (see *Essential Articles* below), pp. 55–78.

Dickens, A. G. *Thomas Cromwell and the English Reformation.* New York, 1959.

Dictionary of National Biography. 63 vols.; London, 1885–1900.

Documents Illustrative of English Church History, ed. Henry Gee and William John Hardy. London, 1921.

Elton, G. R. *Policy and Police.* Cambridge, Eng., 1972.

————. "The Real Thomas More?" In *Reformation Principle and Practice,* ed. Peter Newman Brooks. London, 1980.

————. *Reform and Reformation.* Cambridge, Mass., 1977.

————. *The Tudor Constitution.* Cambridge, Eng., 1960.

Erasmus, Desiderius. *The Colloquies of Erasmus,* trans. Craig R. Thompson. Chicago, 1965.

————. *The Correspondence of Erasmus.* Toronto: University of Toronto Press, 1975– .

————. *The Enchiridion,* trans. Raymond Himelick. Bloomington, Ind., 1963.

————. *Opus Epistolarum Des. Erasmi Roterodami,* ed. P. S. Allen, H. M. Allen, et al. 12 vols.; Oxford, 1906–58.

————. *The Praise of Folly,* trans. Clarence H. Miller. New Haven, 1979.

Essential Articles for the Study of Thomas More, ed. R. S. Sylvester and G. P. Marc'hadour. Hamden, Conn., 1977.

Fisher, John. *The English Works of John Fisher,* ed. John E. B. Mayor, London, 1876.

FitzStephen, William. "Thomas Becket." *English Historical Documents,* vol. 2, ed. David C. Douglas. London, 1953.

Fortescue, John. *A Learned Commendation of the Politique Laws of England,* trans. R. Mulcaster. London, 1573. *Short-title Catalogue* 11195.

Fox, Richard. *Letters, 1886–1527,* ed. P. S. and H. M. Allen. Oxford, 1529.

Foxe, John. *Acts and Monuments of the Martyrs,* ed. Josiah Pratt. London, 1875.

Fraenkel, Pierre. "Johann Eck und Sir Thomas More." *Von Konstanz nach Trient,* ed. Remigius Bäumer. Munich, 1972.

Fulop, Robert Ernest. "John Frith (1503–1533) and His Relation to the Origin of the Reformation in England." Unpublished dissertation, New College, University of Edinburgh, 1956.

Goring, J. J. "The General Proscription of 1522." *English Historical Review,* 1971, pp. 681–705.

Greenblatt, Stephen. *Renaissance Self-Fashioning.* Chicago, 1980.

"Gregory VII on Investiture." *Introduction to Contemporary Civilization in the West,* vol. 1, pp. 268–74. New York, 1969.

Guy, J. A. *The Public Career of Sir Thomas More.* Brighton, Sussex, 1980.

Hall, Edward. *Chronicle.* London, 1809 (facsimile of 1550 edition).

Harpsfield, Nicholas. *The Life and Death of Sir Thomas More,* ed. E. V. Hitchcock. London, 1932.

Hudson, Hoyt Hopewell. *The Epigram in the English Renaissance.* Princeton, 1947.

Hughes, Philip. *The Reformation in England,* vol. 1. New York, 1963.

Hunt, Ernest William. *Dean Colet and His Theology.* London, 1956.

Jenkins, Elizabeth. *The Little Princes in the Tower.* London, 1978.

Kendall, Paul Murray. *Richard the Third*. Garden City, N.Y., 1965.

Lander, J. R. *Government and Community, 1450–1509*. Cambridge, Mass., 1980.

LeClercq, Jean. *The Love of Learning and the Desire for God*. New York, 1962.

Lehmberg, Stanford E. *The Reformation Parliament, 1529–1536*. Cambridge, Eng., 1970.

Letters and Papers, Foreign and Domestic, of the Reign of Henry VIII, ed. J. S. Brewer, James Gairdner, and R. H. Brodie. 21 vols.; London, 1862–1932.

Luther, Martin. *Martin Luthers Werke*. 58 vols.; Weimar, 1883– .

Marc'hadour, Germain. "L'Avenement des Temps Modernes." Review of the book of that title in *Moreana* 6, 27.

———. "The Death Year of Thomas More's Mother." *Moreana* 63, 13-16.

———. *L'Univers de Thomas More*. Paris, 1963.

Merriman, Roger Bigelow. *Life and Letters of Thomas Cromwell*, 2 vols. Oxford, 1902.

More, Thomas. *The Yale Edition of the Complete Works of St. Thomas More*. New Haven and London, 1963– .

    CW 2   *The History of King Richard III*, ed. Richard S. Sylvester.

    CW 3   Part I, *Translations of Lucian*, ed. C. R. Thompson.

    CW 3   Part II, *The Latin Poems*, ed. Clarence H. Miller, Leicester Bradner, Charles A. Lynch, and Revilo P. Oliver.

    CW 4   *Utopia*, ed. Edward Surtz, S. J., and J. H. Hexter.

    CW 5   *Responsio ad Lutherum*, ed. J. M. Headley, trans. Sister Scholastica Mandeville.

    CW 6   *A Dialogue Concerning Heresies*, ed. Thomas M. C. Lawler, Germain Marc'hadour, and Richard C. Marius.

    CW 8   *The Confutation of Tyndale's Answer*, ed. L. A. Schuster, R. C. Marius, J. P. Lusardi, and R. J. Schoeck.

    CW 9   *The Apology*, ed. J. B. Trapp.

    CW 12   *A Dialogue of Comfort Against Tribulation*, ed. L. L. Martz and F. Manley.

    CW 13   *Treatise on the Passion*, etc., ed. Gerry Haupt.

    CW 14   *De tristitia Christi*, ed. C. H. Miller.

———. *The answere to the fyrst parte of the poysened booke wh. a namelesse heretyke hath named the souper of the lorde*. London, 1533 (misdated 1534). *Short-title Catalogue* 18077.

———. *The Correspondence of Sir Thomas More*, ed. Elizabeth F. Rogers. Princeton, 1947.

———. *The History of King Richard III and Selections from the English and Latin Poems*, ed. R. S. Sylvester. New Haven and London, 1976.

———. *The Latin Epigrams of Thomas More*, ed. L. Bradner and C. A. Lynch. Chicago, 1953.

———. *Selected Letters*, ed. Elizabeth F. Rogers, trans. Marcus Haworth, S.J. New Haven and London, 1961.

———. *Sir Thomas More: Neue Briefe*, ed. Hubertus Schulte Herbrüggen. Münster, 1966.

———. *The Supplycacyon of Soulys agaynst the Supplycacyon of beggars*. London, 1529. *Short-title Catalogue* 18092.

———. *The Workers . . . in the Englysh tonge*. London, 1557.

Nelson, William. "Thomas More, Grammarian and Orator." *PMLA* 58 (1943), pp. 337–52.

Ogle, Arthur. *The Tragedy of the Lollards' Tower*. Oxford, 1949.

Pantin, W. A. *The English Church in the Fourteenth Century.* South Bend, Ind., 1962.

Patrologiae Cursus Completus: Series Latina, ed. J. P. Migne. 221 vols.; Paris, 1844–1903.

Perroy, Edouard. *The Hundred Years War,* trans. W. B. Wells. New York, 1965.

Pollard, A. F. "The Making of Sir Thomas More's Richard III." In *Historical Essays in Honour of James Tait.* Manchester, 1933. (EA, pp. 421–31.)

———. *Wolsey,* introduction by A. G. Dickens. New York, 1966.

Quinones, Ricardo J. *The Renaissance Discovery of Time.* Cambridge, Mass., 1972.

Reynolds, E. E. *The Field Is Won.* London, 1968.

———. "An Unnoticed Document." *Moreana* 1, pp. 12–17.

Roy, William. *Rede me and be nott wrothe.* Strasbourg, 1528. *Short-title Catalogue* 21427.

Saint Basil, *The Letters,* with an English translation by Roy J. Deferrari. Cambridge, Mass., 1961. Loeb Classical Library, Volume I.

Scarisbrick, J. J. *Henry VIII.* Berkeley and Los Angeles, 1968.

Short-title Catalogue of Books Printed in England, Scotland, and Ireland and of Books Printed Abroad, 1475–1640, ed. A. W. Pollard and G. R. Redgrove. Oxford, 1946.

Stapleton, Thomas. *The Life and Illustrious Martyrdom of Sir Thomas More,* trans. Philip E. Hallett. London, 1928.

State Papers of the Reign of Henry VIII. 11 vols.; London, 1830–52.

Statutes of the Realm, ed. A. Ludus, T. F. Tomkins, J. Raithby, et al. 11 vols.; London, 1810–28.

Stow, John. *The Annales of England.* London, 1601.

———. *A Summarie of the Chronicles of England.* London, 1590.

Sylvester, Richard, ed. *St. Thomas More: Action and Contemplation.* New Haven, 1972.

Tanner, Lawrence E., and William Wright. "Recent Investigations Regarding the Fate of the Princes in the Tower." *Archaeologica* 84 (1934), pp. 1–26.

Thomas, Keith. *Religion and the Decline of Magic.* New York, 1971.

Thomson, John A. F. *The Later Lollards.* London, 1965.

Tucker, Melvin J. *The Life of Thomas Howard, 1443–1524.* London, 1964.

Tudor Royal Proclamations, ed. P. Hughes and J. Larkin, vol. 1. New Haven, 1964.

Two Early Tudor Lives: The Life and Death of Cardinal Wolsey by George Cavendish; *The Life of Sir Thomas More* by William Roper, ed. Richard S. Sylvester and Davis P. Harding. New Haven, 1962.

Tyndale, William. *An Answer To Sir Thomas More's Dialogue,* ed. H. Waller. Cambridge, 1850.

Unwin, George. *The Guilds and Companies of London.* 2nd ed.; London, 1925.

Watney, John. *Some Account of the Hospital of St. Thomas of Acon in the Cheap.* London, 1892 (2nd ed., 1906).

Wernham, R. B. *Before the Armada.* London, 1966.

Whiting, Bartlett Jere. *Proverbs, Sentences, and Proverbial Phrases from English Writings Mainly before 1500.* Cambridge, Mass., 1968.

Wigmore, John. *Wigmore on Evidence.* 3rd ed., 10 vols.; Boston, 1940.

Wycliffe, John. *Select English Works,* ed. T. Arnold. Oxford, 1869–71.

NOTES

I HAVE KEPT the scholarly apparatus to a minimum. Many of the works I cite—such as *Utopia* and *The History of King Richard III*—are so short that they can be read easily in less than an evening. I have not supposed it necessary to annotate every reference to them. For any scholar acquainted with the correspondence of Erasmus it is sufficient to know only the date of a particular letter to find it in the Allen edition in Latin or in the as yet incomplete English edition of the correspondence being published by the University of Toronto Press. I have tried when possible to use accessible modern English versions of sixteenth-century texts. This means, for example, that I have used Davis Harding's edition of William Roper's *Life* of More rather than the scholarly edition of E. V. Hitchcock published for the Early English Text Society in 1935. When I have had to rely on the original texts as reproduced in the Yale edition of More's works, I have modernized the spelling. In a very few places I have silently replaced an obsolete English word with a modern one. The people who heard Buckingham speak at the Guildhall would have understood the word "rouning," and that is the word More used to describe what they did after the speech. We would say they fell to whispering, and "whispering" is the word I have used instead of "rouning." I have used "heavens" for "welkin," and for the expression "it booted not" I have written "it did no good."

Whenever possible I have used the translations of the correspondence of Erasmus in the Toronto edition. But since that edition is incomplete I have had to turn often to the Allen edition, and here the translations from the Latin are my own. I have usually used the translations of More's Latin in the Yale edition, but where the Yale editors have not yet made translations or where I have disagreed with them, I have made my own.

I could easily have multiplied my notes by ten, but in these days of wildly explosive costs a proliferation of apparatus quickly passes the point of diminishing returns. I have tried to be especially careful to provide a guide to the evidence in those areas where my conclusions may seem controversial.

Scholars in the field will quickly see the great debts I owe to the works of G. R. Elton, Stephen J. Greenblatt, John Guy, J. H. Hexter, Arthur Ogle, Melvin J. Tucker, and to all the editors of the Yale edition of the complete works.

ABBREVIATIONS
(Complete citations will be found in the bibliography.)

A&C	*St. Thomas More: Action and Contemplation.*
A&M	Foxe, *Acts and Monuments.*
BL	More, *The Latin Epigrams.*
CCI	"Gregory VII on Investiture."
Corr.	More, *The Correspondence of Sir Thomas More.*
CSPS	*Calendar of State Papers, Spanish.*
CSPV	*Calendar of State Papers, Venetian.*
CW	More, *The Yale Edition of the Complete Works of St. Thomas More.*
CWEL	Erasmus, *The Correspondence of Erasmus.*
DCD	Augustine, *De civitas dei (On the City of God).*
DNB	*Dictionary of National Biography.*
EA	*Essential Articles for the Study of Thomas More.*
EE	Erasmus, *Opus Epistolarum Des. Erasmi Roterodami.*
EW	More, *The Workes . . . in the Englysh tonge.*
GH	*Documents Illustrative of English Church History.*
KR	*The History of King Richard III and Selections from the English and Latin Poems.*
LP	*Letters and Papers, Foreign and Domestic, of the Reign of Henry VIII.*
PL	*Patrologiae . . . Series Latina.*
SL	More, *Selected Letters.*
SP	*State Papers of the Reign of Henry VIII.*
SR	*Statutes of the Realm.*
ST	Aquinas, *Summa theologiae.*
STC	*A Short-title Catalogue of Books Printed in England, Scotland, and Ireland and of English Books Printed Abroad, 1475–1640.*
TRP	*Tudor Royal Proclamations.*
TTL	*Two Early Tudor Lives.*
WA	Luther, *Martin Luthers Werke.*

PAGE

38 *in service to princes* EW, a₄ᵛ.

39 *invited him there* TTL, 198.

40 *marrying such a man* Erasmus, *Colloquies*, 120–22.

41 *when she married More* Harpsfield, 93.

42 *make her a whore* Augustine, *Against Julian*, 282.

42 *ordination to him forever* CW 6, 53.

CHAPTER 4

45 *Pygmies from Ethiopia* SL, 2.

46 *happy omen for England* SL, 2–3.

46 *tubercular like his father* Lander, 347.

46 *just the right length* CW 6, 81.

46 *his union with Catherine* Hall, sig. iv₅ᵛ.

47 *greater than their source* CW 8, 593.

48 *objected to the union* Scarisbrick, 13.

50 *nobles of the realm* Stow, 447.

50 *sum he had requested* Chrimes, 200–1.

51 *disappointed all his purpose* TTL, 199.

51 *did with some regularity* Lander, 336.

51 *wrote his* Utopia CW 4, 92–93.

51 *More should beware* TTL, 199–200

52 *Informers could be ignored* BL, 138–39.

52 *honor the princely couple* Stow, *Annales* (1601), 808.

52 *learned to be kings* Scarisbrick, 6–7.

53 *typical of roses* BL, 143.

53 *supported on every side* BL, 143.

54 *over bonds and obligations* Guy, 6.

54 *affection of the city* EE 4, 20.

54 *More in these years* Guy, 6.

54 *Canterbury, William Warham* EE 1, 488.

PAGE

56 *died eighteen hundred men* Hall 2, fol. 18.

56 *many for its failure* LP 1, 1422.

56 *capable of getting things done* LP 1, 1323.

57 *is gradually killed off* CW 4, 139.

57 *authority so to advance* Roy, h₄.

58 *his friend, Bishop Richard Fox* Richard Fox *Letters*, 58.

59 *whole story more accurately* BL, 200.

59 *Hervé had five hands* BL, 200–1.

59 *he could not avoid it* BL, 202.

60 *banners a King's coat* LP 1, 2268.

61 *a meaningless word* BL, 198.

61 *no loss to be taken* BL, 219.

62 *the law doth read* TTL, 199.

62 *League had a concession* TTL, 200.

CHAPTER 5

65 *the study of Greek* SL, 2.

67 *know as to experience* Quoted in LeClercq, 16.

67 *soul to true worship* CW 4, 233.

71 *listening to Plato himself* EE 1, 273.

72 *driven to embrace it* More, *Poysened Booke*, n₁.

72 *preaching against images* Hunt, 51–62.

73 *things was from God* ST, 1.47.2.

75 *partner of my endeavors* SL, 6.

76 *auspices of the Catholic Church* CW 6, 84–85.

CHAPTER 6

81 *ripens to Harvest* EE 1, 273–74.

81 *the age of gold* Bainton, 59.

81 *became a despot* EE I, 275, n. 7, ep. 119.

83 *gratifying your lusts* Erasmus, *Enchiridion*, 159.

84 *stinking of Lucian* WA 18, 609.

84 *filthiness and abuse* CW 3 (I), xlvi.

PAGE

84   *and superstitious untruths* CW 3
     (I), 5.
85   *should treat with caution* CW 3
     (I), 6–7.
86   *sixteenth century liked it* CW 3
     (I), xxxvii.
86   *violent and fearsome thing* CW 3
     (I), 98–101.
87   *in all the important things* EE 1,
     422–23.
88   *eager to support scholars* EE 1,
     449–52.
89   *back with impunity* Erasmus,
     Folly, 128–29.
89   *things of the spirit* Erasmus, *Folly*,
     136.
89   *nailed to the cross* Erasmus, *Folly*,
     88–89.
89   *theologians did exist* Erasmus,
     Folly, 95.
90   *of our master-doctors* Erasmus,
     Folly, 121.
91   *with such madness* Erasmus,
     Folly, 137–38.
91   *aloud to More* Campbell, 55.
92   *very costly gifts* Erasmus, *Folly*,
     72.
92   *even the sun itself* CW 4, 157.
92   *returned to Colet* EE 1, 455–56.
92   *doing exceedingly well* EE 1, 458.
93   *epistolary pace of Erasmus* EE 1,
     475.
93   *to live in England* EE 1, 476.
93   *each other every day* EE 1, 488.
93   *fair copy of anything* EE 1, 493.
94   *express his deep regret* EE 1, 472.
94   *day at his house* Guy, 13.
95   *write* The Praise of Folly EE 4,
     16.
95   *from Italy to England* EE 1, 460.
95   *to go on with it* Erasmus, *Folly*,
     144; EE 1, 94.
96   *with Christian moderation* Eras-
     mus, *Folly*, 2.
96   *and greatest editor* Erasmus,
     Folly, x.

PAGE

96   *Croke a little money* EE 1, 467–
     68.
96   *such serious matters* EE 1, 468.
97   *not breaking it* EE 4, 16.

CHAPTER 7

101 *in so great surety* KR, 52–53.
101 *two hours after* KR, 53.
101 *skin and hard bone* KR, 97.
102 *she had not been* KR, 58.
102 *withstood his purpose* KR, 9.
102 *originate with him* CW 2, 166–
     67; Jenkins, ix.
103 *meddle no farther* KR, 83.
104 *to a servile flattery* KR, 84.
104 *body with many others* KR, 54.
104 *her outer petticoat* KR, 55.
104 *of his own mother* KR, 61.
104 *children are bastards* KR, 63–66.
104 *villainy done them* KR, 73.
105 *to his own commodity* KR, 43.
105 *person of your grace* KR, 94–
     96.
106 *to keep her child* KR, 39.
106 *weeping as fast* KR, 41–42.
107 *get her with child* KR, 65.
107 *are still snoring* CW 2, 17.
107 *it made no difference* KR, 20.
107 *by Richard's servants* KR, 23.
107 *a mess of them* KR, 47.
107 *penance for adultery* KR, 56.
108 *a swarm of bees* KR, 78.
108 *speech in the Guildhall* Pollard
     (1933).
109 *nigh to the queen* KR, 59.
109 *information from angels* Perroy,
     243.
111 *but Brackenbury refused* KR, 85–
     86.
111 *most intimate friends* Tucker, 38–
     39.
111 *singular dear friend* TTL, 225.
111 *fortune would be made* See
     Tucker's careful account, 38–39.
111 *family with the usurper* Such is
     Tucker's supposition, 44.

112 *no one knew where* KR, 87–88.

112 *the princes were dead* Tucker conjectures that the princes might have been killed by the end of June—before Richard's coronation on July 6. More indicates that the murders took place immediately after Richard's coronation. Since Howard was Constable of the Tower until July 17, there was indeed plenty of time for Richard to act after his coronation.

112 *to medical examination* Tanner and Wright.

113 *as he had hoped* KR, 86.

113 *suggest the man's name* Kendall, 445–46.

114 *encounter with the usurper* CW 2, 202–3, n. 36/26; EA, 424–25; Tucker, 43.

116 *sanctuary in England* KR, 37–40.

116 *invaders, the Goths* DCD, 1.7.

116 *that God pulleth down* KR, 94.

119 *would have been flattering* EA, 425.

CHAPTER 8

123 *case from top to toe* CW 6, 318.

124 *among his neighbors* CW 6, 326.

124 *have heard none harm* CW 6, 318.

124 *mortuaries in his day* Wycliffe 3, 285.

125 *can own no property* Ogle, 55–57.

126 *called Hunne's case* CW 6, 326.

126 *The pope or Jesus* Pantin, 82.

126 *arise with such patronage* Pantin, 83–87.

127 *themselves from the fire* Cross, 37–39.

128 *those midnight lectures* CW 6, 328.

128 *believed they were wrong* CW 6, 325.

128 *that so made them* CW 6, 330.

128 *condemned the mass* CW 6, 330.

129 *was planted evidence* Ogle, 113–31.

129 *in Hunne's own hand* Ogle, 130–31.

129 *had murdered him* CW 6, 327.

129 *a lack of grace* More, *Supplycacyon,* clv.

129 *fear of worldly shame* CW 6, 326–27.

129 *praise in his* Utopia CW 4, 187.

130 *Our Lady at St. Paul's* CW 6, 327.

130 *to him a spiritual matter* EW, 298.

130 *record of the inquest* Hall, fol. 50–55v.

132 *dignity of his crown* Hall, fol. 55.

132 *Hunne on December 2* Derrett, "Affairs," 224.

134 *such a singular manner* CW 4, 228.

134 *letter to Wolsey* Thomson, 169.

135 *his undeserved trouble* EW, 298.

136 *searching of the truth* CW 6, 318.

136 *who stole a horse* CW 6, 321.

137 *four score and ten* CW 6, 323.

137 *me any more service* CW 6, 324.

137 *Are these stories true?* Ogle says not; p. 95.

137 *Go before you drink* SL, 24.

138 *bare as a bird's arse* CW 6, 324–25.

138 *than half their strength* CW 6, 319.

138 *Horsey must be innocent* CW 6, 325–26.

138 *he [Horsey] should be guilty* CW 6, 326.

139 *he hanged himself* CW 6, 327.

139 *to shameful death also* CW 6, 327.

140 *burned for an heretic* CW 6, 328; Ogle, 102–6.

140 *lodged against him* CW 9, 222–23.

140 *Tunstall excommunicated him* CW 9, 223–24.

CHAPTER 13

190 *six shillings, and three pence* LP 2, 1468.

190 *set on float again* LP 2, 679.

190 *expenses on the embassy* LP 2, 1467.

190 *his "diets" in Flanders* LP 2, 1470.

191 *food during his absence* EE 2, 196.

191 *king at the same time* EE 2, 196–97.

191 *mixed and intermittent* Elton (1960), 89.

191 *than More, Ammonio said* EE 2, 200–1.

192 *sent for so frequently* TTL, 202.

192 *lawyer can be found* Nelson, 340.

192 *release of the ship* TTL, 201.

192 *to forbear his service* TTL, 201.

194 *Any help is good.* CW 6, 233–34.

195 *destitute in English society* Guy, 22.

195 *the Court of Requests* Guy, 20.

197 *were prentices in Cheap* CW 9, 156.

198 *will let you know* EE 3, 111.

198 *practice in the courts* Guy, 26.

198 *get the fee paid* A&C, 90–91.

199 *it to someone else* Corr., 87.

199 *him for his assistance* EE 2, 430.

200 *read in my life* Corr., 280.

200 *with similar effusions* A&C, 105.

200 *the heavens and wept* CW 12, 213–16.

200 *in honor and health* Corr., 299.

200 *whom he is secretary* EE 3, 286; A&C, 108.

201 *the smack of truth* A&C, 109.

201 *More wrote him afterwards* SL, 144–45.

201 *as to imagine them* SL, 94.

202 *undertreasurer of the exchequer* A&C, 94.

202 *£ 173 6s 8d a year* A&C, 95.

202 *four times a year* Guy, 24.

202 *in the surviving records* Guy, 24–26.

202 *to his daughter Cecily* Guy, 25.

202 *she had been wed* Guy, 26.

202 *son John in 1529* Professor Guy has drawn this amazing tale out of the manuscripts that he has so brilliantly studied, 25–26.

202 *important dignitaries to England* LP, 2, 4333; Hall, sig. 14^V.

202 *diplomatic missions abroad* Guy, 16.

202 *Whitehall and Star Chamber* Guy, 14.

202 *Brabant and Flanders* LP 3, 739.

203 *from Germany into England* Moreana 61, 27.

203 The Assertion of the Seven Sacraments TTL, 235.

203 *shall treat at Calais* SP 1, 20; quoted in A&C, 104.

204 *rule in his stead* LP 3, 2549,

205 *honorable and profitable peace* Corr., 263.

205 *avoid calling a Parliament* Goring, 681–705.

206 *so little of consequence* Dickens, 20. Merriman 1, 313.

207 *preservation of the king* TTL, 203–5.

207 *shillings to the pound* Hall, fol. 109^V.

208 *one thing for another* Hall, fol. 109^V.

208 *bringeth hither with him* TTL, 206.

209 *left in a huff* TTL, 204.

209 *fifty pounds or larger* Hall, fol. 110^V.

209 *In this realm* Merriman 1, 313.

209 *to say to him* TTL, 207.

210 *Wolsey dated August 24* LP 3, 3267.

210 *agreed to Wolsey's request* Corr., 278.

PAGE

210   *not agree with him* TTL, 207–8.

211   *chastised himself with whips*
      TTL, 224.

211   *the Coming of Christ* Scarisbrick,
      136.

212   *pension of thirty-five pounds* Guy,
      25.

212   *many a fair penny* Corr., 518.

212   *that of undertreasurer* Guy, 27.

213   *with devotion and integrity* Guy,
      28–29.

213   *in the cloth trade* Guy, 25.

214   *and Francis had talked* LP 4,
      3337.

CHAPTER 14

218   *in Bucklersbury Street* Reynolds
      (1968), 54.

218   *that included several gardens*
      Watney (1892), 268.

218   *property until his death* Watney
      (1906), 127.

218   *day at his house* Guy, 13.

218   *mischance in his house* Corr.,
      422.

218   *he had complete confidence* Corr.,
      422.

219   *no itch at all* CW 8, 605.

219   *home in the evening* Harpsfield,
      94.

219   *ruled by anyone yet* Harpsfield, 95.

220   *weened I had slept* SL, 242.

220   *Dame Alice knew about it* LP, ad-
      dendum 1, 1024.

220   *wood as his pillow* Stapleton, 9.

220   *all the long night* CW 12, 277.

221   *eleven grandchildren as well* Sta-
      pleton, 100.

221   *a little thought to it* Stapleton,
      107.

222   *joyous by literary pursuits* SL, 109.

222   *yourself, my beloved daughter* SL,
      109.

222   *dear to my heart* SL, 110.

222   *sun from the moon* SL, 146.

223   *to such a man* SL, 151–52.

PAGE

223   *could scarcely understand them*
      Corr., 120–23.

224   *to hear a sermon* EE 4, 547–79.

225   *not love you now* BL, 231.

225   *on several royal commissions* Rey-
      nolds (1968), 169.

225   *but never married again* Reynolds
      (1968), 170.

226   *the hearing of cases* Guy, 14.

226   *his father in 1522* Guy, 25.

226   *a suburb of London* Reynolds
      (1968), 173.

226   *her for her accomplishments* SL,
      148–49.

226   *for all she wrote* SL, 155.

227   *prefer to three boys* SL, 155.

227   *was better than virginity* EE 5,
      366–67.

227   *recapture the original meaning*
      Harpsfield, 80–81.

227   *printed about 1526* Margaret
      More Roper, Moreana 7, 9–64.

227   *her body, she recovered* TTL,
      212–13.

227   *with worldly matters after* TTL,
      213.

228   *to avoid the plague* Hall, fol. 176^{v}
      —177.

229   *keep out the wind* CW 4, 123.

231   *prayers and spiritual exercises* TL,
      211.

231   *that Roper mentions elsewhere*
      TTL, 224.

231   *what life could not* SL, 182–83.

231   *not fail to go* TTL, 208.

232   *others were imprisoned there* CW
      9, 118–20.

232   *their complaints before him* TTL,
      220.

232   *by him at Chelsea* Guy, 87.

232   *to amuse the group* Stapleton, 96–
      97.

232   *ran down his ears* CW 8, 900–1.

233   *very great pain therefore* Harps-
      field, 94.

233   *you for whole good* TTL, 211.

PAGE

256   *almost nothing of Greek* EE 3,
       312–30.
257   *any leisure for learning* Corr., 173.
257   *before Christ was born* Corr., 177.
261   *of art than life* EE 4, 9–12.
262   *words but good deeds* EE 4, 234.

                CHAPTER 17

269   *kind of golden age* CWEL 4, 261.
270   *name to the author* EE 3, 238–39.
270   *are some great men* EE 3, 605–7.
270   *only as an extreme Augustinian*
       The monk has accused Erasmus of
       fomenting Luther's heresies, but
       More does not flatly say that Lu-
       ther's works are heretical. SL, 122
       or 172.
270   *sacrosanct Roman See* Corr., 85.
271   *or even the pope* EE 4, 96–107.
274   *grow out at last* EE 5, 330.
274   *Louvain named Nicholas Egmon-
       danus* EE 4, 383–89.
275   *ye know well* CW 8, 815–16.

                CHAPTER 18

278   *had anything heard before* Corr.,
       498.
279   *fine bit of nonsense* CW 6, 56.
281   *subject to his* Responsio For the
       significance of this addition, see
       J. M. Headley in CW 5, 732–74.
281   *something about vehemence* CW
       5, 795.
281   *from prior premises* CW 5, 181.
285   *observe it as one* CW 5, 386–87.
286   *see God in the face* EE 5, 178.
287   *urging him to battle* EE 5, 290–
       93.
287   *as much as it can* EE 5, 295.
287   *now stupidly attack—matrimony*
       CW 5, 671.
288   *persisted in such views* EE 4, 387.
288   *would later define it* CW 6, 311–
       12.
288   *report everything Erasmus said*
       CW 5, 197 and 904–5.

PAGE

289   *my dear darling still* CW 8,
       177.

                CHAPTER 19

294   *never so craftily polished* EW, 73.
295   *soul from the body* EW, 77.
295   *until we experience it* EW, 78.
295   *death drawing on* EW, 77.
295   *that man lies dying* EW, 78.
296   *to eternal damnation* EW, 79 and
       83.
296   *they, too, are damned* EW, 79.
297   *thine own heart* EW, 77
298   *are all equal* EW, 84.
298   *rebuked by an inferior* EW, 87.
298   *pleasures of the flesh* EW, 75.
       the clothes cover EW, 96.
       wrought therein EW, 95.
298   *purse one night yet* EW, 94.
299   *be brought to church* EW, 79.
299   *in an old coat* EW, 84.
299   *where thy money lieth* EW, 78.
300   *suddenly change into pity* EW,
       86.

                CHAPTER 20

303   *disciples and its patrons* EE 4,
       115.
303   *run each other through* CW 5,
       690–93.
305   *later polemical works* Corr., 342.
307   *hands in their blood* WA 6, 347.
307   *of all the slaughter* TRP 1, 182;
       procl. 122.
308   *without care or shame* CW 6, 375.
308   *or changed or impeded* WA 18,
       619.
309   *work to More* Fraenkel (1972)
310   *these books by Cochlaeus* CW 6,
       535–47.

                CHAPTER 21

313   *the demon of music* A&M 4, 621.
313   *could lead to it* Davis, 775–90.
314   *when he married Margaret* Harps-
       field, 84.

PAGE

316   *and pray for him* Harpsfield, 87.

318   *Lost Her Virginity, etc.* Les Admirables Secrets.

CHAPTER 22

326   *to tumult massacre and rapine* Corr., 328.

328   *as saints, wrote perpetually* Corr., 338.

329   *virtue or castigate evil* Corr., 355–56.

330   *the church of Christ* Corr., 357.

330   *had used his name* CW 5, 196–97.

331   *decreased and grew cool* Stapleton, 39.

333   *lose a decision* SL, 163.

335   *Berquin's execution by fire* CW 8, 341.

336   *such people were foolish* EE 7, 5–14.

337   *commonwealth as I do* CW 8, 1379.

342   *changes in the world* CW 6, 235.

344   *thorn was no more* CW 6, 85 and 625.

344   *girl and her affliction* CW 6, 92 and 629.

345   *manifest messenger of hell* CW 6, 346.

345   *people have burned him* CW 6, 426.

348   *house on Easter eve* Dickens, 110.

349   *into the English tongue* TRP 1, 196; see Schuster in CW 8, 1210–11.

CHAPTER 23

352   *example they give us* CW 6, 296.

354   *her under royal protection* A&M 4, 657–58.

356   *only God knoweth* EW, 313.

357   *grant Henry a divorce* Wernham, 113–14.

357   *for peace with him* Wernham, 120–21.

357   *Cambrai in his epitaph* SL, 181.

358   *appear before them again* LP 4, 5702; Scarisbrick, 224–25.

359   *written on the subject* LP 4, 5732.

360   *Henry's sister without permission* TTL, 93.

360   *coin of patience now* Pollard (1966), 234.

361   *before More became Lord Chancellor* John Fisher, English Werks, p. 261.

361   *deny it to others* See Guy, 50–64.

362   *follow his own conscience* EA, 79.

362   *always claimed he did* SL, 231.

362   *and in the Bible* SL, 228–34.

365   *make him a prince* Hall, fol. 187^V.

366   *perilous and infective breath* LP 4, 6075.

367   *at Greenwich by daybreak* TTL, 113–15.

367   *singular dear friend* TTL, 225.

368   *directed by the privy council* LP 4, 6026. CSPS 4, 194.

369   *Fisher to the king* Guy, 117–18.

369   *because it was traditional?* Guy, 118–19.

CHAPTER 24

371   *a prodigious sum* LP 4, 6214.

371   *him with my teeth* TTL, 130.

371   *from the king himself* TTL, 134–35.

372   *of power in England* LP 4, 6513.

372   *a dozen lesser folks* Scarisbrick, 259.

372   *whom they suspect* CSPS 4, 354.

372   *being dismissed from office* CSPS 4, 433.

373   *revolt against the king* Pollard (1966), 291.

373   *tomb of the tyrants* CSPS 4, 522.

373   *something about Wolsey's property* LP 4, 6262.

374   *owed him seven hundred pounds* LP 4, 6586–88.

374   *of the royal council* LP 4, 6666.

374   *to see to it* LP 4, 6484.

395 *death by perjuring himself* CW 6, 201.

395 *a heretical prayer book* CW 8, 13 and 1097–99.

396 *the devil's stinking martyr* CW 8, 16–17.

396 *going to the cross* A&M 4, 619–56.

397 *in the proper form* Guy, 171.

399 *do it more frequently* LP 5, 372.

399 *church, or the law* LP 5, 569.

399 *More scorned Reed* CW 8, 23–24.

399 *connections with Thomas Cromwell* Guy, 169.

399 *possession at the burning* LP 5, 560.

400 *administered the sacrament* CW 8, 24.

400 *Bilney now fully recanted* CW 8, 24–25.

401 *I pray God it may* CW 8, 25.

402 *a synonym for repression* Guy, 172–73.

402 *pelted with rotten fruit* Guy, 173.

402 *they remained long after* Hall, fol. 202.

403 *because he was monk* CW 8, 17.

403 *after escaping from More* LP 5, 574.

404 *at his returning hither* CW 8, 20.

404 *Stephen Vaughan of heresy* Vaughan, DNB.

404 *heresy under his charge* CW 9, 117–18.

404 *try to steal in again* CW 9, 119.

405 *even stolen Segar's purse* CW 9, 119.

405 *I ween better worthy* CW 8, 21.

406 *resigned as Lord Chancellor* See Clebsch, 281–82; CW 9, 88 and 348n.

406 *time, and praying aloud* CSPV 4, 765.

406 *a chatterer, he said* CW 8, 710.

406 *the wretches burn forever* CW 8, 590.

406 *rest of the realm* CW 9, 116.

406 *measures at their command* CW 9, 109–10.

CHAPTER 26

407 *the House of Lords* CSPS 4, 888.

407 *passed on through intermediaries* CSPS 4, 883.

408 *might still be possible* Elton (1977), 149.

409 *get a favorable vote* Lehmberg, 137–38.

409 *it to his city* CSPV 4, 754 and 760.

409 *than he had requested* Lehmberg, 145–49.

409 *from the House itself* Elton (1977), 150–53; Elton (1972), 273; Lehmberg, 138–42.

410 *previously proved false* CW 6, 261.

410 *strongest measures against it* CW 6, 263.

410 *man be unjustly condemned* Fortescue, sig. H_7^v.

411 *taken as self-incrimination* Trapp in CW 9, lxi–lxvii.

411 *helped draft it* Hughes, 238.

412 *to your highness's assent* GH, 157.

412 *translated into church law* GH, 158.

412 *clergy had greatly offended* GH, 168.

413 *subjects and not ours* Hall, fol. 205.

414 *Parliament in January 1532* EA, 79–81.

414 *working against the divorce* LP 5, 986–87.

414 *framing their own statutes* CSPS 4, 951.

414 *intensity of the evil* CSPS 4, 951.

415 *appointed by the king* GH, 176–78.

415 *resignation to Charles V* CSPS 4, 952.

PAGE

444 *feared rather than loved* EE 10, p. 136

444 *More's administration* EE 10, pp. 137–8

444 *service as Lord Chancellor* TTL, 231–32.

444 *they were in prison* EE 11, 73.

445 *shared one soul* EE 11, 221.

445 *for the Catholic faith* EW, 929.

445 *had been misdated 1534* Corr., 466–69.

446 *perfectly cured and suddenly* CW 6, 93

447 *and so greatly disordered* Cranmer, 272.

447 *inspiration and demon possession* Tyndale's *Answer*, Society, 91–92.

447 *victim to a great plague* Cranmer, 274.

447 *many mad follies* LP 6, 967.

447 *information out of people* LP 6, 887.

448 *would ensnare Thomas More* Elton (1972), 274–75.

448 *wrath of the king* LP 7, 238.

448 *wicked woman of Canterbury* Corr., 489.

449 *action on the divorce* Cranmer, 272–74.

450 *souls of great and small* Corr., 464–66.

451 *might flow great loss* Corr., 487.

451 *power of her prayers* LP 6, 1466.

452 *would not hear them* LP 6, 1468.

452 *no harm in it* LP 6, 1467.

453 *acquitted himself handily* TTL, 231–32.

453 *to drive him thereunto* TTL, 230.

453 *grace was much deceived* TTL, 233.

453 *letter to the emperor* CSPS 5, 22.

454 *authority more slenderly touched* TTL, 235.

454 *our crown imperial* TTL, 235.

455 *is not cast off* TTL, 237.

PAGE

455 *which mine heart standeth* Corr., 492.

456 *unto this noble realm* SL, 211.

458 *in the previous century* LP 6, 1425.

458 *one heavy, displeasant look* Corr., 491–501.

459 *at the king's pleasure* Elton (1972), 277.

459 *of this present parliament* Hughes, 270; GH, 244–47.

459 *of Appeals and Dispensations* Hughes, 270; Elton (1972), 224.

459 *for the most part* Elton (1972), 225–26.

459 *and compelled to swear* CSPS 5, 45.

460 *of the king's measures* CSPS 5, 45.

460 *his carnal affections utterly* TTL, 237–38.

CHAPTER 28

463 *leave me to mine* Corr., 501–7.

463 *that More and Fisher took* LP 7, 499.

464 *Cromwell could not allow* LP 7, 500.

464 *regarded as an enemy* TTL, 238.

465 *to the king's mercy* Corr., 508–9.

465 *in the bliss of heaven* Corr., 510–11.

466 *case was Lorenzo Campeggio* CSPS 5, 27.

466 *London for the Parliament* LP 7, 462.

466 *a million of gold* CSPS 5, 40.

466 *wife might be executed* CSPS 5, 40.

467 *it to Margaret More Roper* Corr., 511–13.

467 *carefully worked out together* Corr., 514–32.

468 *for more causes than one* Corr., 527.

468 *to renounce his conscience* Corr., 515.

468   *to think of them so* Corr., 527.

468   *through all Christian nations* Corr., 525.

469   *against the law of God* Corr., 524.

469   *he could bear the worst* Corr., 530.

470   *she had eaten herself* Corr., 529.

472   *judgment, heaven, and hell* CW 12, 4.

472   *we can see for ourselves* CW 12, 21.

472   *their hour of need* CW 12, 92.

473   *out of their head* CW 12, 61.

473   *I fear it very sore* CW 12, 62.

473   *was severed from the body* CW 12, 125.

474   *special revelation of God* CW 12, 141.

475   *all the long night* CW 12, 277.

476   *to be ruled yet* CW 12, 219–20.

476   *against its heretical foes* CW 13, 136–77.

477   *justifies sinners before God* CW 13, 111.

477   *Luther's marriage is condemned* CW 12, 93.

477   *shall we never find* CW 12, 272.

477   *to play the knave* CW 12, 273.

477   *the thousands at once* CW 12, 273.

478   *duresse and hard handling* SL, 243.

478   *a faithful Christian man* SL, 237.

478   *temptation a way out* CW 12, 278–79.

478   *at the hand of God* SL, 237.

478   *sooner rid [of it]* CW 12, 301–2.

479   *to do in writing* Corr., 488.

479   *lighter with hope thereof* Corr., 537.

479   *cold and the damp* CW 12, 277.

479   *suffered before his imprisonment* CW 12, 157.

479   *probably did the same* CW 12, 187.

479   *regime in mortal danger* CSPS 5, 84.

479   *would not go through* CSPS 5, 112.

480   *enjoy their possessions undisturbed* Elton (1972), 400–1.

480   *judge errors and heresies* SR 3, 492.

480   *went beyond the statute* TTL, 240–41.

480   *of anything therein contained* SR 3, 493.

481   *death for high treason* Lehmberg, 203–6.

481   *of all his goods* SR 3, 528.

481   *divers and sundry ways* Elton (1972), 402.

481   *not include this formula* SR 3, 527–28.

481   *our Lord continue it* Corr., 543.

481   *take anything from her* Corr., 540.

482   *in this world also* Corr., 548.

482   *that fell that winter* LP 8, 856.

482   *audience with the king* Corr., 554–55.

482   *great house was confiscated* Stapleton, 214–15.

483   *to light in 1963* Miller in CW 14, 695–97.

484   *resurrected from the dead* CW 14, 191.

484   *priest when morning came* CW 14, 9.

485   *everlasting joy of heaven* CW 14, 13–19.

485   *committing a terrible sin* CW 14, 595.

485   *out over many hours* CW 14, 47.

485   *the thought of pain* Corr., 542.

485   *them when they strike* CW 14, 59.

485   *injury to his cause* CW 14, 63.

485   *with the conqueror's wreath* CW 14, 69.

486   *body and blood of Christ* CW 14, 391.

486   *and blood—Frith's view* CW 14, 393.

486   *meaning what they said* CW 14, 395.

PAGE

511   *rather have comforted him* TTL, 251.

511   *to depart from him* TTL, 251–52.

511   *kissed their father as well* Stapleton, 201.

512   *he hath great cause* Corr., 563–65.

512   *the validity of relics* Acts 19:12.

PAGE

513   *liberty to be present* TTL, 253.

513   *and help thee himself* Hall, fol. 226^v.

513   *me shift for myself* TTL, 254.

EPILOGUE

518   *mock in the communication* Hall, fol. 226^v.

INDEX

Batmanson, John, 241, 257
  TM's reply to (1519), 257–60
Bayfield, Richard, 403
Beanfort, Margaret, 21, 22
Becket, Thomas, xvii, 7, 15, 422,
  482
  tomb, shrine of, Canterbury, 19,
    332–3, 408
Beerbohm, Max, 187
beggars and begging, 16, 94, 165
Bernard of Clairvaux, 66–7, 90–1
Bible
  accessibility of, 236–7
  changes in and accretions to, 69
  role of, in church, 252–3, 283–5
  "sola scriptura," 121, 148–9, 181–2,
    344; TM attacks, 283–4, 486; vs.
    tradition, 149, 283, 286, 306, 327;
    Tyndale on, 319
  in Utopia (as lacking), 178
Bible. N.T. English, 19–20
  Authorized ("King James") Version
    (1611), 312, 318, 322, 323
  Henry orders, then revokes (1530),
    349, 427–8
  in Hunne affair, 128–9
  TM's advocacy of, 347–9; later
    opposition to, 427–8
  Tyndale's, 312, 318–24
  Wycliffe's, 252
Bible. N.T. Greek (Erasmus's), 235,
  236–8
  Dorp on, 145, 146
  TM on, 148, 149, 150, 239, 241,
    256–60
  opposition to, 244, 251–63
  textual notes in, 237–8
  Tunstall on, 239
  Vulgate revision with, 237
Bible. N.T. Latin (Vulgate), 146, 149,
  258
  revised by Erasmus, 237
Bilney, Thomas, 237, 313–14, 338,
  396–401
  death of (1531), 313, 396
  TM on, 339, 346–7
bishops, 142–3
  Answer of the Ordinaries (1532),
    411–13
  vs. Henry VIII, 407, 414–15; on
    divorce, 383; on English Bible, 349;

on oaths, 413; Submission of the
  Clergy (1532), 415
see also clergy
Blount, William, Lord Mountjoy, 80,
  87–8
Boleyn, Anne, 60, 61
  and Cromwell, 494
  Henry VIII and, 213–14, 349, 362–3,
    389, 414, 423, 494, 496; books
    proposed by Anne, 339, 354;
    marriage (see below marriage to
    Henry)
  and Lutheranism, 380, 396
  marriage to Henry (1533), 430–1;
    annulled by Clement VII, 440;
    denial of, as treason, 459; TM on,
    456
  as queen, 440, 456, 459, 479, 491;
    coronation (1533), and TM's
    absence from, 438–40; gives birth to
    Elizabeth (1533), 440–1
  and Wolsey, 360, 361, 372
Boleyn, Sir Thomas, Earl of Wiltshire,
  60, 380, 386, 390, 415, 444
  and TM, 453, 496, 504
Bolt, Robert: Man for All Seasons, 501
Bonvisi, Antonio, 156
book burnings, 302, 303, 323, 337
Bosworth Field, battle of (1485), 17, 60,
  113, 387
Brackenbury, Sir Robert, 111
Brandon, Charles, Duke of Suffolk,
  359–60, 368, 415, 496, 504
  and Wolsey, 367, 372
Bridgett, T. E., xix
Brixius, Germanus, 52
  Antimorus, 245–6, 249
  Burning of the Ship Cordelière, 58–9;
    Erasmus's letter on (1517), 243
  Erasmus's letter to (1520), 249
  TM's epigrams on, 59, 243, 245–6,
    249
  TM's Letter Against (1520), 246–8
  TM's quarrel with, 245–9 passim
Brook, Richard, 194
Buckingham, Duke of, see Stafford,
  Edward; Stafford, Henry
Bucklesbury Street house, London, 88,
  94, 218, 238
bucolic tradition, 3–4, 161
Budaeus, William, 201, 240–1, 248, 249

ABOUT THE AUTHOR

RICHARD MARIUS was born and educated in Tennessee and received his doctoral degree from Yale University. He taught Reformation history for many years at the University of Tennessee and is now head of the Expository Writing Program at Harvard College. He has written two novels, *The Coming of Rain* and *Bound for the Promised Land,* and a biography, *Martin Luther,* and is an editor of several volumes in *The Yale Edition of the Complete Works of St. Thomas More.*

He lives in Belmont, Massachusetts, with his wife and two of his three sons.